SOCIETY,

PERSONALITY,

AND

DEVIANT

BEHAVIOR

SOCIETY, PERSONALITY, AND DEVIANT BEHAVIOR

A STUDY OF A
TRI-ETHNIC COMMUNITY

Richard Jessor

Theodore D. Graves

Robert C. Hanson

Shirley L. Jessor

Institute of Behavioral Science
University of Colorado
Boulder, Colorado

Holt, Rinehart and Winston, Inc.
New York/Chicago/San Francisco
Atlanta/Dallas/Montreal/Toronto
London

Copyright © 1968 by Holt, Rinehart and Winston
All rights reserved
Library of Congress Catalog Card Number: 68-16474
2666501
Printed in the United States of America
1   2   3   4   5   6   7   8   9

Passages from *Delinquency and Opportunity: A Theory of Delinquent Gangs,* by L. E. Ohlin and R. A. Cloward, are reprinted with permission of The Macmillan Company. © The Free Press, a corporation, 1960.

PREFACE

This book is a report of an exploration in behavioral science. It describes an important social problem—deviant behavior, especially excessive alcohol use—and investigation of it in a small rural community.

The need for greater understanding of problem behavior in contemporary society can hardly be overemphasized; it served as a spur to our efforts and helped sustain our commitment to the demands of a lengthy research project. But for us as behavioral scientists, the research provided additional opportunities: to extend to a field situation a social learning theory of personality which had its origin in the clinic and the laboratory; to try to fashion a more comprehensive explanatory scheme by bringing together concepts from psychology and from the disciplines concerned with the social environment; to explore a methodology for field studies which seemed to promise greater rigor; and, finally, to put to test an abstract interdisciplinary theory by confronting it with a concrete pattern of naturally occurring, socially significant behavior. How these opportunities were exploited, and with what measure of success, is what the book is about.

The structure of the book is uncomplicated. After an introductory chapter describing the community, its tri-ethnic composition, and the apparent ethnic variation in deviance and alcohol use, there are four chapters in which the theory of the research is presented. These chapters describe the conceptualization of deviant behavior, of certain sociocultural and per-

v

sonality factors presumed relevant to deviance, and of the way in which the process of socialization links the person with his environment. At the end of Chapter 5 is a summary showing the overall social-psychological framework in schematic form. Chapter 6 begins with a discussion of the methodological orientation which guided the design of the field study, and then turns to a description of the three independent but converging studies that were carried out in the community.

The following four chapters, 7 through 10, deal with what is perhaps, next to theory, the key issue in social research: the development of measures—measures of deviance and of alcohol use, and measures of the sociocultural environment and of personality. There is a good deal of technical detail in these chapters, which would seem essential for the specialist but may be of limited interest to the reader concerned only with the main results of the research. The latter appear in Chapter 11, where the major theoretical ideas are tested, and in Chapter 12, where the socialization research is reported. The final chapter summarizes and also acknowledges at least the more obvious limitations of our work.

Although the book is concerned with deviance and drinking behavior, the formulations have implications, we hope, for other areas of behavior and for social-psychological theory in general. The concepts and the measures we have used to deal with behavior, with personality, with the sociocultural environment, and with socialization may be of interest to others beyond those directly concerned with deviance and alcohol use.

Every social and intellectual enterprise has a historical development; research projects are no exception. The work reported here began nearly ten years ago, and our ideas have grown and developed and shifted to accommodate the course of our experience. While the major formulations have remained the same, there have been changes of emphasis, increased attention to previously slighted variables, and even reconceptualizations of data. Readers familiar with our earlier papers and research reports will be aware of these changes, especially with respect to the ideas about anomie and about social and personal control. We have decided not to burden this report with the dialectics of our own development, but, instead, to present our final thinking and interpretation of data. We take for granted the reader's awareness that the particular ideas presented here are at least some distance from where they began.

The research we describe could not have been successfully completed without the contributions of each of the four authors. Each was involved at every level of the work, from the formulation of ideas to the devising of measures, the collection and analysis of data, and the writing, finally, of portions of the book. The authors formed a working interdisciplinary group: Richard Jessor and Shirley Jessor are psychologists, Theodore Graves is an anthropologist, and Robert Hanson is a sociologist.

With respect to particular responsibilities, Richard Jessor was in charge of the work from its inception at the beginning of 1959. As co-director (with Professor Omer C. Stewart) of the Tri-Ethnic Research Project, he directed the portion of that larger project that is reported here and was responsible for the major theoretical formulations and the design of the research described in this book. He was primary author of Chapters 1 through 6 and of Chapter 13 and was responsible for the final draft of the manuscript.

Theodore Graves joined the Tri-Ethnic Project as a research assistant about six months after it got under way. He wrote his dissertation as part of his work and then became a research associate with major responsibility for the High School Study and, later, for overall data analysis. He is primary author of Chapters 7, 8, 10, and 11. Robert Hanson joined the team as research associate near the end of the second year and assumed the responsibility of devising and elaborating measurement of the socio-cultural environment of the community, particularly of access to opportunity and anomie. He is primary author of Chapter 9, and he drafted a major section of Chapter 1. Shirley Jessor was a research associate from the very beginning of the project. She initiated the Community Survey Study and later assumed principal responsibility for the Socialization Study. She is primary author of Chapter 12, and she wrote the initial draft of Chapter 5. With this division of labor on record, we need to reiterate that this is a joint outcome in the full sense of the term—a product which would have a radically different contour in the absence of any one of the four contributions.

To accomplish work of this sort is to contract a series of debts one can never hope to repay, but merely to acknowledge. We were fortunate in receiving generous support from the National Institute of Mental Health under Grant No. 3M-9156. We were fortunate also in being able to borrow ideas and tools from earlier workers in the behavioral sciences; these we hope to fully acknowledge in the text. And we had the good luck to be able to rely upon colleagues, consultants, and students in ways which made the difference between success and failure. Among colleagues, mention must be made of Omer C. Stewart, who initiated the general idea of a Tri-Ethnic Research Project and directed those aspects of the project concerned with the ethnography and the ethnohistory of the community. Stewart's long experience as an anthropologist, his extensive knowledge of the research community, and his own work in the community were invaluable to us. Kenneth R. Hammond participated in helpful discussions in the earliest phase of the research, and we are grateful also to him.

A number of consultants aided us at different stages of our work, each leaving an imprint. Our greatest debt, one we have waited a long time to acknowledge in this way, is to Julian B. Rotter. Not only has he advised us on this research, but his social learning theory of personality has influenced the course of our thinking from the time, years ago, when for two of us, he was teacher. Clyde Kuckhohn talked with us not long after we began, and we subsequently had special cause to regret his untimely death. We had valuable instruction in social psychology from Melvin Seeman and in measuring drinking behavior from George L. Maddox. Thomas Gladwin served throughout as liaison with NIMH, but his contributions to our work inevitably strayed from the administrative level to that of ideas, for which we were always grateful. Carl L. Anderson also facilitated our relationship with NIMH and had the initiative to expand communication between our project and related research around the country.

Our research assistants taught us more than we dare acknowledge; best of all, they never permitted conceptual complacency. We are much indebted to Braxton Alfred, Paul Chassy, Curtiss Frank, John S. Gillis, Susan Strand Johnson, Carol Joyce, Colin Martindale, James G. Minard, Gabino Rendon, Jr., Carol Guertin Schneider, John Shybut, Robert W. Titley, and Peter Weiss. Two assistants, however, deserve our special thanks: N. John Castellan, for his statistical contributions, and Peter H. Grossman, for his role in the development of the drinking measures.

The collection of interview data in two of our studies required, in addition to the work of the authors and research assistants, the assistance of a number of mature women willing to face the uncertain rigors of field work. For their essential help we are grateful to Mrs. Jean Clark, Margaret Hanson, Bea Hoffman, Helen Power, Betty Reiss, Fabiola Rendon, and Sue Weatherley.

We have been especially fortunate in secretarial assistance. We are indebted to Mrs. Esther Larson, who was project secretary during the initial phase of the research, and to Mrs. Adelyn Grimes, who was project secretary during the later phase. Both served us exceptionally well. Mrs. Pamela Fry imposed order on an earlier draft of the manuscript, and the final typing of the entire manuscript was done with unusual care by Miss Joanne Yamaguchi.

Two acknowledgments have been saved for last, not because they are least but because the debts they mark are pervasive rather than specific. The first of these is to the University of Colorado Institute of Behavioral Science and its director, Ozzie G. Simmons. The Institute, the unit of the university in which our project was located, is a relatively unique organization for the advancement of behavioral science. By providing us with excellent research facilities and with various kinds of assistance, it guaranteed that the work would reach completion. More important, perhaps, have been its ethos and its concern for the pursuit of socially significant knowledge; these have had an enduring influence upon our work. It is a pleasure to acknowledge this book as Publication Number 95 of the Institute of Behavioral Science.

Finally, we turn toward the community this book is about. While our description of the research setting is phrased in the present tense, the reader is reminded that it is the "ethnographic present," the present at the time, nearly seven years ago, when the main data were being collected. During that time we lived in the community for periods of varying length, we participated in the life of the community, and we made some lasting friendships. Our indebtedness, unhappily, cannot be expressed by acknowledgment of the identity of the community or of those living in it who helped us throughout—we have made no mention of its name anywhere in this book, and at no point is identifiable information given about any individual resident. More than for the cooperation and the help we received, however, we are grateful for what the community enabled us to learn; for that opportunity, we hope this book will be taken as a small repayment.

R.J.
T.D.G.
R.C.H.
S.L.J.

BOULDER, COLORADO
January, 1968

CONTENTS

PART ONE

Introduction

CHAPTER ONE

The Setting and the Problem

During the last two decades, there has been a steady acceleration of behavioral science research upon major problems of social life. The involvement has been pervasive, ranging across such widely separated areas as mental illness, racial and ethnic discrimination, drug addiction, acculturation, poverty, crime and delinquency, and the alienation of man in mass society. The interest of the larger society in the application of behavioral science concepts and methods has stemmed from its broadening concern to effect an amelioration of these problems. Among behavioral scientists, concurrently, the conviction seems to have grown that the maturity of their disciplines will be reflected, at least in part, in the degree to which understanding in these areas has been achieved.

The present book has emerged from this context. It is an account of a large-scale effort the aim of which was to attempt to develop systematic understanding of a social problem, the occurrence of deviant behavior, and to evaluate that understanding by means of empirical research.

Despite the large quantity of previous research, the present state of the behavioral sciences does not inspire confidence in the success of such a venture. Neither conceptual nor methodological development has gone far enough to cope adequately with the awesome complexity of social behavior, and the accumulation of empirical knowledge has been far too scattered and segmental to provide a sure basis for scientific insight. What we have been left with, largely, is promise. This promise is based upon the partially successful beginnings in behavioral science thus far; it is nourished also by the knowledge that both the physical and the biological worlds have already yielded to the sustained application of rational investigation. In the light of this appraisal, the central issue for the behavioral scientist is how to proceed in a manner most likely to secure some of the fruits of that promise.

Our own perspective led us to emphasize several characteristics which

3

we considered to be important aspects of any such approach. Each of these will emerge more clearly as a major theme in subsequent chapters of the book, but it should be useful to list them here. First, we felt that potentially fruitful research should begin with and be embedded in theory, "theory" being a term nearly synonymous with what is connoted by the term "understanding." Second, we felt that an adequate theory of any aspect of social behavior should be comprehensive enough to accommodate both the person and his environment. Such a theory should be interdisciplinary, should be capable of simultaneously encompassing both individual and social variation—in short, should be what is termed a "field theory." Third, the nature of the theoretical framework should be such as to enable systematic derivation of measures and relatively unequivocal coordination of concepts to empirical phenomena. In theory formulation which goes beyond sheer intellectual exercise, the luxury of vagueness cannot be afforded; an eye toward ultimately connecting up with the phenomena to be explained should help steer the theoretical enterprise from the beginning.

This book, then, is a report of our attempt to implement such an approach in the study of deviant behavior and excessive alcohol use. Described in it is a five-year research project, a field study, which was carried out in a small tri-ethnic community in southwestern Colorado. More is attempted, however, than simply to describe another research undertaking. In the book, the first concern is the presentation of a social-psychological framework for the study of deviance. In this theoretical formulation, the way in which personal and social variables systematically articulate with each other is conceptualized; the resulting model is one which we hope will have general applications beyond the problem of deviance. The second concern is the development of a methodological orientation to field research which permits the increased degree of control necessary for testing hypotheses and evaluating and extending theory. The third concern is to describe the development of measures and procedures which derive logically from the theory, which serve to implement the methodological orientation, and which may be useful in a variety of other social-psychological investigations. Finally, we are concerned with findings, data which in their own right add something to our knowledge of deviance and alcohol use, but, perhaps more important, data which enable evaluation of the adequacy of understanding or the reach of theory.

Various questions, undoubtedly, have already arisen in the reader's mind: What is meant by a comprehensive or field theory? What social and psychological variables were actually studied? How is deviance defined? In what way can field studies have systematic relevance for theory? These questions must all be answered; they will be considered in the chapters immediately following this one. For the present, however, only two purposes need be accomplished. The first of these is to describe briefly the setting in which the research took place, the community whose nature both influenced and constrained our work. Without some sense of the community, the reader would be disadvantaged in judging the meaning of what has been done and of what has been found.

The second purpose is to describe the "confronting problem" as we saw it at the outset—that is, the extent and distribution of deviance and alcohol use which were apparent characteristics of the community and fairly obvious to anyone with more than a superficial knowledge of the community. In doing this, we wish to avoid the crucial questions of definition which inevitably make technical terms of such expressions as "deviance" and "excessive alcohol-use." It will be enough for the present to look at the confronting problem in the community from a common-sense point of view, for instance, that of an ordinary member of the community itself.

Before describing the community, we should make clear that it was selected as a research site for both conceptual and pragmatic reasons. Its tri-ethnic composition—Anglo-American, Spanish-American, and Indian—promised an unusual natural laboratory. The importance of this characteristic of the community was accentuated by the fact that variation in rate of occurrence of deviance and excessive alcohol use apparently followed ethnic lines. Further, the availability of three separate and relatively nonoverlapping populations within a single community promised separate tests of the adequacy and, therefore, of the generality of the theory. In addition, the community was small enough so that it could be approached ethnographically, and direct observations could be made of the major facets of community life; yet, at the same time, it was large enough so that adequate samples could be drawn for a variety of different purposes. Finally, and of great pragmatic significance, the community was one in which research contact and activity had been going on for some time previous to the initiation of the present research.[1] This meant not only that a backlog of potentially useful information on the community and its members would be available but also—perhaps even more important—the likelihood was higher that our project would be accepted by the community as simply a continuation and enlargement of research efforts to which it was already habituated. Thus, the usual problems attendant upon initiating research in a new community would be minimized.

---

[1] The community, because of its interesting ethnic composition and accessibility to the University of Colorado, had been used as a summer laboratory for training anthropology students in field techniques over the previous years. The course was under the direction of Professors O. C. Stewart and G. W. Hewes of the Department of Anthropology.

THE TRI-ETHNIC RESEARCH COMMUNITY[2]

General Description of the Area

The research community consists of the Anglo-American,[3] Spanish-American, and Indian population of a small town and its surrounding rural area. The town lies in a river valley in southwestern Colorado within the boundaries of an Indian reservation. At the northern end of the river valley, beyond the research area but visible from the main street of the town, snow-capped mountain peaks rise to a height of about 13,000 feet; at the southern end of the valley, also beyond the research area, nearly desert-like conditions prevail, precipitation is minimal, and vegetation is sparse and scrubby. The research town lies about midway between these ecological extremes, at a point where the valley is widest, spreading nearly ten miles across.

East and west from the center of town, reddish mesas covered with piñon and sagebrush rise from the irrigated valley floor. Just beyond the town limits to the north is the Indian Agency, which predates the town itself. While the Indian reservation was established in 1879, it was only after the coming of the railway and the opening of the land to home-steading that, in 1910, a town was finally established; its name was taken from that of one of the reservation Indian chiefs.

In appearance the town is like many others in this part of the Southwest. There are about two hundred residences, twenty businesses, and four churches within the town. Many of the buildings are of adobe mud faced with stucco and roofed with corrugated iron. The paved business street, eight blocks long, includes the bank, the post office, three main general merchandise and grocery stores, a large hardware-lumber company, the office of the weekly newspaper, two liquor stores, three gas station-garages, a barbershop, a drugstore, a pool hall, several cafes, and two bars. The houses in which people live are generally along unpaved streets, muddy

[2] The description of the community in the following pages is presented in general terms, organized for the most part around the main areas of institutionalized social life: economic, social, political, and religious interactions. Beyond reliance upon our own observations and data, we are indebted for source material to a number of our colleagues: Omer C. Stewart (1952); Braxton M. Alfred (1962); and Gabino Rendon, Jr. (1962).

A more *systematic* description of the research community and the three ethnic groups, in terms deriving from our conceptual framework, emerges in Chapter 9, "The Measurement of the Sociocultural System."

[3] Whites, whether of English, German, or Italian extraction, are referred to locally as "Anglos" to distinguish them from the Spanish-Americans in the area, who are also technically "Caucasian." With few exceptions, furthermore, the local Spanish are not "Mexicans," having lived as farmers in the area for many generations.

in winter and dusty in summer. Those of the Anglos tend to be larger, better built, and better maintained. The Spanish and Indian homes, with a few exceptions, are adobe or frame: many are weathered and run-down, especially those along the river and toward the south end of town near the small railroad freight station.

The town has a municipally owned water and gas company, a two-man police force, and a volunteer fire department. It serves as the center for a sanitation district, a soil conservation district, and a number of irrigation ditch companies. It is also a base for the state highway maintenance department and the headquarters for the school district. The grade school and high school are both located in the town, while the junior high school is on the Indian Agency grounds, just north of the town limits.

The Indian Agency grounds contain a complex of buildings and activities which make the Agency area a second focus of interaction in the research community. The area includes the Agency headquarters building, the Tribal Affairs building (which also houses the tribal jail), the junior high school of the community, a recreation center with surrounding park, a clinic building maintained by the U.S. Public Health Service, and several dormitories for Indian students who are not from the local reservation but who attend the community schools. In addition, scattered throughout the grounds are government-owned houses occupied by Agency personnel and school district teachers.

In the countryside surrounding the town and the Agency are the homesteads, farm and grazing lands, woodlands and forests of the residents. Though their homes are generally widely dispersed, in some areas houses are clustered in small hamlets, which may have a general store, post office, gas pump, and, perhaps, an elementary rural school building, sometimes vacated. Spanish-American clustering tends to occur in the southern and eastern parts of the valley, Anglo housing clusters are more evident in the northwest part of the valley, and Indian clustering is present in the central part. Throughout the valley, however, on the reservation and off, in the town and in the countryside, one's neighbor may, with almost equal likelihood, be Anglo, Spanish, or Indian.

The boundary of the research community was defined by the boundaries of the local school district.[4] According to a virtually complete census of the residents within this area—a total of 2719 persons—approximately 46 percent were Anglos, 34 percent were Spanish-Americans, and 20 percent were Indians. Of the total, approximately 29 percent lived in town or on the nearby Agency grounds and 71 percent lived in the surrounding countryside, within a radius of approximately ten miles from the town. Broken down by ethnic group, the figures show about 25 percent of the Anglos lived in town or at the Agency and 75 percent in the

---

[4] There is a discussion of the basis and justification for this decision in Chapter 6.

country; among the Spanish, 37 percent lived in town and 63 percent were rural; of the Indians, 25 percent lived in town and 75 percent in the surrounding countryside. The relatively high proportion of Spanish in the town—they are also the largest group in town in absolute numbers—reflects the fact that many of the Spanish families lost their landholdings during the depression and moved into town, where they received support in the form of welfare assistance.

Economic Aspects of Life in the Community

The economy of the community rests mainly on irrigation agriculture and stock raising. Common crops are alfalfa, wheat, oats, barley, corn, beans, and potatoes. Forage crops for cattle feeding are raised on about two thirds of the irrigated land. The average Anglo farm has over one hundred acres of irrigable land, about twice as much as either the average Spanish or Indian family farm. Some of the Anglo farmers also engage in intensive dairy farming, whereas none of the Indians or Spanish do. In general, the Anglo farms are also more mechanized and are operated more efficiently. The Anglos run the Soil Conservation District, the Marketing District, and the Irrigation District. Voluntary agricultural organizations, such as the Grange and the 4-H Club, tend to have almost exclusively an Anglo membership.

The Spanish contribute a significant proportion of the agricultural production of the valley, but it is less than the Anglo proportion. Although the average Spanish farm is about 90 percent as large as the average Anglo farm, it has less irrigable and more marginal land. Consequently, the Spanish rely more on cash crops such as wheat, plus traditional garden crops and small livestock such as chickens and rabbits for their subsistence. The Spanish have less access to short-term loan capital, their farms are less mechanized, and they obtain less technical assistance from government agricultural agencies.

Since the Indians settled on the reservation in the 1870s, farming and stock raising have been the primary economic activities of most families, but the average farm production has been less than that of similar size farms of either the Anglos or Spanish, despite the generally better quality of the Indian land. Most Indian farmers work "assigned land," land which is owned by the tribe, but some families still own their original allotted lands. Until recently, the tribe itself operated a farm of over one thousand acres on which feed crops were raised and pasture was provided for the sheep and cattle cooperatives organized within the tribe.

In addition to their domination of the agricultural enterprise in the community, the Anglos also constitute the merchant class. Except for a few establishments catering to Spanish and Indian trade specifically, all retail businesses, mostly family operated, are owned by Anglos. The public and professional offices of the community are, for the most part, also held by Anglos.

In the wage-earning class, the Spanish predominate. They are laborers for the construction company which digs irrigation canals and engages in other heavy construction. They are most frequently the wage laborers in the filling stations, the ditch riders and laborers for the Indian Service, the farm hands and herders for the tribe, and the waitresses and fry cooks in the cafes. The Spanish also perform some wage labor for the School District and do housework for private families. Although the Spanish constitute the largest segment of the population of the town, only a few establishments—a pool hall, gas station, barbershop, and two small grocery stores off the main street which cater almost exclusively to a Spanish clientele—are owned or operated by them. A few Spanish receive railroad pensions, and others depend on welfare for subsistence. According to welfare records, between 40 and 50 percent of the Spanish population has at some time received welfare assistance.

An unusual aspect of economic life in the community is reflected in the fact that the Indians now have two sources of income not available to Anglos or Spanish. The most important source since 1954 has been monthly per capita payments from the tribal estate. The land-claims settlement (a federal court judgment in 1950 awarded the tribe about five and a half million dollars), the discovery and production of natural gas on tribal lands, the sale of lumber, and other tribal enterprises have resulted in income to the tribe which has been and is being shared among all legal members of the tribe. Although the amount of the monthly per capita payment has varied, a family of five has in past years received between $4000 and $6000 per year in per capita payments, with provisions made for the protection of the payments received for minors.

The second main source of income for tribal members is that available from within the tribal bureaucracy itself. Members of the tribe earn wages for time spent as officers and members of the tribal council and of the eleven tribal committees, about fifty positions altogether. Since some of the positions require full-time work, and since committee meetings are called weekly or even more frequently, these jobs provide substantial supplemental income for officeholders. Other members work for the tribe as police, dormitory supervisors, recreation hall waitresses, maintenance employees, and the like. In fact, nearly all local Indian wage laborers are employed by the tribe, suggesting an important latent function of the expanding tribal bureaucracy.

Political Participation

In the 1960 presidential election, about 77 percent of the eligible Anglos voted, about 62 percent of the eligible Spanish voted, but only 15 percent of the eligible Indians voted. There is very little Indian participation either in town politics or in political parties. Almost all Indian political activity is confined to the tribal organization. Both the Anglo and Spanish populations, on the other hand, are involved in party politics and in town government, but the Anglos hold the more powerful position.

In town politics, the Anglo merchants control the parliamentary procedures in the town meetings. The mayor has always been an Anglo. In the meetings of the Council, the Anglo members tend to initiate most of the necessary actions of the town government; the Spanish members appear to have operated largely as a veto group which may shift its support to one or the other side when a split develops among the Anglos.

With respect to the Indians, decisions in the past were simply imposed upon them by the federal government through the superintendent of the local Indian Agency. Within the last ten years, however, a dramatic change in the political structure and autonomy of the tribe has occurred. In 1954, a Rehabilitation Plan, required for the successful settlement of the tribe's land-claims case, was approved by Congress and signed by the President. The Plan involved changes in the tribe's constitution, by-laws, and corporate charter, facilitating the achievement of tribal goals in fields such as housing, education, health, and law and order. The Plan specified procedures to deal with a variety of problems such as the land-assignment code, forest and range management, per-capita payments, and tribal administrative organization. During the first ten years of operation, a number of very capable Indian leaders have emerged, and the tribe has managed its affairs with a great deal of autonomy and visible success. The role of the Bureau of Indian Affairs has consequently shifted from that of authoritative director, managing its ward, to that of advisor and technical consultant.

The Schools

The relatively recent construction of all-weather roads in many sections of the present school district has permitted a consolidation of school facilities in the central community. Most of the outlying elementary schools have been closed, and the children take the school bus into town. This has particularly affected Spanish-American children in isolated areas to the south and east who previously had attended what were *de facto* segregated elementary schools, often staffed by Spanish teachers. Only those who went on to high school, therefore, formerly had an integrated school experience.

Most of the Indian children now also attend the consolidated public schools in town, making the school system the most integrated institution in the entire research area. In the fall of 1956, after the Rehabilitation Plan was put into effect, Indian children were taken into the community school district, and school facilities on the reservation became part of the town school plant. The Indians contribute support to the school district through contracts paid by the federal government. Thus far, there is little evidence of general Indian concern for school politics or of active participation by Indians in the local Parent-Teachers' Association, although the education committee of the tribe does maintain contact with school authorities. The Indian children, however, seem to have made a satisfactory adjustment to the town school system. Some of the Indian boys have become stars on the athletic teams, Indian children hold some of the class and student government offices, and, in general, Indians participate with equal status in the various school organizations and activities.

There is little question that the Anglo group dominates the administration of the educational system. The school board is generally composed of important Anglo ranch owners or merchants. Despite deliberate efforts to obtain Spanish and Indian teachers, most school employees—the superintendent, principal, teachers, secretary, custodian, and bus drivers—have been Anglo. The primary support for the athletic teams and band has come from Anglo organizations, such as the local Lions Club.

The Spanish parents, unlike the Indians, do participate in activities of the Parent-Teachers' Association. Within the school, the Spanish children participate on a par with the members of the other two ethnic groups. Spanish boys are members of the athletic teams, and some of the girls are officers in the Cheerleaders' Club. In general, they hold their share of class, club, and student government offices.

Many Indian students have attempted college; all but one, however, have failed to complete their degrees, usually dropping out because of drinking or other problems. As a result, many Indian students have developed the idea that it is not possible for them to succeed in college. Furthermore, most see no economic opportunities for themselves "on the outside" and aspire to no more than a tribal job. "If we could only get *one* Indian through college and into a well-paying professional job to serve as a model for the other Indians . . . ," is a phrase heard frequently in the community. The local Spanish children are better off in this respect. Several have successfully completed and others are presently attending college.

The Churches

Ethnic separatism in the community, while pervasive, is perhaps clearest in religious activity and in death. The largest Anglo church is Presbyterian, and most of the Anglo elite belong to it. The women's societies and youth groups within the church afford arenas of social life almost completely separate from participation by other ethnic groups. Efforts to integrate other ethnic groups have not had much success. The Missouri Synod Lutheran Church, the Baptists, and a small Mormon Community are also exclusively Anglo. A few other denominations, such as the Church of Christ, are represented among the Anglos, but members must go to other towns to attend services. Most Anglos are buried in the community (that is, Protestant) cemetery.

The Catholic Church, in size of membership the largest church in the community, and the Catholic cemetery are both Spanish. The women's societies of this church constitute the only voluntary organizations in the community made up of Spanish members. A small, geographically isolated group of Spanish families are Penitentes, and a few Spanish families are members of the Assembly of God Church.

Although most of the Indians are nominal Catholics and have been baptized in the Catholic Church, there are not more than a dozen Indian families who participate actively in church activities. An obvious barrier to more general Indian participation is the use of the Spanish language in the Catholic Church. A few of the Indians are Protestant, nominal members of the Presbyterian Church; there is a small Baptist Indian mission; and a few Indian families practice the Peyote religion, officially called the Native American Church. Services of the latter, led by visiting priests or officials of the church from surrounding states, are held about six times a year. Indians, despite different religious memberships, have been and prefer to be buried in the reservation cemetery, where lots and maintenance are provided by tribal funds.

Social Organizations

Again, in contrast with the Indians and Spanish, the Anglos have formed a number of voluntary organizations with social, civic, or recreational functions, such as an Anglo women's club affiliated with the National Federation of Women's Clubs and a bridge club, also exclusively Anglo. The Lions' Club, while not exclusively Anglo, draws most of its membership from the Anglo business community. In the rural area are the Grange and the 4-H Club, which tend to be exclusively Anglo. Within the Presbyterian Church are the Ladies' Aid Society and two youth fellowship groups with activities and functions which are primarily social. The Spanish, aside from the two women's societies in the Catholic Church, have no social or cultural organizations. Among the Indians, organized social and cultural affairs are somewhat limited; the annual Sun Dance and Bear Dance are the two significant social events. In addition, however, there are dances once a month in the tribal recreation hall, tribal rodeos, a tribal fair, and a tribal athletic association.

The Communications Media

The weekly town newspaper, supported mainly by Anglo subscribers, reports local happenings and social events. The news reported about minority group members often tends to concern public "trouble" events, such as arrests for assault or drunken driving. School news, however, involving students from all three ethnic groups, is reported in detail, especially athletic events. Since the formation of a public relations position within the tribe, more news about Indian affairs is published in the paper, and there have been substantial increases in the number of minority group subscribers in recent years.

It is interesting to note that almost 90 percent of the Indian households own television sets, while only 12 percent have telephones. These facts, aside from the geographical isolation of some houses from telephone lines, attest, on the one hand, to the recent affluence of tribal members, and, on the other hand, to a traditional preference for isolation and independence. About 60 percent of Spanish households own television sets and 20 percent have telephones; about 80 percent of Anglo households own television sets and over 60 percent have telephones. Another source of news and information for members of the community is the radio-television station in the county seat town about twenty miles away. The daily newspaper in that town contains, as well as state, national, and world news, information about persons and events in the local area.

Although this description may suggest a rather isolated community, that is only the case geographically; and now, with all-weather roads emanating from the town in all directions, even geographic isolation is largely a thing of the past. Like most American communities, this one is intimately linked to the larger society. Mass communications such as television, radio, newspapers, magazines, and movies (a drive-in movie, just north of town, operates during the summer, and a regular movie house, in the county seat town, operates year-round), expose the community residents to the national and international scene. The network of economic, political, and social interchange with the county, state, and nation serves the same function. The county seat, for example, is the base for services of importance to members of the community. No doctors or dentists reside in the research community town, although the Bureau of Indian Affairs has maintained part-time clinics for the Indians. Consequently, health and welfare services stem mainly from arrangements with persons or facilities in the county seat. Geographic mobility also helps tie the community to the outside world, since many members of the community have lived or spent time elsewhere. Beyond the war veterans, this is especially true of teachers, the Agency personnel, and the transient pipeline workers for the gas company, known locally as "roughnecks." Because of the many interconnecting links with the larger society, what happens outside the community does not pass unnoticed; this is as true of events in Washington and in Denver as it is of actions in Hollywood.

In addition, it should be mentioned that this area, like most small communities, is affected by the nationwide movement from the farm to the city. Mobility out of the community, especially among young people, is high, reflecting mainly the lack of local employment opportunity, but stemming as well from an increasing disaffection with rural or small-town life. Among the young, complaints are frequently voiced about how "dead" things are in the community, how little there is "to do," and how living here means being out of the stream of what is really going on in the world.

A great deal of change is presently occurring in the community; some of it is the outcome of tribal development activities in housing and recreation, and some is the result of the potential recreational impact of a huge lake to be created by a new dam at the south end of the river valley. Whether such changes can counter the perceptions of limited opportunity and the disaffection of the people, especially the young, and can stem their exodus, remains to be seen.

Looked at as a whole, the research community is not very different from many others in this part of the American Southwest. The three ethnic groups which make up its population are almost completely intermingled geographically, but the ethnic boundaries are clear, and voluntary social networks tend to be sharply circumscribed by these boundaries. What should emerge most clearly from this sketch is that there is a definite hierarchy in the community, with the Anglos occupying the dominant position and maintaining control over most of the community institutions and resources. The Spanish and Indians occupy minority positions, the Spanish being more accepted by the Anglos and less the object of prejudice and even hostility than the Indians. Economically, however, due to the tribe's substantial assets, the Indians are, as we have seen, significantly more advantaged than the Spanish.

With this general overview of the setting, it is possible to focus attention upon an aspect of community life about which nothing has been said in the description thus far—the occurrence of deviant behavior. It was this aspect of community life which constituted for us the central research concern, and the dimensions of the problem as they appeared at the outset to interested observers should be pointed out.

THE CONFRONTING PROBLEM: THE ETHNIC TOPOGRAPHY OF DEVIANCE

A newcomer to the community is not long in sensing the widespread concern over drinking and a variety of other forms of "trouble." Throughout the years in which the research was being conducted or prepared for, one or more members of the research group lived in the community, participated in the ordinary local activities, and has extended opportunities to observe various aspects of public and private community life. The local concern with problem behavior appeared as a recurrent theme, one which was not limited to the dominant Anglo group. As a matter of fact, the concern of the Indian tribal administration was such that, during the time of our research, it organized two separate workshops on alcoholism, to which a large number of outside experts were invited, in the hope of learning how to cope with what it viewed as a serious and urgent matter.

Direct observation of some aspects of behavior related to alcohol use is, one finds, not at all difficult. This is due largely to the presence of the two bars at opposite ends of the main street in town. One of the bars is almost exclusively patronized by Indians and Spanish-Americans; the other draws some of the Anglo "roughnecks" and a few of the more established Anglo residents, as well as Indian and Spanish customers. A frequent behavior pattern of some patrons, especially members of the minority groups, is to spend the entire evening in the bar until, often thoroughly drunk, they are forced to leave at closing time. During the evening, one or more visits to the other bar might be made.

It is apparent that the bars serve an important social function; there is little else to do in the town at night, and at either of the bars one can meet other people, watch television, and listen to the jukebox as well as drink.[5] For some patrons, it seems equally clear, however, that the bar is a place to get drunk or to keep from getting sober again, a place to get into fights, and a place to find a sexual partner.

One sees a fair amount of drunkenness on the streets as well as in the bars, and during the day as well as at night. The persons who are seen drunk, again mainly Indians, are not only the patrons moving back and forth between the two bars. There is an established pattern of group drinking, usually of cheap, fortified wine, in back alleys of the town, among the weeds of a deserted lot, or along the riverbank, and of subsequent wandering around the town. This pattern also makes its contribution to observable drunkenness on the streets. A third source of public drunkenness is the drinking which takes place in cars while driving around town or around the countryside, a pattern seen mostly among the youth. This public nature of alcohol use contributes to its saliency as a problem in the community. Its public character also guarantees that the problem behavior which is usually associated with heavy alcohol use, such as fighting, drunken driving and car accidents, and neglect of children left at home, will also be exposed to public view. Since it is mainly the members of

---

[5] It is worth noting that the Indians are legally unable to drink alcoholic beverages on the reservation since the tribe has not exercised its option to repeal the longstanding Indian prohibition statute. Indian drinking is legal, however, in town.

the two minority groups, but especially the Indians, who follow these public patterns, the relation between problem behavior and ethnic status does not go unnoticed in the community.

The ethnic concentration of heavy alcohol use and problem behavior is clearly seen in the community, and a general impression of the situation is widely shared. Almost no member of any of the ethnic groups would disagree that the greatest amount of such behavior in the community is contributed by the Indians, the least by the Anglos, and that the rate for the Spanish is somewhere in between. Strong disagreement arises only in the explanations one gets for this situation, that is, in the differing versions of what may be called the community "folk psychology." These versions are of interest because they so clearly reflect more general aspects of community relationships.

Although there are large differences in viewpoint, there is the feeling among some Anglos that the Indians have never and will never be any different. The relatively uncontrolled use of alcohol by Indians is seen to reflect a biological incapability of moderation, and the associated aggression, sexual promiscuity, and other behaviors make clear, in their view, that the Indians are simply not as advanced in civilization as the whites. Explanations of long years of economic deprivation are brushed aside with the statement that the Indians' recent affluence has made no noticeable difference in these regards. In fact, the run-down condition of many of the new Indian houses and cars, purchased with the recently obtained financial resources, is cited as further evidence of the general thesis. Common as such stereotyped attitudes are wherever groups are in a dominant-subordinate relationship, they serve little in the way of providing understanding or suggesting effective solutions within the community and tend, rather, to harden the ethnic divisions. Others among the Anglos show much deeper understanding of the problem. They emphasize, for example, the lack of an integrated family life among the Indians, and they point out that the Indians have been "doled to death."

Among some of the Indians, especially the leaders, however, there is the feeling that their problems are in some way the legacy of the past, of the Indians' generations of exploitation by the whites, and of the long years of dependency on the federal government, not only for subsistence but for decision-making and direction as well. When this legacy has been supervened, the problems currently so salient should, they feel, recede to the level which they occupy in other groups. And on this latter point, there is a quickness to note that the Anglos are themselves not without some measure of the very same problems, and probably more than is generally known, because the Anglos tend, unlike the Indians, to drink in private.

Against this background, it is worthwhile presenting some comparative ethnic data on selected aspects of deviance and alcohol use in order to provide a clearer picture of the obvious confronting problem for the re-search. The technical problems of the measurement of deviance and al-cohol use, and the analysis of more comprehensive behavior data, are presented later, in Chapters 7 and 8; the present purpose is simply to describe further the apparent ethnic topography of problem behavior.

The data shown in Table 1.1 refer to a stratified random sample of

TABLE 1.1
Ethnic Group Percentages for Various Measures of Deviance and Alcohol Use

Measure	Anglo ($N = 92$)*	Spanish ($N = 60$)*	Indian ($N = 66$)*
1. Those having any court convictions for other than motor vehicle violations in the past ten years.	1	12	54
2. Those having any self-report of "serious deviance" (for example, child neglect).	25	29	60
3. Those whose drinking is usually done in bars or cars.	16	17	46
4. Those who sometimes or often drink in the morning.	9	22	33
5. Those reporting having been drunk three or more times last year.	3	15	38
6. Those who report five or more occur-rences of drinking-related deviance (for example, fights while drinking).	14	15	53
7. Those whose over-all alcohol consump-tion pattern is describable as "usually heavy."	2	9	26
8. Those whose Quantity-Frequency index of alcohol intake is above the total group median.	34	50	74
9. Those who report problem and/or heavy drinking in home of orientation.	14	22	37

* All the drinking measures are based on *present drinkers only:* 64 out of 92 Anglos are present drinkers (70%); 46 out of 60 Spanish are present drinkers (77%); and 53 out of 66 Indians are present drinkers (80%). Note that the percentage which drinks in each ethnic group is not strikingly different.

the community adults, both male and female, and derive from either inter-view data or data based upon the examination of court records. The entire study for which this sample was drawn is described in detail in subsequent chapters.

The primary empirical fact with which these data from the community confront us is *the relative position of the three ethnic groups with respect to rates of behavior relevant to deviance.*[6] In Table 1.1, nine separate criteria or indexes of ethnic rates of deviance and alcohol use are presented. Although not all of these measures are independent of each other, and although they constitute only a selected set of available criteria, they are fair representatives of the total situation observable in the community.

The most striking fact is the relatively high position of the Indians on every criterion. While on measure 1, only 1 percent of the Anglos and 12 percent of the Spanish have records of at least one court conviction during the last ten years, fully 54 percent of the Indians do. These court record data are supported by measure 2, based on interview self-reports, which shows an Indian rate of "serious deviance" (for example, having had trouble with the law, or having been contacted by an agency for child neglect), more than twice as high as that of the other two ethnic groups.

Measures 3–9 take on greater meaning if it is kept in mind that the *proportion* of persons who represent present drinkers in each ethnic group is not very different (see footnote to Table 1.1). The measures show, without exception, the higher rate of excessive or deviance-prone use of alcohol by the Indians. The Indians do more of their drinking outside the home, that is, in bars or cars; they more often drink in the mornings; they were drunk more often during the previous year; they have more drinking-related incidents of deviance (such as getting into fights, or trouble with the law because of drinking); their drinking pattern is more often heavy; and their Quantity-Frequency index of alcohol intake is considerably higher. Other available data show that the Spanish, on the average, drink twice as much per unit of time as the Anglos, while the Indians drink, on the average, three times as much as the Spanish. That this use of alcohol is not just a recent occurrence can be seen in the fact that the Indians report more often coming from families of orientation where heavy or problem drinking was present (measure 9). Although these measures obviously vary in degree of refinement, their over-all import cannot be doubted.

The second most striking fact about these data is the consistently intermediate position of the Spanish. Worth noting also is the closer proximity of the Spanish to the Anglos rather than the Indians on most of the measures. It should be emphasized, finally, that there are large differences within groups and extremely wide ranges on nearly every measure. Sex differences on the measures are also ubiquitous, with males showing higher rates than females on all measures within all three ethnic groups.

---

[6] While these data refer to the adult population, the ethnic ordering of deviance and alcohol use holds also for the teen-age population, data for which will be presented later, when the study of the local high school is reported.

The foregoing data, while culled from our own subsequent findings, represent the situation in the community as it was roughly seen at the outset, the field situation to which our research was addressed. They point up very clearly the existence of two kinds of variation in rates of deviance and excessive alcohol use: the variation *between* ethnic groups and the variation *within* each ethnic group. The problem which the research effort faced, therefore, was to provide a social-psychological account of both kinds of variation and to secure empirical support for the validity of that account. How this was done is described in detail in the chapters which follow.

Unfortunately, neither the brief sketch of the locale nor the data just presented can fully animate the dimensions or the tenor of life in this small rural community. Such, however, was not our present objective. Our aim was, instead, to describe enough of the situation and the problem to illuminate our starting point. From here, the road we took was abstract, involving a search for theory and understanding which could eventually tell us something more than was apparent when we began.

REFERENCES

ALFRED, B. M. Demographic description of [the research community]. Tri-Ethnic Project Report, September 1962, mimeo.

JOHNSON, C. A study of modern southwestern Indian leadership. Unpublished doctoral dissertation, University of Colorado, 1963.

MEIER, H. C. Three ethnic groups in a southwestern community. Unpublished master's thesis, University of Colorado, 1955.

RENDON, G., JR. Voting behavior in a tri-ethnic community. Unpublished master's thesis, University of Colorado, 1962.

STEWART, O. C. [Indian tribe] adjustment to modern living. In S. Tax (Ed.), *Acculturation in the Americas*. Vol. 2. *Proceedings, Twenty-Ninth International Congress of Americanists*. Chicago: University of Chicago Press, 1952. Pp. 80–87.

PART TWO

The Theoretical Framework

CHAPTER TWO

The Concept of Deviance

In his instructive discussion of the variety of problems attending the study of deviant behavior, Albert Cohen warns that "a major task before us is to get rid of the notion, so pervasive in sociological thinking, that the deviant, the abnormal, the pathological, and, in general, the deplorable always come wrapped in a single package" (1959), p. 463). If anything, this is an understatement of the degree to which the term "deviant behavior" has acquired myriad and often conflicting connotations. Since deviant behavior is the concern of the present investigation, it is necessary to clarify our use of the term and to specify its properties and reference. The conceptual analysis in this chapter is aimed at this objective. An adequate discussion will require that a number of separate but related issues be addressed and that, ultimately, the interpretation of deviance relied upon in our research be presented.

DEVIANCE AS SOCIALLY DEFINED BEHAVIOR

It would seem useful to begin the discussion by citing several recent definitions of deviant behavior to see what form they take and whether general implications can be drawn from them. Cohen, in his discussion mentioned above, offers a definition of deviant behavior "as behavior which violates institutionalized expectations—that is, expectations which are shared and recognized as legitimate within a social system" (1959, p. 462). Merton states that deviant behavior "refers to conduct that departs significantly from the norms set for people in their social statuses. . . . Deviant behavior cannot be described in the abstract but must be related to the norms that are socially defined as appropriate and morally binding for people occupying various statuses" (1961, pp. 723–724). For Clinard, the term "deviant behavior" is reserved for "those situations in which behavior is in a disapproved direction [from norms], and of sufficient degree to exceed the tolerance limit of the community . . ."

(1963, p. 22). Finally, Erikson states that "deviance can be defined as conduct which is generally thought to require the attention of social control agencies—that is, conduct about which 'something should be done'" (1964, pp. 10–11).

The most salient point upon which these writers agree is that the locus of reference of the term "deviant" is not to something intrinsic to the behavior itself. Reference, instead, is always to a socially defined criterion of evaluation: shared expectations about what behavior is appropriate and what behavior fails to accord with the social norms regulating action in particular situations. This point, that deviance is not an intrinsic property of any behavior, has been emphasized by Sherif: "An item of behavior, taken in and by itself, cannot be labeled either conformity or deviation. There is no such thing as conforming or deviating behavior in the abstract" (1961, p. 159).

It follows from this, of course, that the very same behavior may or may not be regarded as deviant, depending upon its relation to the social norms which prevail at the time and place of its occurrence: drunkenness at a New Year's Eve party may be conforming, while drunkenness on the job may be defined as deviant; extramarital intercourse in contemporary American society departs from social norms regulating sexual behavior, but the same is not true among the Eskimos, where wife-sharing is part of hospitality; killing a stranger during peacetime is almost uniformly agreed to be deviant, whereas the same action in wartime brings acclaim.

While it is important to emphasize that deviance is not a property of the behavior per se, it is equally important to stress that the term "deviant" is used to characterize *behavior, not the actor* manifesting the behavior. All too often, the classificatory leap is made from the appraisal of certain actions as departing from social norms to the labeling of the actor as deviant. This has been most conspicuously the case where theories and concepts of psychopathology have been invoked to explain the occurrence of deviant behavior.

The assumption implicit in such reasoning has been that the presence of personality pathology provides the only sufficiently compelling explanation of why a person would fail to conform to normative expectations. Empirical evidence simply does not support this interpretation, however. It has not been shown that personality disturbance is either a necessary or a sufficient condition for the occurrence of behavior departing from social norms. The actual empirical state of affairs is summed up best by Cohen: "Much—probably most—deviant behavior is produced by clinically normal people" (1959, p. 463).

The shortcoming of an interpretation centering around psychopathology is that, in labeling the *actor* as deviant, it thereby prejudges the explanation of his behavior. It would seem much more useful, theoretically, to reserve the term deviant for describing behavior in relation to norms and then to seek an explanatory framework which can account for the occurrence of such behavior.[1]

To stress this point is certainly not to say that personality in general is irrelevant to deviant behavior, although it has sometimes seemed that the latter view is implied in certain sociological discussions. It should be clear that the dismissal of psychopathology as an explanation no more challenges the *general* relevance of personality factors than the dismissal of, say, poverty as an explanation of deviance challenges the *general* relevance of sociocultural factors. All behavior, deviant or not, can be construed as the outcome of the simultaneous operation of both personality and sociocultural determinants. The inadequacy of psychopathology as an explanation is not that it implicates personality, but that—as with poverty—it is a priori, nonanalytical, and not sufficiently general as an approach to explanation.

DEVIANCE AS DEPARTURE FROM SOCIAL NORMS

A second realm of consensus among the cited definitions is with respect to the fact that the norms invoked in classifying behavior as deviant are *social* in nature. That is, they refer to those shared expectations or standards of appropriateness upon which members of social groups can rely for the orderly regulation of social behavior. As symbolic aspects of the social environment, such norms have a public character and are broadly considered to require adherence; departure from them implies the consequence of some form or degree of social response.

The nature and variation of this social response will be discussed shortly; at this juncture, the aim in stressing the *social* reference of norms is to distinguish social norms from two other types of norms which could also be employed in classifying behavior as deviant: *legal* and *personal* norms. Legal norms are standards of appropriateness which have been codified in statutes and which define legally institutionalized consequences for their violation. While legal norms are obviously not discontinuous from social norms, it is evident that they refer only to some subset of all behaviors departing from social norms. The subset of behaviors usually

---

[1] In the reporting of results in later chapters, groups of subjects are established on the basis of certain criteria; one of the groups will be referred to as the deviant group. It should be understood that this use of the term "deviant" is elliptical for the characterization: "persons who have manifested certain behaviors, or a certain frequency or combinations of behaviors, which depart significantly from prevailing social norms." In accord with the preceding discussion, the focus of classification in our research is stringently maintained on *behavior* rather than on persons.

includes those which are the more extreme departures and which may involve injury to others or serious disruption of the social organization. Stated otherwise, social sanctions tend to apply to a much larger domain of behavior than do legal sanctions. It follows from this that to focus on legal norms in defining deviant behavior would be to restrict attention to no more than a portion of the problem. It would mean also that those extra-legal social processes regulating the larger domain of deviant behavior—the processes of informal social control, for example—would be ignored.

A reliance upon personal norms in defining deviance entails similar shortcomings. Although the day-to-day operations of the varied agencies of socialization do guarantee a fair degree of overlap between social norms and internalized personal norms, there are clearly cases in which disparities exist. For example, a person may impose upon himself far more stringent standards of behavior than would be socially expected, and then experience guilt over his failure to adhere to them. But such departure from personally held norms would not mobilize the social response which would seem to be part of the very meaning of deviant behavior. Contrariwise, where personal norms are lax, behavior cannot be said to depart from them; yet that same behavior may be seen by others as deviant and as justifying the mobilization of sanctions.

Obviously, there is much overlapping of social, legal, and personal norms. In light of the foregoing consideration, however, it would seem possible to deal with deviant behavior most comprehensively, with most consistency among individuals, and with the greatest relevance to operative social processes by focusing on social rather than on either legal or personal norms.

DEVIANCE AS BEHAVIOR IMPLICATING SOCIAL CONTROLS

There is a third major area of agreement in the definitions quoted at the beginning of this chapter, one which involves the *magnitude of departure* from normative standards implied by the concept of deviant behavior. Merton speaks of "conduct that departs significantly" and, a page later, refers to "substantial departures"; Clinard talks of departures "of sufficient degree to exceed the tolerance limit of the community"; and Erikson invokes the agencies of social control in describing deviant behavior as conduct about which "something should be done."

What is apparent in these statements is that it is neither sufficient nor useful to classify as deviant any and every behavior which departs from some expected standards. First of all, social norms do not usually specify only a particular behavior as acceptable. As Sherif has emphasized, "Norm-regulated behavior cannot be represented as a single point" (1961,

p. 180). Instead, "The norm allows for variations and for alternative actions, within certain bounds. Behavior falling within these bounds is within the 'latitude of acceptable behavior' " (Sherif and Sherif, 1964, p. 62). Thus, the problem of specifying behavior as norm departing is complicated by the fact that norms usually accommodate a *range* of behaviors as appropriate. The problem is further complicated by the fact that behaviors which are outside of this range, those which fall in what the Sherifs refer to as the "latitude of rejection," vary also in the magnitude of their distance from the latitude of acceptance.

This variation in normative specification has been caught up by Merton (1957, p. 133) in his differentiation of standards for behavior as prescribed, preferred, permitted, or proscribed. The first two categories would clearly fall within the range specified by the Sherifs as the latitude of acceptance; the third could represent either the least-accepted or the least-rejected behaviors; and the fourth clearly belongs to the latitude of rejection.

Given the range of variation in behavior usually accommodated by social norms, the identification of deviance as a departure from normative standards requires some criterion of magnitude of departure which locates it clearly outside of the latitude of acceptance and within the latitude of rejection. A useful criterion, specified most directly by Erikson, but also implied by both Clinard and Merton, is the degree to which the behavior is likely to evoke a corrective social response from others or to engage the attention or action of social control agencies. In short, the definition by others of the need for a corrective response, or the actual occurrence of social control responses, provides a means of specifying behavior which departs substantially enough from shared expectations of appropriateness to warrant the characterization of "deviant."

Such a social control perspective on the definition of deviant behavior insures that the behavior at issue will be of serious concern to society. It is in this sense that the concept of "deviance" merges with the concept of "social problem." Deviance, as we have defined it, fits well as an instance accommodated by a recent definition of social problems: "Social problems . . . are problems in the sense that they represent interruptions in the expected or desired scheme of things; violations of the right or proper, as a society defines these qualities; dislocations in the social patterns and relationships that a society cherishes" (Nisbet, 1961, p. 4).

In evolving a research definition of the concept of deviant behavior, we have considered several important issues thus far. Before continuing, it should be helpful to summarize their implications to this point. It has been emphasized that deviance is a term reserved for the characterization of behaviors rather than persons; at the same time, deviance is construed not as a property intrinsic to any behavior but as a characterization arrived at by reference to some outside standard of evaluation. Among the alternative possibilities for evaluative reference, the one which places behavior most clearly in the context of ordinary social interaction processes is the social, rather than the legal or personal, norm. Social norms, in practice, generally accommodate a range of behaviors as more or less appropriate, expected, or acceptable. Hence, an evaluation of behavior as deviant requires that it lie outside this range—that it represent a substantial departure from what is socially defined as appropriate. Departures of such magnitude are usually identifiable by the corrective or controlling social responses which they mobilize. In short, deviant behavior is socially defined as "a problem" by society as a whole or by those segments of society that confront it.

THE PROBLEM OF DEVIANCE AS A ROLE

With this much in mind, certain further distinctions become necessary. Although our own emphasis has been placed on deviant behavior rather than on deviant persons, a perhaps intermediate position is reflected in certain contemporary sociological writings. Consideration of this latter view will help further to delineate the conceptual boundaries of our own definition of deviance.

The intermediate position referred to has come out of recent sociological interest in societal reactions to deviant behavior, especially those processes by which society *comes to label as deviant* an actor who has manifested certain behavior. This "social processing" (Toby, 1962, p. 331), involving the application of social controls and including the social labeling of the actor as a deviant, may eventuate in the actor coming to define himself as *playing a deviant role*. Thus, "the criminal is a person who has come to think of himself as a thief or a hoodlum" (Toby, 1962, p. 331).

The distinction being emphasized has been made earlier by Lemert, who differentiates two types of deviation, primary and secondary. Primary deviation refers to deviant behavior which may have occurred for any of a variety of reasons but which, in its occurrence, does not entail for the actor any reorganization of his self-defined roles. The occurrence of primary deviation may result in certain societal reactions which in turn affect the actor. These societal reactions may be corrective and/or "labeling"; in either case, they tend to create problems for the actor. His response to the problems created by societal reaction to his primary deviation may involve further deviance. Lemert refers to this as secondary deviation. "In effect, the original causes of the deviation recede in importance or give way to the central importance of the disapproval and isolating reactions of the community" (Lemert, 1948, p. 28). It is secondary deviation which Lemert feels is peculiarly of interest to the sociologist: "From a narrower sociological viewpoint the deviations are not significant until they are organized subjectively and transformed into active roles and become the social criteria for assigning status" (Lemert, 1951, p. 75).

The importance of societal responses to deviance as a critical factor in either producing or maintaining deviant behavior has been stressed also by Cohen (1959) and by Becker (1964). In a paper by Kitsuse (1964), this recent concern with processes of social and self-definition of deviant roles is clearly represented. He uses in his analysis the example of the social interactions which lead to the social definition of a person as "a homosexual." Ray (1964), in the area of drug addiction, carries the point even further, arguing that the failure of significant others to validate the ex-addict's *new* role, abstainer, can actually contribute to a resumption of his old role: drug addict.

That deviant roles exist and are important in society can hardly be questioned. Their significance for understanding certain social processes of definition cannot be disputed; nor can their contribution to the organization and maintenance of certain forms of deviance. Nevertheless, approaching the study of deviance through a concentration on deviant roles involves a number of important limitations. The first of these stems from the obvious fact that not all deviance can reasonably be interpreted as role behavior. Much that is considered as deviant behavior—all the behavior, for example, which would be assigned to Lemert's category of primary deviation—occurs outside of any stable social or personal role and is neither organized nor defined in relation to such a role. As a matter of fact, such behavior usually occurs in conflict with the *conforming* roles which the actor is seen and sees himself as actually enacting. To the extent to which this is true, only a portion of the general domain of deviant behavior can be accounted for by the study of role-mediated deviance.

A second limitation arises because the very same behavior may or may not occur as part of a deviant role: it can be difficult determining which is actually the case in a particular instance. Thus, while theft as part of a gang, or illicit sexual intercourse by occupants of a house of prostitution, clearly imply deviant role behavior, the same activities by persons outside of such organizations need imply no role mediation at all. Further, as is implicit in Lemert's distinction between primary and secondary deviation, the very same behavior early in a given actor's history may not be role mediated while, later on, after social and personal processing, it may become so. In addition, deviant behaviors vary in their potential for generating role definition. Certain kinds of deviant behavior, such as persistent drug use, since they necessarily depend for their success upon adequate deviant role performance, generally tend to carry personal role definitions along with them; others, sexual promiscuity, or physical aggression, for example, tend not to. Issues such as these create serious problems in documenting the fact that particular deviant behaviors are actually components of established roles. The problems are exacerbated in ecological areas, such as rural settings, where institutionalized deviant role systems may be neither available, apparent, nor well organized.

A third limitation of taking a deviant role approach is that it does not account for the *initial* occurrence of deviant behavior. Lemert, it will be remembered, speaks of primary deviation as arising from a wide variety of causes, with the behaviors being definable "as adjuncts or accessories of socially acceptable roles," and as not producing "symbolic reorganization at the level of general role conception" (Lemert, 1948, p. 28). According to Lemert, it is only *after* its occurrence has led to certain societal reactions that deviant behavior tends to become part of a role—that secondary deviation develops. But the initial occurrence of deviance would seem to constitute in its own right an important subject for study, one which would be abandoned by a concentration on role-mediated or secondary deviance alone.

Finally, the emphasis upon deviant roles tends to obscure the facts that *conforming* behavior is also role-mediated and that social processing occurs to define and support the maintenance of conforming behavior also. Taking these facts into account, it becomes entirely reasonable, when deviance occurs, to focus upon the failure or inadequacy of *conforming* role mediation rather than having necessarily to invoke the additional concept of the development of a deviant role.

Considerations of the sort just discussed led us to approach deviance at the level of behavior itself. By taking behavior as the focus, the necessity of prejudging its etiology, either in relation to occupancy of a deviant role or, as rejected earlier, in relation to a deviant personality, is avoided. In attempting to explain its occurrence, deviant behavior can then be considered as any other class of behavior, including conforming behavior, would be. This point will be elaborated in the final section of the chapter, but at this juncture, one implication of this general position should be emphasized. It is a point made clearly by Albert Cohen: "A theory of deviant behavior not only must account for the occurrence of deviant behavior; it must also account for its failure to occur, or conformity" (1959, p. 463).

THE PROBLEM OF THE SOCIAL FUNCTIONS OF DEVIANCE

In approaching a definition of the concept of deviance, further difficulties have been encountered because of a frequent tendency to associate with it the connotation of something deplorable, morally bad, or socially dysfunctional. While it can be seen from our definition presented thus far that none of these connotations is in any way implied, that the term "deviance" can be employed as an entirely objective description of behavior divested of any morally evaluative implications, it is understandable how such unwarranted surplus meaning may have accrued in the past. The study of deviance has historically been connected with the study of social disorganization and social problems, and the latter studies have frequently dealt with their subject matter as being in need of amelioration. Also, the definition of deviance as behavior eliciting social control responses conveys clearly that *some* segment of society actually does consider the behavior to be inappropriate or wrong. The fact that this perspective need not characterize the behavioral scientist's view often tends, however, to be obscured.

With respect to moral judgments, it should be clear that these lie outside the domain of behavioral science. With respect to the issue of social dysfunction, something more needs to be said.

Merton's concern about the "frequently made assumption that nonconforming and other kinds of deviant behavior are necessarily dysfunctional to a social system and that social dysfunction, in turn, necessarily violates an ethical code" (1961, p. 736) leads him to emphasize the ethical neutrality of the concept of social dysfunction. He further emphasizes that, given the differentiated nature of contemporary society, what may be dysfunctional for one portion of society could well be functional for another. Without addressing the intricacies of the functionalist position in contemporary behavioral science, we may conclude that it is simply not defensible, a priori, to ascribe to deviant behavior consequences which are necessarily dysfunctional for society.

The indefensibility of such an a priori position emerges sharply from several recent discussions of deviance which, in seeking to right the balance, have stressed, instead, the latent *positive* functions of deviance for social structures. In an important paper, Dentler and Erikson (1959) survey some of the empirical evidence for the positive effects of deviance on group structures and functions. One of the propositions which they arrive at is that "deviant behavior functions in enduring groups to help maintain group equilibrium" (1959, p. 100). In a later paper, Coser (1962) cites a series of instances arguing for the same general proposition.

Perhaps the most compelling statement about the contribution of deviant behavior to the maintenance of an intact social order is that of Erikson (1964). His basic point is that "transactions taking place between deviant persons on the one side and agencies of control on the other are boundary-maintaining mechanisms [for the social system]" (1964, p. 13). The following quotation conveys the line of Erikson's reasoning:

> As a trespasser against the group norms, [the deviant] represents those forces which lie outside the group's boundaries: he informs us, as it were, what evil looks like, what shapes the devil can assume. And in doing so, he shows us the difference between

the inside of the group and the outside. It may well be that without this ongoing drama at the outer edges of group space, the community would have no inner sense of identity and cohesion, no sense of the contrasts which set it off as a special place in the larger world.

Thus deviance cannot be dismissed simply as behavior which disrupts stability in society, but may itself be, in controlled quantities, an important condition for *preserving* stability (1964, p. 15).

It would seem, from these commentaries, that the question of whether deviance is to be construed always and everywhere as a social evil does not have a simple answer. Clearly, some instances of the positive social functions of deviance can be identified—increasing group solidarity, defining the boundaries of normative systems, initiating social change. And where deviance does appear to be socially dysfunctional, it may be so only for some differentiated segment of the society, at some particular point in time, rather than for the society as a whole at all stages of its development. In view of these considerations, it would seem wise to define deviant behavior entirely independently of the question of its long-range positive or negative consequences for society. The latter can then become appropriate issues for empirical investigation rather than serving as initial defining criteria. In accord with this view, the concept of deviance which was employed in the present research, although identifying a class of behavior mobilizing social control responses, was, nevertheless, defined neutrally with respect to its ultimate social functions.

THE PROBLEM OF DEVIANCE AS "NORMATIVE" IN THE LOWER CLASS

One of the most recurrent and troublesome issues in approaching conceptual understanding of deviance remains to be addressed. This is the issue of whether what we have called deviant behavior can fairly uniformly be considered as deviant throughout American society, or whether such a characterization would vary sharply across different sectors of the society. Earlier it was stated that the characterization of behavior as deviant depends upon its substantial departure from socially defined norms operative in the situation, departure sufficient to mobilize social control actions. In simpler societies or in homogeneous groups, such a criterion presents few problems since normative standards tend in such circumstances to be quite pervasively shared. On the other hand, contemporary American society, like all industrialized societies, is highly differentiated and heterogeneous and is constituted of well-defined social strata, varying subcultures, and multiple reference groups. It is conceivable, therefore, that the norms regulating deviance are not widely shared under these conditions, that what is defined as deviant in one part of society is not in another, and, even, that there are behaviors which, though characterized as deviant in one sector, may actually represent *conformity* to the norms within a different sector.

This latter position, an expression, perhaps, of what might be called "sociological relativism," has been urged quite strongly in some of the literature on deviance. With respect to American society in particular, the position asserts that the values and norms of lower-class society, or of certain subcultures within it, are different from those of the middle class. Consequently, behavior which departs from middle-class norms may not only *not* be in opposition to but may actually be consonant with lower-class norms. In its extreme, this position would imply that "deviance" is *normative* in the lower class. Such an interpretation would, of course, be in agreement with the greater actual prevalence of deviance known to occur at that social location, and it gains, thereby, an initial degree of credence.

Perhaps the most explicit and forceful exposition of this point of view is that presented by the anthropologist Walter Miller (1958), although the "cultural transmission" approach to delinquency (Sutherland, 1955) and the "delinquent subculture" approach (Cohen, 1955) include somewhat similar implications. Miller's position is that there is a lower-class way of life, and that the lower class has evolved a distinctive cultural tradition of its own, with its own distinctive values and norms or, in his terms, its own characteristic "focal concerns." Differing from those of middle-class culture, the focal concerns of lower-class culture are said to have direct implications for deviance. According to Miller: "Following cultural practices which comprise essential elements of the total life pattern of lower-class culture *automatically* violates certain legal norms" (1958, p. 18, italics added). Further, he argues, the principal motivational support for the practice of illegal acts by members of lower-class corner groups, "as in the case of any persisting cultural tradition, derives from a positive effort to achieve what is valued within that tradition, and *to conform to its explicit and implicit norms*" (1958, p. 19, italics added).

The adoption of Miller's interpretation would have serious implications for any approach to a general theory of deviance. It would, for example, mean that deviance must be defined entirely in *local* terms; that various illegitimate or illegal acts could not usefully be characterized as deviant for members of the lower class since those acts would really represent conformity to prevailing norms; that a *general* theoretical account of such acts would be unattainable since separate accounts would have to be provided for lower-class and for middle-class persons; and that the relatively high prevalence of crime in the lower class would no longer be problematic; it would already be explained simply by reference to cultural tradition and normative adherence.

The tenability of this general position is open to serious question. First of all, the position is based upon the assumption of such a degree of cultural and normative insularity of social classes in contemporary American society as to require a sharp discontinuity between them. The sheer likelihood of such a state of affairs obtaining in the face of the mass communications networks, the homogenizing educational institutions, and the large amount of social and geographic mobility in modern industrialized society would seem small. Second, there is much available evidence of society-wide sharing of a variety of values relative to conformity, such as the generally held stigmatization of manual labor (Merton, 1957, p. 145), the pervasive importance of occupational achievement and education (Antonovsky and Lerner, 1959; Rosen, 1959), and the widespread placing of value on material success (Sherif and Sherif, 1964, p. 199). While this point will be elaborated in the next chapter in relation to Merton's anomie theory, its bearing here is that such evidence of widely shared values across social classes is hardly compatible with the sharp degree of cultural insularity and the associated discontinuity in regulatory norms posited by Miller's position.[2] Third, the fact of the matter is that many, perhaps most, members of lower-class corner group gangs ultimately abandon delinquent behavior upon the assumption of adult roles in marriage or work (see Karacki and Toby, 1962). In this same connection, Matza and Sykes refer to "the frequently observed 'reformation' of delinquents with the coming of adult status" (1961, pp. 717–718). Since such reformation takes place while the individuals remain *within* the lower-class culture, it is obviously insufficient to explain the earlier delinquency simply by its normative consonance with that general culture.

Thus far, only the general implausibility of a sharp discontinuity between middle- and lower-class culture has been argued. It is important, now, to consider more directly whether there actually is compelling empirical evidence for the existence of norms in direct support of deviance in lower-class culture, or even in delinquent subcultures. Sykes and Matza, in a persuasive paper, oppose "the theoretical viewpoint that sees juvenile delinquency as a form of behavior based on the values and norms of a deviant subculture in precisely the same way as law-abiding behavior is based on the values and norms of the larger society . . ." (1957,

[2] A different kind of emphasis upon the essential *continuity* between the middle and lower classes comes from Matza and Sykes (1961). They argue that the frequently cited values of the lower-class delinquent upon "kicks," excitement, and immediate gratification are merely extensions of existing counterparts in the leisure values of the middle class. The latter may be "subterranean," but they nevertheless exist side by side with the overt importance attached to hard work, postponement, and achievement. The Matza and Sykes' description of subterranean middle-class leisure values actually has much in common with the "focal concerns" which Miller employs to characterize lower-class culture as a way of life distinct from middle-class life.

p. 666). The delinquent, in their view, is by no means immune or indifferent to the expectations of the larger society and, in many ways, he appears to recognize the moral validity of these expectations. "The juvenile delinquent would appear to be at least partially committed to the dominant social order in that he frequently exhibits guilt or shame when he violates its proscriptions, accords approval to certain conforming figures, and distinguishes between appropriate and inappropriate targets for his deviance" (1957, p. 666). It is precisely because of this commitment to the dominant order that it becomes necessary for the delinquent to justify his delinquent actions to himself and to others, that is, to employ what these authors describe as "techniques of neutralization" for anticipated social disapproval.

With respect to the possibility of organized neighborhood normative support for delinquent behavior, Maccoby and her colleagues concluded that: "We did not find this to be the case; residents of the high delinquent area were just as quick as the residents of the 'low' area to tell us that minor vandalism and small thefts from stores, etc., were serious and should be dealt with severely." "The residents of a high-delinquency area appear to share the values of the larger society about the 'wrongness' and 'seriousness' of such activities as stealing, damaging property, juvenile drunkenness, etc." (1958, pp. 49–50).

It is possible to pursue this issue even further, to data obtained from deviant or delinquent youth themselves, data bearing directly on the question of whether they hold delinquent values or conform to deviant norms. In a recent study of seventh grade youths from four nonurban areas in Texas, the hypothesis that delinquency might simply be a function of a nondominant value orientation was investigated. Questionnaire data were obtained on the societal values held by the youth. These value data failed to predict either the occurrence or the severity of subsequent deviance among the youth, whose activities were followed over a period of five years. The authors (Kelly and Veldman, 1964), in accounting for this failure, speculate that deviants may actually maintain the *dominant* values, but simply not have sufficient impulse control to obtain their goals in a socially valued way.

Further pertinent data come from an important study by Sherif and Sherif (1964) investigating delinquent behavior among adolescents of differing social class, ethnic, and racial background in three large cities of the Southwest. Certain of their findings are of immediate relevance to the present issue. The data indicate that the youth, irrespective of their background or neighborhood, "showed their awareness of the value of education, and occupational choice, and the necessity of work to secure a good life" (p. 200). Beyond this evidence of the general acceptance of *dominant* cultural values, the data indicate also a widely shared appraisal of regulatory norms: "Students in all areas showed their knowledge

of 'right' from 'wrong' as defined by the law and in the school. . . .
[H]igh school students in different neighborhoods did not differ markedly
in *knowledge* of the limits of acceptable behavior and the points at which
deviation is subject to sanctions by adult authorities" (Sherif and Sherif,
1964, pp. 200–201).

Finally, reference should be made to a relatively unique approach to
research on the values of gang delinquents in Chicago. Data in this research were collected by means of a semantic differential procedure which
involved ratings of concepts or images representing the activities and orientations of the middle class, the lower class, and three kinds of delinquent
subcultures. Subjects were from the white and Negro middle and lower
classes and from gangs. Analyses of the data showed that: "All six populations evaluated images representing salient features of a middle-class style
of life equally highly. . . . In fact, the middle-class images were evaluated
significantly higher by every one of the populations than nearly all other
subcultural images, especially those that are unquestionably illegitimate"
(Gordon *et al.,* 1963, p. 117). In addition, when the various images
were rated along a "smart-sucker" dimension, the "smartness" ratings
of *middle-class* images were found to be higher than those for any other
subcultural images. This finding held for *all* six populations in the study.

In the preceding discussion, an attempt has been made to bring into
question the proposition that there is a sharp discontinuity between middle-
and lower-class culture in American society. A corollary of that proposition—that "deviance" can be construed as generally normative in the
lower class—is also rejected. What the arguments and the empirical evidence cited seem to support, instead, is the alternative view. Certain values,
those attaching importance to success and to its legitimate instrumentalities, for example, are apparently quite widely shared. Also widely shared
are regulatory norms—norms which determine what behaviors are to be
defined as deviant—especially where the behaviors concerned are departures sufficiently serious to implicate processes of social control. The latter
is the criterion we have employed in formulating our research definition
of deviance.[3]

The view that the norms of the lower class directly support deviance—
the view we have been unwilling to accept—may have part of its origin
in the failure to distinguish between *cultural norms about what behaviors*

[3] The position taken here should not be interpreted as asserting complete homogeneity throughout American society. Obviously, as our own findings will show,
there are substantial variations among social class and ethnic groups in numerous
sociological and psychological attributes and orientations. Some of these differences
even have to do with tolerance for deviance. Thus, the study by Gordon and
associates (1963), while showing quite general acceptance of middle-class prescriptive
norms, also indicated that tolerance of deviant behavior tended to be inversely

are expected or valued and the observed prevalence of occurrence of various behaviors. "This dual referent is particularly likely to be found in the work of anthropologists. . . . They draw less sharply the distinction between the statistically normal and the normative" (Yinger, 1960, p. 628). Essentially the same point is made by Gordon and his associates (1963) in considering their own finding that so-called middle-class values are indeed meaningful to members of lower-class gangs.

> The discrepancy between these findings and the values reported for lower-class culture . . . by Miller may be related to his anthropological methodology. The anthropologist often assesses values by inferring them from extended observation of a population's spontaneous behavior, including verbal behavior . . . the values of the populations studied can [therefore] never be reported as other than those implied by their behavior (1963, pp. 127–128).

The unfortunate consequence of such an approach is that it guarantees exceptionless agreement between behavior and norms and, therefore, makes the analysis of norms redundant in the explanation of social behavior. By failing to treat the relationship between norms and behavior as problematic, such an approach also minimizes the contribution to social behavior of determinants other than norms. These other determinants are precisely those which would need to be invoked to account for variation, even opposition, in the relationship between norms and behavior.

An issue such as this, the pervasiveness of values and norms, obviously depends for its ultimate resolution upon empirical evidence in given situations. We took the precaution in our own research of ascertaining the validity of our general position, and we were able to show that the behaviors employed as instances of deviance were, in fact, all seen as "wrong"—that is, as nonnormative, by all groups in the community.[4] Nevertheless, the arguments and research literature cited earlier were necessary for two reasons. The first of these is that it is still necessary in behavioral science research to defend against middle-class bias: the possibility that the theoretical position adopted simply reflects the ethnocentric distortions of middle-class investigators. The preceding discussion should have helped to make clear that both logical and empirical bases for our view exist.

---

related to social level. That such differences obtain in tolerance or acceptability of deviance does *not* mean, however, that deviant behavior is normative—our main point here. As will be shown in the theoretical analyses in later chapters, tolerance of deviance implicates a number of other social and personal processes rather than simply reflecting the content of prevailing norms.

[4] See Chapter 10 for further details regarding this point.

The second, and perhaps more important, reason is theoretical. In seeking a general explanation of deviance which obtains across a heterogeneous population, it is necessary that the definition of deviance be meaningful or appropriate for all sectors of the population sampled. If certain behaviors were to be seen as norm departing in one sector but as actually norm supporting in another, then the interpretation of the research as dealing with deviance would be jeopardized. The second reason, then, for the elaboration of the view that regulatory norms are rather widely shared is to support the interpretation of the present research as dealing with a phenomenon, deviance, which is similarly defined in varying social class and ethnic groups.

EXCESSIVE ALCOHOL USE AS DEVIANT BEHAVIOR

The general position that certain regulatory norms are quite widely shared and pervasively legitimated in contemporary American society seems fairly clear-cut when the area of legally sanctioned criminal or delinquent behavior is at issue. It is perhaps less obvious with respect to the area of morally or socially sanctioned deviance, behavior which, while considered socially inappropriate or illegitimate, is not necessarily illegal. Drinking behavior, a major empirical focus of the present research, apparently spans these two domains. Some uses of alcohol—drinking while driving, for example—are illegal; other uses—such as chronic drunkenness—are usually only illegitimate. Because of our interest in drinking, the relation of alcohol use to the concept of deviance requires special attention.

For most of the kinds of behavior we have been referring to thus far—theft, sexual assault, drug use, physical violence—sheer occurrence is amenable to characterization as deviant in nearly all circumstances. Drinking behavior, however, is so diverse as to defy such labeling unless further specified. The additional information generally required, having to do with such qualifications as age, sex, and religion of the drinker, time and place of the drinking, modes and amounts of alcohol consumed, and correlates and consequences of the drinking, testifies to the complexity and differentiation of norms surrounding the use of alcohol.

At one extreme in American society are the norms of certain fundamentalist religious groups and the American temperance movement which prescribe total and unqualified abstinence from alcohol. Ford (1960) reports that 76.3 percent of a sample of Southern Appalachian households, largely Southern Baptist and Methodist, considered drinking as "always wrong"; among the rural respondents, the percentage reached 87.8 percent. Most states attempt to enforce abstinence for the young through legal prohibition against alcohol sale or purchase where youth under certain age limits are involved. Maddox and McCall (1964) state that "both parental and public law typically support abstinence for the adolescent in principle. Teen-age drinking is deviant behavior in the sense that it is not preferred or encouraged" (p. 62).

That the existence of such legal norms does, in general, have an impact on youth has been shown in a number of studies of alcohol use among minors. Most recently, Campbell (1964) has reported that, of a sample of more than 1500 high school seniors in North Carolina, 91 percent report that both parents prefer that they not drink. The data of Maddox and McCall, collected in the high schools of a midwestern city, showed that: "Most of the teen-agers in this study expressed disapproval of drinking by individuals of their own age. Their disapproval is consistent both with their reported abstinence and with their perception that individuals like themselves are in the majority" (p. 74).

The presence in American society of such abstinence norms, among certain religious groups and for youth, is probably one reason for a much more pervasive ambivalence about alcohol use, even among adults, and even in situations where drinking is regularized, moderate, and overt (see Myerson, 1940). A discerning observer of such situations can hardly fail to note the attendant humor and the accompanying euphemisms ("medicine," "painkiller") which suggest some ambivalence or uneasiness about alcohol use or its latent consequences. In general, however, where drinking occurs and its use is institutionalized or ritualized, the regulatory norms have to do not with abstinence but with *moderation*.[5]

Interesting accounts of legitimized alcohol use, where the regulatory emphasis is upon moderation, are provided for the Cantonese in New York by Barnett (1955) and for the American Jew by Snyder (1958). In both cases, there are clear-cut norms regulating the immoderate use of alcohol and effective social controls to implement them. Snyder cites the widely known ditty, "Shikker iz a Goy," to point up the value placed by the Jews on sobriety and their identification of drunkenness as a characteristic of the Gentile outgroup. The emphasis upon moderation obtains also with respect to sex differences; it is most apparent that, throughout American society, moderation in alcohol use is particularly stressed for women, with more permissive limits considered appropriate for men.

There seem to be three main reasons for social concern about alcohol

[5]Again, the reference for this statement is American society in general. Anthropological studies have identified other cultures where drunkenness is not only not condemned but is positively sanctioned. Heath (1958) reports, for example, that among the Bolivian Camba during festive celebrations, "Drunkenness is consciously sought as an end in itself and consensus supports its value" (p. 445). See also Bunzel's description of the Mexican Chamula (1940) and Simmons' description of the Peruvian community of Lunahuaná (1960).

use as a source of problem behavior and for a regulatory norm of moderation. First, concern stems in part from what are widely thought to be intrinsic properties of alcohol as a drug, properties which ultimately eventuate in loss of self-control. The amount consumed and, perhaps, the rapidity of consumption are seen, therefore, to have, in themselves, potentially negative outcomes. Concern stems, second, from certain of the symbolic or cultural definitions attached to alcohol. Alcohol in various situations has come to signify permitted relaxation of social and personal controls—at social gatherings and on festive occasions, for example. Because of these symbolic definitions, alcohol in situations *not* considered appropriate, such as on dates between teen-agers, during arguments, or on the job, constitutes a potential threat to orderly social interaction and effective role performance. Third, the widely shared observations of an association between alcohol use and socially undesirable correlates and consequences generate social concern. Here the concern refers to the co-variation between alcohol use and other behaviors which are themselves negatively valued: crime, violence, sexual transgression, inability to perform important social roles—in marriage, parenthood, and work—and, ultimately, the relatively complete social and personal failure involved in alcoholism.[6]

The norm of moderation in alcohol use has reference to each of these sources of social concern. Moderation as a regulatory norm for adults has to do, therefore, with amount consumed, appropriateness of the circumstances of consumption, and the avoidance or minimization of the negative correlates and consequences of alcohol use. *It is in relation to this sort of complex criterion[7] that it becomes possible and useful to define certain modes and uses of alcohol as deviant behavior.* These uses would include excessive consumption, recurrent drunkenness, heavy drinking at home, drinking on the job, violence related to alcohol use, and failure at expected role performance, such as holding a job, or sustaining a marriage, due to drinking. It should be noted that these kinds of instances of alcohol

---

[6] Alcoholism as an entity was not a systematic concern of our research for several reasons. First, in a community the size of our research setting, the frequency of alcoholism in the population is too small to serve as an adequate research criterion. Second, the valid determination that a person is an alcoholic is complicated, especially in a context where heavy drinking and recurrent drunkenness are fairly widespread. Third, the largest share of the deviant use of alcohol takes place among those who are clearly not alcoholic in any strict sense of the word. Finally, our general approach to deviance sought to accommodate the deviant use of alcohol without the necessity of recourse to whatever might be the unique factors in the etiology of alcoholism as a particular syndrome. Stated otherwise, our framework sought an account of excessive alcohol use which would be continuous with the account of deviant behavior in general.

[7] For minors, age per se would also have to be included.

use meet the general criterion for defining deviance, that is, the mobilization of some sort of social control responses.[8]

THE THEORETICAL CONCEPTUALIZATION OF DEVIANCE

The discussion thus far has dealt with a variety of issues inevitably engaged in any effort to arrive at a useful research definition of deviance. The preceding analyses of normative reference, role implications, social functions, and the pervasiveness of normative consensus all bear on problems of determining under what circumstances behavior may be reliably and usefully characterized as deviant.

Throughout these considerations, the focus has consistently remained upon *behavior*. There are two main reasons for this in the present enterprise. First, it is the occurrence of deviant behavior which is the confronting problem for society; that is to say, it is behavior which constitutes the set of events that engenders social concern or social response. Thus, behavior is the level at which any satisfactory explanatory scheme must ultimately come to rest. Second, it is behavior which lies uniquely at the intersection of personal and social processes; since one of the major aims of the present research was the elaboration of a unified social-psychological scheme, maintaining the focus on behavior seemed a necessary instrumentality to accomplish that general purpose.

The approach to the explanation of behavior which was relied upon in this research, Rotter's social learning theory (1954), will be described in greater detail in Chapter 4. At this point, it suffices to say that, within this approach, the occurrence of any behavior is construed as the outcome of a selection, choice, or decision process. Alternative behaviors available in the actor's repertoire are "sifted" in order to determine which behavior has, for the person, the highest expectation of maximizing valued consequences in that particular situation. To account for the occurrence of any behavior, therefore, requires knowledge that it has been learned or

---

[8] Data collected in the research community corroborate the presence of a normative emphasis on moderation. Adult subjects were asked to rate the wrongness of various behavior items on a scale with a range of 0–9. The behaviors varied in degree of seriousness of their departure from social norms, including such diverse items as "driving over the speed limit" and "a married woman fooling around with other men." For all three ethnic groups, the items "a woman being a heavy drinker" and "a man being a heavy drinker" were rated near the "very wrong" end of the scale. For two of the ethnic groups, the only items in the list which were rated more severely had to do with marital infidelity; for one of the ethnic groups, a third item, "parents who don't stay home with their kids most of the time," also slightly surpassed the "heavy-drinker" items. In general, then, the immoderate use of alcohol—a man or a woman being a heavy drinker—was clearly considered as deviant by all ethnic groups in the community.

is available to the actor, knowledge of the expectations held by the actor that the behavior will lead to certain outcomes, knowledge of the value placed on those outcomes, and knowledge of the various outcomes which are potentially available in the particular situation. *Within this theoretical perspective, deviant behavior occurs when the expectation of its maximizing valued goal attainment or preferred outcomes is higher than that for conforming behavior.*

Since *all* learned behavior is considered to be goal directed or purposive, deviance and conformity are, in this respect, theoretically homogeneous. Special principles and special conditions, such as psychopathology, are no more required to account for deviance than to account for conformity. Stated otherwise, it becomes clear that, as Albert Cohen noted earlier, a theory of deviance is simultaneously a theory of conformity; an account of the occurrence of deviant behavior is, at the same time, an account of the failure of conforming behavior to occur, and vice versa. The problem for an explanation which adequately accounts for deviance is not, therefore, the postulation of unique behavioral principles or conditions. *It is, instead, the identification of those variables and processes in the person and the sociocultural situation which operate together to make the likelihood of occurrence of deviance greater than that for conformity.*

These variables and processes would be ones which affect: the learning or availability of deviant and conforming behavior in the actor's repertoire (for example, differential opportunity to observe the occurrence of such behavior); the expectations that deviant or conforming behavior will lead to certain outcomes (for example, differential success and failure experience with such behavior in the past); the value placed upon certain outcomes or occurrences (for example, differential parental emphasis upon school achievement and reward for successful school performance); and the availability of various outcomes or goals in specific situations (for example, differential access to legitimate occupational rewards).

Further, these variables and processes should be such as to provide a homogeneous account for three different aspects of the problem: 1) the circumstances under which a given individual will engage in deviant or conforming behavior; 2) the difference between individuals in the same situation, some of whom engage in deviance and others of whom conform; and 3) the distribution in society of deviant behavior, that is, the differential prevalence of deviance at different sociocultural locations. Such an account would, thereby, constitute a *general* theory of deviant behavior, one capable of dealing with intraindividual and interindividual differences in deviant behavior as well as with group differences in the rate of occurrence of deviant behavior.

The central theoretical assertion in the discussion of deviance as behavior is the statement that deviance, like other behavior, is goal directed:

it refers to behaviors which are learned ways of seeking gratification and success and of coping with frustration and failure. The centrality of the assertion derives from the fact that it contains the seeds of a general theory of deviance, one which will be elaborated in the next chapters. At this juncture, the main point of our conceptualization can be stated as follows: When conforming behavior fails to eventuate in important gratifications or consistently falls short of achieving the goals sought, alternative behaviors will be employed to achieve those goals or to adapt to the failure to achieve them; among these alternatives will be behaviors which, while technically effective in achieving those goals, can be socially defined as deviant.

This general point of view is entirely compatible with Merton's theory of social structure and anomie (1957). Bredemeier and Toby (1960) take the same general position: "When . . . feelings of satisfaction are not available through socially acceptable experiences, one may seek to obtain them through socially unacceptable experiences" (p. 10). And it is clearly the stance adopted by Cloward and Ohlin (1960) in their theory of delinquent gangs:

> Efforts to conform, to live up to social expectations, often entail profound strain and frustration. . . . Deviance ordinarily represents a search for solutions to problems of adjustment. . . . Deviance may be understood as an effort to resolve difficulties that sometimes result from conformity. . . . [The] search for solutions . . . may or may not turn out to be non-conforming or delinquent (pp. 38–39).[9]

This conceptualization of deviance as alternative behaviors oriented toward goal attainment, or as responses to or solutions for "problems of adjustment," carries no implication that the *gratifications* which are sought are in any way different, or unique, or themselves "deviant." There is an unfortunate tendency to imply a perverseness in the goals sought through the employment of deviant behaviors. Actually, in general, the opposite seems true. The satisfactions associated with deviance are hardly esoteric. They consist, for the most part, in those very goals or gratifica-

---

[9] The goal-directed nature of deviant behavior, despite its sometimes seemingly directionless appearance, is nicely stated in the following quotation by these authors: "[D]eviance is not purposeless, although it may be random and disorganized. It may not result in a successful solution (in fact, deviant solutions may even bring on additional and more serious problems of adjustment), but action need not be rational in order to be purposeful. The person who gropes blindly for a way of resolving a problem of adjustment is engaging in purposeful action even if the solutions he reaches are senseless and self-defeating" (Cloward and Ohlin, 1960, pp. 38–39).

tions generally emphasized by the culture, characteristic of the socially defined and socially learned "good things in life," and associated with widely shared interpretations of the meaning of success, whether the latter refers to life as a whole or to specific areas of personal and interpersonal performance.

DEVIANT BEHAVIOR AS AN EFFECTIVE MEANS OF GOAL ATTAINMENT

That deviance can be technically effective as a means to widely sought goal attainment is hardly to be questioned. The rewards of much of deviant behavior are quite apparent: sexual gratification, financial gain, power, status, and prestige—in short, the whole range of socially and psychologically defined valued outcomes. This range includes, of course, the valued outcomes of avoiding or suppressing unpleasant states such as fears, worries, anxieties, or feelings of frustration—consequences uniquely associated, for example, with the deviant use of alcohol or drugs.

In this consideration of the effectiveness of deviance in achieving goals, it is useful to distinguish the rewards of deviance which are direct consequences of the deviant activities from those which derive from the symbolic implications of engaging in such activities. This distinction can be seen especially clearly with respect to such deviant behavior as drug use and excessive alcohol use. With respect to the direct outcomes of drug use, it has been pointed out (Leighton, Clausen, and Wilson, 1957) that drugs "may afford release of tension and help create a world in which pressing mundane concerns are of little import. . . . [P]erception may be sharpened so that life seems richer and fuller. . . . Fears of several types . . . may be reduced . . ." (p. 273). In contrast to these direct, physiologically mediated outcomes of drug use are those valued outcomes which are symbolically mediated. Thus, these same writers emphasize that: "When taken in small groups or gangs, drugs may enhance for the individual his sense of group membership, *as much by the shared act of use* as by the intrinsic effects of the drug" (p. 274, italics added).

The literature on alcohol use has been especially explicit on the symbolic mediation of valued outcomes of drinking. Washburne (1956) has emphasized that alcohol can function as a cue for a new social situation in which people define each other differently and in which the individual may not be held responsible for certain aspects of normative adherence. The same reasoning is followed by MacAndrew and Garfinkel (1962):

'Being drunk' may be construed as a state of being-in-the-world to which society grants a provisional relaxation of the individual's institutionalized obligations, and particularly of the demand of accountability which is ordinarily required as a condition of accredited membership in the collectivity and of sanctioned competence (p. 264).

With respect to teen-age use of alcohol, Maddox and McCall (1964) describe the symbolic meanings of alcohol use as including: status transformation; group identification; and, as Washburne and as MacAndrew and Garfinkel have also emphasized, the legitimation of unconventional behavior. Among their subjects: "Alcohol is perceived to be related to the achievement of personally or socially desirable goals" (p. 93). Lemert contributes another aspect of the symbolic use of alcohol in his observation that for the Northwest Coast Indians drinking is "an act of aggression against white authority" (1954, p. 336).

DEVIANCE AS IMPLYING THE FAILURE OF CONFORMITY

The obvious fact that deviant behaviors often constitute technically effective means for achieving valued social and personal goals is, of course, insufficient in itself to account for their occurrence. For while they may be successful in attaining certain goals, they are also, by definition, socially unacceptable and, therefore, sooner or later liable to the negative consequences of guilt, censure, or punishment for the actor. In contrast, conforming behaviors which are technically effective in achieving valued goals are not subject to such negative consequences. On balance, then, for most socialized members of society, conformity should prevail over deviance. It is here, however, that a basic guiding premise of the present research must be invoked. That premise, elaborated in the following chapter, is that conforming behavior is simply not always successful for achieving certain valued goals; and this is especially the case for persons who occupy disadvantaged social locations.

It is this "failure of conformity" which creates the sufficient conditions for engagement in deviance, despite the probable negative sanctions associated with the occurrence of the latter. It is the failure of conformity which creates the "problems of adjustment" or the frustration to which deviance can be construed as an emergent alternative response. Whatever other explanatory interpretations may apply—and deviance, admittedly extraordinarily complex, is not easily explained—our basic proposition is that *much of deviance can be interpreted as a response to the failure of conformity*. This proposition can be stated in more systematic terms. When the expectation that conforming behavior will maximize valued goal attainment becomes low (as a consequence, for example, of a history of failure experiences), *relative to* the expectation that deviant behavior will maximize valued goal attainment, it is under these theoretical circumstances that deviance should occur.

DEVIANCE AS A CATEGORY-TERM

One final point needs to be made before concluding the discussion about the concept of deviance. As used in the present analysis, "deviance" is clearly a category-term, a term for a *class* of behavior. The class is composed of behavioral instances of widely varying form and character, all socially defined as significant departures from shared social norms and considered to have the common function of serving as alternative modes of achieving valued goals when legitimate behavior has not been successful. Which *particular* deviant alternative may be employed in a given situation will, of course, depend upon past learning and the nature of the present situation. Just as with conforming behavior, however, it is assumed that there have usually been learned multiple and mutually substitutable deviant behaviors for achieving particular goals in particular situations. Thus, prestige, which may be out of legitimate reach, can be attained through physical violence, through theft, through excessive alcohol use, or through vandalism. These deviant actions are, in this sense, functionally substitutable for each other.

The intent of this latter discussion is to clarify the aim of our research, the objective of which was to provide an account for the occurrence of deviance *as a category or a class*. Although the importance of explaining the occurrence of particular instances of deviant behavior cannot be minimized, it would seem to be a later step in the evolution of theory. The initial task to which our efforts were directed was, therefore, the explanation of the occurrence of *any* instance of the class of deviant behaviors. It is because of this objective that deviance should be understood as a category-term in our usage.[10]

SUMMARY

The aim, in this chapter, has been to develop an understanding of the concept of deviance employed in the research. A number of different issues have been addressed in the hope of divesting the term of unwanted connotations and limiting its reference to what is empirically manageable. It was emphasized that deviance is not an intrinsic attribute of any behavior but involves, rather, a social evaluation of behavior from the point of view of prevailing norms. The evaluation is of behavior, not of persons or roles. Behavior, to merit the characterization of "deviant," must depart substantially from normative standards; the departure must be of sufficient

---

[10] It follows that conformity was also treated as a class or category-term. In the absence of deviance, conformity is understood to obtain. What *particular* conforming behavior obtains was not a research concern; it was the presence or absence of the *class* of conforming responses which was of theoretical interest.

magnitude to mobilize social control responses. Such behavior, it was argued, is quite pervasively viewed as deviant throughout American society, and the notion that deviance is normative in the lower class was rejected.

As behavior, deviance is not considered to require special principles to account for its occurrence. As with any other goal-directed behavior, its occurrence depends, theoretically, upon its likelihood of maximizing valued goal attainment *relative to* the likelihood for other behavior—in this case, conforming behavior. That deviant behavior can be technically effective in achieving widely shared goals was discussed. That it should occur despite the probability of negative personal and social consequences was made contingent upon the fact that conforming behavior is often unsuccessful in achieving goals in contemporary American society, especially for the socially disadvantaged.

The problem for theory, then, is to identify and to specify the interrelations among the set of personal and social variables which should have an influence upon the relative likelihood of occurrence of these two classes of behavior: deviance and conformity. It is to this task that the following three chapters are addressed. In this effort, the articulation and interrelation of psychological and sociocultural variables in general should gain illumination.

REFERENCES

ANTONOVSKY, A. AND M. J. LERNER. Occupational aspirations of lower class Negro and white youth. *Social Problems,* 1959, *7,* 133–138.

BARNETT, M. Alcoholism in the Cantonese of New York City: An anthropological study. In O. Diethelm (Ed.) *Etiology of chronic alcoholism.* Springfield, Ill.: Charles C Thomas, 1955. Pp. 179–227.

BECKER, H. S. Introduction. In H. S. Becker (Ed.) *The other side: Perspectives on deviance.* New York: Free Press, 1964. Pp. 1–6.

BREDEMEIER, H. C. AND J. TOBY. *Social problems in America.* New York: Wiley, 1960.

BUNZEL, R. The role of alcoholism in two Central American cultures. *Psychiatry,* 1940, *3,* 361–387.

CAMPBELL, E. Q. The internalization of moral norms. *Sociometry,* 1964, *27,* 391–412.

CLINARD, M. B. *Sociology of deviant behavior.* (Rev. ed.) New York: Holt, Rinehart and Winston, 1963.

CLOWARD, R. A. AND L. E. OHLIN. *Delinquency and opportunity.* New York: Free Press, 1960.

COHEN, A. K. *Delinquent boys: The culture of the gang.* New York: Free Press, 1955.

COHEN, A. K. The study of social disorganization and deviant behavior. In R. K. Merton, L. Broom, and L. S. Cottrell, Jr. (Eds.) *Sociology today: Problems and prospects.* New York: Basic Books, 1959. Pp. 461–484.

COSER, L. A. Some functions of deviant behavior and normative flexibility. *American Journal of Sociology,* 1962, *68,* 172–181.

DENTLER, R. A. AND K. T. ERIKSON. The functions of deviance in groups. *Social Problems,* 1959, *7,* 98–107.

ERIKSON, K. T. Notes on the sociology of deviance. In H. S. Becker (Ed.) *The other side: Perspectives on deviance.* New York: Free Press, 1964. Pp. 9–21.

FORD, T. R. Status, residence, and fundamentalist religious beliefs in the Southern Appalachians. *Social Forces,* 1960, *39,* 41–49.

GORDON, R. A., J. F. SHORT, JR., D. S. CARTWRIGHT, AND F. L. STRODTBECK. Values and gang delinquency: A study of street-corner groups. *American Journal of Sociology,* 1963, *69,* 109–128.

HEATH, D. B. Drinking patterns of the Bolivian Camba. *Quarterly Journal of Studies on Alcohol,* 1958, *19,* 491–508.

KARACKI, L. AND J. TOBY. The uncommitted adolescent: Candidate for gang socialization. *Sociological Inquiry,* 1962, *32,* 203–215.

KELLY, F. J. AND D. J. VELDMAN. Delinquency and school dropout behavior as a function of impulsivity and nondominant values. *Journal of Abnormal and Social Psychology,* 1964, *69,* 190–194.

KITSUSE, J. I. Societal reaction to deviant behavior: Problems of theory and method. In H. S. Becker (Ed.) *The other side: Perspectives on deviance.* New York: Free Press, 1964. Pp. 87–102.

LEIGHTON, A. H., J. A. CLAUSEN, AND R. M. WILSON. (Eds.) *Explorations in social psychiatry.* New York: Basic Books, 1957.

LEMERT, E. M. Some aspects of a general theory of sociopathic behavior. *Proceedings of Meetings of Pacific Sociological Society, State College of Washington,* 1948, *16,* 23–29.

LEMERT, E. M. *Social pathology.* New York: McGraw-Hill, 1951.

LEMERT, E. M. Alcohol and the Northwest Coast Indians. *University of California Publications in Culture and Society,* 1954, 2, No. 6, 303–406.

MACANDREW, C. AND H. GARFINKEL. A consideration of changes attributed to intoxication as common-sense reasons for getting drunk. *Quarterly Journal of Studies on Alcohol,* 1962, *23,* 252–266.

MACCOBY, ELEANOR E., J. P. JOHNSON, AND R. M. CHURCH. Community integration and the social control of juvenile delinquency. *Journal of Social Issues,* 1958, *14,* 38–51.

MADDOX, G. L. AND B. C. MCCALL. *Drinking among teenagers.* New Brunswick, N.J.: Rutgers Center of Alcohol Studies, 1964.

MATZA, D. AND G. M. SYKES. Delinquency and subterranean values. *American Sociological Review,* 1961, *26,* 712–719.

MERTON, R. K. *Social theory and social structure.* (Rev. ed.) New York: Free Press, 1957.

MERTON, R. K. Social problems and sociological theory. In R. K. Merton and R. A. Nisbet (Eds.) *Contemporary social problems.* New York: Harcourt, Brace & World, 1961. Pp. 697–737.

MILLER, W. B. Lower class culture as a generating milieu of gang delinquency. *Journal of Social Issues,* 1958, *14,* 5–19.

MYERSON, A. Alcohol: A study of social ambivalence. *Quarterly Journal of Studies on Alcohol,* 1940, *1,* 13–20.

NISBET, R. A. The study of social problems. In R. K. Merton and R. A. Nisbet (Eds.) *Contemporary social problems.* New York: Harcourt, Brace & World, 1961. Pp. 3–18.

RAY, M. B. The cycle of abstinence and relapse among heroin addicts. In H. S. Becker (Ed.) *The other side: Perspectives on deviance.* New York: Free Press, 1964. Pp. 163–177.

ROSEN, B. C. Race, ethnicity, and the achievement syndrome. *American Sociological Review,* 1959, *24,* 47–60.

ROTTER, J. B. *Social learning and clinical psychology.* Englewood Cliffs, N.J.: Prentice-Hall, 1954.

SHERIF, M. Conformity-deviation, norms, and group relations. In I. A. Berg and B. M. Bass (Eds.) *Conformity and deviation.* New York: Harper & Row, 1961. Pp. 159–198.

SHERIF, M. AND CAROLYN W. SHERIF. *Reference groups: Exploration into conformity and deviation of adolescents.* New York: Harper & Row, 1964.

SIMMONS, O. G. Ambivalence and the learning of drinking behavior in a Peruvian community. *American Anthropologist,* 1960, *62,* 1018–1027.

SNYDER, C. L. *Alcohol and the Jews: A cultural study of drinking and sobriety.* New Brunswick, N.J.: Rutgers Center of Alcohol Studies, 1958.

SUTHERLAND, E. H. AND D. R. CRESSEY. *Principles of criminology.* (5th ed.) New York: Lippincott, 1955.

SYKES, G. M. AND D. MATZA. Techniques of neutralization. *American Sociological Review,* 1957, *22,* 664–670.

TOBY, J. Criminal motivation. *British Journal of Criminology,* 1962, April Issue, 317–336.

WASHBURNE, C. Alcohol, self and the group. *Quarterly Journal of Studies on Alcohol,* 1956, *17,* 108–123.

YINGER, J. M. Contraculture and subculture. *American Sociological Review,* 1960, *25,* 625–635.

CHAPTER THREE

The Sociocultural System and Deviance

A GENERAL PERSPECTIVE

Despite much discussion about the significance of interdisciplinary work during the last two decades, no general paradigm for behavioral science research has emerged.[1] Even when such socially significant behavior as mental illness or delinquency has been investigated, the research tends to bear the traditional stamp of the disciplines involved. In anthropology and sociology, the conceptual focus is on the sociocultural system. The traditional research paradigm of these disciplines involves the establishment of relationships between aspects of the sociocultural system and the prevalence or rate of occurrence of some aspect of behavior. In psychology, the conceptual focus is on the individual, and the traditional research paradigm of this discipline seeks relationships between the personality system and some aspect of behavior.

Certain advantages of maintaining a strict disciplinary focus are obvious. Communication among members of the profession is generally facilitated. The possibility of carrying on research which is *systematic* is greater since it has primarily been within, rather than between, disciplines that conceptual elaboration has occurred and that linkages between concepts have been established. Finally, it can reasonably be argued, the development of the discipline is more rapidly promoted by remaining entirely within its conceptual perimeter.[2]

---

[1] For examples of interdisciplinary *conceptual* efforts or discussions in the behavioral sciences, see Parsons and Shils (Eds.), *Toward a general theory of action* (1951), and Gillin (Ed.), *For a science of social man* (1954). Interdisciplinary *research* efforts, however, have usually merely aggregated concepts from the separate disciplines, for example, Hollingshead and Redlich, *Social class and mental illness* (1958).

[2] This latter point has not gone unchallenged, however, as can be seen in the following reminder by a sociologist to his colleagues: "The study of social systems

Although the division of labor represented by the existing social science disciplines has obviously been empirically fruitful, the scope and detail of *explanation* of social behavior has been limited by the corresponding limitations of the separate traditional paradigms. Thus, the sociocultural approach alone provides little understanding of the structures and processes which mediate between a state of society and the occurrence of behavior. What, for example, are the intervening steps between growing up in an urban slum and becoming a delinquent boy? Neither does it account for the individual differences that inevitably obtain in any relationship between society or culture, on the one hand, and behavior, on the other. Why do some boys raised in urban slums become delinquent while others do not? The purely psychological approach, in its turn, fails to provide an account for the location and distribution in society of certain kinds of personality systems. Why, for example, may alienation be more prevalent among lower-class than among middle-class adults? A further explanatory limitation derives from the fact that similar constellations of personality attributes may result in different behavior under different circumstances or at different times. Why do strong needs for peer recognition lead some youngsters to commit crimes while others go out for football? The problem here, as Yinger (1963) has emphasized, is that every behavior is simultaneously personal and situational; a full account of it cannot be achieved without analytic attention to the context of its occurrence.

It can be seen that these respective limitations refer to gaps in the causal chain and reflect the restricted scope of the particular explanatory network within which social behavior is embedded by the separate disciplines. An analysis of the character of these limitations makes clear, however, that the traditional paradigms are, in fact, *logically* complementary. The boundary conditions or the "givens" of each are actually the conceptual focus of the other. More exhaustive explanation becomes possible, therefore, by the development of a more inclusive paradigm, one which can encompass the separate conceptual foci of the sociocultural and psychological approaches and can integrate them into a single and logically coherent system. Such a synthetic framework, joining and articulating concepts from the separate disciplines, should enable the behavioral scientist to traverse a relatively unbroken path among the various concepts, and between them and the data of social behavior. The development of this

---

can often be made much more incisive if one element in the analysis is a psychological theory, that is, a theory of the person as a system. . . . To estimate the influence of one aspect of social structure on another one must, therefore, consider the role of the personality system as the main intervening variable" (Inkeles, 1963, p. 320).

kind of framework was a major aim of our work, and it is this to which the term "social-psychological" refers in the present book.

Social scientists seem increasingly to be accepting this general viewpoint. Kurt Lewin's elaboration of the field theory position in social science (Lewin, 1951) provided the early impetus in this direction. More recently, one can find expression of it in such remarks as the following:

> A full understanding of any social situation and its probable conse-
> quences . . . assumes a knowledge not only of the main facts
> about the structure . . . but also of the main facts about the
> personalities operating in that structure. What is required, there-
> fore, is an integration or coordination of two basic sets of data
> in a larger explanatory scheme . . . (Inkeles, 1959, p. 273).

Closer to our own concern with deviance, the criminologist Cressey has espoused a similar view, pointing out that any theory of social behavior must have two distinct but consistent aspects.

> First, there must be a statement that explains the statistical dis-
> tribution of the behavior in time and space (epidemiology), and
> from which predictive statements . . . can be derived. Second,
> there must be a statement that identifies . . . the process by
> which individuals come to exhibit the behavior in question, and
> from which can be derived predictive statements about the behav-
> ior of individuals (Cressey, 1960, p. 47).[3]

The promise of such an orientation for more comprehensive explanation is unlikely to be realized, however, through the arbitrary aggregation of variables from the several behavioral science disciplines. The variables selected should meet certain logical requirements if a unified, coherent, and systematic framework is ultimately to be achieved. The most general logical requirement is that the concepts, rather than constituting sheer description of self-evident, surface characteristics, should be of sufficient abstractness to be able to reveal certain essential properties or underlying dynamics of social behavior. Low-order, descriptive concepts as used in much of psychiatric nosology, terms such as "juvenile delinquency," concepts such as "broken home," preclude, by virtue of their local and surface character, generalizations of any scope.

A second logical requirement is that the concepts selected from each

---

[3] In a book which appeared after this chapter was written, Yinger presents an excellent elaboration of the field theory perspective in behavioral science and applies this perspective to the analysis of several areas of social behavior. See J. M. Yinger, *Toward a field theory of behavior: Personality and social structure.* New York: McGraw-Hill, 1965.

discipline should suggest or carry implications for concepts in the other disciplines. Thus, with respect to selecting appropriate personality concepts, the possibilities for coordinating them with sociocultural variables becomes of crucial concern. On this point, Child, in discussing relationships between the fields of personality, sociology, and anthropology, has stated: "Relevance to social variations may usefully serve as one criterion for the importance of any dimension of personality. . . . For limited purposes, it might be the most significant one" (1963, p. 268). It is largely due to inadequacy on this ground, for example, that the depth concepts of psychoanalysis, so remote from relevance to social variation, have thus far made only a limited contribution to a useful social psychology.

A third logical requirement is that the concept should have some clear-cut implication for specified behavior since it is only through its own linkage with behavior that it can illuminate the process by which concepts in the other discipline can, in turn, be related to behavior. The deficiency, in this regard, of the personality concepts of Rorschach psychology was at least in part responsible for some of the disappointments of the early culture-personality efforts which relied so heavily upon that instrument.

Fulfillment of these requirements for useful concept formulation should logically eventuate in separate *systems* of abstract concepts from each discipline, each system implying or reflecting the other, and each coordinated with behavior. To the extent that this is true, there should obtain between the personality system and the sociocultural system a formal or structural identity which provides the basis for their systematic or conceptual coordination.[4] This position is similar to that expressed by Levi-Strauss in his analysis of social structure:

> The essential value of these studies [of structure] is to construct models the formal properties of which can be compared with, and explained by, the same properties as in models corresponding to other strategic levels. . . . Their ultimate end is to override traditional boundaries between different disciplines and to promote a true interdisciplinary approach (1953, p. 529).

In such an approach, it is clearly no longer the case that variables are chosen for interdisciplinary study because they are modish—"social class," for example—or, as is the case with "size of household," because they happen to be conveniently available in census data; or because there are in existence tests to measure them, as with "anxiety." Variables or

---

[4] A general position related to this is advanced by Inkeles and Levinson. See their paper "The personal system and the sociocultural system in large-scale organizations," *Sociometry*, 1963, *26*, 217–229.

concepts from anthropology, sociology, and psychology are selected—or invented—because they can contribute to *systems which can be linked logically* and which can, thereby, expand the scope and detail of the explanatory account.

It was with this general perspective in mind that we undertook the delineation of a social-psychological framework for investigating deviant behavior. In this chapter we will present the concepts and the structure of the sociocultural system and describe its linkage to deviance. This will be followed, in the next chapter, by a discussion of the concepts and structure of the personality system and its linkage to deviance; finally, in Chapter 5, there will be a presentation of a socialization scheme connecting the two systems. At that point, the entire social-psychological theory of deviance will have been described, and it will then be possible to assess the degree to which we have been able to fulfill the requirements of this general perspective.

THE SOCIOCULTURAL SYSTEM

Although we have developed our own scheme for presenting the analytic structure of the sociocultural environment, it will be apparent to the reader that our indebtedness to Robert K. Merton for his theory of anomie (1957, Chapters 4 and 5), and to Cloward (1959) and Cloward and Ohlin (1960) for their theory of differential opportunity systems is far-reaching. Both approaches have sought to provide an account of deviance as a *socially induced* phenomenon, thereby accounting for the differential distribution of deviance rates in society. We have also been influenced by a related approach, that of Alexander H. Leighton and his colleagues (1959, especially Chapters 8 and 9; Hughes *et al.,* 1960; D. C. Leighton *et al.,* 1963), which has relied upon a theory of sociocultural disintegration. This theoretically oriented, epidemiological work—while from a somewhat different tradition, and though concerned with a different problem area: the prevalence of psychiatric disorder—has underlying commonalities with Merton's anomie orientation and its extension by Cloward and Ohlin.

The sociocultural system can usefully be differentiated into three substructures: the opportunity structure, the normative structure, and the social control structure. Each person is considered to occupy, simultaneously, positions within each of these substructures and, depending upon the intersection of his three locations in this social space, to be more or less likely to engage in deviant behavior.

These three structures will be discussed in turn, the concepts included in each structure will be presented, and their relationship to other concepts and to deviance will be described. A diagram of the entire sociocultural system and of its relation to deviance will conclude this chapter and will serve as a schematic summary of the discussion.

The Opportunity Structure

The crucial importance of the opportunity structure in relation to deviance is that it can provide the basis for a dynamic—for a source of pressure, or for an instigation toward the adoption of illegitimate means. How this comes about will be elaborated in this section.

By the term "opportunity structure" is meant that set of socially structured and institutionally legitimate channels of access to the achievement of goals emphasized or valued by the American culture. Location in the opportunity structure, therefore, identifies a person or group with respect to *degree of access to culturally valued goals* presently obtaining and/or likely to obtain in the future. The general importance of this aspect of the social environment is conveyed in Max Weber's concept of objective "life-chances" and is forcefully stressed by Nadel's emphasis, in his penetrating analysis of social structure, on degree of command over existing benefits and resources. The latter phrase is meant to indicate control over "both gratifications current and favored in a society and the instrumentalities for their attainment" (Nadel, 1957, p. 117). The notion of position or relative access in the opportunity structure is also, of course, a large part of the conceptual content of the term "social class" as it is employed in contemporary sociology (see Hollingshead and Redlich, 1958).

In his analysis of a prominent facet of American culture, Merton documents the overwhelming emphasis placed on success or achievement values as well as the fact that these values are frequently interpreted in terms of wealth, monetary gain, and material possessions. The notion of the Protestant ethic, with its stress upon the moral obligation to work hard in the pursuit of success, illuminates this emphasis, and its implications are recurrently presented in the educational system, in literature, and through the mass media. Not only is success (especially in terms of wealth) asserted as a dominant goal of American social life but—and this becomes of critical importance—striving for success is enjoined upon *all* members of the society. It "is regarded as appropriate for everyone, irrespective of his initial lot or station in life" (Merton, 1957, p. 167). Examples of the existential possibility of achieving success, despite the humblest of origins or the severest of obstacles, are reiterated in American history and have become an integral part of American folklore, as can be seen in the influence and tenacity of the Horatio Alger myth (see Wohl, 1953).

As Merton points out, however, the institutionalized channels of access for achieving these goals, pervasively emphasized by the culture, are, in actuality, not uniformly distributed throughout society; the lower social strata and certain subgroups, notably racial and ethnic minorities, represent disadvantaged locations with respect to opportunity. It is this malintegration between the pervasive value emphases of the culture and the socially structured limitations on legitimate access to these values which generates pressure toward deviance—that is, pressure toward adopting alternative, even if illegitimate, means to achieve success or to cope with failure. In Merton's terms: "It is the *disjunction* between culturally induced high aspirations and socially structured obstacles to realization of these aspirations which is held to exert distinct pressure for deviant behavior" (1957, p. 174). Pressure is greatest where access to legitimate means to success is most limited, that is, where the disjunction between values and access is greatest. The concentration of deviance rates in the lower socioeconomic strata and among marginal ethnic and racial groups is partly explained, then, in these terms.

The foregoing discussion of how differential location in the legitimate opportunity structure can exert pressure to engage in deviance should not be misinterpreted as simply a statement relating poverty to crime. The relation between poverty and crime is itself not straightforward. In his discussion of crime and aggression in Ceylon, Wood (1961) points to the difference in the relationship of low status to serious crime when status is ascribed as opposed to when it is achieved. Low status, when ascribed, and therefore legitimized by community norms, does not correlate highly with crime. But low status in achieved-status systems does relate to frequency of serious crime. The difference lies, according to Wood, in the fact that expectations which are generated in achieved-status systems never materialize for those at the bottom, thus creating tensions or pressures often leading to crime. Related to this is Toby's point that "resentment of poverty is more likely to develop among the relatively deprived of a rich society than among the objectively deprived in a poor society" (1963, pp. 23–24). These comments bear on the central thesis of the Merton position; it is not disadvantage in the opportunity structure per se which generates pressure toward deviance but, rather, disadvantage in the context of certain social expectations, disadvantage in the face of universal cultural enjoiners that success is possible and that striving for success is obligatory.

> It is only when a system of cultural values extols, virtually above all else, certain *common* success-goals *for the population at large* while the social structure rigorously restricts or completely closes access to approved modes of reaching these goals *for a considerable part of the same population,* that deviant behavior ensues on a large scale (Merton, 1957, p. 146).

The pervasive dissemination of core success values and the broadly shared understanding of the tangible criteria of success are difficult to overestimate in light of the widespread diffusion of contemporary mass media. That the burden of these values has reached into the farthest corners of American society is readily documented. Thus, a recent comprehensive review of the disadvantaged situation of the Negro in America concludes: "The salient feature of Negro Americans is that they have accepted and internalized American culture, but are generally denied the chief rewards and privileges of that culture. High crime rates are but one consequence of this situation" (Pettigrew, 1964, p. 156). Another comparable conclusion comes from a large-scale research venture among urban teen-age groups—Anglo, Negro, and Spanish-speaking—in Oklahoma and Texas. The investigators arrived at the following conclusion from an analysis of data collected to answer specific questions about the value orientations of urban youth:

> There is one clear and striking generalization about the high school youth which holds in all areas and despite their differing backgrounds: Their values and goals earmark them all as youth exposed to the American ideology of success and wanting the tangible symbols of that success. There were no differences between the youth in different areas with respect to desires for material goods. In addition to comfortable housing, the symbols of success for these adolescents included a car in every garage, a telephone, television set, transistor radios, fashionable clothing, time to enjoy them, and money to provide them. It is obvious, however, that present accessibility of these items differed enormously for youth in the different areas (Sherif and Sherif, 1964, p. 199).

The uniformity of emphasis upon success, dispersed throughout American society, sets the stage for the critical importance of occupying an advantaged location in the legitimate opportunity structure. An advantaged location is one which provides control, or the prospect of control, over certain goals—wealth, power, prestige—or over a set of institutionally prescribed means—education, occupation, income—which can lead to achieving these goals. This distinction between goals and means is, of course, somewhat arbitrary, or is, at least, influenced by the vagaries of time sequence. Thus wealth, a goal, is simultaneously a means to other goals, such as power and prestige. Similarly, education, a prescribed and dominant means to success, functions also as a goal the attainment of which constitutes success.

It is obvious, therefore, that what constitutes the legitimate opportunity structure depends upon the cultural definition of success and upon the cultural definition of what is appropriate in the way of striving for success. The complexity of exhaustively defining "position in the opportunity structure" is suggested by the efforts of Meier and Bell (1959) to construct an index of access to means for the achievement of life goals. Their index attempts to map position in the opportunity structure in terms of education, occupation, income, social isolation, marital status, age, religious preference, occupational mobility, and class identification. Additional variables can also be conceived as providing access or as constituting barriers to access in society, depending upon the socially defined meaning they have; thus, being a member of the female sex, or the Negro race, or an ethnic minority has implications for control or possible control over access to culture goals. Moreover, the relation of these variables to access involves subtle interactions which are also socially structured. Advanced age, for example, clearly limits access to economic goals for a low-status person in industrial society, while it can be a source of increased access for a high-status person. While this kind of complexity conveys the magnitude of the problem of defining position in the opportunity structure, approximations based on only a few mapping variables—for example, Hollingshead's (1956) two-factor index of social position, utilizing only education and occupation—have been found widely useful in research.

The fundamental point is that in American society there is a differential distribution of legitimate resources or channels of access to the goals pervasively stressed by the American culture. The topography of access and, therefore, the topography of value-access disjunctions closely parallels the hierarchy of socioeconomic status and membership in minority ethnic or racial groups. This means that value-access disjunctions will be concentrated in the lower social strata and that this socially structured source of pressure for deviance will consequently be concentrated there. With Merton's hypothesis, the import of locating a person or group in the American opportunity structure derives from the fact that position in that structure directly maps degree of pressure toward deviance. Stated otherwise, location in the opportunity structure serves as an *index of degree of instigation to the use of illegitimate means* in adapting to value-access disjunction.

The preceding statement specifies the probabilistic linkage between a sociocultural concept, value-access disjunction in the legitimate opportunity structure, and deviant behavior rates. Of additional concern to us, in view of the general considerations which introduced this chapter, is that a linkage be specified between this sociocultural concept and some parallel aspect of the personality system. Intimations of such a linkage have been implicit throughout this discussion of location in the opportunity structure. A more detailed statement will be postponed for the next chapter, which deals with the personality system; it may be pointed out here, however, that patterned exposure to differential location in the social opportunity structure should eventuate in differential personally held *expectations* of achieving personally valued goals. Such differential expectations will be shown to constitute a personality counterpart of value-access disjunction in the sociocultural system.

We have thus far discussed one facet of the sociocultural system relevant to deviance, and have also mentioned its possible relevance for personality. We may now turn to a second aspect of the sociocultural system on which our research efforts focused, the normative structure, and discuss our conceptualization of the relationship between the normative structure and deviance.

The Normative Structure

In the preceding discussion, attention was given to one aspect of the culture, namely, definitions and emphasis upon the values and goals toward which striving is to be directed or toward which social life should orient itself. Pressure toward deviance was then shown to be a possible resultant of limited access to those culturally defined success values. In the present section, the focus is upon another aspect of the culture, namely, definition and specification of *appropriate modes of goal striving*. This portion of the sociocultural environment, which consists of shared definitions or institutionalized expectations about acceptable behavior, and which includes consequential implications for unacceptable behavior, will be referred to here as the normative structure. Insofar as such a definition implies the regulation of behavior, the normative structure serves the social function of controlling against the occurrence of deviance.

It was in his analysis of suicide as a social rather than an individual phenomenon that Durkheim (1951) articulated the role of social norms in controlling behavior. Stating that certain social needs—wealth, for example—are basically insatiable and that certain social forces—such as rapid industrialization—generate unlimited aspirations, Durkheim argued that the stability of society is dependent upon the regulation or limitation of the expression, in action, of such desires. The social apparatus which functions to maintain the stability of society by regulating man's behavior is the normative order which legitimizes certain behavior and places limits or restraints on other behavior. The breakdown of the regulatory apparatus—that is, the situation in which norms are no longer operative or effective guides to action or no longer serve to limit or constrain the expression of desires—was characterized by Durkheim as a condition of "anomie." In his own terms, "anomie" is a "state of de-regulation" (1951, p. 253).

This general orientation is elaborated by Parsons in the following exposition.

> Not merely contractual relations but stable social relations in general and even the personal equilibrium of the members of a social group are seen to be dependent on the existence of a normative structure in relation to conduct, generally accepted as having moral authority by the members of the community, and upon

their effective subordination to these norms. They not merely regulate the individual's choice of means to his ends, but his very needs and desires are determined in part by them. When this controlling normative structure is upset and disorganized, individual conduct is equally disorganized and chaotic. . . . *Anomie* is precisely this state of disorganization where the hold of norms over individual conduct has broken down (1949, p. 377).

Despite its wide usage in discussions of anomie, the term "breakdown" needs to be recognized as no more than a convenient metaphor, a device for generating further analysis. A brief discussion of the concept of norm can be a useful start in that direction. To begin with, it is important to re-emphasize that norms are not identical with behavior, nor is there usually a simple and direct inferential relationship from behavior to norms. Indeed, the entire orientation of our theory is that behavior, in this case, deviance, is the outcome of a complex interacting system of determinants of which norms constitute only one element. Norms are not simply average or modal behavior; instead, as elaborated in the preceding chapter, norms are to be construed as *socially defined standards or expectations* about what are appropriate modes of action in various social situations.

The emphasis upon social definition of these standards or expectations suggests several other important properties of the concept of norm which will, in turn, enable us to empty the term "breakdown" of some of its connotations. First, the social definition of norms implies that they are relatively widely shared rather than personal or idiosyncratic standards. Second by virtue of this sharing, they carry with them a moral quality, that is, an obligation to others for their fulfillment, an imperative for adherence. Durkheim speaks of the rule of "the collective conscience" in relation to the maintenance of normative controls. Third, intrinsic to the social definition of norms is a pattern of sanctions to be applied in instances of normative violation. The sanction pattern will, of course, vary with the nature of the norms, with how they are qualified in terms of prescription, preference, permission, or proscription (Merton, 1957, p. 133). For example, the character of the minimal negative social sanction for normative departure has been suggested by Seeman[5] as the expression of "surprise."

A number of implications for the meaning of normative breakdown follow from these considerations and provide the first outlines for an operationalization of the concept of anomie. It is possible to think of breakdown in terms of the degree to which these normative expectations

[5] This idea is put forth in a preliminary statement on the concept of social norm by M. Seeman in a dittoed paper (no date). Seeman's paper has been very helpful in this general discussion of the nature of social norms.

are shared—that is, in terms of the degree of social *consensus* which underlies them. Low consensus on patterned expectations about social behavior can, in an interacting group, be considered part of the meaning of, or a referent for, breakdown in norms.[6] In this condition, uncertainty about what is appropriate behavior prevails, and the predictability which norms generally provide for behavior is minimal or absent. At the extreme, low consensus becomes idiosyncratic normative definition, or social chaos.

Another part of the meaning of normative breakdown can be found in the decline and disappearance of the moral authority of norms, "the hold of norms over individual conduct." While they may remain widely shared, and even publicly reiterated, their effective influence upon behavior, by way of regulation or constraint, is lessened or has become attenuated. Instances of this sort are those where norms previously existing as regulative social expectations come to evolve into mere verbally expressed *ideals,* departures from which are increasingly frequent. Changing patterns of premarital sex behavior may exemplify this process—chastity may be changing from a widely shared, regulative standard to a less effective ideal norm. The loss of moral authority and effective influence of previously effective norms is, thus, another possible referent for normative breakdown.

Finally, and obviously related to this loss of authoritativeness of norms, a diminution or decline in the application of sanctions for normative violations may signal normative breakdown. The moral imperiousness of norms derives, in large part, from the fact that adherence to them is rewarding over the long run, even in the negative sense that adherence simply avoids the possibilities of punishment. To the extent that the sanction pattern disintegrates, either in the failure of regular punishment for normative departure or, in the extreme, in the actual reward for transgression, the moral quality of the norms is dissipated, and the "reasonableness" of adhering to them is weakened. The inconsistency, irregularity, or unpredictability of the application of sanctions in support of norms can thus be seen as another possible connotation for the term "normative breakdown." Further discussion of the implications of varying sanction patterns will be undertaken in the section on the social control structure, which follows the present section.

This analysis of some possible dimensions of anomie is, of course, not exhaustive. Further analysis could usefully be made, for example, of the concept of low consensus itself. Low consensus in a group may

---

[6] Low consensus on norms as a referent for normative breakdown implies a pre-existing normative structure supported by general consensus. Low consensus may, of course, be unrelated to the notion of breakdown, as when it obtains in a newly formed or novel social situation.

consist of either generalized uncertainty or *conflicting* views about what is appropriate. The implications of such a differentiation of the idea of low consensus may be important in relation to deviant behavior. Further, low consensus in different *areas* of social life may have importantly different consequences for deviance. But what should emerge clearly from this discussion of norms is that the general referent for anomie is a social or sociocultural property, not a characteristic of an individual. Durkheim, in his consistent effort to eschew psychological reductionism, should not be misread on this point; for him, anomie refers to a state of society, a social fact. Merton, whose elaboration of the anomie concept we will consider shortly, is equally emphatic on the specification of anomie as a sociological rather than a psychological term.

Nevertheless, a certain amount of confusion has developed in this regard in the recent literature. Some of the confusion can be traced to the publication by Srole (1956) of an anomie scale, a set of items designed to measure *personal* beliefs, perceptions, or orientations. Although Srole has suggested that the term "anomia" be used to distinguish the psychological concept measured by his scale from the sociological concept of anomie, no general agreement on usage obtains. This is most clearly seen in the recent book by Mizruchi (1964) who, after a lengthy discussion of the importance of the distinction between the objective (sociological) concept of anomie and the subjective (psychological) concept of anomia, ends ultimately by relying, in his own research, upon the Srole scale as an index of anomie.

While there may well be methodological justification for such usage of the Srole scale as an indirect index or partial reflection of anomie, the result is likely to be a further contribution to conceptual confusion of an important distinction. In addition, certain critical empirical problems are denied investigation by such usage: for example, problems dealing directly with the relationship *between* anomie and anomia, or with the conditions under which anomia can and cannot be considered a psychological counterpart of the sociological concept of anomie. At the base of some of these difficulties lie the unavailability of relatively direct measures of anomie and the consequent tendency to rely upon quite indirect or remote measures, such as the Srole scale. But, as Merton has emphasized, pragmatic considerations of this sort, or of the sort which justifies reliance upon "social bookkeeping data" that happen to be available, are not suitable alternatives to developing theoretically derived indicators of the anomie concept.

Fulfillment of the latter objective would seem to be predicated upon retaining the definition of anomie as a state of the sociocultural environment—more particularly, of the normative structure—and upon defining it in a way which will enable relatively direct, theoretically derived measures of it to be constructed. It was this purpose to which the earlier discussion of normative breakdown was addressed. Its implications for our own measurement of anomie will be apparent in Chapter 9.

Thus far, we have been discussing the nature of a *state* of the normative structure—anomie. It was in his analysis of an important *source* of anomie in American society that Merton made a major contribution toward the formation of a linkage between anomie and deviant behavior. The general form of his hypothesis will be familiar because of its similarity to our earlier analysis of the way in which value-access disjunction generates pressure toward deviance. The present point is the contention by Merton that value-access disjunction not only generates pressure toward deviance but also strains the normative structure and ultimately produces a state of anomie. Anomie occurs particularly

> when there is an acute disjunction between the cultural norms and goals and the socially structured capacities of members of the group to act in accord with them. . . . On this view the social structure strains the cultural values, making action in accord with them readily possible for those occupying certain statuses within the society and difficult or impossible for others. . . . When the cultural and the social structure are malintegrated, the first calling for behavior and attitudes which the second precludes, there is a strain toward the breakdown of the norms, toward normlessness (Merton, 1957, pp. 162–163).

The emphasis of this position is, then, upon the normative attenuation likely to develop when legitimate avenues to the achievement of culturally valued goals are limited or unavailable.

Cloward and Ohlin (1960, pp. 82–86) have listed three important ways in which Merton's theory of anomie is an extension beyond Durkheim's view. First, the formulation is now applicable not only to insatiable strivings or aspirations but to striving even for limited goals, as long as the possibility of achieving them by legitimate means is also limited. Second, the formulation goes beyond a concern with major social crises or rapid industrial change to implicate the ordinary social processes of daily life, wherein aspiration and legitimate opportunity are discrepant. Finally, the formulation enables a differentiated location of anomie in different parts of the sociocultural environment rather than treating it as a state of society in the large.

Since, according to Merton, stress on the normative structure is a function of limited access to valued goals by legitimate means, the "social topography of anomie" should, to some extent, parallel disadvantage in the opportunity structure. A relative concentration of anomie should, therefore, be found in the lower social strata and among marginal racial and ethnic groups. Such a concentration would parallel the known concentration of deviance rates in contemporary American society. Location in the normative structure may then constitute, like location in the legitimate opportunity structure, a second element in a sociocultural theory of deviance rates. While location in the opportunity structure is interpreted in terms of differential *pressure towards* deviance, location in the normative structure is interpreted in terms of differential *control against* deviance.

The stress on the normative structure deriving from the condition of limited access, by legitimate means, to valued goals is one major and potent source of anomie in various sectors of American society. By their failure to provide effective guides to successful action, the institutionalized norms become attenuated in moral validity and reduced in persuasive control over behavior. But *any* factors which serve to attenuate the regulatory function of norms would conduce to anomie, and a number of other socially patterned sources have been identified as having, or would seem logically to have, this consequence. A brief discussion of several of these sources will help to round out the picture of the social processes generating stress on the normative structure.

In his initial discussion of anomie (1957, Chap. 4), Merton describes the situation in which the culture places little emphasis upon norms governing the choice of means. The concern with ends is so all-encompassing that cultural support for prescribed behavior is minimal; only technical efficiency serves as a criterion for the selection of means. The value of normative adherence, per se, is minimal because the culture, in its almost exclusive preoccupation with the *outcome* of action, neglects to emphasize the importance of the *manner* in which the outcome is achieved. Merton feels that this condition applies differentially in American society. He cites, for example, the greater emphasis by lower-middle-class parents than by lower-class parents on training their children to abide by the moral mandates of society. Such a condition, a cultural emphasis upon goals at the expense of means, should also conduce to anomie since support for sheer normative adherence is minimal, and the moral suasion of norms is consequently attenuated. Since concern with means has often stemmed from and been supported by religious institutions in society, the increasing trend toward secularization may well be contributing further to this source of anomie: the de-emphasis upon the intrinsic importance of employing appropriate means.

Another source of anomie lies in the simultaneous presence of multiple or alternative normative structures. Such situations obtain when there exist, side by side, social groups of different culture or origin, such as occurs after varied immigration to large urban centers, or during acculturation contact. Leighton's (1959) use of the notion of "cultural confusion" as an index of social disintegration is apposite here. The attenuation of norms under these circumstances can be seen to derive from the simultaneous presence of alternative, though perhaps not conflicting, norms. The sheer presence of alternatives may serve as an influence tending both to diminish the claim to legitimacy of any particular set of norms and to increase the uncertainty about what is appropriate behavior for members of the various groups.

The prevalence of a high deviance rate alone can readily be seen as another potential source of anomie. Under such circumstances, normative violation becomes a readily apparent characteristic of the social ecology. Beyond providing models for the learning of illegitimate means, as we shall discuss in the next section, exposure to such an ecology should attenuate the regulatory force of norms by demonstrating that norms are actually not as widely shared or as strongly held as might have been thought. Where, in addition, such normative violations do not result in the occurrence of negative sanctions, the effect on anomie should be compounded. Merton comments on this point in discussing the feedback relationship in which anomie leads to deviance and the occurrence of deviance then leads to an increase in anomie: "A mounting frequency of deviant but 'successful' behavior tends to lessen and, as an extreme potentiality, to eliminate the legitimacy of the institutional norms for others in the system" (1957, p. 180).

No attempt has been made to be exhaustive in discussing the various possible sources of anomie, especially because empirical data to substantiate many of these speculations are lacking. The central concern has been to indicate how the normative structure is subject to a variety of stresses and to suggest that these stresses are not homogeneously distributed throughout society. Indeed, *all* of the sources here discussed would seem to be more characteristic of the lower strata of American society than of the higher, and all seemed to be differentially operative in our research community. In any event, the outcome of such stresses—anomie—is the erosion and decline of the moral authority of norms and the increased uncertainty or decreased consensus about appropriate modes of behavior.

The link between location in the normative structure and deviance can be summarized at this point. Location in the normative structure specifies the position of a person or group with respect to *degree of exposure to anomie;* and *anomie conduces to deviance in the sense that it implies the absence or lessening of effective normative control over behavior.* The link between anomie, as an aspect of the sociocultural environment, and some attribute of the personality system—one of our previously stated requirements for concepts in an interdisciplinary scheme—has already been hinted at in our discussion of anomia or alienation. It will be taken up in more detail in Chapter 4, on the personality system.

To this point, we have developed the opportunity structure and the normative structure as two significant aspects of the sociocultural system, and have specified their theoretical relation to deviance. The third critical aspect of the sociocultural system, the social control structure, can now be considered.

The Social Control Structure

The interpretation of limited access in the legitimate opportunity structure as creating pressure toward reliance upon illegitimate means and the interpretation of anomie in the normative structure as constituting a relative failure of normative control against deviance together provide only a partial account of the sociocultural processes eventuating in deviance. Significantly missing are those aspects of the environment *directly* involved in the social management of conformity and deviance. The reference here is to socially patterned opportunities for learning and for performing deviant behaviors and to the nature and operation of sanction systems for encouraging conformity and discouraging deviance. When effective, these aspects serve to control against the occurrence of deviance and, together, they constitute what may be called the social control structure of the social environment.

Our thinking in this area was influenced by the important paper by Cloward (1959) on illegitimate means and the subsequent extension of those ideas in the book *Delinquency and Opportunity* by Cloward and Ohlin (1960). Although our own views are somewhat different from those of Cloward and Ohlin, it should be useful to begin the discussion by describing their major thesis. Whereas Merton was concerned with differential access to legitimate means, a long line of work in the sociology of crime, the Chicago tradition, had been concerned with processes which refer to differential access to *illegitimate* means. The work of Shaw and McKay (1942) on the "cultural transmission" of crime and delinquency and the work of Sutherland (1955) on "differential associations" with criminal behavior patterns have in common a concern with opportunities to learn and perform deviant behavior. Cloward and Ohlin argue that such opportunities, socially patterned and differentially available, influence not only the likelihood of occurrence of deviant behavior but also the specific *form* which the deviant act takes. They point out that Merton's theory, focusing mainly on legitimate means, apparently assumed that illegitimate means were either generally available or, if differentially available, relatively unimportant in generating deviance. The Chicago school, on the other hand, concerned largely with illegitimate means, failed to note the importance of limited access to legitimate means as a source of pressure toward deviance.

Recognizing the complementarity of these two concerns, Cloward and

Ohlin offer the concept of "differential opportunity structures" as a way of bringing them together in an internally consistent fashion. In their view, each person can be thought of as occupying a position in *both* a legitimate and an illegitimate opportunity structure. They state:

> There are marked differences from one part of the social structure to another in the types of illegitimate adaptations that are available to persons in search of solutions to problems of adjustment arising from the restricted availability of legitimate means. In this sense, then, we can think of individuals as being located in two opportunity structures—one legitimate, the other illegitimate. Given limited access to success-goals by legitimate means, the nature of the delinquent response that may result will vary according to the availability of various illegitimate means (1960, p. 152).

In the analysis of Cloward and Ohlin, Merton's theory is significantly extended in at least three important respects. First, by identifying the differential availability of illegitimate means, attention is focused on an important additional factor conducing to deviance rates in general. Second, a concern with differential access to illegitimate means enables the theory to begin to specify which *kind* of deviance will occur as an adaptation to the stress of limited access to legitimate means. While Merton does discuss different forms of adaptation to anomic pressure, and does suggest that these adaptations are differentially distributed in society, his deviant adaptations are abstract and schematic—they each include a variety of different forms of deviance, and their differential occurrence is not systematically derived from an analysis of the social milieu.

The question left unanswered by Merton's discussion of different forms of adaptation to anomic pressure is: Given environmental stress, what determines which one, out of a whole series of possible adaptations, is the adaptation that will occur? This "specificity" problem is a critical issue in any theory where the emphasis is placed upon some form of environmental stress. Leighton (1959), for example, uses a sociocultural disintegration theory of stress to account for the distribution in society of one general form of deviance—psychiatric disorder. But his stress theory alone does not indicate why psychiatric disorder rather than crime should occur as the adaptation to the stress. More particularly, it does not account for which *type* of psychiatric disorder will occur, assuming that psychiatric disorder is the adaptation. The same issues can be raised when Merton's theory of anomie is employed to account for deviance: Why does crime rather than some other form of deviance occur, and why, within the range of criminal adaptations, does confidence racketeering rather than theft, or drug pushing, take place? The basic question remains: *Given stress,* how may an account be provided that suggests which type of adaptation to the stress or pressure will occur? The idea of differential access to illegitimate means, with its emphasis upon opportunities to learn *specific forms* of deviance, is a large step toward an answer, as we will show in more detail shortly.

The third respect in which Merton's theory is extended in the Cloward-Ohlin analysis is that deviance-learning structures are emphasized; this has the effect of bringing closer attention to the general processes of social learning. Since social learning processes are the crucial mediators between patterned exposure in the social environment, on the one hand, and acquisition of characteristic personality and behavior tendencies, on the other hand, increased attention to learning should further our understanding of social behavior in general.

Our own orientation varies in certain respects from the Cloward-Ohlin view. To begin with, the primary concern of their theory is with delinquent gangs or delinquent subcultures, and their discussion of learning and performance structures for deviance is predicated in large measure on the existence of organized and elaborate criminal structures (such as gangs and rackets) in a community, usually in an urban setting. But such stable criminal structures provide only a special case of the more general thesis of Cloward and Ohlin about learning and performance opportunities. Access to illegitimate means, socially patterned and differentially distributed, can refer to far less structured and organized illegitimate means. That is, it can usefully refer to differences in exposure of individuals to the *everyday manifestations* of deviant behavior by other individuals in the environment, or to differences in daily, even fortuitous, opportunities to transgress. This more general view of the idea of access to illegitimate means makes possible an account of deviance which is not necessarily institutionalized in gangs or organized over time.

Further, it has seemed to us important to locate an individual in *three* rather than two sociocultural structures, as Cloward and Ohlin have done. Our separation of the normative structure from the legitimate opportunity structure is, in our opinion, conceptually important since, as we have earlier suggested, anomie is the logical consequence of several *other* factors besides limited access to success goals. In addition, while they can be expected *in general* to co-vary, limited access and anomie *need not* be correlated. Their possible independence has already been noted in such social situations as those in which limited access is institutionalized, as with poverty in caste or other ascribed status systems; or in situations where countervailing solidary social mechanisms, such as religious commitment, are strongly operative. Maintaining a conceptual separation has the further advantage, moreover, of now enabling direct empirical study of variation in the normative structure as a consequence of variation in *both* legitimate and illegitimate access.

Lastly, it is possible to conceptualize the Cloward-Ohlin description of the illegitimate opportunity structure as only part of a broader social control structure in the sociocultural environment. The emphasis in their analysis upon differential opportunity to learn and perform deviant acts suggests immediately the operation and effectiveness of social controls, but does not exhaust the latter. The whole range of social agents and institutions, formal and informal, organized and unorganized, which are involved in the management of deviance-conformity through the administration and regulation of both positive and negative sanctions constitutes another essential aspect of the social control structure. By considering (1) the opportunities to learn deviance; (2) the opportunities to learn the source, nature, and likelihood of sanctions consequential on deviance; and (3) the opportunities to perform deviant acts, all as parts of the social control structure, it is possible to arrive at a broader, still conceptually homogeneous, structure than is implied by the Cloward-Ohlin description of the illegitimate opportunity structure.

The social control structure, as we define it, has, then, these foregoing three facets, each relevant to access to illegitimate means. Location in the social control structure is of theoretical importance since position in that structure should relate to deviance. *To the extent that the social controls supporting legitimate behavior and opposing illegitimate behavior are minimal, irregular, or undependable—to that extent, deviance rates should be higher.* This proposition should hold whether the impetus for deviance derives from limited access in the opportunity structure or from any other source. Further, given pressure toward deviance, the location of a person or group in the social control structure should have, as Cloward and Ohlin have emphasized, implications for the specific kind of deviant behavior—crime, psychosis, drug or alcohol addiction, sexual promiscuity—engaged in as an adjustment to such pressure.

At this point, it can be seen that the social control structure and the normative control structure play similar theoretical roles: When operative and effective, they both serve to constrain against deviant behavior. In this sense, as controls, they might well be considered simply as two components of some larger control structure. Our purpose in attempting to maintain a conceptual separation of these two sources of controls at this stage is largely to facilitate research on their interrelation and on how each major source of controls may influence the other. Obviously, these controls are not independent in operation—we have argued earlier, for example, that failure to apply consistent sanctions (the social control structure) may attenuate the moral validity of norms and generate anomie (the normative structure)—but it is precisely such interdependence which can be empirically investigated by maintaining, at this stage, their analytic separateness.

Exposure to Deviance

The relation of the social control structure to deviance can best be elaborated by considering each of its three components in turn. The first component concerns differential opportunity to learn deviant behavior, or what we have in our research called *exposure to deviance*. The central point here is that a major source of learning of complex social behavior originates in exposure or in the opportunity to *observe* both its occurrence and the functional consequences of its occurrence in the social environment. The relevance of this kind of learning to the likelihood of deviance has been broadly captured by Sutherland (1955) in his formulation of the principle of differential association: Persons become criminals because of an excess of intimate associations with criminal behavior patterns as against associations with noncriminal behavior patterns. Such excess is distributed differentially in society and accounts, according to Sutherland, for the epidemiology of crime. More specifically, for example, Cressey has stated: "The *chances* of being presented with an excess of criminal behavior patterns are better if one is a Negro, a member of the working class, a young male, an urban dweller, and a native American than they are if one is white, middle-class, old, a rural resident or an immigrant" (1961, p. 59).

A recent example of empirical work on Sutherland's proposition is the study by Voss in which adolescents in Honolulu were asked to report the frequency of their own delinquent behavior and, at the same time, to report on frequency of association with delinquent friends. The research supports the conclusion "that adolescents who associate extensively with delinquent friends report more delinquent behavior than those whose contacts with delinquent peers is minimal" (1964, p. 85).

Association with criminal behavior patterns or, more generally, exposure to deviance, is useful in orienting attention to the general process of learning, but a more analytic approach is clearly necessary. Such an approach should be able to account for (1) the learning of kinds of behaviors which are actually often large units constituted of a number of smaller acts organized over time (for example, committing a robbery, or carrying out a seduction); to account for (2) the learning of *styles* of behavior or orientations which themselves may increase the likelihood of deviance (for example, the tendency toward immediate gratification, or short time perspective); and to account for (3) self-conceptions or self-identities which may have relevance for deviance (for example, defining oneself as a potential "troublemaker," or as a potential alcoholic). While a more general social learning theory bearing on these kinds of concerns will be described in the next chapter, on the personality system, and while a number of alternative learning processes, such as conditioning and direct training, would also bear on these concerns, there is a recent interest in imitation and modeling theory which has direct application to the concept of exposure and the consequent *acquisition* of deviant behaviors.

Bandura and Walters (1963) report a large number of investigations which deal with vicarious learning, that is, learning which is mediated by observation and which results in imitation or matching of the behavior of a model. For example, (Bandura, Ross, and Ross, 1961; 1963), one group of nursery school children was exposed to aggressive adult models, while a second group was exposed to models who displayed inhibited and nonaggressive behavior. The aggression, both physical and verbal, was expressed against a large inflated plastic doll. Subsequent to exposure to the models, the children were mildly frustrated, and measures of aggression were obtained in a new setting with the model absent. "The children who observed the aggressive models displayed a great number of precisely imitative aggressive responses, whereas such responses rarely occurred in either the nonaggressive model group or the control group" (Bandura and Walters, 1963, p. 61). Further, the authors conclude that "research demonstrates that when a model is provided, patterns of behavior are typically acquired in large segments or in their entirety. . . . The learner generally produces more or less the entire response pattern, even though he may perform no overt response . . . throughout the demonstration period" (1963, p. 106).

Such studies, in documenting the crucial role of models in the acquisition of behavior, including behaviors which, like aggression, may be involved in deviance, emphasize the importance of the *ecology of deviant behavior models*. An ecology with a high rate of deviance, such as may occur in urban slum areas, or in a disorganized family, should increase the likelihood of acquiring deviant behavior patterns.

In addition to deviant behavior patterns, there are certain general behavior styles or orientations which can be seen as conducive to deviance, such as the tendency to seek immediate gratification. It is interesting to see that such stylistic variables may also be learnable through exposure to models. A recent study by Bandura and Kupers exposed children, in a game situation, to models who exhibited differential patterns of reinforcing or rewarding themselves upon reaching certain performance criteria in the game. The study provided strong support for their hypothesis "that patterns of self-reinforcement can be acquired imitatively through exposure to models . . ." (1964, p. 7). It is possible to construe the tendency to indulge in immediate gratification as such a pattern or style of self-reinforcement.[7] Insofar as this is the case, this study provides some initial support for the learning, by modeling, of such deviance-relevant *styles* of behavior. This consideration adds significantly to the importance

---

[7] A fuller discussion of the relevance to deviance of such styles of behavior as the tendency toward immediate gratification will be presented in Chapter 4, on the personality system.

of the notion of exposure to models and of the nature of the social ecology within which such exposure occurs.

Finally, exposure which results in the learning of self-conceptions or self-identities relevant to deviance needs also to be considered. Coming to identify oneself as "a delinquent" or as "a troublemaker" need not be dependent entirely on such labels being applied to one by others or on actual, direct engagement in such activities. There is interesting research evidence available to suggest that such self-conceptions may come about by generalization, going beyond certain obvious similarities which a person perceives between himself and certain models. The evidence further suggests that such "matching" can occur even when the characteristics of the model are socially undesirable or reprehensible. A series of studies by Stotland and his colleagues (1961a; 1961b) has supported the hypothesis that a person's perception of similarity between himself and a model on some given attribute, or in certain limited respects, can lead to the person's assumption that similarity obtains in other respects as well. Stotland and Patchen (1961) were able to show that persons of little initial prejudice, as measured by an attitude scale, became more prejudiced when exposed to information about the bigotry of a model with whom they knew only that they had in common certain *objective* characteristics, such as college major, part-time job, and father's occupation. It is noteworthy that this generalization to additional assumed similarity by the subjects took place despite the social undesirability of the additional attribute, namely, prejudice. This type of "identity" modeling can also have relevance for deviance. For example, in a high deviance rate ecology, nondeviant persons, seeing themselves as initially similar in certain limited respects to prevalent deviant models—in race, ethnic origin, age, or physical prowess—may generalize to seeing themselves as like those models in additional ways, that is, as being themselves potential deviants. The implications of such a process for reference group theory (see Merton, 1957, Chapters 8 and 9) are apparent.

This discussion of the importance of models as a potent source of learning of deviance accords with, but elaborates the emphasis of Sutherland on differential association and of Cloward and Ohlin on the learning aspects of the illegitimate opportunity structure. While these authors have emphasized the *institutionalization* of training for crime, the present stress on modeling argues that acquisition of deviant behaviors can occur in the routine transactions of daily life whenever the ecology provides exposure to models of deviant behavior, of deviance-prone styles, and of deviance-relevant identities.[8]

---

[8] We have been concerned here with acquisition rather than performance. The actual performance or imitation of a deviant response is influenced by the anticipation of consequences, that is, by expectations that the response will lead to reward

The distribution, in the sociocultural environment, of models for deviance has been described as an aspect of the social control structure. Where controls are strong, the prevalence of such models should be correspondingly restricted, and vice versa. That the distribution of deviance models is strongly socially patterned is supported by the conclusions quoted previously from Cressey (1961) in which the chances of being presented with an excess of criminal behavior patterns were shown to be related to a variety of demographic characteristics. Within the general social ecology, the importance of the family in mediating the presentation of deviance models has also been supported by research evidence. In the follow-up analysis, twenty years later, of the Cambridge-Somerville Youth Study, criminal record data were obtained, at about age twenty-seven, on 253 boys initially studied at age seven. At the time of the follow-up, 56 percent of the sons of fathers who had criminal records themselves had criminal records. In contrast, only 35 percent of the sons of fathers without criminal records themselves had criminal records. The authors studied several additional factors, including criminality of the mother, parental rejection, and consistency of discipline. The importance of the role of family models emerges in the authors' conclusion: "If the father is criminal and the mother is also a deviant model, criminality generally results regardless of parental affection" (McCord and McCord, 1958, p. 73).

The concentration of deviance models within the *lower* strata of society is directly implied by the known distribution of deviance rates.[9] The sociocultural distribution of exposure to models of deviance can be seen, therefore, to parallel the distribution of the other variables we have already considered. In summary, as one aspect of the social control structure, exposure to deviance models may be considered to provide access to illegitimate means. Such exposure is conducive to deviance and to the kind of deviance exhibited and is differentially distributed in the sociocultural environment in a way which accords with the epidemiology of deviance rates.

---

or punishment. To the extent that the social ecology provides exposures to *successful* models for deviance, to that extent, not only acquisition but also *performance* of deviance is more likely. We will elaborate this issue in the next section.

[9] These rates reflect, of course, not only the greater pressure for deviance and the lesser normative control at this location, but also such additional social processes as (1) "downward drift" to this location, by virtue of their deviance, of persons initially at higher social locations, and (2) the "accumulation" at this location of persons whose deviance impedes mobility upward. On this latter point, a thirty-year follow-up of clinic cases seen in childhood showed that patients with police contact had strikingly less upward mobility than those without. "Since anti-social behavior apparently blocks movement out of the lower class, anti-social individuals tend to accumulate in the lower class. Lower class children, therefore, have a disproportionate access to association with anti-social individuals" (Robins, Gyman, and O'Neal, 1962, p. 492).

Relative Absence of Sanction Networks

The second major component of the social control structure has to do with the regulation of the system of sanctions and the socially structured character of their administration. This component is referred to, in our research, as the *relative absence of sanction networks.* The sanction system implies rewards for conforming behavior as well as punishments for deviance—it may operate consistently and predictably or irregularly and minimally; it may involve legal actions or informal social and interpersonal reactions; it may originate in intimate groups, such as the family, or in more remote formal membership groups, such as a professional society. The effective operation of a sanction network is functionally so important to the maintenance of organized social relationships that social disorganization is frequently indexed by the absence or attenuation of this source of control (see Set A of the disintegration indices described in Leighton, 1959).

Stated another way, an individual can be assumed to be under the effective and continued control of social sanctions insofar as he occupies positions in a family or in other social institutions—church, job, and social groups, both formal and informal—which *themselves* are functioning effectively. Being mapped into such positions brings the contingencies of socially mediated rewards and punishments directly to bear on his actions. Where an individual is not mapped into such positions, those contingencies are unlikely to influence his choice of behavior and, hence, they are unable to encourage conformity or to control against deviance.

At the level of the family, the attenuation of sanction networks is suggested by the frequently cited association of broken homes with deviance. One report showed that three fourths, twice the expected ratio, of Negro delinquents in a large eastern city who came before the law in 1948 did not have both of their natural parents living at home (Diggs, 1950). It is assumed that any departure from the integrated, nuclear family structure probably lessens the effectiveness of application of sanctions.

The differential operation of sanctions *at the level of neighborhood* is illustrated by data from an interview study of adults in two areas of Cambridge, Massachusetts. The areas were similar in socioeconomic characteristics but very different in rates of delinquency. The hypothesis at issue was that private citizens in the high-delinquency area would be less likely than those in a low-delinquency area to take remedial action when they saw other people's children engaging in some kind of delinquent or pre-delinquent activity (Maccoby, Johnson, and Church, 1958). A lesser sense of community was shown to obtain in the high-delinquency area: Respondents knew fewer of their neighbors by name, did not know as many people intimately enough to borrow something, and less often felt they had common interests with their neighbors. Responding to hypothetical incidents of abusive language, property damage, fighting or drinking, the low-delinquency area residents reported themselves more ready to "do something about it"—significantly so on the latter two categories. Finally, with respect to real-life incidents in which the respondents actually had had the opportunity to take some controlling action, the residents of the low-delinquency area had somewhat more often actually taken such action. This finding held true even in those incidents in which the residents themselves were not the victim. Maccoby and her associates conclude: "The lack of social integration appears to have certain direct effects in a lowered level of social control of delinquent and pre-delinquent activities" (1958, p. 51), the control to which they refer involving the informal neighborhood regulation of sanctions (see also, in this connection, Reiss, 1951).

In his report on the relative infrequency of drunkenness and alcoholism among the Cantonese of New York's Chinatown, Barnett (1955) draws a compelling picture of the organization of family and group controls around intoxication. One incident illustrates the operation of sanctions *at the level of the informal social group.* When one member of a supper party became intoxicated and fell asleep, another member took a picture of him. The next day a print of the offender was posted on the group's bulletin board with the face cut out, making identification difficult, if not impossible. A notice underneath stated that this was a man who drank too much and did not know how to control himself; if he persisted in disgracing his friends the same print would appear—with the face included! This informal incident relates to a somewhat more formal approach to group sanctions taken by Soviet authorities in the Twenties in efforts to stamp out vice. According to Carter (1946), name, address, and place of employment were taken down on all men found during a raid on a house of prostitution. The next day the names were posted in various public places under the heading "Buyers of the Bodies of Women."

At the level of the large formal group, Snyder (1964) argues convincingly for the importance of membership in a solidary group as an effective preventive against inebriety and alcoholism. Drawing his examples from data on drinking among various religious groups, he emphasizes that integration into the religious community has significant control consequences against inebriety. This control is in addition to that which may be provided by the specific quality of the drinking norms (for example, the ritual orientation to drinking among the orthodox Jews). Such integration relates to the operation of the reward-punishment system. Snyder's interpretation of the role of the formal group gains support from a recent cross-cultural study in which the data on social organization and alcohol use in the

Human Relations Area Files were used. In this analysis, Field (1963) found a strong association between drunkenness and various indicators of the degree of formal organization of society among primitive tribes. The presence of such organizational characteristics as corporate kin groups, a village settlement pattern rather than nomadism, and patrilocal residence at marriage, was associated with less drunkenness. Field suggests that societies with features such as these are likely to be well organized and to have interpersonal relationships structured along hierarchical respect lines; such factors, he argues, are likely in turn to control extremely informal, friendly, and loosely structured sorts of behavior at drinking bouts, thereby reducing drunkenness.

These examples of the operation of sanctioning processes at various levels of social interaction have in common the consideration that the regulation of controls—through the consistent, orderly, and predictable administration of both positive and negative sanctions—depends, at each level, upon the degree of organization of the social unit. Locations in the social control structure can be described by the differential availability of such organized social units in which individuals may participate. The degree to which the behavior of an individual is regulated by such social sanction networks can thus be seen to vary along the continuum running from nonmembership in any such social units at one end, through membership in relatively unorganized social units, to membership in multiple solidary social units at the other end. Location in the latter, as compared with the former, should control against deviance. Effective sanctioning networks limit access to illegitimate means through the positive rewards provided for conformity and the negative consequences administered for transgression; absence of such sanction networks conduces to deviance.

Opportunity to Engage in Deviance

The third component of the social control structure, *opportunity to engage in deviance,* while important to articulate, can be dealt with briefly since it is related to the other components of social control which have been discussed. Where deviance models are prevalent and the application of sanctions is relatively inoperative, it is also likely that the actual opportunity to engage in deviance will be higher. This component of social control has been referred to by Cloward and Ohlin as the "performance structure" aspect of the illegitimate opportunity structure; this is in contrast to the "learning structure" aspect discussed earlier as exposure to deviant models. While their emphasis again is placed upon fairly structured or organized opportunities to perform criminal roles or acts—as might exist, for example, in an organized gang or racket—the notion of opportunity for deviance is, in fact, a more general one. It refers to location in socially defined positions where the actual possibilities of engaging in deviant behavior are greater. This may be due either to greater access to certain deviance-relevant objects, such as drugs and alcohol, or to occupying certain roles—of age, sex, or occupation—less subject to observation and supervision of behavior. Age, for example, is relevant to access to alcohol since availability of the latter is legally regulated in terms of a minimum age for purchase or public consumption. Occupational position, as Lindesmith and Gagnon note, is highly relevant to drug addiction rates; addiction among physicians in virtually all Western nations is especially high. "The simplest and most plausible explanation of the high rate of addiction in the [medical] profession is in terms of availability of drugs. . . ." (Lindesmith and Gagnon, 1964, p. 171).

Opportunity for deviance varies also with exposure to social observation—for example, the anonymity characteristic of the large urban center as compared to the smaller community. It is related also to variation in direct social interference—the accompaniment of females by chaperones in social situations, reliance on curfews, or the presence of police patrols, for example. The general point to be emphasized is that the availability of opportunity for deviance, as with the differential prevalence of deviance models and the relative absence of sanction networks, reflects the operation of the social control structure. The less effective the operation of the social control structure, the greater the availability of opportunities to engage in deviance and, consequently, the higher the deviance rates.

Three components of the social control structure have been discussed, and an attempt has been made to show the connection to deviant behavior of each of these different kinds of access to illegitimate means. The linkage of this portion of the sociocultural system to some corresponding aspect of the personality system will be discussed in the chapter dealing with personality substructures; obviously implied is the degree to which social controls have been internalized.

CONCLUDING SUMMARY

The differentiation of the social environment into three major structures enables us now to specify a sociocultural theory which provides a *logical* account of the distribution of deviance rates in society and which, as will be shown, has implications for coordinate structures in the personality system. The sociocultural theory identifies a major source of *instigation to* deviance—limited access in the legitimate opportunity structure—and two major sources of attenuated *control against* deviance: anomie, in the normative structure, and access to illegitimate means, in the social control structure. The sociocultural system has dynamic properties; the balance of instigation and control is what theoretically determines the level of deviance rates at a given social location during any given period.

The sociocultural system we have described, and its relation to deviance, is shown schematically in Figure 1. For each structure, we have specified the characteristic of the location which is theoretically most conducive to deviance, that is, value-access disjunction, anomie, and access to illegitimate means. The fundamental sociocultural proposition schematized in Figure 1 is the following: *The magnitude of deviance rates at a given location in society will vary directly with the degree of value-access disjunction, anomie, and access to illegitimate means characterizing that location.*

FIGURE 1
The Sociocultural System and Deviance Rates

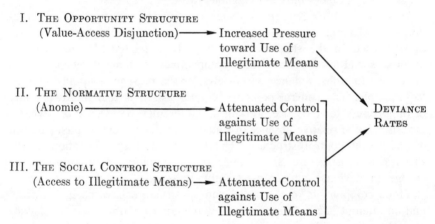

In general, the locations in each structure theoretically most conducive to deviance are those which characterize the social situation of the lower strata and of the marginal racial and ethnic groups in our society. In this sense, then, *the theory accounts for the concentration of deviance rates in these strata by postulating a parallel concentration of the variables theoretically relevant to the occurrence of deviant behavior.*

A corollary of this statement is, of course, that the three major theoretical variables should show some degree of intercorrelation; stated otherwise, there should obtain some degree of congruence of the positions a person occupies in the three sociocultural substructures. This idea of covariation of position is clearly implied in Merton's formulation of the relation of limited access in the opportunity structure to anomie in the normative structure. The correlation of access to legitimate opportunity with access to illegitimate means is spelled out by Cloward and Ohlin as follows: "Social controls and channels to success goals are generally related: where opportunities exist, patterns of control will be found; where opportunities are absent, patterns of social control are likely to be absent, too. The association of these two features of social organization is a logical implication of our theory" (1960, pp. 174–175). It is implicit, then, that our formulation of the sociocultural system calls for some degree of correlation among its elements: Limited access in the opportunity structure, anomie, and access to illegitimate means should all tend to vary together. The degree to which this logical implication holds true empirically will be examined in Chapter 9.

Location of an *individual* with respect to position in each of the three sociocultural structures yields a likelihood estimate of his behaving in a deviant fashion. It is critical to emphasize, however, that such a statement is only a *probabilistic* one. What a rate figure always implies about any individual in a defined population are the *chances* of his showing whatever attribute is of concern. The *inevitability* of a given *individual* showing that attribute, however, can only be argued when it has been shown that the expected effects of occupying certain social locations have indeed *taken place*—the individual *actually has* those personal attributes which were hypothesized to flow from his location in a certain sociocultural position. It is variation in personality system attributes, in other words, which accounts for the individual differences in behavior *among persons all located at the same sociocultural position.*

In the following chapter, the concepts and structure of the personality system will be presented and their coordination to variables in the sociocultural system and to deviance will be detailed.

REFERENCES

BANDURA, A. AND CAROL J. KUPERS. Transmission of patterns of self-reinforcement through modeling. *Journal of Abnormal and Social Psychology,* 1964, *69,* 1–9.

BANDURA, A., DOROTHEA ROSS, AND SHIELA A. ROSS. Transmission of aggression through imitation of aggressive models. *Journal of Abnormal and Social Psychology,* 1961, *63,* 575–582.

BANDURA, A., DOROTHEA ROSS, AND SHIELA A. ROSS. Imitation of film-mediated aggressive models. *Journal of Abnormal and Social Psychology,* 1963, *66,* 3–11.

BANDURA, A. AND R. H. WALTERS. *Social learning and personality development.* New York: Holt, Rinehart and Winston, 1963.

BARNETT, M. Alcoholism in the Cantonese of New York City: An anthropological study. In O. Diethelm (Ed.) *Etiology of chronic alcoholism.* Springfield, Ill.: Charles C Thomas, 1955. Pp. 179–227.

CARTER, H. D. *Sin and science.* New York: Ronald, 1946.

CHILD, I. L. Problems of personality and some relations to anthropology and sociology. In S. Koch (Ed.) *Psychology: A study of a science.* Vol. 5. *The process areas, the person, and some applied fields: Their place in psychology and in science.* New York: McGraw-Hill, 1963. Pp. 593–638.

CLOWARD, R. A. Illegitimate means, anomie, and deviant behavior. *American Sociological Review*, 1959, *24*, 164–176.

CLOWARD, R. A. AND L. E. OHLIN. *Delinquency and opportunity*. New York: Free Press, 1960.

CRESSEY, D. R. Epidemiology and individual conduct: A case from criminology. *Pacific Sociological Review*, 1960, *3*, 47–58.

CRESSEY, D. R. Crime. In R. K. Merton and R. A. Nisbet (Eds.) *Contemporary social problems*. New York: Harcourt, Brace & World, 1961. Pp. 21–76.

DIGGS, MARY H. Some problems and needs of Negro children as revealed by comparative delinquency and crime statistics. *Journal of Negro Education*, 1950, *19*, 290–297.

DURKHEIM, E. *Suicide*. (Trans. J. A. Spaulding and G. Simpson) New York: Free Press, 1951.

FIELD, P. B. A new cross cultural study of drunkenness. In D. J. Pittman and C. R. Snyder (Eds.) *Society, culture, and drinking patterns*. New York: Wiley, 1962. Pp. 48–74.

GILLIN, J. *For a science of social man: Convergences in anthropology, psychology, and sociology*. New York: Crowell-Collier and Macmillan, 1954.

HOLLINGSHEAD, A. B. *Two-Factor Index of Social Position*. Mimeographed, 1956.

HOLLINGSHEAD, A. B. AND F. C. REDLICH. *Social class and mental illness: A community study*. New York: Wiley, 1958.

HUGHES, C. C., M. TREMBLAY, R. N. RAPOPORT, AND A. H. LEIGHTON. *People of cove and woodlot: Communities from the viewpoint of social psychiatry*. Vol. II. *The Stirling County study of psychiatric disorder and sociocultural environment*. New York: Basic Books, 1960.

INKELES, A. Personality and social structure. In R. K. Merton, L. Broom and L. S. Cottrell, Jr. (Eds.) *Sociology today*. New York: Basic Books, 1959. Pp. 249–276.

INKELES, A. Sociology and psychology. In S. Koch (Ed.) *Psychology: A study of a science*. Vol. 6. *Investigations of man as socius: Their place in psychology and the social sciences*. New York: McGraw-Hill, 1963. Pp. 317–387.

INKELES, A. AND D. J. LEVINSON. The personal system and the sociocultural system in large-scale organizations. *Sociometry*, 1963, *26*, 217–229.

LEIGHTON, A. H. *My name is legion*. Vol. I. *The Stirling County study of psychiatric disorder and sociocultural environment*. New York: Basic Books, 1959.

LEIGHTON, DOROTHEA C., J. S. HARDING, D. B. MACKLIN, A. M. MACMILLAN, AND A. H. LEIGHTON. *The character of danger: Psychiatric symptoms in selected communities*. Vol. III. *The Stirling County study of psychiatric disorder and sociocultural environment*. New York: Basic Books, 1963.

LEVI-STRAUSS, C. Social structure. In A. L. Kroeber (Ed.) *Anthropology today*. Chicago: University of Chicago Press, 1953. Pp. 524–553.

LEWIN, K. *Field theory in social science: Selected theoretical papers*. D. Cartwright (Ed.). New York: Harper & Row, 1951.

LINDESMITH, A. R. AND J. H. GAGNON. Anomie and drug addiction. In M. B. Clinard (Ed.) *Anomie and deviant behavior.* New York: Free Press, 1964. Pp. 158–188.

MACCOBY, ELEANOR E., J. P. JOHNSON, AND R. M. CHURCH. Community integration and the social control of juvenile delinquency. *Journal of Social Issues,* 1958, *14,* 38–51.

MCCORD, JOAN AND W. MCCORD. The effects of parental role model on criminality. *Journal of Social Issues,* 1958, *14,* 66–75.

MEIER, DOROTHY L. AND W. BELL. Anomie and differential access to the achievement of life goals. *American Sociological Review,* 1959, *24,* 189–202.

MERTON, R. K. *Social theory and social structure.* (Rev. ed.) New York: Free Press, 1957.

MIZRUCHI, E. H. *Success and opportunity: Class values and anomie in American life.* New York: Free Press, 1964.

NADEL, S. F. *The theory of social structure.* New York: Free Press, 1957.

PARSONS, T. *The structure of social action.* (2nd ed.) New York: Free Press. 1949.

PARSONS, T. AND E. A. SHILS. (Eds.) *Toward a general theory of action.* Cambridge: Harvard University Press, 1951.

PETTIGREW, T. F. *A profile of the Negro American.* Princeton, N.J.: Van Nostrand, 1964.

REISS, A. J., JR. Delinquency as the failure of personal and social controls. *American Sociological Review,* 1951, *16,* 196–207.

ROBINS, N., H. GYMAN, AND PATRICIA O'NEAL. The interaction of social class and deviant behavior. *American Sociological Review,* 1962, *27,* 480–492.

SEEMAN, M. A preliminary statement on the concept of social norm. Dittoed. No date.

SHAW, C. R. AND H. D. MCKAY. *Juvenile delinquency and urban areas.* Chicago: University of Chicago Press, 1942.

SHERIF, M. AND CAROLYN W. SHERIF. *Reference groups: Exploration into conformity and deviation of adolescents.* New York: Harper & Row, 1964.

SNYDER, C. R. Inebriety, alcoholism, and anomie. In M. B. Clinard (Ed.) *Anomie and deviant behavior.* New York: Free Press, 1964. Pp. 189–212.

SROLE, L. Social integration and certain corollaries: An exploratory study. *American Sociological Review,* 1956, *21,* 709–716.

STOTLAND, E. AND M. PATCHEN. Identification and changes in prejudice and in authoritarianism. *Journal of Abnormal and Social Psychology,* 1961, *62,* 265–274.

STOTLAND E., A. ZANDER, AND T. NATSOULAS. Generalization of interpersonal similarity. *Journal of Abnormal and Social Psychology,* 1961, *62,* 250–256.

SUTHERLAND, E. H. AND D. R. CRESSEY. *Principles of criminology.* (5th ed.) New York: Lippincott, 1955.

TOBY, J. The prospects for reducing delinquency rates in industrial societies. *Federal Probation,* 1963, *27,* 23–25.

Voss, H. L. Differential association and reported delinquent behavior: A replication. *Social Problems*, 1964, *12*, 78–85.

Wohl, R. R. The "rags to riches story"; An episode of secular idealism. In R. Bendix and S. M. Lipset (Eds.) *Class, status and power: A reader in social stratification.* New York: Free Press, 1953. Pp. 388–395.

Wood, A. L. Crime and aggression in changing Ceylon. *Transactions of the American Philosophical Society*, 1961, *51*, Part 8. Pp. 1–132.

Yinger, J. M. Research implications of a field view of personality. *American Journal of Sociology*, 1963, *68*, 580–592.

Yinger, J. M. *Toward a field theory of behavior: Personality and social structure.* New York: McGraw-Hill, 1965.

CHAPTER FOUR

The Personality System and Deviance

A GENERAL PERSPECTIVE

The contribution of the psychology of personality to the systematic exploration of complex social behavior has not thus far been impressive. The salient example, the influence of psychoanalytic theory on culture-personality studies, proved not only an empirical disappointment in most respects, but for a time even threatened the foundations of cultural anthropology. Leslie White was moved to the caustic comment that some anthropologists "have sold their culturological birthright for a mess of psychiatric pottage" (1949, p. xix), and Francis Hsu warned his anthropological colleagues: "If we are not careful we shall be in danger of drifting into a nipple-diaper theory of man that will be . . . dangerous and absurd" (1952, p. 250).

The fact is that neither of the two views of human nature dominant in psychology, the psychoanalytic view and the behavioristic view, has taken *systematic* cognizance of the sociocultural environment or of the social nexus of human behavior. The former view, emphasizing biological and early-learned components of personality, and the latter view, emphasizing molecular and peripheral stimulus-response systems, have both failed to yield a satisfactory picture of man as a social being. As a result, the man of contemporary psychology has been described by Asch (1959) as a "quite dwarflike creature" and by·Allport (1955) as a "caricature."

The more recent developments in personality theory outlined by Sanford (1963) hold promise, however, of changing this state of affairs. Among the variety of significant recent trends he discusses, two are of special pertinence to our work. The first of these is the increased attention to and concern for *cognitive* variables of personality—beliefs, values, expectations, attitudes, ideologies, and orientations. This burgeoning interest in the cognitive, reflecting a long overdue recognition of the unique importance of language and symbols in human behavior, represents at the same time a move away from the biological and animal models inherent in psychoanalysis and behaviorism. It represents also a more adequate appraisal of the role of consciousness and rationality in human affairs than was contained in the classical Freudian legacy derived largely from studies of psychopathology. That even psychoanalysis itself is not immune to this emphasis on the cognitive is clearly evident in the vigorous developments currently underway under the rubric of "ego psychology" (see Gill, 1959).

The second significant change in personality theory involves the effort to accomodate *social* influences on personality development and functioning. As Sanford notes, this emphasis logically follows, at least in part, from the previous one: "An accent on cognition usually goes with an accent on the environment . . ." (1963, p. 504). Beliefs, attitudes, values, and expectations are increasingly considered as outcomes or precipitates of experience, the latter term referring to transactions which take place within a socially defined context. It is this context which, in turn, endows the objects and actions of social interchange with their meaning.

The implications of the emphases upon cognitive and social variables are entirely consonant with the concept of "social personality" urged a decade earlier by Inkeles (1953) as that level of personality analysis which has the greatest potentiality for contributing to the study of society. In contrast to the then prevalent notion of "basic personality," with its emphases upon deep-lying, early-learned, and largely unconscious personality dimensions (see Kardiner, 1945), the emphasis of the notion of "social personality" is placed upon socially learned cognitive systems. These beliefs, attitudes, values, and expectations reflect more of the learnings of later life, are more or less available to conscious awareness, and can be expressed fairly directly in speech and action. Their importance for the student of social systems lies in the relatively direct linkage which can be constructed between such dimensions of personality and their correlates in the past and present sociocultural environment. In Inkeles' terms, "these idea systems have crucial relevance to the individual's social action, and consequently for the social system" (1953, p. 584). Such dimensions of personality are likely, then, to meet the criterion of "relevance to social variations" which Child (1963) has suggested as a major one in selecting personality concepts for social-psychological research.

Personality, as with the sociocultural environment, is not usefully dealt with in global or diffuse terms. It requires, instead, differentiation into component structures or variables whose interactions are logically consequential for behavior choices. This is another way of stating that personality is best conceived of as a *system,* a term referring to the organization of the relatively enduring psychological substructures of a person. In the present conception, the occurrence of certain behaviors becomes more likely as the logical consequence of the organization of the personality system.

But personality, it must be noted, does not itself determine behavior directly. The interaction of elements in the personality system eventuates in *tendencies or dispositions* to respond in certain ways. The *actual* response is construed as a joint function of the articulation of the personality and sociocultural systems. The response which occurs reflects *both* the personality-determined dispositions and the socioculturally determined characteristics of the situation to which the response is to be made.

Our orientation, in summary, has stressed the importance of treating personality as a differentiated system made up of component structures which connect with behavior by generating dispositions to respond. The component structures are delineated at the level of the "social personality," referring to cognitive variables which are outcomes or correlates of patterned exposure, over time, to the sociocultural environment. The approach to personality which largely meets these requirements is the approach with which the present research began, namely, Rotter's social learning theory of personality (1954, 1955, 1960, 1967). A brief description of the theory should be useful at this point.

ROTTER'S SOCIAL LEARNING THEORY
OF PERSONALITY

Social learning theory of personality is a formulation which has been developed over the past two decades by Julian B. Rotter and a number of his students and colleagues. The theory is called a "learning" theory because behavior is seen as taking place in a *meaningful* environment (rather than in one defined by the language of physics), and meaning or significance is acquired through past experience. The term "social" is employed to convey the concern of the theory for the interpersonal or societal mediation of the significant learnings and the rewards and punishments experienced by individuals.

The theory is somewhat different from certain other learning theories in psychology in that its immediate conceptual focus is upon human beings rather than animals; it is concerned essentially with cognitive learning or central processes rather than with peripheral motor responses; and the outcome of learning—the personality—is represented in systems of preferences or valuations and systems of expectation or anticipation which mediate goal-directed behavior tendencies. It should be helpful to describe the major terms and formulations of Rotter's theory in order to provide the background for the personality system variables which were used in the present research. All of our psychological variables derive from, are extensions of, or can be interpreted in terms of the basic concepts in Rotter's approach.

The fundamental concepts in Rotter's social learning theory are the following: (1) *expectation* (E), which refers to the subjective probability held by an individual that a specific behavior will lead to the occurrence of certain events or reinforcements; (2) *reinforcement value* (RV), which refers to the degree of preference for the events or reinforcements which are contingently related to behavior; (3) *behavior potential* (BP), which refers to the likelihood of occurrence of a behavior, or the relative strength of the tendency to respond in a certain way; and (4) the *psychological situation* (S), which refers to the immediate context of action described in psychologically relevant terms, that is, in terms reflecting the actor's potential perception or interpretation of his confronting situation.

These basic terms generate the following descriptive formula, which constitutes the foundation for prediction or explanation at the personality level: BP = f(E and RV). The formula reads: The potentiality of any behavior occurring in a given situation is some function (probably multiplicative) of (1) the expectation that it will, in that situation, lead to a particular goal and (2) the value of that goal in that situation. Note that the "S" term is implicit in that each of the other terms in the formula is variable or dependent upon the specific properties perceived in the psychological situation. Action, or actual behavior, then, always involves a process of selection or choice, from a repertoire of behaviors, of that behavior with the highest potential for leading to gratification in a given context.

This model, explicated at the level of a specific behavior potential, expectancy, and reinforcement value, has only limited utility since it deals with only a single behavior in a specific situation in relation to a single reinforcement. For most purposes, a higher-level or broader formulation is needed. The processes of socialization and experience are such that various specific behaviors become functionally related as a consequence of their mutual substitutability in leading to classes of similar goals; and various specific goals become functionally related as a consequence of their interchangeability in reinforcing certain behaviors. Thus, *sets* of functionally related behavior potentials become established through learning; this more generalized behavior concept is called *need potential* (NP). The mean expectancy of obtaining positive gratification which now characterizes a set of related behaviors is referred to as *freedom of movement* (FM).[1] And, the mean or characteristic preference value of a set of similar or functionally related goals is referred to as *need value* (NV).

It is now possible to state the more generalized social learning formula-

---

[1] "We have selected the term *freedom of movement* [rather than mean expectancy] in order to convey the relationship of this concept to some of the frequently used concepts of maladjustment, since freedom of movement deals with expectancy for a variety of behaviors for positive satisfaction. High freedom of movement implies an expectancy of success for many different behaviors in different situations; low freedom of movement implies the opposite" (Rotter, 1954, p. 194). We will elaborate the central significance of this concept shortly.

tion which takes into account these learned relationships among behaviors and goals and yet retains the theoretical logic of the basic formula: NP = f(FM and NV). This formula states that the potentiality of occurrence of a set of functionally similar behaviors (NP) in relation to a set of similar goals is a function of (1) the mean expectancy (FM) for these behaviors actually leading to these goals and (2) the mean value (NV) of the set of goals.

An example at this level of analysis may make the meaning of this formula more concrete. One might, for example, be interested in accounting for why a teen-ager spends most of his free time in peer group interaction rather than in studying or in school-related work. The account would require determining the value the teen-ager placed on various consequences of doing well in school—such as being admired by the teacher, being respected by the other students for good work, being rewarded by his parents for good grades, and being able to go on to college because of his school achievements. The value of these goals or reinforcements, all related to school achievement, would be summarized as need value for academic recognition.

The inquiry would then turn to the assessment of the set of behaviors available to the teen-ager for reaching these goals—for example, studying hard for exams, doing outside reading, turning in extra papers, speaking up in class, taking elaborate lecture notes, discussing issues after class with the teacher. The expectations he holds that these behaviors will lead to academic success are a consequence of his past successes and failures and of his view of the present situation. The expectations characteristic of this set of behaviors, all related to his need value for academic recognition, would be summarized as his freedom of movement for academic recognition. Finally, the probability of occurrence of one or more of the set of behaviors listed above, that is, his need potential for academic recognition, would then be, according to the formula, a function of his freedom of movement for academic recognition and his need value for academic recognition.

A parallel analysis would be carried out for the value placed on the gratifications involved in peer group interactions, for example, affection from the opposite sex, or recognition for leadership, social, or physical skills. The expectations for attaining these goals by some set of available behaviors, such as those exhibiting athletic prowess, would also be determined. The analysis might then lead to the conclusion that the reason why the teen-ager spends so little time at school work is that he places little value on academic recognition; or that, while he has equal freedom of movement for the two sets of goals, he has much stronger need value for peer affection than for academic recognition; or that, despite a high need value for academic recognition, his freedom of movement is so low that he avoids the situation and turns to situations involving peer interaction, where his freedom of movement for attaining his goals is relatively high.

It should be noted that, in this example, we have been operating at an intermediate level of generality, speaking neither of a single goal-directed behavior, such as studying hard, nor of a highly general class of directional behavior, such as recognition behavior. Rather, we have retained some degree of *situational* specification by speaking, in this case, of *academic* recognition. It is possible, of course, to operate at any level of generality, depending upon one's purpose. Thus, an experimentalist might wish to manipulate specific behaviors (for example, studying) in testing a theoretical hypothesis, while a clinical psychologist, with no interest in the particular behaviors involved, might wish to describe the main directions of a person's life (such as "recognition oriented").

The sets of functionally related behavior potentials are the needs or motives in Rotter's theory. At the more general level, they are intended to represent some of the major directions of human activity in our society. Some of the needs which have been used in the theory are, for example, needs for recognition-status, love and affection, dependence, dominance, and independence. It is important to make clear that these needs do not depend upon physiological referents; they are, rather, dispositions to action the nature and organization of which are a consequence of social learning or enculturation by the individual. Insofar as needs represent the precipitate in the individual of social learning, they are considered to reflect in large part the patterned systems of valuation and the patterned systems of success and failure with which the culture, over time, has confronted the individual in his psychological environment.

One further point remains to be emphasized in this general outline of Rotter's theory of personality, namely, the substantial theoretical importance attached to the psychological situation. Each of the terms in the formula is coordinated to the situation, which means that the magnitude of each term varies to some extent as the situation varies. Thus, persons are not seen as bundles of attributes that "will out," irrespective of where they are and when. Rather, *the situation is influential in determining not only the relative strength of behavior tendencies but also the process of choice among them in leading to action.* The situation is describable in terms parallel to those used to describe persons, for example, in terms of the various goals available ("an achievement situation"), or in terms of the accessibility of goals ("a complex or difficult or threatening situation"). The psychological situation is, then, the environment of learned meanings constituted largely of the *social definitions* of the personal and nonpersonal world in which every person is and has been embedded. The psychological situation thus provides a bridge between personality, on the one hand, and the sociocultural environment, on the other.

We have, to this point, summarized some of the main aspects of social learning theory to which we will have recourse in delineating the personality system and its substructures as employed in our research. Anthropologists and sociologists should find these conceptions especially congenial for several reasons. First, the terms in which personality is described are quite obviously parallel to the terms in which the sociocultural system can usefully be described. Such a parallel, in turn, lays the groundwork for a logical coordination between the two systems. Second, the dynamics of personality are located neither in the individual's physiology nor in the earliest learned and least accessible regions of his experience; rather, the strivings reflect the learning of socially patterned and socially reinforced preferences or values. Finally, the general level of personality description is that which is fairly salient in carrying on interpersonal and social behavior—cognitive processes such as beliefs, values, and expectations—and that which, while relatively enduring, is continuously subject to change throughout the life span.

THE PERSONALITY SYSTEM

Our treatment of the personality system is directly analogous to our treatment of the sociocultural environment. Three major component structures of personality, each of which is parallel to its sociocultural counterpart, will be described. The three personality structures are: (1) the perceived opportunity structure, (2) the personal belief structure, and (3) the personal control structure. Further, the relations posited among the personality substructures are formally identical with those assumed among the sociocultural substructures. The coordination of each of the personality substructures to the terms of Rotter's theory will become evident as each is discussed in turn.

The Perceived Opportunity Structure

The principal concern of the perceived opportunity structure is with the values or goals toward which an individual is striving and the expectations which he holds of attaining them. More precisely, the concern is with the *relation between* values or goals, on the one hand, and expectations of attaining them by the set of socially approved or prescribed behaviors, on the other hand. Where expectations fall short, in the psychological sense, of comparability or equivalence with the importance attached to goals, a gap exists. This psychological gap, a value-expectation disjunction, is termed a *personal disjunction,* and it constitutes, at the personality level, a direct analogue of Merton's value-access disjunction at the sociocultural level. Similar to the latter, personal disjunctions generate the dynamic or provide the *source of instigation in the personality system* to employ alternative behaviors for achieving goals. When the alternatives adopted are socially disapproved behaviors, personal disjunctions are construed as having instigated deviance. Some elaboration of these variables and their interaction leading to deviance is necessary.

Need Values

The first variable requiring discussion is need value. Our theoretical concern with the concept of need value is not with linking differences in need value directly to behavior. Rather, the concern with need value is due to its role in establishing, at the personality level, the necessary precondition for the occurrence of deprivation or for the existence of personal disjunctions. Only if an individual actually does value certain goals is it possible for their lack of attainment to be a meaningful frustration for him. Need value is theoretically crucial, then, in setting an individual baseline against which variation in expectation for goal attainment occurs. Such variation, resulting in value-expectation disjunctions, reflects the degree of instigation to deviant behavior.

The conceptualization of need values in Rotter's theory rests upon several important distinctions. First, these values refer to *personally held* preferences for certain goals or events. While such personal preferences may mirror culturally defined and culturally shared values, the reference of the need value concept is to the person and not to the society. Second, need values refer to *motivationally relevant* states of affairs such as values for affection, independence, or recognition. This use of the term is characteristic of contemporary personality formulations (see Murray, 1959; Lewin, 1951; Atkinson, 1958, especially Chapter 42). The general idea of the motivational relevance of the value concept is perhaps best captured in Kurt Lewin's term "valence," which specifies the attractiveness or value of a goal as being directly correlated to the strength of the relevant motive.[2]

Third, need values refer to goals or satisfactions which are *psychologically defined* rather than defined in the common object or event language. To take an example, a car may have extremely high preference value for a teen-ager. In the common object language one may describe his behavior as car oriented, or as car striving, or, more colloquially, as "car crazy." A psychological description, however, would require specification of the satisfactions involved in possessing a car—for example, prestige, affection, social power. The possible range of psychologically defined satis-

---

[2] We have stressed the motivational relevance of the concept of value in order to clarify the difference between our use of the term to refer to preferences for certain goals and the use of the value term in such concepts as "value orientations." In the latter usage, "value" refers to general ideas or beliefs about man and his relations to the world (see Kluckhohn and Strodtbeck, 1961). Such beliefs or value orientations, when used to characterize persons, would belong to the personal belief structure in our scheme.

factions implicated by any objects or events depends upon the meanings which have accrued to them for a given individual. Thus, the object money may implicate, for one person, power, for another prestige, for a third independence. It is this latter psychological level of analysis to which the concept of need value refers. It may also be seen that any given need value, say the need value for recognition, may be implicated by a large variety of objects or statuses or events—wealth, membership in a select social club, owning a "hot-rod," dating the most popular girl, excelling in athletics, or going to the "right" school.

The success values which Merton describes as pervading American society are described, in the main, in the common object language. This is the language of discourse also employed by the man in the street. Thus, when Mizruchi (1964) asked for "signs of success in our society," his respondents mentioned education, friends, home ownership, and money, among their replies.

The importance of the emphasis upon psychological definition of values lies in our concern with degree of personal deprivation. Since the same psychological satisfaction can usually be attained through a variety of mutually substitutable objects—the teen-ager without a car may attain peer group recognition alternatively by athletic accomplishments or by dating the best-looking girl in the class—reliable assessment of personal deprivation can be made only at the level of satisfactions, not at the level of objects attained. In our research on the value aspect of the perceived opportunity structure, we concentrated, then, upon Rotter's concept of need values, values which are personal, motivationally relevant, and psychologically defined preferences.

The major theoretical problem faced, once this definition of need value is reached, is *which* need values and *how many* different need values must be sampled in an individual's repertoire in order to provide an adequate baseline for the establishment of psychological deprivation or personal disjunction? Obviously, specific answers to such questions cannot be made without consideration of the behavioral domain being investigated—in our case, deviance—and of the characteristics of the persons involved—in our case, adults and adolescents in the American culture. In general, however, it would seem to be crucial to sample the need values which are involved in the main interactions of daily life, the deprivation of which should inevitably lead to strong feelings of frustration. Need values of this sort have been specified by numerous personality theorists, and there is an impressive amount of overlap in the lists they provide (see Murray, 1938; McClelland *et al.,* 1953; Child and Whiting, 1950; and Rotter, 1954). Further, it would seem to be crucial, not necessarily to exhaust the need value repertoire, but to sample a sufficient and significant enough portion of it so that attainment or nonattainment could reasonably be presumed to have important consequences for an individual's adjustment or behavior.

Considerations such as these influenced our selection of both number and kind of need values to be sampled. We made the a priori assumption that by sampling need values for recognition, affection, dependency, and independence, we would be working with satisfactions of major relevance and importance in the lives of our subjects. Frustration or nonattainment of these need values should be significant enough to eventuate in instigation to alternative behavior—our fundamental theoretical requirement.[3]

A summary of the nature and role of need values in the perceived opportunity structure should be useful at this point. Need values are personal preferences for goals described in motivational terms. Our interest in need values is not in linking them directly to behavior; theoretically we do not have any basis for anticipating that deviants will differ from non-deviants in their profiles of need values, that is, in the importance they attach to certain kinds of psychological satisfactions.[4] Rather, our interest in need values stems from the theoretical necessity of establishing the conditions generating the occurrence of psychological deprivation or frustration. In order to accomplish this, at least a significant segment of the need value repertoire must be assessed, and the assessment must sample various areas of life in which such satisfactions can be gained. Once this is known, it is then possible, by introducing the concept of expectation for achieving these values, to specify the degree and nature of deprivation at the personality level. It is this latter variable to which our theory directs attention in accounting for instigation to deviance.

A comment by Inkeles relates to our own aims in this regard: "We . . . need to discover the most likely consequences of the deprivation of needs, such as needs for dependence, for affiliation, for self-respect and others to which social situations and systems may systematically deny adequate satisfaction" (1963, p. 380). Leighton's theoretical approach to the underlying basis of psychiatric symptom development is also similar

---

[3] The actual need values investigated varied in the several separate studies which were carried out, but in each study this same theoretical requirement was met. Details on the measurement of need values in the different studies are described in Chapter 10.

[4] Numerous psychological researches have tried to link measures of needs or motives directly to behavior, especially studies of needs on the Thematic Apperception Test or on the Edwards Personal Preference Schedule. Increasingly, however, there is awareness of the importance of multivariable efforts when behavior prediction is the aim (see Rotter, 1960, pp. 305–308). In reviewing some of the implications of single-variable studies, Child concludes that "a theory about multiple influences on a behavioral tendency may reveal consistencies which a common sense approach of looking for apparent [that is, direct] similarities might miss altogether" (1963, p. 606).

to our view of instigation to deviance. Instead of employing need values, he postulates a series of striving sentiments the fulfillment of which he considers essential to a benign psychical condition.[5] He proposes that "interference with striving leads to a disturbance of the essential psychical condition" (Leighton, 1959, p. 146) and may eventuate in psychiatric symptoms. While, in contrast to our own work on need values, these striving sentiments were not directly measured in the Stirling County study, the general paradigm is the same: A set of satisfactions is postulated, and their nonattainment provides a source of instigation to problem behavior.

Expectations

It is possible now to turn to the second major variable in the perceived opportunity structure, the concept of expectation. Given the baseline of need value, the concept of expectation provides the means for determining the degree to which psychological deprivation actually obtains in the personality system.

The concept of expectation, in one form or another, has come in recent decades to occupy a central position not only in psychology but in other behavioral sciences as well. Since the early emphasis on expectation by Tolman, Lewin, and Brunswik, nearly all systematic psychological accounts of behavior include some concept referring to the anticipation of outcomes or future events. It is apparent that the orderly regulation of social life depends heavily upon the anticipatory capabilities of man.

Our own concern with expectations, at this point, is with their implications for behavior. Holding need value constant or stable, the selection of a behavior from a repertoire is entirely dependent, according to Rotter's formula, upon the expectation of attaining the goal by way of that behavior in that situation. The behavior with the highest expectation of success, or the lowest expectation for failure or punishment, is the one which, theoretically, will have the strongest behavior potential. Where the expectation that a particular behavior will lead to a goal is low, alternative behaviors will be more likely to be tried. If expectations are low for the large class of behavior which constitutes socially approved modes of striving, then the alternatives likely to occur should be those which are socially disapproved—namely, deviance.

This concern with low expectations for a *class or set* of behaviors leading to goal attainment refers us to Rotter's concept of freedom of movement. It will be recalled that expectations for classes of functionally related

---

[5] While some of these sentiments, such as "the securing of love" or "the securing of recognition," are similar to the content of our need values, others involve quite different content, for example, "the expression of spontaneity" (see Leighton, 1959, p. 148).

behaviors (need potentials) leading to classes of similar goals (need values) are summarized in Rotter's theory as the freedom of movement for those behaviors. The importance of the concept of freedom of movement has been clearly stated by Rotter and it is worthwhile quoting him fully on this point:

> A crucial part of this theory is that there are specific hypotheses regarding the behavior of an individual with low freedom of movement and high need value for a particular class of satisfactions. When an individual has low freedom of movement and places high value on some class of reinforcements, he is likely to learn behaviors to avoid the failure or punishments that he anticipates in this area and may make attempts to achieve these goals on an irreal level. That is, the person anticipating punishment or failure may avoid situations physically or by repression or may attempt to reach the goals through rationalization, fantasy or symbolic means. The great variety of behaviors commonly regarded as defenses or psychopathological symptoms are here referred to as avoidance or irreal behaviors (1967, p. 491).

This formulation is crucial to our analysis of the perceived opportunity structure and deviance. Rotter has specified a condition—high need value and low freedom of movement—which is a clear-cut analogue of Merton's value-access disjunction at the sociocultural level. In adopting it, however, we have reformulated it in two major ways to make it more appropriate to our purposes. First, Rotter's concern, as a clinician, has been largely with the usual symptoms of psychopathology, which he designates by the rubrics of avoidance or irreal behaviors. While such behaviors frequently do result from the high need value and low freedom of movement condition, they need not do so inevitably. Nor is it necessary that they be considered the most likely kinds of behavior to occur under that condition. Looked at analytically, the high-NV–low-FM condition specifies only *a general state of instigation to alternative behaviors,* that is, to behaviors which may have a relatively higher likelihood of attaining the valued goals or of avoiding or coping with failure. *Which* behaviors will be tried as alternatives depends on a variety of factors which will have influenced the individual's behavioral repertoire through past experience and which vary in the contemporary psychological situation.

It is our contention that the high-NV–low-FM formulation may usefully be applied to the condition where there is low FM for the class of socially approved or conforming behaviors. Depending upon differential past exposure to illegitimate means, and differential present opportunities to engage in illegitimate means, some of the behavioral alternatives instigated by this condition will be departures from normative prescription, that is, will be deviant behaviors. Thus, while Rotter stresses the relation of this general instigating condition to psychopathology, we wish to stress its relation to our concern with deviance.[6] The fundamental dynamics are identical. Whether psychiatric disorder or delinquency emerges would seem to be a function not of the instigating condition itself but *of the alternative behaviors available in the person's repertoire.* These, in turn, depend upon past learning or exposure, including exposure to illegitimate means, and upon the nature of the present situation.

The general process may be illustrated by the example of the teen-ager who has high value for school achievement and low expectation, perhaps because of limited ability, of being able to do well in school by such socially approved behavior as hard work and study. This value-expectation disparity creates pressure either toward the adoption of socially unapproved, but technically effective, alternative behaviors, for example, cheating on an exam, or toward the ultimate repudiation of the school-achievement goal in favor of other, more accessible goals, such as recognition from a peer group that hangs around the pool hall.

A second aspect of our reformulation is equally important. Rotter speaks in the quotation just cited (1967, p. 491) of the *particular* condition of high NV and low FM as the source of instigation. This can be seen, however, as only a special case of a more general proposition, namely, that *any disjunction* or disparity between NV and FM creates the essential precondition for trying those alternatives with *less* disjunction. Given that a need value is above some threshold level, so that it can reasonably be considered of some importance or value, then the possible relation of FM to this NV can be seen as a continuously varying one. Rather than having to define a single categorical condition of high need value and low freedom of movement, *instigation may be treated as a continuous variable* referring to the differential magnitude of NV-FM disjunction or disparity. To parallel Merton, we have called the magnitude of a value-expectation disparity a "personal disjunction." The main point here is that it is possible to generalize Rotter's condition of instigation from a categorical one to a continuously distributed one.[7]

The low-ability teen-ager with high value on academic achievement confronts instigation to alternative behavior; so, also, does the low-ability teen-ager with only moderate value for academic achievement. The differ-

---

[6] There is, of course, no intrinsic necessity for the instigation to alternatives to eventuate solely in social problem behavior. Creative or innovative acts of social value may also be seen as a possible outcome of the high-NV–low-FM condition.

[7] In the research carried out by Rotter and his students, instigation has actually been treated as a continuous variable. In theoretical elaborations, however, the present formulation has not been explicated.

ence between the two is one of degree; it lies in the differential magnitude of personal disjunction and, consequently, in the differential magnitude of instigation to alternative behaviors.

The implementation of this concept of personal disjunction requires a particular methodology which enables the independent assessment of values and expectations *for the same goals* and, at the same time, enables these assessments to be mapped onto a similar scale so that disjunctions can be determined. The development of both questionnaire and interview procedures which sought to accomplish this is described in Chapter 10.

It should be noted that Rotter's concept of low freedom of movement (which concerns expectations only) and our concept of personal disjunctions (which considers *both* values and expectations) are equivalent when need value can be assumed to be at some level of importance. Thus, if it were possible to make the assumption about a set of goals that they were very important or were highly valued by a person, then instigation could be predicted solely from variation in freedom of movement, without having directly to assess need value. Since it is generally the case that most people value the NV's we are presently dealing with—affection, recognition, dependence, independence—a rough approach to assessing differential instigation among persons could be based upon differences in FM alone. It is clear, however, that individuals vary to some extent in the degree to which they actually do value these goals; because of this, the more precise assessment of instigation should be the one which takes into account the *individual's* NV. This is exactly what the concept of "personal disjunctions" is designed to do. And it is for their use in this regard, that is, in constituting personal disjunctions, that the assessment of need values was considered as theoretically necessary in the discussion earlier in this section.

We have now described the important aspects of the perceived opportunity structure, one of the three major components of the personality system. This component is considered to be the analogue, at the personality level, of the legitimate opportunity structure at the sociocultural level. The aspects of the perceived opportunity structure which were discussed—values, expectations, and personal disjunctions—are all considered to be the outcome of social learning and, therefore, to reflect patterned exposure to differential location in the sociocultural opportunity structure. The linkage with the sociocultural opportunity structure is based upon the assumption that location in that structure should involve differential experiences of success and failure which should, in turn, eventuate in differential expectations of achieving valued goals. Location where access is limited should result in lower expectations or in higher personal disjunctions.

It should be pointed out that patterned exposure to limited access involves not only exposure to the actual *experience* of failure to achieve goals but also exposure to the *objective probability* of future failure. Such probability derives from learning the meaning of certain objective factors characterizing one's position in the sociocultural opportunity structure: the meaning of being a Negro, of coming from an immigrant family, of not being able to finish school. In this sense, patterned exposure to the failure of *others,* similarly located and similarly characterized, can be as important in generating pressure for deviance as the *personal* experience of failure or limited access. The role of this kind of exposure is especially critical for teen-agers whose position in the opportunity structure is still uncertain and largely dependent upon the position of others, primarily their parents. Lower-class youth are exposed to obvious examples of the existential barriers to open opportunity which are reflected in the failure of their parents, often despite hard work and persistent effort, to achieve the valued goals of American culture.

The importance of patterned exposure to the failure of others is poignantly caught up in the phrase "models of dissociation" (Antonovsky and Lerner, 1959). These authors use the phrase to describe the circumstances whereby Negro or immigrant parents, in encouraging their children to strive to get an education and to get ahead in life, deliberately use themselves as a negative reference group, that is, as models *not* to be emulated. The fact of the matter is, however, that such models of dissociation, implying the probability of failure, do constitute an important aspect of patterned exposure to value-access disjunction in the opportunity structure; they should, therefore, have an important effect upon *perceived* opportunity in the personality system.

The linkage of the perceived opportunity structure to deviant behavior directly parallels the relation of the sociocultural opportunity structure to deviance rates. To the extent that an individual's perceived opportunity structure is characterized by pervasive value-expectation disparities, that is, by personal disjunctions in a variety of need areas, to that extent does he experience instigation to try alternative behavior, even if the latter are illegitimate, to attain gratification or to cope with failure. What the specific character of the alternative behavior will actually be depends in large part upon other factors, the other two substructures of the personality system, to be discussed in the next two sections.

The Personal Belief Structure

Our efforts to differentiate the personality system in terms of components which can both reflect aspects of the sociocultural system and carry implications for deviant behavior have led us to look beyond sources of personal instigation to sources of personal control. Any conceptualization of personal control immediately involves a wide variety of variables

referring to beliefs, orientations, general values, internalized standards, and attitudes which, in one way or another, constrain (or fail to constrain) against deviance. While, in these terms, all of the variables would have a common function and could, therefore, logically be subsumed within a single personal control substructure, we have preferred to follow the resolution adopted with respect to the parallel question at the sociocultural level of analysis.

It will be recalled from the earlier discussion that both the normative structure and the social control structure were described as generating controls against deviance. They were, in that sense, logically subsumable under a single, higher-order, social control structure. Instead, we chose, for both conceptual and heuristic purposes, to retain the differentiation of control processes into the two separate control substructures. The same choice was implemented at the personality level of analysis with the differentiation of control processes into two separate control substructures: the personal belief structure and what is then called "the personal control structure."

Some of the reasoning behind this choice may make its advantages clearer and help to reduce any sense of conceptual arbitrariness. The complete *elimination* of arbitrariness is not possible, both because of the very fact that the two substructures are allocated a single theoretical function—control—and because the assignment of a particular variable to one or the other of the two substructures can be made convincing only by differentially emphasizing one or another of its properties.

The most compelling *conceptual* reason for maintaining the two control substructures derives from the interpretation of explanatory variables as being closer to or more remote from the class of behavior, the criterion, being predicted. If one were interested, for example, in predicting drinking, one might ask a respondent about his attitude toward alcohol use, its rightness or wrongness, its benefits or mischiefs. Such an attitudinal variable could be interpreted as being conceptually "close" to the behavior being predicted since the variable focuses upon and directly implicates the actual behavior of drinking. On the other hand, one might attempt to predict alcohol use from conceptually more remote variables having less direct implications for the control of drinking—for example, a variable like the general belief in the possibility of exercising an influence over one's future. The latter variable in no way directly implicates the criterion behavior. Rather, it depends for its linkage to drinking upon a more elaborated conceptual analysis.

We have divided the set of personal control variables on this basis of conceptual contiguity to the criterion. The control variables allocated to the personal belief structure are, as will be seen, relatively more remote. The control variables we have gathered under the rubric of the personal control structure were determined by their relatively greater proximity to deviance. This basis for decision is similar to the one employed at the sociocultural level in differentiating control processes into the more remote normative structure and the more proximal social control structure.

A *heuristic* reason for maintaining two separate control substructures derives from the empirical interest which has been accorded certain variables in the previous research literature and from the greater possibility, by keeping them separate, of examining their relationships to each other and to different aspects of the sociocultural environment. Thus, alienation has recurrently been singled out as a psychological correlate of anomie, but the same is not true of tolerant attitudes toward deviance. By keeping alienation, in this example, conceptually separate from tolerant attitudes toward deviance, the empirical assessment of their relationship is facilitated, as is the assessment of how they may co-vary with respect to a third variable, such as anomie.

Finally, on this point, the separation of controls into two substructures at the personality level satisfies the logic of the parallel we have been seeking to establish with the sociocultural analysis, yielding a part-for-part coordination between the two levels. Whether the elegance thereby achieved is compelling depends, of course, on the discussion of the particular rationale for the variables in each of the two substructures, their differential "closeness" to the criteria, and their differential implication by correlative aspects of the sociocultural environment.

This introduction to the discussion of controls at the personal level requires three other points to be made. The first is brief and is simply a reminder: The variables we will be discussing are ones which we have conceptualized as having implications for deviant behavior by way of control or its absence. But this emphasis in no way should be taken as exhausting their meaning or their more generally considered role in behavior. Alienation, for example, while having implications for deviance in our view, obviously has a wide range of relations other than those we have investigated.

The second point is that the variables in the personal belief structure and in the personal control structure, while all cognitive, are not necessarily of the same generality nor the same conceptual type. We have not attempted to distinguish systematically the several concepts of attitudes, orientations, beliefs, or normative values, although such distinctions may be essential for other purposes. Not only is the problem of conceptual separateness a difficult one, but agreement on what differentiates an attitude from a belief, or a belief from a value-orientation, is not well established in the literature. Our use of such terms is, therefore, relatively interchangeable, although we have tended to use the term "orientation," or "belief," for more generalized personal views and the term "attitude," for views more specifically related to a particular category of behavior—in this case, deviance.

The third point is that all of these variables are considered as having their systematic effects upon behavior by affecting the magnitude of the terms in the basic social learning formula, BP = f(E and RV). Thus, for example, a general orientation—that one can influence the course of one's future—can be coordinated to behavior through use of the formula. Such an orientation may raise the expectations of future goal attainment for behaviors such as working hard and being friendly. The higher the E's for these behaviors, the higher their BP's; hence, the more likely is their occurrence as against the occurrence of alternative behaviors, such as loafing and fighting. It is the possibility of just such theoretical coordination which underlies our *systematic* interest in these variables in accounting for deviance.

The personal belief structure, then, consists of those cognitive beliefs or orientations which are relatively remote conceptually from the specific category "deviant behavior." Nevertheless, the presence of such beliefs and orientations contributes to the likelihood of occurrence of deviance by the fact that *a failure of control against instigation to deviance* is implied. The two psychological variables to be discussed in this category are *"alienation"* and the *"belief in internal or external control,"* both of which, as will be shown, reflect patterned exposure to the sociocultural environment.

Alienation

A long and somewhat confusing history surrounds the definition of the concept of alienation. With no hope of resolving differing perspectives on the term, our present aim is simply to make clear our *own* conceptual usage and empirical specification. In order to do this, a brief review of background considerations is necessary.

Two main currents contribute to the whirlpool of ideas eddying around the present status of the alienation concept. One of these has its source in Marx and his concern for the social and personal consequences of complex, industrialized processes of production. He saw the latter as increasingly separating the worker from the product of his labor and from other workers. The other current has its source in Durkheim's concept of anomie and in the use of this term, or one of its variants, to refer to a personal or subjective state having somewhat the same connotations as the term "alienation." Both the term "alienation," and the *psychological* use of the term "anomie" have in common their reference to a personal or individual state which is presumed to reflect a social condition—for

Marx, the fragmentation of productive relations; for Durkheim, normless-ness or de-regulation.

The psychological use of the concept of anomie is clearly conveyed by MacIver: "Anomy [*sic*] signifies the state of mind of one who has been pulled up by his moral roots, who has no longer any standards but only disconnected urges, who has no longer any sense of continuity, of folk, of obligation. . . . The individual's sense of social cohesion—the mainspring of his morale—is broken or fatally weakened" (1950, pp. 84–85). Davol and Reimanis summarize their review of various discus-sions of psychological anomie by speaking of: "an individual's perception of the social order as lacking meaningfulness or usefulness, his withdrawal from society, or his perception of constant conflict between the basic goals in life" (1959, pp. 217–218). And Ansbacher (1959) notes the polar contrast between this concept and Alfred Adler's concept of "social interest," which stresses the opposite of psychological anomie: the individ-ual's sense of social involvement, his identification with the common good, and his commitment to social contributiveness. Thus far, there is fair agreement on the social-isolation–social-connectedness dimension of psy-chological anomie, that is, on the degree to which an individual feels himself mapped into a solidary, organized, and effective social order.

The definition was extended in another direction with the advent of a scale to measure anomie developed by Srole (1956). This 5-item scale is a psychological measure which has been taken "to measure anomie as *subjectively* experienced" (Merton, 1957, p. 165). To avoid continua-tion of the confusion between the sociological state of anomie and its psychological counterpart, Srole has suggested that the term "anomia" be employed for the latter. The scale, by including items stating that "the lot of the average man is getting worse" and implying the bleakness of "the way things look for the future," added a dimension of pessimism about the future to the meaning of psychological anomie, or anomia. In fact, Meier and Bell (1959) interpret Srole's scale largely as a measure of *despair* and cite, in support of their interpretation, a similar view of the scale by Nettler (1957).

Their interpretation, while partly justified, does not seem, however, to exhaust the anomia construct. Rather, the notion of despair or pessi-mism about the future seems a useful addition to or extension of a *syndrome* of feelings or beliefs, the core of which has been conveyed earlier by the social-isolation–social-connectedness dimension. In support of this latter emphasis, a study by Reimanis and Davol (cited in Davol and Reimanis, 1959) shows that the Srole anomia scale is negatively correlated, in an institutional domiciliary population, with measures of desire for social affiliation and of the actual maintenance of contacts with close friends and relatives.

The similarity between these concerns stemming from the Durkheim anomie tradition and the concerns centering on the concept of alienation is made apparent in the penetrating analysis by Seeman (1959) of the various historical meanings attached to the alienation concept. Seeman has distinguished five relatively nonoverlapping meanings of alienation and has undertaken the task of "translating" each meaning into the language of Rotter's social learning theory: *Powerlessness*—the expectancy or probability held by the individual that his own behavior cannot determine the occurrence of the outcomes or reinforcements he seeks; *meaninglessness*—a low expectancy that satisfactory predictions about future outcomes of behavior can be made; *normlessness*—a high expectancy that socially unapproved behaviors are required to achieve given goals; *isolation*—low reward value for goals or beliefs that are typically highly valued in the given society; and *self-estrangement*—the degree of dependence of behavior upon anticipated future rewards rather than upon current intrinsic ones.

Although our own "translations" would be somewhat different (for example, normlessness might better be defined as a low expectancy or uncertainty about what behavior is appropriate in various social situations), Seeman's thoughtful essay has served the function of clarifying the concept of alienation and of coordinating it to Rotter's theory of personality. What emerges from his discussion is that, while the rhetoric of both alienation and psychological anomie can be spoken by the same tongue, there is considerable room for choice in the empirical operationalization of either term.[8]

Our conclusions from reviewing the implications of these considerations were several. First, a term was needed on the psychological level to refer, with minimal confusion, to what could be considered as the subjective counterpart to the objective sociological condition of anomie. For this purpose, we have eschewed all variants of the "anomie" term, such as "anomia," "subjective anomie," and "psychological anomie," in favor of the term "alienation." Second, the psychological term "alienation" should refer to a fairly generalized view or perspective held at a mostly conscious level and describing the individual's appraisal of his general life situation. Third, the term should refer to a *syndrome* of relatively co-varying attributes rather than to any single one. Finally, the core aspect of the syndrome, the aspect which has received the most general emphasis from various scholars and which seems to unify the constellation of associated attributes, is the idea of the sense of social connectedness or isolation.

This latter emphasis is partly captured by Nettler's definition of an

---

[8] Seeman's empirical work (see, for example, Seeman, 1962, 1963, 1966) has concentrated on the powerlessness aspect of alienation which we will consider shortly in the discussion of belief in internal or external control.

alienated person as "one who has been estranged from, made unfriendly toward, his society and the culture it carries" (1957, p. 672). Leighton has also given emphasis to the importance of social connectedness by designating three out of ten of his essential striving sentiments as relevant to this concern: "Orientation in terms of one's place in society and the place of others"; "The securing and maintaining of membership in a definite human group"; and "A sense of belonging to a moral order and being right in what one does, being in and of a system of values" (1959, p. 148).

Our own approach to measuring alienation has given primary weight to the dimension of social isolation. The dimension includes isolation in the sense of being rejected, excluded, or repudiated in social relations; in the sense of lacking commonalities with others, that is, the absence of shared values; and in the sense of lacking a feeling of responsibility for the welfare of others. Recognizing the *syndrome* quality of alienation, however, we have also included items relevant to two other aspects: the feeling of lack of gratification in ordinary day-to-day role activities; and the feeling of pessimism about the future.

The concept of alienation, then, is a part of the personal belief structure referring generally to the individual's sense of social isolatedness and his estrangement from basic life roles. Implicit in the foregoing discussion is the coordination of this personality variable to the sociocultural environment; alienation is considered in our scheme as a personality counterpart of anomie. Alienation has recurrently been described in the sociological literature as a reflection of the vicissitudes of industrialization, rapid social change, and the development of mass society, the very same social conditions invoked as determiners of breakdown in normative consensus and regulation. In denoting a sense of social isolation, a personal loss of identity with larger social units or with other persons, alienation should reflect, or exhibit consonance with, the degree of anomie in the social milieu.[9] In addition, just as the degree of anomie is considered to be influenced by value-access disjunction in the sociocultural system, the degree of alienation is theoretically influenced by personal disjunctions in the personality system.

With respect to its coordination to deviant behavior, alienation is interpreted as indicating the relative absence or failure of personal control. This effect stems from the fact of the social isolatedness or social disconnectedness of the alienated person. Because of his isolation, the usual concerns about group monitoring of his behavior, maintaining his social reputation or social status, and fulfilling the daily requirements of role

---

[9] Yinger (1965) remarks: "Strangely enough, however, none of the research on anomia as an individual fact examines its relationship to anomie as a property of the group" (p. 205). In the present research, an effort *is* made in this direction.

behavior, are, for the alienated person, severely attentuated. Yet it is such concerns which, among the unalienated, function as powerful personal controls against deviance. Insofar as alienation attenuates such personally regulative concerns, alienation may be interpreted as conducing to deviance.

Belief in Internal or External Control

The second variable which we have located in the personal belief structure is one which has emerged directly from Rotter's social learning theory. It is buttressed by a large amount of systematic research involving such diverse concerns as social action-taking behavior, resistance to influence, and various aspects of the learning process (see Rotter, Seeman, and Liverant, 1962; Rotter, 1963; Rotter, 1966). This is the variable of belief in internal or external control (I-E). The I-E variable is defined as a generalized orientation or expectation that the outcomes of one's behavior are *contingent upon what one does* (internal control) *as opposed to being determined by outside forces, such as powerful others, or impersonal random forces, such as luck, fate, or chance* (external control).

The definition of this variable is very similar to the Man-Nature value orientation discussed by F. Kluckhohn and Strodtbeck, with internal control paralleling Mastery-over-Nature and external control paralleling Subjugation-to-Nature (1961, p. 13). Other ethnographic discussions of fatalistic world-views—Saunders (1958) and Edmonson (1957) on the Spanish-Americans of the Southwest; Banfield (1958) and Cancian (1961) on the mountain peasants of southern Italy—have also indicated the usefulness of a concept such as I-E orientation for describing particular cultures. Transcending any specific culture, the culture of poverty, too, has been described as involving the trait of fatalism (Lewis, 1961). This is also consonant with Miller's designation of Fate as one of the "focal concerns" of lower-class culture: "Many lower class individuals feel that their lives are subject to a set of forces over which they have relatively little control. . . . Not infrequently this often implicit world view is associated with a conception of the ultimate futility of directed effort towards a goal . . ." (1958, p. 11).

This latter consequence of a fatalistic outlook, noted clearly by Miller, will be critical to our discussion of the relation between the I-E orientation and deviance. Essentially the same interpretation of fatalism was arrived at by Oeser and Emery in their analysis of gambling as a rejection of the rational manipulation of available cultural means: "This rejection will tend to occur when the individual is faced with environmental determinants over which he has no control, and which, from his point of view, are unpredictable" (1954, p. 41).

The relation of an internal or external control orientation to directed efforts toward goals has been shown in several empirical studies. Gore and Rotter (1963) used a measure of I-E with students in a southern Negro college. The measure successfully predicted the extent to which Negro students would commit themselves to active roles in the civil rights movement. Seeman has used an I-E measure as an empirical specification of powerlessness, one of his interpretations of alienation. He has been able to show that among tuberculosis patients the internal orientation accompanies greater objective knowledge about their condition (Seeman and Evans, 1962), and, among reformatory inmates, greater learning about parole-relevant information (Seeman, 1963).

The coordination of the I-E variable to the sociocultural environment has been indicated by the citations of its use in cross-cultural, folk-urban, and social class description. Further, it appears to be an orientation differentially distributed *within* any society, depending upon the degree of predictability existing at different locations. Hence, like alienation, the belief in external control should vary with the degree of anomie at a particular social location. In this sense, it would be possible to conceptualize the belief in external control as a part of the syndrome of alienation described earlier. And, like alienation, the belief in external control should also reflect the degree of personal disjunctions in the personality system.

The coordination of belief in external control to deviance rests upon the consequence of such a fatalistic outlook noted above by Miller, the feeling of "ultimate futility of directed effort toward a goal." Holding an external or fatalistic orientation makes planned, directed actions less likely. Hence, such a belief represents an absence of control over present behavior by the usual anticipation of consequences and contingencies which attach to it. If what happens is seen as largely a matter of fate (the external control orientation), then persevering in the schedule of conforming behavior which is specified by society, and which is justified because it is supposed to eventuate in rewards, can have little personal conviction.

This general orientation may also lead to attributing the cause of failure or lack of personal goal attainment to arbitrariness in the social system, especially if a visible basis exists, as in racial discrimination, for seeing the deprivation as unjust (see Cloward and Ohlin, 1960, p. 110 and following). "It is as if the unjust deprivation [external control] cancels out the individual's obligation to the established system . . . and encourages him to emulate other role models on the basis of expediency alone" (Cloward and Ohlin, 1960, p. 118). A recent study supports these general interpretations—those inmates designated by custodial personnel as clear-cut "troublemakers" in a federal correctional institution were significantly more external in orientation than inmates designated as "non-troublemakers" (Wood, Wilson, Jessor, and Bogan, 1966).

These two orientations, alienation and belief in external control, constitute our two variables in the personal belief substructure of the personality
system. We have departed from Seeman in two ways: by defining a *general*
orientation called "alienation," consisting largely of felt social isolation;
and by maintaining separation of alienation from the more specific belief
in external control. (Seeman refers to the latter as alienation in the powerlessness sense.) Our stance has the heuristic advantage, it seems to us,
of permitting an *empirical* assessment of the relations between alienation
and belief in external control and between both of them and the larger
network of sociocultural, personality, and deviant behavior variables.

The Personal Control Structure

The third component of the personality system, the personal control
structure, is considered as the psychological counterpart of the social control structure at the sociocultural level. The variables allocated to this
structure are those which reflect more directly the aspects of social control
having to do with exposure to deviant models, absence of sanction networks, and opportunity for deviance. The control variables allocated to
this structure are also those which more directly implicate the behavior
category of deviance than do the variables considered in the personal
belief structure.

Personal control is seen as a critical facet of the behavior process eventuating in transgression. Given the instigation generated by value-expectation disjunction, and given the weakened control provided by alienation
and belief in external control, the personal control structure becomes deci-
sive in regulating deviance. By "personal controls" we will mean the internalization of attitudes and orientations fairly directly regulating any departure from normative prescriptions. Specifically, three variables will be described under this rubric: *tolerance of deviance; tendency toward immediate gratification;* and *short time perspective.*

Tolerance of Deviance

A large part of what is meant by personal control is contained in
the notion of conscience or in the Freudian concept of the superego,
the cognitive agency which is the internalized repository for the socially
defined norms or standards of acceptable conduct. The emphasis upon
internalization is the crucial differential between personal controls and
social controls; the reference of personal control is to *self-administered*
regulations and sanctions for conformity or deviance. These may range,
in the latter case, from minor twinges of conscience to severe and in-
capacitating guilt feelings over actions which do not conform to social
rules for appropriate behavior. To the extent that internalization of the
regulatory norms of the larger society has *not* taken place, to that extent

is deviance more likely. Under such circumstances, the constraints exercised by parallel *personal* standards of right and wrong will be minimal or absent.

This conceptualization of personal control suggests a relatively direct approach to ascertaining the degree to which an individual does have evaluative standards for various behaviors which reflect the standards contained in the larger society's norms and which, it can be assumed, he applies to his own action tendencies. The psychological variable involved here is the subject's attitude toward deviance—that is, the tolerance he holds for various behaviors departing more or less from the normative prescriptions commonly accepted in daily social life. This attitudinal variable thus reflects the degree of personal acceptance or tolerance for transgression and is considered an index of the degree of internalization of social rules.

It can be seen that the relation of this attitudinal variable to actual behavior is mediated by the concept of expectancy. Holding a highly tolerant attitude toward deviance may indicate, for example, a low expectation for punishment for engaging in that behavior. Or a highly tolerant attitude may indicate an expectancy that deviant behavior is required in order to achieve valued goals. Expectations of punishment, in Rotter's theory, operate to inhibit or suppress behavior. Tolerance of deviance, therefore, interpreted as a low expectation for punishment, should conduce to deviance. In this sense, the presence of this attitude indicates a failure of personal control against the occurrence of transgression.

The relation of tolerance of deviance to the sociocultural environment is, like all the personality system variables, mediated by past learning. Holding a highly tolerant attitude toward deviance may reflect a history of exposure to weak or irregularly applied sanctions, to a wide variety of successful deviant role models, and to opportunity to engage in and succeed at deviance. The presence of such circumstances during an individual's development will depend upon his location in the social control structure and, more particularly, upon the family in which he is being socialized. "The child develops appropriate personal controls . . . when the family milieu is structured so that the child identifies with family members who represent roles of conformity with non-delinquent norms and accepts the norms and rules embodied in these roles" (Reiss, 1951, p. 198).

This emphasis upon the central importance of the family milieu in teaching repudiation of deviance is supported by Inkeles: "Inadequate superego development can be expected in the absence of the parent, or where only intermittent, irregular, and inconsistent parental demands are met. . . . [or] where the parental treatment is very harsh. . . . [or] where the parent is extremely weak . . ." (1963, pp. 339–340). He concludes from this analysis that weak superegos should be differentially distributed in society: "It is evident that in marginal slum districts of great cities a high proportion of the children will experience conditions of socialization of the variety conducive to weak superego development" (1963, p. 340).

Immediate Gratification and Short Time Perspective

The second and third variables constituting the personal control structure are the tendency toward immediate gratification and short time perspective. These will be discussed together since they tend to refer to a single orientation in which these two elements co-vary to a high degree. The interest in ability to defer or postpone derives initially from Freud, who considered the renunciation of immediate impulse gratification as a critical step in psychological development. Postponement involves the accommodation of a prolonged time period into the *scheduling* of gratification; it involves taking into account the likely consequences of present behavior extended into future time. *Immediate gratification* may be defined as a generalized tendency, a higher-order behavior potential, to engage in activities leading to relatively immediate positive or valued consequences or reinforcements. *Short time perspective* may be defined as a generalized tendency to consider only a brief time period as the context in which behavior-choices are made. Both of these tendencies have been described in the literature as differentially distributed in society and as relevant to deviance (see Clausen, 1957).

The theoretical linkage of these tendencies to deviant behavior involves the following reasoning. Much of the behavior which is immediately impulse gratifying is of the sort which is socially disapproved and potentially definable as deviant: sex, aggression, or drinking, for example. While such behavior usually gratifies an impulse at the moment, it is often correlated with long-term negative consequences—the teen-age girl can become pregnant, the aggression can lead to expulsion from school, drinking may lead to loss of a job. These negative, long-run consequences usually serve to constrain against immediate gratification, but when an individual is characterized by a short time perspective, he is unlikely to be considering long-run consequences at the time of behavior choice.

The tendency to engage in immediately gratifying activities implies also the *avoidance* of much of the socially sanctioned preparatory activity which is necessary to achieve socially valued goals; for example, the long period of education and hard study needed to be able to get a good job later on and to achieve a satisfactory income. Such conforming activity, which is not immediately gratifying to most people, is supported for most persons by the anticipation of large rewards in the distant future—again, a situation precluded by a short time perspective. The end result of the tendency toward short time perspective and toward immediate gratification is an increased likelihood of deviance through the failure of personal controls. These controls involve deferment and consideration of the long-range consequences, both positive and negative, of behavior choices.

In an important early paper, Lawrence Frank (1939) elaborated the notion of time perspective as follows: "Whole social classes may be described by the time perspectives that dominate their lives as revealed in the range of their planning, their prudential calculations, their forethought, their abstinence, and so on" (p. 297). And further:

> The more remote the focus of his time perspective, the more he will exhibit preparatory or instrumental behavior that uses the present only as a means to the future; the more immediate the focus the more he will exhibit consummatory behavior and react naively and ignore consequences (p. 298).

Numerous other authors have also pointed out the social-class-linked nature of these tendencies. According to LeShan:

> In the lower-lower class, the orientation is one of quick sequences of tension and relief. One does not frustrate oneself for long periods or plan action with goals far in the future. The future generally is an indefinite, vague, diffuse region and its rewards and punishments are too uncertain to have much motivating value. In this social class, one eats when he is hungry (1952, p. 589).

And Miller notes: "Many of the most characteristic features of lower class life are related to the search for excitement or 'thrill'" (1958, p. 11). Cross-cultural differences in time perspective are clearly documented by F. Kluckhohn and Strodtbeck (1961).

The possibility that tendencies toward short time perspective and immediate gratification can be learned by direct exposure to models was discussed earlier in the section on the social control structure. The Bandura and Kupers study (1964) was mentioned as suggesting that certain kinds of self-reinforcement schedules can be learned through modeling. More direct evidence on the relation of modeling and immediate gratification comes from a recent study by Bandura and Mischel (1965). These investigators were able to show that children with already established tendencies toward immediate or toward delayed gratification could be influenced to *change* their tendency by being exposed to an influential model whose behavior was the opposite of theirs. Thus, immediate gratifiers were influenced to become more delayed, and delayed gratifiers were influenced to become more immediate; the influenced changes were sustained over a one-month retest. Such data point up the vulnerability of persons living in disintegrated neighborhoods; despite what may be successful socialization efforts within the home, the availability of models outside the home might bring about a reversal of such orientations as the tendency to delay gratification. Exposure to persons who tend to consider only the momentary implications of their actions and who tend to emphasize pleasure-seeking or "kicks" provides behavior models for the learning of these orientations and for the consequent development of weak personal controls.

With respect to the linkage of the variables to deviant behavior, a variety of studies has shown empirical relations. Barndt and Johnson (1955) found that stories told by delinquents had a significantly shorter action span than those of controls. Siegman (1961) found Israeli youngsters who were delinquent to have shorter time perspectives than a non-delinquent control group. A study by Mischel (1961) investigated delay behavior among delinquent and nondelinquent Trinidadian children. Offered a choice between a smaller five-cent candy reward right away and a larger twenty-five-cent candy reward requiring a week's wait, his delinquent subjects chose the immediate reward significantly more often than the non-delinquents. Finally, Ricks and his colleagues (1964) show an increase in time perspective among delinquent boys given vocationally-oriented psychotherapy.

To sum up, the variables of tendency toward immediate gratification and short time perspective reflect, on the personality level, aspects of location in the social control structure. The variables have been described as differentially distributed in society and as linked with deviance. The coordination to deviant behavior emerges through the consideration of these variables in terms of attenuated personal controls against personal transgressions. Together with the attitudinal variable, tolerance of deviance, these variables constitute the personal control structure. The latter is considered an analogue, in the personality system, of the social control structure in the sociocultural system. Location in a weak social control structure should be reflected, through patterned exposure, in a weak personal control structure.

CONCLUDING SUMMARY

The entire personality system has now been presented, along with the rationale for the three substructures and for the particular variables included within each of them. The system as described is presented schematically in Figure 2. The differentiation of the personality system into substructures enables a *logical* account of the likelihood of occurrence of deviant behavior *for an individual*. The theory of personality specifies a major source of *instigation* to deviance—low expectations for attaining valued goals by conforming behavior—and two major sources of *control* against deviance: certain personal beliefs and certain attitudes and general-

FIGURE 2
The Personality System and Deviant Behavior

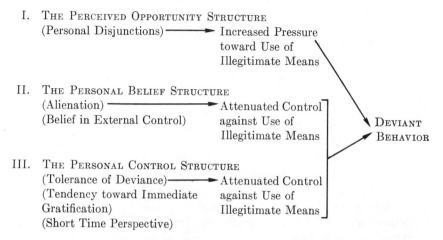

I. THE PERCEIVED OPPORTUNITY STRUCTURE
(Personal Disjunctions) ———➤ Increased Pressure
toward Use of
Illegitimate Means

II. THE PERSONAL BELIEF STRUCTURE
(Alienation) ————————➤ Attenuated Control
(Belief in External Control)   against Use of
Illegitimate Means

DEVIANT
BEHAVIOR

III. THE PERSONAL CONTROL STRUCTURE
(Tolerance of Deviance)————➤ Attenuated Control
(Tendency toward Immediate   against Use of
Gratification)   Illegitimate Means
(Short Time Perspective)

ized tendencies. Like the sociocultural system, the personality system has dynamic properties; the balance of instigation and control is what theoretically determines the likelihood of occurrence of deviant behavior.

In Figure 2, the variables listed within each structure are described in terms of their theoretical conduciveness to deviance. The fundamental personality system proposition schematized in Figure 2 is the following: *The likelihood of occurrence of deviant behavior will vary directly with the degree of personal disjunction, alienation, belief in external control, tolerance of deviance, and tendencies toward short time perspective and immediate gratification characterizing an individual at a given moment in time.*

Each major aspect of the personality system was described as reflecting a correlative aspect of the sociocultural system. The importance of such coordination derives from a logical necessity. For the individual to mediate the relation between the sociocultural environment and deviance rates he must, to some degree, carry or reflect within his personality the consequences of patterned exposure to that environment.

As within the sociocultural system, certain relations are theoretically expected *among* the variables within the personality system. These relations may be summarized as involving some degree of positive intercorrelation. This correlation should obtain either because of a common learning background—thus, tolerance of deviance and short time perspective may be learned together in the same context—or because of a theoretical interdependence—thus, theoretically, high personal disjunctions should generate alienation.

At this point, it is possible to see more clearly the relationships between the sociocultural and the personality models. First, the two models are formally identical. Each proposes a source of stress or pressure or instigation—a dynamic—toward engaging in illegitimate behavior. Each proposes two major sources of control or restraint against the instigation to deviance. *In each model, deviance is conceived of as the resultant or balance of the interaction of pressure and controls.* Second, it can be seen that the structures and variables in each model are analogues of the corresponding structures and variables in the other model. This enables a *logical* linkage between the two models and the attainment of a systematic interdisciplinary scheme. The relatively straightforward and direct relationship between value-access disjunction and personal disjunction, between anomie and alienation, and between access to illegitimate means and tolerance of deviance—each pair of concepts a social-psychological linkage—provides us with a *systematic* basis for examining the mediational role of personality between society and behavior.

In the next chapter, the presentation of our theoretical formulation is extended and completed by articulating the role of socialization as a link between the sociocultural and the personality systems.

REFERENCES

ALLPORT, G. W. *Becoming.* New Haven: Yale University Press, 1955.

ANSBACHER, H. L. Anomie, the sociologist's conception of lack of social interest. *Journal of Individual Psychology,* 1959, *15,* 212–214.

ANTONOVSKY, A. AND M. J. LERNER. Occupational aspirations of lower class Negro and white youth. *Social Problems,* 1959, *7,* 133–138.

ASCH, S. E. A perspective on social psychology. In S. Koch (Ed.) *Psychology: A study of a science.* Vol. III. New York: McGraw-Hill, 1959. Pp. 363–383.

ATKINSON, J. W. (Ed.) *Motives in fantasy, action, and society.* Princeton, N.J.: Van Nostrand, 1958.

BANDURA, A. AND CAROL J. KUPERS. Transmission of patterns of self-reinforcement through modeling. *Journal of Abnormal and Social Psychology,* 1964, *69,* 1–9.

BANDURA A. AND W. MISCHEL. Modification of self-imposed delay of reward through exposure to live and symbolic models. *Journal of Personality and Social Psychology,* 1965, *2,* 698–705.

BANFIELD, E. C. *The moral basis of a backward society.* New York: Free Press, 1958.

BARNDT, R. J. AND D. M. JOHNSON. Time orientation in delinquents. *Journal of Abnormal and Social Psychology,* 1955, *51,* 343–345.

CANCIAN, F. The southern Italian peasant: World view and political behavior. *Anthropological Quarterly,* 1961, *34,* 1–18.

CHILD, I. L. Problems of personality and some relations to anthropology and sociology. In S. Koch (Ed.) *Psychology: A study of a science.* Vol. 5. *The process areas, the person, and some applied fields: Their place in psychology and in science.* New York: McGraw-Hill, 1963. Pp. 593–638.

CHILD, I. L. AND J. W. M. WHITING. Effects of goal attainment: Relaxation versus renewed striving. *Journal of Abnormal and Social Psychology,* 1950, *45,* 667–681.

CLAUSEN, J. A. Social patterns, personality, and adolescent drug use. In A. H. Leighton, J. A. Clausen and R. M. Wilson (Eds.) *Explorations in social psychiatry.* New York: Basic Books, 1957. Pp. 230–272.

CLOWARD, R. A. AND L. E. OHLIN. *Delinquency and opportunity.* New York: Free Press, 1960.

DAVOL, S. H. AND G. REIMANIS. The role of anomie as a psychological concept. *Journal of Individual Psychology,* 1959, *15,* 215–225.

EDMONSON, M. S. *Los manitos: A study of institutional values.* New Orleans: Tulane University Press, 1957.

FRANK, L. K. Time perspectives. *Journal of Social Philosophy,* 1939, *4,* 293–312.

GILL, M. The present state of psychoanalytic theory. *Journal of Abnormal and Social Psychology,* 1959, *58,* 1–8.

GORE, PEARL M. AND J. B. ROTTER. A personality correlate of social action. *Journal of Personality,* 1963, *31,* 58–64.

HSU, F. L. K. Anthropology or psychiatry: A definition of objectives and their implications. *Southwestern Journal of Anthropology,* 1952, *8,* 227–250.

INKELES, A. Some sociological observations on culture and personality studies. In C. Kluckhohn, H. A. Murray and D. M. Schneider (Eds.) *Personality in nature, society, and culture.* New York: Knopf, 1953, Pp. 577–592.

INKELES, A. Sociology and psychology. In S. Koch (Ed.) *Psychology: A study of a science.* Vol. 6. *Investigations of man as socius: Their place in psychology and the social sciences.* New York: McGraw-Hill, 1963. Pp. 317–387.

KARDINER, A. *The psychological frontiers of society.* New York: Columbia University Press, 1945.

KLUCKHOHN, FLORENCE R. AND F. L. STRODTBECK. *Variations in value orientations.* New York: Harper & Row, 1961.

LEIGHTON, A. H. *My name is legion.* Vol. I. *The Stirling County study of psychiatric disorder and sociocultural environment.* New York: Basic Books, 1959.

LESHAN, L. L. Time orientation and social class. *Journal of Abnormal and Social Psychology,* 1962, *47,* 589–592.

LEWIN, K. *Field theory in social science: Selected theoretical papers.* D. Cartwright (Ed.) New York: Harper & Row, 1951.

LEWIS, O. *The children of Sanchez: Autobiography of a Mexican family.* New York: Random House, 1961.

MACIVER, R. M. *The ramparts we guard.* New York: Crowell-Collier & Macmillan, 1950.

MCCLELLAND, D. C., J. W. ATKINSON, R. A. CLARK, AND E. L. LOWELL. *The achievement motive.* New York: Appleton-Century-Crofts, 1953.

MEIER, DOROTHY L. AND W. BELL. Anomie and differential access to the achievement of life goals. *American Sociological Review,* 1959, *24,* 189–202.

MERTON, R. K. *Social theory and social structure.* (Rev. ed.) New York: Free Press, 1957.

MILLER, W. B. Lower class culture as a generating milieu of gang delinquency. *Journal of Social Issues,* 1958, *14,* 5–19.

MISCHEL, W. Preference for delayed reinforcement and social responsibility. *Journal of Abnormal and Social Psychology,* 1961, *62,* 1–7.

MIZRUCHI, E. H. *Success and opportunity: Class values and anomie in American life.* New York: Free Press, 1964.

MURRAY, H. A. *Explorations in personality.* New York: Oxford University Press, 1938.

MURRAY, H. A. Preparations for the scaffold of a comprehensive system. In S. Koch (Ed.) *Psychology: A study of a science.* Vol. III. New York: McGraw-Hill, 1959. Pp. 7–54.

NETTLER, G. A measure of alienation. *American Sociological Review,* 1957, *22,* 670–677.

OESER, O. A. AND F. E. EMERY. *Social structure and personality in a rural community.* New York: Crowell-Collier & Macmillan, 1954.

REISS, A. J., JR. Delinquency as the failure of personal and social controls. *American Sociological Review,* 1951, *16,* 196–207.

RICKS, D., C. UMBARGER, AND R. MACK. A measure of increased temporal perspective in successfully treated adolescent delinquent boys. *Journal of Abnormal and Social Psychology,* 1964, *69,* 685–689.

ROTTER, J. B. *Social learning and clinical psychology.* Englewood Cliffs, N.J.: Prentice-Hall, 1954.

ROTTER, J. B. The role of the psychological situation in determining the direction of human behavior. In M. R. Jones (Ed.) *The Nebraska Symposium on Motivation,* 1955. Lincoln: University of Nebraska Press, 1955. Pp. 245–269.

ROTTER, J. B. Some implications of a social learning theory for the prediction of goal directed behavior from testing procedures. *Psychological Review,* 1960, *67,* 301–316.

ROTTER, J. B. Personality factors in motivation. *Final Report.* To Air Force Office of Scientific Research. December, 1963. Mimeographed.

ROTTER, J. B. Generalized expectancies for internal versus external control of reinforcement. *Psychological Monographs,* 1966, *80,* No. 1, Whole No. 609. Pp. 1–28.

ROTTER, J. B. Personality theory. In H. Helson and W. Bevan (Eds.) *Contemporary approaches to psychology.* Princeton, N.J.: Van Nostrand, 1967. Pp. 461–498.

ROTTER, J. B., M. SEEMAN, AND S. LIVERANT. Internal *versus* external control of reinforcements: A major variable in behavior theory. In N. F. Washburne (Ed.) *Decisions, values, and groups.* Vol. II. New York: Pergamon Press, 1962. Pp. 473–516.

SANFORD, N. Personality: Its place in psychology. In S. Koch (Ed.) *Psychol-*

ogy: A study of a science. Vol. V. New York: McGraw-Hill, 1963. Pp. 488–592.

SAUNDERS, L. English-speaking and Spanish-speaking people of the Southwest. In H. D. Stein and R. A. Cloward (Eds.) *Social perspectives on behavior.* New York: Free Press, 1958. Pp. 157–170.

SEEMAN, M. On the meaning of alienation. *American Sociological Review,* 1959, *24,* 783–791.

SEEMAN, M. Alienation and social learning in a reformatory. *American Journal of Sociology,* 1963, *69,* 270–284.

SEEMAN, M. Alienation, membership, and political knowledge: A comparative study. *Public Opinion Quarterly,* 1966, *30,* 353–367.

SEEMAN, M. AND J. W. EVANS. Alienation and learning in a hospital setting. *American Sociological Review,* 1962, *27,* 772–782.

SIEGMAN, A. W. The relationship between future time perspective, time estimation, and impulse control in a group of young offenders and in a control group. *Journal of Consulting Psychology,* 1961, *25,* 470–475.

SROLE, L. Social integration and certain corollaries: An exploratory study. *American Sociological Review,* 1956, *21,* 709–716.

WHITE, L. A. *The science of culture.* New York: Farrar, Straus, 1949.

WOOD, B. S., G. G. WILSON, R. JESSOR, AND J. B. BOGAN. Troublemaking behavior in a correctional institution: Relationship to inmates' definition of their situation. *American Journal of Orthopsychiatry,* 1966, *36,* 795–802.

YINGER, J. M. *Toward a field theory of behavior: Personality and social structure.* New York: McGraw-Hill, 1965.

CHAPTER FIVE

The Socialization System and Deviance

A GENERAL PERSPECTIVE

The linkage between the sociocultural system and the personality system depends, of course, upon some aspect or process of enculturation. This has been emphasized throughout the foregoing presentation by the use of such terms as "patterned exposure," "modeling," "learning," "mirroring," and "training." Although these terms have been used loosely and relatively interchangeably, their common function has been to denote processes whereby what is initially "outside"—the sociocultural environment—ultimately influences, affects, or shapes what is "inside"—the personality.

While it is true that the process is bidirectional—personalities, in turn, shape their sociocultural environments—the primary vector, and the one which is institutionalized as a major function of society, is toward the members of a culture gradually coming to incorporate and reflect the patterned meanings and structures of their cultural surround. The myriad ways in which the success of this process is insured range from reliance upon deliberate and formally structured training procedures to dependence upon the subtle and incidental learning which characterizes the countless transactions of everyday social life. All, however, implicate the time-binding nature of man which enables him, through the content and experiences which he provides for his children, to pass on the heritage of the culture and to mirror the larger society.

The term "socialization" has come to summarize the variety of processes which transform infants into bearers and instruments of their culture. The concern in this study, however, is not with socialization as an end in itself. Rather, it derives from the critical juncture which such processes must be assumed to occupy if the logic of the over-all social-psychological framework is to be sustained. We look upon socialization in the way Leighton, Clausen, and Wilson (1957) have described it: "as a master concept for coordinating the clinical and sociological approaches . . ." (p. 21); or, in Inkeles' words, as "one of the major points of articulation between psychology and sociocultural studies." (1963, p. 364). Processes of socialization lie at the interface between the sociocultural environment and personality. The relationship between the environment and the person can be made more compelling, therefore, by demonstrating its mediation by way of the process of socialization.

The primary purpose of our own interest in socialization was, therefore, to support the logic of the over-all social-psychological framework by showing that differential location in the sociocultural system leads to different socialization practices, and that these different socialization practices lead to different personality systems which, in turn, have varying implications for deviance.

A number of issues remained to be resolved before socialization could be mapped into the larger theoretical framework. The first had to do with the decision as to what point or stage in development to focus upon.[1] The heavy psychoanalytic commitment of much of the previous work in socialization had targeted the early infancy period as critical in establishing the main outlines of the personality structure. Much of the empirical investigation tended, as a consequence, to concentrate on early parental attitudes and practices dealing largely with basic physical and physiological training. These interests, represented in numerous anthropological studies of national character and of cultural influences on personality, culminated in several agonizing reappraisals of the entire problem and in admonitions such as that by Hsu quoted earlier.

It has become increasingly apparent that the Freudian hypothesis that later personality structure is laid down during infancy is in doubt (see Orlansky, 1949; Caldwell, 1964). It has also become clear that social learning is a continuing process and that much of the learning which is required for successful social role performance and interaction can only occur later in life: during later childhood and adolescence, at least. On this point, Sewell has maintained that "in any but the most static societies the individual cannot possibly be prepared during childhood for the complex roles that he will be called upon to play at later periods in his life" (1963, pp. 173–174).

Efforts to account for personality or behavior at a given stage of life are more likely to succeed if relatively recent rather than remote antecedents are sought. The longer the time gap, the greater the probability

---

[1] For reasons to be made clear in Chapter 6, dealing with the research design, it was only feasible for us to study the socialization of the high school students in the community. The discussion to follow, therefore, takes teen-agers as its focus, considering the relation of socialization to teen-age personality and behavior.

that unknown factors have intervened to displace or transform the meaning and influence of earlier events. Finally, there is the additional methodological problem of increasing unreliability of retrospection as the remoteness of the past which the socializing agent is asked to report on or to describe is increased. For all of the foregoing reasons, it seemed to us inappropriate to focus on the infancy stage.

We chose instead to center our inquiry for the most part on the pre-adolescent period. Since the subjects whose socialization we were investigating were the high school students in the community, the pre-adolescent period seemed to have sufficient proximity in time to make the search for socialization antecedents to their personality and behavior a reasonable one. It is a period of time not so remote as to raise serious problems about recall by their parents. And it would seem to be a period of time in which developments occur which could be particularly critical for teen-age adjustment, especially with respect to acquiring pre-delinquent orientations and behaviors. It is, for example, the period in which family ties often come under strain, in which peer associations begin to gain increasing influence, and in which impending physical maturation confronts the youngster with various, often urgent, problems of personal and social adjustment.

Related to the issue of which period of development to focus upon was the question of *which aspects* of development to focus upon. Given our general orientation toward deviance, it would follow that one focus should be on the factors influencing the variables in the personality system, those variables which were described in the preceding chapter. If, as our contention has been, these personality substructures have particular relevance for the occurrence of deviance, then some knowledge about the socialization factors which have influenced them would be most directly relevant. For this reason, the aspects of socialization which were studied were, in part, those for which we could rationalize a psychological relationship with one or another of our major personality variables: such as need values, expectancies, internal-external control, or tolerance of deviance.

But to concentrate solely on the socialization of *personality* would yield only a partial picture since the general process of socialization into deviance involves also the socialization of *behavior,* that is, the learning of specific response repertoires differentially relevant to deviance. Socialization experiences which can affect the direct learning of deviant behavior— for example, exposure to deviant role models in the home—are, therefore, an equally important class of antecedents to focus on. To sum up this issue, our study of socialization led to inquiry about antecedent processes and experiences which could be coordinated with the larger predictive scheme and with the class of behavior at issue, that is, with personality system variables and deviant behavior.

The agency of socialization on which the research ultimately settled was the family. Granting the partiality of the account which must emerge from this relatively narrow focus, in absolute terms the role of the family as socializer can be seen as primary and pervasive. The family is, after all, the most proximal social system in which patterned exposure occurs; it generally guarantees a continuity of exposure extending back in time to the earliest consciousness of social meanings; and it is the single milieu that encompasses, at pre-adolescence, the widest range of experiences and involvements for the child. Analysis of socialization as it occurs within the family should, for these reasons, reveal a significant amount of information about the influence exerted by the culture on the developing child.

Once a focus upon the family had been determined, the next issue was the selection of particular facets of the large range of family interactions and processes to be investigated. Socialization within the family obviously occurs in a number of different ways, ranging, as noted before, from the deliberate instruction of children to the learning which occurs casually and which is incidental to sharing in the life of the family. The importance of the latter source of learning cannot be overemphasized, although it has not received as much research attention as direct training and the conscious manipulation of rewards and punishments. Merton notes, in this connection, that

> the child is exposed to social prototypes in the witnessed daily behavior and casual conversations of parents. . . . It may well be that the child retains the implicit paradigm of cultural values detected in the day-by-day behavior of his parents even when this conflicts with their specific advice and exhortation (1957, pp. 158–159).

A consideration of the several sources of or instrumentalities for socialization in the family suggests three of major importance. The first, and most obvious, source is the direct training procedures which the parents employ in full consciousness of their use and with some rationalized expectations about their outcome. These may involve the entire disciplinary apparatus wherein deliberate efforts are made to shape conforming rather than deviant behavior by exercising a contingent allocation of rewards and punishments. They may also involve deliberate attempts to shape values, attitudes, and expectations about the world. The second, are the held beliefs, values, and orientations of the parents which, though no self-conscious effort to transmit these to the children may be made by the parents, can be detected by the child as the "implicit paradigms" influencing his parents, and, therefore, relevant to him.

Third, are the behavioral models which the family members may provide without explicit attention being called to them, and sometimes, even, with the attention given them being that of disavowal—for example, the drunken father who cautions his son not to emulate his "weakness." These "social prototypes" constitute an important source of the learning of behaviors through the process of modeling or imitation. Training practices, parental beliefs and orientations, and family models constitute, then, three important instrumentalities of socialization. An understanding of these, taken together, should account for a large portion of the cultural transmission process within the family.

It should be mentioned, finally, that our commitment to investigating possible socialization antecedents of the basic variables in the personality system required of us a considerable amount of what could be called "restrospective psychologizing." In the absence of well-established empirical relations between socialization and its outcome, it was necessary to hypothesize the kinds of socialization experiences which would, psychologically, be likely to eventuate in such outcomes as high need value for affection, or the feeling of external control, or an attitude of strong repudiation of deviance. It was largely a combined reliance upon the general implications of social learning theory, some of the relevant literature, and common sense, that led to the specification of possibly relevant antecedent conditions or experiences. These, in turn, determined the development of interview measures of such conditions.

This is another way of indicating that socialization itself was not our prime concern; rather than beginning with an interest in some aspect of socialization, our starting point was its outcome. From outcome—that is, from teen-age personality and behavior—we deduced possible antecedents which could be measured. It should be noted that, while an effort was made to specify antecedents for each of the variables in the personality system, no assumption was made that these prior conditions would be specific and nonoverlapping. In fact, there is some ground for thinking of these antecedents as forming an interactive system reflecting some *general* property of the family milieu, a family climate or atmosphere, which could have an influence on all of the personality variables to a greater or lesser extent. Overlap among antecedents in accounting for personality outcomes can, of course, be examined empirically; the relevant data are presented in Chapter 12.

Before discussing the specific content of the socialization study, it should be useful to review what is required of it if it is to contribute support to the larger social-psychological framework. First, it is necessary to be able to show that differential location in the sociocultural system results in or is related to *differential socialization practices* or experiences. On this general point, a sizable body of literature exists in which are demonstrated relationships of such sociocultural variables as socioeconomic status, ethnic membership, and parental education to variations in parent-child relationships, disciplinary practices, and teachings about beliefs and goals in the family (see Sewell, 1963; Hoffman and Lippitt, 1960; Bronfenbrenner, 1958; Clausen and Williams, 1963; Sears, Maccoby, and Levin, 1957; Crandall, 1963; Strodtbeck, 1958).

Second, it is necessary to be able to show that these variations in socialization practices do indeed make a difference in the *personality outcomes* among the teen-agers. That is, it is necessary to demonstrate the predictability of teen-age personality from pre-adolescent socialization. On this general point, the literature is abundant, although not necessarily with specific reference to the personality variables in our scheme (see Miller and Swanson, 1958; 1960). Although many of the earlier studies in this domain suffered from methodological and conceptual limitations, the recent work reviewed by Becker (1964) indicates a greater carefulness and refinement of investigation. Most important in recent work is the investigation of *multiple* socialization variables and their interactions in shaping personality, obviously a more appropriate interpretation of the complexities of the socialization problem. "The literature review implies that the research strategy has been one of first establishing the more salient themes and then moving cautiously toward the variation on the themes produced by a more complex interaction of variables" (Becker, 1964, p. 201).

Third, and last, it is necessary to show that variations in socialization practice make a difference in *behavioral outcome,* that is, in likelihood of deviance. Some writers have been dubious about the possibilities of predicting from socialization directly to behavioral variables such as delinquency or maladjustment. Child, for example, stated a decade ago that

> the very behavioral meaning of these variables is so different in various individuals, and the antecedent-consequent sequences which may lead to a person's being assigned to a given position on a scale of adjustment so diverse, that such studies are of little use in furthering our understanding of socialization (1954, p. 658).

The pessimism of Child's statement probably reflects the failures of studies in which the effort was made to tie very *remote* socialization experiences to later behavior. There has been a strong psychological tradition, nevertheless, of attempts to relate family variables to behavior, and particularly, in the older child, to deviance (Healy and Bronner, 1936; Glueck and Glueck, 1962; Bandura and Walters, 1959). The emphasis of these efforts has been on the role of rearing practices, within a particular social context, in influencing proneness to deviance.

These three functions or requirements of the socialization study—to link the sociocultural environment to socialization practices, to link socialization practices to personality, and to link socialization practices directly to deviant behavior—are what can enable the socialization study to strengthen the general social-psychological framework as an explanatory instrument.

THE SOCIALIZATION SYSTEM

The discussion to follow will be organized in terms of three major areas of parental socialization influence. By construing the family as a microcosm of the larger sociocultural environment, it is possible to use somewhat the same divisions of the family environment as were abstracted earlier from the larger sociocultural system. Now, however, the social agents mediating the various influences of society are restricted to the family, or, more particularly, to the parents alone.

The logic of this organization is thus consistent with the larger scheme. In that scheme we posited systematic relations between personality substructures and sociocultural substructures *assuming* the mediating role of patterned exposure or socialization. In the present scheme we are positing systematic relations between the same personality substructures and, now, microcosmic (that is, family) sociocultural substructures which together constitute the system of socialization.

The three areas of parental influence are considered to reflect the corresponding substructures in the sociocultural environment and to influence most directly, but not at all exclusively, the correlative substructures in the adolescent's personality system. It is more critical to emphasize the qualification—the absence of exclusiveness in influence—when talking about the family environment than when describing the larger environment. In the intimacy of the family, the possibility of correlation among the separate sources of socialization influence is obviously greater. It is even possible, as mentioned earlier, to consider the family environment as having a *general* climate: as being a setting with certain overriding characteristics that pervade most or all of the interactions which occur in it. To the extent that this is the case, any given source of parental influence is likely to be related to other sources of influence. Likewise, any given personality outcome is likely to reflect multiple sources of parental influence. Keeping this qualification in mind, it is nevertheless useful to proceed in the manner suggested since it will help to retain a systematic organization for the study of socialization. Also, by retaining separate sources of influence, it becomes possible to examine their relative importance and their interrelations.

The three areas of parental socialization influence to be described are: the parental reward structure, the parental belief structure, and the parental control structure. The rationale for considering these areas as having potential influence upon personality and, therefore, *indirectly* upon deviant behavior will be presented. These areas also have, in some cases, *direct* influence on behavior by specifically providing learnable patterns of deviant responses.

The Parental Reward Structure

The general concern of the parental reward structure is with the *kinds* of rewards provided and the *mode* of their application within the family. While the range of rewards which may be available for a child is extensive, the central importance of the reward category of *affection* has been emphasized by most theorists since it is presumed to underlie and be implicated by nearly all parent-child interactions. More particularly, influence or discipline practices aimed at shaping the child's behavior in parentally desired directions necessarily rely, in one way or another, on the use of affectional rewards.

This interdependence between influence or discipline practices, which reflect the *mode* of reward administration, and affection, which reflects the importance of *kind* of reward, has emerged in numerous studies. Summarizing some of these, Becker (1964) notes:

> It is apparent that the consequences of disciplinary practices cannot be fully understood except in the context of the warmth of the parent-child relation . . . (p. 202). A point of major significance is the fact that the nature of the affectional relations between parent and child is correlated with the use of certain kinds of discipline. In particular, the use of praise and reasoning has been repeatedly found associated with warmth variables, and the use of physical punishment with hostility variables (p. 176).

Affectional interaction in the family and *influence or discipline practices* were, therefore, investigated jointly under the rubric of the parental reward structure. The concept of affectional interaction refers to the amount, intensity, and pervasiveness with which affection characterizes parent-child relationships. It is conveyed not only by the amount of time each parent spends with the child but also by the parents' readiness to respond to the child's needs or problems when they arise, and by the acceptance which the child is given to feel in general and in relation to other children in the family.

The concept of influence or discipline practices refers to the manner in which the parent reacts to the child's behavior both when it is acceptable and nonacceptable. Involved here are the procedures employed to signify satisfaction with desirable behavior on the child's part—these may range from demonstrative expression of affection, to praise, gifts, or ignoring the child; and those procedures employed to signify dissatisfaction with undesirable behavior—these may range from verbal reproof, to love withdrawal, humiliation, or physical punishment. This partial listing of various influence techniques helps to illustrate more clearly the interdependence of discipline and affection within the family milieu.

Affectional interaction and parental influence practices are seen as a major way in which the child's perception of the opportunity structure is shaped. The degree to which affection is provided within the family should influence not only the child's need values for affection but other need values associated with these as well—values for achievement, for example. In addition, the incorporation of affectional rewards with influence practices should have important consequences for encouraging striving behavior and increasing expectations that such behavior will be rewarded.

Influence practices which rely upon verbal statements and explanations should have the additional consequences of generating more veridical expectations for reward and punishment and of making clear to the child the meaning and consequences of his behavior, thereby enabling him to achieve valued goals more readily and more predictably. Within a context of warmth and affection, discipline procedures involving rational explanation and the provision of positive rewards for accomplishments should, in sum, lead to a greater sense of freedom of movement for the child than the opposite kind of reward structure.

Consider, for example, a young person who has learned, over time, that there is little or unpredictable affection and reward to be attained by continued striving for parentally emphasized values such as achievement. He is likely to reduce his expectations of achieving his goals and to experience personal disjunctions for his usual—that is, his socially appropriate—behaviors. The instigation to deviance implicit in this description is the basis for linking the parental reward structure not only to personality dispositions, such as disjunction, but also to deviant behavior. Besides the instigation stemming from personal disjunctions, deviance should be more likely for another reason. In the absence of affection in the home, the child's stake in maintaining acceptance by the parents is minimized. The control against deviance which the possibility of loss of this affectional stake usually maintains is absent.

The parental reward structure may also influence personality substructures other than the child's perception of legitimate opportunity. For example, beliefs in internal or external control are likely to be influenced by the clarity and consistency with which rewards and reproofs are administered and by the degree to which they are accompanied by verbal explanations. Where rewards are infrequent or unpredictable, where little explanation of their occurrence is provided, where punishments are arbitrary, the consequence is more likely to be a belief in external control—a belief that what happens is outside of one's personal control and that contingencies are only loosely connected to one's actions.

In a similar fashion, the adolescent's personal control system is also likely to be influenced by the kind and mode of reward administration. Hoffman (1963a; 1963b) has noted that internalization of standards— conscience—is facilitated by affection and rational explanation. Clarity about what constitutes "right" and "wrong," and affectionally mediated involvement with such standards, tends to safeguard their acquisition and their application by the child to new situations of temptation.

The parental reward structure, constituted of affectional interaction and the set of influence practices, may be seen, then, as having direct implications, over time, for the child's general perception of legitimate opportunity, his beliefs, and his personal controls, and indirect implications, therefore, for the likelihood of deviance. The posited link with deviance has gained empirical support in several studies. Becker's review again is relevant: "Parents of delinquents repeatedly have been shown to have poor affectional relations with their children and to use poor disciplinary techniques" (1964, p. 193). With respect to the other main linkage of concern, various studies have shown that affectional interaction and influence practices vary with parental position in the larger sociocultural environment (see, for example, Sears, Maccoby, and Levin, 1957; Kohn, 1963). The use of verbal and rational discipline techniques has been shown especially to characterize middle-class parents, while the use of physical and impersonal reward and reproof practices tends to characterize parents in lower socioeconomic positions.

The Parental Belief Structure

While in the parental reward structure emphasis was placed upon a set of parental *practices,* the role of parental *beliefs* in the process of socialization is emphasized in the parental belief structure. Beliefs have to do with the general view of, orientations toward, or ideologies about the world which the parents maintain. These beliefs may be assumed inevitably to influence the child, either directly, as his parents teach him, or indirectly, as he senses that they are the guiding paradigms of his parents' behavior. The two belief variables we have considered to be important here are the variables of *alienation* and *belief in external control.* Each of these received attention in the preceding chapter with respect to their conceptual definition and their relation to the sociocultural environment and deviant behavior. The present discussion will center, therefore, on the influence which these two parental beliefs may be presumed to have on the child's personality system.

Alienation, as we said earlier, refers to the sense of social isolation and estrangement from basic life roles. It implies a pessimism about the possibilities of achieving meaningful interpersonal relations and gaining satisfaction from the daily transactions required in the carrying out of social role behavior. Related to this general belief is belief in external control, the orientation that the outcomes of one's behavior are not contingent on what one does but are determined by outside forces, such as powerful other persons, or impersonal random forces, such as fate, luck, or chance. Taken together, these parental beliefs taught to or detected by the child over the course of his earlier development should have important consequences for his personality system. Most directly affected should be the child's *own* beliefs, his *own* sense of alienation or external control. But also affected should be his perception of access to legitimate opportunity and his personal controls.

Alienation and external control as prevailing beliefs or orientations in the parents can be seen to influence the socialization process in two ways. The first is in the transmission to the child of an outlook which, to the degree to which he adopts it, interferes with his prosecution of culturally approved striving behavior and his pursuit of socially mediated rewards. The second is in removing the parents from active participation in, commitment to, and responsibility for the very process of socialization itself. To the extent to which this happens, socialization becomes a much more haphazard process, dependent to a larger extent upon the vagaries of external events and lacking the controls intrinsic to involved parental guidance. Gildea, Glidewell, and Kantor report, in this connection, that "mothers who cannot see themselves as either responsible or potent are more likely to have disturbed children" (1961, p. 86).

The child exposed to alienated, externally controlled parents is more likely, then, to develop similar ideas about isolation from others, the lack of satisfaction in role behaviors—for example, in school work—and the chance-mediated nature of an unpredictable future. Such ideas, as we have argued earlier, should indirectly conduce to deviance. By contrast, the nonalienated parent with a strong belief in internal control should not only convey parallel ideas to his child but should exert further control and guidance by engaged participation in the parental role itself, that is, by the active assumption of responsibility for socialization. The child exposed to such a family milieu is less likely to engage in deviance because the beliefs he has learned are consistent with socially approved means of striving. Continued parental responsibility for his further development serves also as an important inhibitor against his engagement in deviant behavior.

The Parental Control Structure

While functioning, as does the parental belief structure, to socialize control, the parental control structure centers on the aspects of the family milieu more directly concerned with access to or control against deviant behavior itself. The concern of the preceding structure was with the transmission of certain general orientations to the child which have indirect implications for deviance. The present structure incorporates those aspects of the socialization experience which result in the learning of deviance directly or in the failure to develop an internalized set of standards—a conscience—which functions to constrain against deviance.

The parental control structure is analogous, in microcosm, to the community social control structure described in Chapter 3. Its components, now within the family, comprise *the degree of exposure to deviant role models, the degree to which limits are set and sanctions are consistently and pervasively applied, and the opportunities which the parents provide for a child to engage in deviance.* Where parental controls are strong and consistent, the child should develop an attitude of repudiation of deviance; where the reverse is the case, the child should develop an acceptance or tolerance of deviance.

Certain aspects of the parental control structure, such as exposure to deviant role models in the family, may have direct effects on deviant behavior without the necessity of mediation by personality structures. In this connection, the research on imitation and modeling of aggressive behavior discussed earlier (see Bandura and Walters, 1963) should be recalled. Sometimes a child is exposed to two *different* patterns: the parents' actual behavior and their direct teaching of standards. Often these patterns are not consistent, such as in the case of the father who drinks chronically but tries to teach his children to avoid alcohol. In a recent study, Mischel and Liebert (1965) investigated what children tend to learn when exposed to such inconsistency between the actual behavior of models and the teaching of behavior standards by the models. Interestingly enough, the subjects tended to adopt the more lenient alternative for themselves, that is, to follow the line of least resistance. This experiment is a paradigm of a situation often confronted in family settings where parental controls are weak: the actual behavior of the parents provides models for deviance even though the parents try to teach otherwise.

Aspects of the parental control structure, other than the aspect dealing with models for deviance, involve the whole system of regulations brought to bear on the child's potential transgressions—the set of rules for his activities and the strictness with which they are applied; the parent's own general tolerance of deviance which, even if not recurrently proclaimed, the child may be able to detect; the consistency between the parents' views of transgression and regulation; and, less directly, whatever teaching is done about the desirability of a long time perspective and deferring gratification. Each of these aspects has implications for the child's attitudes about deviance. But each also has implications for the actual possibility of engaging in deviance and for the sanctions to which such actions would lead.

The linkage of the parental control structure to the sociocultural environment follows from the discussion in an earlier chapter about how social controls may vary with social location. The focus of the present remarks has been mainly on the relation of the parental control structure—comprised of both beliefs or attitudes and practices—to adolescent personality and behavior. The primary socialization outcome of the parental control structure, with respect to personality, is deemed to be the effect upon the variables in the child's personal control structure—his tolerance of deviance, short time perspective, and tendency toward immediate gratification. With respect to actual behavior, certain direct transmission of deviant response patterns may be expected to follow from the extent to which the parental control structure provides the child with deviant role models (see McCord and McCord, 1958).[2]

CONCLUDING SUMMARY
ON THE SOCIALIZATION SYSTEM

We have, to this point, presented the basic concepts which guided the study of socialization in this research. To enable the socialization study to fulfill the aims set for it in the introduction to this chapter, we have attempted to treat the family milieu as a microcosm of the larger society. And we have made the same kind of abstractions from the family milieu that were used to differentiate the larger sociocultural environment. The three socialization substructures—the parental reward structure, the parental belief structure, and the parental control structure—are considered as analogues, within the family, of their counterparts in the larger sociocultural system. By virtue of this fact, they should bear logical relations to the sociocultural structures and, as the latter themselves do, to the personality structures.

While the effort has been made to delineate three separate socialization substructures, it is again important to assert that they are seen as usually intercorrelated sources of influence. In this sense, they constitute a system which may have characteristic general properties more important than those of any of its parts. With respect to *specific* consequences for the child of *specific* aspects of parental socialization, no single parental practice was deemed to be exclusively influential or determinative in producing

---

[2] While we have stressed in this discussion the direct modeling of behavior patterns, it is quite often the case that children will take the opposite course of action than that provided by the model. Thus, the daughter of an alcoholic becomes an abstainer. In this case, the father functions as a "model of dissociation." The conditions which lead to adopting or to dissociating from a model's behavior have not been clearly delineated. Probably relevant are such factors as the perceived negative consequences of the behavior and the availability of positive alternatives, for example, peer models.

a given personality attribute or deviant behavior. Instead, it was presumed that the various parent socialization practices and attitudes interact to produce a home atmosphere that, in the *benevolent* sense, might be described as rewarding of culturally approved behavior, affectionate, rational, communicative, optimistic, and oriented toward social responsibility or conformity.

It was anticipated that the personality of an adolescent would reflect this atmosphere in various ways: in his perception of legitimate opportunity (for example, his expectations for achievement and acceptance in school and his expectations of later success in education, occupation, and income); in his sense of being able to control his destiny; and in his anticipation that deviant behavior will be punished and should be repudiated. Furthermore, his behavior should show some parallel to this personality structure. He should be more conforming in school and less likely to engage in deviant behavior in general.

The converse picture emerges from the home in which parental rearing practices provide little affectional interaction, the parents are alienated, and there is minimal regulation and only weak repudiation of deviance. This atmosphere should lead, in the adolescent, to lower expectations for achievement by socially approved means, higher disparities between life goals and anticipations of reaching them, and greater tolerance of deviant behavior. The adolescent with these characteristics should be more likely to engage in alternative, possibly deviant, behavior to achieve his life goals.

The socialization system as it has been described is presented in schematic form in Figure 3. In this figure, as in Figures 1 and 2, the variables in the three structures are described in terms that show their conduciveness to deviance. The nature of this model is somewhat different from the models presented in Figures 1 and 2. We have not tried to depict instiga-

FIGURE 3

The Socialization System, Personality, and Deviant Behavior

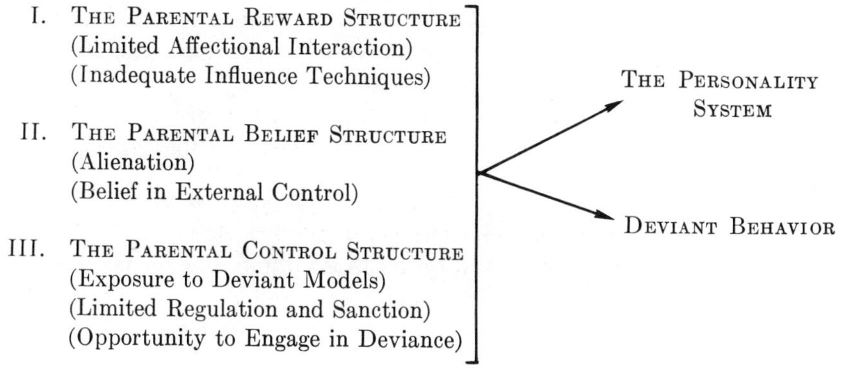

I. THE PARENTAL REWARD STRUCTURE
    (Limited Affectional Interaction)
    (Inadequate Influence Techniques)

II. THE PARENTAL BELIEF STRUCTURE
     (Alienation)
     (Belief in External Control)

III. THE PARENTAL CONTROL STRUCTURE
      (Exposure to Deviant Models)
      (Limited Regulation and Sanction)
      (Opportunity to Engage in Deviance)

THE PERSONALITY SYSTEM

DEVIANT BEHAVIOR

tion and control separately, but, in line with the preceding discussion, to represent the three structures as generating an over-all family situation conducive to deviance. Stated otherwise, the diagram represents the conception of the family milieu as a single context of somewhat intercorrelated aspects.

It may be seen, further, that this context has three kinds of consequences—one for the personality system, one for deviant behavior directly, and one for deviant behavior indirectly, that is, as it is mediated by the personality system. The general proposition schematized in Figure 3 can be stated as follows: *The more fully the variables in the three structures characterize a given family situation, the more likely it will be that the child will develop personality attributes conducive to deviance and will actually engage in deviant behavior.*

CONCLUSIONS FOR THE OVER-ALL THEORETICAL FRAMEWORK

The aim of these chapters has been to present the social-psychological framework which guided the research on deviance and excessive alcohol use to be reported in subsequent chapters. The framework was designed to take into account both personal and sociocultural factors and, further, to show their articulation in a larger interdisciplinary explanatory scheme. Pursuit of the latter objective was facilitated by viewing the sociocultural and personality systems as isomorphic, that is, as conceptual analogues of each other. This perspective provided a logical basis for bringing the two systems together. By joining the two systems logically, it becomes possible to traverse between epidemiological and individual accounts of deviance which are conceptually homogeneous.

Several things can be said about the framework as a whole. First, while our employment of the framework has been limited to deviance and alcohol use, its applicability to other areas of social behavior such as mental health, social mobility, social change, and personal adjustment, should be apparent. Not only are some of the specific concepts likely to be useful in a variety of studies, but the general mode of approach to linking social and psychological concepts would seem likely to prove fruitful in other work.

Second, the framework is seen as a limited but differentiated theory. At least, it accomplishes what Nadel has sketched as the criteria of a conceptual scheme:

> "[T]heory" can also be understood in another, less ambitious, sense, namely as a body of propositions (still interconnected) which serve to *map out* the problem area and thus prepare the ground for its empirical investigation by appropriate methods.

More precisely, the propositions serve to classify phenomena, to analyze them into relevant units or indicate their interconnections, and to define "rules of procedures" and "schemes of interpretation." "Theory" here equals conceptual scheme or logical framework . . . (1957, p. 1).

But the statement of relations among the terms of the framework—enabling both prediction and the provision of a logical account for empirical phenomena—perhaps permits a claim to a somewhat stronger version of the term "theory." The framework seems more consonant with Merton's description of "theories of the middle range[:] . . . special theories applicable to limited ranges of data . . ." (1957, p. 9).

Third, the framework is not to be interpreted as an effort to account for *all* of deviance or delinquency; nor is it an effort to account for the absolute rates of deviance which may characterize a particular residential area. The theory attempts to account for observed variation between groups and within groups, but not for absolute rates of behavior. Our concern at this stage has been to assert (and then to demonstrate) the *relevance* of the concepts in the scheme to the occurrence of the kinds of deviance we have specified and measured. Stated in this way, the scientific burden is to show that the concepts *make a difference* rather than to determine exactly how much of a difference they make. Instead of trying to establish exact parameter values, we have been concerned with the establishment of parameter *relevance*.

Fourth, it follows from the logic of our approach that no *single* variable can be expected to account for a great deal of the variance in deviant behavior. If deviance is considered to be the outcome of an interacting *set* of influences—either sociocultural, or personality, or socialization, or a combination of these—then the role of any single influence must depend in large part upon its relation to other influences. Relations of single explanatory variables to deviance should be small, therefore, relative to relations of sets of explanatory variables dealt with simultaneously.

A final point worth stressing is the primary concern of such a framework for *explanation* rather than prediction. Prediction can often be accomplished with great accuracy in the absence of any valid explanatory scheme. What is meant by "concern for explanation" is the embedding of the social phenomenon of deviance in a logical network of concepts whose properties make its occurrence an inevitable (that is, a logically required) outcome. It has been this latter objective to which these chapters have been addressed: to sketch a coherent set of concepts, to specify their interconnections, and to show how different rates or different likelihoods of occurrence of deviant behavior follow logically from those conceptual relations.

The entire social-psychological framework is now presented in schematic form in Figure 4. The boxes represent the major classes of variables, and the arrows designate the major relations investigated in our research. It should be emphasized that the arrows drawn do not exhaust all of the meaningful relations among the variables. For example, the personality system obviously can have a feedback effect upon the sociocultural system, but that is not shown in the diagram. Only those lines of influence assumed and investigated in our research are shown. It should also be noted that relations among variables *within* a box are left unspecified in this diagram. It will be recalled, however, that in the previous diagrams, Figures 1, 2, and 3, that purpose was accomplished for each of the boxes separately.

FIGURE 4

The Over-all Social-Psychological Framework for the Study of Deviance

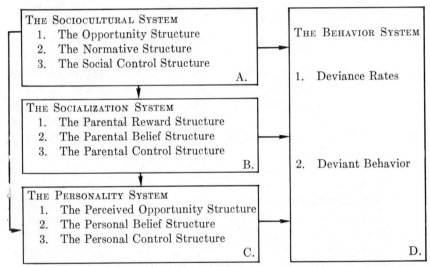

Several important aspects of the framework are represented in Figure 4. First, each of the three "predictor" systems (Boxes A, B, and C) has direct linkage with behavior (Box D). Second, the sociocultural system may have both direct and indirect influence upon the personality system. Third, although not shown by arrows, it can be seen that it would be possible to *combine* the separate sources of influence on deviance and deal with them simultaneously. Indeed, it follows from our discussion at the outset of Chapter 3 that the *joint* use of sociocultural and personality variables— a field theoretical approach—should provide a broader account of deviance than either set of variables alone.

In the previous chapters, each of the three systems influencing deviant behavior was described in some detail. Within each system, the deviance-prone characteristics of each structure were specified. Keeping those characteristics in mind, the major proposition schematized in Figure 4 can be stated: *The more the sociocultural, socialization, and personality systems—separately and together—have the characteristics previously specified as theoretically conducive to deviance, the greater the deviance rate and the greater the likelihood of occurrence, for a given individual, of deviant behavior.*

The implementation of this general framework in a particular research approach will be discussed in the following chapter.

REFERENCES

BANDURA, A. AND R. H. WALTERS. *Adolescent aggression.* New York: Ronald, 1959.

BANDURA, A. AND R. H. WALTERS. *Social learning and personality development.* New York: Holt, Rinehart and Winston, 1963.

BECKER, W. C. Consequences of different kinds of parental discipline. In M. L. Hoffman and Lois W. Hoffman (Eds.) *Review of child development research.* Vol. I. New York: Russell Sage Foundation, 1964. Pp. 169–208.

BRONFENBRENNER, U. Socialization and social class through time and space. In Eleanor E. Maccoby, T. M. Newcomb, and E. L. Hartley (Eds.) *Readings in social psychology.* New York: Holt, Rinehart and Winston, 1958. Pp. 400–424.

CALDWELL, BETTYE. On the effects of infant care. In M. L. Hoffman and Lois W. Hoffman (Eds.) *Review of child development research.* Vol. I. New York: Russell Sage Foundation, 1964. Pp. 9–87.

CHILD, I. L. Socialization. In G. Lindzey (Ed.) *Handbook of social psychology.* Reading, Mass.: Addison-Wesley, 1954. Pp. 655–692.

CLAUSEN, J. A. AND JUDITH R. WILLIAMS. Sociological correlates of child behavior. In H. W. Stevenson (Ed.) *Child psychology: The sixty-second yearbook of the National Society for the Study of Education.* Part I. Chicago: The National Society for the Study of Education, 1963. Pp. 62–107.

CRANDALL, V. J. Achievement. In H. W. Stevenson (Ed.) *Child psychology: The sixty-second yearbook of the National Society for the Study of Education.* Part I. Chicago: The National Society for the Study of Education, 1963. Pp. 416–459.

GILDEA, MARGARET, J. C. GLIDEWELL, AND MILDRED B. KANTOR. Maternal attitude and adjustment in school children. In J. C. Glidewell (Ed.) *Parental attitudes and child behavior.* Springfield, Illinois: Charles C Thomas, 1961. Pp. 42–89.

GLUECK, S. AND ELEANOR GLUECK. *Family environment and delinquency.* Boston: Houghton Mifflin, 1962.

HEALY, W. AND AUGUSTA F. BRONNER. *New light on delinquency and its treatment.* New Haven: Yale University Press, 1936.

HOFFMAN, LOIS W. AND R. LIPPITT. The measurement of family life variables.

In P. H. Mussen (Ed.) *Handbook of research methods in child development.* New York: Wiley, 1960. Pp. 945–1013.

HOFFMAN, M. Child rearing practices and moral development: Generalizations from empirical research. *Child Development,* 1963, *34,* 295–318.

HOFFMAN, M. Parent discipline and the child's consideration for others. *Child Development,* 1963, *34,* 573–587.

INKELES, A. Sociology and psychology. In S. Koch (Ed.) *Psychology: A study of a science.* Vol. 6. *Investigations of man as socius: Their place in psychology and the social sciences.* New York: McGraw-Hill, 1963. Pp. 317–387.

KOHN, M. Social class and parent-child relationships: An interpretation. *American Journal of Sociology,* 1963, *68,* 471–480.

LEIGHTON, A. H., J. A. CLAUSEN, AND R. N. WILSON (Eds.) *Explorations in social psychiatry.* New York: Basic Books, 1957.

MCCORD, JOAN AND W. MCCORD. The effects of parental role model on criminality. *Journal of Social Issues,* 1958, *14,* 66–75.

MERTON, R. K. *Social theory and social structure.* (Rev. ed.) New York: Free Press, 1957.

MILLER, D. R. AND G. E. SWANSON. *The changing American parent.* New York: Wiley, 1958.

MILLER, D. R. AND G. E. SWANSON. *Inner conflict and defense.* New York: Holt, Rinehart and Winston, 1960.

MISCHEL, W. AND R. M. LIEBERT. Effects of discrepancies between observed and imposed reward criteria on their acquisition and transmission. *Journal of Personality and Social Psychology,* 1966, *3,* 45–53.

NADEL, S. F. *The theory of social structure.* New York: Free Press, 1957.

ORLANSKY, H. Infant care and personality. *Psychological Bulletin,* 1949, *46,* 1–48.

SEARS, R. R., ELEANOR E. MACCOBY, AND H. LEVIN. *Patterns of child rearing.* New York: Harper & Row, 1957.

SEWELL, W. H. Some recent developments in socialization theory and research. *Annals of American Academy of Political and Social Science,* 1963, *349,* 163–181.

STRODTBECK, F. L. Family interaction, values, and achievement. In D. C. McClelland, A. L. Baldwin, U. Bronfenbrenner, and F. L. Strodtbeck. *Talent and society.* Princeton, N.J.: Van Nostrand, 1958. Pp. 135–194.

PART THREE

The Approach to a Field Study of Deviance

CHAPTER SIX

Methodological Orientation and the Design of the Research

In every study of human behavior, the particular ways in which knowledge and understanding are pursued represent choices among possible alternatives. The rationalization and justification of those choices necessarily involve methodological considerations. For this reason, our initial attention will be devoted to the methodological orientation which guided the investigations. A discussion of the exercise of controls over observation and inference in field studies occupies the first part of the chapter. For each type of control, its role or application in our research is described. In the second half of the chapter, the specific explication of the research design and the general procedures employed in the several studies is dealt with.

MINIMIZING INFERENTIAL AMBIGUITY

The history of the behavioral sciences—this is perhaps especially true for psychology—has been enlivened by a great deal of dispute over methods. The dialectic in much of the argumentation has been the opposition between the experiment and the field or observational study, support for either approach often involving a pejorative account of the limitations of the other. A closer look at this issue will help to introduce our own position about the methodological status of field studies.

For many workers, the laboratory experiment constitutes the ideal model for truly scientific research and is considered responsible for the remarkable progress and depth of analytic understanding achieved in the physical sciences. Advocates of the experiment point to its intrinsically compelling logical structure, the fact that its principal characteristic, intervention or manipulation under otherwise unvarying circumstances, permits a sharp reduction in inferential ambiguity or the uncertainty surrounding the conclusions drawn from the research. From this perspective, the field

137

observer, the clinician, or the cultural anthropologist seem to be able to generate, by contrast, crude, uncertain, or at most, "preliminary" knowledge.

While there is merit in the claims for the experiment and a certain validity in the criticism of some of the uses of nonexperimental methods, these claims and criticisms have had two unfortunate consequences. First, the performing of experiments has become in itself an honorific activity, independently of any other criteria for evaluating the character of the work—its significance or generality, for example. Second, research on certain kinds of problems or phenomena has been slighted simply because such problems do not seem amenable to the experimental approach. As Kaplan has noted, "in contemporary behavioral science the attitude toward experimentation is in danger of becoming a kind of ritualism" (1964, p. 146).

The advocates of the field study or of naturalistic observation are not without their own rationale. To begin with, they read the history of science differently, taking solace from the powerful contributions made by observation in such fields as astronomy, geology, and biology. Second, they see definite advantages to studying phenomena in their natural settings rather than in the more or less artificial conditions of the laboratory: the possibility of understanding naturally occurring covariation and the likelihood of greater representativeness of the findings. When these are the objectives of research, we are cautioned to keep in mind that "Analytic procedures may remove the influence of other forces from a relationship under observation, but these forces are not removed from nature" (Yinger, 1965, p. 7).

Finally, the point is made that for certain problems or phenomena there is simply no alternative to observation. These include problems where knowledge is insufficiently developed to enable manipulation and phenomena which could not be brought into the laboratory without Procrustean consequences. Thus, Wright has commented that "It is impossible now to make experimental arrangements that allow for the full size and complexity of many events. . . . The strategy in every such case is to capitalize upon experiments in nature by substituting selection for manipulation of variables" (1960, p. 130). In the same vein, while advocating joint recourse to experiments and to field studies, Bandura and Walters note that the latter "have the advantage of permitting observations of the effects of a wide range of stimulus events that cannot be readily reproduced in laboratory situations because of practical or ethical considerations" (1963, p. 45).

The methodological polarization between experiment and field study seems, hopefully, to be waning. One reason appears to be pressure from society for behavioral scientists to contribute more directly to problems of immediate social significance, problems such as mental illness, the effects of segregation, or delinquency. Although experiments are not impossible in these areas, field studies are obviously required in any substantial response to that pressure. These social pressures are related to pressures from those within the behavioral sciences who are concerned that their disciplines keep contact with the complexities of social reality. Thus, Cook (1962) urges that research be directed toward "socially significant events," and Sanford (1965) calls for increased attention to "human problems," "problems that people really worry about." The effect of these pressures has been to increase awareness that, in any comprehensive quest for understanding of complex, large-scale, time-extended social behavior, various *combinations* of methods, related to each other in logically or temporally ordered structures, must inevitably be involved.

Also contributing to the trend toward depolarization has been logical analysis of both the experiment and the field study. Not only does such analysis make clear that a large variety of different methods is included under each of these major approaches, but also, to quote Kaplan, that actually "there is no sharp distinction between observation and experimentation, only a series of gradations and intermediates" (1964, p. 144).

The analysis from which this conclusion emerges shows that the fundamental issue dividing experiment from field study is *not* intervention or manipulation but *the degree to which controls have been applied to the process of observation and inference.* It is the latter, rather than the former, which determines to what extent ambiguity of inference has been minimized. In this light, manipulation may be seen as simply one technology for "instituting controls" (Kaplan's phrase). Admittedly, it is a uniquely powerful technology in that it can sharply reduce ambiguity of inference, especially about the direction of relations between variables. But it is neither the only technology for this purpose nor one which can ever wholly eliminate ambiguity. Questions always remain about the success of the manipulations, the certainty that the manipulations have the intended meaning for the subject, and the possibility of alternative inferences from the findings. Indeed, the strategy of replication reflects a recognition of the ambiguity residual in even the most elegant experiment. Finally, if manipulation is only one technology for minimizing ambiguity, it should be apparent that, through reliance upon other technologies, field studies can also be subjected to the instituting of controls.

The utility of this general point of view is that it affords a criterion of methodological adequacy which is not coterminous with any particular method of research but which may be applied to all research. The criterion—minimizing inferential ambiguity—serves to ask whether controls have been instituted to the fullest degree that the problem and the research situation permitted. This perspective makes clear that the merit of research does not lie in the ritual application of honorific methods but in the optimal matching of methods to the character and requirements of problems. A discussion of the controls over observation and inference which were employed in our own field study should be helpful at this juncture. Five categories of controls were involved and will be elaborated; all of these will be seen to be interrelated—that is, to be separate facets of an over-all methodological orientation.

CONTROL THROUGH SELECTION

It is the salient characteristic of field studies that control over the observation of variation depends upon selection. This means no more than that persons, groups, or situations differing in some attribute or set of attributes of interest to the research need to be found or identified or established. (This is sometimes spoken of as "establishing the independent variable.") The process of locating or establishing the desired variation may be a relatively direct and uncomplicated one where the attributes involved are phenotypic, that is, obvious or apparent; or it may require relatively elaborate search procedures where the attributes are genotypic, that is, abstract or recondite. It is clearly easier, for example, to select for or establish sex differences than differences in sexual identification; it is easier to locate rural-urban variation than variation in social disorganization. Whatever the level of the attribute, however, selection for variation on it should be unequivocal if this type of control is to be successfully achieved. And, as will be seen, for control through selection to be unequivocal requires the implementation of yet *other* kinds of controls.

Selection in our research involved both phenotypic and genotypic levels, the former focusing on an attribute in which variation was apparent, and the latter focusing on a set of abstract attributes on which the existence of variation had to be established. With respect to the first, the community available as the research site, consisting of three relatively nonoverlapping ethnic groups, provided obvious variation in ethnic status. The readily apparent attribute of ethnic status made control through selection—that is, the establishment of groups varying in ethnic status—a relatively straightforward matter. And that aspect of the research which was directed toward determining the correlates or implications of ethnic status could proceed with little difficulty in this regard.[1] Much social research seems

[1] That even the establishment of ethnic status is not entirely uncomplicated is immediately evident when one begins to classify offspring of interethnic marriages. Criteria for classification have to be established which can involve reference to lineage, location in certain membership groups (for example, being listed on the tribal rolls), and even such factors as self-definition and the pattern of voluntary associations.

to be of this order, yielding descriptions of the concomitants of variation in ethnic, social, culture, or sex groups.

With respect to our second and principal interest, however, the achievement of control through selection required a much more complicated procedure for establishing variation; in fact, it constituted a large share of the research effort. The issue here was, of course, the establishment of the existence of variation on the attributes specified by the *theory,* attributes which are a good deal less available to simple observation or enumeration than is ethnic status. Thus, for example, selecting groups varying in "sociocultural pressure toward deviance" or in "access to illegitimate means" became a major research objective.

The achievement of this goal required the development of extensive and detailed measurement procedures to enable the establishment of the independent variables and the selection of comparison groups. This kind of effort ordinarily can be avoided only by remaining at the phenotypic level, where an attribute is apparent in its variation. It is also an effort which can be bypassed through a willingness to rely upon an apparent attribute to serve as an index or map of the more difficult-to-establish abstract attributes. Thus, in our research, it would have been a possible strategy to rely upon ethnic status itself as an index for some of our theoretical attributes—for example, value-access disjunction, or degree of anomie. The difficulty, of course, lies precisely at the level of control: Such a strategy fails to make *direct* measurement of the selection attributes. It thereby fails to establish optimal observational control over their variation; to that extent, inference remains ambiguous. Such a strategy would also have precluded an investigation of variation in the theoretical attributes *within* each of the ethnic groups, thereby constituting a crucial limitation to the concerns of the research.

It can now be seen that to speak of controlling variation by selection, when the attributes at issue are abstract or genotypic, can do little more than separate the field study approach from an approach employing manipulation. To investigate theoretical attributes, control through selection can minimize ambiguity only when those attributes are measured relatively directly and unequivocally. The accomplishment of the latter objective depends upon the institution of *other* types of controls, and it is to some of these that the following sections are addressed.

CONTROL THROUGH STANDARDIZATION

The phrase "control through standardization" means the application of procedures to minimize the operation of subjective, idiosyncratic, or other factors which, in the process of observation and inference, generate unreliability. Standardization includes procedures for maximizing reliability of observation, such as the use of multiple observers, interview schedules, or tests; procedures for maximizing the representativeness of observations, such as sampling methods; procedures for maximizing the reliability of data processing, such as objective scoring systems and established coding guides; and procedures for maximizing the reliability of data interpretation, such as statistical evaluation of the pattern of findings. These are, of course, the familiar controls to which one usually refers in elementary discussions of research; they represent efforts to maintain quality control over observation and inference.

Despite the obviousness of these procedures, control through standardization has often been ignored, especially in complex field studies of naturally occurring social behavior. There are areas in the behavioral sciences that have either failed to develop and apply such procedures to research or have even opposed their application as being inimical to their objectives. Examples can be found in clinical work in psychology, in social psychiatry, and in ethnographic work in anthropology, the efforts of these groups resting mainly upon observation by highly trained individuals. Janowitz notes, for example, that "Anthropologists still seem to believe that their personal direct observation gives them an adequate basis for recording complex social reality" (1963, p. 153). Likewise, Maquet, in urging the use of multiple observers and standardized scales in anthropological research, comments as follows: "Such an effort has not been made in anthropology because research has not been oriented toward this aim. Up to now anthropologists do not seem to have been bothered by the influence of their individual characteristics on the collection of facts" (1964, p. 52). And French remarks that "Cultural anthropologists have spent little time . . . analyzing and perfecting a methodology" (1963, p. 417).

All three authors cited see the anthropology of the future as departing from the tradition of single individuals gathering global observations of isolated and relatively simple societies. It is precisely their concern with the impending transition to intensive research on complex contemporary societies that has led them to criticize the traditional research mode. Given that anthropological research will increasingly deal with variation in degree of attributes rather than their mere presence or absence, that it will increasingly deal with more abstract rather than apparent attributes, and that it will need to cope with complex sets of attributes rather than one or two, observation unassisted and unconstrained by standardization procedures is even more likely than before to fall short of its objectives.

The relationship of control through standardization to the previously discussed issue of control through selection should be apparent. The compellingness of the location and establishment of variation, especially when the attributes are genotypic or abstract, depends almost entirely upon the adequacy of the procedures employed to reduce unreliability and bias in observation. Control through selection in the latter case can rarely be claimed in the absence of control through standardization.

In the light of this commitment, standardization was heavily relied upon in the present research. A large degree of effort was devoted to the construction and use of interview schedules and psychological tests or inventories, the development of objective scoring systems, the employment of sampling procedures, and the application of statistical analyses. It was our belief that resistance to the use of such procedures, as either unnecessary or as "constricting the freedom of observation," was unwarranted; on the contrary, it seemed likely that without them it would be impossible to achieve research objectives of any major complexity. It is interesting in this regard to note Janowitz's skepticism about efforts after holistic analysis in anthropology, efforts which are based almost entirely upon direct observation. He urges, instead, the use of "the quantitative instruments of sociology and social psychology . . . because these methods uncover relations essential for a configurational analysis" (1963, p. 153).

CONTROL THROUGH THE USE OF THEORY

The control to be discussed in this section is that instituted through the use of theory as an explicit framework for research. Although theory is more frequently seen as something to be demonstrated as valid or invalid rather than as providing a source of control over observation and inference, its functions in the latter sense are critical contributions to the process of research.

The key point on which this position turns is epistemological: Observations can never be achieved in "raw" form—no facts exist independently of some interpretive apparatus. In sum, the empirical world is already a conceptual one. This idea of the "theoretical" nature of all observation is nicely expressed in Hanson's (1958) phrase "the theory-laden character of perception," in Bronowski's (1959) comment that "every fact is a field," or in Kaplan's (1964) emphasis on the point that "observation is already cognition." Once this idea is accepted, it becomes clear that research is never without theory of some sort. The issue that the researcher faces is not whether to use theory or not but, at best, how to take advantage of explicit theory, and, at worst, how to avoid being misled by the operation of implicit theory.

Taking advantage of explicit theory means having available a structure of interrelated concepts sufficiently elaborate and articulated to suggest the kind of observations to be made or data to be sought, to specify the nature and properties of the procedures to be employed in making the observations, and to give meaning to the resulting empirical findings. In short, it means taking advantage of the directive role which an explicitly formulated theory can play in every phase of the research endeavor. The recognition of this role implies an "instrumentalist view of tehories—that their significance lies in the action they guide . . . forming concepts and laws, conducting experiments, making measurements, providing explanations and predictions" (Kaplan, 1964, p. 310).

Our own methodological orientation involved the development and use of theory as "a guide to action" or, in terms relevant to the present discussion, as a source of controls over observation and inference. When theory is used to specify the attributes on which control through selection is pursued, and when it specifies the properties of procedures on which control through standardization is based, its function as a source of control becomes apparent. In these areas, theory effects *an increase in the relevance of the observations achieved to the inferences sought;* in this way, it serves to reduce inferential ambiguity, one of the major objectives of the institution of controls.

Kuhn's description of the state of affairs which obtains when scientific work is carried on in the absence of an established theory is apposite here.

> In the absence of a paradigm or some candidate for paradigm, all of the facts that could possibly pertain to the development of a given science are likely to seem equally relevant. As a result early fact gathering is a far more nearly random activity than the one that subsequent scientific development makes familiar[;] . . . early fact gathering is usually restricted to the wealth of data that lies ready to hand. . . . But though this sort of fact-collecting has been essential to the origin of many significant sciences, . . . it produces a morass (1962, pp. 15–16).

This situation is not unfamiliar in all the behavioral, sciences where significant social behavior has been investigated. Speaking again of cultural anthropology, Janowitz points to the "deep imbalance between data collection and theory construction" (1963, p. 151), and French, commenting on his own discipline, states that "anthropologists as a group do not know what they know; they do not know the questions for which they have accumulated answers" (1963, p. 417). While cultural anthropology is not to be singled out for special indictment on this score, it provides an instructive example since theoretical elaboration in that discipline has not gone very much further than asserting the importance to behavior of a single concept, "culture." Without elaboration, it is difficult to realize much in the way of a guide to scientific action from a single, global concept; that is, it is difficult to gain direction in proposition formation, observation, the development of measurement procedures, or the drawing of inference, all of which are served by recourse to theory.

The relatively infrequent reliance upon theory in the study of naturally occurring social behavior may reflect a sense that such behavior is too complex to be manageable at this stage of development of the behavioral sciences, that adequate theory is not as yet available. On the other hand, it may reflect an unfortunate tendency to consider theory unrelated to such research. As Cook notes with dismay, "the feeling has grown that research on socially significant phenomena can not be theoretical; it can only be applied" (1962, p. 67). Neither view seems justified. When theory is seen in the perspective just discussed, its exploitation in research on socially significant phenomena appears to be a necessity.

This question has another facet which should be discussed. We have talked in this section about theory as a source of control. In the preceding chapters, a theoretical formulation was elaborated, a test of whose adequacy was stated to be a major aim of the present research. Is it possible to talk simultaneously about using a theory as a source of control and testing its utility as an explanatory framework?

It seems to us that this is precisely what is logically required. A theory is never adequate in a universal sense; its adequacy is always relative to some set of phenomena or data which constitutes its purview. The appraisal of a theory's adequacy depends entirely upon a confrontation of the theory with just those phenomena, data, or observations for which it claims explanatory relevance. But such a confrontation, to be compelling, requires that the theory enter into the process of securing those observations, that is, *that the control function of the theory be exercised already.* To confront a theory with theoretically irrelevant or theoretically ambiguous data would seem to be logically inappropriate. It was precisely because of our interest in testing the utility of our theory of deviance that we felt it necessary to rely upon that theory as a source of methodological control.

CONTROL THROUGH CONSTRUCT VALIDATION

Control through construct validation is actually a specific aspect of control through the use of theory. It has been selected for further attention for two reasons; first, it is a way of making clearer some of the implications of the preceding topic, and second, it constitutes in its own right an important methodological issue for research in the behavioral sciences. It has to do with the way in which measures—tests, inventories, questionnaires, interviews—of theoretically important concepts are obtained for use in research.

Measures seem often to be adopted because of their sheer availability: their familiarity to the investigator, ease of use, or popularity at the time. This "tyranny of the available" has the unfortunate consequence that measures may take primacy over concepts in the execution of research or that less than adequate measures of concepts may be employed.[2] Countering the influence of availability, and serving to sharpen the entire matter of the relation between measures and concepts, has been the discussion in recent years of the notion of construct validity (Cronbach and Meehl, 1955; Jessor and Hammond, 1957; Loevinger, 1957; Campbell and Fiske, 1959; Campbell, 1960). From the present vantage point, construct validity is considered another aspect of control.

The term "construct validity" means the establishment of evidence for the claim that a score on a particular procedure may be interpreted as a measure of a particular concept. The logical basis for that claim can be seen to require simultaneous evidence from several directions, the convergence of which increases conviction in the inference about what is being measured. First, the evidence comes from the characteristics of the test itself, the degree to which both item content and structure are relevant to the concept at issue. Second, the evidence comes from the degree to which the measure relates to other variables in a way that follows from the properties of the concept or from the place that the concept occupies in a theoretical network. And third, the evidence comes from the demonstration that the measure does *not* relate to variables with which, according to the properties of the concept, it should not.

It can thus be seen that a claim for the construct validity of a measure is an inference the ambiguity of which is minimized by the convergence of several lines of independent evidence. It can also be seen that the acquisition of these lines of evidence must depend upon the application of theory, however crude or refined, to the construction and development of measures. It is theory which specifies the properties of a concept, its relations to other concepts, and its implications for behavior, including test behavior. In the absence of construct validation, the claim that a given test or procedure is a measure of a particular concept remains ambiguous as do, in turn, all other inferences based upon that claim. The absence of the control provided by the use of theory in the construction and development of measures leaves the meaning of the research findings correspondingly limited.

Theoretical derivation of tests is, therefore, fundamentally a strategy for inference. The primary relevance of construct validity for research is the control which it provides against alternative inferences about the meaning of a particular measure; the convergence of multiple, independent lines of evidence strengthens the claim being asserted and lessens the likelihood that an alternative inference can be equally well supported. And, of course, it is the establishment of the meaning of measures which

---

[2] The tyrannical influence of "availability" is not limited to measures alone—consider, for example, the tremendous effect upon psychological research of the availability, as *subjects,* of rats and college sophomores.

is the crucial preliminary step to the testing of theoretical propositions about relations between concepts.

Control through construct validity imposes limitations upon recourse to already available measures. One must ascertain that the available measures were so devised and now have such properties as to be useful and relevant for the purposes at hand. The likelihood of this being the case with measures originally built for very different purposes is often slim, and it is at this point that the choice is confronted of building new instruments to conform to one's concepts or bending one's concepts to the shape of available instruments. In the latter event, control over inference is clearly sacrificed.

In the former choice, a program of test construction and validation is entailed. It was this choice which was made, within the limits of feasibility, in the present research. Of the large battery of inventories, interview schedules, rating procedures, and behavior tests, all were, without exception, constructed for the purposes of the present investigations or adapted from procedures previously devised to measure the same theoretical concepts. To the extent that construct validity was established for our measures, and this was not possible in all cases, to that extent was another source of control achieved and inferential ambiguity lessened.

CONTROL THROUGH MULTIPLE CONVERGING STUDIES

The logic of the preceding discussion is equally appropriate with respect to the present aspect of control, the final one to be discussed. In the foregoing section, the central issue had to do with reducing the ambiguity in the claim that a test is a valid measure of a concept. The reduction in ambiguity, it was argued, is accomplished by the mustering of various converging lines of independent evidence. In the present section, we are concerned with the claim not that a measure but that a theory is valid; here, again, we argue for reliance upon converging, independent evidence.

Despite careful attention to all the sources of control previously discussed, the fact remains that any single test of the adequacy of a theory may be successful for reasons other than are contained in the theory. This means simply that the possibility of chance factors influencing the outcome always exists, that the operation of unknown biases in selection or in measures employed is always a possibility that even the best of controls can never entirely eliminate. This situation is not limited to field studies but obtains also in laboratory experiments. In the laboratory, the strategy available for coping with this possibility, that is, for reducing this source of inferential ambiguity, is replication. By exact repetition of a study in a way which is entirely independent of the previous study, the alternative inference that the original results could be explained by chance or some unknown bias is weakened, and the claimed inference is clearly strengthened.

In field studies, especially in small communities, replication is an extremely difficult strategy to employ; some substitute for its contribution as a control is necessary. The approach we relied upon was what might be called the strategy of multiple, converging studies: The relatively simultaneous execution of *a set of entirely independent studies, each of which tests the theoretical framework and all of which, together, provide, when consistent, convergent validity for that framework.*

Unlike replication, the present strategy does not call for the identical repetition of the research. As a matter of fact, variation in subjects and in kinds of procedures used is actually desirable in the several studies.[3] The connection of the theory to different and independent situations lends, when successful, greater weight to the theory and diminishes the likelihood of equally successful alternative inferences, for example, chance, or some unknown systematic bias. As Kaplan has stated: "[W]hat counts is the range of facts that the theory takes into account, and especially their heterogeneity. . . . What counts in the validation of a theory, so far as fitting the facts is concerned, is the convergence of the data brought to bear upon it, the concatenation of the evidence . . ." (1964, pp. 313–314).

To accomplish this final type of control, three entirely independent studies were carried out in the community, each study putting the theory to test, but each varying in the character of the subjects used, in the particular procedures employed, or in the part of the theory investigated. In all studies, however, the basic concepts remained the same. To the extent that the evidence from these three studies converges in support of the theory, to that extent has control been applied to inferences about the adequacy of the theory.

The discussion of our methodological orientation has been organized around the various sources of control which were employed in effecting a reduction in observational and inferential ambiguity. Controls, when viewed in as broad a sense as we have done, seem to us to constitute the central methodological problem of field studies in the behavioral sci-

---

[3] The logic of this assertion may be seen to follow from Cronbach and Meehl's discussion of construct validity. "Numerous successful predictions dealing with phenotypically diverse 'criteria' give greater weight to the claim of construct validity than do fewer predictions, or predictions involving very similar behaviors. In arriving at diverse predictions, the hypothesis of test validity is connected each time to a subnetwork largely independent of the portion previously used. Success of these derivations testifies to the inductive power of the test-validity statement, and renders it unlikely that an equally effective alternative can be offered" (1955, p. 295). When a theory rather than a measure is at issue, the same logic would seem to apply.

ences.[4] The five sources of control—selection, standardization, theory, construct validity, and multiple, converging studies—are not meant to be exhaustive and are clearly not mutually exclusive; they simply indicate the ones to which we gave attention. Central to all of them, as is obvious by now, is the influence of theory, an influence which, in our view, permeates every aspect of the research process.

In the wisdom of hindsight, our methodological reach exceeded our grasp. While the orientation just discussed quite explicitly and continuously guided our research efforts, it was impossible for us to fulfill all of its demands. Some of our measures were constructed after the fact—that is, after data had been collected with other purposes in mind. Construct validation of measures was simply not pursued in certain cases. Some of our analyses were clearly *post hoc,* and some of our theory developed from such analyses rather than antedating them. It is in the full awareness of these limitations, limitations arising from the inevitable vicissitudes of the field situation and the inevitable shortcomings of the researchers, that we have felt it important, nevertheless, to describe our methodological orientation. Its importance lies not only in the pervasive influence which it had upon our own work, but in making clear that possibilities do exist for instituting *substantial* control—even in field studies in complex social situations.

We turn now to a more concrete description of the way in which the research was actually carried out.

DESIGN OF THE RESEARCH

Our intention to study a significant aspect of social behavior in a small community and, at the same time, to evaluate a theoretical framework for that behavior confronted us with the task of devising multiple converging investigations relevant both to the theory and the ongoing life of the community. Three major studies were planned to give us a reasonable purchase on this objective. Within each study, the design required the establishment of groups varying in degree of deviance-proneness according to the theoretical formulation elaborated in the preceding chapters. These groups were then compared in relation to a variety of measures of deviance and excessive alcohol use in order to assess whether the the-

---

[4] A somewhat related view of the nature of controls has been stated by the anthropologist, Oscar Lewis. "For purposes of this paper the term 'control' is defined rather broadly to include any technique or method which decreases the probability of error in the observation, collection, and interpretation of field data. Different methods may therefore offer different degrees of control. In this sense one can have control without the controlled group of the laboratory experiment. Indeed, the laboratory experiment is only one type of control. In short, anything which increases the chances of getting more objective, meaningful, and reliable data is a control" (1953, p. 457).

oretically expected differences in behavior actually obtain. How the specific groups were set up will be described in later chapters, after the various measures have been dealt with. In the present chapter, the primary aim is to describe the three major studies. Each of these will be presented in turn.

Study I: The Community Survey Study

The aim of the Community Survey Study was to assess the applicability of the theory of deviance to the adult population of the community. For this purpose, a structured, self-contained interview was devised which, with supplemental information from the examination of court records, provided the primary data for analysis.

The Sample

A virtually complete census of the community had been accomplished prior to the inception of this study.[5] The census had been carried out by first mapping every house within the school district boundary line[6] and then by direct interviewing of the head of household or other responsible informant using a brief, standardized census form. The census list included 1286 adults between the ages of twenty and sixty-five. On the basis of this list, stratification by sex and ethnic group was carried out, generating six sex-by-ethnic populations. Sampling was then done randomly within these populations by entering an alphabetized list for each of them at a number determined by the throw of a die, and then selecting every *n*-th name in the list. In this way, each person on a given list had an equal chance of appearing in the sample drawn from that list.

The sampling ratio was determined by considerations of the size of the groups available, the anticipated attrition due to refusal, and the mini-

[5] The census was carried out by a team of interviewers directed and supervised by Dr. Omer C. Stewart, whose work was essential to us for our sampling procedures. We are grateful to Dr. Stewart for this assistance.

[6] While geographical lines are rarely entirely congruent with lines drawn to reflect social-psychological processes, the school district boundary was decided upon as a valid delimitation of the community for several reasons. First, the entire educational system of the community oriented inward from that boundary to the schools which were located, with two small exceptions, in the town at the center of the community. Second, the orientation inward from that boundary followed from the concentration in the town of most of the community's services as described in Chapter 1. Third, the existence in the town of the main churches and of shopping and recreation generated a largely centripetal social orientation. Although the community was not a closed unit, and a large number of outward transactions did occur at its school district boundary, nevertheless, for the reasons mentioned, both a sense of community and a pattern of internal interaction characteristic of a community unit were reasonably encompassed by the school district boundary line. Further information on the community was presented in Chapter 1.

mum number of subjects felt to be needed in each ethnic group for intended analyses broken down by sex and by at least one other dichotomous variable. A one in six sampling ratio was adopted for both the Anglo and Spanish groups. Because of ·their smaller population, greater anticipated refusal rate, greater expected variance, and the need for larger *absolute* numbers in making analytic tests, the Indians were sampled at double that rate, a one in three ratio.[7]

The sampling procedures resulted in the designation of 109 Anglos (56 males and 53 females), 64 Spanish-Americans (34 males and 30 females), and 80 Indians (41 males and 39 females), a total for the community of 253 adults. When the interviewing was launched, an effort was made to reach every designated respondent, to interview persons who had moved away recently if possible, and to consider as a "refusal" only someone who spurned three separate contacts to enlist his cooperation. The results of these efforts were the following: Of the original 253 names, 221 usable interviews were obtained. The 32 not obtained consisted of 10 refusals and 22 who were unavailable because of moves away, being in service, psychosis, or death since the census was completed. A refusal rate of 10 out of 231 persons contacted is approximately 4 percent, a figure gratifying to us because unexpectedly small.

The final samples used in the analyses of data were the following: 93 Anglos (45 males, 48 females); 60 Spanish (30 males, 30 females); and 68 Indians (35 males, 33 females). Of the original designations, this represents a figure of 85 percent for the Anglos, 94 percent for the Spanish, 85 percent for the Indians, and of 87 percent for the community as a whole. These figures seem high enough not to jeopardize the sampling representation, especially when considering that, for those *available* at the time of the study, the figure obtained is actually *96 percent* for the community as a whole.

The use of stratified random sampling from a complete census list, the reliance upon a high sampling ratio, and the success in obtaining a high rate of returns provide a substantial basis for confidence in findings about the adult population of the community drawn from these data.

The Development of the Interview

For each of the concepts in the theoretical scheme, questions were devised which could be used in face-to-face interviewing. Details will be avoided here since each interview measure is described in the subsequent

---

[7] For efforts to establish population parameters for the community as a whole, a procedure was devised to take account of this disproportionate Indian representation, and a program to do this task was written for the IBM 709 by N. John Castellan, Jr. In the present report, however, we are not concerned with population parameters.

chapters. The interview contained measures of each aspect of the sociocultural, personality, and behavior systems. This is what is meant by referring to the Community Survey Study as a self-contained test of the over-all theoretical framework.

The general mode of approach was to consider each concept separately, to formulate multiple questions or items referring to the properties of that concept (or to borrow them from procedures already developed in one of the other studies or in parallel research being conducted outside the community), to have the items judged, sifted and revised by the research team, and then to adopt the measure for incorporation into a draft form of the interview. When this had been accomplished, the form was tried out and revised several times. Ultimately, it was tried with approximately two dozen Spanish-American subjects in a small rural community near the University. On the basis of this latter experience, further revisions were made, and the interview schedule was once more rewritten. The final form consisted of forty-three pages, and administration took a modal time of about two hours. A copy of the interview schedule appears in Appendix 2. Although needed for only a small percentage of the older Spanish group, a translation of the schedule into Spanish was also made. No version was developed for the Indian language because of the difficulties involved and because some English was spoken by every Indian respondent but one; for the latter, an interpreter was used.

The interview schedule was relatively highly structured with most questions having response categories available from which the respondent chose his answers. Where response categories were long or complex, a card showing them was handed to the interviewee to assist him during the questioning. Since the response categories were also read aloud to each respondent, and since they were often similar across measures, they quickly became familiar and easy to use. The order of presentation of measures was designed so that items of an intimate or uncomfortable nature came later, after rapport had been well established. Factual questions were asked at the beginning to help put the subject at ease.

Administration of the Interview

In addition to the four authors, eight other persons conducted the interviews. These were either graduate students in the behavioral sciences or wives of faculty members or professional people. Intensive training in interviewing, involving lectures, role-playing, supervised tryouts, and independent practice, was provided. The entire team of a dozen interviewers went into the community at the same time, and the bulk of the interviewing was completed within a two-week period. At the end of each day's interviewing, completed schedules were checked and assignments made for the next day. Interviewing was done by interviewers of the same sex and, where Spanish was the language used, by Spanish-speaking interviewers. The locus of the interview was wherever a respondent was found willing to take the time required and where there was sufficient privacy—in the kitchen of a home, at a workplace or office, in the fields by a tractor.

Response to the interviews was extremely gratifying. Cooperation was not difficult to obtain, and even information generally considered intimate or private was quite readily given. Respondents were assured of anonymity, but many seemed less concerned with that than with being able, through their answers, to make some contribution to the understanding of social problems. Many also insisted on thanking the interviewers for talking with them and for providing them the opportunity to consider their lives from an unfamiliar vantage point. Because of such cooperativeness, the resulting interviews were, on the whole, of very high quality.[8]

Processing of Interview Data

Interviews were scored or coded and these data were then punched on IBM cards. Processing of data usually involved internal analyses of the separate measures, analyses of convergent and discriminant validity and description of ethnic group and sex differences on the various measures. A series of more than a dozen Research Reports dealing with the various interview measures in themselves was prepared, and the analyses in these reports served as preliminary or descriptive steps prior to applying the data to testing the theory.

Court Records

Because of our continuing concern with the veridicality of self-reports of deviant behavior, and in order to develop a more comprehensive measure of such behavior, the interview was supplemented by an intensive search of court records for all of our respondents. The records of the local justice of the peace courts, the tribal court, the county court, and the district courts were scrutinized for the previous ten years where possible. These data, described in Chapter 8, constitute the only data external to the interview in this particular study.

To sum up, the Community Survey Study was aimed at the twenty- to sixty-five-year-old adults in the community. Subjects, stratified by sex and ethnic group status, were drawn randomly from the total adult population of the school district. Data were collected by interview and bear on the sociocultural, personality, and behavior systems of our theoretical framework. This study constitutes, therefore, an autonomous test of the

---

[8] Some difficulties were experienced, however, with a small number of the older, less acculturated, heavier-drinking Indians in relation to the psychological measures, resulting in a number of incomplete protocols in this respect. See Chapter 10.

theory, one based almost exclusively on interview measures of both the "independent" and the "dependent" variables.

Study II: The High School Study

The aim of the High School Study was, in general, identical with that of the Community Survey Study: to provide an independent test of the over-all theory guiding the research. It focused, however, on a younger age group, the students in the senior high school in the community, and employed a different set of measurement procedures while orienting to the same basic concepts. The primary data for the High School Study were obtained by means of group-administered questionnaires or tests. Additional data were obtained by interview, ratings, records, and observation of controlled behavior choices.

The Sample

The subjects for this study were the entire local student body of the sophomore, junior, and senior classes of the high school in the community, 93 students in all. A 100 percent sample of those enrolled in the high school at the time of testing was obtained.[9] The composition of the student sample was as follows: 42 Anglos (22 male and 20 female); 36 Spanish (15 male and 21 female); and, unfortunately, only 11 local Indians (6 male and 5 female), and four other Indian students, children of nonlocal Indian residents, all male. The small size of the local Indian sample in the high school effectively made this study a bi-ethnic rather than a tri-ethnic one. Enrollment in the three classes was: 38 sophomores (20 males and 18 females); 25 juniors (15 males and 10 females); and 30 seniors (12 males and 18 females).

While the sample obtained in the high school was a total one, it is important to emphasize that it did not provide a total sample of those of high school age in the community. Of the latter, some were attending school elsewhere and some had dropped out of school for one reason or another. With respect to an age-defined population then, the high school sample, even though total within the school, is limited in its representativeness for these reasons. As is apparent, the age range of the subjects in this study is just below the lower limit of the age range covered in the Community Survey Study. It encompassed persons ranging in age from fifteen to twenty-one years, the age period in which behaviors ultimately resulting in delinquency or deviance are often learned or tried out for the first time.

---

[9] A group of Indian students from distant tribes who boarded in the community and attended the same school was not included in the analysis of the data since their homes were all away from the community and the pattern of their lives, determined largely by their residence in dormitories, was uniquely different.

The Development of Procedures

Because of the exceptional cooperation of the school superintendent, principal, teachers, and school board, it was possible to extend the process of development of procedures over a three-year period, collecting the final data only in the third year. During the first year, a set of preliminary measures of the major concepts was devised and applied in the school. The data from this administration were analyzed during the course of the following year, subjected to item analyses, scaling procedures, and comparisons with criteria such as sex, age, grade in school, and achievement scores. On the basis of this work, the measures were revised and readministered during the second year of the research. Analyses of the sort described were again carried out. By the end of the second year, procedures were finally revised and available, and the data for testing the theory were collected in the third year.

The procedures employed fell into five categories. The first of these, *group-administered questionnaires,* was the source of the bulk of the data. Nearly all of the questionnaires were structured to a high degree and provided response categories for the subject. The questionnaires included measures of values and expectations, perceived life chances, internal control, tolerance of deviance, and drinking and deviant behavior. The second category of procedures was an *interview* in which each subject was seen individually for the primary purpose of assessing time perspective and obtaining certain socioeconomic information about the family. The third category consisted of *controlled behavior choices* for the purpose of measuring delay of gratification. The fourth category was made up of *rating procedures.* Ratings of deviant and conforming behavior were obtained for each student from his teachers, the principal, his mother, and other students. Finally, the fifth category consisted of the data available on each student from *school records* such as his grades, achievement test scores, number of times absent, and information on certain aspects of his family situation. These five types of procedures provided nearly all the data employed in the High School Study; they yielded measures of the sociocultural, personality, and behavior systems, and thereby enabled a second independent test of our over-all theoretical framework.

Administration of the Procedures

The final group procedures were formed into three separate booklets each of which required approximately an hour of time. These procedures appear in Appendix 3. The three hours of data were collected from each subject by taking over one of his classes on three successive mornings. The first two authors were able, by each entering a class at 9, 10, and 11 A.M., to test the whole school with the same booklet within a single morning. The same schedule was repeated for three successive mornings. By this approach, communication between students was minimized.

Within the classroom, the examiner was introduced to the students by their teacher, who then left the room. The booklets were passed out, instructions read aloud, and then the examiner paced the students by reading aloud each question, allowing time for an answer, and then reading aloud the next question. Students read the questions in their own booklets, of course, but the pacing was designed especially to assist those who might have had reading difficulties. At the end of the booklet students were asked, each day, to write their evaluations of the procedures. Students were assured of anonymity and were told that their answers would be treated from then on solely by the code number on their booklet rather than by name.

The interviews were carried on in a teacher's room assigned to us for that purpose. Students were excused from class individually for the time required. The ratings were obtained using standardized forms with explicit categories and full rosters of students to be rated. Each teacher and the principal was seen individually, and each student was rated by several persons independently. School records were scrutinized by us at our leisure in the principal's office. Collection of the behavior choice data on delay of gratification involved cooperation of the local drugstore owner for one measure and of the English teacher for another measure.

Cooperation in this study was excellent due probably to several different reasons. First, the school personnel assisted throughout in creating a helpful atmosphere and lending their approval to our work. Second, we were well known to most of the students by our presence in the community over the preceding three years. One of us, the second author, had for some time conducted at his home a weekly "teen club" for whoever wanted to attend. This was a highly successful aspect of our participant observation in the community; it ultimately helped to secure for us the cooperation especially of those youngsters who might most likely have repudiated the whole business of being tested, those seen in the community as pre-delinquent.

There was a third reason for the excellent cooperation. We began the first day of testing by offering to sponsor and pay for a dance for the whole school, and we began the third day of testing by distributing to each student tickets redeemable for merchandise at the local drugstore. While for us these were actually data collection procedures for measuring delay of gratification, they served to evidence a contribution on our part deserving of some return from the student. Finally, the procedures themselves were, on the whole, considered by the students to be intrinsically interesting. This is overwhelmingly shown in the written comments accumulated from the students at the end of each day's testing. Their comments indicated that the students were stimulated by the opportunity to consider things about themselves and their attitudes seldom otherwise addressed. They also emphasized that they were willing to help if it would contribute to understanding of problems of human behavior. There were, of course, some students who did not like the tests and who were confused by what they were about, but most of these insisted that they had answered honestly.[10]

Processing of the Data

All tests were scored and punched on IBM cards. Internal analyses were made and were again evaluated in a series of Research Reports. Ultimately, for each subject, several IBM cards were employed which contained, beyond basic identifying data, all of his scores on all the measures. These data were the ones employed in testing our theoretical propositions.

In summary, the High School Study parallels the Community Survey Study in enabling an independent appraisal of the over-all theoretical framework. It deals with subjects younger in age, and it relies primarily on group-administered test procedures. The advantages of the High School Study lie in the greater degree of standardization and development of procedures which it permitted, the greater use of multiple procedures to converge on a single concept, and the greater variety of types of procedures—questionnaires, ratings, interviews, record data, and behavior choices—which it employed. In addition, certain ancillary problems, such as the analysis of peer-group interaction structures, difficult to study among the adult sample, were amenable to investigation in the high school situation. The major shortcomings of the High School Study are the limitation in the sampling of that age group in the community (despite a total sample of those attending the high school), and the small number of Indian subjects in the sample, making possible only a bi-ethnic rather than a tri-ethnic comparison. The latter limitation does not, of course, affect the testing of the theory independently of ethnic status.

For the kind of control through multiple converging studies which was discussed earlier in this chapter, the results from both the Community Survey and the High School studies should show the expected parallel outcomes.

---

[10] The procedure, interestingly enough, which elicited the most negative reaction was not at all the one dealing with reporting on their *own* drinking and deviant behavior; rather it was the sociometric questionnaire in which names of *other* students had to be written down for such items as "getting into trouble the most around here."

Study III: The Socialization Study

The aim of this third independent study differed from that of the other two. The portion of the theoretical network which it was designed to test was one not implicated directly in either the Community Survey Study or the High School Study. Its focus was on the processes which must be assumed both to antedate the personality and behavior systems and to mediate the relation of the latter to the sociocultural environment. The establishment of this linkage, an aspect of the larger theory, in a manner which is consistent with the findings from the other two studies, would provide convergent support for that theory. The method used in this study to accomplish these aims was a structured interview with parents in the community.

The Sample

The availability of comprehensive personality and behavioral data on the students in the high school made it advantageous to study the character of socialization which they themselves had experienced. This consideration determined that the sample of socializing agents should be constituted from those who had been and continued to be responsible for those youngsters. The sample of respondents for this study was consequently designated as all of the mothers[11] of the high school students resident in the community. Data obtained from such a sample would be entirely independent of that obtained, under separate and earlier circumstances, from their children. It would thereby enable uncontaminated evaluation of relationships between the parent or home attributes and the personality and behavior attributes of their children.

The 93 students in the high school came from 81 local families. Interviews with mothers (or mother-surrogates) in 75 of these families (92.6 percent) were successfully obtained. Of the remaining six, one mother (Anglo) refused to be interviewed, three mothers (2 Anglo and 1 Spanish) had recently moved away, and two mothers, presumably still resident in the community (1 Spanish and 1 Indian), could not be located at the time of the research. In terms of completeness of sampling, these figures are highly satisfactory.

The final composition of the mother sample was the following: 35 Anglo mothers, 27 Spanish mothers, 10 local Indian mothers, and three

---

[11] A small number of fathers was also interviewed but, since we were unable to do a complete sample of both mothers and fathers, we chose to concentrate on the mother as the parent probably having the greater familiarity with their offspring.

other Indian mothers.[12] Their interviews refer to 88 high school-age children, 46 sons and 42 daughters. Because of the small number of local Indian mothers, ethnic comparisons in this study, as in the High School Study, are mainly bi-ethnic.

The Development of the Interview

Since this study is described in detail in Chapter 12, only enough needs to be said here to locate it in the over-all design of the research. Following our theoretical concerns, primary attention was given to assessing the family situation relative to rewards, beliefs, and controls. An interview schedule was drawn up and, as had been done earlier with the Community Survey, was tried out and revised several times. The final version consisted of twenty-four pages, fairly structured in format. A copy of the interview schedule appears in Appendix 4. A complete Spanish language form was also constructed and was available for use when needed. Modal time for administration of the interview was one and one-half hours.

Administration of the Interview

The interviewing was accomplished in the same manner as in the Community Survey Study, described previously. There were five interviewers (one of whom was the fourth author); all were professionally trained married women. Training in interviewing in general, and in the use of this interview in particular, was provided prior to beginning field work. Two of the women, fluent in Spanish, did the bulk of the interviewing of Spanish mothers.

Again, in this study, cooperation was impressive; this cooperation was partly motivated, of course, by the connection of the interview with the offspring of the respondents. Interviewing was usually done in the home and in a situation of privacy. Mothers were told nothing of the data that we had obtained on their children; in fact, none of the mother interviewers had any of that information available to her, thus forestalling a possible source of data contamination.

Processing of the Interview Data

The interviews were all coded or scored and punched on IBM cards for both internal analyses of particular scales and for assessing intervariable relations. Of the latter, three main categories were considered: relations between the sociocultural situation of the family and the socialization practices characterizing it; relations among the various aspects of the so-

---

[12] The characterization "other Indian" refers, as noted earlier, to Indians living in the community who are not members of the local tribe. There was a small number of such persons considered as residents and having children in the local high school.

cialization process; and, finally, relations between the socialization practices used by the parents and the personality and behavior of their children, data on the latter having been independently obtained.

In summary, the Socialization Study was designed to provide convergent support for the general theoretical framework by dealing with the linkages which must be operative if location in the sociocultural system is to be considered influential on the nature of the personality system and, ultimately, on behavior. A one and one-half hour interview, structured to elicit conceptually relevant socialization antecedents of the personality and behavior systems of teen-agers was administered to a nearly complete sample of the mothers of students in the local high school. The success of the Socialization Study and its contribution to the appraisal of the theoretical framework rest ultimately on how fully the findings of this study mesh with those of our other two studies.

SUMMARY

In this chapter, the concern has been to present the methodological stance which guided the research and to outline the over-all design which followed from it. It will be recalled that our concern in the first half of this chapter was with the variety of controls which had been in one way or another instituted over our field research. Five types of controls were discussed: control through selection, through standardization, through the use of theory, through construct validity, and through multiple, converging studies. That discussion was intended to make clear our commitment to a particular way of doing field research and, in general terms, the procedures we followed.

The second half of the chapter described the broad structure of the research design as consisting of three entirely independent studies, each relevant to and having the possibility of generating convergent support for the larger theory. The Community Survey Study focused on adults and relied primarily upon an interview; the High School Study focused on teen-agers and relied on a variety of procedures principal among which were group-administered questionnaires; the Socialization Study, employing an interview, focused upon parents of the students in the high school. The three studies are sufficiently different in the subjects dealt with, the methods used, and the part of the theory implicated that their convergence could constitute powerful support for our theory.

No attempt was made in this chapter to describe the detailed characteristics of specific scales or measures employed in the several studies, nor of the comparison groups established to test the theoretical predictions. This is fully accomplished in the chapters to follow. In Chapters 7 and 8, the measurement of the behavior system is considered, in Chapter 9, the measurement of the sociocultural system, and in Chapter 10, the measurement of the personality system. The data for these next chapters will be drawn only from the Community Survey and the High School studies, which are so closely parallel in nature. In each chapter, the structure and properties of each measure will be developed and its relations to sex and ethnic group status will be presented. Once the measures have been established in this way, the relations proposed by the theory will be examined—this task will be undertaken in Chapter 11. In Chapter 12, the measures and findings of the Socialization Study will be examined, and their relation to the data presented in Chapter 11 will be developed. It will be at that point that the scope of the convergence which emerges across the three studies will be most clearly apparent. And it will be at that point that the role played by the methodological orientation and the research design dealt with in this chapter can best be fully, and finally, appraised.

REFERENCES

BANDURA, A. AND R. H. WALTERS. *Social learning and personality development.* New York: Holt, Rinehart & Winston, 1963.

BRONOWSKI, J. *Science and human values.* New York: Harper & Row, 1959.

CAMPBELL, D. T. Recommendations for APA test standards regarding construct, trait, or discriminant validity. *American Psychologist,* 1960, *15,* 546–553.

CAMPBELL, D. T. AND D. W. FISKE. Convergent and discriminant validation by the multitrait-multimethod matrix. *Psychological Bulletin,* 1959, *56,* 81–105.

COOK, S. W. The systematic analysis of socially significant events: A strategy for social research. *Journal of Social Issues,* 1962, *18,* 66–84.

CRONBACH, L. J. AND P. E. MEEHL. Construct validity in psychological tests. *Psychological Bulletin,* 1955, *52,* 281–302.

FRENCH, D. The relationship of anthropology to studies in perception and cognition. In S. Koch (Ed.) *Psychology: A study of a science.* Vol. 6. *Investigations of man as socius: Their place in psychology and the social sciences.* New York: McGraw-Hill, 1963. Pp. 388–428.

HANSON, N. R. *Patterns of discovery.* Cambridge: Cambridge University Press, 1958.

JANOWITZ, M. Anthropology and the social sciences. *Current Anthropology,* 1963, *4,* 139, 149–154.

JESSOR, R. AND K. R. HAMMOND. Construct validity and the Taylor Anxiety Scale. *Psychological Bulletin,* 1957, *54,* 161–170.

KAPLAN, A. *The conduct of inquiry: Methodology for behavioral science.* San Francisco: Chandler, 1964.

KUHN, T. S. *The structure of scientific revolutions.* Chicago: University of Chicago Press, 1962.

LEWIS, O. Controls and experiments in field work. In A. L. Kroeber (Ed.) *Anthropology today: An encyclopedic inventory.* Chicago: University of Chicago Press, 1953. Pp. 452–475.

LOEVINGER, JANE. Objective tests as instruments of psychological theory. *Psychological Reports*, 1957, *3*, 635–694. Monograph Supplement 9.

MAQUET, J. J. Objectivity in anthropology. *Current Anthropology*, 1964, *5*, 47–55.

SANFORD, N. Will psychologists study human problems? *American Psychologist*, 1965, *20*, 192–202.

WRIGHT, H. F. Observational child study. In P. H. Mussen (Ed.) *Handbook of research methods in child development.* New York: Wiley, 1960. Pp. 71–139.

YINGER, J. M. *Toward a field theory of behavior: Personality and social structure.* New York: McGraw-Hill, 1965.

PART FOUR

Results: Establishing the Criterion Variables

CHAPTER SEVEN

The Measurement of Drinking Behavior

In this chapter and the next, the approach which was taken to the measurement of the behavior system in our theoretical scheme is presented. The term "behavior system" means those functionally related sets of illegitimate behaviors which have been learned as alternative ways of seeking gratification or of coping with frustration and failure, in short, what was conceptualized in Chapter 2 as deviant behavior. In the present chapter, the measurement of the subset of deviant behavior involving alcohol use will be considered; in the chapter to follow, the concern will be with deviant behavior which is not necessarily related to the use of alcohol. This division is one of convenience and tradition; for both subsets, the basic problems of measurement are largely the same.

These problems stem in part from the fact that the behavior at issue is generally considered to be socially undesirable both by the actor and others, a fact which tends to remove the behavior from easy observation or from entirely veridical report. Yet the test of the theoretical scheme can be no better than the adequacy of the measurement of the behavior it is intended to explain. It was in recognition of the crucial character of this point that much of the research effort was directed toward "the criterion problem," that is, toward establishing conceptually relevant and valid measures of deviant behavior.

The approach, in the main, was to seek multiple measures of deviance so that the inadequacies of any particular measure could not seriously jeopardize the theoretical tests. At the same time, multiple measures yield a more differentiated criterion and enable an exploration of the relations among the various aspects of deviance symbolized by the different measures. Finally, multiple measures give greater scope to the definition of deviance and make possible, when combined, a more exhaustive criterion than that yielded by any of the components alone. It should be added that, although the primary aim of these measures was to serve as criteria for testing the adequacy of our explanation of group and individual differences, they also permitted a description of the distribution of deviance in the community which is far more satisfactory than that available to casual observation.

The complexity of the nature of alcohol use has been referred to earlier, in Chapter 2. A full understanding and description of drinking behavior requires simultaneous examination of its various facets: the *amount* consumed, the physical and social *context* of drinking, the *meanings* attached to alcohol by the drinker, the *consequences* which follow upon its use, and the conditions under which drinking was *learned*. Measurement of all of these aspects was undertaken in our investigation, but our present concern is with only a small part of the range and variation in the use of alcohol, that part which can be called excessive, deviant, or deviance prone. To get at this particular aspect of alcohol use, four major criterion measures were developed: a measure of intake, a measure of the personal meanings attached to alcohol, and two measures of the socially undesirable consequences of alcohol use. In this chapter, these measures will be described and elaborated, their relations to each other presented, and their distribution in relation to sex and ethnic groups examined.

THE QUANTITY-FREQUENCY INDEX:
A MEASURE OF INTAKE

Any study of drinking behavior must cope with the problem of obtaining accurate measures of the amount of alcohol ingested by various persons under investigation. Gross statistics on alcohol consumption in the United States, based on liquor sales records, have been available since 1850. When these figures, issued by beverage, are translated into units of absolute (that is, undiluted) alcohol to equate beverages of differing alcoholic content, it appears that American drinking has stabilized at a rate of about two gallons of absolute alcohol per year per person of drinking age (fifteen or over) (McCarthy, 1959, p. 181), or approximately seven tenths of an ounce of absolute alcohol per day—about a pint of beer.

Such gross figures fail, of course, to convey the wide individual and group differences in alcohol intake which obtain in this country. For example, a number of independent surveys suggest that approximately one third of the population of legal drinking age are total abstainers (Riley and Marden, 1947; Maxwell, 1952; and Gallup, 1945 and 1946, cited by Maxwell). In addition, all of these studies found substantial group differences in proportion of abstainers, with female, less-educated, rural, and lower socioeconomic groups consistently having higher abstinence rates.

More refined measurement of alcohol intake is needed, however, if variation *among* drinkers is to be specified. Beginning with a 1946 survey by the National Opinion Research Center which asked not only *if* a person drank but also *how often* he drank, the measurement of alcohol intake has become progressively more detailed and differentiated. Cumulating through the work of a number of investigators (Maxwell, 1952; Straus and Bacon, 1953; Mulford and Miller, 1960a; and Knupfer, *et al.*, 1963) have been procedures for getting at frequency and amount of drinking, for dealing with intake by major type of beverage (beer, wine, and liquor), and for dealing not only with average consumption but with the range of variation in consumption. Our own measurement is built directly upon the preceding work; it was influenced especially by the California study techniques of Knupfer and her co-workers.

In order to preserve the interest in beverage specificity first suggested by Straus and Bacon, frequency data were obtained by us for each of three major beverage types. During the Community Survey interview, subjects were handed a card on which the following categories were printed:

> Three or more times a day
> Two times a day
> About once a day
> Three or four times a week
> Once or twice a week
> Two or three times a month
> About once a month
> Less than once a month, but at least once a year
> Less than once a year
> Never

"Here is a card that says how often people drink," the interviewer told them. "Let's take *wine* first. Which one says how often you usually have wine? Let's look at it." The interviewer then read the frequency categories aloud. These frequency categories are presented in descending order from "Three or more times a day" to "Never." This order of presentation, suggested by the California researchers, is intended to make it easier for fairly regular daily drinkers to admit to their high frequency by suggesting that even higher frequencies among some subjects were anticipated by the interviewers. Actually, in our own Community Survey Study, 8 of the 221 adult subjects did report a drinking frequency of three or more times a day, and three others reported twice a day, so these extreme categories were used occasionally.

Following the frequency question, subjects were asked to report how often they consumed various *quantities* of wine. The format used was identical to that used by Knupfer and her co-workers: "Think of all the times you have had *wine* recently. When you drink wine, how often do you have five or more glasses?

    ——Nearly every time
    ——More than half the time
    ——Less than half the time
    ——Once in a while
    ——Never

When you drink wine, how often do you have three or four glasses? (same categories repeated)
When you drink wine, how often do you have one or two glasses?" (same categories repeated)

The same procedure for assessing frequency and amount consumed was then repeated for beer and for liquor, including mixed drinks. The advantages of such an obviously time-consuming approach are several. First, and most general, by breaking down a complex behavioral syndrome such as drinking into several component parts, the accuracy with which the respondent was able to recall his own behavior may have been increased. Second, it enables a beverage-by-beverage analysis of drinking habits. Third, it differentiates the pattern or regularity of consumption of varying amounts of a beverage enabling a distinction to be made, for example, between a drinker who *always* drinks moderately and one who is *usually* a light drinker but *sometimes* drinks heavily.

For purposes of devising an intake criterion for each individual, it was necessary in some way to arrive at a composite score which could serve to summarize the information on frequency, amount, and range available for each of three beverages differing in alcohol content. The solution was to convert each subject's intake of each beverage into ounces of absolute alcohol, multiply this by the frequency with which each beverage was consumed, add across the three beverage types (wine, beer, and liquor), and convert to *total ounces of absolute alcohol ingested per day*. Because our data included *range* of consumption, as suggested by Knupfer, and because wine, beer, and hard liquor differ in the amount of absolute alcohol contained, this resulted in an extremely complicated scoring procedure. The scoring details are described in Appendix 5.

The resulting score has a number of distinct virtues:

1.   it summarizes, in a single figure, quantity, frequency, and range of consumption of beverages differing in alcoholic content;
2.   this figure, average ounces of absolute alcohol consumed per day, is readily comprehensible and can easily be translated into other meaningful units, such as "beers" or "drinks;"

3. the score permits the calculation of group statistics such as means and medians which are not possible when discrete descriptive categories are employed; and

4. the score is continuously distributed along a single dimension permitting correlational analyses, tests of differences between group means, and other statistical comparisons.

Throughout the pages which follow it will be this figure, *average ounces of absolute alcohol consumed per day,* which we will mean when we refer to an individual's *Quantity-Frequency* or *"Q-F" score.*

Modifications in Quantity-Frequency Measurement for High School Students

The format for collecting Quantity-Frequency data described above was used in the survey interview of a sample of adults in the research community. Comparable data were also sought from high school students in order to provide an independent test of the predictive scheme and to obtain information about drinking behavior from a group at a critical age in their acquisition of drinking patterns. To save research time and energy, much of the data on the students was collected by means of group-administered paper and pencil tests. Simplification of the Q-F procedure was therefore required.

The complex measure of range of consumption developed by Knupfer's group seemed unwieldy when attempts were made to create a format for self-administration; it was consequently eliminated. Since evidence on variations such as "binge" drinking was being obtained by questions on the frequency with which students had been drunk or "pretty high" during the last year (to be discussed below), it was felt little would be lost. The resulting format is quite similar to that employed by Mulford and Miller in their Iowa survey (1960a). Students were simply asked in questionnaires:

How often do you *usually* drink *wine?* Circle one.

a. One or two times a day
b. About three or four times a week
c. About one or two times a week
d. About one or two times a month
e. At *least* one time a year
f. Less than one time a year
g. Never

When you drink *wine,* how much do you usually drink at *one* time? Circle one.

a. A bottle or more
b. About half a bottle, or about five glasses

    c. Three or four glasses
    d. One or two glasses
    e. Less than one glass
    f. Never drink wine

Similar questions were then asked with respect to beer and liquor, with modifications in the quantity categories to equalize roughly the absolute alcohol involved. The full drinking questionnaire used in the high school, the scoring manual, and the manual for converting responses to units of absolute alcohol are contained in Appendix 5.

Despite the modifications in format, the conversion of student responses to average ounces of absolute alcohol consumed per day provides a Q-F score directly comparable to that obtained from adult respondents. Furthermore, all of the advantages of such a distributed score for statistical manipulation, noted above for the adults, have also been retained.

The Q-F score served as our main criterion of alcohol intake in both the Community Survey and High School studies. It should be clear, however, that Q-F itself cannot be construed as a criterion of deviant behavior since it is a measure which ranges from abstinence (Q-F = 0) to an unspecified high level of intake. Only when a decision is made establishing some point in the Q-F distribution as the cutoff for high, excessive, or deviance-prone intake, intake likely to be associated with socially undesirable consequences, does this measure become relevant to our concern with deviance. In a sense, then, the relevance of the Q-F measure to deviance depends largely upon the association which is known to exist between certain high levels of intake and *other* behavior considered to be deviant, for example, frequent drunkenness.

THE PERSONAL-EFFECTS FUNCTIONS
OF DRINKING: A MEASURE OF MEANING

It is not enough to know simply *how much* a person drinks; *why* he drinks is, obviously, of importance also. It is clear that people drink for many reasons and cope with personal pressures in many different ways. The Tri-Ethnic research was guided by a theory which was formulated to explain only a certain *kind* of drinking: the consumption of excessive quantities of alcohol in order to achieve goals otherwise blocked or in order to cope with failure through, for example, the narcotizing effects of the alcohol. What seemed to be needed, therefore, was some indication of the extent to which persons have learned to use alcohol to help solve their problems or to achieve otherwise unattainable goals. Such reasons for or functions of drinking can be seen as a link between the social-psychological pressures exerted on a person, on the one hand, and his excessive or deviance-prone use of alcohol, on the other. It is because of this hypothesized linkage that our research focused upon measuring, in addition to intake, the problem-solving or personal-effects reasons for the use of alcohol.

The variety of reasons for drinking is, of course, limited only by the variety of social learnings associated with alcohol and its properties. Nevertheless, at least in American society, three broad categories of reasons have been emphasized: *social-convivial, social-facilitating,* and *personal-effects reasons.* These categories emerge from the work of Mulford and Miller (1959a, 1960b) and from a provocative recent paper by Fallding (1964). By "social-convivial drinking" is meant drinking for the pleasure of the social interaction which accompanies it, a type of drinking which tends to be symbolic of and dependent upon pre-existing solidarity and trust within the social context in which it occurs. Large quantities of alcohol intake are not considered necessary to the occasion, and moderate levels of alcohol use are characteristic. In a broader perspective, the ritual use of alcohol and alcohol use with meals, both of which also tend to be moderate, would seem to belong in this category; expressed reasons for alcohol use such as "makes get-togethers fun" or "it's a nice way to celebrate special occasions" belong to this category.

To drink for "social-facilitating reasons" is to use alcohol for the purpose of overcoming social inadequacies, such as the sense of uneasiness, apprehension, and anxiety which may obtain in social situations where mutual trust and a sense of social solidarity are not established. Both because of its physiological effects and social definitions attached to its use, drinking alcohol can readily be learned as a way of facilitating group adaptation and achieving a sense of social solidarity. Social-facilitating drinking, unlike social-convivial drinking, involves alcohol as a *necessary* aspect of successful role performance in certain social situations. This dependence on alcohol as a means for successfully coping with social inadequacies probably increases the level of a person's alcohol intake. Regular consumption of relatively large quantities of alcohol can then become a necessary concomitant of adequate social participation by breaking down the barriers to conviviality which otherwise would obtain. Expressed reason for drinking such as "to be part of the group," or "makes you less shy," would be examples of the social-facilitating use of alcohol.

Once a drinker has learned to imbibe alcohol not merely for symbolic purposes but rather as a successful way of coping with certain personal inadequacies, it is not a difficult step to generalize from this learning to alcohol use for coping with other types of personal inadequacies. Thus, drinking can begin to serve *many* purposes: the person is lonesome, sad, has business problems, is concerned about personal failure and inadequacy, or is apprehensive about the opinions others have of him. Such drinking tends to occur in relation to its *personal-effects* on the drinker, effects which may enable him to transcend the problems he faces, to change the situation enough so that the problems are no longer present or relevant, or to narcotize himself so that he is no longer aware of his problems. Drinking of this sort is what is meant by the "personal problem-solving use of alcohol," and both frequent and heavy use of alcohol would seem to be characteristic. Expressed reasons such as "makes you worry less about what other people think of you" or "feeling under pressure, tense" would be examples belonging to this category.

It is this latter category of reasons which was of closest concern to our theoretical framework: Such reasons can be considered indirectly to reflect the degree of pressure on a person toward the use of illegitimate means; and personal-effects drinking, involving the frequent and heavy use of alcohol, is more likely to be associated with the socially disapproved consequences of drinking, such as frequent drunkenness.

It is possible to consider these three major categories of reasons for drinking as forming a unilineal scale, reflecting perhaps a developmental sequence in learning about the various functions of drinking. If this is the case, then a person's position along this scale, from social-convivial drinking to social-facilitating drinking to personal-effects drinking, should be positively associated with his level of alcohol intake and of accompanying alcohol-related problem behavior; Mulford and Miller found this to be the case in a series of studies of alcohol use in Iowa (1959a, 1960b, 1960c, and 1963).

In their studies, a set of twenty reasons for drinking were presented to subjects in an agree-disagree format and were found to satisfy all the requirements of a cumulative Guttman scale. The following eight items, arranged in scale order, are representative of the total set and illustrate well the passage from social-convivial, through social-facilitating to personal-effects drinking (these representative items are those selected by Mulford and Miller):

1. Liquor is customary on special occasions
2. Liquor makes a social gathering more enjoyable
3. Liquor helps me enjoy a party
4. Liquor makes me more carefree
5. Liquor makes me less self-conscious
6. Liquor gives me more confidence in myself
7. Liquor helps me feel more satisfied with myself
8. Liquor helps me forget I am not the kind of person I really want to be

Strong associations were found between a person's position along this "functions" scale, his Quantity-Frequency of alcohol intake, and his report of social problems related to his drinking on each of three independent tests of their hypotheses (Mulford and Miller, 1959a; 1960b; 1960c).

In our own investigation of the personal functions of drinking, an initial effort was made to distinguish between the needs which spur one on to drink and the goals which one seeks through drink. Two questions were therefore asked of adults:

"Now I'd like to know what makes you feel like having a drink. Here are some things other people have said. As I read them, say whether or not each one is true for you."

"Now, which of the following things about drinking would you say are *important* for you? As I read them, say whether or not each one is important for you."

Each of these questions was followed by a list of possible reasons for drinking. Most of the items used by Mulford and Miller in their work were included in this list, but they were freely modified and supplemented in an attempt to tap as wide a range of reasons for drinking as possible. Both format and content were modified somewhat for the High School Study, though most items remained identical.

It became obvious during administration that the two questions for getting at reasons for drinking were being answered as if they composed a single scale. For purpose of item analyses, therefore, responses to both questions were combined and correlations were run between all items and between items and total score. For both the adult and the high school study, these analyses revealed a subset of fourteen items with consistently higher item-total score correlations and impressive inter-item relationships. This subset was distinguished by the "personal-effects" content of the items, that is, they were items which suggested that alcohol was being used to cope with personal psychological problems, particularly those involving negative self-images.[1]

Given our particular theoretical interest in the prediction of social problem behavior, and the association between drinking as a way of coping with personal problems and the drinking of large quantities of alcohol,

---

[1] A second subset, somewhat lower in internal homogeneity, was distinguished by its "psycho-physiological" content—that is, drinking was being engaged in to cope with physical symptoms, such as "feeling tired," which may be presumed to have a strong psychological component.

Cluster analysis provided further corroboration for the nature of the item-sets. In both the Community Survey and High School studies, and also in a study of college students made later, using an expanded list of functions (Carman, 1965), three consistent factors emerged: two highly correlated factors made up of personal-effects items, distinguished by being predominantly "needs" for or "goals" of drinking, and a third factor composed of the psycho-physiological items. In the college study, "social-convivial" and "social-conforming" factors also emerged (see Grossman, 1965, for details on the Tryon cluster analyses, and Jessor, Carman, and Grossman, in press, for a description of the college study).

the subset of fourteen personal-effects items in both the adult and the high school studies was designated a single scale, with the subject's score in each case being the number of items on this scale which he indicated applied to his own drinking. These items and their biserial correlations with total score for both the adult community and the high school are

TABLE 7.1
Personal-Effect Reasons for Drinking: Biserial Item-Total Score Correlations*
For Adult and Adolescent Respondents in the Research Community

Item	Community Survey Study	High School Study
1. Feeling under pressure, tense	.58	.59
2. Having problems	.89	.76
3. Feeling lonely	.72	.65
4. Feeling mad	.74	.75
5. Just feel you have to have a drink sometimes	.52	.80
6. Feeling sad	.84	.57
7. Not getting ahead	.96†	1.00†
8. Makes you less shy	.64	.44
9. Makes you feel more satisfied with yourself	.64	.54
10. Helps you forget your problems	.91	.77
11. Gives you more confidence in yourself	.84	.56
12. Makes you feel happier	.77	.57
13. Helps you forget you're not the kind of person you'd like to be	.89	.17†
14. Makes you worry less about what other people think of you	1.00	.60

* All biserial correlations have been corrected by removing each item's contribution to the total score with which it is correlated (Henrysson, 1963; Castellan and Link, 1963).

† Proportion responding positively is under 10 percent.

presented in Table 7.1. Total score on this measure of the personal-effect reasons for drinking could range from 0–14.[2]

The score achieved by a subject on this measure can be considered an indication of the degree to which alcohol is used for personal problem-

---

[2] Our tendency throughout our research has been to use total scores rather than scale scores, even where Guttman scales can be shown to obtain. Guttman criteria are sufficiently strict so that if a unilinear scale *does* exist, total score is always an excellent approximation of scale score. Where items in a theoretically contrived "scale" do *not* meet Guttman criteria (as appears to be true of many psychometric procedures with quite respectable internal consistency), then total score becomes an expedient and satisfactory way of summarizing the data, one in which all items are given equal weight in testing relations with other variables.

solving purposes. As discussed above, such usage should relate to amount and frequency of alcohol consumed as well as to the consequences following upon its consumption. Although technically not a direct measure of either deviant behavior or drinking behavior, the measure should be related to such behavior in that it should reflect both the instigations to and the goals served by alcohol use.

TIMES DRUNK IN THE LAST YEAR: A MEASURE OF CONSEQUENCES

The excessive or deviant use of alcohol, as discussed in Chapter 2, is often defined by the consequences to which it leads, that is, by the occurrence of behaviors which are themselves seen as a violation of normative expectations. One such consequential behavior is chronic or frequent drunkenness, a behavior pattern highly associated with the frequent consumption of large quantities of alcohol. While drunkenness from time to time or on particular occasions may not be frowned upon, or may even be expected, repeated intoxication is widely considered as deviant or problem behavior. Such behavior is often cited as an excellent example of efforts to cope with personal difficulties, pressures, or failures to achieve goals by avoidance or retreatism, that is, by recourse to the narcotizing properties of large quantities of alcohol.

As a simple way of measuring the frequency of such behavior, all drinkers in the Community Survey sample were asked:

How often have you been drunk in the last month?
How about in the last year?

These items yielded a score which was the number of reported times drunk in the last year. In the High School Study, the language of this question was modified slightly as follows:

How many times have you gotten drunk or pretty high in the last year? Circle *one* only.

a. ten or more times
b. eight or nine times
c. six or seven times
d. four or five times
e. two or three times
f. one time
g. never

Student responses were treated exactly as the adult responses were, that is, a score for number of times drunk in the last year was obtained for each drinker.

DRINKING-RELATED DEVIANCE:
A SECOND MEASURE OF CONSEQUENCES

The association of alcohol with social problem behavior is not limited to drunkenness. Heavy alcohol use may eventuate in behavior seen as a problem by others, whether it involves drunkenness or not. To get at alcohol-related problem behavior other than drunkenness, a number of questions were asked in the Community Survey interview, and a score was derived from the responses to these questions. This drinking-related deviance score reflects the number of instances reported by the subject of drinking-related problems with family, friends, the job, and legal authorities.

Answers to the following questions were combined in the index:

> How often have you had problems with your family because of your drinking?
> How about with your friends?
> How often have you gotten into fights while drinking?
> How often have you had trouble about a job because of drinking?

The number of instances of problems of this sort reported as occurring during the last ten years was summed as a single composite score. In addition, the respondent's answer to the question:

> How many times have you driven a car during the last year when you had a good bit to drink?

was also added into this composite score. Finally, after a series of items designed to get at other aspects of deviant behavior, the respondent was asked:

> What (else) have you gotten into trouble with the law about?
> What happened?

Responses which indicated drinking-related legal problems were also added into the subject's drinking-related deviance score.

In the High School Study, the form and content of questions bearing on drinking-related problem behavior were modified to be appropriate to a self-report questionnaire for teen-agers. Toward the end of the last day's testing, students were asked:

> How many times have you gotten into trouble with your family because of drinking? Circle one.
>
> a.   several times
> b.   once or twice
> c.   never

How many times have you had fights because of drinking? Circle one.

a. several times
b. once or twice
c. never

How many times have you gotten into trouble with the law because of drinking? Circle one.

a. several times
b. once or twice
c. never

At a later point in the questionnaire, along with other questions, these two were asked of the students:

How often have you:
Driven when you've had a good bit to drink? Circle *one*.

| Very often | Several times | Once or twice | Never |

Gone on beer parties? Circle *one*.

| Very often | Several times | Once or twice | Never |

These items were all scored 0–3 or 0–4, and the scores were added across items.

In both the Community Survey Study and the High School Study, an effort was made to assess as wide a variety as possible of problem behaviors likely to be associated with alcohol use. While any particular behavior item may not in itself be of great social concern, the assumption made was that its recurrence and, especially, its accompaniment by *other* problem behaviors would constitute an adequate definition of deviant behavior linked to drinking. This was the rationale for building a drinking-related deviance score as the sum of the occurrences of a variety of deviant behaviors.

THE VALIDITY OF THE MEASURES
OF DRINKING BEHAVIOR

The intimate content of the questions bearing on alcohol intake, drunkenness, and drinking-related problem behavior and the necessary reliance upon self-reporting both create difficulties familiar to many social scientists in their research. Responses may be colored by the subject's understandable desire to protect himself from exposure, to live up to the expectations or norms of a middle-class Anglo interviewer, or to acquiesce in the face-to-face situation where he may perceive himself in a subordinate role. To what extent do such factors influence the data and reduce their validity? To assess the validity of our drinking measures—the problem here is that of the validity of *criterion* variables rather than of *predictors*—three different directions may be pursued. The first of these involves brief recourse to the techniques employed to elicit the data; the second, an analysis of the internal relations among the various criteria in order to ascertain whether they interrelate as expected theoretically; and the third, an examination of sex and ethnic variation on the criterion measures to see whether expected differences actually obtain. Further validation will be forthcoming in the following chapter, after our other measures of deviant behavior have been presented.

Maximizing Veridicality of Drinking Reports

Our efforts to increase the veridicality of the respondents' answers involved a number of obvious and widely used interview practices. At the beginning of the Community Survey interview, the respondent was assured of anonymity, and the same was true in the high school testing. Because our concern was not exclusively focused on drinking and deviance but included also a large number of questions on sociocultural position, psychological attributes, and attitudes, the questions bearing on drinking behavior in both the adult survey and the high school study could be embedded in a broad, unthreatening context. They were also placed late in the interview and in the test battery, following fairly intimate probing on other aspects of life. It was hoped that in this way rapport with the subject might already have become well established, that he would by then be used to being asked intimate questions, and that he would have experienced a nonjudgmental response on the part of the interviewer to his previous answers.

Finally, a number of frequently used techniques of question wording were employed. Respondents were asked, for example, "How many times have you . . . (engaged in some behavior)" rather than "Have you ever. . . ." And response categories were provided which suggested expectations by the interviewers that these behaviors frequently occur. Furthermore, simple acquiescence was not sufficient to complete the task requested of him; the respondent had to give some consideration to the *frequency* with which he engaged in various behaviors.

It cannot be expected that these techniques wholly overcame the tendency for subjects to respond in a socially desirable manner. The need to protect oneself from censure is strong and may operate unconsciously, coloring the answers of even extremely cooperative subjects. The most satisfactory method for evaluating how successful these techniques may have been in overcoming such problems is to compare the self-reports with data gathered from other sources. This will be done in the next chapter. Because of the inevitable effect of social desirability pressures in leading most respondents to consciously or unconsciously underreport their drinking and deviance, it would be naive for either the researcher or the reader to accept the face value of the interview or test scores as wholly accurate representations of the amount of drinking and problem behavior actually taking place in the research community. But such naïveté is not necessary. If we make the assumption that the distorting effects of memory and self-protection have a roughly equal influence upon all respondents, then we should at least be able to *order* the respondents fairly accurately with respect to their drinking behavior. Even without such an assumption, *groups* of respondents can probably be ordered accurately since individual differences in amount of distortion can then be readily assumed to cancel each other out. The actual scores reported by the respondents are simply considered as *symbolic of* the extent of the particular behavior being studied.

A second and perhaps more important symbolic characteristic of these measures should be kept in mind. Each measure of various aspects of drinking and alcohol-related problem behavior can be considered a different operational definition of some underlying broader construct, "the deviant use of alcohol," which has meaning above and beyond what is conveyed by that particular measure. Scores on each measure can thus be considered symbolic of a person's position with regard to this underlying construct. To the extent that these various measures are adequate alternative indices of this construct and touch on various aspects of it, they should correlate with each other. Such convergence among measures, though not necessarily demonstrating the existence of this construct, does increase confidence in their validity.

Interrelationships among the Drinking Measures

An examination of the extent of convergence among the measures of drinking was therefore undertaken. Intercorrelation matrices among the four drinking measures described in the previous sections are shown in Table 7.2 for the adult community and Table 7.3 for the high school students. It is worth recalling at this point that, although the measures are all based on self-report data, they are otherwise fairly distinct operationally. The Quantity-Frequency index is a derived score based on reports of the subject's drinking behavior with regard to each of three beverage types. Frequency of intoxication and of drinking-related problem behavior are both simply frequency statements by the subject, but with regard to quite different categories of activity. The Personal-Effects score is derived from responses to a fairly long list of reasons for drinking presented in an agree-disagree format.

Despite these differences, correlations among the measures are both uniformly high and extremely significant statistically: Where alcohol intake is high, drinking tends to be accompanied by personal-effects reasons and

TABLE 7.2
Agreement among Alternative Measures of Drinking Behavior:
Community Survey Study*

	Product-Moment (Pearson) Correlations			
	Quantity-frequency	Personal effects	Times drunk	Drinking-related deviance
Quantity-frequency of alcohol use				
Personal-effects reasons for alcohol use	.51			
Times drunk during last year	.60	.45		
Drinking-related deviance	.49	.48	.63	

* $N = 221$, for which a correlation of .16 is significant at the .01 level, one-tailed test.

frequent drunkenness and drinking-related deviance. Correlations within ethnic groups, and correlations using only *present drinkers,* drop somewhat and vary among groups as a result of decreases in the number of subjects and in the range of scores being correlated. The over-all picture, however, remains substantially the same as that reported here. Correlations in the High School Study are almost always higher than those for the adult Community Survey, suggesting either that the high school data are more reliable, that there is more common method variance in the high school measures, or, perhaps, that adolescent drinking is a less differentiated phenomenon than adult drinking.

Given the independence of the two samples from which these data were collected, together with the important age difference between them,

TABLE 7.3
Agreement among Alternative Measures of Drinking Behavior:
High School Study*

	Product-Moment (Pearson) Correlations			
	Quantity-frequency	Personal effects	Times drunk	Drinking-related deviance
Quantity-frequency of alcohol use				
Personal-effects reasons for alcohol use	.47			
Times drunk during last year	.71	.57		
Drinking-related deviance	.63	.58	.86	

* $N = 93$, for which a correlation of .24 is significant at the .01 level, one-tailed test.

the similarity in the over-all *pattern* of relationships among these variables is also of interest. Table 7.4 compares a rank-ordering of these correlations from highest to lowest for both the High School and the Community Survey studies. It should be noted that for both groups the highest association is found between drunkenness and drinking-related problems and

TABLE 7.4

Comparisons of Ranked Levels of Association between Measures of Drinking Behavior for Two Independent Samples

Measures Being Compared	High School Study	Community Survey Study
	rank	*rank*
Drinking-related deviance *vs.* times drunk	1	1
Times drunk *vs.* quantity-frequency index	2	2
Quantity-frequency index *vs.* drinking-related deviance	3	4
Drinking-related deviance *vs.* personal-effects	4	5
Personal-effects *vs.* times drunk	5	6
Quantity-frequency index *vs.* personal-effects	6	3

the second highest between alcohol intake (Q-F) and drunkenness. The remainder of the ordering is also identical for the two studies with the exception of one correlation, that between Q-F and Personal-Effects. This dependable and quite stable convergence provides some support for the thesis that each measure reflects a distinct aspect of an underlying and relatively unified behavioral domain, namely, the deviant use of alcohol.

SEX AND ETHNIC VARIATION ON THE DRINKING MEASURES: THE TOPOGRAPHY OF DRINKING BEHAVIOR IN THE COMMUNITY

We are now in a position to assess ethnic and sex differences in drinking behavior in the research community. Since radical sex and ethnic differences in overt drinking behavior are obvious to the most casual community observer, such an assessment serves as concurrent validation of the adequacy of the measures for separating these distinct groups. At the same time, however, these measures can enable us substantially to refine the knowledge yielded by such casual observations.

In Tables 7.5 and 7.6, sex group differences in each of the four measures of drinking are presented. It can be seen that among both the adult respondents to the Community Survey and the high school students, the differences between the sexes are all substantial and in the expected direction: In general, men drink more than women, are more apt to do

TABLE 7.5
**Sex Group Differences on Four Measures of Drinking Behavior:
Community Survey Study**

Measure		Means and Standard Deviations		Significance*
		Males (N = 109)	Females (N = 109)	(Males *vs.* Females)
Quantity-	$\bar{X}$	1.54	0.29	t = 3.48
frequency	σ	(3.56)	(1.14)	$p <$ .001
of alcohol				
use				
Personal-	$\bar{X}$	3.5	1.8	t = 3.80
effects	σ	(3.7)	(2.8)	$p <$ .001
reasons for				
alcohol use				
Times drunk	$\bar{X}$	10.0	1.4	t = 3.43
during	σ	(25.9)	(4.5)	$p <$ .001
previous				
year				
Drinking-	$\bar{X}$	2.3	0.7	t = 3.47
related	σ	(4.4)	(1.9)	$p <$ .001
deviant				
behavior				

* All *t*-tests of group mean differences are two-tailed.

so to cope with feelings of personal inadequacy, get drunk more often, and experience more drinking-related complications. Although these findings may seem obvious, had these measures *not* revealed such differences this would have caused considerable consternation. The ability of the measures to differentiate sex groups successfully is one more piece of evidence for their general validity.

Ethnic-group differences in drinking behavior are of far more immediate interest here since these served as part of the confronting problem which gave rise to our research. Table 7.7 presents ethnic group means and tests of group differences on all four measures of deviant or deviance-prone drinking behavior among adults in the Community Survey Study. The Spanish-Americans report ingesting twice as much alcohol as Anglos, but appear neither to get drunk more frequently nor to have more drinking-related problems. No Anglo-Spanish differences on these three measures are statistically significant. By contrast, the Indians report ingesting nearly seven times as much alcohol as the Anglos, and more than three times as much as the Spanish. They are more apt to drink to solve personal

TABLE 7.6
Sex Group Differences on Four Measures of Drinking Behavior:
High School Study

Measure		Means and Standard Deviations		Significance*
		Males ($N = 47$)	Females ($N = 46$)	(Males *vs.* Females)
Quantity-	$\bar{X}$	0.45	0.07	$t = 4.80$
frequency	σ	(0.51)	(0.19)	$p < .001$
of alcohol				
use				
Personal-	$\bar{X}$	3.4	2.0	$t = 2.18$
effects	σ	(3.1)	(2.8)	$p < .05$
reasons for				
alcohol use				
Times drunk	$\bar{X}$	3.2	0.9	$t = 5.88$
during	σ	(2.5)	(1.1)	$p < .001$
previous				
year				
Drinking-	$\bar{X}$	4.1	1.3	$t = 6.03$
related	σ	(3.5)	(1.9)	$p < .001$
deviant				
behavior				

* All *t*-tests of group mean differences are two-tailed.

problems, they get drunk more than seven times as often as the other two groups, and have about six times as many problems associated with their drinking. The magnitude of these ethnic group differences, it is worth noting, is greater than that between males and females.

Turning to the High School Study, it needs to be kept in mind that high school students are not representative of all of the adolescents in the community since the less conforming students tend to drop out of school. These dropouts also tend to occur more frequently among minority group members, thereby probably decreasing ethnic differences among those who remain in school. The students, furthermore, are exposed in the high school to a longer period of relatively uniform middle-class exhortations which might be expected further to reduce ethnic differences among them. Despite such probable leveling effects, the high school data accord with the adult findings. As can be seen in Table 7.8, Anglo and Spanish differences on all drinking measures are minimal, though there is a general tendency for Spanish students to drink more, with more associated complications. The number of local Indians in the high school—

TABLE 7.7
Ethnic Group Differences on Four Measures of Drinking Behavior:
Community Survey Study

Measure		Means and Standard Deviations			Significance*		
		Anglos (N = 93)	Spanish (N = 60)	Indians (N = 68)	Anglos vs. Spanish	Anglos vs. Indians	Spanish vs. Indians
Quantity-frequency of alcohol use	$\bar{X}$	0.3	0.6	2.0	t = 1.83	t = 3.72	t = 2.95
	σ	(0.8)	(1.3)	(4.5)	N.S.	p < .01	p < .05
Personal-effects reasons for alcohol use	$\bar{X}$	1.1	3.1	4.2	t = 4.46	t = 7.04	t = 1.87
	σ	(1.9)	(3.5)	(3.9)	p < .001	p < .001	N.S.
Times drunk during previous year	$\bar{X}$	2.0	1.5	14.4	t = 0.38	t = 3.82	t = 4.18
	σ	(12.0)	(5.0)	(29.3)	N.S.	p < .01	p < .001
Drinking-related deviant behavior	$\bar{X}$	0.6	0.6	3.4	t = 0.03	t = 5.07	t = 5.16
	σ	(2.4)	(1.8)	(4.8)	N.S.	p < .001	p < .001

* All *t*-tests of group mean differences are two-tailed. Differences not significant at the .05 level or better are indicated as N.S.

11—is too small to permit confident generalizations, but it is still worth noting that, on all measures, their means are higher than those for the Spanish students, and, in the case of drinking-related deviant behavior, this difference is substantial.

These mean scores fail, however, to reveal important differences in the *range* of drinking behavior to be found within each ethnic group. Among the Anglos, for example, *abstinence* is an important alternative pattern of behavior with regard to alcohol use. Twenty-five percent of the adult Anglos sampled reported that they *never* drank, and an additional 5 percent had given it up. This abstinence pattern is also a relatively important one among Spanish: Seventeen percent reported never having drunk alcohol, with 7 percent having given it up at some point. In contrast to both of these groups, only 3 percent of the Indians never drank, though an additional 17 percent claim currently to have given up drinking. These

TABLE 7.8
**Ethnic Group Differences on Four Measures of Drinking Behavior:
High School Study**

Measure		Means and Standard Deviations			Significance*		
		Anglos ($N = 42$)	Spanish ($N = 36$)	Indians ($N = 11$)	Anglos vs. Spanish	Anglos vs. Indians	Spanish vs. Indians
Quantity-frequency of alcohol use	$\bar{X}$ σ	0.2 (0.3)	0.3 (0.4)	0.4 (0.7)	$t = 0.77$ N.S.	$t = 0.99$ N.S.	$t = 0.66$ N.S.
Personal-effects reasons for alcohol use	$\bar{X}$ σ	2.4 (3.1)	2.9 (3.0)	3.3 (3.1)	$t = 0.74$ N.S.	$t = 0.81$ N.S.	$t = 0.31$ N.S.
Times drunk during previous year	$\bar{X}$ σ	1.6 (2.1)	2.3 (2.5)	2.7 (2.0)	$t = 1.35$ N.S.	$t = 1.68$ N.S.	$t = 0.59$ N.S.
Drinking-related deviant behavior	$\bar{X}$ σ	2.1 (2.0)	2.8 (3.1)	4.2 (2.4)	$t = 1.13$ N.S.	$t = 2.64$ $p < .02$	$t = 1.59$ N.S.

* All t-tests of group mean differences are two-tailed. Differences not significant at the .05 level or better are indicated as N.S.

same group differences in abstinence are to be found at the high school level as well. Over 20 percent of both Anglo and Spanish students are abstainers (though the Spanish percentage is composed entirely of females). All of the 11 local Indian students report themselves as drinkers. Clearly, rates of abstinence, as an alternative pattern within each group, distribute themselves ethnically much as do rates of consumption.

Our other data, not dealt with in these tables, elaborate these group differences in drinking behavior. Disregarding frequency of drinking, and pooling both present and former drinkers, about 60 percent of both the Anglo and Spanish adults sampled report never having more than four drinks at a sitting; this can be said of only a quarter of the Indians. Similarly, only 3 percent of the Anglos and 10 percent of the Spanish can be classified as *heavy* drinkers in the sense that they report usually having more than five drinks at a sitting. But 25 percent of the Indians report themselves consistently to exceed these bounds of moderation. Furthermore, these ethnic differences do not appear to be a new phenomenon, a result, perhaps, of the repeal of the Indian Prohibition Act following the Second World War. Only 7 percent of the Anglo and only 3 percent of the Spanish adults reported that one or both of their *parents* had been considered a heavy or problem drinker; but almost 20 percent of the Indian adults reported having parents who drank heavily.

As with the sex differences, these ethnic group differences are in accord with expectations, and the findings are consistent in both the adult and high school studies. The primary ethnic difference lies between the Indians and the other two ethnic groups, with the Spanish generally close or similar to the Anglos in drinking behavior. The Spanish drink more than the Anglos (though the difference is not significant), but the main difference between Spanish and Anglos lies in the *reasons* for their drinking. As seen in Table 7.7, the Spanish are more apt (significantly so) than the Anglos to drink as a way of solving their personal problems. In this particular respect, Spanish respondents appear more like the Indians than the Anglos in their drinking. The underlying *dynamics* of their drinking behavior can thereby be said to differ markedly from their Anglo neighbors, even though the overt *form* of their drinking is in many ways similar. This is a theme which will be returned to in subsequent analyses. In general, the ethnic group findings can be seen to contribute strongly to the validity of the measures of drinking behavior.

SUMMARY

The primary aim of this chapter has been to present the measures of drinking behavior. These were developed to serve as criteria which were to be predicted, in turn, by the sociocultural and personality variables in our theoretical scheme. Consistent with the methodological orientation discussed in the preceding chapter, we sought to devise multiple measures of drinking behavior which would enable us to converge upon the concept of the deviant or deviance-prone use of alcohol. Further, we sought to evaluate these measures in two independent studies to increase confidence in their qualifications to serve as adequate criterion measures.

Specifically, four measures of drinking behavior were developed. The first of these, the Quantity-Frequency index, is a summary measure of frequency, amount, and range of consumption of three beverages: beer, wine, and liquor. The measure expresses the ounces of absolute alcohol consumed per day and serves as the basic measure of *intake*. The second measure has to do with *reasons* for drinking, or the functions served the drinker by alcohol consumption. A scale of fourteen items referring to personal-effects or problem-solving reasons for drinking was developed to reflect the use of alcohol in response to pressures or as a way of coping with failure. The third and fourth measures refer to socially disapproved *consequences* of alcohol use: drunkenness and other forms of drinking-related deviance.

Attempts were made to maximize the validity of these measures by reliance on interview and test procedures designed to increase veridicality of report. Validity of the resulting data was supported by the expected pattern of relationships, all positive and significant, existing among the four measures. Support for the validity of the measures came also from the clear-cut differentiation they provided of both sex and ethnic groups (especially Indian–non-Indian differences) in both studies. Further validation will be presented in the following chapter in relation to our other measures of deviant behavior.

While the findings presented in this chapter have enabled us to establish drinking behavior criteria to employ in our analyses in later chapters, they have also contributed in two other important ways. First, they have provided a detailed and quantitative picture of various aspects of the use of alcohol in a small rural community. The accumulation of knowledge of this sort is important in furthering understanding of the range and variation of this socially significant behavior pattern. Second, the findings illuminate at least part of the internal structure of drinking behavior, showing clear relationships between amount consumed, reasons for consumption, and socially undesirable consequences of alcohol use. The data support the notion of a deviance-prone *syndrome* of alcohol use, one involving high intake for personal-effects reasons.

The discussion, in Chapter 2, of the concept of deviance extended beyond the excessive use of alcohol and its related consequences. A test of the theory requires, therefore, the establishment and availability of criteria *other* than those having to do only with drinking. Chapter 8 is devoted to the description of these criteria and to the development of composite criteria of deviant behavior.

REFERENCES

Carman, R. S. Personality and drinking behavior among college students. Unpublished masters thesis, University of Colorado, 1965.

Castellan, N. J. Jr. and S. W. Link. Biserial-point biserial correlation program for IBM709/7090 (CPA 139). *Behavioral Science*, 1963, *8*, 368–369.

Fallding, H. The source and burden of civilization illustrated in the use of alcohol. *Quarterly Journal of Studies on Alcohol*, 1964, *25*, 714–724.

Grossman, P. Drinking motivation: A cluster analytic study of three samples. Unpublished doctoral dissertation, University of Colorado, 1965. Also Research Report No. 28, Tri-Ethnic Research Project, Mimeographed. Pp. 1–186.

Henrysson, S. Correction of item-total correlations in item analysis. *Psychometrika*, 1963, *28*, 211–218.

Jessor, R., R. S. Carman and P. Grossman. Expectations for need satisfaction and patterns of alcohol use in college. *Quarterly Journal of Studies on Alcohol,* in press.

KNUPFER, GENEVIEVE, R. FINK, W. B. CLARK, AND ANGELICA S. GOFFMAN. Factors related to amount of drinking in an urban community. The California Drinking Practices Study, Report No. 6. Mimeographed. 1963.

MAXWELL, M. A. Drinking behavior in the state of Washington. *Quarterly Journal of Studies on Alcohol,* 1952, *13,* 219–239.

MCCARTHY, R. G. (Ed.) *Drinking and intoxication.* New York: Free Press, 1959.

MULFORD, H. A. AND D. E. MILLER. Drinking behavior related to definition of alcohol: A report of research in progress. *American Sociological Review,* 1959, *24,* 385–389.

MULFORD, H. A. AND D. E. MILLER. Drinking in Iowa: II. The extent of drinking and selected sociocultural categories. *Quarterly Journal of Studies on Alcohol,* 1960, *21,* 26–39.

MULFORD, H. A. AND D. E. MILLER. Drinking in Iowa: III. A scale of definitions of alcohol related to drinking behavior. *Quarterly Journal of Studies on Alcohol,* 1960, *21,* 267–278.

MULFORD, H. A. AND D. E. MILLER. Drinking in Iowa: IV. Preoccupation with alcohol and definitions of alcohol, heavy drinking and trouble due to drinking. *Quarterly Journal of Studies on Alcohol,* 1960, *21,* 279–291.

MULFORD, H. A. AND D. E. MILLER. Preoccupation with alcohol and definitions of alcohol: A replication study of two cumulative scales. *Quarterly Journal of Studies on Alcohol,* 1963, *24,* 682–696.

RILEY, J. W. JR. AND C. F. MARDEN. The social pattern of alcoholic drinking. *Quarterly Journal of Studies on Alcohol,* 1947, *8,* 265–273.

STRAUS, R. AND S. D. BACON. *Drinking in college.* New Haven: Yale University Press, 1953.

CHAPTER EIGHT

The Measurement of Deviance-Conformity

The theoretical formulation we have advanced as an attempt to account for the occurrence of deviant behavior has remained at a general level —that is, its primary concerns have been with the *class* of deviant behavior and the occurrence or nonoccurrence of some member of that class rather than any particular form of deviance. As discussed in Chapter 2, various behaviors within the broad category of deviance can be considered to be functionally equivalent, each serving as a way of attaining goals otherwise blocked, or as a way of coping with the experienced or expected failure to attain those goals. Which particular behaviors are likely to be employed depends upon variation in past learnings and variation in the action situation. For our purposes, at the present stage of development of our formulations, the central issue to be confronted empirically is the occurrence of *any* form of the class of behavior meeting the criteria for deviance elaborated in Chapter 2.

The implication of such a position for the measurement of deviance is clear: It is necessary to assess the occurrence of the widest possible set of deviant behaviors in order to evaluate the adequacy of the explanatory scheme. This implication led us in two important directions as far as developing criterion measures is concerned. First, it led us to try to assess, in addition to behaviors involving or dependent upon the use of alcohol, various other possible behavioral manifestations of deviance. The former were described in the preceding chapter, and the latter will be described in this chapter. Second, it led us to develop *composite* measures of deviance based upon the various separate measures since the important theoretical issue was the occurrence of deviance upon any measure. The nature and construction of the composite measure in each study will also be described in this chapter.

A further advantage of assessing the variety of possible manifestations of deviant behavior is that it can enable us empirically to examine the internal structure of the behavior system, the degree to which functional equivalence obtains not only between persons—some persons drink heavily, while others may engage in theft—but also within a person—sometimes a person resorts to drinking heavily, while at other times he may resort to theft. Attention to this issue will be given when the various measures are examined in relation to each other.

Since the nature of the measures devised, as well as the nature of the information available, varied in the two studies, they will be presented separately: first, the Community Survey Study, second, the High School Study.

THE COMMUNITY SURVEY STUDY

It will be recalled that the Community Survey Study was based upon an interview administered to a stratified random sample of community adults. The data provided by the interview are entirely self-report. Some of the self-report data were presented in the preceding chapter in our measures of alcohol use and deviance related to the heavy and personal-effects use of alcohol. Additional self-report data were obtained in the interview, however, with a view toward assessing deviance *other* than that defined by the heavy use of alcohol or following from such heavy use. The measure based on these additional data is referred to as the *Other-Deviance scale;* it will be described below. One source of data for the Community Survey sample which was not self-report in nature was also available to us, namely, court records. The measure based upon these data will also be described in this section. Finally, the development of a composite measure of deviance will be discussed.

The Other-Deviance Scale

After completion of a section on their drinking behavior, their drinking-related problems, and their reasons for drinking, the respondents in the Community Survey Study were presented with a series of questions asking "How many times have you . . ." engaged in a variety of socially disapproved acts. These ranged from being "stopped for speeding" to having "taken things that didn't belong to you," and included interpersonal quarrels or fights with family or friends, problems on the job, sexual transgressions, child neglect, nonpayment of debts, and any type of reported difficulty with the law in which alcohol was not implicated.

In order to minimize the effect of self-protection, these questions were asked in general rather than specific terms, with the implicit assumption that the subject had at some time engaged in such acts. Thus, respondents were not asked "Have you ever committed adultery," but "How many times have you been in a jam about anything to do with sex?" As with the Drinking-Related Deviance scale, there were three ways in which reports to the items on this scale could have been scored: 1) the total number of occurrences of any kind of trouble reported; 2) the total number of life areas in which problems were reported; and 3) the total number of life areas in which repeated or chronic problems had occurred. Conceptually, these summary scores could perhaps be interpreted as measuring somewhat different things; empirically, it developed that they are not. Correlations among the different types of scoring were all in the .80's. Therefore, the most differentiated scoring, that based on the *total number of reported deviant acts,* was used.[1]

The items in the Other-Deviance scale clearly vary in seriousness or severity or the degree to which they fall outside the range of accepted behavior. Thus, having "trouble with a boss on the job" while possibly indicative of social problem behavior is not in itself as serious as having "trouble with the law." Because of considerations such as these, the items in the Other-Deviance scale were categorized into two subsets, those implying "moderate" problem behavior and those implying "serious" problem behavior. Available to us for making this categorization were data obtained earlier from the same subjects as to the perceived degree of "wrongness" of such behaviors. These judgments, which reflect operative community norms, as well as our own judgments of seriousness, led us to the following allocations: Fights, trouble with the boss, being fired from a job, family quarrels, and being stopped for speeding were considered "moderate" and scored 1.0; stealing, nonpayment of debts, sexual transgressions, child neglect, and legal convictions were considered "serious." On the basis of the community norms, reports of serious problems were assigned a weighting of 1.5. Finally, reports of legal difficulties which resulted in a jail sentence were given a weighting of 2.5. The Other-Deviance scale, therefore, yields both a score for each subset of moderate and serious deviance, and a total score which takes into consideration whether the serious deviance has resulted in jailing. Items entering into the score on this measure are only those for which no alcohol involvement has been mentioned by the respondent or could be determined by us.

Sex and Ethnic Group Differences on the Other-Deviance Scale

It is possible to examine the validity of the Other-Deviance measure in the same way we did with the drinking measures and will do later

---

[1] One problem with this scale, which must be laid to our oversight at the time of its construction, is that for most of the items no specific time limit was placed on the period within which the behavior might have occurred. A similar problem arose with most items in the Drinking-Related Deviance scale. Although the apparent context of the items was a contemporary one, some respondents did report events which had occurred many years ago. All such incidents which could be dated prior to 1952 (ten years before the interview) were discarded from both the Other-Deviance and the Drinking-Related Deviance scales. But not all interviewers systematically obtained the date of occurrence of reported events. When there was doubt as to date, reported incidents were included in the total score.

on with the sociocultural and psychological measures, that is, by looking at the concurrence of the data with expected sex and ethnic group differences. Our expectation would be for higher reports of other deviance from males, in contrast to females, and from Indians, in contrast to non-Indians. These were the outcomes that actually obtained with respect to the drinking measures in the previous chapter. The relevant data are presented in Table 8.1.

As anticipated, males have a higher Other-Deviance total score than females, and Indians have a higher score than either the Spanish or Anglo respondents. Only the Indian–non-Indian differences are statistically significant, however.

The lack of strong sex differences and the failure of the Spanish group to fall in its usual intermediate position raise some question concerning the scale's validity. Group differences were therefore examined for the "moderate" and "serious" subscores alone. These are also presented in Table 8.1. In general, the findings on both subscales are quite similar. The one fairly substantial difference occurs in the relatively high rate of Moderate Other Deviance reported by Anglos. This trend accounts in part for the failure of ethnic group differences in total score to appear as strongly as anticipated. But even when Serious Other Deviance is examined alone, the ethnic differences are still not as strong as were found on the drinking measures. It is doubtful that Anglos would overreport their deviant behavior, at least that classified by us as "serious." Rather it may be argued that Spanish and Indians are possibly *underreporting* their deviance. It is also possible, of course, that this scale is tapping behavioral areas which are not as differentiated across sex and ethnic lines as is the deviant use of alcohol. Further validity evidence will be needed to establish more clearly the adequacy of the Other-Deviance measure and to resolve these alternative possibilities.

The Relation of Other Deviance to the Measures of Drinking

Further validation of the Other-Deviance measure can be sought in its relations to our other measures relevant to deviance, those dealing with alcohol use. Two problems arise in the course of such an examination. First is the fact that, although all Other-Deviance reports implicating alcohol were excluded from the score, it is probable that alcohol was nevertheless involved in many of the actual incidents. Our questioning simply did not enable us to rule out the involvement of alcohol. To the extent that reported Other Deviance was associated with alcohol, even though unmentioned, it creates an overlap between the Other-Deviance measure and the drinking measures, an overlap we intended to avoid. Such overlap would increase the correlations between the measures thus contributing to the impression of some degree of validity.

TABLE 8.1
Sex and Ethnic Group Differences in Other Deviance: Community Survey Study

Group	Means and Standard Deviations			Group	Significance†		
	Moderate	Serious	Total*		Moderate	Serious	Total
Males ($N = 106$) $\bar{X}$	1.7	1.5	4.1	Males *vs.* Females	$t = 1.05$ N.S.	$t = 1.48$ N.S.	$t = 1.65$ N.S.
σ	(2.5)	(2.9)	(5.9)				
Females ($N = 110$) $\bar{X}$	1.3	1.0	2.8				
σ	(2.9)	(2.1)	(5.1)				
Anglos ($N = 92$) $\bar{X}$	1.7	0.9	3.1	Anglos *vs.* Spanish	$t = 2.68$ $p < .05$	$t = 0.25$ N.S.	$t = 1.37$ N.S.
σ	(3.2)	(2.5)	(6.1)				
Spanish ($N = 59$) $\bar{X}$	0.7	0.9	2.1	Anglos *vs.* Indians	$t = 0.30$ N.S.	$t = 2.95$ $p < .05$	$t = 2.33$ $p < .05$
σ	(1.5)	(1.8)	(3.7)				
Indians ($N = 65$) $\bar{X}$	1.8	2.1	5.1	Spanish *vs.* Indians	$t = 3.29$ $p < .01$	$t = 3.29$ $p < .01$	$t = 3.98$ $p < .001$
σ	(2.7)	(2.8)	(5.7)				

* Because of the weighting procedure used, the total score does not equal the sum of the two subscores. Rather, it equals moderate, plus 1.5 times serious, plus a small increase in some cases where the trouble resulted in a jail sentence.

† All t-tests of group mean differences are two-tailed. Differences not significant at the .05 level or better are indicated as N.S.

The second problem is related to the first; to the extent that there is overlap, the possibility of examining the degree to which there is functional equivalence between various kinds of deviance is attenuated. Instead of the correlations between measures reflecting substitutability in the person's striving behavior, they may be reflecting no more than the degree of overlap of the measures. With both of these problems in mind, we may look at the findings which are relevant.

Table 8.2 presents product-moment (Pearson) correlations between

TABLE 8.2

Product-Moment (Pearson) Correlations between the Other-Deviance Measure and Measures of the Deviant Use of Alcohol: Community Survey Study*

	Other Deviance		
	Moderate	Serious	Total
Quantity-frequency of alcohol use	.12	.20	.21
Personal-effects reasons for alcohol use	.06	.23	.20
Times drunk during previous year	.06	.17	.16
Drinking-related deviant behavior	.22	.31	.34

* $N = 221$, for which a correlation of .16 is significant at the .01 level, one-tailed test.

Moderate, Serious, and Total Other Deviance and the various measures of the deviant use of alcohol presented in the last chapter. For the Serious Other Deviance and the Total Other Deviance, all these correlations are statistically significant at the .01 level or better. Also, the two sets of correlations are almost identical; there is little which distinguishes them. (Obviously, responses to the items classified by us as moderate are adding nothing of substance to the total score.) The relations between the measures do suggest some degree of validity for the Other-Deviance measure. Yet the associations, while significant, are low. Such a low level of relationship could conceivably be accounted for entirely by the unknown degree of overlap between Other Deviance and these measures of alcohol use. Another interpretation, of course, is that our efforts to eliminate alcohol involvement *were* successful so that the low but significant correlations reflect our success in tapping an aspect of deviance not gotten at by the drinking measures. The support for this interpretation must be sought in the relations of Other Deviance to measures other than the ones thus far examined.

On the assumption that Other Deviance is an adequate measure of non-drinking deviance, the findings support, somewhat, a "specificity" view of deviance when considered intraindividually. That is to say, the substitutability of alternative forms of deviant behavior within an individual's repertoire is not of major magnitude; the occurrence of one form of deviance does not predict strongly the occurrence of deviance of another type. A caveat is in order, however. These data do *not* suggest that alternative forms of deviance are mutually exclusive; that view would have required negative correlations between Drinking-Related Deviance and Other Deviance.

The Use of Court Records

The difficulties involved in obtaining accurate self-report data in the sensitive area of socially disapproved behavior have been noted in previous sections. A major effort was made, therefore, to circumvent the limitations of self-report criterion data by obtaining outside evidence on the conformity or deviance of the research subjects, evidence independent of their self-reports. This effort was most thorough in the High School Study, as will be reported below, where we had available a circumscribed, interacting group under the constant surveillance and supervision of adult authority, their parents and teachers. In the adult study, the problem was more difficult: we were sampling a large and diffuse group of people, spread over a wide geographical area, who were not in frequent interaction with all other members, and whose activities could thereby more easily escape the scrutiny of others.

External authorities to whom all members of the community are subject, however, are the agents of law enforcement. Their observations of the behavior of community members are recorded in official police and court records. These observations are particularly pertinent for our purposes because part of our interest was in the very types of behavior which these agents are charged with the responsibility for detecting and recording.

A systematic effort was therefore made, after the interviewing was completed, to obtain *all* records of all the criminal *convictions* of respondents in the adult study during the preceding ten years.[2] Records of the following courts were examined: United States Federal Court in the two states, two district courts, seven municipal courts, magistrate and justice of the peace courts, the tribal court, and records of the law and order branch of the Bureau of Indian Affairs. These records cover all courts having jurisdiction over crimes committed within the entire research area, with the exception of a small and sparsely settled section in a neighboring state, not covered at the district court level. In addition, they covered all courts in the two major neighboring population centers, and in most of the area surrounding the study community where crimes by community

---

[2] The focus on convictions rather than arrests was based upon the judgment that convictions were a more reliable indicator of the occurrence of deviance and were less subject to ethnic bias.

members might have occurred. In addition to these court records, prison records (including juvenile) were obtained from four state prisons and from the state mental hospital. United States and State of Colorado probation officers' records were also obtained. These prison and probation records contained complete FBI dockets on each case.

Limitations in our record coverage were mainly of two kinds: oversights by the researchers in recording convictions of members of the research community and incompleteness in the records themselves. At the outset, the effort was made to collect complete court records on all members of the research area for as far back as records were available, since time depth was desired for ethno-historical purposes. This approach demanded work with a census list of some 3000 names, and it inevitably resulted in oversights. At a later stage, the task was limited to the list of 221 subjects in the Community Survey sample and to the ten-year period, 1951–1961. This procedure materially simplified the task and insured more accurate coverage.

Even so, completeness was prevented by gaps in the records themselves. These occurred primarily among justice of the peace courts and early tribal records. Record books covering certain periods were simply missing, and one justice of the peace was known to have burned all his records upon leaving office. Our hope was that coverage was sufficiently complete so that it would be the rare respondent with a criminal conviction during the past ten years who would have escaped our notice.

Of the 221 respondents in our Community Survey sample, 45 (20 percent) had court records of convictions for crimes other than civil suits, minor traffic violations, and game law violations, all of which were excluded from our analysis. These 45 respondents had a total of 247 convictions, ranging up to as many as 15 for one of the respondents. Of the court convictions, 87 percent were determined from the records to be alcohol related.

Collecting records of this kind is expensive and time consuming. It is worth a brief discussion to determine what it added to our criterion measurement. The major contribution of such records is, of course, that they provide an external criterion independent of the subject's own self-reports. Particularly with respect to sensitive areas concerned with socially disapproved activity, such data can avoid the distortions inevitably generated by the desire for self-protection. (Distortions may also be contained in record data, however, a fact which will be dealt with in a later section.) Such data can also provide a basis for evaluating just how strong this self-protection tendency has been among the respondents.

One item in the interview schedule had asked specifically, "What (else) have you gotten into trouble with the law about?", with details being obtained as to what actually happened. Of the 45 subjects later determined to have court records, 26 (58 percent) had reported their police record in the interview. In three of the interviews, the question was refused or unclearly answered; and in 16 of the interviews, legal difficulties were clearly *denied*. These latter included ten women and six men; this represents two thirds of the women who have court records and 20 percent of the men.

What kinds of activities were being denied? For the women, the vast majority were relatively minor convictions for drunk and disorderly conduct, but included three fairly serious or chronic cases of this sort leading, for two subjects, to prison terms in the county jail. Two of the convictions denied by the men were also for drunkenness, but the others included contributing to the delinquency of a minor, rape, negligent homicide as a result of drunk driving, and carrying a concealed weapon. Two of the men who denied court records were chronic deviants. Clearly, record data provided specific information about a significant proportion of our subjects, particularly for the women, which would not otherwise have been obtained.

In addition to the 26 respondents who did report their police records to us, three others for whom we had *no* records also reported convictions. If we can assume that the three who reported convictions which we had *not* found in the records represent 58 percent of all convicted subjects whose court record we missed, then by extrapolation we can estimate that about five members of the Community Survey sample had police records which we had somehow missed. Since records on 45 subjects were found, this suggests that our record coverage was roughly 90 percent complete (45/50). Given the previously mentioned inadequacies of the records at the justice of the peace court level, this degree of coverage is quite encouraging.

Sex and Ethnic Group Differences in Court Convictions

Sex and ethnic differences in mean number of court convictions are shown in Table 8.3. The over-all group differences are similar to what we have found on almost all previous measures of deviant behavior, and they serve, thereby, to strengthen the picture which emerged from the self-report data alone. The Indians exhibit by far the most social problem behavior; the Spanish-Americans, though generally intermediate, are behaviorally more like Anglos than Indians and, as expected, the Anglos show the lowest number of court convictions. Indian–non-Indian differences are in all cases larger than male-female differences, though the *variation* in behavior within ethnic groups is greater than within sex groups.

These radical Indian–non-Indian differences in conviction rate are in complete accord with those found elsewhere in the country *wherever records of court convictions have been compared by ethnic group* (see

TABLE 8.3
Sex and Ethnic Differences in Number of Court Convictions, 1951–1961:
Community Survey Study

Group	Means and Standard Deviations		Group	Significance*
Males (N = 110)	$\bar{X}$	1.9		
	σ	(4.3)	Males *vs.* Females	$t = 3.59$
Females (N = 111)	$\bar{X}$	0.4		$p < .001$
	σ	(1.1)		
Anglos (N = 93)	$\bar{X}$	0.01	Anglos *vs.* Spanish	$t = 2.02$
	σ	(0.1)		N.S.
Spanish (N = 60)	$\bar{X}$	0.4	Anglos *vs.* Indians	$t = 6.41$
	σ	(1.6)		$p < .001$
Indians (N = 68)	$\bar{X}$	3.3	Spanish *vs.* Indians	$t = 5.36$
	σ	(5.1)		$p < .001$

* All *t*-tests of group mean differences are two-tailed. Differences not significant at the .05 level or better are indicated as N.S.

Stewart, 1964). Nor can such gross differences be accounted for simply by an ethnic bias in susceptibility to arrest since *both* Spanish-American and Indian respondents occupy minority group status. Differences in minority group status between these two groups are certainly not great enough to account for differences in conviction rate of a factor of ten. Thus, the record data can be assumed to have some degree of validity as a criterion measure of deviant behavior.

The Relation of Court Records
to Other Measures of Deviance

But every use of public records, such as police files, hospital admissions, or newspaper reports, involves possible bias or distortion since no set of records can be assumed to record accurately the universe of acts which it is supposed to document. With respect to our concern with deviance, as just noted, it has often been pointed out that minority or ethnic group members are more susceptible to arrest and conviction than members of the dominant groups in the community.

There are two general ways of handling this sort of problem whenever records are used. The first is to demonstrate that the records are not systematically distorting the frequency of the event being recorded by comparing them with some alternative measure of the same class of events, an alternative not subject to the same type of distortion—a self-report measure, for example. The second is to control for the variable—for example, ethnic status—along which distortion is believed to occur; the hypothesized relationship can thus be examined *within* ethnic subgroups whose members' behavior should have equal probability of getting into the records. Both of these techniques were used.

Table 8.4 presents the product-moment correlations between records of court convictions and our other measures of problem or problem-related behavior, including alcohol intake, personal-effects reasons for drinking,

TABLE 8.4

Product-Moment (Pearson) Correlations between Records of Court Convictions and Alternative Measures of Deviant Behavior: Community Survey Study*

| | Records of Court Convictions | | | |
	Total Sample ($N = 221$)	Anglos ($N = 93$)	Spanish ($N = 60$)	Indians ($N = 68$)
Quantity-frequency of alcohol use	.35	.34	.07	.27
Personal-effects reasons for alcohol use	.36	.44	.18	.31
Times drunk during previous year	.50	.85	.78	.46
Drinking-related deviant behavior	.47	.88	.69	.38
Total other deviance	.22	.01	.53	.19

* For $N = 221$, a correlation of .12 is significant at the .05 level; for $N = 93$, a correlation of .17; for $N = 60$, a correlation of .21; and for $N = 68$, a correlation of .20, all one-tailed tests.

frequency drunk, drinking-related deviance, and other deviance. It was noted earlier that the vast majority of these court convictions are for drinking-related problems: Eighty-seven percent are clearly indicated to be drinking-related in the records, and others, although not formally reported as such, may also be related to drinking. It is of interest, therefore, to note the relatively high correlations which exist between court records and our two most direct measures of drinking-related problems, Drunkenness and Drinking-Related Deviance, .50 and .47, respectively. The two less direct measures of drinking-related problems, Q-F and Personal-Effects Reasons for Drinking, correlate at a lower level, .35 and .36, respectively. Lowest of all is the correlation with Other Deviance (.22) where, according to our procedures in devising the measure, drinking involvement should be minimal. This order or pattern of correlations contributes to the validity of the record data.

A more stringent test of the validity of court records as an index of deviant behavior can be obtained by examining *intra*ethnic group associations. If the records are subject to systematic bias in the administration of justice, its basis is probably in large part ethnic. But *within* any one ethnic group, members probably have close to an equal probability of being convicted for the same type of behavior. Table 8.4 also presents correlations between record data and the other measures within each of the three ethnic groups. It can be seen that the associations between court convictions, drunkenness, and drinking-related deviance remain high in all three groups, and for Anglos and Indians (the Spanish have one reversal) the over-all ordering of the correlations with the other measures of deviance is also maintained. It would appear, then, that the record data are not simply reflecting ethnic biases in the administration of justice since they are quite capable of differentiating *within* each ethnic group as well.

These correlations, both in their over-all level and their patterned differences, suggest that there probably are not gross distortions present in the record data; self-reports of the same type of behavior are similar in distribution. These records serve, in turn, as an outside validation of the self-report data, suggesting that there probably are not gross distortions in those either. This evidence is important since it strengthens the argument that the low correlations reported earlier between Other Deviance and the self-reports of various aspects of drinking behavior are not simply the result of invalid self-reports. If that were the case, then correlations between drinking measures and court records should also be low. Rather, the situation appears to be that the Other-Deviance scale is tapping areas of behavior within the general domain of deviance which the drinking measures miss. It appears, in short, that all the procedures we have presented thus far can be useful contributors to our repertoire of criterion measures.

The Construction of a Global Deviance Measure

None of the various measures of aspects of adult deviant behavior presented in this or in the previous chapter is without its limitations. Because of the general tendency of respondents to protect their self-image by *underreporting* their engagement in socially disapproved behavior, a major weakness of each measure, taken separately, is that it will probably yield a number of "false negatives," subjects who are in fact deviant in their behavior, but who fail to tell us so. Our court records are subject to the same limitations: many persons have engaged in illegal behavior who have not been caught.

To cope with this problem, and to make use of the diverse information provided by our separate measures, a *composite* measure or index seemed desirable. Considering each measure as an "opportunity" for each respondent to be "registered" as having engaged in deviant behavior, the inadequacy of any measure can be compensated by the other measures. In other terms, the scores on the separate measures can be treated as "symptoms," the detection of any one of which is enough to implicate the underlying attribute of deviant behavior. The "diagnosis" is likely to be more accurate as more possible symptoms are investigated. In accord with such a point of view, a single index was constructed to accommodate the cumulating evidence from the separate measures.

The Global Deviance measure is simply a split of the adult sample into two categories: "deviant" and "non-deviant." Since the predictive scheme does not specify what form of deviance structural and personality pressures might generate, this method of pooling together *all* forms of deviance tapped by the various measures provides an efficient way to test the over-all adequacy of our scheme.

A person was placed in the "deviant" category for any one of the following reasons:[3]

1. if he reported having been drunk fifteen or more times during the previous year;
2. if he reported two or more instances of drinking-related problem behavior;
3. if he reported at least one instance of "serious" other deviance; (a person was not classified as "deviant" if he reported only acts which we had previously scored as "moderate," no matter how many of these might have occurred); or
4. if he had a record of court conviction during the previous ten years for *other than* non-alcohol-related traffic violations, violations of game laws, or civil suits.

Ninety-one of the 221 members of our adult sample (41 percent) fulfilled one or more of these requirements and were thereby classified as "deviant," that is, as having engaged in deviant behavior. Their distribution by sex and ethnic categories is presented in Table 8.5. Of the Anglos, 24 percent have been classified as "deviant," of the Spanish, 30 percent, and of the Indians, 75 percent. This summary classification, therefore, captures the same ethnic ordering which has appeared on the majority of the individual measures: Anglos and Spanish appear similarly low in deviance rates, Spanish tending to be slightly higher than Anglos, with

---

[3] The particular cutting points were made individually for each measure by considering both the nature of the empirical distributions and the meaning of that point in relation to our criteria for deviant behavior described in Chapter 2. It should be emphasized again that allocation to the deviant category means only that the person has engaged in some form of *behavior* defined as deviant.

TABLE 8.5

Proportion of Subjects in Community Survey Study Classified as "Deviant" on the Global Deviance Summary Measure

Group	Number Deviant	Proportion Deviant
Total sample ($N = 221$)	91	.41
Males ($N = 110$)	52	.47
Females ($N = 111$)	39	.35
Anglos ($N = 93$)	22	.24
Spanish ($N = 60$)	18	.30
Indians ($N = 68$)	51	.75
Anglo males ($N = 45$)	17	.38
Anglo females ($N = 48$)	5	.10
Spanish males ($N = 30$)	7	.23
Spanish females ($N = 30$)	11	.37
Indian males ($N = 35$)	28	.80
Indian females ($N = 33$)	23	.70

the Indian group standing out dramatically from the other two by its extremely high rate. Sex group differences are also as would be expected. The low proportion for Spanish males suggests, again, underreporting.

Of the 91 subjects classified as deviant, 6 were so on the basis of *all* four component measures used, 19 were deviant on the basis of three of the four component measures, 22 on two of the four, and 44 on only one measure. If we regard court records as essentially a measure of drinking-related deviance (since only one subject who was classified as deviant on the basis of court conviction had no recorded alcohol involvement), then we note the redundancy among these measures. Only two subjects were classified as deviant on the basis of drunkenness alone, only two on the basis of drinking-related problem behavior alone, and only eight on the basis of court records alone. This is what we might have expected from the level of intercorrelation among these measures.

There is now another basis for evaluating the effort which was put into obtaining court records. Ninety-one percent of all those whom we ultimately classified as deviant on the Global Deviance measure would have been classified that way as a result of some aspect of their self-reports alone. Among the men, only 6 percent (three cases) would have been missed had we not gone to the time and expense to search court records intensively. This is an insignificant figure—probably not worth the effort—which speaks very well for the general adequacy of self-report criterion data. Thirteen percent of the women classified as deviants (five cases) would have been missed without court records, however; this is a figure large enough to have some influence on final hypothesis testing.

Some discussion of the fact that our classification procedure resulted in 41 percent of the sample being classified as "deviant" is in order. It may be asked whether such a percentage is not too high and might not reflect criteria which are essentially unrealistic in relation to actual social life. Several things should be mentioned in this regard. The first thing to emphasize is that the use of the Global Deviance measure in our research will not substitute for the separate criteria of which it is composed. In the tests of the theoretical scheme, in Chapter 11, not only Global Deviance but its components also are used as criteria. Thus, any distortions caused by the construction of this composite index will not escape notice. But this is just a procedural safeguard; the issue of the size of the Global Deviance percentage remains.

It will be recalled that, on the basis of court convictions alone, 48 of our respondents (45 by records, 3 by self-admission) were implicated. This is already a high percentage (22 percent) for a random sample of a community. It is especially high if one considers that a court conviction, as we have defined it to leave out traffic, game, and civil suit violations, reflects a serious form of departure from norms, one involving *legal* sanctions. But our concept of deviance was intended to be much broader than the class of behavior eliciting legal sanctions. If legal transgressions are seen as lying further along a scale of seriousness of normative departure than other types of transgressions, then the high rate of legal transgressions in our community suggests the occurrence of a good deal of less serious departures, but departures nevertheless serious enough to meet the conceptual criteria of deviance discussed in Chapter 2. What is being said is that the high over-all rate of deviance gains validity from the high rate of court convictions for our sample.

Further, the high rate of classified deviants must be recognized as a rate of *persons committing certain acts,* not as deviant personalities. This point was emphasized in Chapter 2. Thought of as deviant personalities, the 41 percent figure is startling; thought of as persons who have engaged in certain behaviors over a ten-year period in a context where pressures toward the use of illegitimate means are strong and role models for deviance are widely present, the figure is no longer startling.

Numerous recent epidemiological studies have yielded unexpectedly high prevalence rate figures for mental illness. It has been clear in those studies that the issue devolves to the nature and stringency of the definitional criteria employed. The same is true in our study; the cutting point for each measure entering into the Global Deviance index was carefully considered in terms of its meaningfulness. Although the final decisions are, of course, open to disagreement, it is our feeling that each one is a reasonable referent for what we intend by the concept of deviance.

Finally, given that both the self-report and the record data undoubtedly *under*estimate the occurrence of deviant behavior, the 41 percent figure, if anything, must be considered *low* in relation to the actual prevalence of deviance in the adult sample.

In summary, the Global Deviance category measure is an attempt to capture, within the confines of a single classification, all of the data available bearing on deviance among the adults in the Community Survey sample. It has the great advantage of being based on extremely wide coverage, including both responses to a large number of questionnaire items and data from court records. In this manner, it not only overcomes much of the underreporting which can naturally be anticipated in such a sensitive behavioral area but also, by its diversity of content, it probably taps a large proportion of the theoretical domain we have defined as deviant behavior.

The deviance measures in the Community Survey Study derive from two sources: self-reports in an interview and court records. In the High School Study, the situation was such as to enable the investigation and use of a greater variety of sources in arriving at criterion measures of deviant behavior, and it is to that phase of our research that we now turn.

THE HIGH SCHOOL STUDY

Because we were working with a circumscribed group of subjects in the high school who were in daily face-to-face contact under the supervision of adult authority, the High School Study presented an unusual opportunity to explore intensively the convergent measurement of a behavioral domain—in this case, deviance.

To take full advantage of this opportunity, criterion data were obtained from five independent sources: teacher ratings, peer ratings, self-reports, parent reports, and school records. A small portion of the self-report data bearing on adolescent drinking behavior has already been discussed in Chapter 7. In this section, the full range of criterion data obtained from all five sources will be presented, and the interrelationships among the measures will be explored. The presentation can serve several purposes: to examine the relative advantage of alternative approaches to the measurement of a difficult behavioral domain; to shed further light on the veracity of self-report data; and to give the reader confidence in the criterion groups ultimately established in the high school for the subsequent testing of hypotheses.

Teacher Ratings of Deviant Behavior

The local high school can be viewed as a relatively unusual laboratory situation in which the behavior of the subjects (students) is constantly being observed and rated (grades, evaluations) by a team of trained observers (teachers) over an extended period of time. Because the school is relatively small—129 students at the time our research was conducted—every student is known to every teacher; a student's behavior cannot escape notice, therefore, through his own anonymity. Like most high schools, specialized classes insure that every student is observed by at least four to six different teachers each year in the intimacy of the classroom situation. This provided an excellent opportunity to explore methodological issues of the following kind:

1. To what extent will multiple observers in a relatively naturalistic situation agree in their ratings of student behavior?
2. What are the relative advantages, if any, of global ratings as opposed to ratings based on specific behavioral check lists?
3. To what extent may halo effects influence teacher evaluations?
4. Do different classes and different teachers have sufficiently varying stimulus value for the students so that their behavior changes radically?

At the end of the 1961–1962 school year, all ten teachers and the principal of the local high school were interviewed separately. Each interview took approximately 50 minutes and was carried out during one of the teacher's free periods. All were most cooperative in giving of time which they might otherwise have used for relaxation or classroom preparation. As part of their task, the teachers were asked to provide two conceptually independent ratings of student behavior: a global rating of general classroom deportment and ratings of the occurrence or nonoccurrence of eight specific violations of school norms.

The Global Deportment Ratings

A behavioral continuum was defined for the teachers: at one extreme, "this student is always on time, neatly dressed, courteous in language, quiet and cooperative in class, always has assignments completed on time, and in every way by his behavior, makes his teachers' jobs easier and more satisfying;" at the other, "this student disrupts orderly classroom routine, and displays such behaviors as whispering, talking, giggling, gum-chewing, attention-getting, etc., and in other ways makes his teachers' jobs more difficult and less rewarding."

Each student's name had been typed on a three- by five-inch card, and the teacher was asked to sort these cards into two roughly equal piles, dichotomizing the distribution of students along this continuum. Then each pile was again dichotomized into high and low ratings by the teacher, thus providing a four-category scale of classroom conformity. Students whom a teacher had not had in class during the current school year were eliminated from his ratings.

The Deviance Check List

As a second task, each teacher-rater was presented with a list of eight specific violations of school norms:

1. Smoking—smoked on school grounds, in rest rooms, etc.
2. Drinking—displayed evidence in class or at school functions of having been drinking.
3. Fighting—got into a fight with another student while at school.
4. Disobedience—refused to carry out the request of teacher or school official, or broke school regulations, including also those cases of resistance where ultimate compliance is obtained.
5. Profanity—used profanity in talking with other students or with teachers.
6. Lying—lied to teacher or other school official, forged excuse, etc.
7. Cheating—cheated on a test, copied homework, etc.
8. Stealing—stole school property or the property of others.

This list had been drawn up in consultation with the school principal two years earlier and had been refined and shortened through experience with its use the previous year. It represents the major behavior problems with which the school must cope. Each teacher then proceeded through a list of all students in the school, and for those whom the teacher had had in class, assigned a score of 0 for each behavior which the student had never, to the teacher's knowledge, displayed during the last year; 1 for each behavior displayed only once or twice; and 2 for each behavior displayed several times. Each student's score was then added across all eight items.

Reliability of Teacher Ratings

Analysis of the reliability of these teacher ratings was undertaken to determine to what extent there was agreement *between* teachers in their ratings of student behavior and how *consistent* the teachers were in their ratings of student behavior when operationally distinct rating procedures were used. Despite various factors likely to increase interteacher agreement, such as coffee-break sharing of evaluations of students, the correlations in Table 8.6 of teacher Global Deportment ratings average only in the high forties. This suggests either relatively low reliability of the raters or relatively large differences in student behavior from one classroom to another.

Further analysis revealed that 15 percent of the students were rated as highly conforming in their classroom behavior by one teacher and highly deviant by another. There would seem to be a high presumption of situational specificity in the classroom behavior of these students since the raters who judged these students as conforming had judged *other* students as highly deviant. In addition, 38 percent of the students varied from highly conforming to moderately deviant or from moderately conforming to highly deviant in these ratings of classroom behavior. Thus, presuming that the teacher ratings are valid, there is, for over 50 percent of the students, evidence of fairly large shifts in behavior from one classroom to another.

Correlations between ratings by various pairs of teachers increased when the rating task was made more specific and the frame of reference was

TABLE 8.6

Teacher Global Deportment Ratings—Interteacher Agreement: Product-Moment (Pearson) Correlations*

Teacher	1	2	3	4	5	6	7	8	9	Principal
1										
2	.31									
3	.65	.62								
4	.42	.34	.14							
5	.46	.47	.23	.58						
6	−†	.73	.63	−	.15					
7	−	.40	.69	−	−	.50				
8	.45	.37	.61	.49	−	.39	.51			
9	.59	.47	−	.32	.58	.15	−	.64		
Principal	.30	.48	.46	.40	.45	.49	.59	.65	.52	

* N's for each correlation vary depending on the number of students the teacher-pair have in common. All comparisons, however, are based on at least 20 students. For $N = 20$, a correlation of .36 is significant at the .05 level, one-tailed test.

† A dash indicates that the teacher-pair had less than twenty students in common.

not the classroom alone but the school at large. Table 8.7 presents data for the behavioral check list procedure. Correlations between raters now average in the high fifties, and several achieve quite substantial agreement. On the global rating procedure, only one correlation was over .7; on the behavioral check list, eleven were over .7—that is, more than one third of all the comparisons.

These correlations are still fairly low for a reliable rating procedure. Nevertheless, they are no lower *between* teacher-raters than for the *teachers themselves,* using these alternative procedures. Table 8.8 presents for each rater correlations between his Global Deportment and his Deviance Check List ratings. These correlations also average in the high fifties. Obviously, "halo effects" were not overly influential in determining these ratings.

TABLE 8.7

**Teacher Deviance Check List Ratings—Interteacher Agreement:
Product-Moment (Pearson) Correlations***

Teacher	1	2	3	4	5	6	7	8	9	Principal
1										
2	.30									
3	.51	.81								
4†										
5	.27	.25	.25							
6	–‡	.45	.72		.24					
7	–	.72	.73		–	.87				
8	.71	.76	.58		–	.25	.68			
9	.51	.73	.92		.47	.38	–	.89		
Principal	.36	.66	.83		.38	.60	.69	.60	.62	

* *N*'s for each correlation vary, depending on the number of students each teacher-pair has in common. All comparisons, however, are based on at least 20 students. For *N* = 20, a correlation of .36 is significant at the .05 level, one-tailed test.

† Teacher 4 failed to use the behavior check list.

‡ A dash indicates that the teacher-pair had less than 20 students in common.

TABLE 8.8

**Internal Consistency of Teacher Ratings—
Global Deportment Ratings versus
Deviance Check List Ratings: Product-Moment
(Pearson) Correlations***

Teacher	Number of Students Rated	Correlation between Ratings
1	81	.57
2	60	.65
3	62	.39
4	75	–†
5	78	.63
6	53	.34
7	38	.70
8	62	.64
9	65	.57
Principal	129	.74

* All correlations are significant at the .01 level or better, one-tailed test.

† Teacher 4 failed to use the behavior check list.

The Final Teacher Rating Measure

To increase the reliability of these teacher ratings and attempt to arrive at a general measure of each student's behavior in the school situation at large, a mean score on global deportment and a mean score on the deviance check list were calculated for each student across the ratings of all his teachers. (Every student was rated by at least four teachers and by an average of between five and six.) These means correlate .78 (Pearson r), suggesting a marked improvement in internal consistency of the rating through the combining of multiple observers. The stability of these mean ratings was then further increased by *combining* the means. Students were ranked on each of the two rating procedures, their ranks added, and the sums of ranks were then reranked. If we consider these two measures as conceptually equivalent to the two halves of a psychometric test and apply the Spearman-Brown prophecy formula,[4] then the reliability of this final rating is about .88. It is this final, combined rating which is referred to when the Teacher Rating of Deviance criterion is mentioned.

Several lessons can be drawn from this methodological exercise. First, retrospective ratings of behavior observed over a protracted period in which subject and rater interact are probably inherently unreliable. Factors such as distortions of memory and the social stimulus value which the rater develops with time for the subject being rated are operative. Thus, student behavior will vary from one classroom to another and will change during the school year, just as client behavior varies from one therapist to another and changes with time. The reliability of such ratings can be improved somewhat by making the task more specific and by clearly delineating behavioral acts that the subject being rated may or may not have exhibited; the check list must, of course, adequately sample the major behavioral indicators of the underlying domain. Finally, the stability of such ratings can be vastly improved by combining in some way the scores of several observers. Even quite unreliable rating procedures can thereby achieve respectable internal consistency and, as will be seen later, convergent validity as well.

Peer Ratings of Deviance: A Sociometric Procedure

The presence of an interacting group of subjects, all of whom knew each other well by the latter part of the school year, provided an excellent opportunity to construct a criterion measure based on peer ratings.

A sociometric questionnaire, reconstructed on the basis of two years of

[4] r for total score equals $\dfrac{2r \text{ (between halves)}}{1 + r \text{ (between halves)}}$

previous testing experience in the local high school, served as the basis for peer ratings. Besides yielding information on cliques and cleavages, cross-ethnic friendship patterns, and other aspects of the student social structure, this questionnaire contained four items designed to yield peer ratings of each other's deviant and conforming behavior:

1. Who are the kids *from around here* you most admire?
   (conformity to personal norms)
2. Which kids *from around here* are most likely to do things *you* think they shouldn't do?
   (violation of personal norms)
3. Which kids *from around here* act the way most adults approve of?
   (conformity to community norms)
4. Which kids *from around here* get into trouble the most?
   (violation of community norms)

For each of these questions, space was provided for two nominations. As with all our testing procedures, the seriousness of the task was impressed upon the students and anonymity was assured them. Nevertheless, as could be expected, a fair number of students did not make any or all of their nominations on the negative questions, since a strong peer ethic against "ratting" on their classmates was obviously involved. It is a measure of the seriousness and maturity of the students and the general rapport of the investigators with them that the vast majority cooperated completely. As will be shown below, these ratings agreed strongly with the judgments of others.

All students in the school were then ranked from "most conforming" to "most deviant" on each question, based on the number of nominations they had received from their peers. High rank thus always indicated high deviance, regardless of the form a particular question took. Intercorrelations (Spearman rho) were then calculated between each pair of items, with the expectation that all should be positive. These correlations are presented in Table 8.9.

The fairly low correlations between items which tap opposite ends of the conformity-deviance continuum are an artifact of the procedure whereby Spearman correlations are corrected for tied ranks. Obviously, a large number of students received *no* nominations on any particular item, whereas many of these same students were the very ones being nominated on items tapping the opposite end of the conformity-deviance continuum. Where correlations are performed, tied ranks based on zero nominations then become matched against ranks based on a *distribution* of nominations.

But this artifact cannot account for the *negative* correlations which the first item ("Whom do you most admire?") yielded. These correlations mean that the same students who were reported as deviant in their behavior were also being admired by their peers. This is an interesting aspect of the high school social structure in the research community which is also reflected in its leadership patterns. It became clear that personal admiration, in this particular context, could not be used, as we had planned, as an indirect measure of socially conforming behavior. This does not mean that our conception of deviance as departure from a community standard accepted even by the students themselves was in error, however; students were well aware of and themselves condemned the deviant behavior of those they admired. This is shown by the fact that question two, "Which kids . . . do things *you* think they shouldn't?" correlates .61 with question four, "Which kids . . . get into trouble the most?"

TABLE 8.9

Intercorrelations (Spearman rho) among Sociometric Ratings of Student Behavior by Their Peers*

		1	2	3	4
1.	Who are the kids you most admire?				
2.	Which kids do things *you* think they shouldn't do?	−.24			
3.	Which kids act the way most adults approve of?	.30	.14		
4.	Which kids get into trouble the most?	−.10	.61	.26	

* Rank ordering is based on the number of nominations received. Low rank = conformity; high rank = deviance. All correlations have been corrected for the large number of ties in the zero, one, and two nomination categories. For $N = 129$, a correlation of .15 is significant at the .05 level, one-tailed test.

Question 1 was therefore eliminated from the peer rating procedure. The three remaining items—with consistently positive correlations, tapping both ends of the conformity-deviance continuum—were then combined by adding each subject's rank on each item and reranking the totals. This weights each item equally and provides a continuous measure which is available for correlational procedures. This measure is referred to as the Peer Rating measure of deviance.

The Validity of Peer Ratings of Deviance

These peer ratings have the advantage as a criterion measure of being based on nominations by a large number of observers (128) on several diverse items. Any distortion which the bias of individual students might introduce has probably been cancelled out by pooling nominations. Teacher ratings have these same virtues and, in addition, the maturity and objectivity which teachers should bring to the task. How well do these two procedures agree?

A product-moment (Pearson) correlation between peer ratings and teacher ratings was .75, indicating substantial agreement between these two completely independent sets of ratings by very different sets of "judges." This correlation testifies to validity for both procedures.

Self-Reports of Deviant Behavior

In addition to the teacher and peer rating procedures, the students were asked to report their own deviant behavior. The procedure constructed for the high school students is very similar in content to that developed by Nye and Short (1957) and Short and Nye (1957), though we were unfortunately unfamiliar with their work at the time the present measure was developed. Twenty items covered various areas of adolescent misbehavior ranging from "faked an excuse from home" to "gotten into trouble with the law." This set of items occurred among the third day's testing procedures, after students had become used to our asking intimate questions about their beliefs, hopes, and expectations, and it followed a lengthy section inquiring about their drinking behavior. Students were asked "how often have you" engaged in each of these socially disapproved acts; in response, they circled one of four categories: "very often," "several times," "once or twice," or "never." Four of the twenty items—such as "gotten home a little later than usual from school" and "gone to a movie the night before a test"—were buffers, items intended to break response sets by insuring student attention to variation in the item content.

Numbers with a 0–3 range were assigned to the response categories, and a respondent's score was obtained by adding up these numbers across all items, except the buffers, and then adding to this sum a score for his responses to three items bearing on drinking-related deviance from the drinking questionnaire.[5] In addition to the total score, three subscores were derived: a Drinking-Related Deviance score (based on five items) already presented in the preceding chapter; a School-Related Deviance score (based on seven items); and an Other-Deviance score (based on seven items).

The intercorrelations among these subscales can serve as a crude indication of the internal consistency of the over-all scale; they can, as well, indicate something about the functional equivalence of alternative forms

[5] We have not attempted a differential weighting of these items in relation to their obviously differential seriousness. Our position is based upon the total-score–scale-score reasoning presented in Footnote 2, Chapter 7, upon our experience with the Other-Deviance scale in the Community Survey Study, and upon the views of Lazarsfeld and Robinson (1940), who have pointed out that as the number of items in a composite score increases, correlations between total scores based on different linear combinations of these items rapidly approach 1.0. If the number of items is greater than six or seven, therefore, weighting items is not worth the effort.

TABLE 8.10
Internal Consistency of Self-Reports of Three Types of
Deviant Behavior—High School Study: Product-Moment
(Pearson) Correlations*

	1	2	3
1. School-related deviance			
2. Drinking-related deviance	.44		
3. Other deviance	.69	.56	

* N = 93, for which a correlation of .24 is significant at the
.01 level, one-tailed test. On this and most subsequent analyses
of high school student data, the N has been decreased by the
elimination of 35 Indian boarding school students and one
uncooperative Anglo boy. Because these Indians do not have
their homes in the research community, data from their
parents could not be obtained economically. Furthermore,
these data would have no parallel in the adult community
survey. Finally, their restricted boarding school life limits
their opportunity to engage in the types of deviant behavior
which the project was investigating. Separate criterion measures appropriate to their condition would therefore have had
to be constructed.

of deviant behavior. These are presented in Table 8.10. Although not
extremely high, the correlations are substantial enough to suggest that
they are governed in part by a single underlying behavioral domain.
Whether this domain is merely something like response set or susceptibility
to social desirability pressures or actually the domain of deviant behavior
as we intended is a *validity* problem which will be examined in the following section.

*The Validity of Self-Report Data on Deviant Behavior
by High School Students*

An estimation of the validity of the self-reports can be approached
in two ways: (1) by examination of the internal characteristics of student
responses to the scale, such as the extent to which deviant acts were
reported, differences in response pattern to different kinds of items, and
responses to "buffer" items; and (2) by comparison between self-report
data and alternative measures of the same behavior.

Table 8.11 shows the full set of items in the order in which they were
presented, together with data on the frequency with which each response
category was used. It is perhaps a reflection of the rapport which the
researchers had built up with the students over three years of work in
the high school and of the seriousness with which students approached
the task that such a high proportion reported various deviant acts. For

TABLE 8.11
Self-Reports of Deviant Behavior by High School Students—
Frequency of Reported Acts*

	Item†	Never	Once or Twice	Several Times	Very Often
S	1. Smoked on the school grounds	35	30	22	6
O	2. Taken things that didn't belong to you	30	48	14	1
B	3. Gone on outings with friends	1	20	34	38
S	4. Faked an excuse from home	41	25	21	6
O	5. Gotten into trouble with the law	72	17	2	2
O	6. Sworn or cursed	7	16	43	27
S	7. Cut-up in the classroom	9	18	48	18
B	8. Gotten home a little later than usual after school	7	21	44	21
D	9. Driven when you've had a good bit to drink	62	23	8	0
S	10. Copied other kids' homework	8	41	41	3
O	11. Made out with your dates	11	5	31	45
O	12. Disobeyed your parents	2	58	29	4
S	13. Cheated on tests	24	48	19	2
B	14. Done things on the spur of the moment	4	25	35	29
O	15. Gotten into fights with other kids	27	42	19	5
D	16. Gone on beer parties	31	17	30	15
S	17. Lied to a teacher	27	51	11	4
O	18. Driven a car without a license	17	26	35	15
S	19. Ditched school	34	42	12	5
B	20. Gone to a movie the night before a test	16	36	31	10
	From drinking questionnaire:				
D	Gotten into trouble with your family because of drinking	74	17	2	‡
D	Had fights because of drinking	69	16	8	‡
D	Gotten into trouble with the law because of drinking	82	9	2	‡

* $N = 93$.

† Coding is as follows: S, item forms part of the school-related deviance subscale; D, item forms part of the drinking-related deviance subscale; O, item forms part of the other-deviance subscale; B, buffer item.

‡ The "very often" category was not used with these items.

example, three quarters of the students reported having cheated on tests, and almost a quarter admitted to an occasional brush with the law. Almost half the students reported engaging "very often" in at least one of the fifteen acts which the students themselves considered to be more than a "little bit wrong,"[6] but no student simply reported himself to have done *everything* "very often." Furthermore, of the 25 students who reported "never" to one of the four "buffer" items, only three did to *more* than one of them, and none to more than two. These distributions provide some face validity for the scale.

A second source of validity information comes from a comparison of self-report with external measures of deviant behavior. Gross disagreements between the latter and the total self-report score are rare. Only one student in the top (deviant) quartile of the teacher or peer ratings places himself in the bottom (conforming) quartile of the self-report distribution (an Indian). More problems of the opposite kind occur. Three boys and a girl who are in the bottom quartile of teacher or peer ratings have reported so much deviant behavior that they fall in the top quartile of the self-report distribution. Three of these four are Anglos. These "false positives" may be perfectly honest, but they are perhaps just "too honest," failing to protect themselves through slight underreporting of their deviance as do most of the respondents.

Ethnic differences in the tendency to underreport deviance are not gross. Of those students falling in the most deviant quartile of *either* the teacher *or* the peer ratings, 38 percent of the Anglos, 47 percent of the Spanish, and 33 percent of the Indians also reported enough deviance *themselves* to fall in the top quartile. With respect to overreporting, however, of those falling in the most conforming quartile of either the teacher or peer ratings, only 15 percent of the Anglos, but 64 percent of the Spanish and 50 percent of the Indians also placed themselves there; it appears that there is some tendency for conforming Anglo students to overreport deviant behavior more than conforming Spanish or Indians.

Direct correlations between these self-report measures and the teacher and peer ratings can shed further light on the issue. These correlations are presented in Table 8.12. Although the correlations are fairly substantial, self-reports of *school-related* misbehavior appear to be relatively poor. They correlate lowest of the three subscores with teacher ratings (.41) which were specifically directed at school behavior. It is of interest that the self-reports of *drinking-related* behavior have the highest relationship to *both* teacher and peer ratings, even higher than the *total* self-report score. Perhaps the fact that the questionnaires were administered to stu-

---

[6] Only the four buffer items, plus "making out with your dates" were considered a "little bit wrong" on an Attitude toward Deviance inventory administered at another point in the testing. All other items were rated more than a "little bit wrong."

TABLE 8.12
Product-Moment (Pearson) Correlations between
Self-Reports of Deviant Behavior and Ratings by
Teachers and Peers: High School Study*

Self-Reports	Teacher Ratings	Peer Ratings
School deviance	.41	.30
Drinking deviance	.64	.62
Other deviance	.45	.39
Total self-report	.59	.51

* $N = 93$, for which a correlation of .24 is significant at the .01 level, one-tailed test.

dents in a classroom situation reduced the validity of self-reports concerning their *school* behavior.

In summary, it would appear that, with the exception of perhaps five or six cases, students have quite readily reported their deviant behavior.[7] In fact, perhaps the greatest distortion comes through *over*reporting, or at least underprotecting oneself. This raises for the first time in our measurement of deviant behavior the possibility of obtaining false positives: students who rate themselves more deviant than would various outside observers. The problem will come up again when we examine ratings by the students' mothers.

Parent Reports of Their Children's Deviant Behavior

Reports of a child's behavior by his parents are subject to many of the problems characteristic of self-report data. It is difficult for a parent to be a neutral observer of his child; for most parents, their children are an extension of themselves, and they would like them seen in a good light; parents will generally protect their children's reputation, consciously or unconsciously, by overlooking and underreporting their faults. On the other hand, some parents have developed hostile and bitter feelings toward their children which may be reflected in the opposite type of prob-

[7] It is interesting to note that in a unique validation study of self-report scales similar to the one used here, Clark and Tifft (1966) come to similar conclusions. They followed up self-report questionnaire responses from university students with interviews and, ultimately, with a polygraph examination procedure to check on the accuracy of the self-reports. "[T]here is a high rank correlation [.80] between the ordering of subjects on the original questionnaire and the final ordering of subjects . . ." (p. 521); "[t]he main finding of this study is that self-reporting of delinquency is rather accurate when a wide range of behaviors is considered simultaneously, but that there is differential validity on specific questionnaire items" (p. 523).

lem, an *over*reporting of the child's misbehavior and an overemphasis on his faults.

Reports of the high school students' deviant behavior were obtained from almost all mothers of students living in the community. Fairly late in the socialization interview, and after a series of questions bearing on the general issue of the child's problem behavior and the parents' techniques for coping with it, the interviewer asked: "For each of the following, please tell me if (name of child) has done this 'very often,' 'several times,' 'once or twice,' or 'never.' " Parents were then presented with a list of specific acts almost identical in content to that which the students themselves had received in their testing. Table 8.13 presents these items in the order administered, together with the frequency distribution of the mothers' responses.

These responses, like the parallel self-report measure, were scored 0–3 and added across all but the buffer item to produce an over-all Parent Report score. Subscores were also computed in the areas of school-related,

TABLE 8.13
**Mothers' Reports of Their High School Children's Deviant Behavior—
Frequency of Reported Acts***

		Item†	Never	Once or Twice	Several Times	Very Often
B	1.	Getting home from school a little later than usual	33	18	25	10
S	2.	Cheating on tests	67	11	8	0
O	3.	Cursing or swearing	39	21	19	7
D	4.	Going on beer parties	69	11	6	0
S	5.	Lying to a teacher	63	15	8	0
O	6.	Getting into fights with other kids	54	19	11	2
O	7.	Taking things that didn't belong to him	75	8	2	1
D	8.	Getting drunk	71	11	3	1
O	9.	Heavy petting on dates	72	3	9	2
S	10.	Ditching school, or playing hooky	52	29	5	0
O	11.	Lying to his parents	51	22	13	0
S	12.	Cutting up in the classroom	41	13	24	8
D	13.	Driving when he's had a good bit to drink	76	7	3	0
S	14.	Copying other kids' homework	64	12	10	0
O	15.	Getting into trouble with the law	73	13	0	0

* $N = 86$.

† Coding is as follows: S, item forms part of the school-related deviance subscale; D, item forms part of the drinking-related deviance subscale; O, item forms part of the other-deviance subscale; B, buffer item.

drinking-related and other deviance. (See code at left edge of the table.) Their intercorrelations in Table 8.14 provide a crude indicator of the internal consistency of the scale. Except for the .13 correlation between Drinking-Related and School-Related deviance, these correlations are fairly high. Furthermore, their order presents a now familiar pattern. Like

TABLE 8.14
**Internal Consistency of Parents' Reports of Three Types of
Deviant Behavior of Their Children: Product-Moment
(Pearson) Correlations***

	School	Drinking	Other
School-related deviance			
Drinking-related deviance	.13		
Other deviance	.65	.45	

* $N = 86$, for which a correlation of .18 is significant at the .05 level, one-tailed test.

the self-report subscales, the lowest correlation is between drinking-related and school-related deviance and the highest between school-related and other deviance.   This might suggest the relative independence of drinking-related deviance within the over-all domain of deviant behavior if it were not for the high correlation between self-reports of drinking-related deviance and teacher or peer ratings.

The Validity of Mother Reports of Their Children's Deviance

Some of the potential difficulties with data obtained from mothers on the deviant behavior of their children have been touched on in the introduction to this section. Since parents, particularly mothers, are common informants in social science research, it is worth looking at the validity of these data in some detail.

The most striking aspect is the small number of instances of child deviance reported. In Table 8.13, the frequency distribution of mothers' reports was presented, and it can be seen that the extreme category is rarely used, except for the buffer (item 1), for "cutting up in the classroom," and for "cursing or swearing." Over-all, the mothers reported less than half as many deviant acts as the students themselves reported. In fact, for 16 students (nearly 20 percent of the interviews, and mainly Spanish and Indians) the mothers reported *no* deviance of any kind on the part of their children. On the other hand, 13 mothers reported the legal difficulties their children had had, which though under two thirds of the rate reported by the students themselves, is still substantial. Much of the behavior reported by the students, though certainly not all, may simply not be *known* to their parents; the children, after all, have a stake in keeping their parents misinformed.

Of the students falling in the most deviant quartile of either the teacher or the peer ratings, 92 percent of the Anglo, 15 percent of the Spanish, and 40 percent of the Indian mothers also reported enough deviance by their children to place them in this quartile. Of those falling in the most conforming quartile of either the teacher or peer ratings, 10 percent of the Anglo, 36 percent of the Spanish, and 100 percent of the Indian mothers also placed their children there. This strengthens our suspicion that the non-Anglo mothers are underreporting their children's deviance more than Anglo mothers.

Although reports which accurately reflect the absolute level of deviant behavior in the community are most desirable, the underreporting by mothers which we have discovered would not be too damaging if it still resulted in an accurate *relative* ordering of their children. To examine the relative accuracy of these mother reports, correlations with ratings by teachers, peers, and the students themselves were calculated and are presented in Table 8.15. Except in the area of drinking, where mother and child seem to have reached the greatest consensus, these correlations tend to be in the thirties or below, statistically significant in most cases, but not very impressive. The school-related deviance subscale again appears to be particularly poor.

In summary, the data on their children's deviant behavior collected from the mothers of the local high school students have many of the

TABLE 8.15
**Product-Moment (Pearson) Correlations between
Mothers' Reports of Their Children's Deviant Behavior
and Ratings by Others**

	Mothers' Reports*			
	School	Drinking	Other	Total
Teachers	.14	.42	.32	.34
Peers	.23	.38	.41	.42
Self-Reports				
School	.11	.28	.22	.23
Drinking	.09	.57	.28	.33
Other	.23	.36	.35	.38
Total	.15	.47	.32	.36

* $N = 86$, for which a correlation of .18 is significant at the .05 level, one-tailed test.

same types of problems as the self-report data collected from the students themselves. The mothers, even more than their children, were prone to underreporting, and this was more true of non-Anglos than of Anglos.

Correlations between these parent ratings and those by the subjects themselves, their teachers, and their peers were not too encouraging. The greatest consensus between mothers and their children seemed to emerge with respect to *drinking* behavior, which may suggest that this is a behavior area surrounded by a great deal of overt concern and affect. In a community where public problem drinking is evident on all sides and a constant topic of general conversation, this would not be too surprising. Correlations between ratings in other behavior areas, and with over-all ratings by teachers and peers, however, were not particularly high. In general, it can be concluded that little was learned from the parents about their children's deviant behavior that had not been learned with greater accuracy from other sources.

School Records as a Measure of Deviance

Two types of objective behavioral records were available for all high school students: rates of absenteeism and the grades each student received in his classes. Although these two sets of records draw on quite distinct forms of student behavior, they both can be interpreted as reflecting a single underlying domain: conformity to or deviance from the demands and expectations of the school. Use of these records in the development of criteria of deviance-conformity will be described at this point.

Occasions Absent

Records of absenteeism, collected daily, may serve as an indirect measure of both a specific form of deviant behavior, playing hooky from school, and a more general negative attitude toward school and its normative expectations. The problem in the use of such records is, of course, to disentangle legitimate absence for reasons of sickness from illegitimate absence for such purposes as to help around the house, go shopping, or, most particularly, play hooky. Because legitimate absence tends to be of relatively long duration while illegitimate absences tend to be short, usually a half day or day at most, the total days absent recorded for any student during the school year tends to overemphasize the former while probably masking the latter.

Our attempt at a solution to this problem was to count the number of *occasions* rather than the number of *days* a student had been absent. An "occasion" was defined as any period of absence bounded on each side by a full day of attendance. This procedure reverses the distortion found in the total number of days absent by underemphasizing relatively long periods of illness and overemphasizing short half-day or day absences. Using this approach, a clear trimodal distribution of absenteeism emerged which had been obscured in the distribution of total days absent.

A product-moment (Pearson) correlation between occasions absent first and second semester was .64. This correlation can serve as an estimate of both the reliability of the measure and the temporal stability of the underlying behavior. Combining the two semesters' absenteeism data yields an objective behavioral index of even greater stability: the Spearman-Brown prophecy $r = .78$.

One item on the self-report behavior questionnaire asked directly: "How often have you ditched school?" Three groups of students were compared for mean occasions absent, those who reported that they had ditched school "very often" or "several times" $(N = 17)$, those who said they had only done so "once or twice" $(N = 42)$, and those who said they had "never" done so $(N = 34)$. There was no difference between the first two groups in mean occasions absent—about eleven—during the school year, but both groups averaged four more occasions absent than the group which claimed "never" to have played hooky. These differences are highly significant statistically and testify both to a degree of validity for occasions absent as a measure of hooky playing and to the validity of the self-report data with which they were compared.

One factor which reduces the value of this measure, and which may account for the lack of difference between the two hooky-playing groups, is that after a student has been absent a certain amount, the principal begins to place pressures upon him to reduce his future absenteeism. Such pressures tend to decrease the distribution of this measure at its upper end. Further evidence bearing on the validity of this measure will be presented below when its association with various other criterion measures is analyzed.

Grade Point Average

An objective measure of academic achievement seemed desirable both as a criterion against which to evaluate feelings of inadequacy or low expectations of personal achievement in the academic sphere and as one measure of conformity to the demands of society for legitimate achievement striving. Given the diversity of the student body being investigated, the most satisfactory measure of academic achievement would have been some form of standardized test. Unfortunately, these were available only for those students having academic difficulties. We were, therefore, compelled to construct some form of index from grades.

Student grades were collected only for academic courses: English, history-government, mathematics, and science of any type. Grades in these courses were assigned a numerical value, and an average "grade point" per semester was calculated. These scores were then adjusted to reflect the greater achievement indicated by students in the college-preparatory sections as opposed to those in the regular sections. Since a one- to two-letter grade spread had been suggested by the teachers themselves, these bounds were used and a two-point weighting was given to college-preparatory grades. The resulting measure of academic achievement has quite good stability over time. Adjusted grade point averages for the first semester correlated with those for the second semester .89 (Pearson r). The two semesters were then combined into a single index. The validity of this index as an indirect measure of the domain of adolescent conformity and deviance will be explored further in the next section.

Interrelations among Deviance Criterion Measures in the High School Study

It is now possible to summarize much of what has been discussed in this section on the High School Study by examining the interrelationships among the six alternative criterion measures just presented. The over-all correlation matrix is presented in Table 8.16.

TABLE 8.16
Agreement among Alternative Measures of Deviant Behavior—High School Study: Product-Moment (Pearson) Correlations*

	Teacher	Peer	Self	Mother	Absence	Grades
Teacher ratings						
Peer ratings	.75					
Total self-reports	.59	.51				
Mother reports	.34	.42	.36			
Occasions absent	.58	.50	.26	.21		
Grade point average	.65	.54	.31	.18	.50	

* $N = 93$, for which a correlation of .17 is significant at the .05 level, one-tailed test.

The highest correlation between any pair of measures is found between teacher and peer ratings: .75. What is especially interesting about these two measures is that their pattern of relationships with all other measures is *identical*. The second highest correlation for both measures is with grade point average (.65 and .54, respectively), then with the students' own self-report (.59 and .51), then with absenteeism (.58 and .50, respectively), and lowest of all, with the mother reports (.34 and .42). This strongly suggests that both ratings are validly measuring the same underlying variable.

No consistent pattern of relationships runs through the self-reports and the mother reports, and their over-all level of agreement is only .36. While statistically significant, this is hardly impressive; it reflects poorly on the validity of both measures. Whereas teacher and peer ratings correlated more highly with grades and absenteeism than with self-reports and mother reports, these latter correlate more highly with the teacher and peer ratings than with grades and absenteeism. This is a radical shift in the relationship of academic factors to these two sets of ratings. We shall return to this point later.

It is interesting to note that correlations between self-reports and other measures are consistently higher than those between mother ratings and these same measures. This strongly suggests that we were obtaining better data from the students themselves than from their mothers, as other evidence has already indicated. These findings further exemplify the limitations inherent in working with mothers to obtain information about their children's misbehavior. A more "neutral" observer is clearly desirable, and, in this case, even the actor himself appears better able than his mother to take such an objective role.

The two academic criterion measures, occasions absent and grades, while quite distinct in the behavior they reflect and completely independent operationally, are identical in their *pattern* of relationships with the other measures. As might be expected, both correlate highest with teacher ratings, since both reflect behavior which the teachers are undoubtedly taking into consideration in making their evaluations. But correlations with peer ratings. are similarly high. The correlations with both self-reports and mother reports are substantially lower in both cases.

The relatively strong relationship between these academic criteria and both the teacher and the peer ratings should be explicitly noted. This relationship raises the possibility that a *"halo effect,"* produced by academic performance, has influenced both teacher and peer ratings. On the other hand, it can be argued that satisfactory academic performance is *in fact* one manifestation of conformity to social demands for teen-age students. Furthermore, most teachers will argue that academic performance is in many cases strongly related to *other* behavioral manifestations of conformity to or deviance from the demands of the school. The .5 correlation between grade point average and occasions absent, two completely independent and objective measures of distinct aspects of school behavior, gives testimony to this point; and the correlation between these two measures is roughly of the same order of magnitude as that between each and the teacher or peer ratings. This further supports the interpretation that a "real" rather than an "artifactual" relationship exists between grades in school and other aspects of student behavior.

It has long been recognized by social scientists that grades in school are heavily influenced by cultural and social class differences in experience, motivation, and parental support. The obtained convergence between grades, various forms of school misbehavior, and drinking by high school students suggests to us the need to broaden our perspective on intellectual performance in school. Academic achievement can be seen to be a part of a larger behavioral syndrome all of which may be mapped by similar social and psychological variables.

Sex and Ethnic Group Differences:
The Topography of Deviance in the High School

We are now in a position to specify the distribution of deviant behavior among high school students in the research community. Table 8.17 presents sex group differences on all criterion measures. As expected, girls

TABLE 8.17
Sex Group Differences in Deviant Behavior: High School Study*

Measure		Means and Standard Deviations		Significance†
		Males ($N = 47$)	Females ($N = 46$)	(Males *vs.* Females)
Teacher ratings	$\bar{X}$	85.1	52.3	$t = 4.65$
	σ	(31.7)	(36.0)	$p < .001$
Peer ratings	$\bar{X}$	80.8	51.4	$t = 4.28$
	σ	(35.0)	(31.1)	$p < .001$
Self-reports	$\bar{X}$	25.4	16.2	$t = 6.24$
	σ	(7.8)	(6.4)	$p < .001$
Mother reports	$\bar{X}$	7.1	4.5	$t = 2.29$
	σ	(5.9)	(4.5)	$p < .05$
Occasions absent	$\bar{X}$	11.4	8.5	$t = 2.46$
	σ	(5.5)	(5.7)	$p < .05$
Grade point average‡	$\bar{X}$	4.0	4.8	$t = 2.63$
	σ	(1.3)	(1.5)	$p < .01$

* $N = 93$.

† All t-tests of group mean differences are two-tailed.

‡ On all measures except grade point average, the higher score is the more deviant.

exhibit less evidence of deviant behavior on all measures than do boys, and these differences are all significant at the 5 percent level or better. When academic achievement is conceptualized as an index of conformity to the expectations and demands of adult society, sex differences in grades are understandable in the same terms as sex differences in the other indices; it is not that girls are smarter than boys, they are perhaps just more conforming.

Ethnic group differences on all these measures are presented in Table 8.18. Here, interesting parallels to the high school data on drinking behavior presented in the preceding chapter emerge. On all measures but self-reports and mother reports, Anglo students appear to be the most conforming, Indian students the most deviant, and Spanish students intermediate. *This ordering is identical to that found in the adult community.* In the high school, however, unlike the adult community, ethnic group differences

TABLE 8.18
Ethnic Group Differences in Deviant Behavior: High School Study*

Measure		Means and Standard Deviations			Significance†		
		Anglos (N = 42)	Spanish (N = 36)	Indians (N = 11)	Anglos vs. Spanish	Anglos vs. Indian	Spanish vs. Indian
Teacher	$\bar{X}$	60.3	71.9	82.4	t = 1.32	t = 2.12	t = 0.96
ratings	σ	(36.4)	(39.9)	(29.0)	N.S.	p < .05	N.S.
Peer	$\bar{X}$	61.1	67.3	71.5	t = 0.74	t = 0.96	t = 0.37
ratings	σ	(35.7)	(38.1)	(31.1)	N.S.	N.S.	N.S.
Self-	$\bar{X}$	20.9	20.7	20.3	t = 0.11	t = 0.22	t = 0.14
reports	σ	(8.0)	(9.6)	(8.1)	N.S.	N.S.	N.S.
Mother	$\bar{X}$	7.2	4.5	5.6	t = 2.11	t = 0.76	t = 0.49
reports	σ	(4.8)	(5.7)	(5.9)	p < .05	N.S.	N.S.
Occasions	$\bar{X}$	8.7	9.7	13.4	t = 0.83	t = 3.26	t = 2.47
absent	σ	(5.2)	(5.4)	(4.1)	N.S.	p < .01	p < .05
Grade	$\bar{X}$	5.0	4.2	3.3	t = 2.68	t = 4.33	t = 2.03
point	σ	(1.4)	(1.4)	(1.1)	p < .01	p < .001	N.S.
average‡							

* $N = 93$.

† All *t*-tests of group mean differences are two-tailed. Differences not significant at the .05 level or better are indicated as N.S.

‡ On all measures except grade point average, the higher score is the more deviant.

may well have been reduced by the leveling effect of selective dropouts and the homogenizing effect of the common experiences shared within the high school. Anglo-Indian differences are statistically significant on teacher ratings, absenteeism, and grades, though Anglo-Spanish differences are significant only with regard to grades.

On the self-reports and parent reports, the trend established by the more objective measures either disappears or is reversed. Spanish mothers, in fact, report significantly less deviant behavior by their sons and daughters than do Anglo mothers. The validity of parent and self-report criterion data in the high school has already been questioned on other grounds; the present data raise further doubts.

A general conclusion about the kinds of distortions likely to occur in self-report and parent-report data on socially disapproved behavior can now be made. What appears to happen is that a *leveling* of individual differences (and therefore of group differences) occurs. Those most deviant tend to underreport the most; those least deviant tend to be overly honest in their reports. This general conclusion is in accord with and helps to explain the lack of social class differences in adolescent deviance which Nye and Short found on the basis of their self-report data (1957). Their conclusion that there are no class differences in adolescent delinquency, running counter to much accumulated evidence from a variety of sources, is, in light of the considerations we have raised, perhaps not justified.

The Construction of Global Deviance
Measures in the High School Study

The evidence which has been accumulated points strongly to the conclusion that our most valid criterion measures among the high school students are the teacher ratings and the peer ratings. Furthermore, these ratings are in certain respects complementary: Teachers and peers each have access to information about student behavior which is not generally available to the other group. A combination of these two ratings, therefore, seemed likely to yield a global rating of deviant behavior for high school students which would have some conceptual similarity to the Global Deviance classification developed for the community adults. It has the advantage, further, of being operationally distinct from any measure to be employed in the predictive scheme.

To accomplish this classification, those students in the upper (deviant) quartile of the teacher ratings and the upper (deviant) quartile of the peer ratings were identified. Any student who appeared in *either* of these two groups was placed in the "deviant" category. With this procedure, no student could be classified as "deviant" because of difficulties with a single teacher or one or two classmates since he could not fall into the upper quartile of either of these two ratings without agreement among a *number* of raters that he belonged there. Yet the complementarity of the two types of ratings is preserved: Misbehavior which comes to the attention of *either* teachers or classmates can result in classification as deviant.

The approach described resulted in 34 students out of 93 being allocated to the Global Deviance category, a percentage of 37. This figure is roughly of the same magnitude as that for the Community Survey sample which, it will be recalled, was 41 percent.

The two criterion measures based on school records—grade point average and occasions absent—also appear to have a respectable degree of validity as more indirect measures of student conformity-deviance. These two indices were, therefore, also combined into a single School Adjustment measure, in order that greater stability and breadth of coverage could be achieved than could be provided by either index alone. For this index, student positions on each measure were rank-ordered, the ranks added, and the sums reranked. The total distribution was then simply dichotomized, and the low group was designated as having Poor School Adjustment. This measure has the advantages of being operationally distinct from the other Global Deviance measure in the high school and of being based on daily observations of the student's behavior over a relatively extended period of time. It thereby avoids the possibility of a student being classified as "deviant" because of atypical but noteworthy behavior displayed close to the time at which our ratings were collected.

These two global measures categorize over 80 percent of the students in the same way. It is not surprising, therefore, that sex and ethnic group distributions on these measures, presented in Table 8.19, are quite similar. On the Global Deviance measure, the obtained sex differences would occur by chance less than once in a thousand and on Poor School Adjustment, less than once in a hundred. On both measures, ethnic differences are found which order groups in the same way as did most individual measures

TABLE 8.19

Sex and Ethnic Group Differences in Two Global Measures of Deviant Behavior: High School Study

	Proportion Deviant	
Group	Global Deviance	Poor School Adjustment
Males ($N = 47$)	.60	.64
Females ($N = 46$)	.13	.35
Anglos ($N = 42$)	.29	.38
Spanish ($N = 36$)	.42	.50
Indians ($N = 11$)	.45	.91
Anglo males ($N = 22$)	.45	.55
Anglo females ($N = 20$)	.10	.20
Spanish males ($N = 15$)	.80	.73
Spanish females ($N = 21$)	.14	.33
Indian males ($N = 6$)	.67	.83
Indian females ($N = 5$)	.20	1.00

in both the high school and the adult community: Anglos are the most conforming, Spanish less, Indians, even less. Here, however, these differences are not statistically significant.

SUMMARY AND CONCLUSIONS

In this chapter, a variety of criteria intended to measure non-drinking-related deviant behavior among adults and high school students in the research community has been presented.

Among adults, a self-report measure was constructed based on the subject's responses to the question "How many times have you . . ." engaged in a variety of non-alcohol related but socially disapproved acts. These ranged from being "stopped for speeding" to having "taken things that didn't belong to you," and included interpersonal quarrels or fights with family or friends, problems on the job, sexual transgressions, child neglect, nonpayment of debts, and any type of non-alcohol-connected trouble with the law. This measure correlated with various drinking measures at about the .2 level, statistically significant, but not substantial, suggesting that the measure may be getting at an aspect of the deviant behavior domain not tapped by the various drinking measures.

Records of criminal convictions of members of the research community for crimes committed at any time during the preceding ten years were collected from essentially all courts in and around the study area. Since 87 percent of these convictions were recorded to be alcohol connected, it is encouraging to have found that, for adults, correlations between number of court convictions and various self-report drinking measures ranged from .35 to .50.

The local high school presented an unusual opportunity to obtain criterion data on adolescent deviance from a number of independent sources. Self-reports of "how often" students had engaged in a series of deviant acts were collected to develop a measure similar to the adult scale in general design, although different in content, making it appropriate to adolescent life. In addition to these self-reports, behavioral ratings were obtained from teachers and peers, mother reports on their children's deviance were elicited in an interview, and school records on absenteeism and academic achievement were compiled. These several and independent sources of data permitted a convergence upon student deviance by which confidence in most of the measures could be established. Correlations among the measures ranged from .75 (teacher *versus* peer ratings) to .18 (mother reports *versus* grade point average), with the majority being .5 or better. Only mother reports of their high school children's deviant behavior exhibited substantial evidence of nonvalidity.

In both the Community Survey and the High School studies, males exhibited far more deviant behavior than did females on all of the measures. Ethnic group differences were also similar within both the adult community and the high school. Except for mother reports of their children's deviance and these students' reports of their own non-alcohol-related deviance, all measures provided the same pattern: Anglos exhibited the least deviant behavior, Indians the most, and Spanish were intermediate. In general, Anglo-Spanish differences, though consistent in direction, were statistically nonsignificant, and the largest difference was between the Indians and the non-Indians.

The variety of measures presented in this report converging on the same general behavioral domain and the demonstrated agreement among these indices provide criterion measurement in which substantial confidence can be placed. To provide a summary indicator of these separate measures, criterion *groups* were established; these were based on as wide a net of measurement as we could cast. Since the explanatory scheme employed in the Tri-Ethnic project does not specify the *type* of deviance which various social and psychological factors might generate, such summary indices should provide the most reliable and inclusive criteria for testing the adequacy of the theoretical scheme.

Among adults, a subject was placed in the deviant category if he reported having been drunk more than fifteen times in the last year, if he reported two or more instances of drinking-related problem behavior, or a serious incident of non-drinking-related deviance, or if he had a court record of criminal conviction during the last ten years for other than traffic or game law violations. In the high school, a subject was placed in the deviant category if he fell in the top quartile of either the teacher ratings or the peer ratings of student deviance. A second summary measure for high school students, Global School Adjustment, was based on combined grade point average and occasions absent. The resulting distribution was dichotomized into "good" and "poor" school adjustment. Thus, the criterion category among adults is not wholly dependent upon self-report data and, in the high school, both criterion indices are completely independent of students' self-reports. Among adult and high school subjects, the percentage falling into these deviance categories ordered the ethnic groups in the same manner as did most of the individual criterion measures; thus, the categories appear to represent adequate summaries of the latter.

Now that reasonably valid measures of several forms of problem behavior have been established, efforts can be directed toward the next task of the research, an examination of the sociocultural and personality variables which were hypothesized to give rise to and support this variety of deviant behavior. In the following two chapters, the measurement of these variables will be described. Only after that, in Chapter 11, will it be possible to assess directly the adequacy of the explanatory scheme.

In that assessment, the measures described in the present and preceding chapters will serve as the criteria to be accounted for.

REFERENCES

CLARK, J. P. AND L. L. TIFFT. Polygraph and interview validation of self-reported deviant behavior. *American Sociological Review,* 1966, *31,* 516–526.

LAZARSFELD, P. F. AND W. S. ROBINSON. The quantification of case studies. *Journal of Applied Psychology,* 1940, *24,* 817–825.

NYE, F. I. AND J. F. SHORT, JR. Scaling delinquent behavior. *American Sociological Review,* 1957, *22,* 326–331.

SHORT, J. F., JR. AND F. I. NYE. Reported behavior as a criterion of deviant behavior. *Social Problems,* 1957, *5,* 207–213.

STEWART, O. C. Questions regarding American Indian criminality. *Human Organization,* 1964, *23,* 61–66.

PART FIVE

Results: Establishing the Predictor Variables

CHAPTER NINE

The Measurement of the Sociocultural System

The social-psychological framework described in the earlier chapters included three sociocultural structures which were theoretically related to deviance. The basic sociocultural proposition specified that the magnitude of deviance rates at a given location in society will vary directly with the degree of value-access disjunction in the opportunity structure, anomie in the normative structure, and access to illegitimate means in the social control structure characterizing that location. In the present chapter, the way each of the sociocultural structures was measured and the relationship of the measures to each other and to sex and ethnic group status are described. Besides contributing in this way to the general problem of measurement of the sociocultural environment, an important task in behavioral science, the chapter prepares the ground for the testing, in Chapter 11, of the basic proposition about the relation of the sociocultural environment to deviance.

Although the Community Survey and High School studies were designed to be conceptually parallel, differences in the subject populations demanded differences in the operations by which each variable was measured. These population differences also permitted a division of labor in the development of measures: The Community Survey Study served as the main vehicle for the construction of *sociocultural* measures and the High School Study for the development and refinement of *personality* measures. Consequently, in this chapter, the approach to measuring each sociocultural structure will be presented, first, for the Community Survey Study, where it was initially developed, and second, for the parallel measure employed in the High School Study. In the following chapter, on the personality system, this order of presentation will be reversed.

THE MEASUREMENT
OF THE OPPORTUNITY STRUCTURE

The importance of location in the opportunity structure follows from the theoretical assumption that it reflects a source of pressure toward deviance. When success goals are emphasized throughout society while the structure of opportunity for the legitimate achievement of such goals is not equally available, then pressure is generated to adopt alternative, even if illegitimate, means to reach those goals. Further, the pressure should be greatest where the access is most limited or, in other terms, where the discrepancy between values and legitimate access to them is largest.

The opportunity structure refers, then, to the differential availability of legitimate channels of access to the valued goals of American culture. These channels include education, income, and group memberships. The person who has had a good education, receives high income from his occupational position, and has membership ties to important community organizations is considered to have legitimate access to culturally emphasized goals such as prestige, wealth, and power; he stands high in the opportunity structure. There is relatively little pressure for him to use illegitimate means as alternatives to attain valued goals. On the other hand, a person who has had a meager education, receives little or no income from employment, and belongs to no important community organizations illustrates the case of an obvious disjunction or discrepancy between the goals of prestige, wealth, or power and the legitimate channels of access which he has to them; he stands low in the opportunity structure. Relatively more pressure for him to employ illegitimate means as alternatives to achieve success goals is conceived to exist.

The opportunity structure is obviously related conceptually to the class structure of American society: Persons higher in position in the class structure can be seen to have most access to the legitimate means of achieving goals, while persons low in the class structure have least access to such means. Consequently, the greatest degree of value-access disjunction, and, therefore, the greatest pressure toward the use of illegitimate means, should be found in the lower positions of the class structure.

With respect to the research community, the general description of the three ethnic groups presented in Chapter 1 indicated that the Anglos as a group have achieved the most power and prestige in the community and are economically dominant. As a group, therefore, and relative to the two minority groups, the Anglos would seem to occupy a position high in the opportunity structure and to be characterized by the least value-access disjunction. With respect to the two minority groups, the Indians appear to have access to a larger number of positions of power and prestige than the Spanish. This is due to the existence of the tribal bureaucratic structure and the opportunities it offers for employment, leadership, and status. In addition, the per capita payments contribute to Indian income and, thereby, to the availability of economic resources. For the Spanish, there are available positions of leadership in the social organizations of the Catholic Church and also a limited number of positions in community education and governmental activities. But with respect to purely economic resources, the Spanish seem most limited, farming a larger portion of marginal, unirrigated land and having the greater share of unemployment.

These readily apparent differences between the ethnic groups are not sufficient for our present purposes, however; what is needed is a more precise and reliable measure of location in the opportunity structure, a measure which can be used to locate an individual as well as a group. The importance of the latter requirement derives from our interest in testing, *within* ethnic groups, the influence of variation in location in the opportunity structure. The problem of measuring an individual's position in the opportunity structure becomes that of determining, directly or indirectly, his access to or restriction from legitimate modes for reaching American success goals.

The Community Survey Study

Measurement of the opportunity structure involved the construction of two indexes applicable to individuals: an index of Socioeconomic Status (SES) and an index of Objective Access (OA) in the opportunity structure. The availability of two types of measures enables a consideration of their convergence upon the concept of location in the opportunity structure or, more precisely, upon the concept of value-access disjunction. Both measures are indexes of *access*, not of values; the assumption, which was discussed in Chapter 3, was that success values are pervasively urged and shared throughout American society. The magnitude of value-access disjunction in such a case—that is, where values are shared—should vary directly with variation in access alone.

The Socioeconomic Status Index

A Socioeconomic Status index based on education and job type (and often including such closely related variables as income and neighborhood) has been widely employed by sociologists as an indicator of class status and opportunity. Among our adult subjects the education of the subject and the occupation of the breadwinner in the household correlated .34.[1] These two variables were then combined in the manner suggested by

---

[1] This level of correlation was maintained within both the Anglo and Indian groups separately, but essentially disappeared among the Spanish. This suggests that education may not be serving as a vehicle for occupational mobility as much as many Spanish probably believe.

Hollingshead (1956) for a two-factor Index of Social Position, with education receiving a weighting of 4 and occupation a weighting of 7.[2]

The Measure of Objective Access

In the second measure of position in the opportunity structure, Objective Access, an attempt was made to map a broader class of factors. In this effort we were influenced by and relied heavily upon the earlier work of Meier and Bell (1959) in which they sought to devise an index of access to the achievement of life goals. Twelve items were devised which on a priori grounds were felt to be relevant within the tri-ethnic community. Because of a later decision not to include sex or ethnicity within any of our measures, so as to be able to test for sex and ethnic differences, these two items were eliminated. Subsequent item analysis and a concern to reduce internal redundancy led to the elimination of two more. The final scale consisted of eight dichotomous variables, yielding OA scores running from 0, no favorable access attributes, to 8, all favorable access attributes. These items, their internal splits, and biserial correlations with total score are presented in Table 9.1.

The conceptual relation of each of these indicators to location in the opportunity structure can be described very briefly as follows. A younger person has more objective access than an older one since he still has a chance to achieve presently unobtained goals in the future and since youth itself is responded to socially as an asset in socio-occupational life, whereas the older person's chances are diminishing, and age tends to be seen as a limitation in many areas of social life. Those elderly persons who have never married or who have lost their spouses have even less access to such life goals as successful child-rearing, family participation, social involvement with others, and even occupational success. Persons who speak English as the natural language of the home are less handicapped in securing a good education and better paying jobs than persons who have learned English as a second language and who use another primary language in the home; for the latter, language signifies a large number of other attributes of minority group status, all conceived to hinder

[2] Education categories were scaled as follows: 1. No school 2. Some elementary school 3. Eighth grade completed 4. Some high school 5. Completed high school 6. Some college or special training after high school 7. Completed college. Each scale score is weighted by 4, yielding a range of 4–28. Occupation categories were scaled as follows: 1. Solely on welfare, allotment, or per capita 2. Unskilled workers 3. Semiskilled workers 4. Skilled workers and foremen 5. Clerks and kindred workers 6. Proprietors, managers (including farmers and ranchers), and officials 7. Professionals. Each scale score is weighted by 7, yielding a score range of 7–49.

The SES score consists of the sum of the weighted scaled education and occupation categories. Thus, a person who has completed high school and runs a retail store would have a score of $5 \times 4 = 20$ plus $6 \times 7 = 42$, which sum to 62.

TABLE 9.1
Items Included in the Objective Access Index: Community Survey Study*

Item	Proportion	Item-Total Score Biserial†
1. Age		
0 = 40 and over	49	.41
1 = under 40	51	
2. Age plus marital status		
0 = 40 and single	09	.69
1 = under 40 and/or married	91	
3. Language spoken in present home		
0 = any other than English	55	.85
1 = English only	45	
4. Occupation		
0 = unskilled or unemployed	34	.76
1 = semiskilled or higher	66	
5. Education		
0 = eighth grade or less	35	.69
1 = at least some high school	65	
6. Between-generation mobility	/	
0 = present job has lower status than father's job	35	
1 = present job has same or higher status than father's job	65	.56
7. Religion		
0 = no affiliation, or affiliation other than "Old-Line Protestant"	70	
1 = "Old-Line Protestant": Episcopalian, Presbyterian, Methodist, Lutheran, Congregational	30	.73
8. Social participation		
0 = no formal group participation, *and* four or less informal visits with friends or relatives per month	49	.55
1 = other	51	

* $N = 221$.

† Biserial correlations have been corrected to remove the effect of each item on total score; see Henrysson (1963). A program for this purpose was written for the IBM 709; see Castellan and Link (1963).

access. A person who has moved up in the occupational hierarchy from the position of his parents, or one who has remained at the same position, is likely to have more skills and resources, and to be seen by others in this way, than one who has moved down from the position of his parents. Those who belong to the higher-status Protestant churches have a greater opportunity to gain and hold community prestige than those who have affiliations with the less prestigeful congregations or those who have no religious affiliation at all. The goals of strong friendships, prestige, and positions of respect and influence are more available to persons who participate in formal or informal social groups than to persons who do not. Finally, both a higher education, which increases the chances of earning higher income, and is itself already an achievement receiving social approbation, and a higher occupational position, which produces a higher income and defines a higher social status, increase the objective chances for gaining valued goals legitimately.

The Objective Access scale consists, in summary, of eight dichotomized variables, each one an attribute of an individual relevant to his degree of legitimate access to socially valued goals. In addition to variables like education and occupation which relate clearly to goals of wealth and power, it includes variables relevant to less tangible but nevertheless socially valued goals such as friendship, status, and prestige. OA scores based upon interview responses were devised for each respondent in the Community Survey Study.[3]

Relation of Value-Access Disjunction to Sex and Ethnic Status

It is possible now to consider the two measures of location in the opportunity structure in relation to ethnic status, a criterion about which rather clear-cut expectations exist and which, therefore, can serve as an indication of initial ("known-group") validity for the measures. The relevant data are presented in Table 9.2. There is no reason to anticipate that males and females should differ in objective access, and, in fact, no differences were found. The sexes have therefore been combined for tests of ethnic group differences in the lower part of the table.

With respect to the measure of Socioeconomic Status, there are clear-cut and significant differences among all three ethnic groups. In the class structure of the community, as measured by occupation and education, the Anglos hold the highest position and come, therefore, theoretically, under the least amount of pressure to use illegitimate means for goal attainment, while the reverse is true for the Spanish. As a group, the Spanish hold the lowest socioeconomic position in the community and, theoretically, are subject, therefore, to the most pressure to use illegitimate means to achieve goals. The Indians stand in an intermediate position on this measure, but are closer to the Spanish than to the Anglos.

---

[3] Since the OA scale includes the components of the SES scale, a test of convergence between them is not meaningful. As Kahl and Davis (1955) have shown, however, most measures of socioeconomic status or class position correlate highly with each other and with such standard objective variables as education and occupation.

The measure of Objective Access also demonstrates that the Anglos have a significantly higher average access position than either the Indians or the Spanish. When additional access factors—notably marital status, social participation, and between-generation mobility—are taken into account, however, there is no longer a significant difference in access position in the opportunity structure between the Indians and the Spanish. In comparison with the majority Anglo group, members of both minority groups show significantly fewer of the attributes associated with the objective possibility of achieving goals through the use of legitimate means.

TABLE 9.2

Sex and Ethnic Differences in Two Measures of Location in the Opportunity Structure: Community Survey Study*

Group		Means and Standard Deviations		Group	Significance of Difference	
		Socio-economic Status	Objective Access		Socio-economic Status	Objective Access
Males	$\bar{X}$	43.3	4.4			
($N = 110$)	σ	(16.7)	(2.0)	Males *vs.* Females	$t = 0.78$ N.S.	$t = 1.10$ N.S.
Females	$\bar{X}$	41.5	4.9			
($N = 111$)	σ	(16.4)	(1.8)			
Angles	$\bar{X}$	43.1	6.0			
($N = 93$)	σ	(13.9)	(1.4)	Anglos *vs.* Spanish	$t = 7.92$ $p < .001$	$t = 10.63$ $p < .001$
Spanish	$\bar{X}$	25.0	3.4			
($N = 60$)	σ	(13.6)	(1.5)	Anglos *vs.* Indians	$t = 4.66$ $p < .001$	$t = 8.59$ $p < .001$
Indians	$\bar{X}$	31.5	3.8			
($N = 68$)	σ	(16.7)	(1.7)	Spanish *vs.* Indians	$t = 2.39$ $p < .02$	$t = 1.39$ N.S.

* $N = 221$. All *t*-tests of group mean differences are two-tailed. Differences not significant at the .05 level or better are indicated as N.S.

These findings from the Community Survey Study corroborate our general expectations about relative positions of the three ethnic groups with respect to value-access disjunction in the community. Whether considering a fairly standard measure of social class position (SES) or a more comprehensive mapping of the various channels of legitimate objective access (OA), the results are essentially the same: The Anglos occupy the position of greatest access to opportunity relative to the two minority groups. Between the two minority groups, the Indians are somewhat more favored than the Spanish in objective opportunity. The results are in accord with prior expectations; theoretically, they imply that the greater pressure toward the use of illegitimate means is upon the minority groups, somewhat more upon the Spanish than upon the Indians.

The High School Study

As a result of the already mentioned division of labor between the Community Survey and the High School studies, less effort was expended initially in developing measures of the sociocultural structures in which the students were embedded. As a result, we found ourselves engaged in more *post hoc* analysis of sociocultural variables in the High School Study than was true for the adult study. Clearly, better and conceptually more relevant data might have been obtained had this division of labor not been operative.

Other important differences between the High School and the Community Survey studies obtain, and this is perhaps the best time to make them clear since their implications will extend not only to the opportunity structure but also to the other sociocultural structures to be dealt with later on.

First, there is much greater heterogeneity in the population of adults as compared to the relative homogeneity that exists among the students. For example, whereas the age range among adults spans about forty-five years, the age range among the students covers only five years. Further, the students interact continuously throughout the school year as participants within the same social institution. No corresponding institution exists for the adults which requires such sustained and compulsory participation from the members of the community. Thus, students spend a large portion of their time in a situation contributing in many ways to the establishment of common values, norms, and social experiences; whereas for the adults in the community, their routine activities tend to deepen the already existing differences. As the years since leaving the common experience of the school system increase, so does the ethnic group separation and the heterogeneity among former classmates.

In addition, certain of the important sociocultural attributes of the high school-age youth inevitably derive from and are defined by the attributes of their parents or their family. Related to this is the fact that the role of the high school student is one which is transitional between the worlds of childhood and adulthood. Standards of success that apply to an adult member of the community are not yet applicable to the student. For example, it makes sense to say that, within the community structure, the high school student *is* a success, at least when compared with the teen-aged school dropout who has moved into the community social system as a competitor for jobs and status. The pressure to engage in the use of illegitimate means to attain goals falls with full force on the dropout, who has, by cutting off his education, lost a significant legitimate means for upward mobility.

These considerations raised an important problem for the measurement of the high school student's location in the opportunity structure. Given that a student can be considered simultaneously to occupy positions in *two* opportunity structures, that of the community at large and that of the high school social system, which position should be measured? Since we have earlier described the community opportunity system, something should be said about opportunity or value-access disjunction within the high school before giving an answer to that question.

The students who achieve success *within* the high school social system are those who attain the prestigeful leadership positions. These include the star athletes, class and student government leaders, high academic performers, and social club leaders. Technically, achievement of these positions does not depend on one's background position in the community opportunity structure. An affluent Anglo student whose background puts him high in the opportunity structure of the community may, for example, lack athletic ability, be a poor student, and suffer the dislike of many of his classmates. Within the world of the high school, he would be frustrated in attempts to follow legitimate paths to high school success goals. Consequently, he would be under pressure to use illegitimate means to attain valued goals of prestige, status, and power in the high school social system. More generally, it might be argued that, while disjunctions between the distant goals of high social status, prestige, or power in the community and present access do exist differentially among the students, it is unlikely that such a potential dynamic is as powerful for the instigation of current deviant behavior as disjunction between aspirations and access *within* the immediate situation, for example, between the desire and ability to be a student political leader, athletic star, cheerleader, top academic performer, or member of a prestigious, "wild" clique.

Although there is considerable validity in this interpretation, our own choice was to locate each student within the opportunity structure not of the school system but of the larger community. The reasons for this go beyond the simple but important one of maintaining the parallel with the Community Survey Study. It was felt that, whatever his position within the school system, each student daily engaged in, was aware of, and was defined by the larger community situation. Such confrontation could not be ignored, either as a more general source of social learning or as a more particular source of pressure toward deviance. The Indian basketball star is not without acute awareness that, when his high school days are over, many of the other students will continue on to college and to good jobs in life without him.

In addition to these considerations, the very chances of success in the high school are at least partly dependent on one's background position in the larger opportunity structure of the community. Those students with a background position low in the community opportunity structure are those most likely to have experienced cultural deprivation in the home, to be relatively unaware of the world of books and scholarship, to suffer a language handicap, and to be deprived of the free time to engage in athletics or extracurricular activities. Furthermore, such students are less likely to have easy access to spending money or a car, which are important in establishing high-status friendships and social leadership. In other words, those most handicapped in ability to use legitimate means toward the attainment of goals within the high school tend to be those whose parents stand in the disadvantaged positions in the opportunity structure of the larger community.

In view of these considerations, the decision was made to define each student with primary reference to the community opportunity structure and to employ a measure of Socioeconomic Status similar to that employed in the Community Survey Study. What this means is that the position in the opportunity structure of a high school student derives from the status and attributes of his *parents*. It is to be expected, therefore, that the relative positions of high school ethnic groups in the opportunity structure will reflect the positions of these groups in the community as a whole. Theoretically, the expectation is that minority group students will be under greater pressure to use illegitimate means in goal attainment than the more socially and economically advantaged Anglo students.

The Socioeconomic Status Measure

Only one indicator of position within the opportunity structure was developed for high school students, but more information was available on which it could be based (see Shybut, 1963). Five separate indicators of SES were combined. These included *father's occupation,* scored exactly as among adults, and *family income,* where 1 = under $2000 per year, 2 = $2000–4000, 3 = $4000–6000, 4 = $6000–8000, 5 = $8000–10,000, 6 = $10,000–15,000 and 7 = over $15,000. A *room/person index,* the ratio of the number of rooms in the subject's house (not including bathrooms) divided by the number of family members occupying them, was also included. Finally, *father's education* and *mother's education,* both scored as among adults, were used. Pearson correlations among these five variables are presented in Table 9.3. Note that these relationships are all substantial, averaging in the forties, though the room/person index seems the weakest. Each of these five measures was then dichotomized at the median, and each student was assigned an SES score equal to the number of measures on which his family fell above the median (range:0–5).

TABLE 9.3
**Product-Moment (Pearson) Correlations among
Five Indices of Location in the Opportunity Structure:
High School Study***

	1	2	3	4	5
1. Father's occupation					
2. Family income	.68				
3. Room/person index	.32	.21			
4. Father's education	.47	.46	.35		
5. Mother's education	.54	.56	.24	.53	

* N = 93, for which a correlation of .17 is significant at
the .05 level, one-tailed test.

Sex and Ethnic Group Differences in Value-Access Disjunction

As among the adults, sex group differences in socioeconomic status are minimal; sex groups have, therefore, been combined. But ethnic differences are dramatic. Anglos have an average SES score of 3.69 (standard deviation, s.d. = 1.37), the mean for the Spanish is 1.53 (s.d. = 1.46) and the Indian mean is 1.82 (s.d. = 1.47). Thus, the three ethnic groups in the high school are ordered in exactly the same way as in the adult community, Anglos highest, and Indians slightly higher than Spanish. Anglo–non-Anglo differences are highly significant statistically (t = 6.70, $p < .001$ for Anglos *versus* Spanish; t = 3.81, $p < .01$ for Anglos *versus* Indians). As with the OA measure in the adult study, the Spanish-Indian difference in the High School Study was not significant (t = 0.57).

In summary, the approach to measuring location in the opportunity structure began with the assumption that success values in American society were quite pervasively shared and that the magnitude of value-access disjunction would, therefore, vary directly with the degree of legitimate access available to a person. Two measures of access were employed among adults: One was a relatively standard index of socioeconomic status based upon occupation and education; the other was an attempt at a more comprehensive mapping of legitimate access to success goals. Among high school students, only an index of socioeconomic status was developed. The results in both studies are essentially identical. The Anglos, as expected, emerge as occupying a substantially higher position in the opportunity structure than the non-Anglos. Among adult non-Anglos, the Indians are somewhat favored over the Spanish, but this difference is statistically significant only for the SES measure; in the high school, the Spanish-Indian difference is also nonsignificant.

The obviousness of these findings should not deprive them of significance. First of all, it is this very obviousness of the outcome, that is, the ordering of the ethnic groups, which is a source of validity for the measures of access. This degree of validity enables us to employ the access measures with some degree of confidence in the major task of the research, that is, as *individual* parameters in the prediction of deviance. Our confidence in the measures derives from two other facts. Within one study, alternative operations yielded similar results; and across two studies with quite different subjects and measures, the results were also essentially identical.

Theoretically, these findings imply greater pressure toward deviance upon the non-Anglo groups, somewhat more upon the Spanish. But actual *engagement* in deviant behavior is dependent not only upon pressure but also upon controls. The nature and operation of the latter are perhaps less familiar in discussions of the social environment and are certainly less obvious to the eye than is the nature and operation of access or opportunity. The problem of measurement of one of these major sources of control, location in the normative structure, will now be taken up.

THE MEASUREMENT OF THE NORMATIVE STRUCTURE

The aspect of the normative structure described in Chapter 3 as most relevant to deviant behavior was the degree of anomie which obtains at and characterizes various locations in that structure. Anomie refers to the relative absence of consensus around the norms for appropriate behavior in various situations. In the absence of normative consensus, the control over behavior usually exerted by norms is lacking, a state of de-regulation (see Durkheim, 1951) exists, and, theoretically, the likelihood of deviant behavior is thereby increased. For our purposes, the relevant problem of measuring location in the normative structure becomes, then, the problem of measuring anomie.

Perhaps the most fundamental consideration in any measurement approach to the concept of anomie stems from Durkheim's insistence upon its essentially sociological character. Merton (1957) has maintained this emphasis in his analytic extensions of the anomie concept, and his most recent elaboration of the nature of anomie is worth quoting in full:

> The first thing to note about the sociological concept of anomie is that it is—sociological. Anomie refers to a property of a social system, not to the state of mind of this or that individual within the system. It refers to a breakdown of social standards governing behavior and so also signifies little social cohesion. When a high degree of anomie has set in, the rules once governing conduct have lost their savor and their force. Above all else, they are deprived of legitimacy. They do not comprise a social order in

which men can confidently put their trust. For there is no longer a widely shared sense within the social system, large or small, of what goes and what does not go, of what is justly allowed by way of behavior and of what is justly prohibited, of what may be legitimately expected of people in the course of social interaction. . . . In a word, the degree of anomie in a social system is indicated by the extent to which there is a lack of consensus on norms judged to be legitimate, with its attendant uncertainty and insecurity in social relations. For if norms are not shared, then one cannot know what to expect of the other, and this is a social condition admirably suited for producing insecure relations with others.

Anomie, then, is a condition of the social surround, not a condition of particular people. People are *confronted* by substantial anomie when, as a matter of objective fact, they cannot rely upon a high probability that the behavior of others will be in rough accord with standards *jointly* regarded as legitimate (Merton, 1964, pp. 226–227).

As we noted in Chapter 3, researchers have not always been guided by these conceptual requirements; the most frequent approach to measurement of anomie has been to rely upon an individual psychological measure, usually of anomia or alienation, as an indirect index of anomie. But, as Yinger notes, "To measure individual responses to a brief test is relatively easy; to devise independent measures of normlessness as a property of a social system is exceedingly difficult" (1965, p. 205). It was the latter, however, which we hoped to accomplish.

A conceptually valid measure of anomie seemed to us to require at least a subset of norms, that is, some domain of normative content, and some assessment of the degree of consensus within an interacting group with respect to that normative subset. The assessment of consensus clearly implicates a property of a social group and cannot be interpreted as having an individual reference. The problems were twofold: to generate a subset of norms and to devise measures of consensus. But a further consideration cannot be avoided, namely, that normative content and the degree of anomie associated with that content varies in different interaction systems. A person may be confronted by substantial anomie while riding the subway in New York City, not knowing what to expect from his fellow passengers, but be confronted with little anomie while attending a religious service with other members of his group, where each knows what he and the others are to do from moment to moment.

It was this latter consideration which led to the delineation of two types of anomie which could be operative within the tri-ethnic community.

These two types of anomie correspond to two cultural structures which can be at least conceptually distinguished in the community. The first of these is the ethnic subculture which refers to and regulates the interactions of the members of the ethnic group and contains norms which are not necessarily well known to or accepted by the members of the other ethnic groups. *Lack of consensus among members of an ethnic group around its own norms is referred to as subcultural anomie.* The local community structure, partly common to all three ethnic groups as a result of their continuous social interaction over several generations, but clearly dominated by the customs, institutions, and expectations of the Anglo majority group, suggests the second type of anomie. *Lack of consensus around the community (Anglo) norms is referred to as community anomie.*

Every citizen in the research community is exposed, to some extent, to both of these structures or interaction systems and to the anomie which obtains in them. The degree of anomie in each structure may vary, of course, from absent to pervasive. At one theoretical extreme, a group would be totally normatively integrated, and behavior would be consistently regulated, when every member was in agreement with every other member on all relevant standards of behavior. If presented with a set of possible alternative choices about how to behave in a given situation, all members of the group would select the same response. The distribution of responses, therefore, would have no variance, since all persons in the group would have given the same modal response. On a set of test items representing the relevant normative content, there would be complete consensus and certainty among members about how one should behave in each problematic situation presented. Under these circumstances, normative regulation of behavior is unquestioned, and anomie is completely absent.

At the other theoretical extreme, total anomie would be represented by a group in which members demonstrate a complete lack of consensus on how to behave in given situations. Given a test with a representative set of normative items describing problematic situations, there would be no modal response patterns for the group, no consensus or certainty, no evidence of normative regulation of behavior within the group. In actual social life, of course, neither theoretical extreme is likely ever to be observed. Rather, we would expect group response patterns to vary in the *degree of consensus* they show around empirically defined modal categories of normative behavior.

It was this reasoning which led to defining the basic requirement for the anomie measure as the assessment of the degree of consensus or group agreement which obtained around a subset of norms. The referent for the assessment of consensus is the group, hence, the measure must indicate some characteristic of the distribution of the group's responses.

The Community Survey Study[4]

The Measurement of Subcultural and Community Anomie

In trying to capture the structural fact of anomie in our measurement, the first task we confronted was the accumulation of a set of items, each describing some ordinary behavior within some common family, sex, social, or occupational role which could be presented to respondents in an interview situation. An item pool was constructed to represent behavior choice situations around which norms could be expected to obtain in a group. All items contain descriptions of behavior in roles common to social life in communities throughout the nation. In other words, it was assumed that the problematic situation described in each item was confronted by all ethnic groups in an American community. Pretesting of these items in another multiethnic community resulted in discarding items on which virtually complete consensus was shown. The remaining set of items, twenty-one in all, generated a large range of variation in consensus for both Anglo and minority ethnic groups in the pretest. It was these twenty-one items, shown in Table 9.4, which were used in the Group Norms measure in the Community Survey interview to assess both subcultural and community anomie. The assumption made was that the twenty-one items were a sample which could reflect the character of consensus in the normative structure as a whole.

For each item presented, the respondent was asked:

> "Would you say this was something (she) (he) Absolutely Should; Should; May or May Not; Should Not; or Absolutely Should Not Do?"

It can be seen that the first two response categories indicate the behavior to be prescribed, the third category indicates it to be permitted, and the last two categories indicate it to be proscribed. The responses of an ethnic group to an item will be distributed in some way across these five response categories or, when collapsed, across the three categories of *prescribed, permitted,* or *proscribed.*[5] That category in which the largest proportion of responses fall is the mode, *and the mode is used in our analyses as the empirical norm for the group on that item.* The remainder of the responses will be distributed in the other categories and will represent *the degree of consensus around the modal category or norm,* our referent

---

[4] For a variety of reasons, including logistical ones, anomie was not measured in the High School Study. The data on the normative structure in this research, therefore, stem entirely from the Community Survey Study.

[5] Our analyses of consensus were carried out in both ways, that is, on a five-category and a three-category distribution. Since the results are essentially identical, only the three-category analysis is presented here.

TABLE 9.4
Measures of Subcultural Anomie and Community Anomie Based on the Group Norms Items of the Community Survey Interview

I Group Norm Item*	II Ethnic Group (Anglo, Spanish, Indian)	III Group Mode (Prescribed, Permitted, Proscribed)	IV Strength of Group Norm (Percent in Modal Category)	V Subcultural Anomie (Variance around Own Group Mode)	VI Uncertainty of Group Norm (Relative Entropy, R)	VII Community Anomie (Variance around Anglo Mode)
1. A teen-age daughter obeys her parents without question. (N.S.)	A	Pre	88	.19	.39	.19
	S	Pre	88	.22	.40	.22
	I	Pre	87	.42	.42	.42
2. The husband by himself makes all important money decisions for the family. ($<.001$)	A	Pro	49	.93	.90	.93
	S	Pre	46	1.81	.89	1.95
	I	Pre	40	1.56	.99	1.89
3. Even with close friends a man keeps his real feelings to himself. ($<.001$)	A	Per	42	.58	.99	.58
	S	Pro	47	1.90	.81	.93
	I	Pre	48	1.56	.97	.84
4. A mother follows closely the teachings of her religion. ($<.01$)	A	Pre	75	.28	.56	.28
	S	Pre	96	.09	.16	.09
	I	Pre	77	.37	.88	.37
5. When a mother has many children and the family is poor, she gives a child away to be raised by relatives. ($<.01$)	A	Pro	76	.41	.62	.41
	S	Pro	86	.34	.45	.34
	I	Pro	58	1.00	.88	1.00

No.	Item		Pre/Pro				
6.	A farmer uses the *old* farming methods because they have usually worked in the past. (<.001)	A	Pro	66	.44	.68	.44
		S	Pro	54	1.51	.77	1.51
		I	Pro	45	1.42	.97	1.42
7.	A policeman ignores a drunk person unless some actual damage has been done. (<.001)	A	Pro	71	.65	.72	.65
		S	Pro	53	1.71	.78	1.71
		I	Pro	47	1.89	.83	1.89
8.	When a girl is dating a man she really likes, she lets him go all the way with her. (<.001)	A	Pro	97	.03	.13	.03
		S	Pro	92	.29	.30	.29
		I	Pro	74	.69	.68	.69
9.	An unmarried young man spends most of his time studying and learning things that will help him get ahead in life. (N.S.)	A	Pre	77	.49	.63	.49
		S	Pre	88	.27	.40	.27
		I	Pre	85	.24	.45	.24
10.	A mother teaches her daughter to work toward a career in addition to being a homemaker. (<.01)	A	Pre	82	.24	.48	.24
		S	Pre	97	.08	.16	.08
		I	Pre	76	.53	.65	.53
11.	A husband helps his wife with the household chores. (N.S.)	A	Pre	55	.65	.80	.65
		S	Pre	73	.42	.65	.42
		I	Pre	66	.44	.68	.44
12.	A government official treats people *better* if they are sent by one of his friends. (<.001)	A	Pro	78	.62	.61	.62
		S	Pre	46	1.86	.87	1.93
		I	Pre	39	1.77	.97	1.77
13.	A teen-age boy drops out of school to help support his parents. (N.S.)	A	Pro	53	.84	.87	.84
		S	Pro	59	1.01	.87	1.01
		I	Pro	56	.82	.86	.82

TABLE 9.4 (*Continued*)

I Group Norm Item*	II Ethnic Group (Anglo, Spanish, Indian)	III Group Mode (*Prescribed*, *Permitted*, *Proscribed*)	IV Strength of Group Norm (Percent in Modal Category)	V Subcultural Anomie (Variance around Own Group Mode)	VI Uncertainty of Group Norm (Relative Entropy, R)	VII Community Anomie (Variance around Anglo Mode)
14. The local priest or minister spends time with people even if they are not members of his church. (<.01)	A S I	Pre Pre Pre	81 71 61	.22 .80 .84	.48 .30 .85	.22 .80 .84
15. A father teaches his children to have a *special* respect for the *oldest* child. (<.001)	A S I	Pro Pre Pre	79 92 56	.62 .24 1.41	.59 .32 .83	.62 3.69 2.39
16. After high school, a girl gets married instead of going on to college. (<.05)	A S I	Per Pro Per	60 49 58	.40 .92 .42	.74 .90 .76	.40 .63 .42
17. A businessman tries to make as much profit as he possibly can. (<.001)	A S I	Pre Pre Pre	42 68 64	1.54 1.14 .60	.98 .70 .76	1.54 1.14 .60
18. When a child is really sick, parents take him to a doctor right away. (N.S.)	A S I	Pre Pre Pre	93 97 100	.13 .08 .00	.26 .16 .00	.13 .08 .00
19. A school teacher watches how he behaves in public more carefully than other people do. (<.001)	A S I	Pre Pre Pre	62 95 79	.69 .20 .35	.90 .18 .57	.69 .20 .35

20.	A husband leaves all child care to the woman in the family. (<.001)					
	A	Pro	87	.23	.42	.23
	S	Pro	66	1.15	.74	1.15
	I	Pro	61	.87	.85	.87
21.	A mother takes a part-time job to make extra money for the family. (<.001)					
	A	Per	48	.52	.81	.52
	S	Pre	39	1.68	.99	.74
	I	Per	53	.47	.92	.47
	Total Variance (Anomie)					
	A			10.57		10.57
	S			17.73		19.19
	I			17.66		18.40

* Chi-square tests of ethnic group differences in distribution of responses for each item were made. The outcome is shown after each item by the *p* level attained. N.S. = no significant difference.

for anomie. The actual measure of the distribution of responses around the modal category which we employed was a variance statistic.[6]

The operationalization of anomie should now be clear. Two group statistics are used: the mode to define the empirical norm of the group and the variance to define the relative amount of group consensus around the norm. Thus, a group response pattern showing a high proportion of responses within the modal category and little variance indicates high group consensus with relatively high certainty, that is, little anomie. A group response pattern showing a relatively small proportion of responses within the modal response category and a large variance indicates low consensus and uncertainty within the group, that is, a high degree of anomie.

Subcultural Anomie. It will be recalled that subcultural anomie was defined as the lack of consensus within an ethnic group with respect to its own norms. Theoretically, the expectation was for greater anomie, that is, less normative consensus, within the two non-Anglo ethnic groups than within the Anglo group. The reasons for this expectation were discussed in Chapter 3 and need be mentioned here only briefly. The greater tendency toward anomie should follow from the greater value-access disjunction to which the minority groups are exposed, from their exposure to an alternative set of norms held by the dominant Anglo group in the community, and from the continued acculturation pressure, to which they are subjected, to change in the direction of the majority group.

It is now possible to examine that expectation in the light of the findings from the Community Survey interview. In Table 9.4, all of the information relevant to this issue, as well as data to which we will turn for later

---

[6] The procedures used in the measurement of anomie reflect the earlier measurement of consensus on role definitions by Gross, Mason, and McEachern in *Explorations in role analysis* (1958).

Variance equals:

$$\frac{\sum_{1}^{2} f_i (\text{Mode} - X_i)^2}{N}$$

where f equals the frequency of a group's response in a category other than the modal category; X equals one of the categories other than the modal category, which varies from the mode by either one or two steps in a three-alternative response pattern; N is the size of the group; and Mode is the category with the largest frequency of response.

For example, in Table 9.4, the distribution of Anglo responses on item 1 is: 80 prescribed (category 1); 9 permitted (category 2); and 2 proscribed (category 3). The variance is:

$$\frac{9(1-2)^2 + 2(1-3)^2}{91} \text{ or } \frac{17}{91} \text{ or } .19$$

considerations, are presented. In column I, the twenty-one normative items used are listed; in column II, the ethnic groups; in column III, the modal category on that item for each ethnic group; in column IV, the "strength" of the group norm, that is, the percentage of the ethnic group respondents accounted for by the modal category; and in column V, the amount of variance around its modal category for each ethnic group.

Consider, for example, item 1. It states, "A teen-age daughter obeys her parents without question." On this item, there was no significant differ-ence in the over-all distributions of responses of the members of the three ethnic groups as measured by the chi-square test: All groups prescribed this behavior with very similar high percentages in the modal category (see column II). The difference in variance is notable, however, with Anglos showing the least variance and the Indians the most variance around their modes which, in this case, happen to be the same. Compare the response pattern of item 1 with that of item 3: "Even with close friends a man keeps his real feelings to himself." The modal category for the Anglos is permitted, that is, "may or may not," while for the Spanish, the modal category is proscribed, that is, "should not," and for the Indians, it is prescribed, that is, "should." There is, thus, an obvious difference in the qualitative direction of ethnic group norms while the strength of the norm in each group, as measured by percent in the mode, is similar (all in the 40–50 percent range). The chi-square test, in this case, shows a significant difference in the response distributions of the three groups. Again, however, the Anglos demonstrate the highest consen-sus as measured by the least variance. The distributions of both the Span-ish and Indians are bimodal, indicating not merely lack of consensus but actual conflict among group members on this particular behavior choice situation.

Before looking at the amount of subcultural anomie characterizing the ethnic groups, their similarity and differences in the quality of the norms themselves should be considered. Inspection of Table 9.4 shows that there was more similarity than difference among the three groups in defining norms, that is, in the modal categories which emerged. The selected mode for the three groups was the same on fifteen of the twenty-one items. Differences in the qualitative direction of normative responses occurred on six items: the husband as money manager (item 2), a man and his friends (item 3), a government official's treatment of clients (item 12), the father-child relationship (item 15), a young woman's career choice (item 16), and a mother as a breadwinner in the family (item 21).

Despite this considerable agreement across the ethnic groups on the *quality* of the norm, the degree of consensus around those norms varies markedly. This is shown not only by the chi-square tests of the response distributions to each item (there are significant differences between the groups on sixteen of the twenty-one items) but also by the basic measure of anomie, the variance statistic showing the extent of lack of consensus.

In column V, Table 9.4, the data show the variances for each item by ethnic group. These variances are summed at the end of that column. The sum of variances for each group on the twenty-one items constitutes a measure of relative subcultural anomie for each group. The Anglos show the least subcultural anomie (10.57), compared with the subcultural anomie measures of the Spanish and Indians, which are significantly larger (about 17.7 for each minority group). The average variance per item for the Anglos is .50, which is significantly less than the average variance per item for either the Spanish or the Indians (both .84). The Anglos show the least variance, that is, highest consensus, among the three groups on ten items, the Spanish, on six items, and the Indians, on five items.

These findings confirm the central theoretical expectation that there would be less anomie in the subcultural normative structure of the Anglo group than in the subcultural normative structures of the two minority groups. Anglos generally experience more agreement on the definition of appropriate behavior in everyday roles; Spanish-Americans and Indians, in the interactions they have with other members of their groups in everyday life, are confronted with more conflict and uncertainty about what is proper or legitimate behavior. Given this greater subcultural anomie, we would expect to find less conformity and more deviant behavior among members of the two minority groups than among the Anglos.

We have argued that the variance statistic measures the amount of consensus among group members and, hence, can be considered a direct measure of "anomie," defined as lack of consensus on norms. Two other measures of the normative structure have been explored and should be discussed here. The first of these, "strength of a group norm," is defined operationally as the percent of the total group responding in the modal category. If all members of the group respond the same way, the norm has complete certainty; no anomie is evident. On the other hand, the percent responding in the modal category where three alternatives are available can be as low as 33.4 percent. Such a low percentage indicates a very weak norm, great uncertainty within the group as to what the norm is, and, therefore, high anomie.

In column IV, Table 9.4, the data show the strength of group norms as measured by the percent of the total group responding in the modal category. Inspection of the table reveals a range of 39–100 percent, almost completely spanning the range of theoretical possibility. Comparing the strength of particular norms across the three ethnic groups, it is apparent that the Spanish and Anglos present a configuration quite different from the Indians. The Spanish show the greatest strength on ten norms, the Anglos on nine, and the Indians on only three of the twenty-one items.

The Indians show the least strength on eleven items, the Anglos on eight, and the Spanish on only two items.

These findings suggest a basis for a further characterization of differences in the normative structures of the three ethnic groups. The Spanish have as high a total variance as the Indians but, at the same time, show more strength than even the Anglos on about half of the norms. This finding suggests conflict in the Spanish group (indicated by bimodal distributions and high variance) on particular norms, perhaps those norms which are undergoing change toward the Anglo norms. For example, item 2 refers to the husband as the sole money decision-maker in the family. On this item, 27 of the Spanish said the husband should be sole decision-maker, whereas 25 said he should not, as compared with the Anglo distribution, where 13 said he should be, 45 said he should not.

The Indians, on the other hand, indicate both relatively low consensus *and* low strength on most norms, suggesting a pattern of more generalized or pervasive normlessness. A possible explanation of this pattern is that the Indian culture has been modified through acculturation to *both* the Spanish and Anglo cultures. The Anglos show a pattern of relatively high consensus with an almost equal distribution of strong and weak norms. When norms are weak (for example, item 3, on male friendship), the disagreement tends to be random in character rather than forming a conflict pattern, as indicated by the nature of the distribution. Thus, on item 3, the Anglo mode is "permission," with variation on either side, yielding a norm which is weak but has relatively low variance. On the same item, both the Indians and Spanish show somewhat stronger modes (for Spanish, proscribed, for Indian, prescribed), but the distributions are bimodal, indicating conflict as manifest in the relatively high variances.

The second of the two additional measures of the normative structure is a measure similar in concept to strength of a norm measured, as just reported, by the percent of the group responding in the modal category. This second measure is the information statistic, R (see Attneave, 1959, p. 9). The measure of relative entropy, R, is presented in column VI of Table 9.4. The R statistic measures the relative degree of uncertainty in a frequency distribution by establishing the ratio of actual uncertainty to maximum uncertainty. The values can range from 0.00 (maximum certainty and perfect predictability) to 1.00 (maximum uncertainty and lack of predictability). Although R takes into account each response, whereas the mode percentage does not, the two measures are highly correlated with each other (.82 in our data), and with the variance statistic. The high association among these three possible, alternative measures of anomie is a source of confidence in the findings. They are measuring essentially the same phenomena and can be substituted for each other without serious loss of information. The mode percentage is easiest to calculate, but is not sensitive to bimodal conflict distributions. Of the three measures, the R statistic is the most inconvenient to calculate. The variance statistic seems, thus, the best measure of anomie of the three since, by definition, it measures degree of consensus and is sensitive both to the amount of central tendency and to conflict indicated by bimodality in the response distributions.

The data, in sum, confirm the theoretical expectation that more sub-cultural anomie would be found in the two minority groups than in the Anglo group. Since the Anglos hold the highest average position in the opportunity structure, followed by the Indians and Spanish, more of the subcultural anomie in the community is concentrated, as expected, in the low-access positions in the opportunity structure. Anomie in the normative structure of a group implies less group regulation of the conduct of members and, hence, the expectation of more deviant behavior among minority group members than among Anglo group members is strengthened. Still to be analyzed, however, is one other type of anomie, community anomie.

Community Anomie.   The notion of community anomie derives from the fact that there is an over-all community interaction system in which members of all three ethnic groups participate. Such interaction occurs in the stores, in the bars and restaurants, on the street, at the school, in town politics, in government offices, during community-wide celebrations and activities, and in inter-ethnic informal groups. The normative structure guiding conduct in these situations, however, tends to be the normative structure of the Anglo majority group. In other words, members of the minority group are under pressure to learn the normative expectations of the Anglo group in these everyday situations. Consequently, the operational definition of community anomie for any group is its degree of consensus with the empirically defined norms of the majority group, that is, with the Anglo modes on the Group Norms scale of the Community Survey interview.

By definition, the amount of community anomie for the Anglos is the same as the amount of Anglo subcultural anomie. For the two minority groups, however, there exists the possibility of differences between them in the amount of community anomie, reflecting possible differences in their degree of acculturation to the norms of the majority group.

Measures of the variance around the Anglo norms are presented in column VII, Table 9.4. The results are very similar to those yielded by the measures of subcultural anomie. The Spanish show the greatest amount of variance (more community anomie relative to Anglos and Indians) on nine items, while the Indians have the highest variance on seven items. The summed measures of lack of consensus for the Spanish (19.19) and for the Indians (18.40) are significantly higher than for the Anglos

(10.57). Across the twenty-one items, the average variance for the Anglos is as before, .50; for the Spanish it is .91, and for the Indians .88; both figures are slightly higher than the variances around their own modes. There is no significant difference between the Spanish and Indians for the community anomie measure.

Consistent with theoretical expectations, members of the two minority groups are confronted with more uncertainty and conflict in *community* interaction situations than are members of the Anglo group. The pressure to learn and to adopt the norms of the majority group probably contributes to the confusion, uncertainty, and conflict in the normative structures of the two minority groups. Since some of the Spanish and Indians have adopted the Anglo norms, uncertainty about proper common role behavior exists for minority group members, not only in interethnic group interaction situations but also in interaction situations within groups. Such a condition of relative normlessness should, of course, provide less control over deviant behavior among members of the minority groups.

Summary: Measurement of the Normative Structure in the Community Survey

Norms are group-defined expectations of appropriate behavior in social situations; they are standards guiding the conduct of group members. Anomie exists to the extent that lack of consensus, disagreement, conflict, and uncertainty about the norms are evident among members of the group as a whole. A conceptually valid operational definition of anomie is the relative lack of consensus among group members, as measured by the total amount of variance, with respect to a set of items of relevant normative content. An additional measure of certainty in the normative structure can be obtained by determining the percent of the group selecting the modal choice of relevant normative content items. Both of these measures indicate a response of the group as a whole, thus yielding sociological measures of anomie.

Two types of anomie were identified which correspond to two conceptually different normative structures confronting members of a tri-ethnic community. *Subcultural anomie* is the relative lack of consensus among members of an ethnic group about appropriate behavior in the common roles of everyday life. *Community anomie* is the relative lack of consensus among group members about the standards for appropriate behavior in common roles of the community, as these standards are defined by the majority Anglo group.

Theoretically, subcultural and community anomie should be greater in the two minority groups than in the Anglo majority group. These predictions were confirmed by the data presented. Anglo respondents demonstrated significantly less variance in their total responses to items of relevant normative content than either of the minority groups. Measures of certainty of particular norms indicated qualitative differences in the normative structures of the two minority groups, despite their similar anomie scores. Among the Spanish, both high certainty and high conflict on particular items were observed. Among the Indians, relatively high uncertainty was common throughout the items. Such a finding suggests a pattern of generalized normlessness among the Indians.

As argued in Chapter 3, more deviant behavior is to be expected among members of a group confronted with confusion and uncertainty in their normative structure. The measures of anomie clearly predict that Anglos should exhibit less deviance than either the Spanish or the Indians, and this is in accord with what is known about Anglo–non-Anglo deviance rates. A prediction of relative Spanish and Indian deviance based on characteristics of their normative structures is less clear-cut, although the more pervasive anomie among the Indians suggests a greater probability of deviant behavior.

We have now considered measures of both the opportunity structure and the normative structure. What remains is to examine the social control structure in order to complete our measurement of the sociocultural environment. Since the normative structure was not measured within the high school, we may turn directly to the presentation of the assessment of social controls.

THE MEASUREMENT OF THE SOCIAL CONTROL STRUCTURE

As elaborated in Chapter 3, the social control structure consists of those socially structured processes which relatively directly govern or regulate the access which a person has to illegitimate means. Access to illegitimate means is considered to be the outcome of the operation of a number of different components of the social control structure. Common to these components is the function they perform in relation to deviant behavior: All increase (or decrease) the likelihood of its occurrence in a relatively direct manner, that is, by facilitating its learning, by reinforcing it, or by providing opportunities for its occurrence. Location of a person within the social control structure indicates, therefore, the degree to which he has access to illegitimate means, a crucial parameter in accounting for the ultimate occurrence of deviance.

The earlier discussion of access to illegitimate means led us to differentiate it into three important components: (1) the opportunity to learn deviant behavior through exposure to deviant role models; (2) the degree of isolation from or integration with agents who apply negative sanctions for deviant acts and positive sanctions for conformity; and (3) the opportunity to perform deviant acts because of the availability of facilitating materials or of situations free from supervision. An effort was made in both the Community Survey and High School studies to devise operations for each of the three components.

As will be seen, not all of the operations are satisfactory, either in conceptual relevance or in regard to their quality as measures. The main reason for this is that our conceptualization of social control developed, in part, along with the research operations rather than entirely preceding them; this meant that data collected for other purposes were later pressed into service as measures when their new implications became clear. This qualification, which applies to certain but not to all of the measures of the components of access to illegitimate means, should be kept in mind in appraising the operations to be reported in the two studies.

The Community Survey Study

Exposure to Deviant Role Models

This measure was designed to assess the first specified component of access to illegitimate means, the differential opportunity to learn deviant behaviors. The period of learning focused upon was the socialization period within the family of orientation; the kind of learning focused upon was that which can occur through exposure to role models who may manifest the behavior of concern, that is, deviance. The assumption made was that the presence within the family of persons who were themselves engaging in deviant behaviors constituted, for the respondent, an opportunity to learn those behaviors which was not afforded the respondent whose family did not include such models.

There are, of course, many types of deviant role models which could be specifically probed for, from the presence of a liar among playmates to the presence of a convicted thief in the family. In the Community Survey Study, detailed probing in these areas was not undertaken. Rather, a simple index was contrived based on a few general questions serving to indicate the extent to which persons have been exposed to deviant role models as part of their family socialization experience.

The measure of Exposure to Deviant Role Models covers, in the time the respondent was growing up, problem drinkers (or heavy drinkers) in his family, parents antagonistic toward one another, whether he grew up in a broken home, or whether any person in the family had been "in trouble" of any kind. These questions were embedded among others in several different parts of the total interview. Together they afford only a global and admittedly crude indicator of the presence of deviant role models in the respondent's socialization experience. When averaged across individuals within each ethnic group, the responses provide a measure of the differential opportunity to learn deviant behavior in the three ethnic groups.[7]

Relative Absence of Sanction Networks

The measure of the second component of the access to illegitimate means variable involved specifying the degree to which a person was mapped into social networks which operate to monitor the behavior of their members, punishing departures from norms and rewarding conformity. It was assumed that persons who are *not* tied into stable interaction networks, that is, those who are socially isolated from responsible sanctioning agents, have greater access to illegitimate means; they not only escape negative sanctions for deviance but are not exposed to positive sanctions for adhering to norms.

An index of the relative absence of sanction networks was constructed; it consisted of five items, each exploring participation (or the lack of it) in formal or informal interaction systems. The absence of a stable family relationship, an informal visiting relationship, membership in formal organizations, significant religious participation, or access to others by telephone, all were considered to indicate relative social isolation or freedom from the actions of possible sanctioning agents.[8] Together, the items

[7] The questions were: (1) "Would you say anyone in your family (of orientation) was thought of as a heavy drinker? Did anyone in your family ever get into any kind of trouble or have problems because of drinking—like with the law, family, friends, work, or health?" (2) "Most parents have arguments and fights. Thinking about when you were eight–twelve, how much of this went on in your home?" (A great deal, a fair amount, or not too much.) (3) "When you were growing up—to around sixteen—were both of your real parents in your home with you, or was one or both of them gone because of death, or divorce, or separation?" (Absence of a parent because of *death* was not counted as a broken home in this index.) (4) "About that age, was anyone in the family in trouble of any kind?" (Probe.) Positive responses to the heavy drinker or problem drinker questions, "fair amount" or "great deal" of family fighting, and family member in trouble questions were each weighted 1, negative responses 0.

[8] The scoring for Absence of Sanction Networks proceeded as follows: With regard to the family, a person who is presently unattached, who does not live with a spouse or in a complete nuclear family of orientation, was assumed to be least subject to family social control and was scored 1; all others were scored 0. Further, a person was assumed to be less subject to sanctions from others and received scores of 1 on each of the following four variables: If he indicated *no informal visiting*, had *no formal group memberships*, reported that he *attended church less than five times during the last year*, and his *family did not own a telephone*. In contrast, persons were assumed to be more subject to sanctions from others and were scored 0 if, in answer to the questions, they indicated some informal visiting, any formal group membership, attended religious services five or more times during the last year, and the family owned a telephone. The decision to

provide an index of a person's access to illegitimate means by virtue of his relative freedom from the operation of social controls.

Opportunity for Deviance

The third component of access to illegitimate means, differential opportunity to engage in deviant behavior, refers, theoretically, to one's actual present access to the materials, instruments, and situations necessary for the performance of deviant acts. For example, the actual availability of a substantial supply of liquor, the ownership or easy access to weapons of violence, access to space free from the supervision of the community, membership in a clique group which practices deviant behavior as a group activity, and similar variables could qualify as direct indicators of the opportunity to engage in deviant behavior.

The measure of Opportunity for Deviance used in this study does not consist of direct and specific variables of the kind mentioned, unfortunately; rather, it is quite crude and consists of four highly indirect items specifying a person's location in the social structure of the community, the assumption being that more opportunity for deviance exists in certain locations than in others. First, it was assumed that males, more so than females, have opportunities to engage in deviance: In general, females are more protected, chaperoned, and restricted than males. Females are more confined to the home, have less access to bars, are expected to be more religious, do not own or know how to use weapons of violence as do most men. Second, it was assumed that *young* adults (less than thirty years old) have more opportunities for deviance than older adults. There is the shared expectation that younger people will "sow their wild oats," and younger people are less involved in responsibilities which restrict their freedom. Older folks are expected to settle down and to become the source of stability and respectability in the community.

Third, it was assumed that town residents, more than rural residents, have more opportunity for deviance. In town, there is always a supply of liquor available, and situations exist for a group to get together to engage in various forms of deviant behavior—getting drunk at a bar, fighting at a dance, or stealing goods from a store. Finally, it was assumed that unemployed persons, more so than employed persons, have an opportunity to engage in deviant behavior. The unemployed are not only under greater pressure to use illegitimate means to attain goals, they also have more free time and are under less supervision.

---

use attendance rather than membership in a religious organization was based on the analysis of the frequency distribution of church attendance. There is a definite break between "regular" attenders and those who attend church only on special occasions, such as Christmas and Easter.

Each of the four items was scored as a dichotomy, the greater opportunity location receiving a score of 1, the more limited opportunity location a score of 0; total score range was, therefore, 0–4.

The Over-all Measure of Access to Illegitimate Means

Since each component has the same theoretical function, to regulate access to illegitimate means, there is a logical basis for combining the three measures into a single, over-all measure of Access to Illegitimate Means (AIM). This measure, composed of the twelve items which entered into the three separate measures, should represent the most comprehensive assessment of location in the social control structure.

The problem which exists in combining the three measures, however, is that it assumes that equal confidence can be placed in them as operations for the concepts involved, a situation which does not, obviously, obtain. The Exposure to Deviant Role Models measure, for example, is based upon only three items, all relating to childhood socialization experiences of the adult respondent. A major weakness of the Opportunity for Deviance measure is the large degree of abstraction between the conceptual meaning and the operational indicators, that is, the lack of measures of specific, concrete access to materials, instruments, and situations permitting the occurrence of deviant behavior. The most conceptually valid of the three component measures would seem to be Absence of Sanction Networks, a five-item scale defining an adult's lack of participation in stable interaction systems. Each of these five items has a direct and conceptually valid relation to the concept of a social control structure.

An examination of the correlations among the component measures reveals them to be essentially unrelated to each other. The tetrachoric correlation between Exposure to Deviant Role Models and Absence of Sanction Networks is —.04; between Exposure and Opportunity for Deviance, —.17; and between Absence of Sanction Networks and Opportunity, .04. It is clear that each measure is tapping a quite different aspect of access to illegitimate means, if it can be assumed at all to be a valid measure of the latter. One's present participation in formal and informal sanctioning networks is related neither to childhood exposure to deviant role models nor to present opportunity to engage in deviant acts. Such low correlations raise questions about the wisdom of combining the component measures into an over-all measure of AIM. These questions will come up again later in considering the relationship of position in the social control structure to position in the opportunity structure and to deviant behavior.

Sex and Ethnic Differences in Access to Illegitimate Means

Assuming a priori that the men and women in the research community came from similar families, we would expect no sex differences in *exposure* to deviant role models while growing up. Table 9.5 shows that this expectation is borne out. Perhaps the slightly higher female exposure rate results from female respondents *defining* "problem drinking" and "getting into trouble" more strictly than male respondents. There is also a nonsignificant tendency for women to be mapped into more sanction networks than men, mainly as a result of their greater church attendance. The significant sex difference in opportunity for deviance (and, thus, also in total score) is almost completely an artifact which is due to the inclusion of sex in the measure. When this item is removed, sex differences disappear.

TABLE 9.5
Sex Differences in Measures of the Social Control Structure: Community Survey Study

Measure		Means and Standard Deviations		Signifi-cance* (Males vs. Females)
		Males (N = 110)	Females (N = 111)	
Exposure to deviant role models	$\bar{X}$	0.45	0.65	t = 1.89
	σ	(0.74)	(0.80)	N.S.
Absence of sanction networks	$\bar{X}$	2.38	2.09	t = 1.89
	σ	(1.16)	(1.14)	N.S.
Opportunity for deviance†	$\bar{X}$	1.82	0.78	t = 9.92
	σ	(0.84)	(0.70)	p < .001
Total access to illegitimate means†	$\bar{X}$	4.63	3.50	t = 4.91
	σ	(1.79)	(1.60)	p < .001

* All *t*-tests of group mean differences are two-tailed. Differences not significant at the .05 level or better are indicated N.S.

† Because this index contains sex as one of its items (men received 1, women, 0), there is a built-in sex difference. When this built-in difference is removed, by subtracting 1 from the male mean, the two groups are actually very similar.

But the situation is quite different when we look at *ethnic group* differences (Table 9.6). Indian respondents report significantly more exposure to deviance in their childhood socialization experience than either Spanish or Anglo respondents. That is, Indians report relatively more problem or heavy drinkers in the home, parental fighting, broken homes, and family members "in trouble" of some kind during the time they were growing up. There were no significant differences between Spanish and Anglos, although the Anglos have a lower mean score.

In the Absence of Sanction Networks measure, there are significant differences among all three ethnic groups. The relatively high average Indian score indicates lack of participation in formal groups, visiting rela-

TABLE 9.6

**Ethnic Differences in Measures of the Social Control Structure:
Community Survey Study**

Measure		Means and Standard Deviations			Significance*			
		Anglos $(N = 93)$	Spanish $(N = 60)$	Indians $(N = 68)$	Anglos *vs.* Spanish	Anglos *vs.* Indians	Spanish *vs.* Indians	
Exposure to deviant role models	$\bar{X}$	.40	.50	.79	$t = 0.84$	$t = 3.00$	$t = 2.07$	
	σ	(.70)	(.70)	(.88)	N.S.	$p < .01$	$p < .05$	
Absence of sanction networks	$\bar{X}$	1.71	2.13	3.04	$t = 2.50$	$t = 8.40$	$t = 5.39$	
	σ	(1.09)	(.98)	(.92)	$p < .02$	$p < .001$	$p < .001$	
Opportunity for deviance	$\bar{X}$	1.05	1.47	1.48	$t = 2.81$	$t = 2.83$	$t = 0.06$	
	σ	(.84)	(.91)	(.99)	$p < .01$	$p < .01$	N.S.	
Total access to illegitimate means	$\bar{X}$	3.15	4.10	5.28	$t = 3.59$	$t = 8.85$	$t = 4.25$	
	σ	(1.54)	(1.63)	(1.48)	$p < .001$	$p < .001$	$p < .001$	

* All t-tests of group mean differences are two-tailed. Differences not significant at the .05 level or better are indicated N.S.

tionships, religious services, stable family relationships, and telephone communication. This relatively greater freedom from social sanctioning networks theoretically confronts the average Indian with less control against deviance than the average Anglo or Spanish. Although the Spanish are subject to more social sanctioning than the Indians, the average Spanish experiences less such social control than does the average Anglo. Anglos are most closely linked with others in stable interaction relationships and are thereby subject to the greatest amount of sanctions against deviant behavior and rewards for conformity.

The Opportunity for Deviance measure shows that Anglo group members fill a complex of positions in the social structure least likely to afford an opportunity actually to engage in deviant behavior. As a group, there is relatively less unemployment, more rural residence, and a somewhat older adult population among Anglos. There are no significant differences on this measure between the Indians and the Spanish.

Finally, when we look at total score on this index, significant differences in AIM between all three ethnic groups are found. This confirms the theoretical expectation that the Anglo majority group members occupy a position in the social control structure with the least access to illegitimate means. The Spanish have significantly less access to illegitimate means than the Indians, primarily because of their relatively greater participation in church activities and social groups, and, secondarily, because of lesser likelihood of exposure to deviant behavior during their socialization experience; the Indians occupy the position in the social control structure with the greatest access to illegitimate means.

The results of the measurement of the social control structure in the Community Survey Study are in full accord with the earlier theoretical analysis. It was anticipated that social controls would be weaker or less operative in the lower socioeconomic strata or among marginal racial or ethnic groups, and this is what has emerged. The findings imply, other things equal, that the greater rates of deviance should occur in the two minority groups, with the Spanish showing less deviance than the Indians. With these findings and implications in mind, it is possible to turn to the measurement of the social control structure in the High School Study.

The High School Study

While performing student roles within the school, all students are within the same social control structure and subject to the same formal sanctions for conformity and deviance. To investigate differential location with respect to social control requires, therefore, that the reference be to a structure outside of the school, one such as membership in clique groups, or the family social control structure. It was upon the latter, the family social control structure, that our investigation was focused in the High

School Study, although some relevant sociometric data on friendship groups will also be presented. As in the Community Survey Study, three components of access to illegitimate means were measured, and a combined over-all Access to Illegitimate Means measure was constituted from the component items. Each of the component measures will be described in turn.

Exposure to Deviant Role Models

Unlike the Community Survey approach, the high school measure of Exposure to Deviant Role Models is not based on information reported by the respondent himself. Rather, the mother of each student was interviewed (as part of the Socialization Study; see Chapter 12) about the home situation of the student. In addition, available court records on all community members were scrutinized for this purpose. Three items were finally included in the index of Exposure to Deviant Role Models, each one related directly to the presumed opportunity to learn deviant behavior from an available model. A student was considered to have had more exposure to deviance if a family member had a court record, if the mother reported that a family member had been in "serious trouble," and, for a student who had, according to his mother, engaged in deviant conduct of some kind, whether one or more deviant models were reported to have been available in his experience.[9] Scores range from 0–5.

The high school measure of Exposure to Deviant Role Models is different from the adult survey measure in that it emphasizes role models which are part of *current* socialization experience. In the Community Survey Study, adults were questioned about role models in their earlier socialization experience, exposure far removed from present behavior.

Relative Absence of Sanction Networks

While the measure of Absence of Sanction Networks in the Community Survey was based on the respondent's report of amount of participation in both informal, visiting, or friendship groups and in formal associations such as church groups and organized social clubs, the measure of Absence of Sanction Networks for a high school student is operationally defined

---

[9] Scoring proceeded as follows for Exposure to Deviant Role Models: (1) Court record on a family member—1; no court record—0; (2) mother reports at least one member of the family who has been in serious trouble—2; none ever in serious trouble—0; and (3) for students who have been identified as having been in trouble with the law, or in "serious trouble," or who have been punished at home for some kind of deviant behavior (for example, heavy drinking, drunken driving, stealing, or truancy as opposed to "misbehavior," such as cursing, or teasing sibs), two or more available deviant models (for example, an older brother with a court record and a friend who had been picked up by the police for speeding)—2; one available model—1; no known models—0. A student's score on Exposure to Deviant Role Models is the sum of his scores on the three items.

by items referring to the amount of control exercised over him *in his home,* as reported by his mother. Six items, each related either to stability of the control situation or to the degree of control, are combined in a single index of Absence of Sanction Networks. The theoretical assumption guiding the selection of these variables is that the more freedom from parental control a student has, the less his conformity will be rewarded and his deviance punished.

The first variable in the index is an assessment of the amount of current regulation of the student's behavior according to the rules parents impose about such matters as time to be home at night, drinking behavior, dating, and driving. Absence of regulatory rules implies that a student is not subject to sanctions for deviance from his parents. The second variable covers the "strictness" characteristic of each parent in dealing with the student's earlier behavior. Thus, this item is a rough indicator of the general character of sanction experience in the student's background. If parents have been strict, the student will presumably have learned to expect sanctions for deviant acts. The third variable refers to the relative tolerance by the mother of deviant acts by a teen-ager. If the mother herself has a relatively tolerant attitude toward deviance, then her child is more likely to feel that his own anticipated deviant act may escape punishment.

The fourth variable is derived from the index of Parental Harmony (described in Chapter 12). The index refers to the amount of agreement or disagreement between parents on how to rear children, specifically, the high school student concerned. The assumption is that if parents disagree about controls over the student, there is less certainty that sanctions will be imposed. The fifth variable, a measure of family stability, assumes that a student has more freedom from control if the family has been unstable, that is, broken by divorce or separation, than if the family interaction system has remained stable during the time the student has been growing up. The sixth and last variable refers to the training in self-control received by the student in his home. If the student has been trained in "immediate gratification" as opposed to "delayed gratification," the latter calling for self-discipline and long-range planning for the future, it is assumed that the student will learn to be less sensitive to the consequences of his behavior, that is, he will not have learned to consider possible future sanctions from others.

The sum of a student's scores on the six variables constitutes his Absence of Sanction Networks score, a score intended to reflect the degree to which his behavior is subject to the operation of sanctions by his family. Score range on this measure is 0–12.

While the present measure concentrates only on the family, in contrast to the parallel measure in the Community Survey Study which dealt with a variety of formal and informal groups, it should be emphasized that the comprehensiveness of the information on parental regulatory standards and procedures provides more direct knowledge of sanctions than was available in the adult study.[10]

Opportunity for Deviance

Opportunity for Deviance is, theoretically, one's access to the materials, means, and situations necessary for the performance of a deviant act. As in the Community Survey, detailed information on such direct access to deviance was not obtained from the students. In both studies, however, the assumption has been made that certain locations in the social structure provide more objective opportunity for deviance than others. Among high school students, it was assumed, first, that in the home and community older students are granted more freedom than younger students to pursue their goals without supervision or direct monitoring of their behavior. Consequently, the older students can be considered to have more objective opportunity to engage in deviant behavior. Second, students who live in town were considered to have more access to the situations, means, and materials for deviance than students who live relatively isolated from each other in the rural surround. The scoring for this measure was simply 2 for town residence, 0 for rural residence, and 2 for age nineteen or above, 1 for age seventeen or eighteen, and 0 for age sixteen or younger. Total score range, consequently, was 0–4.

Clearly, this measure is, a priori, the weakest of the three. It is based on only two items, and both are rather far removed from the concept to which they are intended to refer.

The Over-all Measure of Access to Illegitimate Means

As in the Community Survey Study, the three component measures were combined to constitute a more comprehensive measure of Access

---

[10] Scoring of the variables of Absence of Sanction Networks proceeded as follows: (1) *Parental regulation:* absence of regulation—2; regulation—0, as judged by the mother's response to the question: "What kinds of rules do you set for him now about what he's not supposed to do?" probed for various areas such as time for being in at night, drinking, dating, and driving; (2) *Parental strictness:* both parents reported by the mother as being "easy" in discipline of the child as he was growing up—2; one parent reported by the mother as being "easy" in discipline—1; at least some "strictness" reported for each parent—0; (3) *Mother's attitude toward deviance:* high tolerance toward teen-age deviant behavior—2; moderate tolerance toward deviant behavior—1; and low tolerance of deviant behavior—0; (4) *Parental harmony:* below the median of all parents—2; "single-parent family"—1; above the median in parental harmony—0; (5) *Family stability:* the family has been broken by divorce or separation—2; family broken by death of a parent—1; stable family—0; and (6) *Self-control training:* an "immediate gratification" response by the mother to one or both of two questions about teaching planning for the future to the child—2; planning for the future taught, as indicated by the mother's answers to both questions—0.

to Illegitimate Means comprised of the eleven items entering into the component scores. While all of these items connect, theoretically, with the concept of access to illegitimate means, thereby providing a logical basis for their combination, our confidence in the various items is, again, hardly equivalent. Thus, the same questions about the wisdom of constructing such a composite index arise here as arose at a similar juncture in the Community Survey Study.

An important difference between the two studies does obtain in this respect, however. When the relations among the three component measures are examined, the picture is sharply different from that in the Community Survey Study, where essentially zero relationships obtained. By contrast, the Pearson correlation between Exposure to Deviant Role Models and Absence of Sanction Networks in the High School Study is .52, Exposure and Opportunity for Deviance correlate .28, and Absence of Sanction Networks and Opportunity also correlate .28. Thus, the empirical pattern of relationships provides support for combining of the measures. It does not, nevertheless, generate confidence in measures clearly seen to be weak; their adequacy remains to be examined in relation to outside criteria.

Sex and Ethnic Differences in Access to Illegitimate Means

With the description of the measures and of their interrelations in mind, we may turn now to an examination of the relationship of sex and ethnic status to social control. In Table 9.7, the sex group means for each of

TABLE 9.7
Sex Group Differences in the Social Control Structure: High School Study

Measure		Means and Standard Deviations		Significance* (Males vs. Females)
		Males $(N = 44)$	Females $(N = 41)$	
Exposure to deviant role models	$\bar{X}$	1.25	0.68	$t = 1.74$
	σ	(1.69)	(1.31)	N.S.
Absence of sanction networks	$\bar{X}$	4.50	2.98	$t = 2.83$
	σ	(2.87)	(2.07)	$p < .01$
Opportunity for deviance	$\bar{X}$	1.34	1.37	$t = 0.09$
	σ	(1.22)	(1.26)	N.S.
Total access to illegitimate means	$\bar{X}$	7.11	5.02	$t = 2.38$
	σ	(4.67)	(3.35)	$p < .05$

* All t-tests of group mean differences are two-tailed. Differences not significant at the .05 level or better are indicated N.S.

the three component measures and for the composite measure of Access to Illegitimate Means are presented.

On both Exposure to Deviant Role Models and Absence of Sanction Networks, girls have lower scores than boys, in the latter case, significantly lower. No sex difference in Opportunity for Deviance was found, but the other two differences were great enough to produce a significant sex difference on the total score.

Ethnic differences are reported in Table 9.8. Our expectations are supported by these data. In all three component measures and on the composite AIM score, the Anglo students show the least access to illegitimate means, the Indians the most, and the Spanish students are in between, but consistently closer to the Anglos than to the Indians. Despite the small number of local Indians in the sample, Anglo-Indian differences are large enough to be statistically significant in every case, and on the total AIM index, all three groups are different statistically.

Because of the sex differences found, ethnic-by-sex differences were also determined for Anglos and Spanish (the Indian subgroups were too small) to check these findings; the results are reported in the lower half of Table 9.8. All Anglo-Spanish differences were again in the expected direction, though none attained statistical significance.

These findings are completely congruent with those from the community survey and provide a powerful example of convergence between the two studies. The measures of location in the social control structure used in the High School Study were not the same as those employed in the Community Survey Study. Although in each study, Access to Illegitimate Means was made up of the same three component parts, the actual operations employed differed. Given this variation, and the difference between the two populations, the consistency of the results between the two studies is impressive. Both studies show the Anglos to be located in a position in the social control structure with least access to illegitimate means. At the same time, both studies show the Indians to have the greatest access to illegitimate means. The Spanish occupy, in both studies, a middle position, one closer to the Anglos, however, than to the Indians. The implications of these findings for deviance rates are clear; the ethnic topography of social control is completely consonant with the ethnic topography of deviant behavior shown in Chapters 7 and 8.

Ethnic Group Cleavage in the High School

Before leaving the discussion of social controls in the High School Study, the focus should be shifted from our almost exclusive concern, thus far, with the family environment. Most students are exposed to social control structures other than that provided by their parents. An informal social control structure exists for students outside the formal school system,

TABLE 9.8
Ethnic Group Differences in the Social Control Structure: High School Study

Measure		Means and Standard Deviations			Significance*		
		Anglos (N = 39)	Spanish (N = 32)	Indians (N = 10)	Anglos vs. Spanish	Anglos vs. Indians	Spanish vs. Indians
Exposure to deviant role models	$\bar{X}$	0.38	0.97	3.20	$t = 1.76$	$t = 7.64$	$t = 5.14$
	σ	(1.07)	(1.62)	(1.03)	N.S.	$p < .001$	$p < .001$
Absence of sanction networks	$\bar{X}$	3.05	3.84	5.40	$t = 1.31$	$t = 2.75$	$t = 1.69$
	σ	(2.19)	(2.78)	(2.46)	N.S.	$p < .02$	N.S.
Opportunity for deviance	$\bar{X}$	0.95	1.50	2.10	$t = 2.00$	$t = 2.33$	$t = 1.19$
	σ	(1.15)	(1.16)	(1.45)	$p < .05$	$p < .05$	N.S.
Total access to illegitimate means	$\bar{X}$	4.41	6.31	10.70	$t = 2.02$	$t = 6.01$	$t = 3.61$
	σ	(3.13)	(4.50)	(2.91)	$p < .05$	$p < .001$	$p < .01$

Measure		Anglo Males (N = 21)	Spanish Males (N = 13)	Anglo Females (N = 18)	Spanish Females (N = 19)	Anglo Males vs. Spanish Males	Anglo Females vs. Spanish Females
Exposure to deviant role models	$\bar{X}$	.52	1.62	.22	.53	$t = 1.75$	$t = 1.02$
	σ	(1.36)	(1.98)	(0.55)	(1.17)	N.S.	N.S.
Absence of sanction networks	$\bar{X}$	3.29	4.92	2.78	3.10	$t = 1.67$	$t = 0.47$
	σ	(2.61)	(2.87)	(1.59)	(2.54)	N.S.	N.S.
Opportunity for deviance	$\bar{X}$	.95	1.62	.94	1.42	$t = 1.55$	$t = 1.30$
	σ	(1.24)	(1.19)	(1.06)	(1.17)	N.S.	N.S.
Total access to illegitimate means	$\bar{X}$	4.81	8.15	3.94	5.05	$t = 2.04$	$t = 1.13$
	σ	(3.80)	(5.08)	(2.10)	(3.69)	N.S.	N.S.

* All t-tests of group mean differences are two-tailed. Differences not significant at the .05 level or better are indicated N.S.

namely, that of his clique group, the companions with whom he spends his leisure time. By becoming a member of one group, a particular student may be setting out on the road to trouble; by becoming a member of another clique, he may engage in activities which provide no access to deviant behavior, and, in fact, he may even suffer sanctions from group members should he propose the performance of a deviant act. Since access to illegitimate means has been shown to vary with ethnic group membership, it was of special interest to determine whether the informal friendship groups outside the school are composed of members of a single ethnic group or not.

Two sociometric studies of the high school student population, the second being a replication of the first a year later, clearly demonstrated that ethnic cleavages exist in the informal social groups among high school students (Minard, 1960, 1961). It is true that members of all three ethnic groups participate more or less on a par in the formal organizations of the high school—such as on the athletic teams, in the band and pep club—that the recognized high school leaders come from all three ethnic groups, and that a pattern of cross-ethnic friendships exists among many of the students. Nevertheless, on sociometric preference questions ("Of all the students in your class, name the two students you would choose to sit next to in class"); on anticipated-response questions ("Which students in your class would most likely choose to sit next to you?"); and especially on actual behavior questions ("Which kids from around here do you actually spend most of your free time with after school?"), ethnic cleavages—though varying with the type and content of the question— were clearly demonstrated. Of most interest for the description of informal social control structures are the questions about out-of-school companions.

In Table 9.9, the cleavage analysis on a preference question and on an actual behavior question about after-school companions is shown. The chi-square for cleavage analysis was developed by Proctor and Loomis (1951, pp. 561–585). The chi-square is high for a given ethnic group if the group members have *not* chosen other ethnic persons, if the ethnic group members have *not been chosen* by members of different ethnic groups, or if *both* have occurred. The results presented in Table 9.9 clearly show that the high school students *choose to or actually do spend free time with members of their own ethnic group,* whatever choice the analysis is made on. That this finding is stable is further substantiated by the replication study one year later; the same pattern of cleavage was again observed (see Minard, 1961, p. 25 and elsewhere).

The implication of the sociometric analysis is that, in their leisure time activities, Anglo students associate mainly with other Anglos, Spanish with other Spanish, and Indians with other Indians. This means that, to the extent that informal friendships or clique groups constitute sources of social control, the students tend to be exposed to informal controls from members of their *own* ethnic group. Such a situation should tend to perpetuate the ethnically related character of social controls shown in both the High School and Community Survey studies—that is, Indian

TABLE 9.9

Ethnic Group Cleavage in the High School as Illustrated by Analysis of Sociometric Questions for Juniors and Seniors*

Choice	Comparison	$\chi^{2\dagger}$	Probability

Question: "Who are the four kids *from around here* you would *choose* to mess around with when you're out of school?"

Choice	Comparison	$\chi^{2\dagger}$	Probability
First	Anglo/other	11.66	.001
	Spanish/other	7.96	.01
	Indian/other	20.37	.001
Second	Anglo/other	20.53	.001
	Spanish/other	21.73	.001
	Indian/other	28.12	.001
Fourth	Anglo/other	21.24	.001
	Spanish/other	28.73	.001
	Indian/other	10.04	.01

Question: "Which kids *from around here* do you *actually* spend most of your free time with after school?"

Choice	Comparison	$\chi^{2\dagger}$	Probability
First	Anglo/other	24.83	.001
	Spanish/other	22.00	.001
	Indian/other	28.40	.001
Second	Anglo/other	27.40	.001
	Spanish/other	19.37	.001
	Indian/other	23.48	.001
Fourth	Anglo/other	14.95	.001
	Spanish/other	(*N* too small to test)	
	Indian/other	19.78	.001

* From Minard, 1960, pp. 12, 13, and 14. Both local and non-local Indians are included in this analysis. The third choice data are eliminated from the table for economy.

† For a description of the procedure for obtaining the chi-square for cleavage, see Proctor and Loomis, 1951, pp. 569–581.

student clique groups should reflect the control structure of the larger Indian group; the Anglos and the Spanish, likewise. Thus, informal groups tend to reinforce, rather than to attenuate, the situation previously shown to obtain with respect to social control in the three ethnic groups.

RELATIONS AMONG THE SOCIOCULTURAL STRUCTURES

The theoretical framework presented in Chapter 3 referred to the socio-cultural *system,* that is, it assumed the existence of organized relationships among the component sociocultural structures. More particularly, the elaboration of the sociocultural formulation resulted in the expectation of a positive association or correlation between positions in the several sociocultural structures. Stated otherwise, the theory leads one to anticipate that value-access disjunction, anomie, and access to illegitimate means should co-vary: Where one is relatively high, the others should also be relatively high; where one is relatively low, the others should similarly be low. Such relationships follow logically from the assumptions made in Chapter 3 and from the underlying consideration that social processes interact through time.

These expected relationships can now be examined in the light of the empirical findings. Two modes of approach can be employed. The first of these is to examine directly the interrelationships between the variables representing the separate sociocultural structures; correlations can be used for this purpose where there are measures for each individual. It will be recalled, however, that the measures of anomie are *group* measures. In view of this, direct examination of interstructure relationships can be carried out only between the opportunity structure and the social control structure for both the Community Survey Study data and the High School Study data. The second mode for approaching the question is indirect and relies upon the findings we have presented with respect to the ethnic groups. In this latter approach, the relative position of each ethnic group in each sociocultural structure can be examined to see whether the three positions occupied by each ethnic group are *consonant'* or *similar.* This analysis can also be made for each of the two studies.

Relations between Access to Opportunity and Access to Illegitimate Means

The data relevant to the first approach are presented in Table 9.10. Correlations are shown between the measures of value-access disjunction in the opportunity structure and the various measures of access to illegitimate means in the social control structure. Both the Community Survey Study and the High School Study findings are included.

Considering first the main composite variable in the social control structure, it can be seen that Total AIM is related to both SES and OA among the adults and to SES among the high school students. While the relationships are generally low, they are both consistent and statistically significant, suggesting that, as anticipated, a low position in the opportunity structure is associated with greater access to illegitimate means in the social control structure.

Looking more closely at the component measures of Access to Illegitimate Means, it can be seen that Exposure to Deviant Role Models relates strongly in the High School Study, while in the Community Survey Study no relation exists; in the latter case, the models were far removed in time, while in the former, they referred to the present. The reverse is true in the Absence of Sanction Networks component: There are stronger relations with the opportunity structure in the Community Survey Study than in the High School Study. Part of the high relation with OA (.46) reflects the fact that social participation is one of eight components of the OA score. The same type of spurious result occurs in the high relation of Opportunity for Deviance (which includes unemployment) with SES (.43) in the adult study. Such problems of overlap of items do not, how-

TABLE 9.10

Pearson Correlations between Measures of Value-Access Disjunction and Access to Illegitimate Means

Measure	Community Survey ($N = 219$)*		High School Study ($N = 85$)†
	SES	OA	SES
Exposure to deviant role models	$-.06$	$-.10$	.43
Absence of sanction networks	.26	.46	.23
Opportunity for deviance	.43	.12	.14
Total access to illegitimate means (AIM)	.27	.28	.35

* For $N = 219$, a correlation of .12 is significant at the .05 level, one-tailed test.

† For $N = 85$, a correlation of .18 is significant at the .05 level, one-tailed test.

ever, attenuate the import of these findings, which demonstrate a small but significant relationship between two of the three structures comprising the sociocultural system.

Ethnic Group Analysis of Relations among Sociocultural Structures

The concern in this approach is to assess the consonance of relative positions occupied by the three ethnic groups in each of the three sociocultural structures. What is required is briefly to review the ethnic group analyses previously presented for each of the three structures considered. The picture is completely clear when the Anglos are compared with the non-Anglo groups. The Anglos have been shown to occupy the least deviance-prone position in each of the sociocultural structures: They have greatest access to legitimate opportunity and, hence, are least pressured to adopt illegitimate means; they are confronted by the least anomie and, thus, are subject to the strongest normative controls; and they have least access to illegitimate means, which indicates that they are exposed to effective and operative social controls. Theoretically, the relations of the three positions in the different structures are entirely consonant.

Among the non-Anglo groups, consonance is also apparent. The Indians and Spanish occupy more deviance-prone positions in all three structures than the Anglos. When each of the minority groups is considered separately and compared with the other, the consonance is less pronounced than that which obtains for the Anglos, however. Although the Spanish occupy a somewhat lower position in the opportunity structure than the Indians, they do not show greater anomie than the Indians. In fact, a closer analysis of the anomie measures makes it clear that the Spanish actually have greater normative consensus than the Indians. This is not the consonance theoretically expected between limited opportunity and anomie; on the other hand, the actual Spanish-Indian difference in opportunity is neither large nor clear-cut, and to seek consonance with it is perhaps to ask too much of crude measures.

For both Indians and Spanish, consonance exists between the normative structure positions and the social control structure positions. As just noted, the Spanish occupy a less deviance-prone position in the normative structure than the Indians; the same holds true when their positions in the social control structure are considered, the Spanish clearly being subject to the operation of more effective controls than the Indians.

This analysis supplements the direct, correlational analysis presented earlier. What emerges from both approaches is some degree of support for the theoretical formulations which proposed that, over time, a consonance or homogeneity obtains among the several positions occupied by a person or group within the sociocultural system.

SUMMARY AND CONCLUSIONS

The purpose of this chapter was to elaborate the approach employed in measuring the sociocultural environment. Measures of the three components of the sociocultural system—the opportunity structure, the normative structure, and the social control structure—were described and evaluated. Within the opportunity structure, two measures of value-access disjunction were devised, a measure of socioeconomic status and a measure which more comprehensively maps objective access to socially valued goals. The two measures showed the Anglos to have greater access to opportunity than the non-Anglos. This finding drew strong convergent support from both the Community Survey and High School studies.

With respect to the normative structure, two types of anomie were differentiated: subcultural anomie and community anomie. A measure was devised to assess anomie as a social-structural feature. The results showed the Anglos to have the least anomie of either type. The Spanish and Indians were similar in consensus measures, but the Spanish hold certain norms strongly while the Indians are characterized by a more generalized normlessness. These findings did not draw convergent support from the High School Study since, unfortunately, a similar investigation was not carried out there.

In terms of access to illegitimate means in the social control structure, measures of exposure to deviant role models, integration into sanctioning networks, and differential opportunity to engage in deviance sharply differentiated the three ethnic groups. Again, the Anglos are in the least deviance-prone position, the Spanish are next, and the Indians show the most access to illegitimate means. The data from both studies converge impressively upon this relationship.

The findings of this chapter are important for several reasons. First, they show the possibility of developing theoretically relevant measures of the social environment. The three sociocultural structures elaborated in Chapter 3 were all, in one way or another, operationalized, and the methods were shown to have at least some initial value.

Second, the findings gain added support because of the convergent methodology employed. The measurement of the same variables in two separate studies, where populations and procedures were different, provided for convergent support which serves to strengthen conviction in the validity of the findings.

Third, the data enabled a partial test of a theory of relationships among sociocultural variables; the degree of consonance shown between the various social locations occupied by a person or group provides support not only for Merton's formulation about the relation of limited access to opportunity to normative breakdown, but also for the more general propositions advanced in Chapter 3.

Most important, perhaps, is the bearing these findings have on our theory of deviance. By the pattern of relations shown with respect to ethnic group status, these data provide a first confirmation of the sociocultural portion of the theory of deviance. The confirmation is, of course, indirect; more direct assessment of the relation of the sociocultural variables to deviant behavior will be presented in Chapter 11. Nevertheless, the confirmation is important. *What has been shown is that the ethnic topography of positions in the three sociocultural structures is strongly in accord with the ethnic topography of deviance.* The Anglos have the least value-access disjunction, the least anomie, and the least access to illegitimate means; and they make the least contribution to rates of deviant behavior. The converse applies to the Indians who have, with the Spanish, high value-access disjunctions, but also have the highest anomie and the greatest access to illegitimate means; they contribute the largest share to deviance rates. Intermediate in position on all sociocultural variables except position in the opportunity structure, the Spanish are also intermediate in deviance rates.

These findings, then, constitute a sociocultural "explanation," in admittedly indirect terms, of the differences between the ethnic groups in rates of deviant behavior. Accounting for between-ethnic group variation was stated at the outset as a major objective of the research; the present data represent the first step in that direction. A second step would require a demonstration that these ethnically related sociocultural differences are reflected in ethnically related personality differences. That step is taken in the following chapter.

REFERENCES

ATTNEAVE, F. *Applications of information theory to psychology.* New York: Holt, Rinehart and Winston, 1959.

CASTELLAN, N. J., JR. AND S. W. LINK. Biserial-point biserial correlation program for IBM 709/7090 (CPA 139). *Behavioral Science,* 1963, *8,* 368–369.

DURKHEIM, E. *Suicide: A study in sociology.* Trans. by John A. Spaulding and George Simpson. New York: Free Press, 1951.

GROSS, N., W. S. MASON, AND A. W. MCEACHERN. *Explorations in role analysis.* New York: Wiley, 1958.

HENRYSSON, S. Correction of item-total correlations in item analysis. *Psychometrika,* 1963, *28,* 211–218.

HOLLINGSHEAD, A. B. The two-factor index of social position. Privately printed by the author, Yale University, 1956.

KAHL, J. A. AND J. A. DAVIS. A comparison of indexes of socio-economic status. *American Sociological Review,* 1955, *20,* 317–325.

MEIER, DOROTHY AND W. BELL. Anomia and differential access to the achievement of life goals. *American Sociological Review,* 1959, *24,* 189–202.

MERTON, R. K. Anomie, anomia, and social interaction: Contexts of deviant behavior. In M. B. Clinard (Ed.) *Anomie and deviant behavior.* New York: Free Press, 1964. Pp. 213–242.

MERTON, R. K. *Social theory and social structure.* (Rev. ed.). New York: Free Press, 1957.

MINARD, J. G. Report on preliminary testing program: Sociometric preferences in the junior and senior classes of the local high school. Research Report No. 4, 1960, Tri-Ethnic Research Project, University of Colorado. (Ditto) Pp. 1–129.

MINARD, J. G. Social structure and student behavior in a tri-ethnic high school. Research Report No. 6, 1961, Tri-Ethnic Research Project, University of Colorado. (Mimeo.) Pp. 1–120.

PROCTOR, C. H. AND C. P. LOOMIS. Analysis of sociometric data. In Marie Jahoda, M. Deutsch, and S. W. Cook (Eds.) *Research methods in social relations with special reference to prejudice.* New York: Holt, Rinehart and Winston, 1951. Pp. 561–585.

SHYBUT, J. Demographic characteristics of the high school population of a tri-ethnic community, with comparisons among ethnic groups. Research Report No. 19, 1963, Tri-Ethnic Research Project, University of Colorado. (Mimeo.) Pp. 1–29.

YINGER, J. M. *Toward a field theory of behavior: Personality and social structure.* New York: McGraw-Hill, 1965.

CHAPTER TEN

The Measurement of the Personality System

In Chapter 4, the discussion of the personality system relevant to deviance-conformity resulted in the articulation of three structures: the perceived opportunity structure, the personal belief structure, and the personal control structure. Each personality structure was considered to be analogous to a corresponding structure in the sociocultural system. The measurement of the latter was dealt with in the preceding chapter; the measurement of the former can now be considered. In the present chapter, therefore, the operations by which each personality structure was measured will be described, and sex and ethnic group differences on the personality measures will be presented. Relations among the measures of the three structures will also be dealt with, as will relations between the sociocultural structures and the personality structures. With the completion of this chapter, the criterion and the predictor variables will have been presented, and it will then be possible to address the central task of the research: putting the over-all social-psychological framework to a direct empirical test.

THE MEASUREMENT OF THE PERCEIVED OPPORTUNITY STRUCTURE

What was sought in our effort to measure the perceived opportunity structure was some index of the extent to which each individual felt that he was able to achieve his personal goals within the situation in which he lived. This necessitated a measure of personal *goals or values,* a measure of subjective *expectations* concerning the possible attainment of these particular goals, and, finally, a derived measure to get at the gap or discrepancy between goals and anticipations of their attainment: a measure of *personal disjunctions.*

Clearly, this is a more complex approach than was undertaken in the parallel assessment of *objective* opportunity reported in the preceding chapter. The comparison is instructive. In the sociocultural measure we assumed (in accord with Merton) that the value placed on achievement goals by members of various sectors within the research community was roughly similar. The measure was, therefore, directed simply at the degree of objective opportunity available to each community member for achieving those shared goals. In the investigation of *perceived* opportunity, however, we have attempted to assess personal values directly rather than to assume their similarity across groups. As a result of this effort, therefore, we will be able to examine empirically the extent to which the earlier assumption of their general equality was in fact justified.

The High School Study

In this chapter, each structure is begun with the High School Study since most of the personality measures were first developed and refined in the high school research.

The Measurement of Personal Values

The personal values selected for assessment among high school students involved two general need or goal areas, that of achievement and recognition in academic activities (ACR) and that of love and affection in social interactions (SLA). These two need areas originate in Rotter's social learning theory (see Chapter 4) and were considered central to the goal strivings of high school-age subjects.

To measure the value placed upon these two areas of striving, a thirty-item rating scale procedure was developed and refined by item analyses over a three-year period.[1] Of these items, fifteen were referents for academic recognition and fifteen were referents for social love and affection. For each referent, the subject indicated the magnitude of the value he placed upon it by marking along a linear rating scale. The form employed in the inventory was the following:

How strongly do I like:
To get along well with most of the kids?

The full set of items is presented in Table 10.1, and their correlations

[1] Our first version of a value measure, based upon work by Liverant (1958), was forced-choice in format. This approach was later abandoned in favor of a rating scale procedure in order to facilitate the assessment and comparison of values in "absolute" rather than relative terms.

TABLE 10.1
Pearson Correlations of Personal Value Items with Total Score:
High School Study (N = 129)

Item	SLA	ACR
How strongly do I like:		
1. To get along well with most of the kids.	.65	
2. To be in on the fun that goes on around here.	.63	
3. To get at least a "B" average this year.		.64
4. To have friends want to do things with me during vacation.	.57	
5. To be well prepared for class discussion.		.56
6. To win a scholarship to some college.		.74
7. To have many friends in different groups.	.66	
8. To know that the teacher actually likes me as a person.	.61	
9. To come out near the top of the class on six-weeks tests.		.70
10. To be able to get my ideas across in class.		.64
11. To be thought of as a best friend by several of the kids.	.70	
12. To get on the honor roll during the year.		.78
13. To be well liked by most of the people around here.	.76	
14. To be in the top half of the class at graduation.		.66
15. To be asked to take part in many social activities.	.67	
16. To be able to answer other kids' questions about schoolwork.		.52
17. To have groups show real pleasure when I join them.	.74	
18. To be one of the most popular kids in the class.	.64	
19. To be thought most likely to amount to something by my teachers.		.63
20. To understand new material quickly in class.		.65
21. To go out of my way to help others.	.65	
22. To be voted the best-liked kid in my class.	.73	
23. To be encouraged by my teachers to go on to college.		.72
24. To do well in Math and Science courses.		.54
25. To have other kids enjoy having me around.	.81	
26. To be considered a bright student by my teacher.		.74
27. To openly express my appreciation of others.	.55	
28. To have good enough grades to go on to college if I want to.		.71
29. To be thought of as a good student by the other kids.		.73
30. To do things with the group just because I like being with them.	.59	

with total score for all items in the same need area are also shown. The internal homogeneity of the two subscales is suggested by the fact that these correlations are in all cases above .50.

Sex and Ethnic Group Differences in Personal Values

We are now in a position to examine empirically whether the minority group members are any less oriented toward these particular success goals than their Anglo neighbors. The data are presented in Table 10.2. As might have been expected, girls place significantly higher value on social love and affection goals than boys in the high school and somewhat more value on academic recognition as well.

Turning to ethnic group differences, however, there is no evidence that non-Anglos value these major personal goals less than Anglos. In fact, Spanish-American students in the high school place significantly *higher*

TABLE 10.2
Sex and Ethnic Group Differences in Personal Values: High School Study

Measure		Means and Standard Deviations		Significance* (Male *vs.* Female)
		Males (N = 47)	Females (N = 46)	
Academic recognition	$\bar{X}$ σ	6.4 (1.5)	6.9 (1.2)	$t = 1.65$ N.S.
Social love and affection	$\bar{X}$ σ	6.3 (1.4)	7.1 (1.3)	$t = 2.79$ $p < .01$

		Means and Standard Deviations			Significance*		
		Anglos (N = 43)	Spanish (N = 36)	Indians (N = 11)	Anglos *vs.* Spanish	Anglos *vs.* Indians	Spanish *vs.* Indians
Academic recognition	$\bar{X}$ σ	6.2 (1.5)	7.2 (1.0)	6.2 (1.3)	$t = 3.43$ $p < .001$	$t = 0.07$ N.S.	$t = 2.31$ $p < .05$
Social love and affection	$\bar{X}$ σ	6.4 (1.5)	7.3 (1.1)	6.0 (1.9)	$t = 2.86$ $p < .01$	$t = 0.75$ N.S.	$t = 2.14$ $p < .05$

* All *t*-tests of group mean differences are two-tailed. Differences not significant at the .05 level or better are indicated N.S.

value on academic recognition goals than do Anglo students; the same is true for social love and affection goals. This finding is fully in line with our results from earlier years; in fact, in the first year of testing, when a forced-choice format was employed, both Spanish and Indian subjects ranked academic recognition goals above social love and affection goals, whereas the Anglos reversed this preference order (Graves, 1960). The data suggest, then, that at least among adolescents in the research community, and with respect to these particular goals, the minority group members are no less oriented toward "success" than their more advantaged

Anglo neighbors. We will return to this general issue again in the discussion of the Community Survey Study.

The Measurement of Expectations

The same thirty items, but presented in a different order, were administered to the same students the following day in order to obtain measures of their *expectations* of achieving the goals referred to in the items. An introduction to the expectation inventory emphasized the distinction between values and expectations and made clear to the student how this task differed from that of the previous day. Again, a linear scale was provided, and the students were now asked to check, for each item, how strongly they *expected* each goal to occur. The format was as follows:

How strongly do I expect:
To get at least a "B" average this year?

| 0 | 100 |

SURE IT WILL   EVEN CHANCE   SURE IT *WILL*
NOT HAPPEN   "FIFTY-FIFTY"   HAPPEN

Depending on the scale interval checked, students were given a scale score of 0–9 on each item. Each student again received two total scores: his mean expectancy score for academic recognition goals and for social love and affection goals.

The internal homogeneity of the expectancy questionnaire is very similar to that for the values questionnaire. Except for one item, "to be able to get my ideas across in class," which had only a .31 correlation with total ACR score, the product-moment correlation between item and total score is within a few points of those presented in Table 10.1. Again, all but that one item have correlations above .5.

The Validity of the Values and Expectations Questionnaires

The validation of these two questionnaires was approached in fairly standard fashion:[2] Do the need area subscales correlate with alternative measures of similar constructs more highly than with alternative measures of dissimilar constructs? If so, then the scales can be said to display some initial validity.

Two additional measures were used for this analysis. The first was

[2] Several studies outside of the framework of the Tri-Ethnic Project have since employed these value and expectation inventories and have generated additional validation information. See, for example, Carman (1965) and Opochinsky (1965). The former was concerned with alcohol use and complications among college students; the latter was concerned with selective interpersonal impression formation. Both studies support the utility of the inventories.

grade point average, an objective index of academic achievement. The development of this measure was described in Chapter 8. The second was a sociometric measure of social status, which was used as an indirect index of the degree to which social love and affection goals were actually being attained by each student from his peers in school.

Three items in the sociometric questionnaire were used in the construction of the social status index:

1. Who are the four kids *in this school* you would choose to mess around with?
2. Of all the kids *in this school,* name the four that other kids like best.
3. Which of the kids *in this school* are the ones nobody seems to care about?

As with the sociometric index developed for peer ratings of deviant behavior (see Chapter 8), students were rank-ordered for each item in terms of a dimension of "best liked" to "least liked." Their ranks were added and reranked to provide a rather stable and internally consistent composite index reflecting number of nominations received as being "liked" by others.

The over-all correlation between the Social Status index and Grade Point Average is only .20, indicating that, at least among high school students in the research community, social status and academic achievement are relatively independent.

Given such a degree of independence, it is then pertinent to ask, are value and expectation scores with respect to academic achievement more strongly related to an index of actual achievement in this need area (Grade Point Average), than they are to an index of successful interpersonal peer relations (the Social Status index)? By the same token, are value and expectation scores with respect to social love and affection more strongly associated with the Social Status index than with Grade Point Average?

The evidence bearing on these points is presented in Table 10.3. It can be seen first that the Pearson correlation values are almost all quite low; the only exception is the substantial and gratifying .51 correlation between Grade Point Average and Expectations for Academic Recognition. Since we are seeking relationships between measures of different but related constructs, low correlations are to be expected in general. The consistent *direction* of difference between pairs of correlations (these are indicated in the table by signs) is particularly noteworthy. In each case, values or expectations within the academic recognition need area correlate more highly with grades than they do with social status. Similarly,

TABLE 10.3
**Pearson Correlations of Values and Expectations to Actual
Achievement in Two Need Areas: High School Study***

Measure	Social Status Index		Grade Point Average
Personal values			
Social love and affection	.18	>	.00
	V		∧
Academic recognition	.11	<	.13
Expectations			
Social love and affection	.27	>	.03
	V		∧
Academic recognition	.18	<	.51

* $N = 129$, for which a correlation of .15 is significant at the .05 level,
one-tailed test.

in each case, values or expectations within the social love and affection
need area correlate more highly with social status than they do with grades.
This same directional consistency holds within the Anglo and the Spanish
ethnic groups examined separately (the local Indian group is too small
to provide stable data), within the total male group, and, with one exception among the eight comparisons, within the total female group as well.
This consistency suggests that these measures are actually differentiating
between alternative need areas.

It should be noted also that the correlations between Grade Point Average or Social Status and the appropriate *expectations* scores are consistently
higher than the analogous correlations with the appropriate *values* scores.
This is also true within the Anglo group, the Spanish group, the total
male group, and the total female group, with one exception, where the
correlations are identical. The measure of expectations thus seems somewhat more discriminating than the measure of values.

Despite this evidence of both convergent and discriminant validity, a
good deal of measurement effect appears to be in operation, reducing
the observed distinctions between these two need areas. Although the
Grade Point Average measure and the Social Status index correlated only
.20, mean expectations of achieving academic recognition correlated .59
with mean expectations of achieving social love and affection. Mean personal value scores for goals within these two distinct need areas were
even more highly related: .75.

Finally, the mean value score and expectation score for academic recognition correlated .41; for social love and affection, they correlated .53.
Having no alternative measure of these constructs, we cannot estimate
whether this level of relationship reflects a relative lack of independence
of values and expectations or simply the shortcomings of our measures

of them. The correlations are, nevertheless, sufficiently low to make a derived score based on the interaction of values and expectations both feasible and potentially useful.

The Measurement of Personal Disjunctions

In theory, deviant behavior should be positively related to the actual or perceived inability to achieve personal goals through the use of socially acceptable means. In the sociocultural system measurement, this means-goals disjunction was simply estimated in terms of each subject's position with respect to his access to legitimate means. In that procedure, it was assumed—and left unmeasured, as we have already noted—that all subjects were striving for much the same types of personal goals within the opportunity structure. In our measurement of the personality system, measures of personal goals, as well as measures of expectations for their achievement, were devised. This joint measurement permitted the construction of a *composite* measure of value-expectation discrepancy or means-goals disjunction in which *both* measured values and measured expectations played a part.

There are a number of different ways in which values scores and expectations scores could be combined to get at the gap between them. Several of these were explored (Castellan, 1963), but by far the most straightforward procedure, and that which, empirically, proved to be most satisfactory as well, was simply to subtract the expectation score from the value score *in each case where disjunction occurs,* that is, for each of thirty items where the value score was greater than the expectancy score. These differences were then added across all items in each of the two need areas. The resulting value-expectation discrepancy scores constitute our personal disjunction measure.[3]

Measurement theory leads one to raise several issues with regard to this procedure. For example, there is no empirical or theoretical basis for assuming that the values scale and the expectations scale are in any sense comparable, start from the same zero point, or have equal intervals either within each scale or across scales. All such dubious assumptions were made by us when we simply subtracted a score on one scale from a score on another scale, adding these differences across a series of disparate and clearly unequal items. Nevertheless, the measure seems to capture, better than anything else we devised, the essence of the construct under investigation. The decision as to the merit of the procedure will ultimately be an empirical one, whether it works in the sense of being successfully mapped into a system of empirical relationships specified by the theory.

[3] In a recent paper, Phillips (1964) independently reports an identical procedure in his measurement of what he calls "Expected Value Deprivation," a construct identical to our "Personal Disjunction."

Alternative Measures of the Perceived Opportunity Structure

On the first day of the final year's testing, students were asked to respond to a series of questions bearing on their perceived chances for satisfying personal goals in the future. This Life Chances inventory was a revision of a form developed during the previous year's testing and reported in Guertin (1962).

A major difference between this inventory and the values and expectations questionnaires just described is that the latter focused on relatively immediate goals in the peer group and in the high school situation, whereas the Life Chances inventory was designed to tap more distant goals and expectations. The temporal frame of reference given the student was age twenty-five, and questions were asked about his goals and expectations in three areas: education, job type, and income. For example, students were asked, "What job would you like to have when you are about twenty-five years old? Give the name of a job or occupation and say what you would be doing on the job." Following this, they were asked, "Assuming that wages will be about the same as they are now, about how much money will you be making if you have this job?" Students were then asked to note various barriers which might stand in the way of their getting this job, to estimate their general chances of getting this job, and to state realistically what job they actually *expected* to have at age twenty-five and the income they actually *expected* to be making. The amount of schooling each student actually expected to finish was also obtained, as well as the importance he placed on higher education.

A Life Chances Disjunction index (LCD I) was then constructed as follows: For each of the three areas of education, income, and job type, students were scored 0, 1, 2 on the basis of the amount of disjunction exhibited in that area. Although the definition of each scoring category was more complex than can be briefly stated here, the categories were basically as follows:

Education: 0—expected to complete four years of college
1—expected some post-high-school training
2—expected no post-high-school training

Income: For each student, the yearly income *realistically expected* at age twenty-five was subtracted from the income he thought he would make on the job he really wanted to have. The distribution of these differences was then dichotomized, and students were given a disjunction score as follows:
0—no difference
1—$120–2399 difference
2—$2400 difference

Job Type: 0—student actually expected at age twenty-five to have the same job he really wanted

1—student was not sure of having the job he really wanted at age twenty-five

2—student was pretty sure he would *not* have the job he really wanted at age twenty-five

These three scores were then summed to produce the Life Chances Disjunction index I (LCD I), with a range of 0–6.

A second Life Chances Disjunction score (LCD II) was based on answers to five items placed toward the end of the inventory: When you think about your future realistically, how sure are you of:

1. Being a respected member of the community in which you will be living?
2. Having a happy family life?
3. Being a leader in church groups, clubs, or other organizations?
4. Being able to settle down in whatever part of the country you want?
5. Doing better in life than your parents did?

Students were asked, for each item, to circle one of three response categories: "very sure," "pretty sure," or "not too sure." On the assumption that all five goals would be generally valued, the student's answer to each item was scored 0, 1, or 2, and scores on all five items were summed to yield a disjunction index. It may be seen that this index, LCD II, involves social recognition goals (items 1 and 3) and social love and affection goals (item 2), as well as achievement goals (items 4 and 5). Its content is thus broader and more diverse than that of LCD I.

Intercorrelations among Measures of Perceived Opportunity

Wherever feasible, the research strategy has been a convergent one, employing multiple measures of each major construct. We have thus far in this chapter presented six alternative measures of the perceived opportunity structure among high school students in the research community: expectations of obtaining academic recognition and social love and affection goals; disjunctions between each of these expectations and the values students placed on the relevant goals; and the two Life Chances Disjunction indexes, focusing on the same types of goals, but more distant in future time. The degree of convergence among these measures can now be examined.

Product-moment intercorrelations are presented in Table 10.4. To interpret this table correctly one must recognize that the high correlations between disjunction scores and their corresponding expectations scores are artifactual. (These correlations are properly negative: The higher the

TABLE 10.4

Pearson Correlations among Six Measures of the Perceived Opportunity Structure: High School Study*

	1	2	3	4	5	6
1. Expectations—academic recognition						
2. Expectations—social love and affection	.55					
3. Disjunctions—academic recognition	−.71	−.22				
4. Disjunctions—social love and affection	−.47	−.54	.67			
5. Life chances disjunction—Index I	−.30	.14†	.26	−.04†		
6. Life chances disjunction—Index II	−.33	−.13	.08	.03	.17	

* $N = 93$, for which a correlation of .17 is significant at the .05 level, one-tailed test.

† These two correlations are the only ones not in the expected direction.

expectations, the lower the disjunctions.) Since disjunctions are derived scores based in part upon expectations, they can be considered alternative scoring of the same data, taking value scores into account. It becomes an empirical question, then, of whether variability in value scores among subjects is sufficiently meaningful that a measure of perceived opportunity is improved by taking them directly into account as the disjunction measure does.

The bottom two lines of Table 10.4 are, therefore, the more interesting ones. Here, expectations and disjunctions measures are correlated with the operationally distinct measures of perceived life chances. Significant relations obtain for both expectations and disjunctions in the area of academic recognition. Neither expectations nor disjunctions in the *social love and affection* need area are related to the two perceived Life Chances Disjunction indexes. This, incidentally, is further evidence that separate need areas are actually being measured. Further, the derived disjunction measure appears no more strongly correlated with the two Life Chances Disjunctions measures than is the simple expectations measure; it appears thus far, that nothing was actually gained by attempting to take into account possible differences in personal values for various academic goals. Additional evidence on this matter can come from considering the two kinds of measures in relation to other criteria, however.

Sex and Ethnic Group Differences in Perceived Opportunity

In Table 10.5, sex group means on the six alternative measures of the perceived opportunity structure just discussed are presented. On no measure do these differences achieve the magnitude required for statistical significance. Although high school girls in the research community value love and affection goals more highly than do the boys (Table 10.2), they also have somewhat higher expectations of achieving these goals as well. Consequently, their derived disjunction scores are quite similar

TABLE 10.5
Sex Group Differences in Six Measures of the Perceived Opportunity Structure:
High School Study*

Measure		Means and Standard Deviations		Significance (Male *vs.* Female)
		Males	Females	
Expectations				
Academic recognition	$\bar{X}$	4.6	4.8	$t = 0.71$
	σ	(1.7)	(1.8)	N.S.
Social love and affection	$\bar{X}$	5.4	5.9	$t = 1.75$
	σ	(1.5)	(1.3)	N.S.
Disjunctions				
Academic recognition	$\bar{X}$	3.4	3.6	$t = 0.45$
	σ	(2.0)	(2.2)	N.S.
Social love and affection	$\bar{X}$	2.1	2.5	$t = 1.24$
	σ	(1.3)	(1.6)	N.S.
Life chances disjunction				
Index I	$\bar{X}$	2.9	2.6	$t = 0.86$
	σ	(1.5)	(1.9)	N.S.
Index II	$\bar{X}$	3.6	3.4	$t = 0.29$
	σ	(2.2)	(2.4)	N.S.

* $N = 92$. All t-tests of group mean differences are two-tailed. Differences not significant at the .05 level or better are indicated N.S.

to those of the boys. Because of this lack of sex group differences in the perceived opportunity structure measures, males and females have been combined in all subsequent analyses of these data.

Table 10.6 presents ethnic group means on the same six measures, and here, group differences are substantial. It is important to note where the areas of perceived deprivation lie for the two minority groups. The Spanish students perceive their limitations in the area of academic achievement, job success, and the like; in the area of social love and affection goals, however, they see themselves by and large as no worse off than Anglo students. By contrast, not only do Indian students feel themselves deprived with respect to academic recognition but, unlike the Spanish, they have the lowest expectations of social love and affection goals as well. Although the size of our Indian sample is so small that we must make inferences with great caution, on five of the six measures reported here, it is shown that, for the Indian students, in most of the need areas tapped, a sense of limited opportunity for personal achievement is more pervasive than for their neighbors.

With respect to the relative merits of the expectation and disjunction measures, the evidence remains equivocal: Expectations are more discrimi-

TABLE 10.6

Ethnic Group Differences on Six Measures of the Perceived Opportunity Structure: High School Study

Measure		Means and Standard Deviations			Significance*		
		Anglos $(N = 43)$	Spanish $(N = 36)$	Indians $(N = 11)$	Anglos vs. Spanish	Anglos vs. Indians	Spanish vs. Indians
Expectations							
Academic	$\bar{X}$	5.0	4.7	3.6	$t = 0.73$	$t = 2.62$	$t = 2.08$
recognition	σ	(1.7)	(1.7)	(1.5)	N.S.	$p < .05$	N.S.
Social love	$\bar{X}$	5.5	6.3	4.6	$t = 2.86$	$t = 1.68$	$t = 3.12$
and affec-tion	σ	(1.4)	(1.0)	(1.7)	$p < .01$	N.S.	$p < .01$
Disjunctions							
Academic	$\bar{X}$	2.6	4.2	4.4	$t = 3.84$	$t = 2.42$	$t = 0.30$
recognition	σ	(1.7)	(1.8)	(2.3)	$p < .001$	$p < .05$	N.S.
Social love	$\bar{X}$	2.2	2.3	3.2	$t = 0.41$	$t = 1.37$	$t = 1.22$
and affec-tion	σ	(1.2)	(1.2)	(2.5)	N.S.	N.S.	N.S.
Life chances disjunc-tion							
Index I	$\bar{X}$	2.4	3.2	2.5	$t = 2.12$	$t = 0.10$	$t = 1.55$
	σ	(1.6)	(1.8)	(1.9)	$p < .05$	N.S.	N.S.
Index II	$\bar{X}$	3.0	3.5	5.6	$t = 0.91$	$t = 2.88$	$t = 2.29$
	σ	(2.0)	(2.4)	(2.8)	N.S.	$p < .05$	$p < .05$

* All *t*-tests of group mean differences are two-tailed. Differences not significant at the .05 level or better are indicated N.S.

nating than disjunctions in the love and affection area, but the reverse is true with respect to recognition.

The Community Survey Study

The approach to the measure of perceived opportunity among adults in the research community was conceptually similar to that just presented for high school students, but quite different in format. *Four* general need areas were explored: affection, dependence, recognition, and independence. These four areas were also borrowed from Rotter (1954) as being fairly representative of the range of human motivational strivings. Interview items were constructed which referred to these needs within each of three different *life* areas: family, friendships, and work. Thus, within the family life area, for example, subjects were asked how *important* to them was "the love and affection you get in the family," "having somebody in the family you can count on to help you," "the good opinion of the family for the things you do well," and "being able to do things in the family in your own way." Subjects rated each item as "very important," "pretty important," "not too important," or "not important at all" to them; these were then scored 0 to 3. Similar items were devised for friendship interactions and for the area of work. Eight additional questions, two within each of the four need areas, were also asked; they were couched in general terms and not related to any particular life area. This approach provided a total of twenty *value* ratings, all of which were sufficiently universal in content to be applicable to all three ethnic groups in the community.

In order to get at personal *expectations,* subjects were instructed as follows: "We were talking just now about what you think is *important* in life. Now we are changing over to talk about what you expect and not any more about what you want. We all want certain things, but we don't really *expect* them all." The same items were then presented in an expectancy format—realistic expectations of achieving these goals by the subject were stressed. The respondent's answers ranged along the scale: "very sure," "pretty sure," "not too sure," and "not sure at all." In addition to these twenty expectancy ratings in the four need areas across the three life areas, subjects were also asked to make four global expectancy ratings, such as the following: "When you think about what you really expect in the future, how does it look to you from here: 'very good,' 'pretty good,' 'not too good,' or 'not good at all?'" All of these responses were scored 0 to 3 and summed across items.

The measure of *personal disjunctions,* as among high school students, was a derived score based both on the level of valuation and the level of expectation with respect to a given goal. A "disjunction" was counted for each of the twenty items which the subject had rated as either "very important" or "pretty important" *and* which he was "not too sure" or "not sure at all" of being able to obtain. In addition, he was given one disjunction for each of the four global items for which his future expectations ratings were either "not too good" or "not good at all." Thus, each subject could obtain up to a total of 24 on this disjunction index.

Sex and Ethnic Group Differences in Perceived Opportunity

In Table 10.7, sex group means on values, expectations, and disjunctions, calculated for the community as a whole, are presented. As can be seen at a glance, these means are remarkably similar. What small differences there are in the direction we might expect, such as women placing a higher value on affection and a lower value on independence than men. But none of these differences attains statistical significance. Sex groups have been combined, therefore, for the subsequent ethnic analyses.

TABLE 10.7
Sex Differences in Values, Expectations, and Disjunctions:
Community Survey Study

Measure	Means		Significance*
	Males (N = 100)	Females (N = 104)	
Need Values			
Affection	12.1	12.3	N.S.
Dependency	12.0	11.9	N.S.
Independence	9.7	9.2	N.S.
Recognition	11.7	11.4	N.S.
Expectations			
Affection	10.1	10.2	N.S.
Dependency	10.6	10.9	N.S.
Independence	9.3	8.9	N.S.
Recognition	9.9	9.8	N.S.
Total	47.6	47.2	N.S.
Disjunctions			
Affection	0.8	0.8	N.S.
Dependency	0.8	0.7	N.S.
Independence	0.7	0.8	N.S.
Recognition	1.0	0.9	N.S.
Total	4.3	4.5	N.S.

* All *t*-tests of group mean differences are two-tailed. Differences not significant at the .05 level or better are indicated N.S.

In Table 10.8, the ethnic group data, broken down by need area, on the personal values of our adults subjects are presented. It can be seen that in all cases, with the exception of a somewhat reduced value placed on affection goals by the Indians, *the personal values held by the three ethnic groups on this measure are essentially identical.* This finding is in full agreement with the previously described parallel finding among the high school students in the community; and it further justifies the assumption made in the preceding chapter that personal values are fairly uniformly held by members of the three ethnic groups.

Table 10.9 presents the data on both expectations and disjunctions, the basic measures of perceived opportunity among adults. Given the demonstrated absence of group differences in personal values, these two measures can now be seen as alternative operational approaches to the same construct: feelings of personal deprivation within the perceived opportunity structure.

Two things are clearly evident in the table. First, the Spanish and Indians are surprisingly similar in their feelings of personal deprivation or value-expectation disjunction. Second, with the exception of relatively high

TABLE 10.8
Ethnic Group Differences in Personal Values: Community Survey Study

Need Value Ratings		Means and Standard Deviations			Significance*		
		Anglos (N = 93)	Spanish (N = 60)	Indians (N = 57)	Anglos *vs.* Spanish	Anglos *vs.* Indians	Spanish *vs.* Indians
Affection	$\bar{X}$	12.5	12.5	11.4	$t = 0.05$	$t = 3.02$	$t = 2.69$
	σ	(2.1)	(2.1)	(2.2)	N.S.	$p < .01$	$p < .01$
Dependency	$\bar{X}$	11.7	12.2	12.0	$t = 1.11$	$t = 0.70$	$t = 0.46$
	σ	(2.6)	(2.3)	(2.0)	N.S.	N.S.	N.S.
Independence	$\bar{X}$	9.4	9.6	9.3	$t = 0.53$	$t = 0.28$	$t = 0.70$
	σ	(2.5)	(3.0)	(2.8)	N.S.	N.S.	N.S.
Recognition	$\bar{X}$	11.5	11.7	11.5	$t = 0.61$	$t = 0.13$	$t = 0.44$
	σ	(2.5)	(2.4)	(2.3)	N.S.	N.S.	N.S.

* All t-tests of group mean differences are two-tailed. Differences not significant at the .05 level or better are indicated N.S.

expectations for personal recognition among the Spanish, the Spanish and Indian subjects consistently have lower expectations and more disjunctions than their Anglo neighbors in all need areas, and most Anglo–non-Anglo differences are highly significant statistically. In these data, the disjunctions measure seems somewhat more discriminating than the expectations measure.

The measurement of perceived opportunity has been carried out in the High School Study by questionnaires and in the Community Survey Study by interview. In each study, the paradigm was similar: to measure values and expectations separately and to derive a measure of the discrepancy or disjunction between them. The data from the two studies converge markedly. With respect to personal *values,* no ethnic differences emerge. With respect to expectations for achieving those values, or with respect to personal disjunctions, ethnic differences are clear: The Anglos perceive the greatest degree of opportunity compared to the two minority groups; between the latter there is similarity in general, but a tendency is indicated in both studies for the Indians to perceive less opportunity or more limitations than the Spanish.

THE MEASUREMENT OF THE PERSONAL BELIEF STRUCTURE

The personality variables to be discussed in this section refer to general cognitive orientations or beliefs presumed to reflect or parallel the concept of anomie in the normative structure. In Chapter 4, the relationship of

TABLE 10.9
Ethnic Group Differences in Perceived Opportunity: Community Survey Study

Measure		Means and Standard Deviations			Significance*		
		Anglos (N = 91)	Spanish (N = 58)	Indians (N = 55)	Anglos vs. Spanish	Anglos vs. Indians	Spanish vs. Indians
Expectations							
Affection	$\bar{X}$	10.8	9.6	9.5	$t = 3.16$	$t = 3.27$	$t = 0.16$
	σ	(2.0)	(2.5)	(2.5)	$p < .01$	$p < .01$	N.S.
Dependency	$\bar{X}$	11.5	10.1	10.2	$t = 3.37$	$t = 3.39$	$t = 0.19$
	σ	(2.2)	(2.4)	(2.1)	$p < .01$	$p < .001$	N.S.
Independence	$\bar{X}$	9.5	8.7	8.9	$t = 1.65$	$t = 1.47$	$t = 0.32$
	σ	(2.6)	(3.0)	(2.4)	N.S.	N.S.	N.S.
Recognition	$\bar{X}$	10.0	10.3	9.1	$t = 0.82$	$t = 2.03$	$t = 2.54$
	σ	(2.4)	(2.5)	(2.4)	N.S.	$p < .05$	$p < .05$
Total†	$\bar{X}$	49.9	45.8	45.1	$t = 2.78$	$t = 3.53$	$t = 0.45$
	σ	(8.3)	(9.1)	(7.8)	$p < .01$	$p < .001$	N.S.
Disjunctions							
Affection	$\bar{X}$	0.4	1.2	1.1	$t = 4.04$	$t = 3.88$	$t = 0.31$
	σ	(0.9)	(1.2)	(1.1)	$p < .001$	$p < .001$	N.S.
Dependency	$\bar{X}$	0.4	1.0	1.1	$t = 3.60$	$t = 4.00$	$t = 0.27$
	σ	(0.7)	(1.1)	(1.1)	$p < .001$	$p < .001$	N.S.
Independence	$\bar{X}$	0.5	1.0	0.9	$t = 2.91$	$t = 3.29$	$t = 0.30$
	$\dot{\sigma}$	(0.8)	(1.2)	(0.8)	$p < .01$	$p < .01$	N.S.
Recognition	$\bar{X}$	0.8	1.0	1.1	$t = 1.17$	$t = 1.82$	$t = 0.68$
	σ	(1.1)	(1.1)	(1.2)	N.S.	N.S.	N.S.
Total†	$\bar{X}$	2.8	5.7	5.7	$t = 4.66$	$t = 5.14$	$t = 0.03$
	σ	(3.1)	(4.0)	(3.3)	$p < .001$	$p < .001$	N.S.

* All t-tests of group mean differences are two-tailed. Differences not significant at the .05 level or better are indicated N.S.

† Because of the addition of four global items, the total score does not equal the sum of the four subscores.

two such "belief" variables—belief in internal *versus* external control, and alienation—to the sociocultural environment and to deviance-conformity was elaborated. In the present section, our approach to the measurement of these two beliefs will be described, and data will be presented with respect to sex and ethnic group differences on the resulting measures.

The High School Study

Within the High School Study, only the concept of belief in internal *versus* external control (I-E) seemed suitable for measurement. The item content of the Alienation scale used in the Community Survey Study (see below) seemed to imply many years of confrontation with the difficulties of life and, therefore, seemed inappropriate for use with adolescents. A good deal of research has been conducted around the I-E concept over the last several years; much of this work is summarized in a recent monograph by Rotter (1965). The I-E concept refers to a dimension running from internal control—a belief that one has control over and can influence the consequences of one's behavior, that is, the rewards and punishments one receives for one's actions; to external control—the belief that what happens to one is governed largely by fate, luck, chance, or powerful external forces both human and supernatural.

The Measurement of Internal-External Control

On the basis of an early version of a forced-choice I-E inventory constructed by Dr. Shephard Liverant, a series of tryouts, item analyses, and revisions was carried out. This work eventuated in a twenty-five-item scale used in the final data collection in the High School Study.

The test format was forced choice and involved pairing one statement expressing a belief in personal control and responsibility against another, roughly equated for social desirability, expressing a belief in external control in the same general life area. These item pairs can vary widely in life area and in level of abstraction; within each pair, however, an attempt was made to match statements in both these regards. For example, the first item in the final version of the inventory reads:

I more strongly believe that:

1. a. No matter how much a person tries, it's hard to change the way things are going to turn out.
   b. A person can pretty well make whatever he wants out of his life.

This item expresses a general belief at a rather high level of abstraction. By contrast, the next item reads:

2. a. It's really easy to have friends: a person just needs to try to be friendly.
   b. Sometimes making friends is a matter of being lucky enough to meet the right people.

In this item, a quite specific area of activity is being tapped: making friends. In addition, five buffer items were inserted to attempt to break any set the students might develop concerning the nature of the construct we were attempting to measure. For example, the third item in the inventory reads:

3. a. I don't spend much time thinking about the past.
   b. I often think about the things I did as a child.

Item-total score biserial correlations for the final version of this inventory yielded two items with no correlation; these were therefore eliminated from all subsequent analyses. Correlations for the remaining twenty-three items averaged about .40, which suggests a fair degree of internal homogeneity for the test. The I-E inventory is scored so that the higher the score the greater the belief in *external* control.

An Alternative Measure of Internal-External Control

In line with a general convergent strategy, an alternative measure of internal control was constructed; it was based upon five items embedded within a twenty-seven-item, semiprojective Incomplete Sentences Blank (ISB) administered at the beginning of the second testing day. The ISB also contained items relevant to other personality attributes in our scheme (see below).

The five items used to provide responses for an alternative index of internal-external control beliefs were: "luck," "figuring out people," "figuring out the future," "the future," and "the breaks." A scoring manual for this procedure was prepared (Gillis, 1962) which assigned three-point scores to each item, and yielded 97 percent inter-rater agreement over a subset of responses.

Correlations between this semiprojective ISB score and scores on the forced-choice I-E Inventory were positive and significant both in the 1960 and in the 1961 testing. Given the radical difference in method, this convergence is encouraging evidence for the concept, despite the fact that the correlation level, about .20 both years, is very low. An interesting difference between the results of these two tasks is also worth mention. On the forced-choice procedure, where the socially desirable response is probably readily apparent, mean over-all scores for the test were consistently well in the direction of *internal* control. By contrast, on the more ambiguous incomplete sentences procedure, the over-all mean score both years was in an *external* direction.

Sex and Ethnic Group Differences in Internal-External Control

The data from the twenty-three-item forced-choice inventory of internal-external control are presented in Table 10.10. Since the sex difference is nonsignificant, the data from both sexes have been combined in the subsequent ethnic group analysis. With respect to the latter, it can be seen that no ethnic group differences obtain on this measure within the High School Study. In view of the ethnographic literature on fatalism among the Spanish and in the lower social classes and marginal groups, this finding raises a question about the validity of the I-E scale. The lack of anomie measures in the high school prevents an examination of the consonance of this belief finding with parallel findings about the high school normative structure.

TABLE 10.10
Sex and Ethnic Group Differences in Internal-External Control: High School Study

		Means and Standard Deviations		Significance* (Male *vs.* Female)
		Males (N = 47)	Females (N = 46)	
Internal-Exter-nal Control†	$\bar{X}$	6.4	5.6	$t = 1.12$
	σ	(3.8)	(3.0)	N.S.

		Means and Standard Deviations			Significance*		
		Anglos (N = 42)	Spanish (N = 36)	Indians (N = 11)	Anglos *vs.* Spanish	Anglos *vs.* Indians	Spanish *vs.* Indians
	$\bar{X}$	6.3	5.9	5.5	$t = 0.52$	$t = 0.80$	$t = 0.39$
	σ	(3.8)	(3.2)	(2.6)	N.S.	N.S.	N.S.

* All *t*-tests of group mean differences are two-tailed. Differences not significant at the .05 level or better are indicated N.S.

† High score indicates high external control.

The Community Survey Study

The Measurement of Internal-External Control

For the adult sample in the Community Survey Study, a shorter version of the I-E inventory was adapted for use in an interview situation. The items retained the forced-choice format and were similar in content to those employed in the high school. The final set in the interview I-E scale consisted of twelve items with an average item-total score biserial correlation of .40, identical to that obtaining in the high school questionnaire.

The Measurement of Alienation

The most frequently cited and investigated psychological correlate of anomie has been the variable, or the complex of variables, variously referred to as anomia, psychological anomie, or alienation. Our preference for the latter term, and our conceptualization of its meaning, have been discussed in Chapter 4. To approach the measurement of alienation we followed the Srole scale model (1956) but more than doubled the number of items to include other properties of the alienation concept specified by Seeman (1959).

The final items in our alienation scale, thirteen in number, are presented in Table 10.11. For each item, subjects in the interview were asked to

TABLE 10.11
Internal Characteristics of the Alienation Scale: Community Survey Study*

Item	Proportion alienated	Item-total score biserial correlation
1. I often feel that people around here are not too friendly.	.29	.49
2. Trying to figure out how to get ahead in life is just too complicated.	.29	.73
3. Most of the time I feel the work I'm doing is important and useful.	.06	.31
4. In spite of what some people say, things are getting worse for the average man.	.49	.50
5. I often feel left out of things that are going on around here.	.26	.62
6. Most of the people I know have different ideas than I have about the kind of life they want for their children.	.50	.68
7. When people around here are having a hard time, it's up to me to try and help out.	.17	.23
8. Nowadays children don't give their parents the respect they should.	.79	.32
9. It's hard to know just how to treat people around here since you don't know what they expect.	.48	.77
10. It's hardly fair to bring children into the world, the way things look for the future.	.36	.63
11. I get the feeling that the people around here see most things the way I do.	.42	.34
12. It's not really my concern if other people are in trouble.	.32	.53
13. If I had my choice, I'd live my life very differently.	.35	.57

* $N = 221$.

"strongly agree," "agree," "disagree," or "strongly disagree" with the statement, and were given a score of 0–3 accordingly. The six components of alienation explored in this scale, and the items related to each component, are as follows:

1.   Feelings of social isolation in the sense of being rejected, excluded, or repudiated in social relations: items 1 and 5.
2.   Feelings of social isolation in the sense of lacking commonalities with others; absence of shared values: items 6 and 11.
3.   Feelings of social isolation in the sense of lacking a feeling of responsibility for the welfare of others: items 7 and 12.
4.   Feelings of helplessness, of frustration and despair: items 2 and 9.

5. Feelings of hopelessness, of futility about the future: items 4 and 10.
6. Feelings of lack of gratification in one's ordinary role activities: items 3, 8, and 13.

Despite the high diversity in conceptual content, item-total score biserial correlations averaged over .50, higher than for the conceptually more homogeneous Internal-External Control inventory; unidimensionality, however, could not be demonstrated for the scale as a whole (Titley, 1963). Temporal stability of this measure also appears to be substantial: Test-retest reliability for a small sample of subjects with an eleven-month time gap was over .80.

Scales of this sort are clearly subject to the operation of varied response sets, particularly those of acquiescence and social desirability. Our efforts to cope with factors such as these, which attenuate inferences from test score to attribute, were several, but they were only partially successful. In the Internal-External Control inventory, the forced-choice format tends to control for acquiescence effects, but our attempts to match items on social desirability ultimately resulted in only about 30 percent of the high school or adult subjects selecting the external (socially less desirable) half of the items on the average. In the Alienation scale, we used multiple response categories to lessen acquiescence and were also able to "reverse" three of the items (numbers 3, 7, and 11) without having them sound too trite or distorted. As for controlling social desirability on this scale, we were unable to do more than rely on the respondent's frankness and willingness to express his real feelings.

Fortunately, social desirability effects should operate to minimize the number of "agree" responses to all but the three reversed items on the Alienation scale. Thus, for the remaining ten items, acquiescence and social desirability response sets are operating in opposite directions and may tend to counteract each other. Unfortunately, these two types of response set may both operate to the disadvantage of minority group respondents. They may be more prone to acquiescence, while being less aware of the social desirability value of the items. Both tendencies would serve to increase their alienation score. Final judgment on the adequacy of the scale must await, therefore, presentation of data bearing on the empirical relationship of this measure to others within the theoretical network.

The relationship between the two belief variables, Internal-External Control and Alienation, can now be examined. A product-moment (Pearson) correlation between the two measures in the adult sample was .45 ($N = 210$), indicating a significant association between them, as would be expected from their content. As a matter of fact, Seeman (Seeman and Evans, 1962; Seeman, 1963) has used a very similar version of the I-E scale as his measure of the "powerlessness" component of alienation. It should be pointed out, on the other hand, that the two scales are not so strongly associated as to suggest they are simply measuring the same thing. This will become even clearer later on, when we can examine *the very different pattern of relations* which the two measures have with other variables in our network.

Sex and Ethnic Group Differences in the Personal Belief Structure

In the Community Survey Study, as in the High School Study, sex differences on the personal belief measures are minimal, and the sexes can be combined for further analyses.

Among the adults, *unlike* the high-school students, ethnic group differences are clear. This can be seen in Table 10.12, where, on both personal belief measures, the Anglos have the least deviance-prone scores; and there are significant Anglo-Spanish differences. In addition, the Anglo-Indian difference is also significant on the Alienation measure. The

TABLE 10.12
Sex and Ethnic Group Differences in Personal Beliefs: Community Survey Study

Measure*		Means and Standard Deviations		Significance† (Male *vs.* Female)
		Males ($N = 104$)	Females ($N = 106$)	
Internal- External Control	$\bar{X}$	7.0	7.8	$t = 1.16$
	σ	(4.9)	(4.8)	N.S.
Alienation	$\bar{X}$	17.4	17.7	$t = 0.61$
	σ	(3.8)	(4.1)	N.S.

		Means and Standard Deviations			Significance		
		Anglos ($N = 92$)	Spanish ($N = 58$)	Indians ($N = 60$)	Anglos *vs.* Spanish	Anglos *vs.* Indians	Spanish *vs.* Indians
Internal- External Control	$\bar{X}$	6.0	10.1	7.0	$t = 5.39$	$t = 1.53$	$t = 3.78$
	σ	(3.9)	(5.5)	(4.5)	$p < .001$	N.S.	$p < .001$
Alienation	$\bar{X}$	15.7	19.3	18.7	$t = 6.28$	$t = 6.08$	$t = 0.94$
	σ	(3.5)	(3.9)	(3.4)	$p < .001$	$p < .001$	N.S.

* High score indicates high external control and high alienation.

† All *t*-tests of group mean differences are two-tailed. Differences not significant at the .05 level or better are indicated N.S.

stronger belief in internal control and the lesser sense of alienation among the Anglos should follow from their position in the normative structure, that is, from having the least anomie in their sociocultural environment, and from their greater access to opportunity.

Of interest is the fact that on both measures, the Spanish are more alienated than the Indians, and on the Internal-External Control measure, significantly more so. This is apparently contrary to the anomie findings, where the Spanish group displayed a less pervasive degree of anomie than their Indian neighbors. But it is in line with data on the ethnic group differences in the socioeconomic opportunity structure in the community, where the Indians occupy a somewhat more favored position than the Spanish. In retrospect, it seems reasonable that internal control should be related to the actual economic power each group wields. By contrast, feelings of social isolation, reflected in the Alienation measure, should be more strongly influenced by the actual status relationships which obtain in the community.

Partitioned chi-squares (Castellan, 1965) were run for each of the thirteen alienation items, comparing Anglos with non-Anglos and Spanish with Indians. It is interesting to note, first, that eight of the thirteen items revealed significant Anglo–non-Anglo differences, including at least one item within each of the six aspects of alienation described earlier. This suggests the value of having cast a wide net when constructing the measure and decreases the importance of the lack of unidimensionality which was found. Alienation appears to be a multifaceted phenomenon, but ethnic group differences emerge on each of the aspects measured.

Only three items significantly differentiated the Spanish from the Indian subjects, items 2, 10, and 11. Items 2 and 10 have economic overtones ("trying to figure out how to get ahead in life is just too complicated," and "it's hardly fair to bring children into the world, the way things look for the future"), and in both cases, Spanish subjects are more alienated than Indians. By contrast, item 11 involves social isolation in the sense of a lack of normative consensus (disagreement to the statement: "I get the feeling that the people around here see most things the way I do"); and here, it is the Indians who are more alienated, just as it was the Indians who displayed the more pervasive anomie.

In summary, in the Community Survey Study, the I-E and Alienation measures correlated significantly, as expected, but not highly enough to suggest that they could substitute for each other. On both measures, the expected Anglo-non-Anglo differences emerged. The greater alienation and feelings of external control of the Spanish are in line with the ethnographic literature and with their disadvantaged position in the opportunity structure as well. Their more extreme position on these measures, compared to the Indians, does not fit, however, with the finding of less pervasive Spanish anomie than Indian anomie. In the High School Study, there were no ethnic differences in belief in internal-external control. Since I-E might be expected to reflect not only position in the normative structure but also position in the opportunity structure, the absence of ethnic group differences in the high school may suggest a lack of validity of the I-E scale.

THE MEASUREMENT OF THE PERSONAL CONTROL STRUCTURE

The third structure in the personality system which required the development of measures has to do with the personality analogues of the social controls described in the preceding chapter, those personality attributes which are closely involved in the regulation of deviant behavior. Such attributes, while expected to reflect the operation of social controls, once established, acquire a degree of autonomy and continue to exercise a regulatory function even in the absence of external controls. In this research, two general types of personal controls were measured: (1) attitudes toward deviant behavior, that is, how *wrong* the subject feels it is to engage in various types of deviance; and (2) a more abstract behavioral tendency to think and plan ahead, to defer gratification, and, in other such ways, to take into account, when contemplating various actions, their possible future consequences. Both types of controls, when effective, should, as pointed out in Chapter 4, serve to inhibit the occurrence of deviant behavior.

The High School Study

The Measurement of Attitudes toward Deviance

A wide range of alternative approaches to attitude measurement has been experimented with in psychology, each approach involving somewhat different inferences to underlying attitudes and somewhat different risks of contamination or distortion (Campbell, 1950; Cook and Selltiz, 1964). In the high school, we approached the problem in two ways, one involving a self-report procedure, the other, a semiprojective incomplete sentences procedure.

The self-report procedure was quite straightforward. "We're interested in how wrong you think different kinds of actions are," the students were told in a questionnaire. "Most people think that something like murder is *very* wrong, while something like bragging may be considered only *a little bit wrong* or *not wrong at all.* You can show how wrong you think something is by circling a number from 0 to 9." They were then shown the following scale:

No Wrong		A Little Bit Wrong			Wrong			Very Wrong	
0	1	2	3	4	5	6	7	8	9

After further instruction in the use of this scale and an example, subjects were given twenty items covering various types of socially defined deviant acts ranging from "smoking on the school grounds" (item 1) to "taking things that don't belong to you" (item 2). These items were identical in content to those used for the self-report of deviant behavior discussed in Chapter 7, and their administration on the final day of testing immediately preceded that behavior questionnaire. As in the behavior questionnaire, a "mild" and a "severe" item were given at the outset to provide a range within which the student could anchor his judgments. Four "buffer" items which would not normally be considered "wrong" by most people were also interspersed in order to help avoid response sets.

Internal Consistency of the Attitude Scale. That the students took this task seriously is attested to by the range of responses to items with differing content. This can be seen in Table 10.13, in which each item

TABLE 10.13
Internal Characteristics of the Attitudes toward Deviance Measure: High School Study*

Item		Mean "Wrongness"	Item-Total Score Pearson Correlation
1.	To smoke on the school grounds.	4.8	.65
2.	To take things that don't belong to you.	8.0	.51
3.†	To go on outings with friends.	0.1	.07
4.	To fake an excuse from home.	4.4	.60
5.	To get into trouble with the law.	8.0	.55
6.	To swear or curse.	5.4	.58
7.	To cut-up in the classroom.	4.0	.61
8.†	To get home a little later than usual after school.	1.0	.33
9.	To drive when you've had a good bit to drink.	7.0	.58
10.	To copy other kids' homework.	4.6	.65
11.‡	To make out with your dates.	1.1	.05
12.	To disobey your parents.	7.0	.44
13.	To cheat on tests.	6.8	.71
14.†	To do things on the spur of the moment.	1.7	.17
15.	To get into fights with other kids.	5.5	.69
16.	To go to beer parties.	5.3	.68
17.	To lie to a teacher.	6.0	.54
18.	To drive a car without a license.	5.4	.62
19.	To ditch school.	4.3	.68
20.†	To go to a movie the night before a test.	2.3	.33

* $N = 93$.

† Original buffer item.

‡ Subsequently treated as an additional buffer item.

is presented, with its mean rating and its correlation with a raw total score which did not include the four predesignated "buffers."

It can be seen that the four buffer items range in mean score from 0.1 to 2.3, all within the "a little bit wrong" category. "To make out with your dates" is also considered by these students as no more than "a little bit wrong" ($\bar{X} = 1.1$) and should be treated as a fifth buffer. (Recall from Chapter 8, Table 8.11, that this was also the item students most often reported having engaged in "very often." This probably reflects part of the sexual revolution in the United States with which the authors were not yet "in tune".) But all other items are solidly in the "wrong" to "very wrong" categories, ranging from a mean score of 4.0 to 8.0. This differentiation and variability support the general face validity of the scale.

Relatively high correlations *among* items were also found, suggesting that, despite this variability in response, some underlying general "attitude toward deviance" is being assessed. For the fifteen deviance items, the correlation of each item with the other fourteen ranged from .24 to .40 and averaged .33. By contrast, correlations of the five buffer items (treating "making out with your dates" as a buffer now) with themselves average only .07 and, with the other fifteen, only .10, with a range from −.04 to .21. These distributions are completely nonoverlapping and suggest that the fifteen deviance items are, in fact, getting at something common to them but quite different from whatever is being measured by the five buffers. This conclusion is further supported by the item-total score correlations (shown in Table 10.13) which average over .6 for the fifteen deviance items, but under .2 for the five buffers.

This scale has been further analyzed, including the construction of subscales paralleling those devised for the self-reports of deviant behavior (see Chapter 8), but total score, based on the largest number of items, consistently proved to be a better predictor than any subscore and, therefore, has been the one retained here (see Gillis, 1963).

Because of their susceptibility to deliberate distortion, the validity of self-report scales of this kind is always subject to question. The seriousness with which students seemed to take our research, together with the internal characteristics of the scale just reported, have given us some confidence in these data. In line with a general convergent strategy, however, we also constructed an "attitudes toward deviance" score from four items embedded within the twenty-seven-item Incomplete Sentences Blank (ISB) procedure. These items were "Most drinking," "Making out," "Getting drunk," and "Police officers." Responses to these items were scored from 0–3, in accord with a scoring manual written by Gillis (1962). A clearly positive attitude toward drinking, getting drunk, or "making out" received 0; a qualified positive statement was scored 1; neutral completions, or those in which no attitude was clearly implied, were scored 2; and clear negation was scored 3. For "Police officers," the responses were scored in the same general manner, but with respect to positive or negative attitudes toward the authority figure rather than toward any specific deviant act.

Table 10.14 presents Pearson correlations between scores on these four ISB items and the self-report attitude items most like them in content. The correlations range from .22 to .44, a range almost identical to that for the correlations *among* the self-report attitude items alone. Given the fact that the two procedures were administered on different days and that the tasks were quite distinct, these findings are gratifying and convey validity for both procedures. The over-all correlation of .43 for the two total scores further supports this conclusion.

TABLE 10.14
**Self-Report Attitudes toward Deviance Items versus
Attitudes toward Deviance Items on the Incomplete Sentences Blank:
High School Study***

Measure	Pearson Correlation
To go on beer parties *versus*	
Most drinking	.22
Getting drunk	.44
To make out with your dates *versus*	
Making out	.32
To get into trouble with the law *versus*	
Police officers	.32
Total Attitudes toward Deviance score *versus*	
Four-item ISB attitude score	.43

* $N = 93$, for which a correlation of .17 is significant at the .05 level, one-tailed test.

Sex and Ethnic Group Differences in Attitudes toward Deviance

In Table 10.15, sex and ethnic group differences in attitudes toward deviance in the high school are presented. As might be expected, on both measures, females are far stricter than males, and this difference is highly significant statistically. This finding is in accord with the sex differences in the social control structure presented in the previous chapter.

These sex differences prevent combining males and females when examining ethnic differences. In the lower part of Table 10.15, the direct self-report measure shows Anglo males to be somewhat stricter than Spanish or Indian males, whereas on the semiprojective technique, they are the least strict. None of these differences is large enough to be statistically significant, however, and no inferences from them are justified. By contrast

TABLE 10.15
Sex and Ethnic Group Differences in Attitudes toward Deviance:
High School Study*

		Self-Report Scale	Incomplete Sentences Blank
Males (N = 47)	$\bar{X}$	77.6	6.8
	σ	(20.5)	(2.9)
Females (N = 46)	$\bar{X}$	97.4	8.9
	σ	(19.9)	(2.3)
Males *vs.* females	t	4.74	3.76
	p	<.001	<.001
Anglo males (N = 23)	$\bar{X}$	77.7	6.1
	σ	(23.5)	(3.5)
Spanish males (N = 15)	$\bar{X}$	75.7	7.7
	σ	(18.7)	(2.5)
Indian males† (N = 6)	$\bar{X}$	73.5	6.7
	σ	(17.1)	(1.4)
Anglo males *vs.* Spanish males	t	0.30	1.62
	p	N.S.	N.S.
Anglo females (N = 20)	$\bar{X}$	90.0	8.4
	σ	(21.4)	(2.5)
Spanish females (N = 21)	$\bar{X}$	100.9	9.4
	σ	(15.7)	(2.1)
Indian females (N = 5)	$\bar{X}$	112.6	8.6
	σ	(21.2)	(2.3)
Anglo females *vs.* Spanish females	t	1.85	1.42
	p	N.S.	N.S.

* All *t*-tests of group mean differences are two-tailed. Differences not significant at the .05 level or better are indicated N.S.

† This does not include 4 local BIA Indian males included in the total male group.

Anglo females are the most permissive of the three female groups on both measures. But the relative position of Spanish and Indian females shifts from one measure to the other, and again, differences are not large enough to reach statistical significance. We can conclude that no systematic ethnic differences in attitudes toward deviance are evident in the high school.

The Measurement of Time Perspective

Two other variables within the personal control system were also investigated. These are *time perspective,* or the degree to which an individual thinks about and is concerned with various past implications and future consequences of his actions, and *delay of gratification,* or the tendency to work for long-range goals, even in the face of short-term negative consequences. These two orientations would appear conceptually to be at about the same general level of abstraction: high-order personal attributes which have a degree of cross-situational applicability, and, therefore, help produce the relative consistency of behavioral choice which we recognize by the term "personality." The measurement of time perspective will be described in this section, and the measurement of delay of gratification, in the section to follow. The theoretical linkage of both of these variables to the sociocultural environment and to deviance-conformity has already been elaborated in Chapter 4. Inspiration for the measurement of time perspective used in both the High School and Community Survey studies came from earlier work by Wallace (1965).[4] In individual interviews students were asked to look ahead and then to tell us ten things that they thought they would do or thought might happen to them. This procedure was then repeated to collect ten past events that the subject had already done or that had already happened to him. After all twenty events had been collected, the subject was asked to estimate how long from now each future event would probably happen and how long ago it was that each past event had occurred. The assumption underlying this technique is that a legitimate inference can be drawn from this sample of past and future events to the temporal extension of the subject's psychological field as a whole; thus, we have called this technique the "Life Space" sample. Operationally, future time perspective is defined as the *median* time from the present of the ten future events expected, and similarly for past time perspective.[5]

Sex and Ethnic Group Differences in Time Perspective

The data from the Life Space sample for both future and past time perspective are shown in Table 10.16. Because of skewing in the time distributions, medians have been used as the measure of central tendency, although *t*-tests of mean differences were also computed. With respect

[4] Actually, eight distinct types of measures were devised and explored over a two-year period. A full discussion of these measures, their interrelationships, and their correlation with various behavioral criteria is being prepared for publication elsewhere. (Most of this material is available in Graves, 1961.) From this experience, the most promising technique was selected for use in both the High School and Community Survey studies. This selection was made on the basis of the measure's internal characteristics, its relative freedom from the influence of factors such as verbosity, which might introduce systematic bias, and its appropriateness for the data-collecting approach we had adopted.

[5] Several more complex scoring procedures have been explored, but all correlate highly with the median, and its simplicity recommends it. A full discussion of this scale and its internal characteristics is available in Graves (1961).

to sex groups, none of the differences is statistically significant, and both sexes were combined for further analyses.

The ethnic group comparisons in Table 10.16 show that the Anglo students have the most extended time perspective in *both* the future and the past. The differences between the Anglos and Spanish are small and nonsignificant, however. The main difference lies between these two groups

TABLE 10.16
Sex and Ethnic Group Differences in Time Perspective—The Life Space Sample: High School Study

Measure	Median		Significance* (Males *vs.* Females)
	Males (N = 46)	Females (N = 46)	
Past time perspective			
All 10 events	16 mos.	1 yr.	t = 1.07
First 5 events	2 yrs.	1 yr.	N.S.
Future time perspective			
All 10 events	33 mos.	30 mos.	t = 0.44
First 5 events	30 mos.	25½ mos.	N.S.

	Median			Significance*		
	Anglos (N = 42)	Spanish (N = 35)	Indians (N = 11)	Anglos *vs.* Spanish	Anglos *vs.* Indians	Spanish *vs.* Indians
Past time perspective						
All 10 events	18½ mos.	12 mos.	10 mos.	t = 1.79	t = 4.87	t = 3.02
First 5 events	30 mos.	12 mos.	5 mos.	N.S.	p < .001	p < .01
Future time perspective						
All 10 events	39 mos.	36 mos.	4 mos.	t = 0.68	t = 5.40	t = 4.03
First 5 events	33 mos.	27 mos.	3 mos.	N.S.	p < .001	p < .01

* All *t*-tests of group mean differences are two-tailed. Differences not significant at the .05 level or better are indicated N.S.

and the Indians, both Anglos and Spanish having significantly longer future and past time perspective than the Indians. How much these findings are influenced by the differential dropout of the non-Anglo students or by the leveling effect of the high school experience is difficult to say.

It is interesting to note that the data suggest that time perspective is extended fairly symmetrically into *both* the past and future. In light of this, it makes sense to speak of "extended" *versus* "restricted" time perspective rather than to characterize groups as "future oriented" or "past oriented." Such terms as the latter, frequently employed in ethnographic accounts, gain support from neither these data nor the adult data, as will be seen shortly.

The Measurement of Delay of Gratification

Measures of delay of gratification were developed only for the High School Study, where a degree of manipulation of the natural environment was possible (see Shybut, 1963). Previous research in this area has generally been undertaken with relatively young children, and has usually involved a single type of measure: the subject's choice between a small reward at the time of the experiment (one piece of candy, a nickel, a small toy) or a larger reward a few days later (a larger piece of candy, a dime, a larger toy). Working within this same general paradigm, we attempted to converge on the problem through the use of multiple measures. These included a projective procedure, two verbal choice procedures, and two behavioral choice procedures. Since the verbal choice procedures did not prove to be adequate measures, space will not be taken to describe them.

The Projective Procedure: the Windfall Essay. As part of a regular composition assignment in English class, and without knowledge that this was actually part of our research, all students in the school were asked to write a story about a hypothetical event in which the subject himself was the key figure. As a result of pretests in similar schools, the following format had been arrived at:

> Write a complete story suggested by the following theme: It was a weekday afternoon in a small southwestern town. A teenage boy (or girl) returned home from school to find a letter waiting for him (or her). Quickly he (or she) opened it and read the letter inside. "Dear Sir:" it read, "You will remember entering your name in our nationwide contest. The drawing has just been held and your name was the one selected. You will find a check for $1000 enclosed with this letter."
>
> Now begin your story and be sure to tell a complete story about what the boy (or girl) did with the money. A complete story would have a beginning, a middle, and an ending. In your story tell about any important things which you think would have happened. You will probably want to include answers to these questions in your story:
>
> 1. What did the boy (or girl) think about after getting the money?

2.   What did he decide to do with the money?
3.   Why did he decide to do this?
4.   How did things work out?

In the pretest, the content of these stories was easily classified into delayed *versus* immediate gratification, with interscorer agreement of better than 90 percent (see Shybut, 1963).

The Behavioral Choice Procedures: The Dance Vote and the Thank-You Ticket.   Two behavioral choices were devised to provide a contrast between a relatively immediate but less valued reward and a relatively delayed but more valued reward. The choices were made to appear as "natural" events in the social ecology, and they reflect the possibilities which exist even in field studies for intervention and manipulation. Because of their interest in this regard, the procedures will be described in full.

The Dance Vote.   At the beginning of the first day of testing, the subjects were each given a ballot, and the following instructions were presented to the class verbally:

"Because of your help with our research last year and this year, we want to do something in return. As a matter of fact, we are going to sponsor a dance for the whole high school. We'll pay for everything. We are not sure of the kind of dance you'd like, so we are going to give you a choice. To make sure that this is your *own* choice, we'll do this by secret voting. So let's not talk to each other about it.

"What we can do is this. We can throw a record-hop *this* Saturday night in the multi-purpose room at the grammar school, or we can give you a band-dance on Saturday night a month from now, April 28th, when we have had time to make the final arrangements. For the record-hop we'll have all kinds of records, door prizes, refreshments, and decorations. For the band-dance we can arrange to get the Zuni-Midnighters to play for you.

"In order for us to make the necessary arrangements, we have to know your decision right away. So, if you want a record-hop this Saturday night, put an 'X' in the box next to 'Record-hop this Saturday night' on the voting sheet in front of you. If you want a band-dance on Saturday night a month from now, that's April 28th, put an 'X' in the box next to 'Band-dance on Saturday night a month from now, April 28th.' Mark only *one* choice. Now tear off your vote, and I'll collect it from you."

The ballots were then collected by the experimenter.

The Thank-You Ticket.   The second behavioral choice procedure was provided at the beginning of the third and final day of testing. Attached to each student's questionnaire booklet was a ticket on which were printed the words, "Thank-You Ticket, Tri-Ethnic Research Project," and other information. The following instructions were verbally presented to the class:

> "We really appreciated your help this year, so we are going to give each one of you a ticket worth some money. You can turn in the ticket for whatever you like at the (a local) Drug Store. Because there are so many kids in the school, you probably couldn't all fit into the store at one time. Therefore, we have decided to make the ticket worth more if you wait before turning it in. So, starting today (Wednesday) through Friday (March 30), your ticket is worth 25 cents. Then Saturday through Tuesday (March 31–April 3) your ticket will be worth 35 cents. Then Wednesday through Friday (April 4–April 6) your ticket will be worth 50 cents. Your last chance to turn in your ticket will be Friday, April 6.

> "We want each one of you to have something for yourself. You won't be able to get together and get something as a group. You can only use your own ticket. How much the ticket is worth on the different dates is printed right on the ticket. You can turn it in *any time you wish.*

> "Now would you sign your full name at the top of the ticket, where it says 'signature.' Then, when you buy something with the ticket you'll sign it again on the bottom, right in the store. This is so nobody else can use your ticket.

> "It's not a lot of money, but everybody in the school will get something for himself this way. Remember, you can turn the ticket in anytime, and it's worth more the longer you wait."

At the local drugstore where tickets were to be exchanged, a clerk in charge was instructed to keep a record of the incoming tickets by placing each ticket turned in into an appropriately dated envelope. Each envelope was distinctly marked with a date, one for each of the nine days during which the tickets were redeemable. The tickets were signed and marked with a date as they were turned in for exchange; the envelopes with the tickets were picked up daily by one of the authors. All subjects who did not return their tickets until they achieved their maximum value, that is, until the last three days, were scored as "delayed" gratifiers on this measure; all others were scored "immediate."

The Delay of Gratification Index. The proportion of students who displayed a delay choice on the three measures were the following: Windfall Essay .52; Dance Vote .82; and Thank-You Ticket .86. It can be seen that the preponderance of choices was in the delay direction.

In order to examine the degree of convergence among these alternative measures, and in anticipation of constructing some form of combined Delay of Gratification index, tetrachoric correlations among the three measures were run. These revealed that the dance vote, the thank-you ticket, and the essay all correlated with each other at a significant level, ranging from .15 (dance vote *versus* ticket) to .58 (essay *versus* ticket). They were then combined into a single index; to form the index, we simply classified subjects according to *the number of procedures out of three* on which they had displayed a delay choice.

Sex and Ethnic Group Differences in Delay of Gratification

As in the Attitudes toward Deviance measure, marked sex differences in this aspect of the personal control system were again found, with males displaying a greater tendency for engaging in immediate gratification. It can be seen, in Table 10.17, that only 30 percent of the males were delayed on all three measures, whereas 52 percent of the females were. A chi-square test comparing these frequencies with those in the two other categories combined, (where males were found with consistently higher frequency than females) yielded a value of 3.87, which would occur by chance less than five times in a hundred.

TABLE 10.17
Sex and Ethnic Group Differences in Delay of Gratification:
High School Study*

Group	Proportion in Each Delay Category		
	All Delay	1 Immediate	2 Immediate
Males (N = 44)	.30	.48	.23
Females (N = 46)	.52	.33	.15
Anglo Males (N = 23)	.17	.57	.26
Spanish Males (N = 15)	.47	.40	.13
Indian Males (N = 4)	.50	.25	.25
Anglo Females (N = 20)	.45	.40	.15
Spanish Females (N = 21)	.62	.24	.14
Indian Females (N = 5)	.40	.40	.20

* $N = 90$.

These sex differences require us to look at ethnic differences initially cross-cut by sex. But these reveal that both Anglo boys and Anglo girls are more immediate gratifiers than Spanish boys and Spanish girls, respectively. (The Indian group is too small for meaningful comparison, but appears to be more like the Anglo than the Spanish group on this measure.) This consistency of direction again makes it possible to combine sex groups within ethnic groups. A chi-square test of these Anglo-Spanish differences, comparing those in the All Delay pattern with those in the other two patterns combined, was again significant at better than the .05 level ($\chi^2 = 4.17$). This finding is opposite to what was expected and does not accord with the literature describing lower class and marginal ethnic groups as oriented toward immediate gratification. While this serves to challenge the validity of the Delay of Gratification index at this juncture, its ultimate validity must be determined by examining its relation to the other measures, both of personality and behavior, in our theoretical scheme.

The Community Survey Study

The Measurement of Attitudes toward Deviance

Two measures of Attitudes toward Deviance were used with the community adults. The first is quite similar to the one used in the high school. Respondents were told, "I would like to know how *wrong* you think different things are. Sure, there are always exceptions; like, to protect yourself, killing may be all right, but *usually* people feel killing is wrong. I would like to know how *you* feel in general about these things." The respondent was then handed a card on which the following scale was printed:

No Wrong	A Little Bit Wrong		Wrong			Very Wrong		
0	1	2	3	4	5	6	7	8	9

The interviewer continued, "For instance: Driving over the speed limit. How wrong do you feel that usually is?" Eleven other items ranging widely in content and severity then followed.

In Table 10.18, these items, their average rating, and their correlation with total score are presented. All items have an average rating well within the "wrong" category, with the two heavy drinking items, the two post-marital sex items, and the child neglect items all being rated within the "very wrong" range. This suggests some respondent variation in judging these items, though it is not as great as that found among the students. Notable also are the substantial item-total score correlations, which range between .59 and .75. Inter-item correlations were also obtained: All were

TABLE 10.18
Attitudes toward Deviance Scale: Community Survey Study*

Item	Mean "Wrongness" Rating	Item-Total Score Pearson Correlation
1. Driving over the speed limit.	5.5	.63
2. A woman being a heavy drinker.	7.3	.73
3. A person who doesn't work steady when he could.	6.0	.64
4. A man's having sex relations before marriage.	5.7	.67
5. A person getting into fights.	5.4	.68
6. A husband and wife separating.	5.8	.59
7. A man being a heavy drinker.	7.3	.72
8. A woman's having sex relations before marriage.	6.7	.74
9. A man fooling around with other women after he's married.	8.1	.75
10. Parents who don't stay home with their kids most of the time.	7.2	.60
11. Someone not making good on money he owes.	6.8	.63
12. A married woman fooling around with other men.	8.0	.72

* $N = 221$.

positive, ranging between .2 and .8, with an average of over .4. This finding may, in part, be the result of response set, but it can also be interpreted as suggesting that, despite item-by-item variation, each item is tapping some underlying common attitude toward socially judged problem behavior.

A second Attitude toward Deviance scale, Illegitimate Means Acceptance, confronted the respondent with a series of illegitimate actions employed by individuals occupying different economic, age, and sex statuses in American society. All actions were aimed at acquiring monetary or other forms of achievement goals. Sixteen items were presented, and subjects were asked to judge "how wrong" these actions were along a scale identical in form to that used in the more general attitude scale discussed above. In Table 10.19, the items, their mean "wrongness" rating by ethnic group, and the correlation of each item with total score are presented. The mean ratings for the total sample range from just over 4 at the lower end of the "wrong" category—for kids not being completely honest about their background and qualifications when applying for a job (items 2 and 7)—to over 7, well within the "very wrong" category—for items relating to the manipulative use of sex, cheating in sports, and use of other people's grazing land (items 3, 4, 8, and 11). Interestingly, there is no difference in the ratings of acts by rich or by poor protagonists, though legal transgressions were more highly disapproved than moral ones.

Despite this item specificity, correlations between each item and total

TABLE 10.19
Illegitimate Means Acceptance Scale: Community Survey Study*

Item	Mean "Wrongness" Rating	Item-Total Score Pearson Correlation
1. When he files his income tax report, a rich man reports less income than he really has.	6.7	.57
2. A girl says she has more education than she really has so that she can get a job and earn some spending money.	4.3	.62
3. A big rancher grazes his stock on other people's property without their permission.	7.6	.47
4. The wife of an ordinary worker makes up to her husband's boss so that her husband will get a good raise in pay.	7.1	.59
5. A young girl out of a job buys a lot of clothes on time, knowing she will not make any payments.	6.8	.71
6. A store owner makes a public contribution to a church he doesn't believe in just so he can get extra business from the church members.	5.4	.55
7. When he applies for a very important job, a young college graduate doesn't tell his real religion.	4.2	.54
8. A highly rated boxer loses a fight on purpose in order to get a big pay-off from gamblers.	7.3	.62
9. A poor man accepts $10 from a politician to vote the way the politician asks him to.	6.3	.62
10. A man who can barely support his family gets a $5 bill when he is given change at the grocery store instead of the $1 bill he was supposed to get. He notices the mistake but says nothing about it.	6.1	.75
11. A pretty girl from a poor family lets herself get pregnant when she is dating a boy from a wealthy family, hoping that he will marry her.	7.5	.68
12. The son of a new businessman in town makes up stories about how much money his father has so he can impress his classmates.	5.7	.62
13. A man out of work breaks into a food store at night to get food for his family.	5.5	.42
14. A girl from a hard-up family secretly takes spending money from her father's billfold.	6.8	.65
15. The town favorite in a rodeo contest illegally fixes his gear so that he will have a better chance to win.	6.5	.68
16. A well-to-do woman makes a large contribution to a local club to make sure that she gets to be president of it.	5.5	.70

*$N = 221$.

score average better than .6, with a range from .42 to .75. Inter-item correlations also were all positive, averaging about .35. Again these findings may in part be a product of response set, but they can also be interpreted as indicating that some underlying common attitude is being assessed.

Although these two alternative measures of attitudes toward deviance differ widely in content—one couching acts in terms of situationally specific conditions while the acts in the other were phrased in quite general terms—they are not operationally very distinct. Both require the subject to rate "how wrong" the acts are, considered along an identical scale. Given this degree of similarity in method, the .68 Pearson correlation obtained between their total scores, although substantial, should be interpreted more like the convergence on a construct made by multiple items in the same test than the convergence of operationally distinct measures.

Sex and Ethnic Group Differences in Attitudes toward Deviance

The means for males and females on these two measures of attitudes toward deviance are presented in Table 10.20. As was found in the high school, males are significantly more permissive in their attitudes than are females; this is true for both measures. This finding again precludes their combinations for an examination of ethnic group differences. Therefore, in the remainder of the table, sex by ethnic group means and *t*-tests of these mean differences are given.

Contrary to the outcome among the high school students, ethnic differences among the adults are pronounced. Anglo males are more permissive than Spanish males, while adult Anglo females are more strict than Spanish females on measures of attitudes toward deviance. But, most apparent, *both* groups are *less* permissive in their attitudes, on both measures, than the Indians. This finding is generally significant within both sex groups.

The Measurement of Time Perspective

The other measure of the personal control structure in the Community Survey Study, besides the measure of attitudes, is that of time perspective. The technique used was the procedure for the Life Space sample, but for the interview it was necessary to shorten it from the ten events asked for in the High School Study to only five events. An analysis of the high school data had indicated that the median of the first five future events given correlates over .7 with the median for all ten future events given; for past events the corresponding correlation is over .8. Hence, the shortened time perspective measure in the interview is probably quite comparable to a longer version in the data it yields.

TABLE 10.20
Sex and Ethnic Differences on Two Measures of Attitudes toward Deviance:
Community Survey Study

Group	Attitudes toward Deviance*			Illegitimate Means Acceptance*		
	$\bar{X}$	σ	Significance†	$\bar{X}$	σ	Significance†
Males ($N = 103$)	74.1	(20.9)		95.5	(23.7)	
Females ($N = 108$)	84.6	(16.5)		102.7	(26.6)	
Males *vs.* Females			$t = 4.05$			$t = 2.08$
			$p < .001$			$p < .05$
Anglo Males ($N = 43$)	70.7	(17.3)		97.3	(24.9)	
Spanish Males ($N = 29$)	85.9	(19.3)		103.0	(21.7)	
Indian Males ($N = 31$)	67.9	(23.1)		86.0	(21.2)	
Anglos *vs.* Spanish			$t = 3.42$			$t = 1.03$
			$p < .01$			N.S.
Anglos *vs.* Indian			$t = 0.56$			$t = 2.09$
			N.S.			$p < .05$
Spanish *vs.* Indian			$t = 3.28$			$t = 3.05$
			$p < .01$			$p < .01$
Anglo Females ($N = 48$)	88.0	(14.6)		113.6	(23.1)	
Spanish Females ($N = 29$)	87.2	(15.3)		98.0	(27.3)	
Indian Females ($N = 31$)	77.2	(18.1)		90.1	(25.0)	
Anglos *vs.* Spanish			$t = 0.22$			$t = 2.57$
			N.S.			$p < .05$
Anglos *vs.* Indian			$t = 2.80$			$t = 4.20$
			$p < .01$			$p < .001$
Spanish *vs.* Indian			$t = 2.33$			$t = 1.17$
			$p < .05$			N.S.

* For both measures, a high score indicates high *repudiation* of deviance.

† All *t*-tests of group mean differences are two-tailed. Differences not significant at the .05 level or better are indicated N.S.

Sex and Ethnic Group Differences in Time Perspective

In Table 10.21, the time perspective data by sex and ethnic group for the adult sample are presented. As in the High School Study, sex differences are not significant, and the sexes were combined for the ethnic group analysis. With respect to the latter, the Anglos again evidence the most extended time perspective. Unlike the high school results, the adult Spanish are now significantly shorter in time perspective than the Anglos, in both the future and the past direction, and Spanish-Indian differences are not now significant.

Another difference between adults and adolescents is of interest. Within

TABLE 10.21
**Sex and Ethnic Group Differences in Time Perspective—The Life Space Sample:
Community Survey Study**

	Median		Significance* (Males vs. Females)
	Males (N = 94)	Females (N = 102)	
Past time perspective	4 yrs.	2½ yrs.	$t = 1.18$ N.S.
Future time perspective	2½ mos.	3 mos.	$t = 1.10$ N.S.

	Median			Significance*		
	Anglos (N = 89)	Spanish (N = 54)	Indians (N = 56)	Anglos vs. Spanish	Anglos vs. Indians	Spanish vs. Indians
Past time perspective	6 yrs.	18 mos.	26½ mos.	$t = 3.38$ $p < .01$	$t = 1.33$ N.S.	$t = 1.58$ N.S.
Future time perspective	6 mos.	1½ mos.	1½ mos.	$t = 2.34$ $p < .05$	$t = 1.57$ N.S.	$t = 0.68$ N.S.

* All *t*-tests of group mean differences are two-tailed. Differences not significant at the .05 level or better are indicated N.S.

all three ethnic groups, the high school students have a longer future time perspective and a shorter past time perspective than subjects in their parents' generation. This may reflect the difference in the relative size and extension of the universe of possible events from which subjects draw their sample, though all the medians seem too short to be much affected by this. It may also reflect a change in interest from one generation to the next, with modern youth more oriented toward the possibilities of the atomic age than their parents ever were. Or, finally, it could represent a developmental cycle in time perspective through which everyone passes. Longitudinal research on the subject is obviously needed.

The measurement of the personal control structure of the personality system, to summarize briefly, has involved, first, measures of attitudes toward deviant behavior and, second, a measure of extended time perspective. In the high school only, the tendency to delay gratification was also assessed. In each study, analyses were made to establish the quality of the measuring instruments and the degree to which confidence could be placed in their results. The results of the measurement of personal control, as with perceived opportunity and personal beliefs, are generally in accord with expected ethnic group differences.

While no ethnic differences emerged on attitudes toward deviance in the High School Study, there were significant differences in the Community Survey Study. The lack of high school differences follows the same lack of differences in personal beliefs reported in the previous section. However, the permissive attitude of the Indians, and the similarity between Anglo and Spanish adults in repudiating deviance, strongly accords with the social control structure findings reported in the previous chapter. The significantly more extended time perspective of the Anglos in both of the studies provides further support for expected ethnic group differences, although the ordering of the two non-Anglo groups is not clearly established. In the high school, the measurement of delay of gratification was accomplished successfully, but the greater delay of the Spanish students compared to the Anglos was unexpected.

INTERRELATIONS AMONG THE PERSONALITY MEASURES

What has been presented in the chapter thus far can be summarized and extended by examining the pattern of relations *among* the many measures of the personality system which were developed. On theoretical grounds, the direction of relationship of each measure to deviance-conformity has been specified. It is to be expected, therefore, that all the measures should relate to each other positively if the theoretical framework is correct. Also of interest is the examination of the degree to which the measures *within* a particular personality structure correlate more highly than they do with measures *outside* the structure. Such analyses can, at the same time, shed light on two questions: Whether the separate structures are indeed useful conceptual unities to postulate, and whether a particular measure is a "good," that is, relatively unique measure of a particular structure.

The data for the Community Survey Study are presented in Table 10.22. It can be seen immediately that all but two of the twenty-one correlations are in the expected direction, sixteen of them significantly so. This provides strong support for the potential utility of the theoretical scheme with respect to the personality formulations. The high correlation between Expectations and Disjunctions is, as will be recalled, artifactual; however, the important role of perceived opportunity is clearly demonstrated in the significant relations of both of these measures to all the other measures. The high relation between the Attitudes toward Deviance measure and the Acceptance of Illegitimate Means measure is probably due in large part, as noted earlier, to common method variance.

TABLE 10.22
Interrelations among Personality Variables: Community Survey Study*

Structure	Variable	Pearson Correlations					
		1	2	3	4	5	6
Perceived Opportunity	1. Expectations						
	2. Disjunctions	.76					
Personal Belief	3. Alienation	.35	.48				
	4. Internal control	.28	.43	.45			
Personal Control	5. Attitudes toward deviance	.37	.22	.03	.02		
	6. Acceptance of illegitimate means	.30	.27	.14	.23	.68	
	7. Future time perspective	.14	.15	.06	.20	−.09	−.14

* N = 221, for which a correlation of .12 is significant at the .05 level, one-tailed test. The signs preceding these correlations have been modified so that in all cases a positive correlation indicates that the measures co-varied as would be anticipated from the general theory.

With respect to the question of the conceptual unity of each structure, the evidence does not support a specificity position. For example, the correlation of the Disjunctions measure in the Perceived Opportunity structure with both Personal Belief structure measures is as high as the correlation *between* the latter. Whether this reflects the fact that the beliefs we chose to measure are precisely those likely to be related to the perception of opportunity, or whether it implies that our conceptual separation between the two structures is empirically untenable, is not capable of resolution in the present research. A similar problem arises from the fact that the highest correlation of Future Time Perspective, a Personal Control structure measure, is with Internal-External Control, a Personal Belief structure measure. Beyond the fact that this correlation is a low one, however, there is a question about the adequacy of the Time Perspective measure, since all of its correlations are low, and since it generated the only two negative correlations in the entire matrix. In sum, the Community Survey Study data are not unequivocal on the matter; what is clear, at least, is that evidence *for* specificity of conceptual structures is not present.

The same inquiry can be pursued with respect to the High School Study data. The relevant correlations are presented in Table 10.23. Again, the vast majority of the correlations (all but one, in fact) are in the expected direction; this time, however, only nine of the twenty-one achieve statistical significance. As among adults, the correlation between Expectations and Disjunctions is artifactually high, but both measures correlate higher with the independent measure of Life Chances Disjunctions than with any other personality measure in the matrix. This argues for the conceptual unity of the Perceived Opportunity structure. These measures within the Perceived Opportunity structure are, incidentally, not as strongly and consistently related to all of the other personality measures employed as they were in the adult study.

Among students, belief in Internal Control is significantly correlated with Attitudes toward Deviance, whereas among adults it is not; and it is not significantly correlated with Future Time Perspective, whereas

TABLE 10.23
Interrelations among Personality Variables:
High School Study*

Structure	Variable	Pearson Correlations					
		1	2	3	4	5	6
Perceived Opportunity	1. Expectations AcR						
	2. Disjunctions AcR	.71					
	3. Life chances disjunctions I	.30	.26				
Personal Belief	4. Internal-external control	.14	.05	.08			
Personal Control	5. Attitudes toward deviance	.22	−.08	.12	.19		
	6. Delay of gratification	.24	.10	.09	.19	.10	
	7. Future time perspective	.16	.08	.24	.10	.05	.20

* $N = 93$, for which a correlation of .17 is significant at the .05 level, one-tailed test. The signs preceding these correlations have been modified so that in all cases a positive correlation indicates that the measures co-varied as would be anticipated from the general theory.

among adults it is. Future Time Perspective is significantly correlated with Delay of Gratification, as, conceptually, it should be, though the relationship is low. Neither latter measure, however, relates significantly to Attitudes toward Deviance, calling into question the conceptual unity of the Personal Control structure.

What emerges from these analyses, in summary, is general support for the variables posited by the over-all conceptual framework. Correlations among the variables are, on the whole, in the direction specified by the theory and, in both studies, a non-chance number of these correlations is significant. On the other hand, the correlation matrices do not provide support for the existence of the conceptual unities implied by the postulation of three separate structures. How much the lack of support stems from the particular selection of measures to represent the structures and the adequacy of those measures cannot be determined from the present research. Specific investigations will need to be designed for this particular problem; in the meantime, however, the utility of the structures in generating potentially useful measures seems beyond argument.

RELATIONS BETWEEN THE SOCIOCULTURAL SYSTEM AND THE PERSONALITY SYSTEM

It is possible now to examine the final issue to be considered in this chapter: the relationship between the sociocultural structures and the structures in the personality system. The data are presented in Table 10.24. Because the Normative structure involves characteristics of each

TABLE 10.24
**Interrelations between Sociocultural and Personality System Variables:
Community Survey Study***

		Sociocultural Variables				
		Opportunity Structure		Social Control Structure		
Personality Variables		Socio-economic Status	Objec-tive Access	Expo-sure to Deviant Role Models	Absence of Sanc-tioning Net-works	Total AIM
Perceived Opportunity Structure	Expectations	.13	.22	.09	.29	.24
	Disjunctions	.26	.41	.17	.36	.30
Personal Belief Structure	Alienation	.43	.50	.00	.25	.15
	Internal control	.38	.50	.06	.28	.11
Personal Control Structure	Attitudes toward deviance	.05	.08	.04	.24	.24
	Illegitimate means acceptance	.19	.28	.01	.31	.28
	Future time perspective	.19	.23	.02	.11	.00

* $N = 221$, for which a correlation of .12 is significant at the .05 level, one-tailed test. The signs preceding these correlations have been modified so that in all cases a positive correlation indicates that the measures co-varied as would be anticipated from the general theory.

ethnic *group* rather than of individuals within those groups, there are no measures within this structure which can be related to the measures in the Personal Belief structure. Ethnic group differences in the personality measures, already discussed in relation to ethnic differences in anomie, must serve instead.

All but the two zero correlations in the matrix are in the theoretically expected direction, and twenty-four of these thirty-five correlations (69 percent) are statistically significant. In general, then, the data support the linkages postulated between the sociocultural environment and personality. Further, a larger number and a wider variety of society-person relationships are demonstrated here than are usually considered in most studies of this sort.

It is apparent from looking at the table that the relation of the Disjunction measure to the sociocultural measures is stronger than is true for the Expectations measure. Also apparent is the poor status of the Exposure to Deviant Role Models measure, something we were alerted to already in the preceding chapter. With one exception, its correlations with personality are close to zero. As we shall see in the following chapter, its relation to deviance is also low. The problem, as discussed in the preceding chapter, seems to reside in our poor measurement of an obviously important concept in the Community Survey Study.

With respect to *specificity* in the linkage between a particular sociocultural structure and its analogous personality structure, the evidence is again not strong. For example, correlations between measures of the Opportunity structure and measures of the Perceived Opportunity structure are lower than between the Opportunity structure and the Personal Belief structure. Similarly, the Social Control structure measures relate more highly to Perceived Opportunity structure measures than to Personal Control structure measures.

The corresponding High School Study data are presented in Table 10.25. The picture is not as supportive as that emerging from the adult study. Of the twenty-eight correlations, twenty are in the theoretically expected direction but only eleven of these are significant. Further, six are in a direction opposite to the one which would have been expected, though none of these is statistically significant.

Four of the six negative correlations involve the Internal-External Control measure, which did not relate to any sociocultural measure. It will be recalled from Table 10.23 that this measure did not correlate well with the other personality measures either. Together, these findings raise serious questions about the adequacy of this measure in the high school. The Exposure to Deviant Role Models measure, on the other hand, has stronger relations to personality in the high school than it had among adults, again reflecting the better status of this measure, since it deals

TABLE 10.25
**Interrelations between Sociocultural and Personality System Variables:
High School Study***

Personality Variables		Sociocultural Variables			
			Social Control Structure		
		Socio-economic Status	Exposure to Deviant Role Models	Absence of Sanctioning Networks	Total AIM
Perceived	Expectations AcR	.18	.24	.26	.22
Opportunity	Disjunctions AcR	.27	.13	.16	.17
Structure	Life chances disjunctions	.28	.11	.06	.11
Personal Belief Structure	Internal-external control	−.06	−.15	−.04	−.14
Personal Control Structure	Attitudes toward deviance	−.10	.05	.06	.00
	Delay of gratification	−.13	.18	.00	.04
	Future time perspective	.22	.37	.05	.20

* $N = 93$, for which a correlation of .17 is significant at the .05 level, one-tailed test. The signs preceding these correlations have been modified so that in all cases a positive correlation indicates that the measures co-varied as would be anticipated from the general theory.

with contemporary models for the student, while the adult measure deals with remote models who were reported to be present in the family while the subject was growing up.

With respect to the specificity issue, the data are not strongly supportive. The Opportunity structure tends to be more highly related to Perceived Opportunity measures than to measures in the other structures, but the Social Control structure relates as well if not better to Perceived Opportunity than to Personal Control.

In summary, what again emerges is general support for the theoretical links between the sociocultural situation and personality, but little or no support for *specificity* in that relationship. All the relationships between society and personality are sufficiently low, it should be noted, that variables from each system can be expected to play a supplementary role in any multivariable predictive analysis in relation to behavior.

SUMMARY AND CONCLUSIONS

In this chapter, a series of measures was presented which were used in an attempt to assess the psychological analogues of the sociocultural variables whose measurement was presented in the preceding chapter. Variables within three personality structures were measured: the Perceived Opportunity structure (an analogue of the objective Opportunity structure), the Personal Belief structure (an analogue of the Normative structure), and the Personal Control structure (an analogue of the Social Control structure). Attempts were made to develop multiple measures of each construct and to devise parallel measures appropriate for adults and adolescents, in line with a general convergent strategy.

The Perceived Opportunity Structure

A series of psychological measures of the Perceived Opportunity structure for both high school students and adult members of all three ethnic groups in the research community was presented. The measures involved, first, direct investigation of the personal value structure by asking subjects to rate the importance of various goals along a scale. Second, subjects were asked to provide their personal expectations for the achievement of the same set of goals on which value ratings had been obtained. Finally, disjunction scores, based on the joint relationship between values and expectations, were derived; the higher the value placed on a goal and/or the lower the expectation of achieving that goal, the higher the disjunction score.

Sex group differences among both high school students and adults on all these variables were minimal and rarely attained statistical significance. High school girls did place significantly more value on social love and affection goals than did boys. With regard to personal values, ethnic group differences also tended to be small. Those which did occur, among both adults and adolescents, showed the minority group members to be *more* strongly oriented toward achievement goals than their Anglo neighbors. This finding is in agreement with research by others and provides some justification for the assumption that achievement values are relatively uniformly distributed throughout the American social structure. *What differentiates these three ethnic groups, apparently, is not what they want from life, but what they actually expect to get.*

The unequal distribution of objective opportunity for personal goal achievement was documented in the preceding chapter; both the Indian and Spanish groups within the research community occupy disfavored positions. In this chapter we have shown that this disfavored position is also *perceived* by the minority group members and has become a part of their personality structure. On measures of both expectations and disjunctions with regard to achievement goals, the two minority groups, both adults and adolescents, consistently felt themselves more disfavored than did their Anglo neighbors.

The Personal Belief Structure

In this section we presented two belief measures: alienation and internal-external control. Only the latter was administered in both the high school and among the community adults. The measures were designed to tap a number of related orientations; these included belief in internal-external control, the sense of social rejection, the absence of shared values, the absence of a sense of responsibility for others, feelings of helplessness, frustration or despair, hopelessness or futility, and lack of gratification in one's ordinary role activities.

No ethnic group differences on the I-E scale were found in the high school. Among adults, Anglo–non-Anglo differences on the alienation scale were found which parallel the differences in *anomie* also found in the community. Adult Spanish-Indian differences in alienation, however, were not in line with the differences in normative consensus. Rather, the Indians seemed to feel less hopeless with respect to future achievement within the economic sphere (where they also enjoy greater objective access), but were slightly more alienated than Spanish within the area of social relations, where they are also somewhat disfavored in the community at large.

The Personal Control Structure

Two types of variables were measured within this personality structure: (1) attitudes toward deviance, a variable theoretically quite proximal to the behavior under investigation, and (2) time perspective, including the tendency to delay gratification, which serves as an indirect control against deviance by decreasing the probability that immediately gratifying and, in American society, typically deviant acts are selected.

The attitudes toward deviance measure within both the high school and the adult community required each subject to rate various deviant acts by how wrong he felt they were. Future time perspective was measured by asking subjects to provide a series of future events they expected to do or to have happen to them, and then computing the median time from the present at which these events were expected to occur. Delay of gratification was measured only in the high school, by means of a series of procedures, including a "windfall" essay, and two natural "experiments": a vote for a record dance now or a band dance later, and a "thank you-ticket" which increased in monetary value the longer it was held.

On measures of attitudes toward deviance and delay of gratification, (but conspicuously *not* on time perspective) substantial sex differences were found. Women in all three ethnic groups and at both age levels were consistently less tolerant of deviant behavior than men, and high school girls in all three ethnic groups were more willing than boys to delay gratification. These are the *only* personality variables investigated in this study where such sex differences were found. Given the substantial sex differences in all types of deviant behavior, on the one hand, and in the social control structure into which the sexes are differentially mapped, on the other, this finding assumes important significance.

Among adults, significant ethnic differences in attitudes toward deviance were also found, with Anglos and Spanish tending to be similarly strict, in contrast to the Indians. Again we are confronted by the finding which has repeatedly emerged in this study, that the Spanish, despite substantial socioeconomic differences from Anglos, are more similar to them in personality and behavior than they are to the Indians. The impact of their integrated social control structure, particularly the probable influence of the family and of the Catholic Church, appears profound.

Within the high school, no reliable ethnic difference in attitude toward deviance emerged, but on Delay of Gratification, the Spanish showed more delay than the Anglos. The integrated high school, with its uniform exposure to middle-class Anglo morality, is probably having an important leveling effect on attitudes.

On time perspective, Anglo adults appeared to contrast with both Spanish and Indians in having an *extended* time perspective, whereas in the high school, Anglos and Spanish both have an extended time perspective, in contrast to the Indians, who have an extremely restricted time perspective. The patterning of the time perspective data is, again, not the same as that for other variables placed within the Personal Control structure.

While the findings are complex in their patterning, the over-all weight of evidence in this chapter supports the theoretical expectations following from the knowledge of ethnic group differences both in deviant behavior rates and sociocultural position. The Anglos show greater perception of opportunity, greater conformity-prone personal beliefs, and less deviance-prone personal controls than the non-Anglos. The trend also is for the Indians to be most deviance-prone on these variables and for the Spanish to be in between, but the relative positions of these two groups is not clearly established on all measures. At the group level, then, the personality measures contribute support to the proposed explanation of differential deviance rates among the ethnic samples.

The relationships among these personality variables and between the personality and the sociocultural variables were presented directly. Most of the correlations were positive, as anticipated by theory, and usually they were statistically significant, though less often so among the high school students than among adults. These findings provide general support for the over-all theory. The distribution of these correlations, however, was not such as to provide great confidence in the conceptual unity of the separate personality structures or in the specificity of the relationship between a particular personality structure and its conceptually parallel sociocultural structure. Finally, all correlations were sufficiently low so that various personality and sociocultural measures can be expected to fulfill supplementary roles in a multivariable scheme for the prediction of deviant behavior. The latter will be examined in the following chapter.

REFERENCES

CAMPBELL, D. T. The indirect assessment of social attitudes. *Psychological Bulletin,* 1950, *47,* 15–38.

CAMPBELL, E. Q. The internalization of moral norms. *Sociometry,* 1964, *27,* 391–412.

CARMEN, R. S. Personality and drinking behavior among college students. Unpublished masters thesis, University of Colorado, 1965.

CASTELLAN, N. J. JR. Expectations, values, and personal disjunctions: The development and analysis of two test procedures. Tri-Ethnic Research Report No. 16, 1963, mimeo. Pp.1–31.

CASTELLAN, N. J. JR. On the partitioning of contingency tables. *Psychological Bulletin,* 1965, *64,* 330–338.

COOK, S. W. AND CLAIRE SELLTIZ. A multiple-indicator approach to attitude measurement. *Psychological Bulletin,* 1964, *62,* 36–55.

FRANK, C. Acceptance of illegitimate means—a measure of dominant culture anomie. Tri-Ethnic Research Report No. 15, 1963, mimeo. Pp. 1–37.

GILLIS, J. The construction and development of an incomplete sentences blank and scoring manual for assessing several psychological variables. Tri-Ethnic Research Report No. 10, 1962, mimeo. Pp. 1–30.

GILLIS, J. Issues in the measurement of attitudes toward deviance and their relationships with behavior. Tri-Ethnic Research Report No. 11, 1963, mimeo. Pp. 1–37.

GRAVES, T. D. Report on a preliminary testing program—local high school. Tri-Ethnic Research Report No. 1, 1960, mimeo. Pp. 1–46.

GRAVES, T. D. Time perspective and the deferred gratification pattern in a tri-ethnic community. Unpublished doctoral dissertation, University of Pennsylvania, and Tri-Ethnic Research Report No. 5, 1961, mimeo. Pp. 1–284.

GUERTIN, CAROL. Perceived life-chances in the opportunity structure: A study of a tri-ethnic high school. Unpublished masters thesis, University of Colorado, and Tri-Ethnic Research Report No. 7, 1962, mimeo. Pp. 1–122.

LIVERANT, S. The use of Rotter's social learning theory in developing a personality inventory. *Psychological Monographs,* 1958, *72,* No. 2 (Whole No. 455).

OPOCHINSKY, S. Values, expectations, and the formation of impressions. Unpublished doctoral dissertation, University of Colorado, 1965.

PHILLIPS, B. S. Expected value deprivation and occupational preference. *Sociometry*, 1964, *27*, 151–160.

ROTTER, J. B. *Social learning and clinical psychology.* Englewood Cliffs, N.J.: Prentice-Hall, 1954.

ROTTER, J. B. Generalized expectations for internal *versus* external control of reinforcements. *Psychological Monographs*, 1966, *80* (Whole No. 1). Pp. 1–28.

SEEMAN, M. On the meaning of alienation. *American Sociological Review*, 1959, *24*, 783–791.

SEEMAN, M. Alienation and social learning in a reformatory. *American Journal of Sociology*, 1963, *69*, 270–284.

SEEMAN, M. AND J. W. EVANS. Alienation and learning in a hospital setting. *American Sociological Review*, 1962, *27*, 772–783.

SHYBUT, J. Delayed gratification: A study of its measurement and its relationship to certain behavioral, psychological and demographic variables. Unpublished masters thesis, University of Colorado, 1963.

SROLE, L. Social integration and certain corollaries: An exploratory study. *American Sociological Review*, 1956, *21*, 709–716.

TITLEY, R. W. The measurement of alienation: An analysis of the alienation scale on the community survey. Tri-Ethnic Research Report No. 13, 1963, mimeo. Pp. 1–50.

WALLACE, M. Future time perspective in schizophrenia. *Journal of Abnormal and Social Psychology*, 1956, *52*, 240–245.

PART SIX

Results: Testing the Theory

CHAPTER ELEVEN

A Multivariable Approach to the Explanation of Deviance

In the preceding four chapters we have described the variety of measures needed for an empirical assessment of the theoretical formulation advanced earlier. These measures have been designed to represent the three systems referred to by our conceptual scheme: first, the behavior system, involving measures of excessive alcohol use and other forms of deviance; second, the sociocultural system, involving measures of access to opportunity, anomie, and social controls; and third, the personality system, involving measures of perceived opportunity, alienation, and personal controls. An attempt has been made thus far to evaluate the quality of the measures by considering their internal structure, the pattern of their relations with other measures, and the sex and ethnic group differences they have yielded. These analyses completed, the ground is now prepared for a direct examination of the relation between the sociocultural and personality measures (in conventional terms, our "predictors"), on the one hand, and the drinking and deviant behavior measures (our "criteria"), on the other.

This direct examination will proceed as follows. First, the observed relationship, measure-by-measure, of each major variable in the sociocultural and personality systems to a series of deviance criterion measures will be described. Next, the way in which the use of *multiple* sociocultural variables together, or the use of *multiple* personality variables together, improves the prediction of the deviance criteria will be shown. The following step will be to demonstrate the *interactive effect* of using sociocultural and personality variables *together;* this will be done by showing that each system of variables continues to be predictive when the other is held constant. Finally, and as a logical consequence of these preceding demonstrations, we will show how maximum explanatory power is achieved through *combining variables* from both the sociocultural and the personality system in what is increasingly being referred to as a "field theoretical" approach (see Yinger, 1965). The latter will represent the empirical implementation of the conceptual stance adopted in the early part of this book.

SOCIOCULTURAL VARIABLES
AND THE PREDICTION OF DEVIANCE

To review briefly, the hypotheses concerning the relationship between sociocultural variables and deviant behavior were as follows:

1. *The Opportunity Structure*

    The more favorable a person's position within the objective opportunity structure, the more possible it is for him to achieve his personal goals through socially legitimate means and, consequently, the less the pressure towards deviance.

    a. High socioeconomic status will be associated with low prevalence of deviant behavior.

    b. High objective access will be associated with low prevalence of deviant behavior.

2. *The Normative Structure*

    The more effective and operative the consensus on a group's norms, the lower will be the rates of deviant behavior of its members.

    a. Low degree of anomie in an ethnic group, in the form of high consensus with respect to definitions of appropriate behavior, will be associated with low deviance rates.

3. *The Social Control Structure*

    Limited access to the opportunity to learn and to engage in deviant behavior, including being subject to the operation of effective social rewards for conformity and punishments for deviance, will limit the occurrence of deviant behavior.

    a. Low exposure to deviant role models in the home will be associated with a low prevalence of deviant behavior.

    b. Being mapped into stable social groupings through which social sanctions are provided will be associated with a low prevalence of deviant behavior.

    c. A structural position which provides limited opportunities for engaging in deviant behavior will be associated with low prevalence of such behavior.

Measures of each of the above have been operationally defined for both the Community Survey Study and the High School Study in Chapter 9. At this point, the criterion measures of alcohol use and deviance employed in the Community Survey Study can usefully be reviewed:

1. *Never Drinker*—these are persons who, though they may have tried alcoholic beverages at some point in their lives, have never established a regular pattern of alcohol consumption. As abstainers, they represent the opposite end of a dimension of alcohol

use from that represented by heavy or chronic drinkers. (*Former* drinkers are not included in this category and, because of many complications in measuring their drinking behavior, have not been included in any of the drinking criterion groups.)

2. *Quantity-Frequency Index*—this measure is based on the average amount of absolute alcohol consumed per day, with the distribution then split at a natural break very near the median. High Q-F on this empirical basis is thus not *necessarily* high in any meaningful sense of the term; it is roughly equivalent to an average of two or more drinks per week. However, within this high categories are all the Q-F scores representing extremely high alcohol intake rates.

3. *Times Drunk*—this is simply the number of times the subject reported he had been drunk during the previous year. The obtained median was zero, but we specified the "high" group as reporting having been drunk at least twice.

4. *Other Deviance*—these are self-reports of a series of socially proscribed acts which are not known to be related to drinking. Any admission of acts falling within that subset which most persons would consider "serious" resulted in the subject being classified as deviant.

5. *Global Deviance*—this is the most comprehensive criterion category and the one in which the definition of deviance would most clearly meet the conceptual requirements specified in Chapter 2. A subject was classified as a global deviant for any *one* of the following:

   a. if he reported having been drunk *fifteen* or more times during the previous year;
   b. if he reported *two* or more instances of drinking-related problem behavior;
   c. if he reported at least *one* instance of serious other deviance;
   d. if he had a record of a court *conviction* during the previous ten years for other than a non-alcohol-related traffic violation, violation of game laws, or civil suits.

It can be seen that each criterion measure is categorical, one category representing the group having engaged in behavior which can be classified as deviant or deviance relevant, the other representing the group which has not. The most comprehensive category is Global Deviance, which subsumes a variety of behaviors classifiable as deviant and which has the added virtue of not being based entirely on self-report.

The hypotheses relating the sociocultural measures to deviance for the Community Survey sample are examined measure-by-measure in Table 11.1; the table has been constructed as follows. The distribution of scores

TABLE 11.1

Relationships between Sociocultural Variables and Measures of Deviant Behavior: Community Survey Study*

Structure	Variable		Behavioral Measures†				
			Never Drinker	Quantity-Frequency‡	Times Drunk‡	Other Deviance	Global Deviance
Oppor-tunity	Socio-economic status	+§ −‖ sig.¶	22 12 N.S.	43 59 $p < .05$	10 36 $p < .001$	28 32 N.S.	32 51 $p < .01$
	Objective access	+ − sig.	21 14 N.S.	44 60 $p < .05$	16 32 $p < .05$	28 33 N.S.	37 51 $p < .05$
Norma-tive**							
Social Control	Exposure to deviant role models	+ − sig.	18 17 N.S.	45 62 $p < .05$	16 35 $p < .01$	27 36 N.S.	36 51 $p < .05$
	Absence of sanction networks	+ − sig.	23 10 $p < .05$	42 64 $p < .01$	15 35 $p < .01$	22 43 $p < .01$	27 64 $p < .001$
	Oppor-tunity for engaging in de-viance	+ − sig.	21 11 N.S.	40 69 $p < .001$	17 34 $p < .01$	29 33 N.S.	37 51 $p < .05$
	Total access to illegiti-mate means	+ − sig.	22 11 $p < .05$	38 72 $p < .001$	11 43 $p < .001$	23 43 $p < .01$	29 63 $p < .001$

* $N = 221$.

† Percent above cutting points is given for each criterion.

‡ Only *present* drinkers are included in these analyses.

§ Low deviance-prone group (+) on this predictor.

‖ High deviance-prone group (−) on this predictor.

¶ Level of significance (sig.) of chi-square test of difference in proportions (one-tailed tests). Differences not significant at the .05 level or better are indicated N.S.

** No individually distributed measures were used. See Chapter 9 for a discussion of ethnic group differences in anomie and in rates of deviance.

on each sociocultural *predictor* measure was dichotomized as near its median as possible. Then, on the basis of the expected relationships reviewed above and the score obtained, each subject was assigned to either the low deviance-prone group $(+)$ or the high deviance-prone group $(-)$ on that measure. Then the *proportion* of subjects *within* the low deviance-prone group and *within* the high deviance-prone group which had been independently classified as "deviant" on each *criterion* measure was determined. The table presents these proportions for each sociocultural measure across all the criterion measures. The reader can readily judge the strength of the association between each predictor and each criterion by looking at *the magnitude of the difference* between the proportion of deviants in the low $(+)$ deviance-prone group and the proportion in the high $(-)$ deviance-prone group. The chi-square significance of these differences is entered below each comparison.[1]

Two matters regarding this table require some explanation. First, since anomie has been defined as a group attribute and no individually distributed measures of it were constructed, tests of association cannot be run with the measures of the normative structure. The consistency between ethnic group differences in anomie and ethnic differences in deviance rates has already been noted, however, in Chapter 9.

Second, Never Drinkers are considered, of course, as *non-deviant* with respect to excessive alcohol use; thus, the theoretically expected associations with this criterion are all opposite in direction from those expected for the other four criteria. For this one criterion measure, the proportion in the $(+)$ category *should* be greater than that in the $(-)$ category.

Every one of the thirty tests presented in Table 11.1 shows group differences in deviance rates in the anticipated direction, and over two-thirds of these tests achieve at least the .05 level of statistical significance. The Global Deviance criterion measure, which includes all types of deviant behavior, whether drinking related or not, is associated significantly with every one of these key sociocultural measures. Among these latter measures, Absence of Sanction Networks seems the predictor component most consistently related to the several different definitions of deviance or deviance-relevant behavior, achieving significant association with all five criteria.

These findings provide clear-cut support for the theoretical relations postulated and for the adequacy of the measures involved. The support is not contingent upon any particular criterion measure; it ranges across

---

[1] The reason for presenting these data in the form of categories and proportions is purely heuristic; correlations would have served the same purpose and would have had the advantage of utilizing the full range of the measures. The simplicity and clarity achieved through the method of presentation adopted here will become increasingly apparent, however, as we move from single to multivariable analysis.

all of them and is most compelling in relation to the criterion measure which is theoretically soundest and in which we would have placed our greatest confidence, the Global Deviance criterion.

The High School Study provided an opportunity for an independent replication of these findings. The results from that study are presented in Table 11.2, which was constructed in a manner identical to Table

TABLE 11.2

Relationships between Sociocultural Variables and Measures of Deviant Behavior: High School Study*

Structure	Variable		Behavioral Measure†				
			Never Drinker	Quantity-Fre-quency‡	Times Drunk‡	Poor School Adjust-ment	Global Deviance
Oppor-tunity	Socioeconomic status	+ §	16	49	49	49	31
		− ‖	19	53	62	50	43
		sig. ¶	**	N.S.	N.S.	N.S.	N.S.
Norma-tive††							
Social Control	Exposure to deviant role models	+	24	47	37	32	22
		−	11	58	68	69	57
		sig.	**	N.S.	$p < .05$	$p < .01$	$p < .01$
	Absence of sanction networks	+	26	48	48	36	26
		−	13	55	52	56	44
		sig.	**	N.S.	N.S.	$p < .05,$	$p < .05$
	Opportunity for engaging in deviance	+	23	49	41	40	33
		−	14	56	63	57	41
		sig.	**	N.S.	N.S.	N.S.	N.S.
	Total access to illegitimate means	+	23	50	47	36	30
		−	13	55	55	61	45
		sig.	**	N.S.	N.S.	$p < .05$	N.S.

* $N = 93$.

† Percent above cutting point is given for each criterion.

‡ Only *present* drinkers are included in these analyses.

§ Low deviance-prone group (+) on this predictor.

‖ High deviance-prone group (−) on this predictor.

¶ Level of significance (sig.) of chi-square test of difference in proportions (one-tailed tests). Differences not significant at the .05 level or better are indicated N.S.

** Expected cell frequencies are too small to permit a legitimate test.

†† No individually distributed measures were used.

11.1. Although the various measures are as conceptually parallel to the adult measures as possible, the actual *content* of both predictors and criteria differ. The operational definitions of the five deviance or deviance-relevant behavioral criteria used in the High School Study will be briefly reviewed:

1. *Never Drinker*—this category is composed of all students who reported that they "never drank," though a few of these may have been "tasters." Since teen-agers are still in the process of acquiring adult drinking patterns, this category also includes, of course, subjects who have *not yet begun* to drink.

2. *Quantity-Frequency Index*—with minor simplification for group administration, this index is identical to that for adults, and the median split is only a fraction of an ounce lower.

3. *Times Drunk*—for high school students, this index was based on self-report of "times drunk or pretty high" during the last year. Again, the distribution was split at two or more times.

4. *Poor School Adjustment*—this non-drinking criterion combines the components of grade point average and occasions absent, the resulting distribution having then been cut at the median. Based completely on school records revealing fairly objective types of behavior, this index is operationally independent of self-reports and relatively independent of peer and teacher ratings as well.

5. *Global Deviance*—this criterion is based completely on peer and teacher ratings of each student's behavior. A position in the most deviant quartile of *either* group's ratings resulted in the student being allocated to this criterion category. Like Poor School Adjustment, this measure is also operationally independent of the self-report measures.

Of the twenty-five relationships presented in Table 11.2, all but one (SES as a predictor of Never Drinking) are in the theoretically expected direction. The magnitude of these group differences is not very impressive, however; only six achieve statistical significance. As among the adults, strong associations tend to be found on the most comprehensive criterion, the Global Deviance measure, while the various drinking measures are only poorly predicted. While the consistency of the results of the High School Study with those of the Community Survey Study is further support for the sociocultural formulations, the role of these social factors is apparently weaker at the high school level than at the adult level. One exception to this generalization is the measure Exposure to Deviant Role Models, which produces half of the significant associations in the table.

PERSONALITY VARIABLES
AND THE PREDICTION OF DEVIANCE

Having demonstrated fairly consistent associations in the theoretically expected direction between a number of key sociocultural variables and deviant behavior, we can now turn to a parallel analysis for the *personality* measures. Briefly stated, our hypotheses concerning associations between personality attributes and deviant behavior were as follows:

1. *The Perceived Opportunity Structure*
    The greater the *perceived* opportunity for the achievement of personally valued goals by legitimate means, the less will be the psychological pressures for recourse to alternative means, including deviant behavior.
    a. High expectations, particularly within the achievement or recognition sphere, will be associated with a low prevalence of deviant behavior.
    b. Low disjunction scores, particularly within the achievement or recognition sphere, will be associated with a low prevalence of deviant behavior.

2. *The Personal Belief Structure*
    The greater the generalized belief in internal control and the sense of efficacy, predictability, social integration, and meaningfulness in life (all the opposite of alienation), the greater will be the psychological control against engaging in deviant behavior.
    a. Low alienation scores will be associated with a low prevalence of deviant behavior.
    b. A high score on feelings of internal control will be associated with a low prevalence of deviant behavior.

3. *The Personal Control Structure*
    Internalized standards of conduct repudiating the use of deviant behavior, as well as a generalized orientation toward considering the long-term consequences of one's actions and a tendency to delay gratification in the pursuit of long-range goals, will serve as psychological controls against engaging in deviant behavior.
    a. Nonpermissive attitudes toward deviance will be associated with a low prevalence of deviant behavior.
    b. An extended future time perspective and a tendency toward delay of gratification will be associated with a low prevalence of deviant behavior.

Tests of these hypotheses, measure-by-measure, are presented in Table 11.3 and 11.4, for the Community Survey Study and the High School Study, respectively. As with the sociocultural measures just discussed,

TABLE 11.3

Relationships between Personality Variables and Measures of Deviant Behavior: Community Survey Study*

Structure	Variable		Never Drinker	Quantity-Frequency‡	Times Drunk‡	Other Deviance	Global Deviance
				Behavioral Measures†			
Perceived Oppor-tunity	Expectations	+§	25	49	19	21	25
		−‖	13	54	27	41	57
		sig.¶	$p < .05$	N.S.	N.S.	$p < .01$	$p < .001$
	Disjunctions	+	23	47	15	21	23
		−	15	56	30	41	57
		sig.	N.S.	N.S.	$p < .05$	$p < .01$	$p < .001$
Personal Belief	Alienation	+	22	47	20	25	32
		−	14	56	28	38	52
		sig.	N.S.	N.S.	N.S.	$p < .05$	$p < .01$
	Internal control	+	16	49	21	31	39
		−	21	56	28	32	45
		sig.	N.S.	N.S.	N.S.	N.S.	N.S.
Personal Control	Attitudes toward deviance	+	28	43	19	21	30
		−	8	58	27	42	55
		sig.	$p < .001$	$p < .05$	N.S.	$p < .01$	$p < .001$
	Future time perspective	+	20	59	23	30	38
		−	15	46	24	33	43
		sig.	N.S.	N.S.	N.S.	N.S.	N.S.

* $N = 221$.

† Percent above cutting points is given for each criterion.

‡ Only *present* drinkers are included in these analyses.

§ Low deviance-prone group (+) on this predictor.

‖ High deviance-prone group (−) on this predictor.

¶ Level of significance (sig.) of chi-square test of difference in proportions (one-tailed tests.) Differences not significant at the .05 level or better are indicated N.S.

each major personality measure has been dichotomized at its median. The percentage of subjects falling within each criterion category was then calculated, first for the low deviance-prone (+) group having the personality characteristic which should inhibit the occurrence of deviant behavior, and second for the high deviance-prone (−) group having the personality characteristic conducive to deviance. By examining the difference between these two percentages, a quick index of the relative power of each predictor against each criterion measure can again be obtained.

TABLE 11.4

Relationships between Personality Variables and Measures of Deviant Behavior: High School Study*

Structure	Variable		Never Drinker	Quantity-Frequency‡	Times Drunk‡	Poor School Adjustment	Global Deviance
			Behavioral Measures†				
Perceived Opportunity	Expectations (AcR)	+§	23	44	47	36	23
		−‖	11	56	61	63	50
		sig.¶	**	N.S.	N.S.	$p < .01$	$p < .01$
	Disjunctions (AcR)	+	20	57	51	41	33
		−	15	45	58	57	40
		sig.	**	N.S.	N.S.	N.S.	N.S.
	Life chances disjunctions	+	22	34	43	42	22
		−	12	64	64	56	50
		sig.	**	$p < .01$	$p < .05$	N.S.	$p < .01$
Personal Belief	Internal control	+	16	49	57	48	34
		−	18	52	52	51	39
		sig.	**	N.S.	N.S.	N.S.	N.S.
Personal Control	Attitudes toward deviance	+	27	31	39	45	20
		−	8	68	68	53	51
		sig.	**	$p < .01$	$p < .01$	N.S.	$p < .01$
	Delay of gratification††	+	22	41	41	41	30
		±	17	59	59	51	37
		−	12	53	67	65	47
		sig.	**	N.S.	N.S.	N.S.	N.S.
	Future time perspective	+	23	56	50	39	32
		−	12	45	57	58	40
		sig.	**	N.S.	N.S.	$p < .05$	N.S.

* $N = 93$.

† Percent above cutting points is given on each criterion.

‡ Only *present* drinkers are included in these analyses.

§ Low deviance-prone group (+) on this predictor.

‖ High deviance-prone group (−) on this predictor.

¶ Level of significance (sig.) of chi-square test of difference in proportions (one-tailed tests). Differences not significant at the .05 level or better are indicated N.S.

** Expected cell frequencies are too small to permit a meaningful test.

†† This measure divided subjects into *three* groups: high delayers (+), intermediate delayers (±), and low delayers (−). The high group was run against the other two groups for the chi-square tests.

Among adults, all but two of the associations (Internal Control *versus* Never Drinking, and Future Time Perspective *versus* the Quantity-Frequency index) are in the predicted direction, with over a third of the tests reaching at least the .05 level of significance. The most comprehensive criterion measure, Global Deviance, was significantly associated with all of the personality measures except for Internal Control and Time Perspective. The various drinking measures emerge as fairly difficult to predict at any substantial level from single variables. Finally, the derived Disjunction measure seems to be little more powerful than the simple measure of expectations, confirming our suspicions based on internal analysis of these measures in the last chapter.

Turning to the High School Study, all but four of the thirty-five tests in Table 11.4 are in the expected direction, two of the four failures being the result of a single predictor (Internal Control) and the others of a single criterion measure (the Quantity-Frequency index). As in the adult community study, the Global Deviance criterion was, in general, more strongly associated with these personality measures than were any of the less comprehensive criteria; and again, as among adults, Time Perspective and Internal Control were among the least successful of all the predictor variables, while Attitudes toward Deviance and Life Chances Disjunctions were the most successful. Finally, the derived Disjunction measure appears to be less discriminating than Expectations alone.

The parallel between these measure-by-measure findings among both the adults and the high school students in the same community is striking. Both the sociocultural and the personality measures among both adults and adolescents were more strongly associated with the Global Deviance measure than with the less comprehensive criteria. This finding provides strong empirical support for the decision, made on theoretical grounds at the beginning of this research, to focus not simply on excessive drinking behavior but rather on the larger class of deviant behavior of which excessive drinking can be considered but one form. Regardless of particular operational definition or conceptual comprehensiveness, however, all of the measures of deviant behavior presented here have been found to map into the network of associations with sociocultural and personality variables in precisely the way which the conceptual scheme led us to anticipate. Given the fact that the operational definitions of the predictor and criterion variables in the two studies were generally distinct, while the variables remained conceptually the same, the parallel findings within two independent and different populations provides strong support for the inferences to be drawn from those findings.

The approach thus far has been to examine each measure by itself, without taking into consideration the multiple measures available for each subject. While the results have been encouraging, they can be considered to represent only a limited test of the formulations. The reason for this lies in the theoretical position, stated earlier, that deviance is the complex outcome of *multiple variables operating simultaneously*. Thus, we have spoken of the importance of knowing about a person not only the amount of pressure toward deviance to which he is subject but also the kinds of controls which are operative in his situation. Viewed from this vantage point, no single variable can be expected to account, alone, for any great part of the variance in the occurrence of deviance; the proper study of deviance requires simultaneous consideration of the several variables specified theoretically within the structures of the sociocultural system, within the structures of the personality system, and, ultimately, within the larger system which comprises these two. The implementation of this kind of approach is begun in the following section.

A MULTIVARIABLE APPROACH TO EXPLANATION

The logical implications of the conceptual scheme require that the evaluation of each system, sociocultural and personality, should deal simultaneously with the three structures making up the system. In operational terms, the requirement would be for a measure from each of the three structures in each system to be dealt with together. Thus, to evaluate the sociocultural system formulations, a *triad* of sociocultural measures— made up of a measure of the Opportunity structure, a measure of the Normative structure, and a measure of the Social Control structure— should be tested against the deviance criteria; the personality system formulations should be tested in the same way. It is in this way that the location of a subject in "sociocultural space" or in "personality space" can be dealt with, since that location lies at the intersection of his positions on the measures of the three component structures.

To pursue this "triangulation" approach required some sort of multivariable analytic procedure. A typical method employed for such purposes is, of course, multiple-regression analysis (Blalock, 1960). This approach was not pursued for two reasons. First, if adequate prediction formulas for drinking and deviance are ultimately to be derived, they should be preceded by a thorough, and hopefully theoretically guided, specification of the major relevant independent variables. The present research is only a first approximation to this task. Second, such formulas should be based on broad experience with large and diverse samples if their stability and generality are to be established. Our intensive work in a small community is not appropriate for such a task.

We turned instead to a simpler procedure which has several advantages and can readily be described. The procedure, which we will refer to as "pattern analysis," builds directly on the analyses presented in the preceding measure-by-measure approach. In that approach, each predictor measure was dichotomized at the median, thus creating a theoretically high deviance-prone group and a theoretically low deviance-prone group for each measure. These two groups were then compared on the various criteria in terms of the proportion of previously classified "deviants" they contained; the hypothesis at test was that there should be a lower percentage of "deviants" in the low deviance-prone group than in the high deviance-prone group for each measure.

Following out this type of analysis, it is possible to constitute groups of subjects in terms of their high or low deviance-prone position on *three* predictor measures considered simultaneously, instead of on one. Thus, a group can be constituted which is made up of subjects who are *low deviance prone on all three measures;* theoretically, it should have the lowest percentage of deviants among its members. A group can be constituted which is *high deviance prone on all three measures;* it should have the highest proportion of deviants among its members. And other groups can be constituted based on various patterns of high and low deviance-prone scores on the three measures. For three dichotomized measures considered simultaneously, there are, of course, eight possible patterns of scores on which groups of subjects may be constituted.

The basic virtue of this procedure, beyond its simplicity and the readiness with which it can be grasped by the reader, is that it keeps real groups of persons constantly in view. Each pattern group is a concrete set of persons having a clear-cut set of attributes (its positions on the three predictors) and a clear-cut rate of deviance (the proportion of its members previously classified as "deviant" on any particular criterion). Comparing pattern groups on their percentages of deviants is thus simple and straightforward, and one can see at once not only the difference between the deviance rates of various pattern groups but also the "absolute" rate associated with a given pattern—that is, what proportion of its members have been classified as deviant. In one sense, therefore, the pattern analysis procedure combines the advantages of a quantitative approach with those of a clinical approach.[2]

---

[2] This form of analysis has been anticipated and employed by a number of previous investigators, although the particular format presented here is our own. We were initially led in this direction by a paper by Gould and Schrag (1962). It is also interesting to note that a very similar approach has been taken in the study of innovativeness by Rogers and Havens (1962). Historically, the general approach was employed in different form in the early efforts to predict parole recidivism (see Bruce, *et al.,* 1929, and Glueck, 1929). This note obviously does not attempt to be exhaustive, since many investigators have used some variant of this form of analysis in presenting their findings.

Multivariable Sociocultural Patterns and the Prediction of Deviance

The measure-by-measure analyses in the preceding section and in the preceding two chapters provide some empirical basis for selecting the most promising measures to represent each of the three structures in the sociocultural and personality systems. The predictor measures finally chosen were the ones which presented the least conceptual overlap and were empirically best established. Although our aim was to select one measure within each structure, this could not be accomplished for the sociocultural system since we do not have an *individual* measure of the Normative structure. (Anomie, it will be recalled, was defined and measured as a property of an interacting *group.*) We have therefore compromised for the sociocultural system and have selected one measure from the Opportunity structure (Socioeconomic Status), and two measures from the Social Control structure (Exposure to Deviant Role Models and Absence of Sanction Networks).

These measures have been arranged in a pattern analysis in Table 11.5. The table was prepared as described above. The distribution of scores on each predictor variable had already been dichotomized at the median, and each person, depending on his score, had been assigned to either a low deviance-prone (+) group or a high deviance-prone (−) group on each predictor measure. When this is done for three variables simultaneously, each person can fall, as noted, into any one of eight possible patterns and can have from zero to three high deviance-prone attributes. The proportion of persons in each of these eight patterns who had already been independently classified as "deviant" on each criterion was then calculated.

Line A of Table 11.5 shows the theoretically optimal pattern of these three sociocultural variables: the pattern which should have the *lowest* deviance rate. Persons who have low scores on Absence of Sanction Networks, low Exposure to Deviant Role Models, and high Socioeconomic Status should have the lowest proportion of deviants among them. In fact, the table shows that, of the 43 persons falling into this pattern, only 6, or 14 percent, had been independently classified as deviant on the Global Deviance criterion. This is by far the lowest proportion of deviants to be found for any of the eight patterns in the table.

By comparing lines in the table such that two measures at a time are held constant and only the third one shifts from plus to minus, the effect of this third variable can be easily specified. For each variable, there are four such comparisons which can be made. Consider the Absence of Sanction Networks measure. Comparing line A in the table with line C, one can examine the effect of a shift from plus to minus on this measure while the other two measures remain the same: The percentage of deviants

TABLE 11.5
Sociocultural Variable Patterns and the Global Deviance Criterion Measure: Community Survey Study

Pattern	Sociocultural Variables			Subjects in each Pattern	Global Deviance Criterion Measure		
	Socioeconomic Status	Absence of Sanction Networks	Exposure to Deviant Role Models		Number Deviant	% Deviant	Combined % Deviant
I. Optimal Pattern— minimum expected deviance	A. +	+	+	43	6	14	14
II. One Variable Departure— toward greater expected deviance	B. +	+	—	30	8	27	
	C. +	—	+	19	9	47	33
	D. —	+	+	32	10	31	
III. Two Variable Departure— toward greater expected deviance	E. +	—.	—	16	12	75	
	F. —	+	—	23	10	43	59
	G. —	—	+	36	22	62	
IV. Three Variable Departure— maximum expected deviance	H. —	—	—	20	15	75	75

increases from 14 to 47. Comparing line B with line E, an increase from 27 to 75 percent is shown; line D with line G, an increase from 31 to 62 percent; and, finally, line F with line H, an increase from 43 to 75 percent. These four comparisons show the contribution of the Absence of Sanction Networks measure to the prediction of deviance while the other two variables are held constant. Clearly, it is a powerful measure: The average percentage increase in deviance rate over these four comparisons is 36 percent. The average percentage increase for Exposure to Deviant Role Models over its four comparisons is 16 percent; and that for

Socioeconomic Status over its four comparisons is only 12 percent. Of the twelve comparisons possible in the table, all but one (E with H) reveal a substantial increase in deviance rates.

From our experience with this type of analysis for all of our major deviance and drinking criteria, we have found that, although some overlap does occur in the proportion of deviants among the three patterns with one departure from optimal (lines B, C, and D), and the three patterns with two departures from optimal (lines E, F, and G), these overlaps, as in Table 11.5, are relatively few and small in magnitude, and they probably result from the small samples we have employed. For purposes of simplifying the subsequent tables, therefore, we have combined all the "one departure" patterns (lines B, C, and D in Table 11.5) into a single, more stable group; and we have done the same with the "two departure" patterns (lines E, F, and G in Table 11.5). The percentage figures shown in the far right-hand column of Table 11.5 are the deviance rates for these combined patterns.

This procedure clearly does not exploit the unique or differential contribution of the individual variables in their different interactions. Its assumption, essentially conservative, is that the important variation lies in the *number* of deviance-prone scores a person has (out of the three possible) rather than in which *particular* scores he has. This assumption is, of course, all that our theory was able to specify, since we had no a priori basis for assuming that any given variable in a structure was more or less important than any other. Nor could we assume, on the basis of our theory, that any structure within a system was more important than another; nor that either system, sociocultural or personality, was more or less important. What has been specified by the theoretical formulations in the early chapters has been only the *relevance* of these variables; the present procedure of dealing with the *number* of deviance-prone scores is fully in accord with this position.

Given these assumptions, and returning to the right-hand column of Table 11.5, it can be seen that, as a group's sociocultural pattern departs from the theoretical optimum, the chances of being classified as a "deviant" increase rapidly. Thus, with only *one* variable departing from optimal, the proportion of deviants has risen from 14 percent to 33 percent; with *two* departures, it rises to 59 percent, and, in the group where *all three* sociocultural scores are deviance prone, the proportion of deviants is 75 percent. These striking findings constitute a direct confirmation of theoretical expectations.

The magnitude of this trend in the pattern analysis is so large and its *social* significance so obvious that a demonstration of its *statistical* significance is perhaps irrelevant. Nevertheless, it is possible to test for the significance of the obtained trend, and, in the process, to determine whether the distribution shows any significant departure from a linear model. To do this, the critical ratio for the linear regression of successive patterns against deviance is first calculated; this yields a value of 5.55 which indicates a highly significant linear trend in the data. Second, in order to estimate the extent, if any, of departure from linearity in the data, we calculate the over-all χ^2 value for the 2×8 contingency table: $\chi^2 = 31.50$. Then, since the square of the critical ratio previously calculated, 30.76, is distributed as χ^2, it serves to indicate the proportion of the over-all χ^2 value which is accounted for by the linear regression. Therefore, by subtracting 30.76 from the over-all χ^2 value of 31.50, we find that only 0.74, or an insignificant portion of the original χ^2 value, is accounted for by a *departure* from a linear trend.[3]

To summarize, this statistic indicates that there is a highly significant tendency for groups with progressively less favorable sociocultural characteristics, according to the theoretical scheme, to have an increasing proportion of deviants among their number. Furthermore, there are only small and statistically nonsignificant departures from this linear trend to be found in the data.

The combined form of pattern analysis just discussed can now be presented for the sociocultural measures against *all* of the five deviance or deviance-relevant criteria being employed in the Community Survey Study. These data are shown in Table 11.6. It can be seen immediately that

TABLE 11.6
Sociocultural Variable Patterns and Deviance:
Community Survey Study

Sociocultural Pattern*	Behavioral Measures†				
	Never Drinker	Quantity-Frequency‡	Times Drunk‡	Other Deviance	Global Deviance
Optimal (N = 43)	21	33	3	12	14
1 Departure (N = 81)	21	37	9	30	33
2 Departures (N = 75)	12	72	42	38	59
3 Departures (N = 20)	0	63	47	45	75

* Sociocultural variables used: Socioeconomic status, Exposure to deviant role models, and Absence of sanction networks.

† Percent above cutting points is given for each criterion.

‡ Only *present* drinkers are included in this analysis. *N*'s in the four patterns, from Optimal down, are therefore reduced to 33, 54, 57, and 19, respectively.

[3] See Maxwell, A. E., *Analyzing Qualitative Data*. London: Methuen, 1961. Chapter 4.

for every criterion measure, a strong linear trend is present, with a small departure only on the Quantity-Frequency criterion. Thus, simultaneous consideration of three sociocultural measures results consistently in the prediction of deviant or deviance-prone behavior at a socially meaningful level, whatever criterion of deviance is employed. The combination of measures has clearly improved prediction over that presented earlier, which was obtained on a measure-by-measure basis.

That these findings are not simply an artifact of particular methods or subjects can be demonstrated by examining the parallel findings among the high school students in the research community. In the High School Study replication, the sociocultural measures differ operationally, the subjects differ, their age level and range differs markedly, and the criterion measures differ, particularly in the use of outside raters, that is, teachers and peers, to establish the deviance groups. Only the conceptual framework remains the same.

The three sociocultural variables used are as conceptually similar to those used among adults as possible and include Socioeconomic Status of the student's parents, Exposure to Deviant Role Models in the home, and Absence of Sanction Networks. The formation of the pattern table, as presented in Table 11.7, is identical to the previous one.

Just as in the adult study, strong linear trends are found in the prediction of most of the behavioral criteria, particularly the Global Deviance measure. Problems do appear in the prediction of the Never Drinker and

TABLE 11.7
Sociocultural Variable Patterns and Deviance:
High School Study

Sociocultural Pattern*	Behavioral Measures†				
	Never Drinker	Quantity- Frequency‡	Times Drunk‡	Poor School Adjustment	Global Deviance
Optimal ($N = 19$)	16	38	31	26	11
1 Departure ($N = 30$)	30	67	52	43	37
2 Departures ($N = 20$)	15	35	53	60	40
3 Departures ($N = 15$)	7	64	64	60	60

* Sociocultural variables used: Socioeconomic status, Exposure to deviant role models, and Absence of sanction networks.

† Percent above cutting points is given for each criterion.

‡ Only *present* drinkers are included in this analysis. N's in the four patterns, from Optimal down, are therefore reduced to 16, 21, 17, and 14, respectively.

Q-F criteria in this group, perhaps because drinking for these subjects is not yet a stable behavioral pattern. For example, many "never drinkers" simply have not yet *started* to drink; the conceptual scheme may be less predictive of the age of onset of drinking than of its excessive use. In general, in any case, the High School Study tends to reinforce the findings from the Community Survey Study.

Multivariable Personality Patterns and the Prediction of Deviance

In a manner identical to that just described, a parallel pattern analysis can also be constructed from personality system measures. For the Community Survey Study, one measure from within each of the three personality structures was selected: Disjunctions from the Perceived Opportunity structure, Alienation from the Personal Belief structure, and Attitudes toward Deviance from the Personal Control structure. Multivariable patterns were then generated, resulting in groups of subjects who exhibit varying personality profiles with respect to deviance proneness.

The optimal personality pattern, the one theoretically least conducive to deviance, is one where subjects have relatively *few* disjunctions with respect to the achievement of their goals, *low* alienation from society and its norms, and relatively *high* repudiation of deviance. The opposite pattern should provide the greatest psychological proneness to engaging in deviance, with intermediate patterns grading in between.

These patterns are presented in Table 11.8. As can be seen, Never-

TABLE 11.8
Personality Variable Patterns and Deviance:
Community Survey Study

Personality Pattern*	Behavioral Measures†				
	Never Drinker	Quantity-Frequency‡	Times Drunk‡	Other Deviance	Global Deviance
Optimal (N = 43)	41	30	13	14	16
1 Departure (N = 56)	12	52	11	25	27
2 Departures (N = 63)	16	56	17	30	51
3 Departures (N = 42)	10	60	26	57	69

* Personality variables used: Personal disjunctions, Attitudes toward deviance, and Alienation.

† Percent above cutting points is given for each criterion.

‡ Only *present* drinkers are included in this analysis. N's in the four patterns, from Optimal down, are therefore reduced to 23, 46, 46, and 35, respectively.

Drinkers tend, as expected, to accumulate in the optimal personality pattern, while among those subjects who *do* drink, the heaviest alcohol intake (Q-F) is reported by those in the personality patterns most suggestive of strain. Similarly, drunkenness, despite a small reversal, is more common among those subjects with psychological profiles theoretically conducive to deviance, as are various forms of serious, but non-drinking-related deviance. The measure of Global Deviance, which takes into consideration *both* drinking- and non-drinking-related deviant behavior, also displays a strong association with the personality patterns. Only 16 percent of those having the optimal personality pattern had been independently classified on this index as "deviant," whereas 69 percent of those with the least optimal pattern had been so classified. The linearity of relationship between these personality patterns and the criterion measures should be noted; subjects in intermediate patterns display intermediate rates of deviant behavior.

Again, the convergent High School Study permits us to examine the generality of these findings. Unfortunately, there is no direct parallel to the alienation measure among high school students, and we have already discovered that belief in Internal Control, at least as we have attempted to measure it, was essentially unrelated to deviance among *both* adults and adolescents. The Life Chances Disjunctions measure, however, can serve as a reasonable alternative to Alienation for the high school subjects. It is conceptually and operationally distinct from expectations for academic recognition, having its referent much farther in the future. Thus, a high score reflects relative hopelessness on the part of the student about his future life chances and is thereby conceptually bordering on certain aspects of alienation. The high school personality patterns were therefore generated from Expectations for Academic Recognition, Life Chances Disjunctions, and Attitudes toward Deviance.

As can be seen in Table 11.9, there is a strong association between the patterns on these three variables and never-drinking; and among those teen-agers who *do* drink, relatively heavy drinking and drunkenness appear to be strongly associated with a pattern of psychological disjunction and tolerance of deviance. Similarly, a high degree of conformity to the demands and expectations of the high school is shown, as expected, for those displaying the optimal psychological pattern. Finally, the Global Deviance measure, based on peer and teacher ratings of a student's behavior both within school and outside, is strongly associated with these psychological patterns: Seventy-two percent of those exhibiting the theoretically most deviance-prone personality pattern have been independently classified as "deviant"; only 7 percent of those with the optimal personality pattern are so classified, and the in-between patterns are intermediate in their rates of deviance. Thus, again, as it did for the sociocultural

TABLE 11.9
Personality Variable Patterns and Deviance:
High School Study

Personality Pattern*	Behavioral Measures†				
	Never Drinker	Quantity-Frequency‡	Times Drunk‡	Poor School Adjustment	Global Deviance
Optimal (*N* = 15)	40	22	33	40	7
1 Departure (*N* = 35)	17	38	45	34	20
2 Departures (*N* = 25)	12	50	50	60	52
3 Departures (*N* = 18)	6	88	88	72	72

* Personality variables used: Life chances disjunction, Attitudes toward deviance, and Expectations for academic recognition.

† Percent above cutting points is given for each criterion.

‡ Only *present* drinkers are included in this analysis. *N*'s in the four patterns, from Optimal down, are therefore reduced to 9, 29, 22, and 17, respectively.

findings, the High School Study provides compelling and consistent support to the Community Survey Study with respect to the empirical success of the personality formulations and the personality measures.

Field-Theoretical Patterns and the Prediction of Deviance

In the previous sections, it has been shown that a set of sociocultural variables and a set of conceptually parallel personality variables are equally capable of accounting for deviance rates at a fairly high level of efficiency. The question can then be legitimately raised: Are these two classes of variables essentially redundant, so that it does not really matter within which system a researcher chooses to work, or, on the other hand, are they *supplementary* systems which account for *different* sectors of the variance in deviant behavior? If the latter is the case, then prediction can be increased by working within *both* systems simultaneously. The latter position is essentially that held by "field theorists" in contemporary behavioral science.

To examine this issue empirically, two representative sociocultural measures and two conceptually parallel personality measures were selected so that one set could be held constant while the other was varied. (Only two variables were employed within each system, making a total of four, because of the small *N*'s which were available.) The two variables used within the sociocultural system were Socioeconomic Status, from the Opportunity structure, and Total Access to Illegitimate Means, from the Social Control structure. This latter variable combines into a single index: Exposure to Deviant Role Models, Absence of Sanction Networks, and Opportunity for Deviance. The two parallel personality variables were total Personal Disjunctions, from the Perceived Opportunity structure, and Attitudes toward Deviance, from the Personal Control structure.

In Table 11.10, the results of this analysis are presented. The table was constructed as follows. First, considering only the left half of the table, the sample was divided into three groups: those who had *low* deviance-prone scores on both sociocultural measures (line I), those who had *high* deviance-prone scores on both of these measures (line III), and those with a mixed sociocultural pattern (line II). Rates of Global Deviants were then calculated for these three groups; they ranged from 19 percent for the optimal pattern to 60 percent for the high deviance-prone pattern, with the proportion of deviants in the combined mixed-pattern falling in between at 50 percent. Then, *within each* of these three sociocultural groups, each group was further subdivided into those who *also* had an optimal *personality* pattern with respect to deviance (A) (*low* personal disjunctions and *high* repudiation of deviance), those with a mixed personality pattern (B), and those with a personality pattern conducive to the occurrence of deviant behavior (C).

By this procedure, it was possible to examine the effect of the personality measures at *each* of three different levels of sociocultural deviance proneness. At each sociocultural level, it is clear from the table that variation in *personality* deviance proneness makes a consistent and substantial difference. In line I, for example, where the sociocultural environment is relatively benign, only 19 percent of this group is deviant. But when this group is broken down further, into subgroups A, B, and C on the personality measures, the deviance rates for the latter three groups range from 7 percent to 19 percent to 46 percent, respectively. Though the *N*'s involved are small, the linearity of the results is impressive.

What this example shows is that variation occurs in deviance rates as a function of personality variation *when the sociocultural environment is controlled*. This same effect is shown for Group II and Group III when each is broken down into A, B, and C groups. The small reversal between the A and B subgroups of Group III is possibly due to the small *N*'s involved.

The right-hand half of Table 11.10 duplicates this procedure, now controlling for the personality measures and constructing subgroups A, B, and C on the basis of *sociocultural* variation. Again we find that subjects with similar personality pressures for or constraints against the display of deviant behavior vary in their *actual behavior* depending on the variation in the sociocultural position within which they find themselves located.

This consistent and impressive finding further accents the value of taking *both* classes of variables, sociocultural *and* personality, into account within our over-all social-psychological scheme.

The table makes clear, in dramatic fashion, the central point of the field-theoretical position: *the interdependence of social and psychological variation.* Having demonstrated that both classes of variables are mutually contributing to an account of deviance rates, we can now justify combining them into a single, four-variable "field" pattern analysis. An optimal pattern based on these four variables would describe a person having relatively *high* socioeconomic status and relatively *low* access to illegitimate means (that is, relatively *strong* sanction networks bearing upon him, relatively *low* exposure to deviant role models, and relatively *little* opportunity for engaging in deviant behavior) at the sociocultural level, and, at the personality level, relatively *little* feeling of psychological disjunction and relatively *strong* repudiation of deviance.

As can be seen in Table 11.11, only 7 percent of those displaying this optimal pattern had been independently classified as "deviant" on the Global Deviance criterion. Among those displaying the opposite or deviance-prone syndrome of social and personality attributes, 84 percent were independently classified as "deviant" in some aspect of their behavior. Drinking, as measured by Q-F, drinking-related deviance, and non-drinking-related deviance all exhibit this same linear relationship to these field patterns. Furthermore, in every case but that of the association between the personality patterns and non-drinking-related deviance reported earlier, this field-theoretical approach yields an improvement over the results achieved by either sociocultural or personality variables alone; in several instances, the improvement is substantial. It would appear from these data that an interdisciplinary explanatory network is well worth the effort in terms of empirical returns.

The question must be raised as to whether the associations reported up to now are perhaps an artifact of the substantial sex and ethnic differences known to exist in some of the predictor and in all of the criterion measures. Although sex and ethnic groups are unequally distributed among the various patterns, as theory would lead one to expect, it can be shown that deviance rates are also linearly related to both sociocultural and personality variable patterns *within* the sex and ethnic groups as well. Table 11.12 presents a typical example taken from our comprehensive analysis of this question. Here the field pattern's association with Global Deviance has been broken down into its sex and ethnic components for the Community Survey Study. The small number of subjects in these various components would require the combining of adjacent extreme patterns in order to achieve reasonable stability in deviance rates, as, for example, combining the three and four departure patterns for the

TABLE 11.10
Field Theoretical Pattern Analysis:
Community Survey Study

Controlling Sociocultural Variation

Socioeconomic Status	Access to Illegitimate Means		Personal Disjunctions	Attitudes toward Deviance	Global Deviants (%)
I. +	+				
(19% deviant)		A.	+	+	$\left(\frac{2}{28}\right)$ 7
		B.	±	∓	$\left(\frac{6}{32}\right)$ 19
		C.	−	−	$\left(\frac{6}{13}\right)$ 46
II. ±	∓				
(50% deviant)		A.	+	+	$\left(\frac{4}{22}\right)$ 18
		B.	±	∓	$\left(\frac{20}{35}\right)$ 57
		C.	−	−	$\left(\frac{19}{29}\right)$ 66

Controlling Personality Variation

Personal Disjunctions	Attitudes toward Deviance		Socioeconomic Status	Access to Illegitimate Means	Global Deviants (%)
I. +	+				
(16% deviant)		A.	+	+	$\left(\frac{2}{28}\right)$ 7
		B.	±	∓	$\left(\frac{4}{22}\right)$ 18
		C.	−	−	$\left(\frac{3}{6}\right)$ 50
II. ±	∓				
(39% deviant)		A.	+	+	$\left(\frac{6}{32}\right)$ 19
		B.	±	∓	$\left(\frac{20}{35}\right)$ 57
		C.	−	−	$\left(\frac{8}{20}\right)$ 40

TABLE 11.10 (*Continued*)

III.	–	–			III.	–	–		
(60% deviant)					(67% deviant)				
A.	+	+	$\left(\dfrac{3}{6}\right)$	50	A.	+	+	$\left(\dfrac{6}{13}\right)$	46
B.	±	∓	$\left(\dfrac{8}{20}\right)$	40	B.	±	∓	$\left(\dfrac{19}{29}\right)$	66
C.	–	–	$\left(\dfrac{16}{19}\right)$	84	C.	–	–	$\left(\dfrac{16}{19}\right)$	84

TABLE 11.11
Field Theoretical Patterns and Deviance:
Community Survey Study

Field Pattern*	Never Drinkers	Quantity-Frequency‡	Times Drunk‡	Other Deviance	Global Deviance
	Behavioral Measures†				
Optimal (N = 28)	43	15	0	7	7
1 Departure (N = 54)	17	43	2	17	19
2 Departures (N = 54)	11	51	19	39	54
3 Departures (N = 49)	16	61	18	45	55
4 Departures (N = 19)	0	84	53	47	84

* Field variables used: Socioeconomic status, Access to illegitimate means, Total personal disjunctions, and Attitudes toward deviance.

† Percent above cutting points is given for each criterion.

‡ Only *present* drinkers are included in this analysis. N's in the five patterns, from Optimal down, are therefore reduced to 13, 42, 43, 33, and 19, respectively.

TABLE 11.12
Field Theoretical Patterns by Sex and Ethnic Groups
against the Global Deviance Criterion:
Community Survey Study

Field Pattern*	Males %	Males N	Females %	Females N	Anglos %	Anglos N	Spanish %	Spanish N	Indians %	Indians N
Optimal	0	(5)	9	(23)	0	(21)	0	(4)	67	(3)
1 Departure	25	(28)	15	(26)	19	(37)	14	(14)	67	(3)
2 Departures	56	(32)	50	(22)	29	(17)	44	(16)	81	(21)
3 Departures	50	(20)	59	(29)	64	(14)	32	(19)	75	(16)
4 Departures	93	(15)	25	(4)	100	(2)	60	(5)	92	(12)

* Field variables used: Socioeconomic status, Access to illegitimate means, Total personal disjunctions, and Attitudes toward deviance.

† Percent of deviants is given for each pattern.

women. Nevertheless, a substantial degree of linear relationship is achieved within each of these breakdowns. The weakest association is found among the Indians, where deviance rates in general are so high as to make discrimination among them difficult. But even here, they accumulate in the less benign patterns, as theory would lead one to expect, and a small degree of association is still achieved. The other breakdowns show a substantial relationship between the field patterns and criterion behavior; for Anglos and for males, this match is nearly perfect.[4] Further attention will be given to this issue in the final chapter of the book.

The associations found within the two sex groups or within the three ethnic groups can each be regarded as replications of the over-all study and can thereby increase our confidence in the results. Again, however, further independent convergence on these findings is available from the High School Study, where both subjects and measures differ. The high school field patterns are presented in Table 11.13. The four interacting variables which comprise these patterns are conceptually similar to those

TABLE 11.13
Field Theoretical Patterns and Deviance:
High School Study

Field Pattern*	Behavioral Measures†				
	Never Drinkers	Quantity-Frequency‡	Times Drunk‡	Poor School Adjustment	Global Deviance
Optimal ($N = 11$)	36	29	14	27	9
1 Departure ($N = 19$)	21	60	47	42	27
2 Departures ($N = 28$)	21	32	41	43	36
3 Departures ($N = 22$)	9	65	70	55	50
4 Departures ($N = 5$)	0	100	80	100	100

* Field variables used: Socioeconomic status, Access to illegitimate means, Expectations for academic recognition, and Attitudes toward deviance.

† Percent above cutting points is given for each criterion.

‡ Only *present* drinkers are included in this analysis. *N*'s in the five patterns, from Optimal down, are therefore reduced to 7, 15, 22, 20, and 5, respectively.

[4] Because of ethnic differences on all predictor variables, we thought that high-low cuts based on each ethnic group's *own* medians might improve prediction, particularly among the Indians. Although when using this procedure the present pattern trends persist, in general, no real improvement was found.

employed in the adult community survey, though their measurement, it will be recalled, is quite different. As can be seen, substantial success in the prediction of both drinking and deviance has been achieved, despite the small number of subjects available. For every criterion, this field pattern has resulted in an improvement in over-all prediction. The High School Study would appear, thus, to provide strong corroboration of the findings obtained in the adult Community Survey Study.

SUMMARY

This chapter has presented the heart of our empirical data and the direct tests of the guiding hypotheses. In the first section, the associations of each major variable in the theoretical scheme with five distinct measures of deviant behavior were presented. Consistent trends in the predicted direction were demonstrated both among adults, in the Community Survey Study, and adolescents, in the High School Study, and the parallels between the results of these two studies were striking. Nevertheless, the *level* of the measure-by-measure associations was often low and relatively disappointing in its social and psychological significance.

When predictor measures were *combined* into multivariable "pattern" analyses, however, these associations were sharply increased. On the basis of their scores on three separate sociocultural measures or on three conceptually related personality measures, subjects were allocated to distinct groups which varied in their *theoretical* propensity for engaging in deviant behavior. The *actual* proportion of deviants (as defined by each of five criterion measures) within each of these groups was then calculated, and consistent trends in these rates were found in the theoretically expected direction. The statistical significance of the trends was now very high, and their social and psychological significance obvious to any observer. The findings were clearly replicated in the High School Study.

The sociocultural and personality variable patterns separately accounted for deviance rates at about the same level of effectiveness. The question therefore arose: Are these two classes of variables essentially redundant, so that it does not really matter within which system a researcher chooses to work, or are they *supplementary* systems which account for *different* sectors of the variance in deviant behavior, so that prediction is increased by working with *both* systems simultaneously?

Our data made clear that *both* sociocultural and personality variables are needed for an adequate understanding of deviant behavior. When one set of variables was controlled, the other continued to show predictive power. This led us, then, to combine them into a more complex *field* pattern analysis, which produced an even greater range of deviance rates: from 7 percent in the group with optimal social-psychological characteristics to 84 percent at the other extreme on the main criterion measure,

Global Deviance. Again, this finding was replicated in the High School Study, where the Global Deviance rate ranged from 9 to 100 percent. These findings also persisted *within* sex and ethnic groups analyzed separately, although with some reversals and relatively weakly for the Indians.

The multiple replications of the same empirical findings within different age, sex, and ethnic groups, while using operationally distinct predictor and criterion variables, enables a great deal of confidence in the meaningfulness and the potential for generalization of our results. The conclusions which can be drawn from these findings will be elaborated in the final chapter. At this point, the third study in the over-all design, the study of socialization, can be taken up in order to learn what contribution it makes to an understanding of the social-psychology of deviant behavior.

REFERENCES

BLALOCK, H. M., JR. *Social statistics.* New York: McGraw-Hill, 1960.

BRUCE, A. A., E. W. BURGESS AND A. J. HARNO. Factors determining success or failure on parole. In J. W. Wignore (Ed.) *The Illinois Crime Survey,* Chicago: Blakely Printing Co., 1929. Pp. 516–540.

GLUECK, E. T. Predictability in the administration of criminal justice. *Harvard Law Review,* 1929, *42,* 297–329.

GOULD, L. C. AND C. SCHRAG. Theory construction and prediction in juvenile delinquency. *Proceedings of the Social Statistics Section, American Statistical Association,* 1962. Pp. 68–73.

MAXWELL, A. E. *Analyzing qualitative data.* London: Methuen, 1961. Chapter 4.

ROGERS, E. M. AND A. E. Havens. Predicting innovativeness. *Sociological Inquiry,* 1962, *32,* 34–42.

YINGER, J. M. *Toward a field theory of behavior: Personality and social structure.* New York: McGraw-Hill, 1965.

PART SEVEN

Results: The Study of Socialization

CHAPTER TWELVE

The Measurement of Socialization and the Prediction of Deviance

The data presented in the preceding chapter represent the convergence of evidence from only two of the three studies carried out in the effort to evaluate a theoretical framework for the explanation of deviance. The Community Survey Study and the High School Study have each provided strong empirical support for the sociocultural and personality propositions specified within that framework. It is now possible to turn to the third study, the Socialization Study, to describe its measures and findings, and to examine the degree to which the evidence it yielded converges with that of the other two.

It will be recalled that, in the discussion of the socialization system in Chapter 5, the importance was stressed of examining directly those processes which, over time, are assumed to mediate the relationship between society and person. Evidence about one of these processes, socialization, can provide information about whether this crucial theoretical link actually fulfills the systematic role it is assumed to play. To the extent that it can be empirically demonstrated to do so, the over-all formulation would be strengthened.

In light of this concern with socialization as a linking system between society and the person, the Socialization Study was designed to permit the achievement of two major objectives: first, to demonstrate a relationship between variation in sociocultural location and variation in the character of socialization and, second, to demonstrate a relationship between variation in the character of socialization and variation in the subsequent personality and behavior of offspring. Such a study has the additional consequence of indirectly introducing a time dimension into otherwise cross-sectional research; it should thereby permit somewhat greater conviction about causal inferences among the variables in the over-all network.

The fulfillment of these objectives required an analysis of socialization within the family in terms which could be related systematically to both the sociocultural and the personality systems. That analysis, described in detail in Chapter 5, resulted in the interpretation of the various processes of socialization as constituting a system composed of three major, interacting, and overlapping structures: the parental reward structure, the parental belief structure, and the parental control structure. Each structure was conceptually linked, on the one hand, to the sociocultural environment and to personality attributes and deviant-conforming behavior, on the other. In the present chapter, it is precisely these conceptual linkages which will be examined and evaluated in the light of our subsequent empirical findings. First, however, the way in which each of the socialization structures was measured will need to be described in detail.[1]

THE MEASUREMENT OF THE SOCIALIZATION SYSTEM

The data for the Socialization Study derive from an interview of approximately one and a half hours in length conducted with 75 mothers each of whom had at least one child currently enrolled in the local high school. The focus of the interview was on both preadolescence and early adolescence, periods of time close to the present, less subject to the distortion of long-term recall and more likely to connect with the problematic concerns of our research—that is, with the occurrence of deviant or conforming behavior. The interview was constructed to provide information about direct training procedures involving deliberate parental efforts at shaping the child's attitudes or behavior; to assess, also, certain beliefs and value orientations of the parent which may well be transmitted as implicit paradigms to the child; and, finally, to learn something about the behavioral models or social prototypes provided within the family. Both English and Spanish versions of the interview were available, and cooperation of respondents was excellent.

As described in Chapter 6, the 75 mothers interviewed constituted a 93 percent sample of the population of mothers of local high school students. The 75 interviews refer to a total of 88 students: 40 Anglos, 34 Spanish, and 14 Indians. Of the 88 students, 46 were sons and 42 were daughters. It was the independently measured personality attributes and behavior patterns of these 88 children that served as the criteria to be predicted from the measures of socialization obtained from their mothers. A copy of the interview form appears in Appendix 4.

The Parental Reward Structure Measures

It will be recalled that the parental reward structure was constituted of variables assumed to be important antecedent influences of the child's

---

[1] The Socialization Study was frankly more exploratory in nature than the two studies already described. This was due in part to our relatively limited resources for undertaking it and to our less developed understanding in this area.

perception of opportunity, that is, his expectations of achieving valued goals. Both the influence or discipline practices which the parents employ and the affectional context in the family were specified as relevant in this regard. Though these variables are generally found to be correlated (see Becker, 1964, pp. 176–202), we attempted to devise separate measures of them in order to be able to examine directly their relationship within our sample.

Parental Influence Practices

The reference of this variable is to the specific procedures employed by the parents for signifying satisfaction with desirable behavior or dissatisfaction with undesirable behavior on the part of the child.

In order to gain reliable information about the actual rewarding and reproving practices engaged in by the mothers, we employed a procedure in which a series of alternative practices was described. The mothers were asked to indicate the frequency with which they engaged in each of these practices when reacting to "good" and to "bad" behavior on the part of their child. It was hoped that this kind of approach might help the mother to describe not only her predominant mode but her entire array of influence practices. The various alternatives, presented to the mothers as commonly used influence techniques, had been selected from the literature and were also based upon developmental information obtained earlier from the Community Survey Study in our community.

Reward Mode. To assess the mother's mode of signifying satisfaction with desirable behavior, referred to as her Reward Mode, the following procedure was employed. The mother was presented with these instructions:

> "I'm going to read you some things that other people say they do when their kids behave *well.* For each of these, tell me whether this is something you often do, sometimes do, hardly ever do, or never do."

She was then handed a card listing eight alternatives which were also read aloud by the interviewer. For each alternative, the mother indicated her frequency of use and, at the end, indicated also which practice was employed most often. The eight alternatives, in the order presented, were the following:

> "Tell him that you liked what he did."
> "Buy him something he likes."
> "Don't do anything in particular, since kids are supposed to behave well."
> "Show that you are pleased by a hug or warm smile."
> "Don't do anything, but promise something special for him later on."

"Tell him he should have behaved that way before."
"Give him money to spend for himself."
"Do something special with him."

A scoring system was developed which involved a judgment of each influence practice in terms of its optimality for increasing freedom of movement for the conforming (that is, "good") behavior involved. These judgments were based in part upon previous research about the relation between influence techniques and socially desirable behavior and in part upon psychological analysis of the relation of reward to strength of reinforcement, viewed from the standpoint of social learning theory. The subjectivity and relatively a priori character of these judgments, however, need to be emphasized.

In the scoring of the eight practices, three were rated as *optimal* modes of reward in that they included direct, immediate, personal, rational, or affectional responses. These were: "Tell him that you liked what he did," "Show that you are pleased by a hug or warm smile," and "Do something special with him." Three practices were scored as having *intermediate* value as rewards; these represented impersonal or delayed rewards: "Buy him something he likes," "Don't do anything, but promise something special for him later on," and "Give him money to spend for himself." And two practices were scored as *least optimal* in that they represented lack of reward or near-punishment: "Don't do anything in particular, since kids are supposed to behave well," and "Tell him he should have behaved that way before."

By combining optimality with frequency of use of each practice, a total Reward Mode score, with a 0–15 range, was established. The highest score (15) represents a reward pattern using *only* optimal responses and with high frequency. The use of *only* the least optimal rewards and with high frequency results in the lowest score (0). Various combinations of optimal, intermediate, and least optimal rewards, with varying frequency, yield scores between these extremes.

Reproof Mode. To assess the mother's mode of signifying dissatisfaction with undesirable behavior, referred to as her Reproof Mode, a procedure parallel to that measuring Reward Mode was devised, with a parallel approach to scoring and an identical score range, 0–15. The question this time was the following:

"Now I'm going to read you some things that other people do when their kids behave *badly*. For each of these tell me whether this is something you often do, sometimes do, hardly ever do, or never do."

Of the nine alternatives presented, two, because they are direct and relatively nonthreatening, were judged as relatively *optimal:* "Explain to him why he shouldn't do it" and "Scold him." Four were judged *intermediate* because of their greater severity or because they manipulate the affectional relationship: "Send him off to be by himself," "Don't let him do something he wants to do or take away something he likes," "Tell him that you or your husband are going to punish him later," and "Show him that he is hurting or disappointing you." The three practices scored as *least optimal* were the ones which were severe or humiliating, or which involved extended rejection of the child: "Deliberately ignore him until he behaves well," "Make him feel ashamed in front of everybody," and "Give him a spanking or whipping."

With respect to the judgments of optimality of reproof practices, relevant research was again relied upon. For example, Glueck and Glueck (1950) report that parents of non-delinquents use reasoning more often than parents of delinquents; Sears, Maccoby, and Levin (1957) found that physical punishment increased the incidence of aggression in children; and Bandura and Walters (1959) report the same for adolescents. Yet the subjectivity of these evaluations, reflecting the current lack of established knowledge in this area, must again be acknowledged.

In general, our hope in devising both the Reward Mode and the Reproof Mode scores was to have a quantitative measure which would enable us to begin to explore, albeit crudely, the role of parental influence practices in the larger socialization system. The relation of these two measures to each other, and to other measures in the parental reward structure, will be presented after the other measures in this structure have been described.

Affectional Interaction

The referent of this variable in the parental reward structure is to amount, intensity, and pervasiveness of affection characterizing the mother-child relationship (beyond the affection dispensed as a reward for "good" behavior). The basic assumption was that the greater the degree of affection in the home, the greater the expectations of future success on the part of the child, and the greater the parental possibility of shaping desired behavior. Lack of affection, hostility, and rejection, conversely, have been shown to be related to various forms of deviant or maladaptive behavior in children (see, for example, Bandura and Walters, 1963). Two measures of affectional interaction seemed feasible within the framework of our interview: the degree of maternal responsiveness to the child's needs and the amount of interaction between mother and child in terms both of the time spent together and the character of the activities engaged in.

Responsiveness to Child's Needs. Open-ended questions were asked of the mother with reference to how she usually responded when the child confronted her with help-seeking or problem-solving requests. The focus of the questions (with one exception) was on the mother's *behavior,* what she usually did, and the answers were coded in terms of whether her response was affectionate and sympathetic (scored 2) or primarily task oriented (scored 1), or unsympathetic and uninvolved (scored 0). The questions were:

1. "What did you usually do when S was worried about not doing well in school?"
2. "What did you usually do when S complained about too many chores to do?"
3. "What did you usually do when S came to you for help with his personal problems?"
4. "What did you usually do when S asked you to do something or go someplace with him and you were very busy?"
5. "What did you usually do when S said that other kids didn't want to play with him?"
6. "In general, what do you think is the most important thing a family can do for a child while he's growing up?"

The situations represent natural everyday parent-child interactions that provide the possibility for expression of maternal concern and affection. The scoring attempted to reflect the degree to which affection actually was expressed; the possible score range was 0–12.

Mother-Child Interaction. For this second measure, mothers were asked whether they had been absent from the child for long periods, how often they spent time with the child when he was younger, what they did together, and how often they spend time with him now and in what kinds of activities. The more frequent and diverse the activities, the higher the score (range, 0–10).

In summary, two major variables in the parental reward structure have been described in terms of the operations used to measure them. The first variable—parental influence practices—includes measures of the quality and frequency of both rewards and reproofs administered by the mother. The second variable—affectional interaction—includes a measure of maternal responsiveness to child's needs and of the quantity and quality of affectionate interaction between mother and child.

In view of the nature of these variables, and on the basis of previous research (see Becker, 1964), some degree of relationship between the variables would be expected. Correlations among the four measures in the parental reward structure, enabling an examination of this question, are presented in Table 12.1. First, it will be noted that Reward Mode and Reproof Mode, the two measures of the influence practices variable, have a small but significant correlation. There is a tendency for mothers

TABLE 12.1
Pearson Correlations among Measures of the Parental Reward Structure*

	Reward mode	Reproof mode	Responsiveness to child's needs
Reward mode			
Reproof mode	.29		
Responsiveness to child's needs	.21	.11	
Mother-child interaction	.24	.04	.37

* N's vary between 66 and 73, depending on the number of mothers who had a complete score on both variables being correlated. For N's of this size, a correlation of .20 is significant at the .05 level or better, one-tailed test.

who choose from the optimal array of reward practices to choose also from the optimal array of reproof practices. Second, the two measures of affectional interaction, Responsiveness to Child's Needs and Mother-Child Interaction, are also correlated significantly, and the correlation again is low in magnitude. In addition, it can be seen that the highest correlations in the table are those between measures of the same variable, as one would wish. With respect to the initial question of the relation between influence practices and affectional interaction, the answer is, however, ambiguous. Reward Mode relates almost as strongly to the two measures of affectional interaction as it does to Reproof Mode. But Reproof Mode, itself, shows no relationship whatsoever to the affectional interaction measures. Further comparisons with additional criteria will be needed before deciding on the adequacy of these measures.

The Parental Belief Structure Measures

In contrast with the previously discussed parental reward structure, which deals with the effect on the child of parental *practices,* the present concern was with the effect on the child of *beliefs* held by parents. It is assumed that the parents' general views and premises about the world constitute another important dimension in the socialization process. These exert an influence on the child which may be direct, through overt parental transmission of their held beliefs, or may be indirect, the beliefs serving as implicit paradigms which may be perceived and modeled by the child.

Two parental belief variables were selected for measurement in the socialization study because of their role in the over-all theory. They are *alienation* and the *belief in internal or external control.* The emphasis in the present structure was on the relation of these parental beliefs to the child's personality and behavior. There are, of course, many other beliefs—religious, social, or humanitarian—which might be considered influential, but it seemed most relevant to confine the present study to those belief variables which had previously been highlighted in the Community Survey and High School studies and which had been linked both to society and behavior.

Alienation

The nature and measurement of this concept have been described in detail in earlier chapters. To review briefly, alienation was measured in this study by a thirteen-item, Likert-type scale, exactly the same scale as was used in the Community Survey Study. The score range is 0–39, with the higher score reflecting greater alienation. Because of the fact that 11 mothers in the Socialization Study had also been interviewed in the earlier Community Survey Study, there was an opportunity to examine test-retest reliability on this measure. The correlation between scores on two occasions approximately a year apart was .84 for these 11 subjects, quite satisfactory considering the length of time involved.

Alienation as a parental belief was considered to operate as an *indirect* influence upon the child, an aspect of the parent's cognitive orientation, her perspective on life, the future, and relations with others which, while not necessarily taught to the child, could well be sensed by him as an implicit paradigm after which his own outlook should be modeled. In contrast, our concern with the following belief variable, belief in internal-external control, was with the possibility of direct parental teaching of this outlook to the child.

Belief in Internal-External Control

The nature of this variable, as well as its conceptual linkages to society and behavior, has also been described in detail in earlier chapters. In general, the variable refers to the degree to which a person believes that what happens to him is largely a consequence of his own behavior as opposed to being a matter of fate, luck, chance, or the control of powerful others. Our concern in the present study was with the degree to which certain socialization processes could influence the development of this belief in the child. The process we chose to examine was the relatively direct, overt teaching of a belief in internal or external control by the parent.

The teaching of internal-external control as a set of antecedent conditions was operationalized, in this study, through a series of open-ended questions about how children's inquiries have been (or would be) answered. The responses the mothers gave to five such questions were coded, in turn, as to whether they were predominantly internal, mixed, or external in content. An open-ended rather than a forced-choice technique, though more difficult to score, was used to provide more freedom of response and to disguise the examiner's purpose.

The following instructions were used: "Now let's talk about something quite different. We've been talking about a lot of different things, like rules and things. We're also interested in how parents answer some of their children's questions. Kids ask all kinds of questions."

Five items were then presented:

1. "They ask why some people are much better liked than others. What did you say was the reason?"
2. "They ask why some kids do so much better in school than others. What did you say was the reason?"
3. "They wonder why marriages break up. What did you say was the reason?"
4. "They want to know why some people do things that get them into trouble with the law. What did you say was the reason?"
5. "They ask why there is so much misery in the world—poverty, illness, war, prejudice. What did you say was the reason?"

The responses to each item were scored 2 for an internal response, 1 for a mixed response, and 0 for an external response. The range for the teaching of internal-external control measure was, therefore, 0–10, with a high score reflecting a high *internal* orientation.

A sample of eighteen interviews, including a total of ninety items, was chosen to assess interscorer reliability; resulting agreement between two scorers was 81 percent. When disagreements were discussed and criteria made clearer, agreement was substantially improved.

In summary, two measures assessing the variables in the parental belief structure—mother's alienation and mother's teaching of belief in internal or external control—have been described. The first variable—alienation—is presumed to comprise an orientation that may indirectly affect the young person's beliefs and expectations; the second variable, the direct teaching of internal or external control, was viewed in terms of its possible effects on the child's own constellation of similar beliefs.

The correlation between the two variables in the mother sample was .04, an absence of relationship which is contrary to what was anticipated. On theoretical grounds, one would have expected alienated mothers to tend to teach external control and unalienated mothers to teach internal control. Since the Alienation measure has received validation in other parts of the research and also has demonstrated its reliability, the measure of Teaching of Internal-External Control seems the one more likely to be jeopardized by this finding. One of its obvious shortcomings is the restricted variance in its distribution of scores. Empirically, it turns out to be a measure generally unrelated to any of the other socialization variables. On the other hand, mother's teaching of internal-external control does relate directly and significantly to the child's score on the high school measure of internal-external control ($r = .38$). As a method of measurement, the approach employed seems to be a useful one, but it is clear that a good deal more development is necessary before confidence can be placed in it.

The Parental Control Structure Measures

The third and final aspect of the socialization system which was conceptualized has reference to the conditions in the family which are concerned more directly with access to or control against deviant behavior itself. The parental control structure encompasses a complex set of variables considered likely to influence the possibilities for the direct learning of deviant behaviors, for actually engaging in deviant behaviors, and for developing the kind of moral orientation which fails to inhibit the occurrence of deviance. The parental control structure should, therefore, have implications for the learning of personality attributes more directly relevant to the control or support of deviant behavior than the variables in the preceding structures, and for the actual learning and performance of deviant behaviors. Three main components of the parental control structure were delineated; their measurement will be described.

Exposure to Deviant Role Models

The presence within a family of a member who behaves or has behaved in a fashion definable as deviant does not inevitably imply a higher probability of the child also manifesting deviant behavior. What can be assumed is that *opportunities* are present for the learning, through modeling, of deviant behaviors, or even of the attitudes and beliefs that may be directly associated with such behavior. Whether the child *actually* imitates or, on the other hand, dissociates himself from such a model, probably depends on the influence of the other components in the control structure as well as upon the variables in the reward and belief structures. McCord and McCord (1958) found, for example, that young people were more prone to imitate criminal or deviant parents when their parents were erratic in discipline or were rejecting.

The measure of exposure to deviant role models derived from interview questions in which mothers were asked if their child could have learned any unacceptable behavior from a family member and if any member of the family had ever been in serious trouble.

Recognizing the problem of achieving accurate reports about deviance in the family, we also made use of court records which were available on the families. Records of deviance for an immediate family member were used either to corroborate the mother's information or to provide additional information to be added to the score. The total score on exposure to deviant role models combined the mother's report with court records, weighting for the number of models as well as for the frequency of records of deviance. The score range was 0–6, the *higher* the score, the greater the exposure in the family to deviant role models.

Limited Regulations and Sanctions

The second component of the parental control structure is concerned with a variety of aspects of the family milieu involved in the family's direct or indirect efforts to lessen the likelihood that nonconforming behavior will occur. Primarily, it has to do with the presence and consistency of application of rules and regulations for the child, the parent's own attitudes toward deviant behavior, and the stability of the home environment. All of the aspects are interpretable in terms of contributing to a well-regulated family environment, which should inhibit deviance, or to a poorly regulated environment, which should fail to do so.

Rules and Regulations for a Teen-ager's Behavior. The mother was asked what rules she *now* has for eight activities for her teen-ager including: time for being in at night; amount of dating or smoking; time spent watching television and doing homework; restrictions related to associating with certain boys or girls, drinking, and driving a car. A score of 0 is given for a moderate or highly regulated milieu *or* for no rules deemed necessary because the adolescent is reported by the parent as responsibly self-regulating. A score of 2 is given for a relative absence of rules.

Strictness-Laxness. The score for strictness-laxness is based simply on the mother's own evaluation of both parents' strictness or easiness, over time, in relation to regulating their child. A score of 0 was assigned to "some strictness," a score of 1 if at least one parent was described as "easy" or "very easy-going," and a score of 2 if both parents were described as "easy-going."

Mother's Attitudes toward Deviance. The mother's ratings of the degree of acceptability to her of a variety of teen-age behaviors was considered to be an indirect measure of the degree to which she has been regulating her child's behavior through an attitude of tolerance or intolerance of deviance. The assumption was made that the mother who shows a tolerance of deviant behavior has also been less likely, within the family, to control or inhibit its expression.

An attitude scale, comparable to the one administered to the high school students, was read to the mother in the interview. She was asked to rate, for each of thirteen behaviors: "How wrong you think it is for a teenager to do these things?" Response categories ranged from "very wrong" (3), "wrong" (2), "not too wrong" (1), to "not wrong at all" (0). The behaviors include school-related deviance (cutting up in the classroom, copying other kids' homework, cheating on tests, lying to a teacher, playing hooky); drinking-related deviance (getting drunk, driving when he's had a good bit to drink); and other deviance (taking things that don't belong to him, getting into fights with other kids, cursing or swearing, lying to his parents, heavy petting on dates). The total empirical distribution of scores (ranging from 23–39) was trichotomized, and a score of 2 assigned to high tolerance of deviance, 1 to moderate tolerance, and 0 to low tolerance.

Lack of Interpersonal Harmony and Consistency. Any inconsistency of agreement between parents as to the appropriate standards for the child's behavior and what to do when he misbehaves may further attenuate family control by reducing clarity of expectations and consistency of enforcement. The inconsistency and disharmony score was based on answers to questions about parental disagreement on child rearing, the content of the disagreement, the prevalence of arguments about child rearing, and more general interparental disagreement.

The following seven questions contribute to the score:

1. "What about the ideas you and your husband have about how to bring up S, would you say they are very much the same, different in some ways, or very different?"
2. "What do you disagree about in how to bring up S?"
3. "When you do disagree, do you sometimes get into arguments about it?"
4. "Do you think S knows that you and your husband disagree about how to bring him up?"
5. "What other kinds of things do you and your husband disagree about, not to do with children?"
6. "Compared to most people you know, how would you say you and your husband get along?—very well, pretty good, fair, not too well."
7. "What kinds of things do you and your husband do together?"

The total raw score (0–13) was dichotomized at the median, with an assigned score of 0 reflecting relative harmony and consistency, and a score of 2 reflecting relative disharmony and inconsistency between parents.

Broken Home. This item was included as an indirect and inferential measure of weakened controls, the assumption being the simple one that a single parent has relatively greater difficulty in assuming and carrying out successfully the full management and regulation of the child. The score reflects also the basis for the broken home in order to weight the disharmony preceding the break (0 = stable home; 1 = home broken by death; and 2 = home broken by separation or divorce).

Parental Teaching of Immediate Gratification. An orientation toward deferment of gratification in the service of future valued goals operates as a personal control against deviance; hence, the role the parents play in teaching such an orientation can contribute to the regulation of deviant behavior. A brief assessment of such teaching was made by asking two questions of the mother: 1) "Some people tell their children that the future is too hard to plan for and it's better to get what you can out of life in the present. How do you feel about this?" and 2) "Some people tell their children that the only way to get what you really want in life is to try and work out the future way in advance. How do you feel about this?"

A score of 0 was given for orientation toward planning on at least one of the questions, and a score of 1 for an immediate gratification response to both items.

The measurement of the second major variable in the parental control structure, Limited Regulations and Sanctions, thus cumulated scores across six different measures or conditions each of which may be considered an "item" of the larger index or measure. What unifies the diversity among these "items" is their interpretation as contributing to or reflecting the degree of operation of regulations and sanctions. The total score range on this composite measure was 0–11, the higher the total score, the more deviance prone the family environment—that is, the more limited the presence and operation of regulations and sanctions against deviance. A home characterized as limited in regulation is one in which there are few or inconsistent rules for behavior, a tolerant attitude toward deviant behavior, a lax approach to enforcement against transgression, and an orientation toward immediate gratification.

Opportunity for Deviance

In the third and final component of the parental control structure, the actual opportunity available to the child to engage in deviance is dealt with. Opportunity was assessed simply—and most indirectly and tenuously—by way of the child's residence and age. A town child, as contrasted to a rural child, was considered to have more opportunity for the observation and practice of deviant behavior; an older child, in contrast to a younger child, was considered to have greater access or more opportunities to engage in certain illegitimate activities, such as driving a car and drinking in a bar.

For the opportunity score, residence and age were combined to provide a total opportunity score of 0–4. The age variable was trichotomized so that youths below seventeen got a score of 0, those aged seventeen to nineteen got a score of 1, and those nineteen or above got a score of 2. A dichotomy of 0 for rural and 2 for town residence was used.

It is now possible to ask the same question about these three components of the parental control structure that was asked about the components of the reward and belief structures, namely, to what extent does a relationship exist among them? The answer can be found in Table 12.2. It will be seen in this table that all three components of the parental control structure correlate significantly with each other. The relation between Limited Regulations and Sanctions and Exposure to Deviant Role Models is of moderate magnitude, whereas the relations of these two measures with Opportunity for Deviance is low. The correlations with the latter variable empirically bear out the relatively tenuous basis upon which it was constructed. In terms of its length, its sampling of widely varying aspects of the home control situation, and its correlation with

TABLE 12.2
Pearson Correlations among Measures of the Parental Control Structure*

	Exposure to deviant role models	Limited regulations and sanctions	Opportunity for deviance
Exposure to deviant role models			
Limited regulations and sanctions	.52		
Opportunity for deviance	.26	.24	

* *N*'s vary between 66 and 73, depending on the number of mothers who had a complete score on both variables being correlated. For *N*'s of this size, a correlation of .20 is significant at the .05 level or better, one-tailed test.

Exposure to Deviant Role Models, the measure in the parental control structure in which most confidence belongs would seem to be Limited Regulations and Sanctions.

Relations among Socialization Structures

We have to this point provided a description of the three major structures comprising the socialization system and have detailed the way in which these structures and their components were measured. Within two of the structures, some degree of relationship has been demonstrated between the main components of the structures. This was not the case for the parental belief structure, in which mother's alienation and mother's teaching of belief in internal-external control were shown statistically not to be related at all. A further problem can now be investigated, namely, the degree to which relationships exist, not between the components of a structure, but between the major structures themselves. Whereas, for both conceptual and empirical reasons, separate structures have been delineated, much research in socialization has been carried out describing the environment of the home as having a single, overriding character, climate, or atmosphere which pervades all aspects of family life (see, for example, Baldwin, Kalhorn, and Breese, 1945; Schaefer, 1959; and Lorr and Jenkins, 1963). Stated otherwise, the question to be answered is whether the three structures of the socialization system—rewards, beliefs, and controls—can be considered simply as different aspects of a larger *syndrome* representing a generalized home climate, or whether they can be better treated as relatively independently varying characteristics.

To approach an answer to this generality-specificity question, the variable in which we had most confidence was selected from each of the three structures to represent that structure, and the intercorrelations among these variables were then determined. Choice of the representative variables from each structure was based upon its theoretical import, the content of the measure, and the previously noted empirical findings about its relationship to other measures within the same structure.

All of the correlations shown in Table 12.3 are significant and in the theoretically expected direction. The content and the structure of the three

TABLE 12.3
Pearson Correlations between Measures of the Three Socialization Structures*

	Mother-child interaction	Mother's alienation	Limited regulations and sanctions
Mother-child interaction			
Mother's alienation	.44		
Limited regulations and sanctions	.46	.52	

* N's vary between 66 and 73, depending on the number of mothers who had a complete score on both variables being correlated. For N's of this size, a correlation of .20 is significant at the .05 level or better, one-tailed test. All signs have been changed so that a positive correlation means the correlation is in the direction anticipated by the theory.

measures are different enough to minimize the likelihood of the correlations simply being inflated by method variance. The tendency shown in the table is for an alienated mother to engage in less affectional interaction with her child and to impose fewer regulations and sanctions. Conversely, affectional interaction, a sense of relatedness to others and involvement in daily role behaviors, and well-regulated family controls against deviance constitute a clear pattern. The correlations are of sufficient magnitude to provide some degree of support for a generality point of view emphasizing the climate of the home situation or the syndrome quality of socialization. On the other hand, the magnitude of these correlations is only moderate and certainly insufficient to rule out some degree of specificity in the variation of the component socialization structures. What emerges, primarily, from this correlation matrix is the possible existence of measurable *patterns or syndromes of socialization processes relevant to the deviant-conforming behavior of children.*

We have thus far dealt with the way in which measurement of the socialization system was carried out. Socialization was construed as a linking system between the sociocultural system, on the one hand, and the personality and behavior systems, on the other. To serve as an effective bridge, the structures of the socialization system had to be logically relevant to the structures in these other systems. To this end, the socialization system was viewed as a microcosm of the larger society, and its structures—the parental reward structure, the parental belief structure, and the parental control structure—were developed as analogues of the corresponding structures in the sociocultural system. Their relations to the personality and behavior attributes of the adolescent would, therefore, follow the same logic which coordinated the sociocultural system to those attributes.

Measurement, hampered by the lack of established knowledge of the socialization antecedents of adolescent personality and behavior, was admittedly crude. It depended in large part upon our own analytic efforts to identify relevant antecedent exposure or influence. In addition, it was not possible, for reasons of both time and resources, to develop fully the measures employed and, thereby, to establish a stronger antecedent basis for confidence in them. The confidence, as will be seen shortly, comes largely from their later success in predicting our criteria. This is just another way of restating the exploratory nature of the Socialization Study noted earlier.

It is possible now to turn to the central concern of the Socialization Study, the demonstration of its systematic role as a bridge between society and the person. The first objective will be to examine the relation of socialization to variation in sociocultural location; an examination of the relationship of socialization to variation in the personality and behavioral attributes of the teen-age children will follow.

SOCIOCULTURAL VARIATION AND SOCIALIZATION

If location in society is to have an influence on the personality and behavior of its members, some part of that influence must be mediated, over time, by the way in which persons are differentially socialized at different locations. A large amount of previous research has pointed to the influence of sociocultural factors on child rearing (Sewell, 1963; Hoffman and Lippitt, 1960; Bronfenbrenner, 1958; Clausen and Williams, 1963; Crandall, 1963; Sears, Maccoby, and Levin, 1957; Strodtbeck, 1958). Our aim in this section is to demonstrate that differences in socialization, in terms of our own measures, do exist at different social locations, and that such differences are consistent with our over-all theoretical formulations about the nature of deviant behavior.

Ideally, it would have been desirable to locate each of our families in each structure of the sociocultural system in order to appraise the issue at hand. Since this was not possible, due to the absence of the appropriate information, a less systematic and less comprehensive approach was employed. For each family, we had available the measure of socioeconomic status (SES) based upon five items: father's job type, father's education, mother's education, a room/person index, and family income. This enabled us to locate the family within the opportunity structure of the sociocultural system.

Our second item of sociocultural information was, of course, ethnic status. Variation in socialization as a function of ethnic status is a matter of some interest in its own right. For our present purposes, however, ethnicity may be considered an indirect (and, therefore, crude) index of location in the sociocultural system as a whole. It will be recalled that the findings of the Community Survey Study ordered the three ethnic groups with respect to favorableness of location in society, the Anglos having most access to opportunity, the least anomie, and least access to illegitimate means; the Indians having most anomie and access to illegitimate means, and being in the middle in access to opportunity; and the Spanish being perhaps lowest in opportunity, but being in the middle on anomie and access to illegitimate means. These findings suggested a rough ordering of the three groups with respect to sociocultural proneness to deviance. By looking at the relation of ethnic status to socialization, it becomes possible to examine the relation of this ordering to the ordering of scores on the socialization measures.

Socioeconomic Status and Socialization

Findings are presented first with respect to the measure of location in the opportunity structure: socioeconomic status. Ethnic status will be considered in the following section. In Table 12.4, the correlations of each of our socialization measures with SES are shown.

In general, the table supports the existence of a relationship between sociocultural location and socialization. All of the correlations show the expected direction of relationship, and a non-chance number of the correlations is statistically significant.

Looking more closely at the correlations, we can see that within each socialization structure at least one measure relates significantly to SES. Considering the parental reward structure, Reward Mode, as an influence practice, shows a statistically significant relationship; with respect to Affectional Interaction, Responsiveness to Child's Needs and Mother-Child Interaction are both significantly related to SES. In the parental belief structure, Alienation is significantly related, as expected, to sociocultural position, and this finding replicates that of the Community Survey Study.

TABLE 12.4

**Pearson Correlations of Parent Socialization Measures with a
Sociocultural Location Measure***

Socialization Measure	Socioeconomic Status
Parental reward structure	
Influence practices	
Reward mode	.20
Reproof mode	.17
Affectional interaction	
Responsiveness to child's needs	.42
Mother-child interaction	.28
Parental belief structure	
Mother's alienation	.44
Teaching of internal-external control	.07
Parental control structure	
Deviant role models	.40
Limited regulations and sanctions	.24
Opportunity for deviance	.09

* N's vary between 66 and 73, depending on the number of mothers who had a complete score on both variables being correlated. For N's of this size, a correlation of .20 is significant at the .05 level or better, one-tailed test. All signs have been changed so that a positive correlation means the correlation is in the direction anticipated by the theory.

As noted before, Teaching of Internal-External Control shows a near zero relationship. Turning finally to the parental control structure, one can see that, except for Opportunity for Deviance, the measures relate significantly with SES, Deviant Role Models having the stronger association.

To sum up these findings, it can be said that not only does there exist an association between location of a family in society and the nature of the socialization which characterizes it but also that the association is entirely consistent with what would be expected from our theoretical formulation. The lower the position in the opportunity structure (as measured by SES), the less optimal the influence techniques, the less affectional interaction, the greater maternal alienation, the greater the presence of deviant role models, and the more limited the exercise of regulations and sanctions—in short, the more theoretically deviance prone the socialization. While these findings are encouraging in establishing the first evidence for an important linkage, it must once again be emphasized that the correlations are generally quite small.

The other source of evidence which can be brought to bear on the very same issue can now be considered, in the hope of somewhat strengthening the linkage just demonstrated.

Ethnic Status and Socialization

Whenever ethnic groups are compared, the question arises of the degree to which observed differences between them reflect simply tradition-mediated differences embedded in the history of the group or, instead, reflect variation in common processes to which all the groups are more or less exposed. Our emphasis here, as it has been elsewhere in this book, is mainly upon ethnicity as a probabilistic index of location in the sociocultural and personality systems. To speak of ethnic groups as being minority groups or marginal groups is to refer largely to the limited opportunity, greater anomie, and greater access to illegitimate means which characterize the social environment of that ethnic group. Further, it refers to the probable consequences for the personality and for behavior of existence in and exposure to that environment. It follows from such reasoning that ethnic status, indirectly and perhaps tenuously, may, nevertheless, be used to reflect over-all location in the sociocultural system. It follows also that the Anglos, being the socioculturally favored group, should evidence less deviance-prone socialization on our measures than the Indians, with the Spanish in between. The relevant data are to be found in Table 12.5.

The most impressive thing to be noted in Table 12.5 is that, with but two minor exceptions, the mean scores on all the variables are ordered across ethnic groups in the manner expected. The Anglo scores are the most favorable, or theoretically the least deviance prone; the Indian scores are the most deviance prone; and the Spanish scores are in between. One of the exceptions occurs in relation to the Teaching of Internal-External Control measure, a measure previously shown to be poor; the other exception occurs in the Spanish-Indian ordering on Reproof Mode.

The second noteworthy aspect of Table 12.5 is that the expected Anglo-Spanish differences are statistically significant on all four of the measures within the parental reward structure and on Mother's Alienation within the parental belief structure. Within the parental control structure, the results are perhaps even more interesting. Except for Opportunity for Deviance (a highly indirect measure, it will be recalled, composed of age and residence), the measures do not differentiate the Anglo families from the Spanish families in a statistically significant way. The Spanish scores, as expected, are in the more deviance-prone direction, but they are essentially of the same order of magnitude as those of the Anglos. The real change in magnitude lies in the Indian scores, markedly different from both the Anglos and Spanish.

What is interesting about these latter results is that they are exactly in line with what was found in the Community Survey Study. There, the Spanish social control structure was shown to be very close to that of the Anglos, and it was precisely the Spanish-Indian difference in social

TABLE 12.5
Ethnic Group Differences in Socialization Practices

Socialization Practice		Means and Standard Deviations			Difference*		
		Anglo ($N = 32$–39)	Spanish ($N = 25$–32)	Indian ($N = 7$–10)	Anglos vs. Spanish	Anglos vs. Indians	Spanish vs. Indians
Parental reward structure							
Influence practices							
Reward mode	$\bar{X}$	9.6	7.6	6.7	$t = 2.41$ $p < .05$	$t = 2.43$ $p < .05$	$t = 0.80$ N.S.
	σ	(3.5)	(2.8)	(3.1)			
Reproof mode	$\bar{X}$	11.0	9.2	10.9	$t = 2.13$ $p < .05$	$t = 0.10$ N.S.	$t = 1.29$ N.S.
	σ	(3.2)	(3.2)	(3.5)			
Affectional interaction							
Responsiveness to child's needs	$\bar{X}$	8.0	6.1	6.0	$t = 4.27$ $p < .001$	$t = 2.63$ $p < .05$	$t = 0.15$ N.S.
	σ	(1.8)	(1.7)	(2.0)			
Mother-child interaction	$\bar{X}$	8.2	6.7	6.5	$t = 3.54$ $p < .01$	$t = 2.18$ N.S.	$t = 0.26$ N.S.
	σ	(1.3)	(1.8)	(2.4)			
Parental belief structure							
Mother's alienation	$\bar{X}$	14.7	18.2	19.4	$t = 4.22$ $p < .001$	$t = 3.42$ $p < .01$	$t = 0.88$ N.S.
	σ	(4.0)	(3.1)	(3.9)			
Teaching of internal control	$\bar{X}$	5.9	6.3	5.9	$t = 0.68$ N.S.	$t = 0.07$ N.S.	$t = 0.45$ N.S.
	σ	(2.0)	(2.5)	(2.3)			
Parental control structure							
Deviant role models	$\bar{X}$	0.4	1.0	3.2	$t = 1.76$ N.S.	$t = 7.64$ $p < .001$	$t = 5.14$ $p < .001$
	σ	(1.1)	(1.6)	(1.0)			
Limited regulations and sanctions	$\bar{X}$	3.1	3.8	5.4	$t = 1.31$ N.S.	$t = 2.75$ $p < .05$	$t = 1.69$ N.S.
	σ	(2.2)	(2.8)	(2.5)			
Opportunities for deviance	$\bar{X}$	1.0	1.5	2.1	$t = 2.00$ $p < .05$	$t = 2.33$ $p < .05$	$t = 1.19$ N.S.
	σ	(1.2)	(1.2)	(1.5)			

* All t-tests of group mean differences are two-tailed. Differences not significant at the .05 level or better are indicated N.S.

control which seemed responsible for the marked difference in deviance between the Spanish and Indians. In short, the lack of Anglo-Spanish parental control structure differences on the measures used in the present study is exactly what would have been predicted from the knowledge generated from different measures in the Community Survey Study. Our across-the-board expectation of Anglo-Spanish differences in the present study was clearly too crude an interpretation of the implications of ethnic status, and ignored the earlier findings.

In summary, the data relating socialization to ethnic status are strongly corroborating of the linkage between sociocultural location and socialization. Anglo mothers tend to use the more optimal influence practices, to provide more affectional interaction, and to be less alienated than Spanish mothers. On the question of controls, the Anglo and Spanish mothers are highly similar, with the Spanish mothers slightly more deviance prone in their socialization. On nearly all measures, the Indian mothers' scores are the most deviance prone. These differences accord fully with what is known about the sociocultural differences between these groups shown by the Community Survey Study and are consistent with the correlations presented earlier in relation to SES. It should be noted finally that these differences in deviance-prone socialization conform also to the ethnic group topography of deviance in the community.

The data presented in this section have, therefore, provided the first basis for considering socialization as a linkage system in a theory of deviance—they have shown socialization to vary with variation in sociocultural location. The next matter of concern, linking socialization to personality and behavior, will be addressed in the following section.

SOCIALIZATION AND VARIATION IN PERSONALITY AND BEHAVIOR

The aim of the present section is to examine the degree to which measures of parental socialization are predictive of the personality and behavior of adolescent children. The children in this case are the 88 students in the local high school. The personality attributes to be predicted are those already measured in the High School Study, and the same is true of the behavioral criteria. In the case of both personality and behavior, then, we are concerned with deviance, that is, with the prediction from socialization to deviance-relevant personality variables and to deviant-conforming behavior.

The Prediction of Deviance-Prone Personality Attributes

It will be recalled that the socialization measures were constructed to reflect antecedent conditions thought to be specifically related to the personality measures in our theoretical scheme. The three structures in the socialization system—parental rewards, beliefs, and controls—are parallel to the three structures in the personality system—perceived opportunity, personal beliefs, and personal controls. We will be interested, therefore, in examining the parallel relations between socialization and personality. As we have already seen, the variables within the socialization system are moderately intercorrelated, suggesting a home climate or a syndrome quality to socialization. In view of this, it is to be expected that any particular socialization variable may relate to a variety of personality variables and not only to the one it was specifically constructed for. We will be interested in examining, therefore, the nonparallel relations between socialization and personality as well. Our first approach will be to consider the prediction of personality from *single* socialization variables. This will be followed by a multivariable approach using the pattern analysis technique introduced in the preceding chapter.

Prediction from Single Socialization Measures

In Table 12.6, the correlations between each of the socialization mea-

TABLE 12.6

**Pearson Correlations between Parent Socialization Measures
and Key Personality Measures of Their High School-Age Children**

Socialization Measure*	Personality Measure		
	Expectations AcR	Life-Chances Disjunction	Attitudes toward Deviance
Parental reward structure			
Influence practices			
Reward mode	.11	.04	.08
Reproof mode	.10	.29	.02
Affectional interaction			
Responsiveness to child's needs	.23	.06	−.03
Mother-child interaction	.27	.18	.11
Parental belief structure			
Mother's alienation	.32	.23	.08
Teaching of internal control	.07	.16	.15
Parental control structure			
Exposure to deviant role models	.30	.07	.05
Limited regulations and sanctions	.24	.05	.10
Opportunity for deviance	.11	.05	−.16

* N's vary between 66 and 73, depending on the number of mothers who had a complete score on both variables being correlated. For N's of this size, a correlation of .20 is significant at the .05 level or better, one-tailed test. All signs have been changed so that a positive correlation means the correlation is in the direction anticipated by the theory.

sures dealt with thus far and the three personality measures used as predictors in the High School Study are presented. Of the latter, Expectations for Academic Recognition is a measure representing the child's perceived opportunity structure; Life Chances Disjunctions is a measure also representing the child's perceived opportunity structure, but hopefully representing also his personal belief structure, in that it has similarities to Alienation;[2] and Attitudes toward Deviance is the representative measure of the personal control structure. All of the personality measures have been described and developed in Chapter 10.

Two of the four parental reward structure measures are significantly associated with the child's Expectation for Academic Recognition score, and in the direction expected. The more responsiveness and affectional interaction by the mother, the higher the child's expectations of achieving goals in that area. It should be noted that the correlations, while significant, are small, and they account for only a very little of the variance in the personality measure. With respect to the question of specificity of socialization-personality relations, two things are worth noting. First, the parental reward structure variables generally do *not* relate significantly to the other personality measures (except for Reproof Mode and LCD; the latter, however, is really a perceived opportunity measure). This is an indication of specificity. On the other hand, Mother's Alienation, a parental belief measure, predicts the Expectation score and the LCD score just as well as do the reward measures. This is an indication of a form of generality.

With respect to the prediction of the adolescent's Attitudes toward Deviance, none of the parental measures is significantly associated, and Opportunity for Deviance is clearly in the opposite direction.

What seems clear from Table 12.6 is that there is support for the relationship between socialization and personality, but that it is very modest in magnitude and apparent mainly in the parental reward and, secondarily, the parental belief structures. While this is encouraging, it certainly makes obvious the limited capability of any *single* socialization variable for predicting an attribute of the child's personality. Such a conclusion is not a surprising one to arrive at for at least two reasons. Adolescent personality attributes are obviously the outcome of a variety of experiential antecedents, including the whole range of peer group and school

---

[2] The Internal-External Control measure is not used to represent the child's personal belief structure since it has not demonstrated its utility in either the Community Survey Study or the High School Study. Its pattern of relations with other variables has been either close to zero or negative. Interestingly enough, the one sizeable relation it does have is one which was specifically sought: Mother's Teaching of Internal Control correlates .38 ($p < .005$) with child's Internal Control score. In general, however, we have no basis for confidence in our measure of this concept in the present study.

group interactions, none of which entered into our measurement. Further, it would seem likely that a particular personality outcome could more readily be predicted by considering not a single antecedent at a time but rather multiple socialization variables simultaneously. It is the latter to which we may now turn our attention.

Prediction from Multivariable Socialization Patterns

The procedure of pattern analysis was described in detail and used extensively in the presentation of results in the preceding chapter. The pattern analysis procedure will enable us to consider groups of mothers varying in the degree to which the *syndrome* of socialization practices they have employed was or was not theoretically optimal. Given the limited size of our sample, it is possible to consider simultaneously no more than three socialization measures. Each mother, depending upon her score, is allocated to the optimal side or the deviance-prone side of a dichotomized score distribution for each socialization predictor. For three measures considered simultaneously, there will be four groups of mothers: one group having all three measures optimal; one group having one departure from optimality, that is, only two of the three measures optimal; one group having two departures from optimality, that is, having only one of the three measures optimal and the other two deviance prone; and a final group having three departures from optimality, that is, on all measures, this group scores deviance prone. These groups should then vary directly in the percentage of their teen-age children who score on the deviance-prone side of the dichotomized personality criterion variables.

The pattern analysis procedure necessitates the selecting of variables to enter into the multivariable patterns. We selected socialization variables to constitute meaningful psychological clusters, sampling from among those variables in whose individual measurement we had the greatest confidence. Obviously, there is always the possibility of maximizing significant findings by arbitrary selection of predictor variables and trial-and-error exploration. A large number of multivariable patterns were investigated; some worked well and some poorly. We wish to present in this chapter only two predictor syndromes; the two presented are among the best representatives of the other psychologically meaningful combinations of variables which are possible.

Two socialization configurations, abstracting different qualities of the home atmosphere, were analyzed in relation to the three personality criterion variables. The first socialization cluster explores a syndrome in which the combined effects of Reward Mode, Mother-Child Interaction, and Mother's Alienation are operative. This configuration of warmth, affection, optimism, and involvement should maximize the experience of having been personally rewarded for one's efforts, having maternal companionship and interest available, and having a mother who feels engaged and useful. It should therefore result in a greater feeling of effectiveness on the part of the child in securing his goals, both in and after school years, and should minimize disjunctions between major life goals and his expectations of achieving them.

The three personality criterion variables to be predicted from this socialization cluster were selected to parallel the pattern analyses in the High School Study in which prediction from these same personality variables were made to deviant behavior. The personality criterion variables are Expectations for Academic Recognition, Life Chances Disjunctions, and Attitudes toward Deviance. The only student belief variable available, Internal-External Control, was not successfully predicted by any socialization cluster and is not included here.

The data for this first cluster, in Table 12.7, provide clear-cut and

TABLE 12.7
Pattern Analysis by Total Group:
Parent Socialization Patterns versus Adolescent Personality Measures

Socialization Pattern*	Adolescent Personality Measure†		
	Expectations for Academic Recognition	Life-Chances Disjunctions	Attitudes toward Deviance
Optimal ($N = 17$)	18	35	29
1 Departure ($N = 24$)	38	50	67
2 Departures ($N = 19$)	68	53	42
3 Departures ($N = 11$)	73	64	73

* Socialization variable cluster I: Reward mode, Mother-child interaction, and Mother's alienation.

† Percent above cutting points is given for each personality variable. The percentages refer to the proportion of adolescents in each socialization pattern that is above the cutting point in the theoretically "deviance-prone" direction on the personality variables.

compelling support for the associations expected. Moving from the optimal pattern—theoretically favorable scores on all three parent socialization variables—to the least optimal pattern—theoretically *un*favorable scores on all three parent variables—a clear linear progression is found with respect to the percentages on the first two personality attributes. In the optimal parental socialization pattern, only 18 percent of the students have low Expectations for Academic Recognition, whereas 73 percent of those in the least optimal parent socialization pattern have low Expectations for Academic Recognition. For the Life Chances Disjunctions measure, a comparable situation obtains. In addition, for each of these personality variables, the intermediate patterns are all perfectly ordered.

This cluster of parent socialization variables has successfully accounted for students' scores on measures evaluating their expectations for achievement and disparities between their major life goals and their expectations of achieving them. Since the other criterion measure, Attitudes toward Deviance, is more remote conceptually from the combination of parent practices used in the present cluster, it is reasonable that it was not as successfully predicted from this particular configuration. Further evidence of such specificity will be seen in the next configuration.

In constructing the second configuration of parental socialization variables, attention was specifically turned to the most likely precursors, among the theoretical variables, of an adolescent's tolerance or repudiation of deviance. An individual's attitudes toward deviant behavior can be considered to be some reflection of his exposure to rewards for conforming behavior and punishments for deviant behavior, these experiences becoming internalized in the form of attitudes. A regulated household coupled with affectionate companionship should produce a greater intolerance of deviance than one where regulation is absent.

Cluster II, in Table 12.8, provides support for these expectations. With the theoretically optimal socialization pattern, only 36 percent of the students are above the median in their tolerance of deviant behavior. The percentage of those tolerant of deviance increases stepwise to the least optimal pattern in which now 80 percent of the children of these mothers show a high tolerance of deviance. This pattern of affection coupled with

TABLE 12.8
Pattern Analysis by Total Group:
Parent Socialization Patterns versus Adolescent Personality Measures

Socialization Pattern*	Adolescent Personality Measure†		
	Expectations for Academic Recognition	Life-Chances Disjunctions	Attitudes toward Deviance
Optimal ($N = 11$)	18	36	36
1 Departure ($N = 31$)	35	39	45
2 Departures ($N = 19$)	68	74	58
3 Departures ($N = 10$)	70	50	80

* Socialization variable cluster II: Reward mode, Mother-child interaction, and Limited regulations and sanctions.

† Percent above cutting points is given for each personality variable. The percentages refer to the proportion of adolescents in each socialization pattern that is above the cutting point in the theoretically "deviance-prone" direction on the personality variables.

controls also predicts the two other criterion measures, although not as well or as consistently as did Cluster I.

To summarize thus far, these pattern analysis findings make a strong case for the relation of socialization to personality. What emerges clearly is an orderly relation between the degree of deviance-prone socialization to which a child has been exposed and the likelihood of his scoring on the deviance-prone side of a personality attribute considered to be an outcome of such socialization.

Multivariable Pattern Analyses within Ethnic Groups. A question that arises in considering the pattern analysis data, as it did earlier in the Community Survey and High School studies, is the role of ethnicity. Are the results, based as they are on total group analysis, simply a function of ethnic differences so that the persons in the optimal pattern are all Anglo mothers and those in the least optimal pattern Spanish and Indian mothers? Is this, in other words, *just* a prediction of ethnic status, or do the socialization variables provide explanation which applies as well *within* each ethnic group? To answer the question as to the explanatory capability of these measures *within ethnic groups,* a pattern analysis by ethnic group was undertaken for both the Anglo mothers and Spanish mothers (the Indian mother sample is too small). Since the N's were so reduced for many of the patterns, the extreme patterns were collapsed with the adjacent ones so as to result in a dichotomy: favorable patterns (optimal and one departure), and unfavorable patterns (two and three departures).

In Table 12.9, the pattern analyses for Anglos and Spanish on the two socialization clusters are reported.

It can be seen readily that the over-all pattern analysis outcome is upheld within each of the two ethnic groups. In all instances (except predicting Attitudes toward Deviance for Anglos on Cluster I), the step progression is demonstrated within *both* ethnic groups. Those adolescents, either Spanish or Anglo, who have had the more optimal socialization experiences are less likely to have unfavorable scores on the personality variables, and those adolescents, Spanish or Anglo, with the more *un*-favorable socialization experience more frequently have the deviance-prone scores on the personality variables.

It is now possible to summarize what has been learned from the Socialization Study with respect to the linkage between socialization and personality. When parent socialization variables were considered singly and correlated with child personality attributes, there was evidence of significant association. This association was most apparent when the socialization measures involved the parental reward structure. The associations that were demonstrated were, however, all low in magnitude. Thus, support for the socialization-personality linkage was present but not substantial.

When the family was dealt with in terms of several of its socialization

TABLE 12.9
Pattern Analyses by Ethnic Groups:
Parent Socialization Patterns versus Adolescent Personality Measures

Socialization Pattern	Expectations for Academic Recognition		Life-Chances Disjunctions		Attitudes toward Deviance	
	Anglo	Spanish	Anglo	Spanish	Anglo	Spanish
I. Reward mode, mother-child interaction, mother's alienation						
A. Optimal and 1 departure†	28	33	41	44	52	44
B. 2 and 3 departures‡	80	62	60	62	40	50
II. Reward mode, mother-child interaction, limited regulations and sanctions						
A. Optimal and 1 departure†	19	45	35	45	42	36
B. 2 and 3 departures‡	88	57	75	64	75	57

*Adolescent Personality Measure**

* Percent above cutting points is given for each personality variable.

† For Cluster I, the N's in this category are: Anglo, 29; Spanish, 9. For Cluster II, the N's in this category are: Anglo, 26; Spanish, 11.

‡ For Cluster I, the N's in this category are: Anglo, 5; Spanish, 16. For Cluster II the N's in this category are: Anglo, 8; Spanish, 14.

characteristics simultaneously, however, the evidence became more impressive. Multivariable pattern analyses provide powerful support for the association between parental socialization and the personality of the child. And such support holds not only for the total mother-child sample but also *within* the Anglo and the Spanish groups. Considering all the evidence together, a compelling case has been made for the socialization-personality linkage.

The Prediction of Deviant Behavior

In terms of the earlier discussion of socialization as a linking system between society, on the one hand, and personality and behavior, on the other, there remains to be demonstrated only the relationship of the parental socialization measures to adolescent deviant-conforming behavior. Since socialization is predictive of personality attributes, and these same attributes were already shown in the High School Study to be predictive of deviance-conformity, it is to be expected that the demonstration will be successful. The organization of this section will follow that of the preceding one, considering, first, single-variable prediction of behavior, then employing a multivariable pattern analysis approach, and then examining the pattern analyses within ethnic groups. This section will thus complete the presentation of the empirical findings of the Socialization Study.

Prediction from Single Socialization Measures

As just indicated, an important goal of the Socialization Study was to assess the relationship between socialization practices of parents and the occurrence of deviant behavior in their adolescent offspring. In some ways, this task should be easier than attempting to predict the *personality attributes* of the offspring. Since parents are generally oriented toward producing more conforming behavior in their children and directly reinforce behaviors that are observable, what they do is likely to have more discernible and direct outcomes in the child's behavior than in his genotypical or underlying personality attributes.

The various behavioral criteria to be evaluated in relation to the parental socialization measures have all been described in detail in previous chapters. For the examination of single socialization measures in relation to behavior, the same criteria used in the High School Study will be employed: the Quantity-Frequency of Alcohol-Use; Times Drunk; Poor School Adjustment; and Global Deviance criterion measures. Correlations with these criteria are shown in Table 12.10.

As in the High School Study, the Q-F measure of alcohol use is not well predicted. While the direction of correlation is as expected—the less optimal the socialization practices, the higher the Q-F—only one measure, Mother-Child Interaction, reaches significance. With respect to the other behavioral criteria, however, the picture is quite different, the three criteria implicating deviance being significantly related to a number of different socialization measures. (Note again the failure of the Teaching of Internal Control measure.) The correlations with the behavior criteria, it should be noted, are generally better than they were with the personality criteria. The magnitude of the relations is again very modest, but the evidence is sufficiently consistent to generate initial confidence in the socialization-behavior linkage.

Prediction From Multivariable Socialization Patterns

Using the same two clusters of socialization variables which were employed in predicting personality outcomes, we are able to examine the degree to which behavioral criteria are associated with *patterns* of socialization practices. These data are presented in Tables 12.11 and 12.12.

The cluster of socialization measures used in Table 12.11 includes Reward Mode, Mother-Child Interaction, and Mother's Alienation. It can be seen that this set of measures is related strongly to three of the behav-

TABLE 12.10
**Pearson Correlations of Parent Socialization Measures
with Behavioral Measures of Their High School-Age Children***

Socialization Measure	Adolescent Behavioral Measure			
	Q-F	Times Drunk	Poor School Adjustment	Global Deviance
Parental reward structure				
Influence practices				
Reward mode	.12	.13	.15	.25
Reproof mode	.13	− .03	.12	.20
Affectional interaction				
Responsiveness to child's needs	.13	.24	.12	.16
Mother-child interaction	.28	.31	.36	.41
Parental belief structure				
Mother's alienation	.16	.23	.17	.25
Teaching internal control	.05	− .04	− .10	− .11
Parental control structure				
Exposure to deviant role models	.17	.27	.45	.39
Limited regulations and sanctions	.18	.21	.37	.33
Opportunity for deviance	.08	.36	.27	.14

* *N*'s vary between 66 and 73, depending on the number of mothers who had a complete score on both variables being correlated. For *N*'s of this size, a correlation of .20 is significant at the .05 level or better, one-tailed test. All signs have been changed so that a positive correlation means the correlation is in the direction anticipated by the theory.

TABLE 12.11
**Pattern Analysis by Total Group:
Parent Socialization Patterns versus Adolescent Behavior Measures**

Socialization Pattern*	Adolescent Behavior Measure†				
	Never Drinkers	Q-F‡	Times Drunk‡	Poor School Adjust- ment	Global Deviance
Optimal (*N* = 17)	29	50	25	35	12
1 Departure (*N* = 24)	17	55	45	33	33
2 Departures (*N* = 19)	11	41	59	58	37
3 Departures (*N* = 11)	18	78	89	82	73

* Socialization variable cluster I: Reward mode, Mother-child interaction, and Mother's alienation.

† Percent above cutting points is given for each behavior measure.

‡ Only *drinkers* are included in these two analyses. *N*'s in the four patterns from Optimal down, are therefore reduced to 12, 20, 17, and 9, respectively.

TABLE 12.12
Pattern Analysis by Total Group:
Parent Socialization Patterns versus Adolescent Behavior Measures

Socialization Pattern*	Adolescent Behavior Measure†				
	Never Drinkers	Q-F‡	Times Drunk‡	Poor School Adjust- ment	Global Deviance
Optimal (N = 11)	18	33	22	9	0
1 Departure (N = 31)	26	52	48	48	32
2 Departures (N = 19)	11	53	53	47	37
3 Departures (N = 10)	11	78	89	90	80

* Socialization variable cluster II: Reward mode, Mother-child interaction, and Limited regulations and sanctions.

† Percent above cutting points is given for each behavior measure.

‡ Only *drinkers* are included in these two analyses. *N*'s in the four patterns from Optimal down, are therefore reduced to 9, 23, 17, and 9, respectively.

ioral criteria in the table: Times Drunk in the Last Year, Poor School Adjustment, and the key criterion, Global Deviance. The two criterion measures which refer to alcohol use without necessarily implicating deviance—Never Drinkers and Q-F—are not clearly associated with this pattern of socialization predictors.

The cluster of socialization measures shown in Table 12.12 has substituted a parental control measure, Limited Regulations and Sanctions, for the parental belief measure, Alienation, used in the preceding cluster. The contribution of this substitution is substantial. Not only is the Q-F criterion now shown to be related to socialization, but the three criteria predicted by the preceding cluster are now even more sharply predicted than before. This is seen clearly with respect to Global Deviance, where the percentages run from 0 to 80 in linear fashion, and with respect to Poor School Adjustment, where they run from 9 to 90. Such spread in percentages is indeed impressive. This cluster, emphasizing affection and controls, seems to be a powerful socialization pattern in relation to behavior, as it was in relation to personality. Where affection and controls are both optimal, the probability of deviance is very low; where affection and controls are both deviance prone, the probability of deviance is quite high. Taken together, these patterns confirm the predicted linkage between socialization and behavior.

Multivariable Pattern Analyses within Ethnic Groups

The pattern analyses were also carried out separately within the Anglo and the Spanish mother groups to demonstrate that the over-all results

are not simply a reflection of ethnic variation. Patterns were again collapsed due to small N's. It can be seen in Table 12.13 that the over-all
results continue to hold when considered for each of the two ethnic groups
separately, the combined optimal and 1-departure pattern generally showing lower percentages of adolescent deviant scores than the combined
2- and 3-departure pattern.

The evidence presented in this section is consistent. Whether considered
as single measures or as syndromes of measures, whether considered for
the total group of mothers or for separate ethnic groups of mothers, the
parental socialization measures have shown compelling relationships with
the behavioral criterion measures on the high school children.[3] In the

TABLE 12.13
Pattern Analyses by Ethnic Groups:
Parent Socialization Patterns versus Adolescent Behavior Measures

	Adolescent Behavior Measure*								
Socialization Pattern	Never Drinkers		Quan- tity— Fre- quency†		Times Drunk†		Poor School Adjust- ment		Global Deviance	
	A‡	S	A	S	A	S	A	S	A	S
I. Reward mode, mother-child interaction, and mother's alienation										
A. Optimal and 1 depar- ture§	24	22	55	43	32	43	28	44	17	33
B. 2 and 3 departures‖	0	25	60	58	40	75	60	56	60	50
II. Reward mode, mother-child interaction, and limited reg- ulations and sanctions										
A. Optimal and 1 depar- ture§	23	36	50	43	30	57	27	45	15	36
B. 2 and 3 departures‖	12	14	71	58	43	67	50	57	50	50

* Percent above cutting points is given for each behavior measure.

† Drinkers only.

‡ A, Anglo; S, Spanish.

§ For Cluster I, the N's in this category are: Anglo, 29; Spanish, 9. For Cluster II,
the N's in this category are: Anglo, 26; Spanish, 11.

‖ For Cluster I, the N's in this category are: Anglo, 5; Spanish, 16. For Cluster II
the N's in this category are: Anglo, 8; Spanish, 14.

[3] It is interesting to note that two major differences occur in the rearing of
girls as opposed to boys. Mothers report spending significantly more time in interaction with offspring when they are daughters than when they are sons. Also, mothers
report exerting more control and regulation over daughters than sons. These findings

socialization clusters used, maternal affection and family controls have been emphasized. The data suggest that these aspects of the family environment have strong implications for the conformity or the deviance of adolescent offspring.

SUMMARY AND CONCLUSIONS

The Socialization Study was undertaken to provide, if possible, an additional source of convergent evidence in support of the general theoretical framework. The preceding two studies, the Community Survey Study and the High School Study, were directed at showing the relationships between the sociocultural system, the personality system, and deviant-conforming behavior. In this they were successful, and their parallel outcomes yielded important convergent support for the guiding formulations. Implicit in those studies was the assumption of certain mediational processes whereby personality and behavior are influenced and shaped, over time, by location in the sociocultural system. This assumption, however, remained untested. A direct examination of these mediational processes was deemed important both to provide more analytic understanding of the relations among the variables and to converge upon the larger theoretical formulation from a direction different than that of the preceding two studies.

The mediational process selected for investigation was the system of socialization within the family, and the aim of the research was to demonstrate empirically the bridging role played by the socialization system in linking the sociocultural environment to personality and behavior. Because of the availability of comprehensive personality and behavioral measures on the adolescent students in the local high school, the decision was made to study the system of socialization to which *they* had been exposed. An interview was devised, and a 93 percent sample of the mothers of the local high school students, 75 mothers in all, was interviewed about the socialization of their children. The time focus of the interview was upon the preadolescent and early adolescent stages, in the belief that experiences and influences during these periods could more reliably be reported and were likely to be more directly relevant to adolescent personality and behavior than those of an earlier period.

The interview was directed at measuring aspects of socialization likely

---

accord with Bronfenbrenner's (1961) report of greater affection and control available in the family for girls than for boys. The congruity of our data with other reports in the literature about sex differences is encouraging for the validity of the socialization interview. Furthermore, these differences in socialization between boys and girls are compatible with well-known sex differences in deviant behavior shown in numerous studies and in our own High School Study as well. The boys receive somewhat less affection and control than the girls, and the boys have higher rates of deviance in our study.

to reflect sociocultural variation and, at the same time, variation in personality and behavior. To this end, socialization was construed as a system made up of interrelated structures which were analogues or parallels of the previously delineated structures in the sociocultural and personality systems. Three structures were considered to be important for measurement: parental reward, parental belief, and parental control.

The measurement of socialization was recognized as a complex problem, and our own efforts remained crude and exploratory. An attempt was made to deal not only with parental practices, but also with other influences likely to affect the developing child, such as the implicit paradigms conveyed by the parent's beliefs and the models for behavior present within the family. The parental reward structure dealt with influence practices and affectional interaction together, these aspects considered related influences upon the child's perception of opportunity and conforming behavior. The parental belief structure dealt with the mother's alienation and her teaching of internal-external control, the former an indirect and the latter a direct influence upon the child's own beliefs. Finally, the parental control structure dealt with the presence of deviant role models in the family, the actual opportunity available to engage in deviance, and the degree to which regulations and sanctions were operative and enforced within the family. This latter structure, while obviously also relevant to the child's attitudes, was considered to be the structure most directly regulating the actual occurrence of deviant or conforming behavior.

Although analyses of the various measures were carried out, their full development as measures was precluded by considerations of both time and resources. In that respect, the central findings of this study must be held with a degree of tenuousness despite, as has been seen, their strong and consistent convergence with the findings of the other two studies. Analyses showed that low relationships tended to obtain between the different measures within each socialization structure, and that the relations *among* the three socialization structures were moderate: high enough to suggest that family socialization has a syndrome or climate quality as regards these particular variables, but low enough to suggest that different aspects of that syndrome are indeed being measured.

The central findings of this study have to do with establishing the bridging character of the socialization system—that is, the sociocultural-socialization linkage, on the one hand, and the linkage of socialization to personality and to behavior, on the other. With respect to the first of these, it was shown that the various socialization measures relate as theoretically expected to the family's location in the opportunity structure, indicated by the socioeconomic status of the family. It was also shown that the socialization measures order the ethnic groups in exactly the way that would have been expected from their over-all positions in the socio-cultural system. With respect to the latter linkages, evidence was presented for single socialization measures and for patterns of measures showing significant and, in the case of the patterns, compelling relations between socialization and both adolescent personality and adolescent behavior. These relationships hold within both the Anglo and the Spanish ethnic groups, as well as for the mother sample as a whole.

The evidence accumulated strongly supports the role of socialization as a bridge between society and the person in the time-extended process leading to deviance or conformity. The measures of affectional interaction between mother and child, the mother's mode of rewarding the child's conforming behavior, her exercise of regulatory control over the child, and her alienation, all emerge as significant and relevant to the child's development during adolescence. They tend to influence his personality in a way that makes deviance or conformity more or less likely and, through that process and also directly, to shape his eventual behavior in a deviant or conforming direction. From the point of view of our results, the benign family environment is characterized by warmth and affection, rational discipline, regulations, the absence of models for deviance, and the presence of a nonalienated mother.

Besides its convergence with the Community Survey Study and the High School Study, the Socialization Study contributes in a somewhat unique way to our objectives. It is the only study of the three in which there is some sort of time dimension at least indirectly involved, the other studies clearly being cross-sectional in nature. The unique contribution has to do, then, with the possible support for directional inferences from the obtained relationships among our variables. Obviously, the present basis for this is weak; the Socialization Study, while temporally extended through interviewing mothers about events and experiences antecedent to the present, was also, literally, a cross-sectional study. In addition, there are complex feedbacks in the process of socialization. Obviously, the proper approach to the question requires a longitudinal study of the socialization of deviant behavior. Nevertheless, the findings of the Social-ization Study do give some additional confidence in the directions implied in the explanatory scheme by showing that orderly relations obtain between measures of reported antecedents and measures of outcomes.

The limitations of this particular study have been noted several times. Not only were the measures not fully developed and established prior to employing them in tests of relationships, but what was measured consti-tutes only a limited portion of the complex socialization network in which any child develops. Beyond selecting only certain aspects within the family socialization system, no attention was paid to outside sources of influence on the developing child: peers, teachers, and the mass media. All the data derive, in addition, from only one agent of family socialization, the mother; the critical roles played by fathers and siblings were ignored. For a more adequate study of socialization, these limitations must be transcended.

Despite these shortcomings, however, it must be reemphasized that there is internal consistency among the findings of the Socialization Study, and they are clearly in accord with the findings of the other two studies. The latter convergence, especially, provides more confidence in our conclusions than would otherwise be possible; at the same time, it enables the Socialization Study to contribute strong support to the over-all theoretical framework.

REFERENCES

BALDWIN, A. L., JOAN KALHORN, AND FAY H. BREESE. Patterns of parent behavior. *Psychological Monographs,* 1945, *58,* No. 3 (Whole No. 268).

BANDURA, A. AND R. H. WALTERS. *Adolescent aggression.* New York: Ronald Press, 1959.

BANDURA, A. AND R. H. WALTERS. *Social learning and personality development.* New York: Holt, Rinehart and Winston, 1964.

BECKER, W. C. Consequences of different kinds of parental discipline. In M. L. Hoffman and Lois W. Hoffman (Eds.) *Review of child development research.* Vol. I. New York: Russell Sage Foundation, 1964. Pp. 169–208.

BRONFENBRENNER, U. Socialization and social class through time and space. In Eleanor E. Maccoby, T. M. Newcomb, and E. L. Hartley (Eds.) *Readings in social psychology.* New York: Holt, Rinehart and Winston, 1958. Pp. 400–424.

BRONFENBRENNER, U. Some familial antecedents of responsibility and leadership in adolescents. In L. Petrullo and B. M. Bass (Eds.) *Leadership and interpersonal behavior.* New York: Holt, Rinehart and Winston, 1961. Pp. 239–271.

CLAUSEN, J. A. AND JUDITH R. WILLIAMS. Sociological correlates of child behavior. In H. W. Stevenson (Ed.) *Child psychology: The sixty-second yearbook of the National Society for the Study of Education.* Part I. Chicago: The National Society for the Study of Education, 1963. Pp. 62–107.

CRANDALL, V. J. Achievement. In H. W. Stevenson (Ed.) *Child psychology: The sixty-second yearbook of the National Society for the Study of Education.* Part I. Chicago: The National Society for the Study of Education, 1963. Pp. 416–459.

GLUECK, S. AND ELEANOR GLUECK. *Unraveling juvenile delinquency.* Cambridge: Harvard University Press, 1950.

HOFFMAN, LOIS W. AND R. LIPPITT. The measurement of family life variables. In P. H. Mussen (Ed.) *Handbook of research methods in child development.* New York: Wiley, 1960. Pp. 945–1013.

LORR, M. AND R. L. JENKINS. Three factors in parent behavior. *Journal of Consulting Psychology,* 1963, *17,* 306–308.

McCord, Joan and W. McCord. The effects of parental role model on criminality. *Journal of Social Issues,* 1958, *14,* 66–75.

Schaefer, E. S. A circumplex model for maternal behavior. *Journal of Abnormal and Social Psychology,* 1959, *59,* 226–235.

Sears, R. R., Eleanor E. Maccoby, and H. Levin. *Patterns of child rearing.* New York: Harper & Row, 1957.

Sewell, W. H. Some recent developments in socialization theory and research. *Annals of American Academy of Political and Social Science,* 1963, *349,* 163–181.

Strodtbeck, F. Family interaction, values, and achievement. In D. McClelland, A. Baldwin, U. Bronfenbrenner, and F. Strodtbeck (Eds.) *Talent and society.* Princeton, N.J.: Van Nostrand, 1958. Pp. 135–194.

PART EIGHT

Conclusions

CHAPTER THIRTEEN

Overview and Appraisal
of Theory and Findings

The preceding chapters have sought to inform the reader about what we have done and how we went about our work. They have described the initial problem which we assumed as the explanatory objective, the concepts we used in a theoretical formulation, the stance we took with respect to field research, the measures devised and the studies in which they were employed, and, finally, the results that were obtained. A review of these various aspects should be useful at this point; discussion of problems and issues raised by the research and some of its limitations and implications will follow.

A BRIEF OVERVIEW

The research began with the task of accounting for the differential rates of occurrence of problem behavior, especially heavy alcohol use, among three ethnic groups in a small rural community in southwestern Colorado. Although members of the community were ready with their own "explanations," and although there were several obvious vantage points from which an investigation might begin, it seemed clear that the situation provided a natural laboratory in which a general theory of deviance-conformity might be developed and put to test. The accomplishment of such an objective required a conceptual analysis of the behavior involved and of the factors, in both the person and the situation, which might be important influences upon it.

Our first concern was to recognize the essential continuity between deviance and conformity and to assume that an explanation focused at either pole must have implications for the other. What this implied was that deviant behavior, like any other, was best treated as learned, purposive, goal oriented, in short, as adaptive action requiring no special principles to account for its occurrence beyond those required for social behavior in general. The central issue became that of explaining not deviance per se but the occurrence of deviant rather than some other, that is, conforming, behavior. Stated otherwise, the problem was to account for selection or choice among possible adaptive alternatives. In this light, the selection of deviant behavioral adaptations, despite the ultimate possibility of negative sanctions, appeared to be more likely when other alternatives had come to be seen by the actor as promising him little in the way of success. The view that it would be useful to interpret deviance as reflecting, at least in part, the failure of conformity was adopted.

Our second concern was to recognize the complexity inherent in the concept of deviance. One source of complexity stems from the diversity of behavior which the concept subsumes. Any number of actions, all significantly departing from normative prescription, can be learned as alternative adaptations when conforming behavior fails to secure personal goals. The recognition of this source of complexity suggested the need to go beyond a concern with heavy alcohol use alone to include other adaptations which might be functionally equivalent. A test of a theory of deviant behavior seemed to us to require an assessment of the class of deviant alternatives rather than a focus upon any particular one. A second source of complexity is that which inheres in all social behavior: the fact that deviance and conformity represent the outcome of multiple influences and determinants in both the person and his situation.

These views about deviant behavior directed our analysis of both personality and the sociocultural environment, an analysis demanding multiple determinants likely to reflect the failure of conformity and the availability of deviant alternatives. For the major personality formulations, we drew upon Rotter's social learning theory (1954); for the sociocultural concepts, we borrowed from Merton (1957), and Cloward and Ohlin (1961). Complementary, analogous conceptualizations of the person and of the environment, systematically coordinated to each other and to deviance, were consequently developed.

The sociocultural environment was articulated as a system made up of three major structures: the opportunity structure, the normative structure, and the social control structure. Location in the opportunity structure was construed as a source of pressure toward the adoption of illegitimate means, with low access to opportunity implying a relatively high degree of pressure. Locations in both the normative structure and the social control structure were defined as sources of controls against the adoption of illegitimate means, with high anomie in the normative structure and high access to illegitimate means in the social control structure implying a low degree of control. Deviance as a sociocultural outcome was, therefore, considered to be the resultant of sociocultural pressure and controls, neither factor alone yielding a sufficient explanation.

The same conceptual approach was applied to the person. Personality was construed as a system made up of three structures parallel to those constituting the sociocultural system: a perceived opportunity structure, providing a source of pressure toward deviance, and a personal belief structure and a personal control structure, both representing personal controls against engaging in deviance. The resultant of personal pressure and control was seen to determine, now at the personality level, the likelihood of deviant behavior, neither factor alone being sufficient.

Although these two conceptual systems, sociocultural and personality, constitute separate theories of deviance, their formal similarity and parallel concepts enabled their assimilation into a single, interdisciplinary, explanatory scheme. This was our basic objective: to construct a field theory of deviant behavior in which the interaction of sociocultural and personality determinants could be dealt with systematically.

To make the field theory a more convincing synthesis, it seemed important to consider how the sociocultural environment comes, over time, to influence the development of personality. To this end, socialization was construed as a system lying at the interface between society and the person. It also was articulated into three structures, ones likely to reflect the sociocultural system and, at the same time, to be relevant to the personality system. The structures of the socialization system, analogues of the structures in the other two systems, were the parental reward structure, the parental belief structure, and the parental control structure.

A test of the adequacy of the explanatory formulation was seen to rest on its ability to yield, simultaneously, an account of differences between ethnic groups in rates of occurrence of deviance and an account of individual differences within the community and within ethnic groups in the occurrence-nonoccurrence of deviance. The logic of the approach was that the same factors used to explain individual behavior could be applied to explaining differences between groups of individuals, in our case, ethnic groups. The implication of this logic for the meaning of the concept of ethnic status will be elaborated later on.

Second to, and influenced by, our concern for theory was our commitment to developing a research methodology appropriate to the testing of theory in field studies. Although field studies are usually seen as part of the context of exploration and discovery, it was our view that they are also appropriate to the context of justification. To fulfill this latter role, to be relevant to the testing of propositions, field studies require design in which consistent efforts to minimize inferential ambiguity are made. For us this meant, beyond the usual concern for standardization and reliable measurement, the logical derivation of measuring procedures from concepts, the development of multiple measures of concepts, and the use of multiple, converging studies, each independent of the others but converging upon the validity of the over-all social-psychological framework. To the extent that such a methodological orientation could be successfully implemented, to that extent, it seemed to us could theory-testing be compelling in field research.

Three separate and independent studies were carried out in the community. The first of these was a community survey study in which data were collected by individual interview from a random sample of adults between the ages of twenty and sixty-five, stratified by sex and ethnic group. The interview included measures of the sociocultural system, the personality system, and the behavior system, that is, deviance-conformity and alcohol use. Information on the latter was supplemented by an exhaustive search of relevant court records but, in the main, this study provided a self-contained test of the theory based upon self-report interview data. The second study focused upon a younger age group in the community, the students in the local high school. It involved a wide range of procedures, including self-report group questionnaires, interviews, sociometrics, behavior tests, teacher ratings, and school records. Yielding sociocultural, personality, and behavior measures, it enabled a second, independent test of the over-all framework.

The third study dealt with socialization and was an attempt to study the linkage between the sociocultural system, on the one hand, and the personality and behavior systems, on the other. In the socialization study, data were collected by individual interview from the mothers of the students in the high school, and measures based upon these data were used to predict the personality and behavior measures independently obtained from their children in the high school.

All three studies provided some degree of support for the theory guiding the research, and the convergence of the findings from the separate studies constitutes a strong basis for inference. Among the ethnic groups, the Anglos were shown to occupy the most favorable position in the opportunity structure: They have the greatest objective access to valued goals by legitimate means and are, consequently, under the least pressure to adopt alternative, often illegitimate, means. With respect to the normative structure, they were also shown to occupy the most theoretically favorable position: They have the greatest degree of consensus around group norms, that is, the least anomie, and are subject, therefore, to the greatest normative control against the adoption of illegitimate means. Finally, with respect to the social control structure, their position is also the most favorable: .They have least access to illegitimate means and are, therefore, subject to the strongest social controls. Taken together, the findings show the Anglos to occupy the point of intersection in sociocultural "space" which should be theoretically least conducive to deviance, the point, relative to the other two ethnic groups, at which pressures toward deviance are lowest and controls against deviance are highest. These findings are consistent with the data showing that the Anglos, among the three ethnic groups, make the least contribution to deviance rates in the community.

Considering the other two ethnic groups, the Spanish and the Indians, the findings are more complex and make clear the utility of a theory which deals simultaneously with both pressures and controls. In terms of pressures toward deviance, the Indians actually have a somewhat more favorable position in the opportunity structure than the Spanish, at least when access to opportunity is defined exclusively in terms of socioeconomic status. With respect to controls, however, the Spanish clearly occupy the theoretically more favorable position. The measure of normative controls suggests that anomie is more pervasive and generalized among the Indians than among the Spanish; and with respect to social controls, the picture is sharpest, the Spanish having least exposure to deviant role models and being mapped into solidary sanctioning networks such as the Catholic Church, the family, and informal groups significantly more than are the Indians. Despite equal or even greater pressures toward deviance, the Spanish are subject to the operation of much stronger and more consistent controls than the Indians. These findings are consonant with the data showing the Indians to contribute most to the deviance rates in the community, with the Spanish intermediate between them and the Anglos. The intermediate position of the Spanish rates is actually much closer to that of the Anglos than it is to that of the Indians, suggesting the possibly more important role played by social controls, relative to pressures, in influencing the occurrence of deviance.

The findings just described support the sociocultural aspect of the theory in dealing with ethnic group differences in deviant behavior. The results bearing on the personality aspect of the theory are also supportive. The Anglos have the greatest *perception* of opportunity, that is, the highest expectations of achieving goals, or the least personal disjunctions. They are also least alienated with respect to the personal belief structure, and they have the strongest personal controls. The trend with respect to the two minority groups is for the Indians to hold the more deviance-prone position on the personality measures compared to the Spanish, although the relative position of the two groups is not clearly established on all of the measures. With respect to personal control measures, however, as was the case with social controls, the Spanish, despite their low position in the economic opportunity structure, are closer to the Anglos than they are to the Indians.

The support provided for the over-all social-psychological framework by the outcome just described gains reinforcement from the fact that it emerges from two independent studies in the community, one dealing with adults and the other with adolescents of high school age. These two studies, using different age groups, different measures, and different settings, yet generating congruent empirical data, yield the kind of convergence toward which the methodological planning was oriented. Further convergence stems from the socialization study. Ethnic group differences in parental reward structure, parental belief structure, and parental control structure measures follow from the sociocultural position of the family and accord with the personality and behavior measures of the high school children.

Showing that ethnic group differences in deviance rates were consonant with the relative positions of the three ethnic groups on the theoretical variables in the sociocultural and personality systems was a major objective. A second major objective was to provide an account of individual differences by reference to the same theoretical framework. This involved a more direct test of the theory, an assessment of the direct relation of sociocultural and personality measures to the occurrence of deviant behavior.

Each of the measures in the sociocultural and personality systems was related, singly, to each of the multiple criterion measures of deviance and alcohol use. What these analyses showed was that, with some exceptions, the measures related in the direction which the theory implied but that the degree of relationship of each measure was generally small. Given our conceptualization of deviance as the complex outcome of both pressures and controls, low, single-measure correlations were not unexpected. The next step, therefore, was to deal simultaneously with multiple measures, and this was done by a pattern analysis procedure in which each individual was characterized by the "syndrome" of scores he had obtained with respect to measures of both pressures and controls. This pattern analysis procedure, which captures the intent of the theoretical interpretation, was more successful.

Considering the community as a whole, strong linear relations were shown to obtain between the sociocultural syndrome (which included measures of objective opportunity and social controls) and various criteria of deviance. The same was shown to be true for the relations between the personality pattern (which included measures of perceived opportunity, alienation, and personal controls) and deviance and drinking criteria. Most impressive, however, was the "field" pattern, which incorporated both sociocultural and personality measures (objective opportunity, social controls, perceived opportunity, and personal controls) into a single predictor pattern. The relation of the field pattern to the several criteria was shown to account for variance not accounted for by either the sociocultural or the personality patterns alone, and it tended consistently to yield the best prediction of the various deviance criteria in both the Community Survey Study and the High School Study. Treating the community adults as a whole and the high school students as a whole, the multivariable pattern analyses provided compelling evidence in support of the theoretical framework.

The final step in the direct assessment of the theory was to examine it, as above, *within* each of the ethnic groups. The pattern analyses retained the predictiveness they had shown for the community as a whole when they were applied within both the Anglo and Spanish groups, and for both sexes, but they were strongly attenuated in their ability to predict deviance within the Indian group. This attenuation seemed to be due in part to the high deviance rate characterizing the Indians and making differential within-group prediction extremely difficult. More will be said on this point in the discussion of limitations of the research.

To conclude this overview, a further point needs to be made. The measurement of deviance and deviance-prone behavior, such as heavy alcohol use, proved to be a task of great complexity, but one clearly meriting the attention it received. By retaining separate measures of various aspects of deviance and drinking behavior, we were able not only to assess the interrelations among them but also to use them as multiple, separate criteria in theory-testing. Further, by constructing a global index of deviance which combined various separate measures, we were able to approach most closely the kind of criterion the theory was directed at. This global deviance criterion was best and most consistently predicted by the sociocultural and personality measures.

In summary, these three studies in the Tri-Ethnic Research Project, the Community Survey Study of adults, the High School Study of adolescents, and the Socialization Study, yielded convergent, empirical support for the theoretical framework as an explanation of both group and individual differences in deviance and alcohol use. Such convergence suggests that inferences about the nature of deviance in this community, inferences of the sort contained in the theory, can be drawn with some degree of security.

LIMITATIONS OF THE RESEARCH

The preceding overview has focused upon the larger pattern of our findings. Each of the earlier chapters in which the original discussion of the data took place has indicated what bounds need to be placed on such summary generalizations. There were, however, a number of important limitations in our work stemming from the nature of the situation in which it was done, from our approach, and from our findings; these merit at least brief discussion at this point.

Perhaps the most salient question has to do with the character of the research context—a small, rural, southwestern community—and the constraints which it imposes upon generalizing from the findings. As with the study of any community, its representativeness of some universe is always in doubt, especially when the community has been selected, as in our case, for its particular ethnic composition. While there are obviously many other communities like the one in which we worked, it is difficult, on any sampling basis, to lay claim to inferences which go beyond its boundaries. This means, in the most severe terms, that our explanation of deviance applies only to this community, or perhaps to others which are demonstrably similar, and greater generalizability must wait upon extension and replication.

An aspect of this limitation which should be emphasized, and which illustrates the point, is that deviance in the research community cannot be said to be institutionalized in any formal sense. While there are informal peer groups, there do not appear to be gangs of the sort that characterize large urban centers, nor the formalized criminal organizations among adults frequently found in cities. Although the measures of deviance and deviance-prone behavior were comprehensive, they dealt with behavior which is most accurately described as only informally structured. The applicability of the findings is, therefore, in question where deviance can be shown to be a relatively institutionalized, formally supported and rewarded pattern of behavior.

A second major limitation has to do with the fact that the entire theory was not available at the outset of the research, but was in part developed during the process of investigation. This is most true of the social control formulations which, although considered from the beginning, were not specified in sufficient detail to guide the initial data collection. As the importance of social controls began to emerge, data already in hand were used to measure those concepts. While this was generally a feasible thing to do, it was obviously only poorly accomplished in certain respects—for example, in the measurement of opportunity to engage in deviance. Despite the support for the final social control formulations, support which obtained in the separate studies, their partially *post hoc* nature leaves this portion of the theory somewhat less securely established.

A third shortcoming is that certain of our measures simply did not work out. A primary example was the predictive failure of the internal-external control measure. A great deal of effort had gone into the development of this procedure, since the concept of internal-external control seemed theoretically important in linking personality with deviance, and since it was the kind of concept which could be readily coordinated with sociocultural variation. Its failure remains unclear to us, especially since it failed in both the High School and the Community Survey studies to show the expected relationships. These negative findings are not in accord with the success which the same or very similar measures have had in other studies (Rotter, 1966; Seeman, 1963; Wood, Wilson, Jessor, and

Bogan, 1966), or with the importance which social-psychological analysis would assign to the concept. Further work is called for, and our data in this regard are disconcerting.

An additional shortcoming which we regret very much is our failure to explore in greater depth the role of peer groups and the impact of peer socialization. As informal influences conducing to or constraining against deviance, it is obvious they exert a strong influence. In the High School Study, sociometric data could have been employed to this end rather than serving simply as a criterion measure of deviance. In the Socialization Study, inquiry about peer associations could have been profitably undertaken. In both cases, the peer group network in which each youth is embedded would have been available for analysis, and the relation of peer support to the occurrence of deviance might have been better understood.

The inability of our approach to predict the particular *form* of deviant adaptation engaged in is a further limitation of note. It will be recalled from the early chapters that the importance of measuring access to illegitimate means, especially the exposure to deviant role models component, was argued as the direction to take in coping with precisely this problem: with why, for example, one person may adapt to failure and frustration by mental illness, another by narcotics use, and a third by crime or heavy alcohol use. What would seem to be required is an analysis of exposure to various, alternative, deviant adaptations, an appraisal of the possibility of learning them through modeling, and an assessment of the conditions which may endow them differentially with the likelihood of success. In our own work, this type of detailed analysis was not made. Instead, we relied on a crude measure of exposure to any form of deviance, and this limitation precluded a contribution to the understanding of the selection of specific forms of deviance. Our approach, dealing with the *class* of deviant behaviors, was relevant to our concern with testing a general theory, but it meant that an important problem was not confronted.

The fact that our predictor measures in both the sociocultural and personality systems, when dealt with singly, generally had only low or moderate relationships to the criterion measures should also be commented on at this point. How much this reflects inadequate development of measures is difficult to say. Despite a tremendous expenditure of resources on the construction and refinement of measures, it is clear to us that we could have benefited from even more effort in this respect.

The recognition that, despite our efforts, the measures remained relatively crude, supported the decision to dichotomize the measures in devising the pattern analysis procedure. Although that decision seems to discard the possibility of greater discrimination, it does acknowledge the crudeness and attempts, by dichotomizing, to assure that variation on each predictor is securely established. It was the latter which was of primary concern to us in that our aim at this stage of theory development was to establish parameter *relevance* in prediction rather than to estimate parameter values.

A further shortcoming relates to the fact that the empirical findings do not clarify the issue of the conceptual unity of the separate theoretical structures posited within both the sociocultural and the personality systems. Alternative measures within each structure sometimes related better to measures in other structures than they did to each other; also, structures within one system sometimes related to structures in the other system which were *not* their conceptual analogue better than to the one that was. These data are not clear-cut: they support both a generality point of view and a specificity point of view about the functional unities implied by the separate structures. This issue will require further empirical and conceptual analysis. Empirically, there is a need to develop minimally overlapping measures which represent most precisely the conceptual content of each particular structure. Conceptually, the issue turns on the degree to which the structures within a system can be argued to be theoretically uncorrelated. The latter situation would be difficult to defend, either for the sociocultural system or the personality system, since the very notion of system implies a correlation among structures; and this is generally what we found. Whether relations within systems can obtain without jeopardizing the specificity of relations between analogous structures in different systems will only be known when further data are in hand. In the meantime, the theoretical structures postulated for the environment and for the person have thus far been of major heuristic value.

A final limitation to which attention must be called was the relatively poor prediction of deviance within the Indian group. While the pattern analyses showed effectiveness in accounting for variation in deviant behavior within both the Anglo and Spanish groups, only directional trends were obtained for the Indians. There are a number of possible explanations for this. It is possible, for example, that the interview procedures (and the reliance on non-Indian interviewers) were less appropriate to the Indian respondents than to the others in obtaining information on values, expectations, beliefs, and attitudes.

It is also possible that the measures were insufficiently sensitive to important factors differentially operative in the different ethnic groups. For example, while measures of values showed no ethnic group differences of any magnitude, it could be the case that measures focused upon other aspects of the orientation of minority groups to the dominant group could have revealed important differences. One such aspect, of obvious concern to the anthropologist, is acculturation. This concept did not enter directly into our theoretical framework; yet, a secondary analysis of some of our data interpreted in terms of the process of acculturation does seem to enhance prediction within both minority groups (see Graves, 1967). The analysis is *post hoc,* and the measures of acculturation are possibly tenuous, but the results attained are consistent and coherent, and they certainly suggest that the concept of acculturation may have utility in a community such as the one studied here.

One apparent problem in the attempt to account for differences in deviance within the Indian group is the fact of the high rate of Indian deviance, which makes discrimination an extremely difficult task. Given the general clustering of the Indian group at the upper end of the deviance criteria and at the deviance-prone end of the predictors, better prediction of individual differences within the Indian group would require predictors and criterion measures of much greater sensitivity. It is possible, too, that such a high rate of deviance, with the attendant patterning of learning and modeling which it implies, tends to make most of our predictors relatively unimportant determinants of deviant behavior. This difficulty in prediction within the Indian group should not, however, obscure the fact that, at the group level, an association between sociocultural and personality deviance proneness, on the one hand, and rates of deviant behavior, on the other, has been shown to exist.

The shortcomings of the research which have been noted do not constitute an exhaustive list. They are meant to represent some of the kinds of limitations which attenuate the strength of the findings and to alert the reader to the necessary caution in considering their implications, a few of which can be considered now.

SOME CONCLUSIONS AND IMPLICATIONS

Not too long ago, Henry Murray expressed the opinion that "no theoretical system constructed on the psychological level will be adequate until it has been embraced by and intermeshed with a cultural-sociological system" (1959, p. 20). At the most general level, this view was a starting point for us, and the outcome of our work impels us to return to it as a conclusion. The explanatory usefulness of a field theory of behavior has been shown to extend beyond the limits of its psychological and sociocultural component systems. When the latter are "intermeshed," certain previously recalcitrant problems become more docile, problems such as why everyone at the same social location does not behave the same way, or why the epidemiology of certain behaviors is patterned in a particular way in the social structure. Beyond these practical consequences, however, there is the fundamental gain of being able, through reliance upon a field theoretical system, to generate more detailed intelligibility about social behavior.

To make this point about the over-all theory is not to diminish the importance of the particular concepts within the embracing systems. Conclusions about certain of the concepts we have used can, as a matter of fact, be drawn with a fair degree of confidence. It is clear, for example, that the notion of *expectation* constitutes one of our most powerful concepts for describing persons with respect to deviance proneness. Differences in values were relatively minor, whether those values were defined in the common language referring to success or whether they were defined in motivationally relevant terms. What emerged as crucially important were differences in expectation for achieving what was valued. That expectations play a central role in the selective course of human behavior seems clear from the data. This conclusion has greater impact when it is realized that the measures of expectation were conceptually remote from the behavior at issue; unlike another of the psychological measures, tolerance of deviance, which also turned out to be an important predictor, but which dealt directly with deviance, the expectations measures never implicated deviance in the actual measurement procedure.

The conclusion about the important role of expectations in social behavior is in accord with the literature cited earlier, in Chapter 4, and would seem to have pervasive implications for efforts to deal with problem behavior. Social intervention focused upon raising expectations that socially desirable behavior can lead successfully to valued goals would be a tactic consonant with those implications. That such expectations follow, in part at least, from the position occupied in the opportunity structure is suggested by the research and makes the latter a prime target for concentration in organizing efforts at remediation.

To move to a consideration of the concepts employed to describe the sociocultural environment, certainly *social controls* have emerged as central. The critical part played by social controls was nowhere clearer than in the differentiation it yielded between the two minority ethnic groups. Both groups are subjected to strong pressures toward deviance, yet the Spanish, embedded in a persisting structure of religious, family, and interpersonal sanctions, contribute far less to the deviance rates than the Indians, for whom the control structure is fragmented or weak. The meaning of controls in our research is in large part the degree to which a person is mapped into solidary groups that reward conforming behavior, punish departures from group norms, and provide relatively few models for deviance. Other things equal, the strengthening of family and both formal and informal group ties would seem to be relevant to efforts toward reducing deviance.

The latter point is probably also relevant to increasing the degree of normative consensus or agreement about what is appropriate in the way of behavior. The research has demonstrated the possibility of relatively direct measurement of anomie and, although the data derive, unfortunately, from only one study, suggests that such lack of normative consensus may be relevant to deviance. The strengthening of social ties, and the corollary development of interpersonal communication, may be as important in reducing anomie as in strengthening social controls.

The analyses of deviance have been instructive in themselves. The use of multiple raters (for example, teachers, or peers) and multiple sources of data (for example, self-reports, records, teacher ratings, or peer nominations) enable increased reliability and convergent validity to overcome the possible shortcomings of self-reports. It should be noted, in regard to the latter, that our own experience justifies reliance upon self-report data, especially where the concern is with rank-ordering a group of subjects on degree of deviance. The convergence, in our research, between self-report data and external criteria of deviance was impressive.

The findings about alcohol use make the complexity of deviance most evident. Comprehensive understanding of alcohol use required knowledge of how it was learned, the context of its use, the amount drunk, the meaning or psychological functions of drinking, and the consequences of its use. Two persons drinking moderate amounts of alcohol may be doing so in very different ways: one by himself, as a way of overcoming a feeling of being nervous or tense; and the other in a group, as a way of expressing his feeling of community with his companions. The difference between these two patterns is not only likely to have different consequences but to be differentially related to sociocultural and personality pressures and controls as well.

What the research has indicated is that at least several aspects of alcohol use are explicable in terms of the sociocultural and personality concepts in the over-all scheme. This was most apparent where the alcohol use was heavy and for personal-effects, problem-solving reasons (although the scheme did show predictiveness, even for the amount of alcohol drunk). The demonstration that excessive alcohol use is related to differential pressures and controls, both sociocultural and personality, has important implications, not only for understanding this form of problem behavior but also for possible remedial measures.

A final implication of the research requiring mention has to do with the meaning of the concept of ethnicity. Our work has contributed to a social-psychology of ethnicity or ethnic status. Instead of dealing with ethnic status in terms of some set of unique traits or in terms of a peculiar cultural legacy distinctive of a particular group, we have dealt with it as representing a position in social-psychological space. A unitary set of sociocultural, personality, and behavior measures has been applied to all three ethnic groups. The result of this approach was an analysis of ethnic status in the language of the theoretical scheme. Thus, what it means to be an Indian in this community is to have limited opportunity, to be confronted by relatively pervasive anomie, to be subject to weak social controls, and the like. Ethnic status, then, is merely a descriptive term, but one probabilistically implying a bundle of theoretical attributes.

This interpretation of the concept of ethnicity is analogous to what Oscar Lewis has urged with respect to another descriptive concept: poverty. In developing the notion of "the culture of poverty," Lewis has gathered together a number of traits often considered to represent distinctive characteristics of ethnic, national, or regional groups and has argued that these characteristics are

> both an adaptation and a reaction of the poor to their marginal position in a class-stratified, highly individuated, capitalistic society. It represents an effort to cope with feelings of hopelessness and despair that arise from the realization by the members of the marginal communities in these societies of the improbability of their achieving success in terms of the prevailing values and goals (1966, p. 21).

Lewis' distinction between poverty and the culture of poverty is analogous to the distinction we are suggesting between ethnic status and the social-psychology of ethnic status. It happens that poverty and ethnic or marginal status often go together; that is probably what accounts for the fact that the content of Lewis' culture of poverty and the content of our social-psychology of ethnic status have so much in common.

The implications of this discussion seem important. They suggest that the deviance rates of the three ethnic groups characterize them not by virtue of their ethnic status, but largely by virtue of their social-psychological status; place Anglos in the situation of Indians, and deviance rates should increase markedly. Such a view departs sharply from that part of the community psychology which, for example, considers deviance and drunkenness an inherently Indian trait. Further, this view would seem important in any considerations of change; insofar as the problem is seen not as a problem of ethnicity but as a problem of the attributes associated with it, the latter become the obvious target of change efforts.

Finally, this perspective provides a rationale for considering, as a single unit or as a whole, communities which are made up of different ethnic groups. Precisely this has been done in some of the major analyses presented here. Although the groups are descriptively different, the rationale suggests that they can be treated homogeneously in terms of their position on a set of variables applicable to all members of the community, variables which, in essence, summarize much of the social and psychological meaning of ethnic status.

A final word: Our work has captured, obviously, neither the quality of daily life nor the succession of events which pattern the course of time in the community; that task belongs to the sensitive ethnographer.

Instead, as indicated in Chapter 1, the path we chose to follow was an abstract one, and it is now possible to see where it has led. The ideas developed and the data generated have given us a beginning sense of understanding. Hopefully, they may have application to other social problems as well and, ultimately, may contribute in a small way to the amelioration of the human condition. It would be difficult, at this stage, to ask more of behavioral science.

REFERENCES

CLOWARD, R. A. AND L. E. OHLIN. *Delinquency and opportunity.* New York: Free Press, 1961.

GRAVES, T. D. Acculturation, access, and alcohol in a tri-ethnic community. *American Anthropologist,* 1967, *69,* 306–321.

LEWIS, O. The culture of poverty. *Scientific American,* 1966, *215,* 19–25.

MERTON, R. K. *Social theory and social structure.* Rev. Ed. New York: Free Press, 1957.

MURRAY, H. A. Preparations for the scaffold of a comprehensive system. In S. Koch (Ed.) *Psychology: A study of a science.* Vol. 3. New York: McGraw-Hill, 1959. Pp. 7–54.

ROTTER, J. B. *Social learning and clinical psychology.* Englewood Cliffs, N.J.: Prentice-Hall, 1954.

ROTTER, J. B. Generalized expectancies for internal versus external control of reinforcement. *Psychological Monographs,* 1966, *80,* Whole No. 609. Pp. 1–28.

SEEMAN, M. Alienation and social learning in a reformatory. *American Journal of Sociology,* 1963, *69,* 270–284.

WOOD, B. S., G. G. WILSON, R. JESSOR, AND J. B. BOGAN. Troublemaking behavior in a correctional institution: Relationship to inmates' definition of their situation. *American Journal of Orthopsychiatry,* 1966, *36,* 795–802.

Research Reports, Theses, and Publications Related to the Tri-Ethnic Research Reported in This Volume

A. TRI-ETHNIC PROJECT RESEARCH REPORTS

1. GRAVES, T. D. *Report on a preliminary testing program in the local high school—values, expectations, and internal-external control.* April 1960. Ditto. Pp. 1–46.

2. JESSOR, SHIRLEY. *Report on a preliminary testing program in the local high school—the incomplete sentences blank.* May 1960. Ditto. Pp. 1–42.

3. WEISS, P. *Report on a preliminary testing program in the local high school —essays.* July 1960. Ditto. Pp. 1–48.

4. MINARD, J. G. *Report on a preliminary testing program in the local high school—sociometric preferences in the junior and senior classes.* February 1961. Ditto. Pp. 1–95.

5. GRAVES, T. D. *Time perspective and the deferred gratification pattern in a tri-ethnic community.* August 1961. Mimeo. Pp. 1–284.

6. MINARD, J. G. *Social structure and student behavior in a tri-ethnic high school: A replication and extension.* September 1961. Mimeo. Pp. 1–114.

7. GUERTIN, CAROL. *Perceived life-chances in the opportunity structure: A study of a tri-ethnic high school.* June 1962. Mimeo. Pp. 1–122.

8. HANSON, R. C. AND P. CHASSY. *Three types of anomie: Theory and measurement.* Spring 1962. Mimeo. Pp. 1–13.

9. RENDON, G., JR. *Voting behavior in a tri-ethnic community.* August 1962. Mimeo. Pp. 1–110.

10. GILLIS, J. S. *The construction and development of an incomplete sentences blank and scoring manual for assessing several psychological variables.* September 1962. Mimeo. Pp. 1–30.

11. GILLIS, J. S. *Issues in the measurement of attitudes toward deviance and their relationships with behavior.* February 1963. Mimeo. Pp. 1–37.

12. CHASSY, P. AND R. C. HANSON. *Measuring anomie—an analysis of the group norms items on the community survey.* March 1963. Mimeo. Pp. 1–39.

13. TITLEY, R. W. *The measurement of alienation: An analysis of the alienation scale on the community survey.* March 1963. Mimeo. Pp. 1–49.

14. SHYBUT, J. *Delayed gratification: A study of its measurement and its relationship to certain behavioral, psychological and demographic variables.* March 1963. Mimeo. Pp. 1–130.

15. FRANK, C. *Acceptance of illegitimate means—a measure of dominant culture anomie.* April 1963. Mimeo. Pp. 1–37.

16. CASTELLAN, N. J., JR. *Expectations, values, and personal disjunctions: The development and analysis of two test procedures.* April 1963. Mimeo. Pp. 1–30.

17. STRAND, SUSAN. *The development of a self-report measure of deviant behavior: An analysis of the Other Deviance scale on the community survey.* April 1963. Mimeo. Pp. 1–42.

18. GROSSMAN, P. H. *The establishment of alcohol consumption criterion groups: Rationale and associated characteristics.* April 1963. Mimeo. Pp. 1–39.

19. SHYBUT, J. *Demographic characteristics of the high school population of a tri-ethnic community, with comparisons among ethnic groups.* April 1963. Mimeo. Pp. 1–29.

20. RENDON, G., JR. *Objective access in the opportunity structure: The assessment of three ethnic groups with respect to quantified social structural variables.* June 1963. Mimeo. Pp. 1–41.

21. HANSON, R. C. AND G. RENDON, JR. *The location of ethnic groups in the sociocultural structure of a tri-ethnic community.* August 1963. Mimeo. Pp. 1–39.

22. TITLEY, R. W. *Alienation: A study of its social, psychological and behavioral correlates.* August 1963. Mimeo. Pp. 1–65.

23. JESSOR, R. AND SHIRLEY JESSOR. *Social-psychological factors in deviance in a tri-ethnic community.* August 1963. Mimeo. Pp. 1–23.

24. HANSON, R. C. AND T. D. GRAVES. *Objective access, anomie and deviance in a tri-ethnic community.* August 1963. Mimeo. Pp. 1–22.

25. JESSOR, R. *Theory and method in the study of deviance in a tri-ethnic community.* Pp. 1–20.
    HANSON, R. C. *The sociocultural context of deviance.* Pp. 1–20.
    GRAVES, T. D. *Social-psychological processes in differential patterns of deviance.* Pp. 1–15.
    JESSOR, SHIRLEY. *Cultural factors and socialization into deviance.* Pp. 1–19.
    (These four papers are bound together.) November 1963. Mimeo.

26. SHYBUT, J. *Delayed gratification: Further relationships to behavioral, psychological, demographic and developmental variables.* January 1964. Mimeo. Pp. 1–48.

27. GROSSMAN, P. H. *The assessment of alternative definitions of alcohol involvement in relation to sociocultural and psychological variables.* March 1964. Mimeo. Pp. 1–68.

28. GROSSMAN, P. H. *Drinking motivation: A cluster analytic study of three samples.* May 1965. Mimeo. Pp. 1–186.

29. GRAVES, T. D. *The measurement of drinking and deviant behavior.* March 1966. Mimeo. Pp. 1–245.

30.   GRAVES, T. D. *Acculturation, access and alcohol in a tri-ethnic community.* October 1966. Mimeo. Pp. 1–57.

B. THESES

CARMAN, R. S. *Personality and drinking behavior among college students.* Unpublished masters thesis, University of Colorado, 1965.

GRAVES, T. D. *Time perspective and the deferred gratification pattern in a tri-ethnic community.* Unpublished doctoral dissertation, University of Pennsylvania, 1962.

GROSSMAN, P. H. *Drinking motivation: A cluster analytic study of three samples.* Unpublished doctoral dissertation, University of Colorado, 1965.

GUERTIN, CAROL. *Perceived life-chances in the opportunity structure: A study of a tri-ethnic high school.* Unpublished masters thesis, University of Colorado, 1962.

KUYKENDALL, D. L. *Frustration and attribution of blame in middle and lower class delinquents.* Unpublished doctoral dissertation, University of Colorado, 1965.

OPOCHINSKY, S. *Values, expectations, and the formation of impressions.* Unpublished doctoral dissertation, University of Colorado, 1965.

RENDON, G., JR. *Voting behavior in a tri-ethnic community.* Unpublished masters thesis, University of Colorado, 1962.

SHYBUT, J. *Delayed gratification: A study of its measurement and its relationship to certain behavioral, psychological and demographic variables.* Unpublished masters thesis, University of Colorado, 1963.

SHYBUT, J. *Delay of gratification and severity of disturbance among hospitalized psychiatric patients.* Unpublished doctoral dissertation, University of Colorado, 1965.

C. PUBLICATIONS

CASTELLAN, N. J., JR. On the partitioning of contingency tables. *Psychological Bulletin,* 1965, *64,* 330–338.

CASTELLAN, N. J., JR. On the estimation of the tetrachoric correlation coefficient. *Psychometrika,* 1966, *31,* 67–73.

GRAVES, T. D. Acculturation, access, and alcohol in a tri-ethnic community. *American Anthropologist,* 1967, *69,* 306–321.

JESSOR, R. Issues in the phenomenological approach to personality. *Journal of Individual Psychology,* 1961, *17,* 27–38.

JESSOR, R. A social learning approach to culture and behavior. In T. Gladwin and W. C. Sturtevant (Eds.) *Anthropology and human behavior.* Washington, D.C.: The Anthropological Society of Washington, 1962. Pp. 94–114.

JESSOR, R. Toward a social psychology of excessive alcohol-use. In C. R. Snyder and D. R. Schweitzer (Eds.) *Proceedings of the Research Sociologists' Conference on Alcohol Problems,* Southern Illinois University, April 30–May 1, 1964. Pp. 60–79.

JESSOR, R., S. LIVERANT, AND S. OPOCHINSKY. Imbalance in need structure and maladjustment. *Journal of Abnormal and Social Psychology,* 1963, *66,* 271–275.

JESSOR, R., R. S. CARMAN, AND P. H. GROSSMAN. Expectations of need satisfaction and drinking patterns of college students, *Quarterly Journal of Studies on Alcohol,* in press.

SHYBUT, J. Time perspective, internal versus external control, and severity of psychological disturbance. *Journal of Clinical Psychology,* in press.

WOOD, B. S., G. G. WILSON, R. JESSOR, AND J. B. BOGAN. Troublemaking behavior in a correctional institution: Relationship to inmates' definition of their situation. *American Journal of Orthopsychiatry,* 1966, *36,* 795–802.

Community Survey Interview Schedule

(NOTE: The format of the original interview schedule has been altered somewhat and shortened to conserve space. Certain abbreviations are spelled out to make the scales meaningful to the reader.)

SCHEDULE NO:

UNIVERSITY OF COLORADO
TRI-ETHNIC RESEARCH PROJECT
COMMUNITY SURVEY
October 1961

Respondent: _____
            First   Middle   Maiden   Last
Telephone Yes_____ No_____
Residence Town_____ Rural_____
Date:
Time: Start_____ Finish_____ Total_____
Place:
Interviewer:
Others present?_____Yes _____No
    (If yes, relation to respondent)
Completed?_____Yes _____No
    (If no, list omissions)
Remarks?

SCALE 1: Objective Access

11. May I ask your age?_____
12. How many years have you lived around here?
    _____years (or, since_____year came to this area)
13. About how many other places, not around here, have you lived for a year or more?_____places

14. Are you married?
    1. _____married (Ask 14A and 15A)
    2. _____single (Ask 14B)
    14A. Is your husband (wife) living here now?
        1. _____yes
        2. _____no. If no, ask: Why is that? (Specify details)
    15A. Have you ever been divorced, separated, or widowed?
        1. _____no
        2. _____yes. If yes, specify complete history:
    14B. Have you ever been married?
        1. _____no
        2. _____yes. (If yes, ask 15B)
    15B. Were you divorced, separated, widowed, or what? (Get complete history if more than one marriage.)
        _____divorced
        _____separated
        _____widowed
        _____other (Specify)
16. How many people altogether are living in this house?
    16A. Who are they?—not their names, but how they are related to you: how many sons and daughters, brothers or sisters, and so on? (Specify in detail: husband, wife, wife's sister, husband's father, etc. Make sure the total listed fits with question 16.)

    _____   _____
    _____   _____
    _____   _____
    _____   _____
    _____   _____

17. Were you in the armed services?
    1. _____no
    2. _____yes. (If yes, ask 17A)
    17A. What was your last job in the service?
18. (For husbands) Was your wife in the armed services?
    (For wives) Was your husband in the armed services?
    1. _____no
    2. _____yes. (If yes, ask 18A)
    18A. What was your wife's (husband's) last job in the service?
19. When you were growing up—to around 16—were both of your real parents in your home with you, or was one or both of them gone because of death, or divorce, or separation?
    1. _____both real parents home
    2. _____one or both gone (Specify)
110. How many brothers and sisters did you have in your family? This includes even those that may have died.
    _____brothers
    _____sisters
111. What language was *usually* spoken in your home when you were growing up? (If two are mentioned, ask: which one was used most?)

1. _____English   3. _____(Indian tribe)
2. _____Spanish   4. _____Other (Specify)_____
          5. _____Two languages equally
                Specify: _____

_____

111A. What *other* language was spoken in your home when you were growing up?
       1. _____English   3. _____(Indian tribe)
       2. _____Spanish   4. _____Other_____

112. What language is *usually* spoken in your own home now?
       1. _____English   3. _____(Indian tribe)
       2. _____Spanish   4. _____Other (Specify)_____
             5. _____Two languages equally
                   Specify: _____

_____

112A. What other language is spoken in your home?
       1. _____English   3. _____(Indian tribe)
       2. _____Spanish   4. _____Other_____

113. How many rooms are there in this house, not counting the bathroom?
       _____rooms

114. How many of these rooms are used for sleeping?_____

115. Do you have a TV?   1. _____no   2. _____yes.

116. Do you (does your husband) own a car?   1. _____no
                                                2. _____yes

117A. What is your (for married women: your husband's) occupation?*
       What kinds of things do you (does your husband) do on this job?
       *If *unemployed* or *retired,* ask: What is (was) your (your husband's) usual occupation?
       *If *farmer* or *rancher,* ask: Are you the owner or a tenant?
       1. _____tenant
       2. _____owner (If owner, ask a and b)
          (a) In comparison with other farms (ranches) around here, is your farm (ranch) about average, somewhat smaller, or larger than the average?
               1. _____average   2._____smaller
               3. _____larger
          (b) Do you make most of your income from working on your farm (ranch)?
               1. _____yes
               2. _____no. (If no, ask:)
                     What else do you do to get income?

117B. (For married women) Do you work regularly?
       (For married men) Does your wife work regularly?
       1. _____no.   2. _____yes.
       If yes, 1. _____Part-time?   2. _____Full-time?
       What does she (do you) do?

117C. What is the last grade or year *you* completed in school? (Circle appropriate category.)

1. No school
2. Some elementary
3. Elementary completed (8th grade)
4. Some high school

*5. Completed high school
6. Some college or special training after high school
7. Completed college

*(If "completed high school") Did you have special training of any kind after h.s.? (If yes, circle 6, instead of 5.) *What kind?*

118A. What was your (your husband's) first full-time job after you (he) stopped going to school?

119A. Who supported the family while you were growing up?

119B. What was (this person's) your father's occupation?

120. What is your religious preference? (Specify denomination)

120A. How often do you attend church service?

_____Per week _____Per month _____Per year

121A. Do you belong to any clubs, associations or other such groups in this area?

1. _____no   2. _____yes

If yes, which ones? (Then ask 121B.)

a. _____   c. _____
b. _____   d. _____

121B. (If yes) About how many times a *month* do you attend meetings of (each listed group?)

_____a. _____b. _____c. _____d.
_____Total mo. attendance

121C. About how many times a month do you get together with friends, neighbors, or relatives for visits or parties at their place or your place?

_____times a month

121D. Who are the three persons or families you visit with most?

_____
_____
_____

122. Sex (Check)   1. _____M   2. _____F

SKIP TO NEXT PAGE

123. Ethnic Status_____
124. *Objective Access TOTAL SCORE*

SCALE 2: Reinforcement Value

Now I'd like us to talk about what's important to you in life. Different people consider different things important and satisfying to them. What I'm interested in is *your* opinion, what *you* consider most important to you.

I. *RV*
    A. *Family*
        Let's start off by talking about *family life.*

        Rank order. Here are some things that other
        people have said are satisfying in *family life.* Of
        these four things typed on this card, which would
        you say would be *most important* to you in fam-
        ily life?

    *A   The love and affection you get in the family.
    *D   Having somebody in the family you can count
          on to help you.
     *R   The good opinion of the family for the things
          you do well.
     *I   Being able to do things in the family in your own
          way.

    * (These letters stand for need relatedness: Affection; Dependence; Recognition;
Independence.)

        Most important_____ Next_____ Next_____
        Least_____   21._____

        Ratings. Now I'm interested in just how impor-
        tant you would say *each* of these would be to you.
        Let's start with the *first one* on the card, "the love
        and affection you get"; would you say that is
        (3) very important
        (2) pretty important
        (1) not too important
        (0) not important at all to you
        Repeat for each statement.

        A_____   D_____   R_____   I_____   22._____

    B. *Work*
        Now let's talk about *work.*
        Rank order. Here are some things other people
        have said are important in work. (If housewife,
        ask: "Suppose you were working at a job.") Tell
        me which of these would you say would be *most
        important* to you.
    D   To be helped out in getting the job done.
    I   Being able to make your own decisions about
         your work.
    A   Being liked by the people you work with.
    R   Being respected by people because of the way you
         do your work.

Most important_____ Next_____ Next_____
Least_____   23._____

Ratings. Now, how important would you say each
of these would be? Let's start with the first one on
the card: "To be helped out in getting the job
done." Would you say that's
(3) very important
(2) pretty important
(1) not too important
(0) not important at all to you

Repeat for each statement.

D_____ I_____ A_____ R_____   24._____

C. *Friends*
Rank order. Here are some things that other
people have said would be important to them in
their *friendships*. Which of these would you say
would be *most important* to you?

I Having friends who let you do things in your
own way.
A The feeling of knowing people who really like you.
D Having someone you can turn to for help when
you have a problem.
R Being admired and respected by your friends.

Most important_____ Next_____ Next_____
Least_____   25._____

Ratings. How important would you say each of
these would be to you? Let's start with the first
one on the card: "Having friends who let you do
things your own way." Would you say this would
be

(3) very important
(2) pretty important
(1) not too important
(0) not important at all to you.

Repeat for each statement.

I_____ A_____ D_____ R_____   26._____

II. *NV RATING*
I'd like to ask you a few more questions about
what's important to you. Turn over the card a moment

because I'm going to ask, for each of these questions, whether something is very important, pretty important, not too important, or not important at all to you. (Circle response.)

How important is it to you to get advice when you have a hard decision to make or a problem to work out?

(3)VI   (2)PI   (1)NTI   (0)NIA   D28.____

How important is it to you to know that people respect you for the way you do things?

(3)VI   (2)PI   (1)NTI   (0)NIA   R29.____

How important is it to you to know that people you like would want to spend time with you?

(3)VI   (2)PI   (1)NTI   (0)NIA   A210.____

How important is it to you to say what you think even if other people don't agree with you?

(3)VI   (2)PI   (1)NTI   (0)NIA   I211.____

How important is it to you that people you know have a high opinion of you?

(3)VI   (2)PI   (1)NTI   (0)NIA   R212.____

How important is it to you to know you can count on some people to help you if you need it?

(3)VI   (2)PI   (1)NTI   (0)NIA   D213.____

How important is it to you to be free to do things in your own way?

(3)VI   (2)PI   (1)NTI   (0)NIA   I214.____

How important is it to you to feel that the people you like also like you?

(3)VI   (2)PI   (1)NTI   (0)NIA   A215.____

SCALE 3: *Expectations*

We were talking just now about what you think is important in life. Now we are *changing over* to talk about what you *expect* and *not* any more about what you want. We all want certain things, but we don't really *expect* them all. I'd like for us to talk now about the kinds of things you really expect. So it's important to try to be as *realistic* as possible and talk about how you really *expect* things to be for you.

I. *GENERAL Freedom of Movement*
When you think about what you *really* expect in the future, how does it look to you from here?
(3) very good
(2) pretty good
(1) not too good
(0) not good at all   31._____

II. *LIFE AREA Freedom of Movement*
   A. *Family*
      32. Think about your *family* for a minute. How sure do you feel that things can work out the way you want them as far as your *family* or *family life* is concerned?
         (3)   very sure
         (2)   pretty sure
         (1)   not too sure
         (0)   not sure at all   32._____
      33. *Ranking.* Here are some things people have said *they expect* to happen in their family; look at this card and tell me which of these *you expect* most. Remember, *not* what you want, but what you *really expect* to happen *most often.*
      A To get affection from others in the family.
      D To be able to count on the family for help when you need it.
      R To have the good opinion of your family for the way you do things.
      I To be able to do things in the family pretty much the way you want.
         Expect most_____ Next_____
         Next_____ Least_____   33._____
      34. *Rating.* Now, let's go over these again. This time I would like you to say how *strongly* you expect each of these to happen. How strongly do you expect "to get affection from others in your family?"
         (3)   very strongly
         (2)   pretty strongly
         (1)   not too strongly
         (0)   not strongly at all.
         Repeat for the three others in order.
         A_____ D_____ R_____ I_____   34._____

   B. *Work*
   Let's talk about *work* now.
      35. How sure do you feel that things can turn out the way you want as far as your *job* or

work is concerned?

(3)　very sure
(2)　pretty sure
(1)　not too sure
(0)　not sure at all.　　　　　　　　　　35.＿＿＿＿

36. *Ranking.* Now these are some things people have said they expect to happen on their *jobs* or in their *work*. Which of these (on this card) do *you* expect most? Remember, not wish, but what you *expect* will happen most often.

D　To be helped out in getting the job done.
I　To have the chance to do things the way you think is best.
A　To be *liked* by others you work with.
R　To get respect for the way you do your work.

Expect most＿＿＿＿　Next＿＿＿＿
Next＿＿＿＿　Least＿＿＿＿　　　　　　36.＿＿＿＿

37. *Rating.* Now, let's go over these again. How *strongly* do you expect "to be helped out in getting the job done?"

(3)　very strongly
(2)　pretty strongly
(1)　not too strongly
(0)　not strongly at all

Repeat for the three others in order.
D＿＿＿　I＿＿＿　A＿＿＿　R＿＿＿　　37.＿＿＿＿

C. *Friends*

38. How about in your *friendships*? How sure do you feel that things can work out the way you want as far as your friendships are concerned?

(3)　very sure
(2)　pretty sure
(1)　not too sure
(0)　not sure at all　　　　　　　　　38.＿＿＿＿

39. *Ranking.* Here are some things other people have said they expect in their friendships. Which of these do you *expect, not* want, most? That is, which do you expect to happen most often?

I　That friends will pretty much let you do things in your own way.
A　That friends will show real liking for you.
D　That friends will help you out when you have a problem.

    R   That friends will respect and admire you.
Expect most_____ Next_____
Next_____ Least_____   39._____

310. *Rating.* How *strongly* do you expect each
of these (above)?
(3)   very strongly
(2)   pretty strongly
(1)   not too strongly
(0)   not strongly at all
Repeat for each statement in order.
I____   A____   D____   R____   310._____

III. *NEED Freedom of Movement*

Now turn over the card for a moment. When you can't
make up your mind what to do, how sure are you that
you can get help by turning to someone else? Would
you say: Very Sure, Pretty Sure, Not Too Sure, Not
Sure At All?
(3)VS (2)PS (1)NTS (0)NSA   D311._____

How sure do you feel that the way you do things will
be respected by others?
(3)VS (2)PS (1)NTS (0)NSA   R312._____

How sure do you feel that people you like want to
spend time with you?
(3)VS (2)PS (1)NTS (0)NSA   A313._____

How sure do you feel that you can pretty much say
what's on your mind even if other people don't agree
with you?
(3)VS (2)PS (1)NTS (0)NSA   I314._____

How sure are you that people you know will have a
high opinion of you?
(3)VS (2)PS (1)NTS (0)NSA   R315._____

If you were to get into some serious trouble, how sure
are you that people you know well would help you
out?
(3)VS (2)PS (1)NTS (0)NSA   D316._____

How sure do you feel that you can have the freedom
to do things in your own way?
(3)VS (2)PS (1)NTS (0)NSA   I317._____

How sure do you feel that people you like also will
like you?
(3)VS (2)PS (1)NTS (0)NSA   A318._____

SCALE 4: Internal-External Control

I. *OPEN END*

We've been talking about what you *want* and what
you *expect*; now I'd like to talk a little about *why you*

think things happen the way they do. For instance:
What do you think *mostly decides* whether or not a
person gets ahead on his job? I mean, what is the main
reason why a person gets ahead on a job?*   41._____

    * (If S gives responses where I or E remains unclear, ask, "Well, what do you
think is the main reason why (S's response) is that way?")
Can you explain that a little more?
What do you think *mostly decides* whether or not a
marriage breaks up?   42._____
Can you explain that a little more?
What do you think *mostly decides* whether a person is
liked or not?   43._____
Can you explain that a little more?
What do you think *mostly decides* whether or not a per-
son gets into trouble with the law?   44._____
Can you explain that a little more?

II.   *FORCED-CHOICE*

    I'm going to read some questions now, each of which
has two parts, a and b. I'd like you to tell me for each
question which part you believe is more true. In some
cases you may believe both parts are true or neither
part is true. But for every question I'd like you to choose
the part, a or b, which *you* believe is *more* true. Okay?
(Circle a or b CLEARLY)

      a)   If you've got ability, you can always get a good
job.   45._____
or b)   Getting a good job depends partly on being in the
right place at the right time.

      a)   Some of the good and some of the bad things in my
life have happened by chance.   46._____
or b)   What's happened to me has been my own doing.

      a)   Live in the present; the future will take care of
itself.   81._____
or b)   The future must be planned and prepared for.

      a)   It's really easy to have friends; a person just needs
to try to be friendly.   47._____
or b)   Making friends depends on being lucky enough to
meet the right people.

      a)   The best way to get along is to keep in mind the
lessons you learned in the past.   82._____
or b)   What's already happened is dead and gone, and it's
better not to spend too much time thinking about it.

      a)   You need the right breaks for a marriage to be
happy.   48._____
or b)   You can always have a happy marriage if you work
hard at it.

a) I dislike having to sit around waiting for somebody.   83._____

or b) I've plenty of time; I don't mind waiting.

a) Getting into trouble depends completely on the kind of life you lead.   49._____

or b) If the breaks are against you, you can get into trouble.

a) Sometimes, no matter how clearly you've thought something out, other people just don't get it.   410._____

or b) If you know what's on your mind, you can get it across to other people.

a) When I make plans, I am almost certain that I can make them work.   411._____

or b) I have usually found that what is going to happen will happen regardless of my plans.

a) The way a person's life turns out is completely in God's hands.   412._____

or b) What happens in this life depends on how you live it.

a) I don't spend much time thinking about the past.   84._____

or b) I often think about the things I did as a child.

a) With the right approach, racial and religious prejudice can be wiped out.   413._____

or b) People being the way they are, some form of racial or religious prejudice will probably always be with us.

a) I like to do things on the spur of the moment.   85._____

or b) I prefer to have things all planned out in advance.

a) Working hard and steady is the way to get ahead in a job.   414._____

or b) Getting ahead in a job depends on what kind of boss you happen to have.

a) No matter how hard a person tries, some people just don't like him.   415._____

or b) When a person isn't liked, it's because of the way he does things.

a) It's worth doing some things, even if they're not pleasant, in order to get what you want later on.   86._____

or b) It's better to do the things you want when you want to, than to worry about what could happen later on.

a) In the long run, we ourselves are responsible for bad government.   416._____

or b) There's not much the average person can do about how the government runs.

a) It's very important to have your life laid out pretty far in advance.   87._____

or b) It's really not possible to see your life more than a year ahead.

a)   Sometimes family troubles just can't be avoided.   417._____

or b)   A family will be happy only if everyone really does his part.

a)   It's best to give most attention to what's happening now in the present.   88._____

or b)   There's so much we can learn from older people that we should pay more attention to the way they've done things.

a)   Most people who get in trouble start out looking for it.   418._____

or b)   Often trouble starts because a person happens to be in the wrong place at the wrong time.

a)   No matter how much a person tries, it's hard to change the way things are going to turn out.   419._____

or b)   A person can pretty well make whatever he wants out of his life.

a)   If a person wants to get something done, the only place to turn is to himself.   420._____

or b)   Nowadays, people are forgetting the helpfulness of prayer.

a)   It's best to spend money when you have it, and let the future take care of itself.   89._____

or b)   It's better to put money aside so you'll have it when you really need it.

a)   Often I seem to have little influence over what other people believe.   421._____

or b)   When I'm right, I can usually convince others.

SCALE 5: Group Norms (Anomie)

Let's go on to some other kinds of questions. I will read some examples of how some people act in certain situations. People feel differently about these. I'd like to know how *you* feel about a person doing these things; whether he Absolutely Should, Should, May or May Not, Should Not, or Absolutely Should Not. (Note that these are on card.)

A teen-age daughter obeys her parents without question. Would you say she   51._____
1. AS   2. S   3. MMN   4. SN   5. ASN

The husband, by himself, makes all important money decisions for the family. Would you say he   52._____

Even with close friends, a man keeps his real feelings to himself. Would you say   53._____

A mother follows closely the teachings of her religion.   54._____

When a mother has many children and the family is poor, she gives a child away to be raised by relatives.   55._____

A farmer uses the *old* farming methods because they have usually worked in the past.

56.____

A policeman ignores a drunk person unless some actual damage has been done.

57.____

When a girl is dating a man she really likes, she lets him go all the way with her.

58.____

An unmarried young man spends most of his time studying and learning things that will help him get ahead in life.

59.____

A mother teaches her daughter to work toward a career in addition to being a homemaker.

510.____

A husband helps his wife with the household chores. Would you say he
1. AS   2. S   3. MMN   4. SN   5. ASN

511.____

A government official treats people *better* if they are sent by one of his friends.

512.____

A teen-age boy drops out of school to help support his parents.

513.____

The local priest or minister spends time with people even if they are not members of his church.

514.____

A father teaches his children to have a *special* respect for the *oldest* child.

515.____

After high school, a girl gets married instead of going on to college.

516.____

A businessman tries to make as much profit as he possibly can.

517.____

When a child is really sick, parents take him to a doctor right away.

518.____

A school teacher watches how he behaves in public more carefully than other people do.

519.____

A husband leaves all child care to the women in the family.

520.____

A mother takes a part-time job to make extra money for the family.

521.____

SCALE 6:   *Alienation*

I am going to read some things now that other people have said about how they *really feel*. I'd like you to think about these and tell me, for each one, how *you* feel. After I read each one, I'd like you to tell me whether you strongly agree, agree, disagree, or strongly disagree. (Circle answer CLEARLY)

I often feel that people around here are not too friendly.	SA A D SD	61._____
Trying to figure out how to get ahead in life is just too complicated.	SA A D SD	62._____
Most of the time I feel the work I'm doing is important and useful.	SA A D SD	63._____
In spite of what some people say, things are getting worse for the average man.	SA A D SD	64._____
I often feel left out of things that are going on around here.	SA A D SD	65._____
Most of the people I know seem to have different ideas than I have about the kind of life they want for their children.	SA A D SD	66._____
When people around here are having a hard time, it's up to me to try and help out.	SA A D SD	67._____
Nowadays children don't give their parents the respect they should.	SA A D SD	68._____
It's hard to know just how to treat people around here since you don't know what they expect.	SA A D SD	69._____
It's hardly fair to bring children into the world, the way things look for the future.	SA A D SD	610._____
I get the feeling that the people around here see most things the way I do.	SA A D SD	611._____
It's not really my concern if other people are in trouble.	SA A D SD	612._____
If I had my choice, I'd live my life very differently.	SA A D SD	613._____

SCALE 7: Illegitimate Means Acceptance

Hand card to respondent showing the following scale:

No Wrong	A little bit wrong	Wrong	Very wrong
0	1 2 3	4 5 6	7 8 9

Now I'm interested in how *wrong* you think different kinds of actions are. Most people think that something like murder is *very* wrong while something like bragging may be considered only *a little bit wrong* or *not wrong at all.*

If you think there is *no* wrong in an action, say 0; if it is only *a little bit wrong,* and depending on degree, say 1, 2, or 3; if you think it is clearly pretty wrong but not *very* wrong, say 4, 5, or 6; if it is *very* wrong, say 7, 8, or 9, depending in each case on how wrong you think it is.

When he files his income tax report, a rich man reports less income than he really has. How wrong would you say that is, from 0 to 9? 71._____

A girl says she has more education than she really has so that she can get a job and earn some spending money. 72._____

A big rancher grazes his stock on other people's property without their permission. 73._____

The wife of an ordinary worker makes up to her husband's boss so that her husband will get a good raise in pay. 74._____

A young girl out of a job buys a lot of clothes on time, knowing she will not make any payments. 75._____

A store owner makes a public contribution to a church he doesn't believe in just so he can get extra business from the church members. 76._____

When he applies for a very important job, a young college graduate doesn't tell his real religion. 77._____

A highly rated boxer loses a fight on purpose in order to get a big pay-off from gamblers. 78._____

A poor man accepts $10 from a politician to vote the way the politician asks him to. 79._____

A man who can barely support his family gets a $5 bill when he is given change at the grocery store instead of the $1 bill he was supposed to get. He notices the mistake but says nothing about it. 710._____

A pretty girl from a poor family lets herself get pregnant when she is dating a boy from a wealthy family, hoping that he will marry her. 711._____

The son of a new businessman in town makes up stories about how much money his father has so he can impress his classmates. 712._____

A man out of work breaks into a food store at night to get
food for his family.   713.____

A girl from a hard-up family secretly takes spending money
from her father's billfold.   714.____

The town favorite in a rodeo contest illegally fixes his gear so
that he will have a better chance to win.   715.____

A well-to-do woman makes a large contribution to a local
club to make sure that she gets to be president of it.   716.____

SCALE 8: *Time Perspective*

Now let's talk about something else.   810.

I'd like you to look back for a minute, and then tell me five
things that you've done or that have already happened to you.
These don't have to be important things, just anything at all
that comes to mind. (Pause) Anything you've done, or anything that's happened to you.

(After each response say, "OK, some more things now.")

(If S gives a *process* item, like "went to school," say "Now
that's something that (you did) (happened to you) over a
period of time. I'm interested in more specific things that happened at some *particular* time. OK?")

   Events.
1.
2.
3.
4.
5.
(Record Process Items Here)

(GO ON TO NEXT PAGE)

Now I want to go back and find out how long ago it was that
these events happened. How long ago was it when . . .
(event 1.)?   813.

(Repeat for each event listed.)

That's fine. Now I'd like you to look ahead, and tell me five
things that you *think* you'll do or *think* will happen to you.
Again, these don't have to be important things, just anything
at all that comes to mind. (Pause) Anything at all that you
think you'll do or think will happen to you.   811.

(After each response, say, "OK, some more things now.")

(If S gives a process item, like "live in town," say, "Now that's something you'll be doing over a period of time. We're really interested in more specific things that you think will happen at some particular time. OK?")

(Laugh off and reject "death" as something that happens to everyone if this is given.)

> *Events*

1.
2.
3.
4.
5.

(Record Process Items Here)

Now I want to know how long it is from now that you expect these things to happen. How long from now do you expect . . . (event 1.)? 812.____

(Repeat for each event listed.)

(RETURN TO PRECEDING PAGE AND ASK 813.)

SCALE 9: *Attitudes Toward Deviance*

Let's talk about some more things that people do. I would like to know how *wrong* you think different things are. Sure, there are always exceptions; like, to protect yourself, killing may be all right, but *usually* people feel killing is wrong. I would like to know how *you* feel in general about these things.

(Hand card to respondent.)

For instance:
Driving over the speed limit. How wrong do you feel that usually is? 91.____

No Wrong	A little bit wrong	Wrong	Very wrong
0	1 2 3	4 5 6	7 8 9

How about a woman being a heavy drinker? How wrong do you feel that usually is? 92.____

How about a person who doesn't work steady when he could? 93.____

How about a man's having sex relations before marriage? 94.____

How about a person getting into fights? 95.____

How about a husband and wife separating? 96.____

How about a *man* being a heavy drinker?   97._____

How about a woman's having sex relations before marriage?   98._____

How about a man fooling around with other women after he's married?   99._____

How about parents who don't stay home with their kids most of the time?   910._____

How about someone not making good on money he owes?   911._____

How about a married woman fooling around with other men?   912._____

  a) Now I'd like to go back over these 12 things with you (hand card list to respondent) and have you say which of them you think is the *most* wrong. Which is next most wrong? And which is third most wrong?   913._____

    (Try to *avoid* accepting ties.)
      Most wrong item #_____
      Next most wrong item #_____
      Third most wrong item #_____
  b) Now, which one of them would you say was the *least wrong* of all of them?
      Least wrong item #_____

SCALE 10: *Drinking*

    Well, we've been going over a lot of different things, but now I'd like to concentrate on just one thing in more detail. The thing I'd like us to talk about now is drinking; what I mean is alcoholic drinks like liquor, wine, and beer. Of course, whatever you say will be kept private.

    First of all, I'd like to know: 101._____

  A. Do you ever have a drink of liquor, wine or beer? (check)   101A._____

      YES_____ NO_____

(If YES, go on to 102—top of next page)
(If NO, ask:)

  B. Have you ever?   101B._____

      YES_____ NO_____

(If YES, skip down to D and E)
(If NO, ask:)

  C. Why do you think you never did?   101C._____

(IF NEVER-DRINKER, SKIP TO 1016—TOP OF PAGE 34)

  D. About when did you stop drinking?   101D._____
  E. Why did you stop?   101E._____

(For Former Drinker, always select words or phrases in parentheses.)

Here's a card that says how often people drink.   102._____
Let's take *wine* first. Which one says how often you usually
(had) have wine? Let's look at it. (Read statements aloud.)
_____Three or more times a day
_____Two times a day
_____About once a day
_____Three or four times a week
_____Once or twice a week
_____Two or three times a month
_____About once a month
_____Less than once a month, but at least once a year
_____Less than once a year
_____Never

(IF *Less than once a year* OR *Never,* SKIP *to* 104, TOP OF
NEXT PAGE.)

A.   (Think of the time when you *used* to drink wine.) Think
     of all the times you have had wine recently. When you
     (drank) drink wine, how often (did) do you have more
     than half a bottle—say five glasses or more?   103A._____
     _____Nearly every time   ⎫   (IF EITHER OF THESE,
     _____More than half the time ⎭   SKIP TO 104, TOP OF
                                             NEXT PAGE.)

     _____Less than half the time
     _____Once in a while
     _____Never

B.   When you (drank) drink wine, how often (did) do you
     have about three or four glasses?   103B._____
     _____Nearly every time   ⎫   (IF EITHER OF THESE,
     _____More than half the time ⎭   SKIP TO 104, TOP OF
                                             NEXT PAGE.)

     _____Less than half the time
     _____Once in a while
     _____Never

C.   When you (drank) drink wine, how often (did) do you
     have only one or two glasses?   103C._____
     _____Nearly every time
     _____More than half the time
     _____Less than half the time
     _____Once in a while
     _____Never

     Now, let's talk about *beer.* How often (did) do you
     usually have beer? (Read statements aloud.)   104._____
     _____Three or more times a day
     _____Two times a day
     _____About once a day
     _____Three or four times a week
     _____Once or twice a week

_____Two or three times a month
_____About once a month
_____Less than once a month, but at least once a year
_____Less than once a year
_____Never

(IF *Less than once a year* OR *Never,* SKIP TO 106, TOP OF NEXT PAGE.)

A. (Think of when you *used* to drink beer.) Think of all the times you have had beer recently. On a single occasion, how often (did) do you have five or more beers?   105A._____
   _____Nearly every time   } (IF EITHER OF THESE,
   _____More than half the time } SKIP TO 106, TOP OF
                                           NEXT PAGE.)

   _____Less than half the time
   _____Once in a while
   _____Never

B. On a single occasion, how often (did) do you have about three or four beers?   105B._____
   _____Nearly every time   } (IF EITHER OF THESE,
   _____More than half the time } SKIP TO 106, TOP OF
                                           NEXT PAGE.)

   _____Less than half the time
   _____Once in a while
   _____Never

C. On a single occasion how often (did) do you have only one or two beers?   105C._____
   _____Nearly every time
   _____More than half the time
   _____Less than half the time
   _____Once in a while
   _____Never

   Now, how about liquor—whiskey, vodka, mixed drinks, and things like that? How often (did) do you usually have liquor?   106._____
   _____Three or more times a day
   _____Two times a day
   _____About once a day
   _____Three or four times a week
   _____Once or twice a week
   _____Two or three times a month
   _____About once a month
   _____Less than once a month, but at least once a year
   _____Less than once a year
   _____Never

(IF *Less than once a year* OR *Never,* SKIP *to* 108, TOP OF NEXT PAGE.)

A. (Think of when you *used* to drink liquor.) Think of all the times you have had liquor recently. When you (had) have liquor, how often (did) do you have five or more drinks?   107.A_____

_____Nearly every time   ⎞ (IF EITHER OF THESE,
_____More than half the time⎰ SKIP TO 108, TOP OF
                                 NEXT PAGE.)

_____Less than half the time
_____Once in a while
_____Never

B. When you (had) have liquor, how often (did) do you have three or four drinks?   107B._____

_____Nearly every time   ⎞ (IF EITHER OF THESE,
_____More than half the time⎰ SKIP TO 108, TOP OF
                                 NEXT PAGE.)

_____Less than half the time
_____Once in a while
_____Never

C. When you (had) have liquor, how often (did) do you have only one or two drinks?   107C._____

_____Nearly every time
_____More than half the time
_____Less than half the time
_____Once in a while
_____Never

Where (did) do you do *most* of your drinking?   108._____
(Do NOT READ CATEGORIES. CHECK ONE ONLY)

_____home   (If more than one
_____friends' homes   place mentioned,
_____bars and restaurants   repeat question,
_____other (specify)   stressing MOST)

Where else (did) do you drink?   109._____
(CHECK ALL OTHERS MENTIONED)

_____home
_____friends' homes
_____bars and restaurants
_____other (specify)

Who (did) do you do *most* of your drinking with?   1010._____
(READ CATEGORIES. CHECK ONLY ONE)

_____family   (If more than one
_____friends   category mentioned,
_____anybody around   repeat question,
_____alone   stressing MOST)
_____others (specify)

Who else? (CHECK ALL OTHERS MENTIONED)   1011._____
_____family
_____friends
_____anybody around

_____alone

_____others (specify)

(Did) do you ever drink in the morning? Would you say
OFTEN, SOMETIMES or NEVER? (Circle one)   1012._____

How about afternoons?

    OFTEN   SOMETIMES   NEVER   1013._____

How often (did) do you drink with meals?

    OFTEN   SOMETIMES   NEVER   1014._____

(Did) do you usually drink on weekdays or only on
weekends?   1015._____

    _____weekdays

    _____weekends

ASK OF EVERYONE

Before you'd call someone a heavy drinker,   1016._____

a)   How much would he have to drink at one time?
    (drinks, bottles, glasses of a certain beverage)

b)   How *often* would he drink? (per week)

c)   How would he act?

(NEVER-DRINKER—SKIP TO 1018—TOP OF NEXT PAGE)

How did you happen to have your first drink?   1017._____

a)   About how old were you then?

b)   Where was that?

c)   Who were you with?

d)   Did your family know about it?

    _____YES _____NO

e)   (If YES)   What did your family think about it?

      (If NO)   What would your family have thought
                about it?

ASK OF EVERYONE

Did anyone in your family drink at all?   1018._____

    _____YES _____NO

(If NO, go on to 1021, bottom of this page, unless Never
Drinker. If NO from Never Drinker, skip to 1031, top of
page 38.)

(If YES from anyone, ask:) Who were they?

Would you say anyone in your family was thought of as a
heavy drinker?   1019._____

    _____YES _____NO

(If YES, ask:) Who?

Did anyone in your family ever get into any kind of trouble
or have problems because of drinking—like with the law,
family, friends, work, or health?   1020._____

    _____YES _____NO

(If YES, ask:) Who? What kind of trouble?

(FOR NEVER DRINKERS, SKIP TO 1031, TOP OF PAGE 38.)

About how old were you when you first started drinking
regularly?   1021._____

(FOR FORMER DRINKERS, SAY: "Think back to the time when you used to drink in answering the next few questions.")

How often (were you) have you been drunk in (an average) the last month?   1022._____

How about in (an average) the last year?

How often (did you have) have you had problems with your family because of your drinking? (If asked, FAMILY means *present* family)   1023._____

How about with your friends?   1024._____

How often (did you get) have you gotten into fights while drinking?   1025._____

Any accidents?   1026._____

How often (did you have) have you had trouble about a job because of drinking?   1027._____

Has drinking had any effect on your health?   1028._____

Now I'd like to know what (made) makes you feel like having a drink. Here are some things other people have said. As I read them, say whether or not each one (was) is true for you.   1029._____
(CHECK YES RESPONSES ONLY.)
YES
_____Just to be sociable
_____Hot weather
_____Feeling under pressure, tense
_____Pain
_____Hard work
_____Having problems
_____Feeling lonely
_____Having nothing else to do
_____Feeling mad
_____Just feel you have to have a drink sometimes
_____Feeling sad
_____Not getting ahead
_____Feeling tired
Now, which of the following things about drinking would you say (were) are *important* for you. As I read them, say whether or not each one (was) is important for you.   1030._____
(CHECK YES RESPONSES ONLY)
YES
_____Is something people do on special occasions
_____Sometimes helps you feel better
_____Makes you less shy

_____Makes you feel more satisfied with yourself
_____Helps you relax
_____Helps you get along better with people
_____Helps you forget your problems
_____Makes get-togethers more fun
_____Gives you more confidence in yourself
_____Makes you feel happier
_____Helps you forget you're not the kind of person you'd like to be
_____Makes you worry less about what other people think of you

ASK OF EVERYONE

Around here, what do you think is the *main* reason why people drink?   1031._____

Do you think anything needs to be done about the drinking around here? (If yes, specify)   1032._____

SCALE 11: *Other Deviance*

I'd like to ask you about some other things now.
How many times have you gotten into a fight in the last year?   111._____

How many times have you had trouble with a boss on a job?   112._____

How many times have you been fired from a job?   113._____

How many times have you driven a car during the last year when you had a good bit to drink?   114._____

(For married) How many times in your (present) marriage have you had such serious quarrels that your (husband, wife) talked about leaving you?   115._____

How many times have you been stopped for speeding?   116._____

How many times have you not made good on money you owed?   117._____

How many times have you taken things that didn't belong to you?   118._____

How many times have you been in a jam about anything to do with sex?   119._____

(For married with children) How many times have you been contacted by an agency for not taking good care of your children?   1110._____

What (else) have you gotten into trouble with the law about? What happened? (Find out whether respondent was jailed or not for each incident.)

What else have you gotten into trouble with the law about?
What happened?   Jail?   1111._____

(Ask again until respondent says "nothing else.")

SCALE 12:   *Developmental Background*

Well, let's do the last one now. I think you'll find these questions interesting—they're about your experiences as a child. We all have different experiences as we grow up, and thinking back on them helps us in understanding. So think back now to the time when you were a child, not a very young child, but when you were around 8 or 9 to 12 or 13 years of age.

121.   When you were a youngster, around 8 to 12 years old, what was your life like?
       a)   What did you do?

122.   Who brought you up? That is, who had the main responsibility for raising you when you were age 8–12?

123.   What did your (parents) (people who raised you) think were the most *important things* to teach you—for you to learn?

124.   Did your parents plan activities for you in advance ( ) or did they prefer to do things on the spur of the moment ( )?

125.   What kinds of things *that you did then* did your (parents) (people who raised you) *not* like?

126.   When they didn't like something you did, how did they *usually show you* they were displeased or didn't like it?

127.   Who usually did the punishing?

128.   (Omit this for subjects with one rearer)
       Then, which of your (parents) (people who reared you) would you say was more strict with you?

129.   What kinds of things that you did then did your (parents) (people who raised you) seem to *like best?*

1210. When they *liked* something you did, how did they *usually* show you that they were pleased?

1211. (Omit this for subjects with one rearer)
       Most parents have arguments and fights. Thinking about when you were 8–12, how much of this went on in your home?
       A great deal ( )   A fair amount ( )
       Not too much ( )

1212. Around that age, do you remember feeling that the family had a real problem about not having enough money?   Yes( )   No( )

1213. Did your (parents) (people who raised you) seem to feel that the chances of getting ahead for the family were
pretty good ( )   not too good ( )
or pretty bad ( )?

1214. How important did your (parents) (people who raised you) feel it was for you to *do well* in school?
Very important ( )   Pretty important ( )
Not too important ( )

1215. Sometimes kids find that their *teachers* have *different ideas* than their parents have about what one should and shouldn't do. How about you?

1216. Did you ever feel ashamed of anyone in your family —parents, sisters, brothers or relatives?

1217. About that age, was anyone in the family in *trouble* of any kind?   No ( )   Yes ( )
If yes, *who* and *what kind* of trouble?

1218. When you were about 8 to 12 years old, did you feel that you were different from the kids you knew?
If yes, in what way?

1219. How do you (or would you) *raise your children differently* from the way you were brought up?

1220. Summing up, what would you say has been the one single thing that has given you the most happiness in your life?

END OF COMMUNITY SURVEY INTERVIEW SCHEDULE

High School Questionnaires

VOTING SHEET
(Delay of Gratification Measure)

Record-hop this Saturday night.   _____

Band-dance on Saturday night a month from now,
April 28th.   _____

PERSONAL VALUES QUESTIONNAIRE

We're interested in learning something about the kinds of things teenagers like or consider important. What we want to know is how strongly you like to do different things or to have different things happen. Now, how strongly you like something can be shown by putting a check mark somewhere along a line that runs from NEITHER LIKE NOR DISLIKE, at one end, to LIKE VERY MUCH, at the other end.

When you like something *very* much, you can show this by marking a check ($\checkmark$) in one of these spaces toward the end that says LIKE VERY MUCH. If you don't care about something, one way or the other, you can show that by marking a check in one of the spaces toward the other end. If you feel somewhere in between about something, put your check somewhere toward the middle of the line. Your check can be in any of the spaces along the line, depending on how you really feel.

Let's take an example:

40. How strongly do I like:

To have kids ask me to help start a new club?

NEITHER LIKE   LIKE   LIKE VERY
NOR DISLIKE   MUCH

If you think about this for a minute, you can see that some kids would like this very much; some kids wouldn't care one way or the other, and some kids would be in between. Think about the way *you* feel. Now put your check mark in one of the spaces along the line that best shows how strongly *you* like this.

On this questionnaire we're not asking about what actually *does* happen to you, or what you *expect* to happen. We want to know how much you would *like* these different things to happen.

Each question should be answered by itself. Don't worry about how you have answered the others.

REMEMBER!

There are no right or wrong answers. Just put your check marks to show how strongly *you* really like each thing.

A   1.   How strongly do I like:
         To get along well with most of the kids?

NEITHER LIKE   LIKE   LIKE VERY
NOR DISLIKE   MUCH

(This same format was used with the remaining 29 items, presented three to a page. The following items were used. The letter in front of each item number indicates whether it was an Affection (A) or a Recognition (R) item.)

A   2.   To be in on the fun that goes on around here?
R   3.   To get at least a B average this year?
A   4.   To have friends want to do things with me during vacation?
R   5.   To be well-prepared for class discussion?
R   6.   To win a scholarship to some college?
A   7.   To have many friends in different groups?
A   8.   To know that the teacher actually likes me as a person?
R   9.   To come out near the top of the class on six-weeks tests?
R 10.   To be able to get my ideas across in class?
A 11.   To be thought of as a best friend by several of the kids?
R 12.   To get on the honor roll during the year?
A 13.   To be well-liked by most of the people around here?
R 14.   To be in the top half of the class at graduation?
A 15.   To be asked to take part in many social activities?
R 16.   To be able to answer other kids' questions about school work?

A 17.   To have groups show real pleasure when I join them?
A 18.   To be one of the most popular kids in the class?
R 19.   To be thought most likely to amount to something by my teachers?
R 20.   To understand new material quickly in class?
A 21.   To go out of my way to help others?
A 22.   To be voted the best-liked kid in my class?
R 23.   To be encouraged by my teachers to go on to college?
R 24.   To do well in math and science courses?
A 25.   To have other kids enjoy having me around?
R 26.   To be considered a bright student by my teachers?
A 27.   To openly express my appreciation of others?
R 28.   To have good enough grades to go on to college if I want to?
R 29.   To be thought of as a good student by the other kids?
A 30.   To do things with the group just because I like being with them?

PERCEIVED LIFE CHANCES INVENTORY

In this questionnaire, we're interested in learning something about how kids see their futures. Almost everyone spends some time thinking about what life will be like for them. Please answer these questions about your *own* future as realistically and honestly as you can.

1. a. What job would you like to have when you are about 25 years old? Give the *name* of a job or occupation and say what you'd be doing on the job.

    _____

    _____

    b. Assuming that wages then will be about the same as they are now, about how much money will you be making if you have this job?

                                        week
                        $_____per month. (Circle *one*.)
                                        year

    c. There are many things which might keep a person from getting the job he would like to have. What are the things you feel might stand in the way of *your* getting this job?

    d. Taking account of the things you have just written—the things that could stand in your way—what do you think your chances are of *really* having this job some day? Circle *one*.
        Excellent   Good   Fair   Poor

2. a. You have written some things which might stand in the way of your getting the job you would *like* to have. Taking account of things like this, and really being honest about it, what job do you really *expect* to have when you are 25? (Again, give the *name* of a job and say what you will be doing.)

    _____

    _____

    b. Assuming wages then will be about the same as they are now, about how much money will you be making if you have this job?

week

$_____per month. (Circle *one*.)

year

c. Do you think you'll be married by age 25? Circle *one*.

Yes No Uncertain

FOR BOYS ONLY

1. If you think you'll be married at 25 (Yes or Uncertain), do you think your wife will *also* have a job then, besides being a housewife? Circle *one*.

Yes No Uncertain

2. If Yes or Uncertain, how much money do you think *she* will be making?

week

$_____per month. (Circle *one*.)

year

FOR GIRLS ONLY

If you think you'll be married by 25 (Yes or Uncertain), how much money do you think your *husband* will be making?

week

$_____per month. (Circle *one*.)

year

3. a. People have many different reasons for choosing certain jobs. Read the list of reasons A through G below. Now put a check *after* each reason under the heading that best describes *how important* that reason would be to you in choosing the *ideal* job. Don't put any marks in the parentheses yet.

			Very Important	Important	Not Important
( )	A.	Pays good money	_____	_____	_____
( )	B.	Lets me make full use of my abilities	_____	_____	_____
( )	C.	Gives me a chance to work with other people	_____	_____	_____
( )	D.	Lets me do creative and original things	_____	_____	_____
( )	E.	Gives me a chance to be helpful to others	_____	_____	_____
( )	F.	Is a steady job	_____	_____	_____
( )	G.	Gets respect from other people	_____	_____	_____

b. Of all the reasons listed above, think of which one you consider the *most* important in choosing the ideal job. Now put a 1 in the parentheses in front of that reason. Then put a 2 in the parentheses before the reason you would consider *second most* important. Put a 3 in the parentheses before the third most important, a 4 before the fourth most important, and so on. When you finish, you will have a different number in each parentheses.

4. What do you *really* expect to do after you leave high school? Place a check mark after each statement under the heading which best describes *when* you plan to do it.

	Right away	Later on	Not at all
Get a job	____	____	____
Go to a business or trade school	____	____	____
Go to college	____	____	____
Go into the service	____	____	____
Get married	____	____	____

5. How important do you think it is these days for a person to get a college degree, as far as chances for jobs are concerned?

    Circle one

    Very
    important   Important   Not too
    important   Unimportant

6. How much schooling do you really expect to *finish?*
    a. Finish High School. Circle *one.*
        Very Sure   Pretty Sure   Not too Sure
    b. Finish Business or Trade School. Circle *one.*
        Very Sure   Pretty Sure   Not too Sure   Not Going
    c. Finish *at least* 2 years of College. Circle *one.*
        Very Sure   Pretty Sure   Not too Sure   Not Going
    d. Finish 4 years of College. Circle *one.*
        Very Sure   Pretty Sure   Not too Sure   Not Going

7. What are the most important reasons that might *keep* you from going to college?

8. Read the following two statements.
    ____A. In order to get ahead, it's most important to have a good education.
    ____B. In order to get ahead, it's most important to have practical experience.

    Now put a check before the statement you *most* strongly believe to be true.

9. What do your *parents* or the people who are raising you want you to do after you finish high school? Place a check under the heading that tells *when* they want you to do each thing.

	Right away	Later on	Not at all
Go to college	____	____	____
Go to a trade or business school	____	____	____
Get a job	____	____	____
Get married	____	____	____
Go into the service	____	____	____

10. How *often* have you talked with your parents or the people who are raising you about your plans for the future? Circle *one.*
     Many times   Four or five times   Once or twice   Never

11. When you think about your future *realistically,* how sure are you of:
     a. Being a respected member of the community in which you'll be living. Circle *one.*
         Very Sure   Pretty Sure   Not too Sure

b. Having a happy family life? Circle *one*.
Very Sure   Pretty Sure   Not too Sure

c. Being a leader in church groups, clubs, or other organizations? Circle *one*.
Very Sure   Pretty Sure   Not too Sure

d. Being able to settle down in whatever part of the country you want? Circle *one*.
Very Sure   Pretty Sure   Not too Sure

e. Doing better in life than your parents did? Circle *one*.
Very Sure   Pretty Sure   Not too Sure

FOR BOYS ONLY

12. Below is a list of jobs. Circle the L (for like) or D (for dislike) before each job, to show whether you would like (L) or dislike (D) having this job. *Answer every one.*

L   D   1.   Auto mechanic
L   D   2.   Bank teller
L   D   3.   Brick layer
L   D   4.   Construction laborer
L   D   5.   Cook in restaurant
L   D   6.   Doctor
L   D   7.   Engineer
L   D   8.   Farm owner
L   D   9.   Farm hand
L   D   10. Miner
L   D   11. Own your own business
L   D   12. Ranch owner
L   D   13. Ranch hand
L   D   14. Salesman
L   D   15. School teacher
L   D   16. Supervisor or foreman in charge of group of men
L   D   17. Truck driver
L   D   18. Welder

FOR GIRLS ONLY

12. Below is a list of jobs. Circle the L (for like) or D (for dislike) before each job to show whether you would like (L) or dislike (D) having this job. *Answer every one.*

L   D   1.   Airline stewardess
L   D   2.   Bank teller
L   D   3.   Beauty operator
L   D   4.   Cook in restaurant
L   D   5.   Dishwasher in restaurant
L   D   6.   Doctor
L   D   7.   Housewife
L   D   8.   Housekeeper (in someone else's home)
L   D   9.   Maid in hotel
L   D   10. Movie actress
L   D   11. Nurse

L	D	12.	Own your own business
L	D	13.	Salesgirl
L	D	14.	School teacher
L	D	15.	Secretary
L	D	16.	Telephone operator
L	D	17.	Wacs, Waves, or WAF
L	D	18.	Waitress

INTERNAL-EXTERNAL CONTROL INVENTORY

We're going to ask some questions now, each of which has two parts, a and b. For each question, we want to know which part you believe is *more* true. In some cases you may believe *both* parts are true. In some cases you may think *neither* part is true. But, for every question, we want you to choose the part which you believe is *more* true.

Be sure to choose the one you actually *believe* to be more true, rather than the one you think you *should* choose or the one you would *like* to be true.

There are no right or wrong answers. This is a measure of your *own* beliefs.

Read both parts of each question. Then circle the letter *a* or *b*, whichever part *you* believe is *more* true. Each question should be answered by itself. Don't worry about how you have answered the others. Be sure to answer *all* the questions.

REMEMBER!

There are no right or wrong answers. Make the choice which *you* believe to be *more* true.

I more strongly believe that:

1. a.   No matter how much a person tries, it's hard to change the way things are going to turn out.
    b.   A person can pretty well make whatever he wants out of his life.
2. a.   It's really easy to have friends; a person just needs to try to be friendly.
    b.   Sometimes making friends is a matter of being lucky enough to meet the right people.
3. a.   I don't spend much time thinking about the past.
    b.   I often think about the things I did as a child.
4. a.   In the long run, we ourselves are responsible for bad government.
    b.   There's not much the average person can do about how the government runs.
5. a.   Most people who get in trouble start out looking for it.
    b.   Often trouble starts because a person happens to be in the wrong place at the wrong time.
6. a.   Taking a true-false test is a lot like gambling; if you're lucky, you make the right choices.
    b.   The kid who studies can always do well on any test the teacher gives.

I more strongly believe that:

7. a.   There's not much use in trying to change a person's basic attitudes.
    b.   With the right approach, you can usually influence the way a person thinks.

8. a. When I make plans, I am almost certain that I can make them work.
   b. I have usually found that what is going to happen will happen regardless of my plans.
9. a. If people don't like you, it means that you don't know how to get along with others.
   b. It's impossible to figure out how to please some people.
10. a. Getting a job depends partly on being in the right place at the right time.
    b. If you're a good worker, you can always get a job.
11. a. It's very important to have your life laid out pretty far in advance.
    b. It's really not possible to see your life more than a year ahead.
12. a. Not everyone can be popular; so there's no use worrying about it.
    b. In the long run, popularity comes to those who work for it.

I more strongly believe that:

13. a. Getting into trouble depends completely on the kind of life you lead.
    b. If the breaks are against you, you can get into trouble.
14. a. Sometimes no matter how much you've thought something out, you can't get it across to people.
    b. If you know what's on your mind, it's easy to explain it to others.
15. a. The way a person's life turns out is in God's hands.
    b. What happens in this life depends on how you live it.
16. a. Sometimes, when I don't understand something in school, it's because the teacher doesn't explain it well.
    b. Not paying attention in class is the main reason for not understanding the work.
17. a. A major cause of wars is that people do not take enough interest in world events.
    b. I feel more and more helpless in the face of what is happening in the world today.
18. a. My own efforts alone determine how successful I am as a leader.
    b. Without the right breaks you can't expect to be an effective leader.

I more strongly believe that:

19. a. Live in the present; the future will take care of itself.
    b. The future must be planned and prepared for.
20. a. If you aren't popular, you haven't learned how to get along with others.
    b. Popularity depends a lot on what group you happen to get into.
21. a. Human nature being what it is, people can't change very much.
    b. If they work at it, people can make what they want of themselves.
22. a. There is no guarantee that a marriage will be happy; it depends in part on the breaks.
    b. You can always have a happy marriage if you work hard at it.
23. a. Becoming successful is sometimes a matter of getting the right breaks.
    b. Getting ahead in life depends entirely upon a person's ability.
24. a. The best way to get along is to keep in mind the lessons you learned in the past.
    b. What's already happened is dead and gone, and it's better not to spend too much time thinking about it.

I more strongly believe that:

25. a. Sooner or later man will have nature completely under his control.
    b. There are some things in this world that man will probably never learn to control.
26. a. How well you do in school depends on how hard you work.
    b. The grades you get in school depend partly on how much brains you were born with.
27. a. If you get into trouble, it's your own fault.
    b. Many people are victims of circumstances beyond their control.
28. a. I like to do things on the spur of the moment.
    b. I prefer to have things all planned out in advance.
29. a. No matter how hard a person tries, some people just don't like him.
    b. When a person isn't liked, it's because of the way he does things.
30. a. Working hard and steady is the way to get ahead in a job.
    b. Getting ahead in a job often depends on what kind of boss you happen to have.

(Delay of Gratification Items)

31. A high school English class won an essay contest. The teacher offered to take the entire class on a half-day sightseeing trip to (a nearby place) *today* or a full-day trip to (a distant place) a week *from now,* when he had a little more time. Imagine that *you* are in that class. Which trip would *you* choose? Circle *one.*
    a. half-day trip to (a nearby place) *today*
    b. full-day trip to (a distant place) *a week from now.*
32. One summer a high school kid got a pretty good job. The boss said it could be kept in the Fall part-time after school if the kid stuck with it and did the work well. But then a chance came to take a two-week trip to Denver with a friend. The kid thought about it for a while and then decided: Circle *one.*
    a. to *skip* the trip in order to keep the job
    b. to *take* the trip and try to get another job afterwards.

SECOND DAY'S PROCEDURES

INCOMPLETE SENTENCES

Complete these sentences to express *your real feelings.* Do every one. Be sure to make a complete sentence.

1. My fondest wish_____
2. A teen-ager_____
3. Making sense out of life_____
4. In a couple of days_____
5. Luck_____
6. Figuring out people_____
7. Getting ahead_____
8. Some parents_____
9. By the end of the school year_____
10. The most important thing_____

11. Next week_____
12. Most drinking_____
13. Figuring out the future_____
14. Grown-ups_____
15. When I graduate_____
16. Making out_____
17. Other kids_____
18. Five years from now_____
19. Family-life_____
20. The future_____
21. Overcoming my background_____
22. At age sixty_____
23. Getting drunk_____
24. The breaks_____
25. When I'm 30_____
26. Police officers_____
27. What counts in life_____

EXPECTATIONS QUESTIONNAIRE

In this questionnaire we want to learn something about the things teenagers *expect* to do or to happen. What we want to know is how strongly you *expect* different things. Now, how strongly you expect something can be shown by putting a check mark somewhere along a line that runs from SURE IT WILL HAPPEN, at one end, to SURE IT WILL NOT HAPPEN, at the other end.

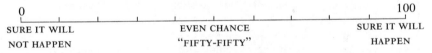

0		100
SURE IT WILL	EVEN CHANCE	SURE IT WILL
NOT HAPPEN	"FIFTY-FIFTY"	HAPPEN

When you are very sure something will happen, you can show this by marking a check (√) in one of the spaces toward the end that says SURE IT WILL HAPPEN. When you *don't* expect something to happen, you can show that by making a check in one of the spaces toward the other end, SURE IT WILL NOT HAPPEN. If you think the chances are about even, put your check somewhere toward the middle of the line. Your check can be in any of the spaces along the line, depending on what you *really* expect.

Let's take an example:

35. How strongly do I expect:
    To have kids ask me to help start a new club.

0		100
SURE IT WILL	EVEN CHANCE	SURE IT WILL
NOT HAPPEN	"FIFTY-FIFTY"	HAPPEN

If you think about this for a minute, you can see that some kids would expect this very strongly, some kids wouldn't expect this at all, and some kids would be in between. Think about what *you* expect. Now put your check mark in one of the spaces along the line that best shows how strongly *you* expect this to happen.

On this questionnaire we're not asking about what you would *like* to have happen. Answer each question in terms of what you really *expect*. We want you to be as realistic as possible.

Each question should be answered by itself. Don't worry about how you have answered the others.

REMEMBER!

There are no right or wrong answers. Just put your check to show how strongly *you* really expect each thing.

A　1.　How strongly do I expect:
　　　To be well-liked by most of the people around here.

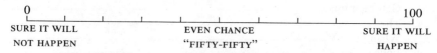

0										100
SURE IT WILL			EVEN CHANCE						SURE IT WILL	
NOT HAPPEN			"FIFTY-FIFTY"						HAPPEN	

(This same format was used with the remaining 29 items, presented three to a page. The following items were used. The letter in front of each item number indicates whether it was an Affection (A) or a Recognition (R) item.)

R　2.　To be in the top half of the class at graduation.
A　3.　To be asked to take part in many social activities.
R　4.　To be able to get my ideas across in class.
A　5.　To be thought of as a best friend by several of the kids.
R　6.　To get on the honor roll during the year.
R　7.　To be able to answer other kids' questions about school work.
A　8.　To have groups show real pleasure when I join them.
A　9.　To be one of the most popular kids in the class.
R　10.　To be thought most likely to amount to something by my teachers.
R　11.　To understand new material quickly in class.
A　12.　To go out of my way to help others.
A　13.　To have friends want to do things with me during vacation.
R　14.　To be well-prepared for class discussion.
R　15.　To win a scholarship to some college.
A　16.　To get along well with most of the kids.
A　17.　To be in on the fun that goes on around here.
R　18.　To get at least a B average this year.
A　19.　To have other kids enjoy having me around.
R　20.　To be considered a bright student by the teachers.
A　21.　To openly express my appreciation of others.
R　22.　To have good enough grades to go on to college if I want to.
R　23.　To be thought of as a good student by the other kids.
A　24.　To do things with the group just because I like being with them.
A　25.　To be voted the best-liked kid in my class.
R　26.　To be encouraged by my teachers to go on to college.
R　27.　To do well in math and science courses.

A 28. To have many friends in different groups.
A 29. To know that the teacher actually likes me as a person.
R 30. To come out near the top of the class on six-weeks tests.

SOCIOMETRIC QUESTIONNAIRE

On this next part, read each question carefully. Then think of the kids who fit the question best. Write their full names in the spaces provided. No one but us will ever see your choices. Like all of our research, everything is confidential. Your answers will not be shown to anyone—not to the teachers, not to the other kids—not to anyone.

Remember!

1. Write in the full name of each person.
2. Put your *first* choice after number 1 in each question, your *second* choice after number 2 in each question, etc.
3. Make *all* the choices for each question.
4. You can choose the same person on more than one question if he fits the question best.

1. Who are the four kids *in this school* you would choose to mess around with:
   1.   2.
   3.   4.
2. Which kids *in this school* have worked out their plans for the future most clearly:
   1.   2.
3. Of all the kids *in this school,* name the four that other kids like best:
   1.   2.
   3.   4.
4. Who are the kids *from around here* you most admire:
   1.   2.
5. Which kids *from around here* are most likely to do things *you* think they shouldn't do:
   1.   2.
6. Which kids *from around here* act the way most adults approve of:
   1.   2.
7. Which kids *from around here* get into trouble most:
   1.   2.
8. Which kids *in this school* are the most likely to amount to something:
   1.   2.
9. Which kids *from around here* do you *actually* mess around with the most:
   1.   2.
   3.   4.
10. Which of the kids *in this school* are the ones nobody seems to care much about:
    1.   2.
11. Which kids *from around here* are thought of as the outstanding leaders:
    1.   2.

THIRD DAY'S PROCEDURES

> Signature . . . .
> 'THANK YOU' TICKET—TRI-ETHNIC PROJECT
> CASH VALUE
> March 28–30 . . . . 25 cents
> March 31–April 3 . . . . . . 35 cents
> April 4–6 . . . . 50 cents
> (NON-TRANSFERABLE)
> Signature . . . .
> Good ONLY at (local) Drug Store

DRINKING QUESTIONNAIRE

In this questionnaire, we are interested in learning something about the use of alcoholic beverages by teenagers around here. Many scientists have been interested in this and have been studying teen-age drinking in high schools all over the country.

We're going to ask you a number of questions about your own experiences with wine, beer, and liquor. Some of these questions may seem funny to you; but we hope you will answer seriously and carefully. All your answers will be kept completely private. It's important for this study that your answers be accurate and honest.

For each question you will be asked either to write a sentence or two or to circle a letter. Everyone should answer every question. If you have any questions, don't wait; but raise your hand right away.

Drinking Questionnaire

1. About how old were you when you had your *first* drink—not just a taste?
2. Where did you have your *first* drink? Circle the letter in front of the answer that applies to you.
   a. at home
   b. at a friend's home
   c. at a relative's home
   d. at some other adult's home
   e. at a party
   f. in somebody's car
   g. at a bar
   h. out in the country
   i. at a dance
   j. _____ (If some other place, write in here.)
   k. never had a drink
3. Who were you with? Circle one letter.
   a. alone
   b. friends
   c. a date
   d. parents
   e. brother(s) or sister(s)

     f.   other relatives

     g.   other adults

     h.   _____(If some other persons, write in here.)

     i.   never had a drink

4.   How did you get the stuff to drink?

5.   How did you feel about your first drink?

6.   Did your parents or whoever was raising you know about it? Circle one.

     a.   yes

     b.   no

     c.   never had a drink

7.   Whether they knew about it or not, how did they feel about your having your first drink? Circle one.

     a.   didn't care

     b.   thought it was okay

     c.   were against it

8.   How often do you *usually* drink *wine?* Circle one.

     a.   1 or 2 times a day

     b.   about 3 or 4 times a week

     c.   about 1 or 2 times a week

     d.   about 1 or 2 times a month

     e.   at *least* 1 time a year

     f.   less than 1 time a year

     g.   never

9.   When you drink *wine,* how much do you usually drink at *one* time? Circle one.

     a.   a bottle or more

     b.   about half a bottle or about 5 glasses

     c.   3 or 4 glasses

     d.   1 or 2 glasses

     e.   less than 1 glass

     f.   never drink wine

10.   How often do you *usually* drink *beer?* Circle one.

     a.   1 or 2 times a day

     b.   about 3 or 4 times a week

     c.   about 1 or 2 times a week

     d.   about 1 or 2 times a month

     e.   at *least* 1 time a year

     f.   less than 1 time a year

     g.   never

11.   When you drink *beer,* how much do you usually have at *one* time? Circle one.

     a.   7 or more bottles

     b.   5 or 6 bottles

     c.   3 or 4 bottles

     d.   1 or 2 bottles

     e.   less than 1 bottle

     f.   never drink beer

12.   How often do you *usually* drink *liquor?* Circle one.
    a.   1 or 2 times a day
    b.   about 3 or 4 times a week
    c.   about 1 or 2 times a week
    d.   about 1 or 2 times a month
    e.   at *least* 1 time a year
    f.   less than 1 time a year
    g.   never

13.   When you drink *liquor,* how much do you usually have at *one* time? Circle one.
    a.   7 or more drinks
    b.   5 or 6 drinks
    c.   3 or 4 drinks
    d.   1 or 2 drinks
    e.   less than 1 drink
    f.   never drink liquor

14.   Where do you *usually* do *most* of your drinking? Circle *one* only.
    a.   at home
    b.   at 3.2 places
    c.   in somebody's car
    d.   at dances
    e.   at parties
    f.   at friends' homes
    g.   in bars
    h.   at relatives' homes
    i.   _____(If another place, write it in here.)
    j.   never drink

15.   Now circle all the other places where you *sometimes* drink.
    a.   at home
    b.   at 3.2 places
    c.   in somebody's car
    d.   at dances
    e.   at parties
    f.   at friends' homes
    g.   in bars
    h.   at relatives' homes
    i.   _____(If other places, write them in here.)
    j.   no other places
    k.   never drink

16.   Who do you *usually* drink with *most* often. Circle *one* only.
    a.   friends
    b.   parents
    c.   brother(s) or sister(s)
    d.   other relatives
    e.   alone
    f.   a date
    g.   _____(If someone else, write in here.)
    h.   never drink

17. Now circle *all* the others you sometimes drink with.
    a. friends
    b. parents
    c. brother(s) or sister(s)
    d. other relatives
    e. alone
    f. a date
    g. _____(If someone else, write in here.)
    h. no one else
    i. never drink
18. *When* do you usually drink? Circle *one*.
    a. weekdays
    b. weekends
    c. both
    d. holidays or special occasions
    e. never drink
19. What kinds of things make *you* feel like having a drink?
20. Circle the letters next to all the different kinds of things which make *you* feel like having a drink:
    a. just to be friendly
    b. hot weather
    c. feeling under pressure
    d. pain
    e. hard work
    f. just to find out what it's like
    g. having problems
    h. feeling lonely
    i. just because I'm not supposed to
    j. having nothing else to do
    k. feeling mad
    l. just feel you have to have a drink sometimes
    m. to act like an adult
    n. feeling sad
    o. not getting ahead
    p. feeling tired
    q. never drink
21. Circle the letters next to all the different kinds of things about drinking that are *important to you:*
    a. helps you feel better
    b. makes you less shy
    c. makes you feel like one of the crowd
    d. makes you feel more satisfied with yourself
    e. helps you relax
    f. helps you get along better with people
    g. helps you forget your problems
    h. makes get-togethers more fun
    i. gives you more confidence in yourself
    j. makes you feel happier

     k.   helps you forget you're not the kind of person you'd like to be

     l.   makes you worry less about what other people think of you

     m. never drink

22. How many times have you gotten drunk or pretty high in the last year? Circle *one* only.

     a.   10 or more times

     b.   8 or 9 times

     c.   6 or 7 times

     d.   4 or 5 times

     e.   2 or 3 times

     f.   1 time

     g.   never

23. Have you ever gotten drunk or pretty high *before* last year? Circle one.

     a.   yes

     b.   no

24. Whether or not they know about it, how do your parents or the people who raise you feel about your drinking *now?*

     a.   don't care

     b.   think it's okay if not too much

     c.   are against it

25. How many times have you gotten into trouble with your family because of drinking? Circle one.

     a.   several times

     b.   once or twice

     c.   never

26. How many time have you had fights because of drinking? Circle one.

     a.   several times

     b.   once or twice

     c.   never

27. How many times have you gotten into trouble with the law because of drinking? Circle one.

     a.   several times

     b.   once or twice

     c.   never

28. Before *you* would call someone a *heavy beer drinker,* how much *beer* would you say he would have to drink? Circle one.

     a.   1 bottle or less

     b.   2 or 3 bottles

     c.   4 or 5 bottles

     d.   6 or 7 bottles

     e.   8 or 9 bottles

     f.   10 bottles or more

29. Before *you* would call someone a *heavy wine drinker,* how much *wine* would you say he would have to drink? Circle *one.*

     a.   1 glass or less

     b.   2 or 3 glasses

     c.   4 or 5 glasses

     d.   half a bottle

e. a full bottle

f. a half-gallon or more

30. Before *you* would call someone a *heavy liquor drinker,* how much *liquor* would you say he would have to drink? Circle *one.*

    a. 1 or less drinks

    b. 2 or 3 drinks

    c. 4 or 5 drinks—a half pint

    d. 6 or 7 drinks

    e. a pint

    f. a quart or more

31. How *often* would you say a *heavy* drinker would drink? Circle *one.*

    a. 3 or more times a day

    b. 1 or 2 times a day

    c. 3 or 4 times a week

    d. 1 or 2 times a week

    e. 1 or 2 times a month

    f. a few times a year

32. What makes *you* decide that a person is drunk—how does he act?

33. Around here what do *you* think is the main reason people drink?

34. Do you think drinking is a problem around here? Circle one.

    a. yes

    b. no

If you think drinking *is* a problem around here, what do you think needs to be done about it?

35. If you *don't* drink, what are your reasons for *not* drinking?

ATTITUDES TOWARD DEVIANCE QUESTIONNAIRE

We're interested in how wrong you think different kinds of actions are. Most people think that something like murder is *very* wrong while something like bragging may be considered only *a little bit wrong* or *not wrong at all.* You can show how wrong you think something is by circling a number from 0 to 9.

No Wrong	A Little Bit Wrong	Wrong	Very Wrong
0	1 2 3	4 5 6	7 8 9

If you think there is *no wrong* in an action, circle the 0. If it is only *a little bit wrong,* circle the 1 or 2 or 3. If it is *wrong* but not *very* wrong, circle 4 or 5 or 6. If it is *very* wrong, circle 7 or 8 or 9. In each case, circle the *one* number that shows exactly how wrong *you* think it is.

Circle one number:

1. To smoke on the school grounds.

No Wrong	A Little Bit Wrong	Wrong	Very Wrong
0	1 2 3	4 5 6	7 8 9

(This same format was used with the remaining 19 items, presented 5 to a page. The following items were used.)

2. To take things that don't belong to you.

3. To go on outings with friends.

4. To fake an excuse from home.

5. To get into trouble with the law.
6. To swear or curse.
7. To cut-up in the classroom.
8. To get home a little later than usual after school.
9. To drive when you've had a good bit to drink.
10. To copy other kids' homework.
11. To make out with your dates.
12. To disobey your parents.
13. To cheat on tests.
14. To do things on the spur of the moment.
15. To get into fights with other kids.
16. To go on beer parties.
17. To lie to a teacher.
18. To drive a car without a license.
19. To ditch school.
20. To go to a movie the night before a test.

BEHAVIOR QUESTIONNAIRE

We're interested now in how often kids *do* different things. This also is something social scientists need to know more about for teenagers, just like drinking. Again, no one else will ever see your answers, and your name will be separated from your answer sheet. So we hope you'll be honest and frank in your answers. *How often have you:*

1. Smoked on the school grounds? Circle *one.*

   Very　　Several　Once or
   Often　　Times　　Twice　　Never

   (This same format was used with the remaining 19 items, presented 5 to a page. The following items were used.)
2. Taken things that didn't belong to you?
3. Gone on outings with friends?
4. Faked an excuse from home?
5. Gotten into trouble with the law?
6. Sworn or cursed?
7. Cut-up in the classroom?
8. Gotten home a little later than usual after school?
9. Driven when you've had a good bit to drink?
10. Copied other kids' homework?
11. Made out with your dates?
12. Disobeyed your parents?
13. Cheated on tests?
14. Done things on the spur of the moment?
15. Gotten into fights with other kids?
16. Gone on beer parties?
17. Lied to a teacher?
18. Driven a car without a license?
19. Ditched school?
20. Gone to a movie the night before a test?

Socialization Interview Schedule

UNIVERSITY OF COLORADO—TRI-ETHNIC RESEARCH PROJECT

SOCIALIZATION SCHEDULE—FINAL FORM

August 1962

Student's name_____

Respondent: _____

  First   Middle   (Maiden)   Last

Age_____ Sex_____ Relation to S. _____

Date_____ Time: Start_____ Finish_____ Total_____

Place_____ Others present? _____

Name of S's father_____

  First   Middle   Last

Is S's father living at home? Yes_____ No_____ (If no, how long away)_____

If no, Separated? _____ divorced? _____ dead? _____ other? _____

Have you remarried_____ How long ago_____ Husband's name_____

Number of children in family in order of age (including any that died)

	Name	Age	Sex		Name	Age	Sex
1.				7.			
2.				8.			
3.				9.			
4.				10.			
5.				11.			
6.				12.			

What other adults have been living in the home while S. was growing up? Name and relationship for each.

Has S. always lived with you? Yes____ No_____

If no, Why not?

      When not?

Schools S. has attended:

Ethnic Group_____

Completed? Yes_____ No_____ (If no, list omissions and reasons.)

Interviewer's name_____

Comments on interview:

SCALE 1: *Achievement*

11. What about the progress S. has been making in *school* during the last few years—how have you felt about it?
12. Have you said anything to him about it?
13. How far would you like him to go with his schooling?
14. What kind of *job* would you like him to get after he finishes his schooling? (If parent answers service, ask first job after service.) Why?
15. How does your husband feel about how S. is doing in school?
16. How far would your husband like him to go with his schooling?
17. What kind of *job* would your husband like S. to have after he finishes his schooling?
18. What do you see as standing in the way of S. getting as much schooling as you'd like him to have?
19. What do you see as standing in the way of S. getting the kind of job you'd like him to have?
110. How much schooling does S. himself want to get?
111. What kind of a job do you think S. himself would like to have when he finishes his schooling?
112. Think ahead ten years from now, what kind of life would S. be leading for you to feel that he's made a success of things?
113. How often have you talked with S. about his plans for the future?
     Many times   Four or five times   Once or twice   Never
114. When you talk about the future what kinds of things do you talk about?
115. Some people tell their children that the future is too hard to plan for and it's better to get what you can out of life in the present. How do you feel about this?
116. Some people tell their children that the only way to get what you really want in life is to try and work out the future way in advance. How do you feel about this?
117. What kind of job do you *really* expect S. will have when he's 25 or so—not what you'd like, but what you really expect?
117a. (For girls) If S. is married at 25, what kind of job do you expect her husband will have?
118. When you think about other families and their kids in this country, would you say your children have
     Just as good a chance   Less chance   Better chance
     to get what they want out of life?
119. What has S. done in the last few years that made you especially proud of him?

SCALE 2: *Affection*

Instructions: Another thing we're interested in is how parents handle different kinds of situations in bringing up their children. If you'll think back over the years from the time S. was a young child, around 6 years old, till now, try and remember what you *usually* did in the following situations. (If parent reports this never happened, say and record "what *would* you do?")

21. What did you usually do when S. was worried about not doing well in school?

22. What did you usually do when S. complained about too many chores to do?

23. What did you usually do when S. came to you for help with his personal problems?

24. What did you usually do when S. asked you to do something or go someplace with him and you were very busy?

25. What did you usually do when S. said that other kids didn't want to play with him?

26. In general, what do you think is the most important thing a family can do for a child while he's growing up?

B.

Instructions: I'm going to read you some things that other people say *they* do when their kids behave *well*. (Hand card to parent. Circle response.) For each of these, tell me whether this is something you Often do, Sometimes do, Hardly ever do, or Never do.

27. Tell him that you liked what he did.

    Often   Sometimes   Hardly ever   Never

Buy him something he likes.

    Often   Sometimes   Hardly ever   Never

Don't do anything in particular, since kids are supposed to behave well.

    Often   Sometimes   Hardly ever   Never

Show that you are pleased by a hug or warm smile.

    Often   Sometimes   Hardly ever   Never

Don't do anything, *but* promise something special for him later on.

    Often   Sometimes   Hardly ever   Never

Tell him he should have behaved that way before.

    Often   Sometimes   Hardly ever   Never

Give him money to spend for himself.

    Often   Sometimes   Hardly ever   Never

Do something special with him.

    Often   Sometimes   Hardly ever   Never

27a. Let's go back now over the things you do often. I'd like to know which *one* you do *most* often. (Read statements rated *often*. Star response.)

28. Now I'm going to read you some things that other people do when their kids behave *badly*. (Hand card and circle response.) For each of these, tell me whether this is something you Often do, Sometimes do, Hardly ever do, or Never do.

Scold him.

    Often   Sometimes   Hardly ever   Never

Send him off to be by himself.

    Often   Sometimes   Hardly ever   Never

Give him a spanking or whipping.

Often   Sometimes   Hardly ever   Never
Explain to him why he shouldn't do it.
Often   Sometimes   Hardly ever   Never
Make him feel ashamed in front of everybody.
Often   Sometimes   Hardly ever   Never
Show him that he is hurting and disappointing you.
Often   Sometimes   Hardly ever   Never
Don't let him do something he wants to do or take away something he likes.
Often   Sometimes   Hardly ever   Never
Deliberately ignore him till he behaves well.
Often   Sometimes   Hardly ever   Never
Tell him that you or your husband are going to punish him later.
Often   Sometimes   Hardly ever   Never

28a. Let's go back now over the things you do often. I'd like to know which *one* you do most *often*. (Read statements rated *often*. Star response.)

29. Of all the different kinds of things you do when S. behaves poorly, which works best for you? Can you tell me about it?

210. Which doesn't work well at all for you? Can you tell me why?

C.

211. When he is pleased with something that S. does, what does your husband usually do?

212. And when he doesn't like the way S. is acting, what does he do?

D.

213. What about the ideas you and your husband have about how to bring up S.—would you say they are: (Circle response.)
Very different   Different in some ways   Very much the same

214. What do you disagree about in how to bring up S.?

215. When you do disagree, do you sometimes get into arguments about it?

216. Do you think that S. knows that you and your husband disagree about how to bring him up?

217. What other kinds of things do you and your husband disagree about, not to do with the children?

218. Compared to most people you know, how would you say you and your husband get along?

219. In general, would you say you and your husband get along: (Circle response.)
Very well   Pretty good   Fair   Not too well?

220. What kinds of things do you and your husband do together?

221. Different couples have different ways of showing that they like each other. Some show their fondness for each other in front of the family, some only show their liking when they are with each other. Which of these is most like you and your husband? (If only child, go on to item 226.)

222. Which of your children, would you say, has been the easiest to bring up? Why?

223. Which of your children, would you say, has been the hardest to bring up? Why?

224. Do you think that S. feels that you like (any of the other children) in the family better than you like him? (If yes) Why do you suppose he feels that way?

225. Do you think that S. feels that your husband likes (any of the children) in the family better than he likes S.? (If yes) Why do you suppose he feels that way?

E.

226. Have you or your husband been away from S. for any long period of time while he was growing up?

227. Did you have any jobs outside the home while S. was growing up?
   If yes, when?
   Who took care of S.?

228. What kinds of things did you and S. do together when he was younger?

229. What kinds of things do you do together now?

230. How often do you do things with S.?

231. How about your husband, what kinds of things did S. and he do together?

232. What kinds of things do S. and your husband do now?

233. How often does your husband do things with S.?

234. Do you think S. would like you and your husband to spend more time with him now?

235. When you do things with S. do you usually do these pretty much on the spur of the moment or do you plan ahead of time?

SCALE 3: Controls

Let's talk some more about the kinds of things parents have to punish kids for.

31. What was the latest thing S. did that you punished him for? Tell me about it.
   How did you punish him?

32. What is the most serious thing S. has done recently that you had to punish him for? Tell me about it.
   How did you punish him?

33. What other things does S. do that you have to punish him for? Tell me more about it.
   How do you punish him?
   (Probe to "exhaust" list.)

B.

34. Why do you think he does things like that?

35. Where did he learn to do those things—from whom?

36. How about from his friends, could he have learned any of these things from them?

37. How about from his brothers or sisters, could he have learned it that way? (Omit, if S. is an only child)

38. How about from relatives, could he have learned it that way? (If yes, specify who and what.)

39.   How about from his parents, could he have learned it that way? (Specify)
310. Now, who do you hold up to S. as a good example for him to follow? Why?
311. Who does S. himself look up to? Why?
312. Is there anyone *you* mention as an example of how *not* to behave? Why?

A. (continued)

313. Let's go back a moment to when S. was younger—about 6 to 8 years old. Did he have to be punished more then, less then, or about the same as now?
314. What kinds of things did he used to do when he was younger that you punished him for?
315. Let's come back to the present. What kinds of rules do you set for him *now* about what he's not supposed to do?
      a)   time for being in at night
      b)   amount of dating
      c)   time spent watching TV
      d)   smoking
      e)   time spent on homework
      f)   against going around with certain boys or girls
      g)   drinking
      h)   driving a car
316. Does S. seem to accept these rules or does he seem to resent any of them? Does he try to get around them in any way?
317. Do you feel it's harder nowadays to keep kids in line and out of trouble than it used to be?

C.

318. Overall, how strict would you say you were with S. when he was growing up. Would you say you were
      Very strict   Strict   Not strict but not easy either   Easy   Very easy
      with S. when he was growing up? (Circle one.)
319. How about your husband, how strict was he with S. when he was growing up? (Circle one.)
      Very strict   Strict   Not strict but not easy either   Easy   Very easy

D.

320. For each of the following I'd like you to tell me how wrong you think it is for a teen-ager to do these things.

Very wrong	Wrong	Not too wrong	Not wrong at all
3	2	1	0

      a)   how about getting home from school a little later than usual _____
      b)   how about cheating on tests . . . . _____
      c)   cursing or swearing . . . . _____
      d)   going on beer parties . . . . _____
      e)   lying to a teacher . . . . _____
      f)   getting into fights with other kids . . . . _____
      g)   taking things that don't belong to him . . . . _____
      h)   getting drunk . . . . _____
      i)   heavy petting on dates . . . . _____

    j)   ditching school—or playing hooky .... ＿＿＿

    k)   lying to his parents .... ＿＿＿

    l)   cutting up in the classroom .... ＿＿＿

    m) driving when he's had a good bit to drink .... ＿＿＿

    n)   copying other kids' homework .... ＿＿＿

E.

321.   What sort of serious trouble has S. gotten into?

322.   (If yes) Has anyone in the family gotten into the same kind of trouble?

323.   Has anyone in the family gotten in any (other) kind of serious trouble?

324.   For each of the following, please tell me if S. has done this

       Very often   Several times   Once or twice   Never

          3   2   1   0

    a)   how about getting home from school a little later than usual ＿＿＿

    b)   cheating on tests .... ＿＿＿

    c)   cursing or swearing .... ＿＿＿

    d)   going on beer parties .... ＿＿＿

    e)   lying to a teacher .... ＿＿＿

    f)   getting into fights with other kids .... ＿＿＿

    g)   taking things that don't belong to him .... ＿＿＿

    h)   getting drunk .... ＿＿＿

    i)   heavy petting on dates .... ＿＿＿

    j)   ditching school—or playing hooky .... ＿＿＿

    k)   lying to his parents .... ＿＿＿

    l)   cutting up in the classroom .... ＿＿＿

    m) driving when he's had a good bit to drink .... ＿＿＿

    n)   copying other kids' homework .... ＿＿＿

    o)   gotten into trouble with the law .... ＿＿＿

SCALE 4:   Internal-External Control

Now lets talk about something quite different. We've been talking about a lot of different things like rules and things. We're also interested in how parents answer some of their children's questions. Kids ask all kind of questions. (If parent says child has never asked such a question for any item, record this and ask "what *would* you say?")

41.   They ask why some people are much better-liked than others. What did you say was the reason?

42.   They ask why some kids do so much better in school than others. What did you say was the reason?

43.   They wonder why marriages break up. What did you say was the reason?

44.   They want to know why some people get into trouble with the law. What did you say was the reason?

45.   They ask why there is so much misery in the world—poverty, illness, war, prejudice. What did you say was the reason?

B.

Let's talk a little now about the kinds of things that have happened while

S. was growing up. Some of the important things that happen to kids are things they never expected. (If yes, specify.)

46. Think back while S. was growing up.
    a) Did S. ever do very poorly in school when he didn't expect to at all?   No   Yes
    b) Was S. ever in an accident or suddenly taken very ill?   No   Yes
    c) Was someone close to S. ever in an accident or suddenly taken ill?   No   Yes
    d) Did the family ever have a real loss of income when it wasn't expected, like your husband losing his job, crops failing, or something like that?   No   Yes
    e) Did anyone S. felt close to ever die when nobody expected it?   No   Yes
    f) Did S. ever lose an animal he was very attached to?   No   Yes
    g) Did S. ever have something very important promised to him that then didn't work out?   No   Yes
    h) Was there ever anyone S. liked or admired very much who let him down?   No   Yes
    i) Did S. ever have to be suddenly sent away to live with someone else for a while?   No   Yes
    j) Did S. ever have a close friend who suddenly had to move away?   No   Yes
    k) Did the family ever have to move to a new place suddenly?   No   Yes
    l) Did S., himself, ever make important plans that just fell through?   No   Yes
    m) Did S. ever have something really wonderful happen to him when he wasn't expecting it?   No   Yes
    n) What other important things happened that S. didn't expect while he was growing up?   No   Yes

C.

Let's talk about some of the things you expect of S.

47. What kinds of responsibilities does S. have—what duties does he have?
48. How long has he been expected to do these things?
49. At what age did S. do the following things? (If no, find out "at what age would you permit this?")
    a) At what age was S. permitted to go around town alone?
    b) At what age was S. permitted to decide how late he could stay out at night?
    c) At what age was S. permitted to drive a car?
    d) At what age was S. given spending money to do with as he pleased?
    e) At what age was S. expected to earn some of his own spending money?
    f) At what age was S. permitted to go with his friends to (nearby city) or places like that?
    g) At what age was S. permitted to go on dates?

h) About how old was S. when he first showed interest in the opposite sex?

i) How about a decision like dropping out of school. At what age would you allow S. to decide that for himself?

410. Does S. take part in important family decisions, like how the money is spent, where to go on a trip, whether to move to another place, etc.?

411. What kinds of things do you feel a boy, girl, of this age should still have decided for him by his parents?

SCALE 5: *Alienation*

I'd like to ask you some questions now about how you, yourself, feel about some things. I am going to read some things now that other people have said about how they *really feel*. I'd like you to think about these and tell me, for each one, how *you* feel. After I read each one, I'd like you to tell me whether you Strongly agree, Agree, Disagree, or Strongly disagree. (Hand card. Circle response.)

I often feel that people around here are not too friendly.	SA A D SD	51.....
Trying to figure out how to get ahead in life is just too complicated.	SA A D SD	52.....
Most of the time I feel the work I'm doing is important and useful.	SA A D SD	53.....
In spite of what some people say, things are getting worse for the average man.	SA A D SD	54.....
I often feel left out of things that are going on around here.	SA A D SD	55.....
Most of the people I know seem to have different ideas than I have about the kind of life they want for their children.	SA A D SD	56.....
When people around here are having a hard time, it's up to me to try and help out.	SA A D SD	57.....
Nowadays children don't give their parents the respect they should.	SA A D SD	58.....
It's hard to know just how to treat people around here since you don't know what they expect.	SA A D SD	59.....
It's hardly fair to bring children into the world, the way things look for the future.	SA A D SD	510.....
I get the feeling that the people around here see most things the way I do.	SA A D SD	511.....

It's not really my concern if other people are in trouble.	SA A D SD	512.
If I had my choice, I'd live my life very differently.	SA A D SD	513.

SCALE 6:   Summary

We asked a lot of questions about S. There are just a few more and then we will be finished.

61.   If you could do it all over again as a parent, how would you bring up S. differently?

62.   In what ways would you like S. to change?

63.   In what ways do you feel you could have been a better mother?

64.   In what ways do you feel your husband could have been a better father to S.?

65.   How have you raised S. differently than your parents raised you? (If only child, go on to item 67.)

66.   How have you raised S. differently than you've raised the other children?

67.   There are many things that one could talk about in bringing up children. Are there things that we haven't gotten around to?

68.   What has been the most satisfying thing to you in having a family?

INTERVIEWER: Turn page for additional factual information.

Face Sheet–2

There are a few other factual things we need to know.

Mother's education_____

Mother's occupation_____

Father's education_____

Father's present occupation _____

Father's 1st job after schooling_____

(If father away from home 5 years or more, ask spouse's education, occupation and 1st job.)

Present annual income:

Under	$ 2,000	_____
Between $ 2,000 and	4,000	_____
Between 4,000 and	6,000	_____
Between 6,000 and	8,000	_____
Between 8,000 and	10,000	_____
Between 10,000 and	15,000	_____
Over $15,000		_____

Procedures Used for Devising Quantity-Frequency Indexes of Alcohol Use in Both the Community Survey and the High School Studies

THE COMMUNITY SURVEY STUDY

Scoring Guide for the Quantity-Frequency Measures

Definitions and Assumptions

1. The unit by which drinking frequency will be coded is occurrences per day.
2. While the absolute alcohol content in ordinary wines customarily ranges between 12% and 14%, some wines are fortified to the point of 20%. We will use a 15% figure in computing the absolute alcohol content of wines drunk.
3. The State of Colorado limits alcohol content of beer to 4% and, since there is no 3.2% beer available in the community, we will use the 4% figure in estimating absolute alcohol content of beer drunk.
4. Alcohol content of liquor (whiskey, vodka, etc.) is one half of stated "proof." Since most liquor ranges between 80 and 100 proof, we will use the median figure of 90 proof, half of which is 45, which is the alcohol content of liquor of that proof.

   (These figures, 15 percent, 4 percent, and 45 percent, are close to those used in a subsequent State of Colorado report. "To compute the absolute alcohol equivalents, the following average percents of absolute alcohol by volume are used: beer, 4.5 percent; wine, 17 percent; distilled spirits, 45 percent" (p. 73). *Facts about alcoholism and the use of alcohol in Colorado*. Alcoholism Publication No. 2. Alcoholism Division and Records and Statistics Section: Colorado State Department of Public Health, March, 1966. Pp. x + 79.)
5. Wine glasses, while traditionally 3.5 oz., do not always realistically reflect the size of the container from which wine is consumed. Wine is drunk directly from the bottle and from tumblers of all sizes. We will use the estimate of 4 oz. to represent the amount of wine defined by "a glass of wine."
6. There is no draught beer sold in the community; so "beers" refers to bottles of beer. Individuals usually drink cans or bottles of beer which contain 11 or 12 oz. We will use the latter figure.
7. Whether drunk plain or mixed, a drink of liquor usually contains 1 shot of liquor, which is traditionally 1½ oz.

8. Responses of "1 or 2" drinks will be scored as 1.5 drinks.
    Responses of "3 or 4" drinks will be scored as 3.5 drinks.
    Five or more drinks will be scored as 6 drinks.

Frequency Items

The following is a table of the Raw and Adjusted Raw Frequency scores of the Frequency item for each beverage. Raw scores are based on a times per day unit; adjusted scores are rounded.

Item Choices	Raw Scores	Adjusted Raw
3 or more times a day	3.00	3.00
2 times a day	2.00	2.00
About once a day	1.00	1.00
3 or 4 times a week	.50	.50
Once or twice a week	.214	.20
2 or 3 times a month	.084	.10
About once a month	.033	.05
Less than once a month but at least once a year	.008	.01
Less than once a year	.00	.00
Never	.00	.00

The Frequency item for each beverage (items 102, 104 and 106 in the Community Survey Schedule—see Scale 10 in Appendix 2) receives its appropriate Adjusted Raw Score.

Quantity Items

The determination of Quantity estimates of consumption for each beverage is figured in terms of absolute alcohol (AA) content per ounces consumed, weighted by frequency of level of consumption. This determination is arrived at as follows:

Community Survey
  Scale 10

Item #	# of Drinks	# of Ounces	Amt. of AA
Wine (15% AA content, 4 oz. per drink)			
103A	6	24	3.60
103B	3.5	14	2.10
103C	1.5	6	.90
Beer (4% AA content, 12 oz. per drink)			
104A	6	72	2.88
104B	3.5	42	1.68
104C	1.5	18	.72
Liquor (45% AA content, 1.5 oz. per drink)			
105A	6	9.00	4.05
105B	3.5	5.25	2.36
105C	1.5	2.25	1.01

Each of the above items consists of 5 frequency choices which receive the following frequency weight values:

> 0—Never
> 1—Once in a while
> 1—Less than half the time
> 2—More than half the time
> 2—Nearly every time

For each respondent, the value associated with his choice among the 5 listed for each item is multiplied by the amount of AA associated with that item. The products for all items for each beverage are summed and then divided by the sum of the values associated with the choices within items. The resultant value is an average quantity of AA intake for each beverage, per sitting. The following is a table of all possible quantity scores for each beverage:

	Beer	*Wine*	*Liquor*
A_2	2.88	3.60	4.05
A_1 & B_2	2.08	2.60	2.92
A_1 & B_1 & C_0	2.28	2.85	3.20
A_1 & B_1 & C_1	1.76	2.20	2.47
A_1 & B_1 & C_2	1.50	1.88	2.11
A_0 & B_2	1.68	2.10	2.36
A_0 & B_1 & C_0	1.68	2.10	2.36
A_0 & B_1 & C_1	1.20	1.50	1.69
A_0 & B_1 & C_2	1.04	1.30	1.46
A_1 & B_0 & C_0	2.88	3.60	4.05
A_1 & B_0 & C_1	1.80	2.25	2.53
A_1 & B_0 & C_2	1.44	1.80	2.02
A_0 & B_0 & C_2	.72	.90	1.01
A_0 & B_0 & C_1	.72	.90	1.01
A_0 & B_0 & C_0	0	0	0

Quantity-Frequency Index

The Q-F Index is composed of the summed products of the Frequency Adjusted Raw Score for each beverage and the average quantity of AA intake for each beverage for each respondent. The values of the index range between 0 and 31.60. The scorer, therefore, has merely to select the appropriate quantity score for each beverage from the above table, multiply it by the appropriate frequency score and sum the products across the beverages.

The following case can serve as an example. A subject reports that he drinks wine once or twice a week. He therefore receives an adjusted frequency score of 0.20. He then reports that he never drinks more than half a bottle of wine at one sitting (A_0), sometimes drinks 3 or 4 glasses of wine at a sitting (B_1), but usually drinks only 1 or 2 glasses (C_2); his consumption pattern for wine is A_0 & B_1 & C_2, and his quantity score from the table is 1.30. This is then multiplied by the adjusted frequency score of 0.20 to yield a wine Q-F of 00.26 when rounded to two places. This process is then repeated for the other two beverages, and the three Q-F scores summed to yield a total Q-F from all beverages.

THE HIGH SCHOOL STUDY

Scoring Guide for Quantity-Frequency Measures

Definitions and Assumptions:

(Same as for Scale 10, Community Survey; see preceding material)

Frequency Items:

The following is a table of frequency values to be assigned to frequency responses for each beverage based on a times per day unit (see Appendix 3, Third Day's Procedures, items in Drinking Questionnaire):

Response Choices	Values
a. 1 or 2 times a day	2.00
b. about 3 or 4 times a week	0.50
c. about 1 or 2 times a week	0.20
d. about 1 or 2 times a month	0.05
e. at least 1 time a year	0.01
f. less than 1 time a year	0.00
g. never	0.00

The frequency item for each beverage (items 8, 10, & 12) receives its appropriate frequency value score.

Quantity Items:

The determination of quantity estimates of consumption for each beverage is figured in terms of absolute alcohol (AA) content per ounces consumed. The following is a table of levels of consumption and AA content for each beverage (items 9, 11, & 13):

Total & Absolute Alcohol Contents

Quantity levels	Wine		Beer		Liquor	
	oz.	AA	oz.	AA	oz.	AA
a.	30.	4.50	96.	3.84	12.00	5.40
b.	18.	2.70	66.	2.64	8.25	3.71
c.	14.	2.10	42.	1.68	5.25	2.36
d.	6.	0.90	18.	0.72	2.25	1.01
e.	2.	0.30	6.	0.24	0.75	0.34
f.	00.	0.00	00.	0.00	0.00	0.00

For each respondent, the AA values associated with his response for each beverage constitute his quantity scores.

Quantity-Frequency Index

The Q-F Index for a beverage is the product of the frequency value and quantity score for that beverage. The Total Q-F Index is the sum of the products taken across beverages.

NAME INDEX

SUBJECT INDEX